STRUCTURED INEQUALITY IN THE UNITED STATES

Critical Discussions on the Continuing Significance of Race, Ethnicity, and Gender

STRUCTURED INEQUALITY IN THE UNITED STATES

Critical Discussions on the Continuing Significance of Race, Ethnicity, and Gender

SECOND EDITION

Edited with Commentary by

Adalberto Aguirre, Jr., PhD
University of California, Riverside

David V. Baker, PhD
Riverside Community College

Foreword by

Edna Bonacich

PEARSON
Prentice
Hall

Upper Saddle River, New Jersey 07458

Library of Congress Cataloging-in-Publication Data

Structured inequality in the United States : critical discussions on the continuing
significance of race, ethnicity, and gender / edited with commentary by Adalberto
Aguirre, Jr, David V. Baker. — 2nd ed.
    p. cm.
  Includes index.
  ISBN-13: 978-0-13-225682-7 (alk. paper)
  ISBN-10: 0-13-225682-7 (alk. paper)
  1. Equality—United States. 2. Discrimination—United States. 3. Minorities—United
States. 4. United States—Social conditions—1945– I. Aguirre, Adalberto. II. Baker,
David V.
  HN90.S6S85 2007
  305—dc22
                                2006100017

Editorial Director: Leah Jewell
Executive Editor: Jennifer Gilliland
Editorial Assistant: Lee Peterson
Marketing Manager: Kate Mitchell
Marketing Assistant: Laura Kennedy
Production Liaison: Marianne
  Peters-Riordan
Manufacturing Buyer: Brian Mackey

Cover Art Director: Jayne Conte
Cover Design: Bruce Kenselaar
**Composition/Full-Service Project
  Management:** Karpagam Jagadeesan/
  GGS Book Services
Printer/Binder and Cover Printer:
  Courier Companies, Inc.

Credits and acknowledgments borrowed from other sources and reproduced, with
permission, in this textbook appear on appropriate page within text.

Pearson Education LTD.
Pearson Education Singapore, Pte. Ltd
Pearson Education, Canada, Ltd
Pearson Education–Japan
Pearson Education Australia PTY,
  Limited

Pearson Education North Asia Ltd
Pearson Educación de Mexico, S.A. de C.V.
Pearson Education Malaysia, Pte. Ltd
Pearson Education, Upper Saddle River,
  New Jersey

10 9 8 7 6 5 4 3 2 1
ISBN-13: 978-0-13-225682-7
ISBN-10: 0-13-225682-7

*We dedicate this book to the memory of our
friend and colleague, Professor Maurice Jackson,
who impressed upon us that teaching about
structural discrimination is important
for our students.*

Brief Contents

Contents

Foreword

To many people in the United States, the problem of racism and racial inequality appears to have been solved. Most believe that the civil rights legislation and the government's war on poverty policy initiatives of the 1960s eliminated racism and racial inequality. *Structured Inequality* challenges these general perceptions by presenting thoughtful social, scientific, and jurisprudential discussions and political commentaries on the more important societal problems connected with racial, ethnic, gender, and class inequality. The selections presented in this book take a critical approach to examining the consequences of structured inequality in the United States for people of color and women. To this end, the authors of *Structured Inequality* provide a comprehensive and critical review of the research literature regarding social inequality. They use this review to develop a conceptual framework for the ideas discussed in each section of the book and to demystify the notion that "all is well" with regard to race in the United States.

Professors Aguirre and Baker have organized *Structured Inequality* with the understanding that the structure and dynamics of social inequality are difficult for students to understand. The authors' goal is to further student knowledge and understanding of how and why structured inequality undermines the hopes and aspirations of millions of people of color and women. The authors have organized *Structured Inequality* as an instructional vehicle for helping students realize that racism, sexism, and class inequality are systemic ideologies that plague U.S. society to its core. To enhance students' understanding of race, ethnicity, gender, and class inequality in the United States, the editors have carefully selected critical discussions that expose the social realities of inequality. The authors of *Structured Inequality* are convincing and straightforward in promoting a discussion on race, ethnicity, gender, and class that is necessary to our collective understanding of the social complexities of U.S. society.

Structured Inequality provides students with a sound theoretical approach to the topic and exposes them to how social scientists analyze social problems from a critical vantage point. One of the book's strengths is its focus on major social institutions—education, criminal justice, family, health and medicine, economics, politics, and the cultural community—to document the persistence of structured inequality within the various institutions of society. In sum, the book offers a clear and concise analysis of the social history of racial, ethnic, gender, and class distinctions in U.S. society and their effect on determining group access to valued resources. The authors of *Structured Inequality* present an innovative approach to the study of structured inequality, an approach that helps students understand the cultural and social roots of social inequality. *Structured Inequality* is a valuable instructional resource for those of us committed to helping students understand the oppressive and exploitive social conditions experienced by people of color and women in U.S. society.

Professor Edna Bonacich
Los Angeles, California

Preface

Writing a book that examines *how* and *why* race, ethnic, and gender inequality continue to characterize our social institutions is a particularly challenging task. For one, when we discuss the ideas disseminated in this book with each other and our professional colleagues, we find that the topics of race, ethnicity, and gender within the context of structured inequality often produces extremely complex moral arguments. For another, when we present the idea to our students that the United States social system continues to systematically disenfranchise racial, ethnic, and gender groups from mainstream American society, we discover that race, ethnic, and gender relations are topics oftentimes regarded as too burdensome for discussion. One of our students once asked bewilderingly, "Why are we studying racism? I thought Martin Luther King took care of all that." This statement reflects a prevailing notion among many American college students that United States society no longer systematically denies persons of color and women full and equal participation in its major social institutions. Our teaching experiences have shown us that college students presume that the aims of the civil rights campaigns of the 1960s alleviated the gross social inequalities suffered by persons of color and women in the United States. This thinking troubles us. Yet we understand that the continued debate regarding the liabilities of affirmative action programs and whether majority white group members are the *new* victims of "reverse discrimination" encourages this perception about race relations in the United States. As one scholar explains, for example:

> There is a myth that white males are being hurt and displaced by Affirmative Action programs. Current statistics show that white males constitute only 33 percent of the U.S. population but yet they represent 80 percent of tenured professors in the Nation. They represent 80 percent of the U.S. House of Representatives and 90 percent of the Senate. [Ninety-two] percent of the Forbes 500 Corporations are controlled by them.[1]

C. Wright Mills observed in *The Sociological Imagination* that the study of race, ethnic, and gender inequality in the United States is the sociologist's quest for an introspective understanding of equality in American society. Our purpose in this book, then, is to introduce students to some of the more notable discourse regarding the continued and consistent patterns of institutionalized discrimination and forms of racist and sexist ideology in United States society. But this book involves more than simply noting that institutionalized racism remains pervasive throughout every segment of United States. We think it's important that students understand that United States society is plagued by what sociologist Joe R. Feagin defines as *systemic racism*—"the system of racist domination and oppression and its consequent racial inequality that has been created, maintained, and legitimated by those who subscribe to the white supremacy ideology."[2] To further students' understanding of structured inequality in United States society, then, we have selected *critical* discussions on inequality that uncover the *social realities* of inequality in the United States and which contradict the societal notion that racism and sexism are simply artifacts of our country's historical past and far removed from modern America. We hope this book will convince our readers that the discussion of race is a necessary requirement for understanding the sociological complexities of our society. Unfortunately, we conclude that American society is intrinsically racist and sexist.

We have divided this book into eight chapters. In Chapter 1, we present our conceptualization of the sociological context for the study of racial, ethnic, and gender inequality in the United States. We are concerned that students understand the relationship between social inequality, discrimination, and racial and ethnic oppression. Underlying the readings adopted for this chapter is that inequality is systemic to United States society. In Chapter 2, we rely upon the work of noted scholars of education to explain that the American education institution amounts to a powerful instrument of racial and ethnic oppression that historically and contemporaneously limits opportunity of persons of color in the United States to realize their full human potential. Here, we focus attention on the changing demographics of student populations, racial segregation in public schools, educational segregation strategies, the invidious distinctions in education, violence and victimization in schools, minority faculty in higher education, and the particular case of inequality in education for American Indians. In Chapter 3, we are troubled by the fact that the United States criminal justice system has fails to meet its Constitutional mandate of "fairness" and "evenhandedness in its processes and procedures. The selections in this chapter reinforce concerns that women and persons of color suffer the consequences of selective law enforcement, institutional judicial bias, status deficiencies in criminal justice, and imposition of the death penalty. Chapter 4 involves discussions on the dimensions of domestic violence, poverty and family violence, and child victimization as outcomes of the inequality suffered by American families. We focus on inequality in the American economic institution in Chapter 5 and discuss issues of inequality associated with occupational segregation, unemployment, racial divisiveness in the workplace, safety in the workplace, child labor, housing discrimination, and poverty. Chapter 6 brings forth compelling scholarship on undocumented immigration, reparations for past injustices, felony disenfranchisement law, the crisis of human trafficking of women and children, and the brutality of America's militaristic imperialism. In Chapter 7, we focus on inequality in the medical institution and call attention to the lack of access that persons of color and women have to affordable health care, rising health care costs as related to corporate interests and medical malpractice, women's health issues eugenics, and criminalization of the mentally ill. Inequality in the cultural community is the topic of Chapter 8. In it, we focus on those societal problems that continue to disrupt communities of color—such as the link between the media and racist ideology, the cultural damage associated with hate crime, homelessness, and we ask whether civil rights is dead in the United States and whether U.S. soceity has adequately vendicated the civil rights injustices of the past. The structural dynamics of race, ethnicity, and gender as mechanisms of stratification and disenfranchisement trouble us, and we hope that this book facilitates student understanding of the society in which they live out their lives.

Adalberto Aguirre, Jr.

David V. Baker

ENDNOTES

1. *Noted in Gwendolyn Zoharah Simmons, "Racism in Higher Education," University of Florida Journal of Law and Public Policy,* 14 (2002): 29–43, at 39.
2. Joe R. Feagin, "Excluding Blacks and Others From Housing: The Foundation of White Racism," *Cityscape: A Journal of Policy Development and Research*, 4 (1999): 79.

About the Authors

Adalberto Aguirre, Jr., received his bachelor's degree from the University of California, Santa Cruz, and a master's and a doctorate in sociology and linguistics from Stanford University. He is a professor of sociology and chair of the sociology department at the University of California, Riverside. His research interests are in sociolinguistics, the sociology of education, and race and ethnic relations. Professor Aguirre has written extensively for such professional journals as *Social Problems*, *Social Science Journal*, *Social Science Quarterly*, *International Journal of Sociology of Language*, and *La Revue Roumaine de Linguistique*. He is the author or coauthor of *An Experimental Sociolinguistic Investigation of Chicano Bilingualism*; *Intelligence Testing, Educational and Chicanos*; *Language in the Chicano Speech Community*; *American Ethnicity: The Dynamics and Consequences of Discrimination*; and *Chicanos in Higher Education: Issues and Dilemmas for the Twentieth Century*. Professor Aguirre is also the editor of *Radical Pedagogy*.

David V. Baker received his bachelor's degree in political science from California State University, Northridge, a master's degree, and a doctorate in sociology from the University of California, Riverside, and a juris doctorate from California Southern Law School. He is an associate professor of sociology at Riverside College in Riverside, California. He has held visiting lectureships at the University of California, Riverside, Chapman University, California States University, San Bernardino, and California State University, Fullerton. His research and teaching interests are in race and ethnic relations with an emphasis on exploring systemic racism in the American criminal justice system. He has contributed works to *Ethnic Studies*, *Social Justice*, *The Justice Professional*, *Criminal Justice Abstracts*, *Social Science Journal*, *The Journal of Law and Social Challenges*, and *Criminal Justice Studies: A Critical Journal of Crime, Law and Society* where he is an associate editor. He is also coauthor of *Social Problems: A Critical Power-Conflict Perspective*.

Professors Aguirre and Baker are coauthors of *Race, Racism and the Death Penalty in the United States*; *Perspectives on Race and Ethnicity in American Criminal Justice*; and *Notable Selections in Race and Ethnicity*.

CHAPTER 1

Structured Inequality in American Society

INTRODUCTION

In law professor Derrick A. Bell's short story, *The Chronicle of the Space Traders*, aliens from a far-off star land at the beachhead of the Atlantic coast of the United States. The Space Traders offer to the people of the United States "gold, to bail out the almost bankrupt federal, state, and local government; special chemicals capable of unpolluting the environment, which was becoming daily more toxic, and restoring it to the pristine state it has been before Western explorers set foot on it; and a totally safe nuclear engine and fuel, to relieve the nation's all-but-depleted supply of fossil fuel." All the Space Traders want in return is "to take back to their home star all of the African Americans who lived in the United States."[1] To Michael Olivas, the conquest, exploitation, colonization, enslavement, and immigration of American racial history illustrate poignantly the reality of the Space Traders' story.[2] Indeed, the European explorers who arrived at American shores planted the seeds of inequality on their initial contact with the indigenous people of the Americas. The European explorers did not simply "discover" America; they arrived on the North American continent with political models especially designed to *conquer* and *subjugate* land and people. The treaties between the Indian nations and the white government of the United States were instruments of colonization used to exterminate and dislocate American Indians from their land.[3]

As a result, treaties became instruments of subjugation for depriving American Indians of their land and freedom. One commentator notes that "by the time Europeans began colonizing the Americas, they had established and adhered to a number of accepted legal norms concerning territorial acquisition and possession."[4] Besides genocide and cultural annihilation, Eric Kades argues that "[o]ne of the most critical deprivations that the American Indians suffered at the hands of the United States was the loss of their lands. Within two centuries of the first European settlements in North America, the newcomers held title to almost every acre of the continent."[5]

Chief Justice John Marshall's unanimous opinion in *Johnson v. M'Intosh* established the legal rationale for the U.S. land grab of Indian territory.[6] The case involved an appeal to determine title to Indian-occupied territories wherein the plaintiff had purchased land in 1773 and 1775 from the Illinois and Piankeshaw Indian nations. Marshall's opinion on the legality of the conveyances made it clear that "the discovery of the Indian-occupied lands of this nation vested absolute title in the discoverers, and rendered the Indian inhabitants themselves incapable of transferring absolute title to others."[7] Put another way, by "conquering" Indian lands, Europeans, rather than Indian nations, were vested with absolute title over Indian lands—the so-called *discovery rule*. U.S. courts continue to follow Marshall's thesis in *M'Intosh* as a fundamental principle of American property law.[8]

The sociolegal significance of *M'Intosh* continues to divide historians. Some scholars argue that because the U.S. government has consistently subscribed to a policy of making voluntary payments to Indian tribes—the United States reportedly paid over $800 million for Indian lands—the conquer and systematic subjugation of Indians and their culture is somehow legitimated.[9] For example, consistent with the reparation viewpoint, Felix Cohen asserts that "[t]he notion that America was stolen from the Indians [is] one of the myths by which we Americans are prone to hide our real virtues and make our idealism look as hard-boiled as possible."[10] In contrast, Kades argues that,

> A recent work classifies M'Intosh as part of a discourse of conquest, which denies fundamental human rights and self-determination to indigenous tribal peoples. This discourse asserts the West's lawful power to impose its vision of truth on non-Western peoples through a racist, colonizing rule of law. [T]he United States acquired a continent "in perfect good faith" that its wars and acts of genocide directed against Indian people accorded with the rule of law. [T]he West's archaic, medievally derived legal discourse respecting the American Indian is ultimately genocidal in both its practice and its intent.[11]

Thus inequality became instrumental in privileging *white society* early in the forging of American society. Indian nations inevitably became pawns in a game designed to promote the social presence and interests of white persons in North America. White society deprived Indian nations of their land to establish a system of rights rooted in the belief that "equality" in white society depended on the "inequality" of Indian nations. That is, for white society to privilege itself in North America, Indian nations had to be deprived of their basis for existence—their sacred lands. In this process of accommodation, white society became more equal as Indian nations became notably more unequal. By the time the framers of the Constitution decided to define the rights and liberties of persons, inequality had become the hallmark of racial and ethnic relations in American society. As sociologist Joe R. Feagin reminds us, the U.S. Constitution explicitly or implicitly recognized racial subordination:

> First, as a result of the compromise between Northern and Southern representatives to the Constitutional Convention, Article I required the counting of each slave as three-fifths of a person for the purposes of determining legislative representation and taxes. . . . In addition, a section of Article II permitted the slave trade to continue until 1808. The Constitution also incorporated a fugitive slave provision, requiring the return of runaway slaves to their owners.[12]

Feagin adds that "neither the Declaration of Independence, with its great 'all men are created equal' phrase, nor the Constitution, with its revolutionary Bill of Rights, was seen by its white framers as applying to a large proportion of the population."[13] As such, the framers of the Constitution were fully aware of the differentiating effects race would have on the allocation of social and political rights to persons within states. Ironically, racial and ethnic minorities perceive the Constitution as the vehicle for obtaining equal rights and for limiting the scope of their rights.[14]

ATTRIBUTING BLAME FOR RACE AND ETHNIC INEQUALITY

To understand the dilemma inequality poses for a society that espouses equal rights for all, sociologists have developed a set of conceptual approaches to the study of inequality—in particular, race and ethnic inequality.[15] *Assimilation theory* is the most prominent approach within the social sciences regarding the study of racial and ethnic relations. Assimilation theory underlies the racial ideology of the American people. The social sciences use the theory to examine the experiences of immigrant groups that have become part of the United States, either voluntarily or involuntarily. Studies focusing on the assimilation of European immigrants have lauded their success in making social, educational, political, and economic advances in U.S. society. In contrast, studies on nonwhite immigrant groups have noted that their limited advances in U.S. society are the result of defective biological or cultural factors. The perceived deficiencies of nonwhite immigrant groups by white society, in particular, has resulted in a generalized characterization of these groups that is demeaning and reinforcing of negative stereotypes held by white persons for racial and ethnic populations in the United States.[16]

Some researchers have blamed racial and ethnic populations for their oppressed situation.[17] For example, in response to the explosion of racial violence in the United States during the 1960s, the federal government established social science commissions to investigate the social problems inundating the black community. President Lyndon B. Johnson established the Commission on Civil Disorders to investigate what had happened, why the riots had occurred, and what policies the federal government could implement to prevent further outbreaks. Louis L. Knowles and Kenneth Prewitt's critique of the Kerner Commission findings, however, illustrates the federal government's apparent failure to sort out the underlying "causes behind the conditions" of civil unrest. In *Institutional and Ideological Roots of Racism*, Knowles and Prewitt argue that the commission did not go far enough in its investigation to discover the root causes of racial violence in the United States. To these scholars, the commission simply attributed civil unrest to a *black pathology*—a blaming-the-victim thesis. Essentially, Knowles and Prewitt attribute racial disorder in America to its "historical roots of institutional racism" that have prevented persons of color from attaining equality in U.S. society. Scholars who question the assimilationist thesis find it an inadequate explanation for the continued subjugation of persons of color in the United States. We contend that the thesis is simply incongruent with the objective historical experiences of Chicanos, American Indians, and African Americans. Regarding the use of an assimilation model to study racial and ethnic populations in the United States, Carlos Arce notes,

Unfortunately, most major assimilation studies focus exclusively on European immigrant groups that arrived by way of the Eastern seaboard . . . very little empirical research has sought to test the applicability of the assimilation model for groups such as Chicanos and American Indians, who created stable, complex civilizations here long before the arrival of European settlers.[18]

Assimilation theory stands in stark contrast with the ill treatment that many white Americans and the federal government have imposed on Muslims and persons of Arab descent since the terrorist attacks of September 11, 2001. In the aftermath of the disaster, white Americans increased their bias-motivated violence and hatred toward Sikhs, Indians, and Pakistanis.[19] Many of the hate-crime victims suffered bodily injury from white perpetrators using baseball bats, metal poles, and guns as weapons. Especially targeted for hate violence have been men wearing turbans and beards. The hate violence continues today. In 2003 alone—nearly three years after September 11—Muslims and Arabs living in major metropolitan areas across the country reported more than a thousand incidents of harassment, violence, and discrimination.[20] The federal government has also acted with ill intent toward Muslims and Arabs. Immediately following the events of September 11, Congress hastily passed the USA Patriot Act, a draconian measure intentionally subverting the constitutional liberties and civil rights of immigrant groups. The act gives law enforcement far-reaching powers that avoid constitutional guarantees of due process and equal protection of the law. As a result, the Department of Justice has targeted thousands of Muslims and Arabs for arrest, searches, seizures, and physical detention without access to legal counsel and the courts. One scholar explains the similarity of the ill treatment of "Muslim-looking" Americans to the abuses suffered by other persons of color in the United States. In this regard, Stubbs puts forward compelling evidence of America's scapegoating of Muslims and Arabs for the September 11 atrocities and questions the ability of the U.S. legal system to guarantee individual liberties and civil freedoms for all Americans following the attacks. He writes,

The prospect of having citizens tried, convicted and executed in secret in response to an ill-defined "war on terror" without some independent judicial oversight smacks of the tyranny of the infamous 'Star Chamber' of centuries past. To make matters worse, to have one weakened group of citizens singled out as social scapegoats is not only unpatriotic and unfair, it is simply uncivilized. We must be vigilant and treat our neighbors as ourselves.[21]

A SOCIOLOGICAL CONTEXT FOR THE STUDY OF RACIAL, ETHNIC, AND GENDER INEQUALITY IN THE UNITED STATES

In this book, we take an impassioned yet realistic look at the patterns and contexts of structured inequality for persons of color and women in U.S. society. From our perspective, social inequality is both the means and the ends of a racially stratified society. *Race* and *gender stratification* establish a graded hierarchy of superior and inferior ranks in society. Society allocates access to valued resources and opportunities according to one's placement in the social hierarchy. For example, those at the top of the social hierarchy (*whites* and *males*) have access to a larger share of social opportunity and resources than those near the bottom of the social hierarchy (*nonwhites* and *females*). The resources valued in a society are usually those that allocate privilege: material wealth, social status or social prestige, and political power.

The dynamics of a stratified system are rooted in a disproportionate distribution of valued resources and result in two culturally distinct groups of people: a culturally dominant group and a culturally subordinate group. The dominant group maintains its social position by controlling the production of valued resources, which they are able to do because they have better access to a larger share of opportunities and resources. For example, by means of property ownership, the dominant group can decide who will have access to valued resources such as jobs and home mortgages. In contrast, members of the subordinate group are unable to improve their rank within the social hierarchy because they lack access to the necessary resources.

STRUCTURED SOCIAL INEQUALITY

The term *structured social inequality* defines a social arrangement patterned socially and historically that is rooted in the ideological framework that legitimates and justifies the subordination of particular groups of people. In other words, social inequality is institutionalized. For example, one can find a record of consistent patterns of institutionalized discrimination in U.S. society that reflects a racist and sexist ideology. Because of this discrimination, U.S. society has systematically denied persons of color and women full and equal participation in major social institutions such as education, employment, health care and medicine, and politics. The discrimination and segregation experienced by persons of color and women in the U.S. educational system has resulted in a pattern of limited occupational and economic growth for each group. Thus the dynamics of discrimination and segregation have confined these populations to a subordinate position in U.S. society. Yet participation in these institutions is essential for social mobility, that is, the transition from one social position to another in the stratified system. In a sense, the subordinate position of persons of color and women in U.S. society amounts to a caste system. Closure and rigidity in rank, and institutionalization and acceptance of rigid ranks characterizes the structured social relationship of persons of color and women to U.S. society. The selections included in this book illustrate the extent to which racial, ethnic, and gender stratification in the United States is institutionalized.

STRUCTURED DISCRIMINATION

Persons of color and women in U.S. society are victims of structured discrimination. Whereas social inequality reflects the procedural nature of unequal access to resources in society, structured discrimination identifies the existence of racial, ethnic, and gender bias. Together, social inequality and structural discrimination define the sociocultural relationship of persons of color and women to society. For example, the limited access persons of color and women have to valued resources constrains their ability to alter their social position in society. In addition, because their social position is a subordinate one, persons of color and women are unable to promote their interests as either a group of individuals or as a class of individuals. As a result, persons of color and women are ignored by social institutions that control access to valued resources because they do not possess the resources required for participation within those social institutions. In the end, persons of color and women are the victims of racist and sexist ideologies that serve as the basis for an unequal distribution of access to valued resources.

Social control, then, is one dynamic in societal systems of intergroup domination and subordination. In U.S. society, the dominant group seeks to control the group life of subordinate group members through various institutional apparatuses of social control. The *legal system* is one institutional mechanism of social control in the United States. As Richard Quinney explains in *Class, State and Crime*, "the coercive force of the state, embodied in law and legal repression, is the traditional means of maintaining the social and economic interests of the dominant group."[22] The U.S. legal system maintains the social arrangement between the dominant group and subordinate groups. Because the power to define social behaviors as *crime* resides with the dominant group, any social behavior engaged in by members of subordinate groups that the dominant group perceives as a threat to their interests *is* crime. Robert Staples explains the arrangement this way:

> The ruling caste defines as those acts as crimes that fit its needs and purposes and characterizes as criminal individuals who commit certain kinds of illegal acts, while similar acts are exempted from persecution and escape public disapprobation because they are not perceived as criminal or a threat to society.[23]

RACIAL AND ETHNIC OPPRESSION

The intersection between racial ideology, racial prejudice, and structured racial inequality is *racial oppression*. Racial oppression is the cumulative product of discriminatory acts built into social structures and legitimated or sanctioned by cultural beliefs and legal codes.[24] In *Racist America*, Joe R. Feagin explains that racism is *systemic* to the social arrangement of white dominion over black people in the United States— systemic white racism is at the very core of American society. The deeply embedded racist relations of American society are produced and "reproduced" and privileging white Americans while concomitantly leaving black Americans disenfranchised. Feagin defines systemic racism as including "the complex array of antiblack practices, the unjustly gained political-economic power of whites, the continuing economic and other resource inequalities along racial lines, and the white racist ideologies and attitudes created to maintain and rationalize white privilege and power. Systemic here means that the core racist realities are manifested in each of society's major parts."[25]

THE PERSISTENCE OF INEQUALITY

The ideologies of racism and sexism remain pervasive in contemporary society because they are deeply ingrained in U.S. culture. To Mario Barrera, "racial ideologies become embodied in the thought of future generations who have no conception of the exact context in which they originated, and are thus transformed into broad-based racial prejudice even among people whose interests are not served by it."[26]

Oliver Cox adds to this viewpoint by arguing that racial prejudice has become part of our cultural heritage and that "as such both exploiter and exploited for the most part are born heirs to it."[27] Moreover, social historian Leon Litwark has noted that racism in American society remains pervasive because "new civil rights laws have failed to diminish the violence of poverty, to reallocate resources, to redistribute wealth and income and to penetrate the corporate boardrooms and federal bureaucracies."[28] These observations reinforce the notion that the prejudices associated with the ideologies of racism and sexism in contemporary American society are irrational forms of racial and gender folklore at work. In *Women of Color: Fighting Sexism and Racism*, sociologists Nijole V. Benokraitis and Joe R. Feagin remind us that *gendered racism* (the intersection between race and gender) remains deeply rooted in the core culture of the United States.[29] As a result, women of color are victimized by negative imagery in the mass media, by educational and workplace discrimination, by sexual harassment, and by gender-related violence.

SUMMARY

Social differences between persons developed during the historical maturation of the Untied States. These social differences matured as forms of social, political, educational, and economic inequality. The persistence of racial, ethnic, and gender inequality in a society ostensibly committed to individual rights is a direct challenge to the historical romanticism surrounding the arrival of immigrants to the United States seeking freedom and opportunity. Race, ethnicity, and gender have played a significant historical role in determining the individual rights of certain racial and ethnic groups in U.S. society.

ENDNOTES

1. Derrick Bell Jr., *Faces at the Bottom of the Well: The Permanence of Racism* (New York: Basic Books, 1992).
2. Michael Olivas, "The Chronicles, My Grandfather's Stories, and Immigration Law: The Slave Traders Chronicle as Racial History," in Richard Delgado and Jean Stephancic, eds., *Critical Race Theory: The Cutting Edge* (Philadelphia: Temple University Press, 2000).
3. Robert Robbins, "Self-Determination and Subordination: The Past, Present, and Future of American Indian Governance," in M. Annette Jaimes, ed., *The State of Native Americans: Genocide, Colonization, and Persistence* (Boston: South End Press, 1992).
4. Gary Morris, "International Law and Politics: Toward a Right to Self-Determination for Indigenous Peoples," in M. Annette Jaimes, ed., *The State of Native Americans: Genocide, Colonization, and Persistence* (Boston: South End Press, 1992).
5. Eric Kades, "The Dark Side of Efficiency: *Johnson v. M'Intosh* and the Expropriation of Indian Lands," *University of Pennsylvania Law Review*, 148 (2000): 1065–1190.
6. Ibid. According to Kades, the defendant in the case, William McIntosh, spelled and signed his last name with a "c," but the Supreme Court used an apostrophe.
7. *Johnson v. McIntosh*, 21 U.S. (8 Wheat.) 543 (1853), in John E. Cribbet, Corwin W. Johnson, Roger W. Findley, and Ernest E. Smith, eds., *Property: Cases and Materials*, 7th ed. (New York: The Foundation Press, 1996). See also Note, "Indian Title: The Rights of American Natives in Land They Have Occupied Since Time Immemorial," *Columbia Law Review*, 75 (1975): 655; Eric Kades, "History and Interpretation of the Great Case of *Johnson v. M'Intosh*," *Law and History Review*, 19 (2001): 67–116.
8. *Tee-Hit-Ton Indians v. United States*, 348 U.S. 272 (1954).

9. Felix Cohen, "Original Indian Title," *Minnesota Law Review*, 32 (1947): 34.

10. Ibid.

11. Kades, "The Dark Side of Efficiency."

12. Joe R. Feagin and Clairece Booher Feagin, *Racial and Ethnic Groups* (Englewood Cliffs, NJ: Prentice Hall, 1993), p. 4. See also William Wiecek, *The Sources of Antislavery Constitutionalism in America, 1760–1848* (1977), cited in A. Leon Higginbotham Jr., *Shades of Freedom: Racial Politics and Presumptions of the American Legal Process* (New York: Oxford University Press, 1996), pp. 220–221.

13. Feagin and Feagin, *Racial and Ethnic Groups*.

14. Oliver Fiss, "Racial Discrimination," in Leonard W. Levy, Kenneth L. Karst, and Dennis J. Mahoney, eds., *Civil Rights and Equality* (New York: Macmillan, 1986).

15. J. Milton Yinger, "Ethnicity," *Annual Review of Sociology*, 11 (1985): 151–180.

16. Richard Delgado and Jean Stephanic, "Images of the Outsider in American Law and Culture: Can Free Expression Remedy Systemic Social Ills," *Cornell Law Review*, 77 (1992): 1258–1291.

17. Charles Valentine, *Culture and Poverty: Critique and Counterproposals* (Chicago: University of Chicago Press, 1968); William Ryan, *Blaming the Victim* (New York: Vintage Press, 1968); Caroline Hodges Persell, "Genetic and Cultural Deficit Theories: Two Sides of the Same Racist Coin," *Journal of Black Studies*, 12 (1981): 19–37.

18. Charles Arce, "A Reconsideration of Chicano Culture and Identity," *Daedalus*, 110 (1981): 177.

19. *The Civil Rights Coalition for the 21st Century*, "New Report Explores Backlash of Hate, Intolerance Six Months After Terrorist Attacks" (March 11, 2002), http://www.civilrights.org/issues/hate/details.cfm?id=7753.

20. Geneive Abdo, "Muslims Say Fellow Americans Are Lashing Out," *Chicago Tribune*, July 15, 2004, p. 14; Peter Slevin, "Arab Americans Report Abuse," *Washington Post*, July 29, 2004, p. A05.

21. Jonathan K. Stubbs, "The Bottom Rung of America's Race Ladder: After the September 11 Catastrophe Are American Muslims Becoming America's New N. . . . S?" *Journal of Law and Religion*, 19 (2004): 115–151.

22. Richard Quinney, *Class, State and Crime: On the Theory and Practice of Criminal Justice* (New York: Longman, 1977).

23. Robert Staples, "White Racism, Black Crime and American Justice: An Application of the Colonial Model to Explain Crime and Race," *Phylon* 36 (1975): 14–22.

24. Jonathan H. Turner, Royce Singleton Jr., and David Musick, *Oppression: A Socio-History of Black-White Relations in America* (Chicago: Nelson-Hall, 1984).

25. Joe R. Feagin, *Racist America: Roots, Current Realities, and Future Aspirations* (New York: Routledge, 2001), p. 6.

26. Mario Barrera, *Race and Class in the Southwest* (South Bend, IN: University of Notre Dame, 1979).

27. Oliver Cox, *Caste, Class and Race: A Study in Social Dynamics* (New York: Doubleday, 1948).

28. Leon Litwack, "Professor Seeks Revolution of Values," *The University of California Clip Sheet* 62 (May 1987), p. 21.

29. Nijole V. Benokraitis and Joe R. Feagin, "Women of Color: Fighting Sexism and Racism," in *Modern Sexism, Blatant, Subtle, and Covert Discrimination*, 2nd ed. (Englewood Cliffs, NJ: Prentice Hall, 1995).

The Earliest Perceptions: The Right of the Discoverer [Conqueror]

Johnson v. McIntosh
Supreme Court of the United States Decided: February 28, 1823 21 U.S. (8 Wheat.) 543

But the tribes of Indians inhabiting this country were fierce savages, whose occupation was war, and whose subsistence was drawn chiefly from the forest. To leave them in possession of their country, was to leave the country a wilderness; to govern them as a distinct people, was impossible, because they were as brave and as high-spirited as they were fierce, and were ready to repel by arms every attempt on their independence.

Mr. Chief Justice MARSHALL delivered the opinion of the Court. The plaintiffs in this cause claim the land, in their declaration mentioned, under two grants, purporting to be made, the first in 1773, and the last in 1775, by the chiefs of certain Indian tribes, constituting the Illinois and the Piankeshaw nations; and the question is, whether this title can be recognised in the Courts of the United States? The facts, as stated in the case agreed, show the authority of the chiefs who executed this conveyance, so far as it could be given by their own people; and likewise show, that the particular tribes for whom these chiefs acted were in rightful possession of the land they sold. The inquiry, therefore, is, in a great measure, confined to the power of Indians to give, and of private individuals to receive, a title which can be sustained in the Courts of this country.

As the right of society, to prescribe those rules by which property may be acquired and preserved is not, and cannot be drawn into question; as the title to lands, especially, is and must be admitted to depend entirely on the law of the nation in which they lie; it will be necessary, in pursuing this inquiry, to examine, not singly those principles of abstract justice, which the Creator of all things has impressed on the mind of his creature man, and which are admitted to regulate, in a great degree, the rights of civilized nations, whose perfect independence is acknowledged; but those principles also which our own government has adopted in the particular case, and given us as the rule for our decision.

On the discovery of this immense continent, the great nations of Europe were eager

Source: *Johnson v. McIntosh*, 21 U.S. (8 Wheat.) 543.

to appropriate to themselves so much of it as they could respectively acquire. Its vast extent offered and ample field to the ambition and enterprise of all; and the character and religion of its inhabitants afforded an apology for considering them as a people over whom the superior genius of Europe might claim an ascendancy. The potentates of the old world found no difficulty in convincing themselves that they made ample compensation to the inhabitants of the new, by bestowing on them civilization and Christianity, in exchange for unlimited independence. But, as they were all in pursuit of nearly the same object, it was necessary, in order to avoid conflicting settlements, and consequent war with each other, to establish a principle, which all should acknowledge as the law by which the right of acquisition, which they all asserted, should be regulated as between themselves. This principle was, that discovery gave title to the government by whose subjects, or by whose authority, it was made, against all other European governments, which title might be consummated by possession. The exclusion of all other Europeans, necessarily gave to the nation making the discovery the sole right of acquiring the soil from the natives, and establishing settlements upon it. It was a right with which no Europeans could interfere. It was a right which all asserted for themselves, and to the assertion of which, by others, all assented. Those relations which were to exist between the discoverer and the natives, were to be regulated by themselves. The rights thus acquired being exclusive, no other power could interpose between them.

In the establishment of these relations, the rights of the original inhabitants were, in no instance, entirely disregarded; but were necessarily, to a considerable extent, impaired. They were admitted to be the rightful occupants of the soil, with a legal as well as just claim to retain possession of it, and to use it according to their own discretion; but their rights to complete sovereignty, as independent nations, were necessarily diminished, and their power to dispose of the soil at their own will, to whomsoever they pleased, was denied by the original fundamental principle, that discovery gave exclusive title to those who made it.

While the different nations of Europe respected the right of the natives, as occupants, they asserted the ultimate dominion to be in themselves; and claimed and exercised, as a consequence of this ultimate dominion, a power to grant the soil, while yet in possession of the natives. These grants have been understood by all, to convey a title to the grantees, subject only to the Indian right of occupancy. The history of America, from its discovery to the present day, proves, we think, the universal recognition of these principles. . . .

No one of the powers of Europe gave its full assent to this principle, more unequivocally than England. The documents upon this subject are ample and complete. So early as the year 1496, her monarch granted a commission to the Cabots, to discover countries then unknown to Christian people, and to take possession of them in the name of the king of England. Two years afterwards, Cabot proceeded on this voyage, and discovered the continent of North America, along which he sailed as far south as Virginia. To this discovery the English trace their title. In this first effort made by the English government to acquire territory on this continent, we perceive a complete recognition of the principle which has been mentioned. The right of discovery given by this commission, is confined to countries "then unknown to all Christian people;" and of these countries Cabot was empowered to take possession in the name of the king of England. Thus asserting a right to take possession, notwithstanding the occupancy of the natives, who were heathens, and, at the same time, admitting the prior title of any Christian people who may have made a previous discovery. The same principle continued to be recognised. . . .

Thus has our whole country been granted by the crown while in the occupation of the

Indians. These grants purport to convey the soil as well as the right of dominion to the grantees. In those governments which were denominated royal, where the right to the soil was not vested in individuals, but remained in the crown, or was vested in the colonial government, the king claimed and exercised the right of granting lands, and of dismembering the government at his will. . . .

These various patents cannot be considered as nullities; nor can they be limited to a mere grant of the powers of government. A charter intended to convey political power only, would never contain words expressly granting the land, the soil, and the waters. Some of them purport to convey the soil alone; and in those cases in which the powers of government, as well as the soil, are conveyed to individuals, the crown has always acknowledged itself to be bound by the grant. Though the power to dismember regal governments was asserted and exercised, the power to dismember proprietary governments was not claimed; and, in some instances, even after the powers of government were revested in the crown, the title of the proprietors to the soil was respected. . . .

Further proofs of the extent to which this principle has been recognised, will be found in the history of the wars, negotiations, and treaties, which the different nations, claiming territory in America, have carried on, and held with each other. . . . Thus, all the nations of Europe, who have acquired territory on this continent, have asserted in themselves, and have recognised in others, the exclusive right of the discoverer to appropriate the lands occupied by the Indians. Have the American States rejected or adopted this principle?

By the treaty which concluded the war of our revolution, Great Britain relinquished all claim, not only to the government, but to the "propriety and territorial rights of the United States," whose boundaries were fixed in the second article. By this treaty, the powers of government, and the right to soil, which had previously been in Great Britain, passed definitively to these States. We had before taken possession of them, by declaring independence; but neither the declaration of independence, nor the treaty confirming it, could give us more than that which we before possessed, or to which Great Britain was before entitled. It has never been doubted, that either the United States, or the several States, had a clear title to all the lands within the boundary lines described in the treaty, subject only to the Indian right of occupancy, and that the exclusive power to extinguish that right, was vested in that government which might constitutionally exercise it. . . .

The magnificent purchase of Louisiana, was the purchase from France of a country almost entirely occupied by numerous tribes of Indians, who are in fact independent. Yet, any attempt of others to intrude into that country, would be considered as an aggression which would justify war. Our late acquisitions from Spain are of the same character; and the negotiations which preceded those acquisitions, recognise and elucidate the principle which has been received as the foundation of all European title in America.

The United States, then, have unequivocally acceded to that great and broad rule by which its civilized inhabitants now hold this country. They hold, and assert in themselves, the title by which it was acquired. They maintain, as all others have maintained, that discovery gave an exclusive right to extinguish the Indian title of occupancy, either by purchase or by conquest; and gave also a right to such a degree of sovereignty, as the circumstances of the people would allow them to exercise. The power now possessed by the government of the United States to grant lands, resided, while we were colonies, in the crown, or its grantees. The validity of the titles given by either has never been questioned in our Courts. It has been exercised uniformly over territory in possession of the Indians. The existence of this power must negative the existence of any right which may conflict with, and control it. An absolute title to lands cannot exist, at the same time, in different persons, or in different governments. An absolute, must be an exclusive title, or at least a title which excludes all others not compatible with it. All our institutions recognise the absolute title of the crown, subject only to the Indian right of occupancy, and recognise the absolute title of the crown to extinguish that right. This is incompatible with an absolute and complete title in the Indians.

We will not enter into the controversy, whether agriculturists, merchants, and manufacturers, have a right, on abstract principles, to expel hunters from the territory they possess, or to contract their limits. Conquest gives a title which the Courts of the conqueror cannot deny, whatever the private and speculative opinions of individuals may be, respecting the original justice of the claim which has been successfully asserted. The British government, which was then our government, and whose rights have passed to the United States, asserted a title to all the lands occupied by Indians, within the chartered limits of the British colonies. It asserted also a limited sovereignty over them, and the exclusive right of extinguishing the title which occupancy gave to them. These claims have been maintained and established as far west as the river Mississippi, by the sword. The title to a vast portion of the lands we now hold, originates in them. It is not for the Courts of this country to question the validity of this title, or to sustain one which is incompatible with it.

Although we do not mean to engage in the defense of those principles which Europeans have applied to Indian title, they may, we think, find some excuse, if not justification, in the character and habits of the people whose rights have been wrested from them. The title by conquest is acquired and maintained by force. The conqueror prescribes its limits. Humanity, however, acting on public opinion, has established, as a general rule, that the conquered shall not be wantonly oppressed, and that their condition shall remain as

eligible as is compatible with the objects of the conquest. Most usually, they are incorporated with the victorious nation, and become subjects or citizens of the government with which they are connected. The new and old members of the society mingle with each other; the distinction between them is gradually lost, and they make one people. Where this incorporation is practicable, humanity demands, and a wise policy requires, that the rights of the conquered to property should remain unimpaired; that the new subjects should be governed as equitably as the old, and that confidence in their security should gradually banish the painful sense of being separated from their ancient connections, and united by force to strangers. When the conquest is complete, and the conquered inhabitants can be blended with the conquerors, or safely governed as a distinct people, public opinion, which not even the conqueror can disregard, imposes these restraints upon him; and he cannot neglect them without injury to his fame, and hazard to his power.

But the tribes of Indians inhabiting this country were fierce savages, whose occupation was war, and whose subsistence was drawn chiefly from the forest. To leave them in possession of their country, was to leave the country a wilderness; to govern them as a distinct people, was impossible, because they were as brave and as high spirited as they were fierce, and were ready to repel by arms every attempt on their independence. What was the inevitable consequence of this state of things? The Europeans were under the necessity either of abandoning the country, and relinquishing their pompous claims to it, or of enforcing those claims by the sword, and by the adoption of principles adapted to the condition of a people with whom it was impossible to mix, and who could not be governed as a distinct society, or of remaining in their neighborhood, and exposing themselves and their families to the perpetual hazard of being massacred. Frequent and bloody wars, in which the whites were not always the aggressors, unavoidably ensued. European policy, numbers, and skill, prevailed. As the white population advanced, that of the Indians necessarily receded. The country in the immediate neighborhood of agriculturists became unfit for them. The game fled into thicker and more unbroken forests, and the Indians followed. The soil, to which the crown originally claimed title, being no longer occupied by its ancient inhabitants, was parceled out according to the will of the sovereign power, and taken possession of by persons who claimed immediately from the crown, or mediately, through its grantees or deputies.

That law which regulates, and ought to regulate in general, the relations between the conqueror and conquered, was incapable of application to a people under such circumstances. The resort to some new and different rule, better adapted to the actual state of things, was unavoidable. Every rule which can be suggested will be found to be attended with great difficulty. However extravagant the pretension of converting the discovery of an inhabited country into conquest may appear; if the principle has been asserted in the first instance, and afterwards sustained; if a country has been acquired and held under it; if the property of the great mass of the community originates in it, it becomes the law of the land, and cannot be questioned. So, too, with respect to the concomitant principle, that the Indian inhabitants are to be considered merely as occupants, to be protected, indeed, while in peace, in the possession of their lands, but to be deemed incapable of transferring the absolute title to others. However this restriction may be opposed to natural right, and to the usages of civilized nations, yet, if it be indispensable to that system under which the country has been settled, and be adapted to the actual condition of the two people, it may, perhaps, be supported by reason, and certainly cannot be rejected by Courts of justice. . . .

The absolute ultimate title has been considered as acquired by discovery, subject only to the Indian title of occupancy, which title the discoverers possessed the exclusive right of acquiring. Such a right is no more incompatible with a seisin in fee, than a lease for years, and might as effectually bar an ejectment. . . .

It has never been contended, that the Indian title amounted to nothing. Their right of possession has never been questioned. The claim of government extends to the complete ultimate title, charged with this right of possession, and to the exclusive power of acquiring that right. The object of the crown was to settle the seacoast of America; and when a portion of it was settled, without violating the rights of others, by persons professing their loyalty, and soliciting the royal sanction of an act, the consequences of which were ascertained to be beneficial, it would have been as unwise as ungracious to expel them from their habitations, because they had obtained the Indian title otherwise than through the agency of government. The very grant of a charter is an assertion of the title of the crown, and its words convey the same idea. The country granted, is said to be "our island called Rhode-Island;" and the charter contains an actual grant of the soil, as well as of the powers of government. . . .

After bestowing on this subject a degree of attention which was more required by the magnitude of the interest in litigation, and the able and elaborate arguments of the bar, than by its intrinsic difficulty, the Court is decidedly of opinion, that the plaintiffs do not exhibit a title which can be sustained in the Courts of the United States; and that there is no error in the judgment which was rendered against them in the District Court of Illinois.

Judgment affirmed, with costs.

STUDY QUESTION

Do you think that Chief Justice John Marshall's characterization of Native Americans in *Johnson v. McIntosh* as "high-spirited" and "fierce savages" legitimated his argument?

The Report of the National Advisory Commission on Civil Disorders: A Comment

Louis L. Knowles and Kenneth Prewitt

The [racist] policy can be understood only when we are willing to take a hard look at the continuing and irrefutable racist consequences of the major institutions of American life.

The contemporary document perhaps most indicative of the ideology of official America is the influential "Kerner Commission Report." This is an important work. It is being widely read, and we cite from it frequently in the pages to follow. However, since our analysis operates from a premise fundamentally different from the Report, a few comments at this point will help introduce the substantive chapters to follow.

The Report asks: "Why Did It Happen?" A painful truth is then recorded: "White racism is essentially responsible for the explosive mixture which has been accumulating in our cities since the end of World War II." Unfortunately, the Report too quickly leaves this truth and emphasizes the familiar list of "conditions" of "Negro unrest." Paraded before the reader are observations about the frustrated hopes of Negroes, the "belief" among Negroes that there is police brutality, the high unemployment in the ghetto, the weak family structure

and social disorganization in the Negro community, and so on.

It is the immediate conditions giving rise to civil disorders which the Report stresses, not the *causes behind the conditions.* Perhaps what is needed is a National Advisory Commission on White Racism. If a group of men sets out to investigate "civil disorders," their categories of analysis are fixed and, from our perspective, parochial. In spite of their admission that "white institutions created [the ghetto], white institutions maintain it, and white society condones it," the categories with which the commission operated screened out the responsibility of white institutions and pushed the commission back to the familiar account of "black pathology."

In the important section "What Can Be Done," this fault is even more clearly seen. Certainly it is true that much accumulated frustration would be relieved if the sweeping recommendations concerning administration

---

Source: "The Report of the National Advisory Commission on Civil Disorders," in Institutional Racism in America, Louis L. Knowles and Kenneth Prewitt, eds. (Englewood Cliffs, NJ: Prentice-Hall, 1969).

of justice, police and community relations, housing, unemployment and underemployment, welfare thinking, and so forth were implemented. The Report merits the closest attention for its statement that issues of race and poverty must receive the highest national priority, and for its further argument that what is needed is a massive commitment by all segments of society. What disappoints the reader is that the section "What Can Be Done" only accentuates the shortsightedness of the section "Why Did It Happen." The recommendations are directed at ghetto conditions and *not* at the white structures and practices which are responsible for those conditions. Thus, while it is true that improved communication between the ghetto and city hall might defuse the pressures building up in the black community, the issue is not "better communication" but "full representation." Black people should not have to communicate with city hall; they should be represented at city hall.

The shallowness of the Report as social analysis is again reflected in its discussion of black protest movements. The Report does not uncover a critical social dynamic: militancy is first of all a response to white resistance and control, not its cause. The naiveté of the Report, and its ultimate paternalism, is nowhere better shown than in its attempt to draw parallels between the black power movement and the philosophy of Booker T. Washington. Accommodation stood at the center of Washington's thought; accommodation is explicitly and forcefully rejected by the ideology symbolized in the "black power" slogan. As Carmichael and Hamilton wrote, "Black people in the United States must raise hard questions which challenge the very nature of the society itself: its longstanding values, beliefs, and institutions."

What we miss in the Kerner Commission Report is the capacity to ask "hard questions." The Commission members are to be saluted for their instinct that "white racism" is the culprit. They are to be faulted for their inability or unwillingness to pursue this theme. We do not have access to the professional resources available to the Kerner Commission, and therefore our study lacks the statistical detail of the national report. But we have tried to push the analysis of the race question into areas where the Report dared not tread: into the heart of institutional, which is to say white, America.

A new realization is dawning in white America. Under the insistent prodding of articulate blacks plus a few unusual whites, the so-called "Negro Problem" is being redefined. Just possibly the racial sickness in our society is not, as we have so long assumed, rooted in the black and presumably "pathological" subculture but in the white and presumably "healthy" dominant culture. If indeed it turns out that "the problem" is finally and deeply a white problem, the solution will have to be found in a restructured white society. Institutional racism is a term which describes practices in the United States nearly as old as the nation itself. The term, however, appears to be of recent coinage, possibly first used by Stokely Carmichael and Charles V. Hamilton in their widely read book, *Black Power*. It is our goal to work with this term until we feel we have come to some full understanding of it, and to present an analysis of specific practices appropriately defined as "institutionally racist." Our strategy is to be self-consciously pragmatic. That is, we ask not what the motive of the individuals might be; rather we look at the consequences of the institutions they have created.

TOWARD A DEFINITION

The murder by KKK members and law enforcement officials of three civil rights workers in Mississippi was an act of individual racism. That the sovereign state of Mississippi refused to indict the killers was institutional racism. The individual act by racist bigots went unpunished in Mississippi because of policies, precedents, and practices that are an integral part of that state's legal institutions. A store clerk who suspects that black children in his store are there to steal candy but white children are there to purchase candy, and who treats the children differently, the blacks as probable delinquents and the whites as probable customers, also illustrates individual racism. Unlike the Mississippi murderers, the store clerk is not a bigot and may not even consider himself prejudiced, but his behavior is shaped by racial stereotypes 'which have been part of his unconscious since childhood. A university admissions policy which provides for entrance only to students who score high on tests designed primarily for white suburban high schools necessarily excludes black ghetto-educated students. Unlike the legal policies of Mississippi, the university admission criteria are not intended to be racist, but the university is pursuing a course which perpetuates institutional racism. The difference, then, between individual and institutional racism is not a difference in intent or of visibility. Both the individual act of racism and the racist institutional policy may occur without the presence of conscious bigotry, and both may be masked intentionally or innocently.

In an attempt to understand "institutional racism" it is best to consider first what institutions and not what they do in a society. Institutions are fairly stable social arrangements and practices through which collective actions are taken. Medical institutions, for instance, marshal talents and resources of society so that health care can be provided. Medical institutions include hospitals, research labs, and clinics, as well as organizations of medical people such as doctors and nurses. The health of all of us is affected by general medical policies and by established practices and ethics. Business and labor, for example, determine what is to be produced, how it is to be produced, and by whom and on whose behalf products will be created. Public and private schools determine what is considered knowledge, how it is to be transmitted to new generations, and who will do the teaching. Legal and political institutions determine what laws regulate our lives, how and by whom they are enforced, and who will be prosecuted for which violations.

Institutions have great power: to reward and penalize. They reward by providing career opportunities for some people and foreclosing them for others. They reward as well by the way social goods and services are distributed by deciding who receives training and skills, medical care, formal education, political influence, moral support and self-respect, productive employment, fair treatment by the law, decent housing, self-confidence, and the promise of a secure future for self and children. No society will distribute social benefits in a perfectly equitable way. But no society need use race as a criterion to determine who will be rewarded and who punished. Any nation that permits race to affect the distribution of benefits from social policies is racist.

It is our thesis that institutional racism is deeply embedded in American society. Slavery was only the earliest and most blatant practice. Political, economic, educational, and religious policies cooperated with slaveholders to "keep the nigger in his place." Emancipation changed little. Jim Crow laws as well as residential and employment discrimination guaranteed that black citizens remained under the control of white citizens. Second-class citizenship quickly became a social fact as well as a legal status. Overt institutional racism was widely practiced throughout American society at least until World War II.

With desegregation in the armed forces and the passage of various civil rights bills, institutional racism no longer has the status of law. It is perpetuated nonetheless, sometimes by frightened and bigoted individuals, sometimes by good citizens merely carrying on "business as usual," and sometimes by well-intentioned but naive reformers. An attack on institutional racism is clearly the next task for Americans, white and black, who hope to obtain for their children a society less tense and more just than the one of the mid-1960's. It is no easy task. Individual, overt racist acts, such as the shotgun slaying of civil rights workers, are visible. Techniques of crime detection can be used to apprehend guilty parties, and, in theory, due process of law will punish them. To detect institutional racism, especially when it is unintentional or when it is disguised, is a very different task. And even when institutional racism is detected, it is seldom clear who is at fault. How can we say who is responsible for residential segregation, for poor education in ghetto schools, for extraordinarily high unemployment among black men, for racial stereotypes in history textbooks, for the concentration of political power in white society?

Our analysis begins with attention to ideological patterns in American society which historically and presently sustain practices appropriately labeled "institutionally racist." We then turn attention to the procedures of dominant American institutions: educational, economic, political, legal, and medical. It is as a result of practices within these institutions that black citizens in America are consistently penalized for reasons of color.

Quite obviously the social arrangements which fix unequal opportunities for black and white citizens can be traced back through American history—farther back, as a matter of fact, than even the beginning of slavery. Our purpose is not to rewrite American history, although that needs to be done. Rather our purpose in this initial chapter is to point out the historical roots of institutional racism by examining the ideology used to justify it. In understanding how deeply racist practices are embedded in the American experience and values, we can come to a fuller understanding of how contemporary social institutions have adapted to their heritage.

HISTORY AND IDEOLOGY

Some form of white supremacy, both as ideology and institutional arrangement, existed from the first day English immigrants, seeking freedom from religious intolerance, arrived on the North American continent. From the beginning, the early colonizers apparently considered themselves culturally superior to the natives they encountered. This sense of superiority over the Indians, which was fostered by the religious ideology they carried to the new land, found its expression in the self-proclaimed mission to civilize and Christianize—a mission which was to find its ultimate expression in ideas of a "manifest destiny" and a "white man's burden."

The early colonists were a deeply religious people. The church was the dominant social institution of their time, and the religious doctrines brought from England strongly influenced their contacts with the native Indians. The goals of the colonists were stated clearly:

> Principal and Maine Ends [of the Virginia colony] . . . ware first to preach and baptize into Christian Religion and by propagation of the Gospell, to recover out of the arms of the Divell, a number of poore and miserable soules, wrapt up unto death, in almost invincible ignorance . . . and to add our myte to the Treasury of Heaven.

Ignorance about the white man's God was sufficient proof in itself of the inferiority of the Indian and, consequently, of the superiority of the white civilization.

The mission impulse was doomed to failure. A shortage of missionaries and an unexpected resistance on the part of the Indian (who was less sure that the white man's ways were inherently superior) led to the dismantling of the few programs aimed at Christianization. It became clear that conquering was, on balance, less expensive and more efficient than "civilizing."

Thus began an extended process of genocide, giving rise to such aphorisms as "The only good Indian is a dead Indian." It was at this time that the ideology of white supremacy on the North American continent took hold. Since Indians were capable of reaching only the stage of "savage," they should not be allowed to impede the forward (westward, to be exact) progress of white civilization. The Church quickly acquiesced in this redefinition of the situation. The disappearance of the nonwhite race in the path of expansionist policies was widely interpreted as God's will. As one student of America's history has written, "It apparently never seriously occurred to [spokesmen for Christianity] that where they saw the mysterious law of God in the disappearance of the nonwhite races before the advancing Anglo-Saxon, a disappearance which apparently occurred without anyone's willing it or doing anything to bring it about, the actual process was a brutal one of oppression, dispossession, and even extermination."

In short, what began as a movement to "civilize and Christianize" the indigenous native population was converted into a racist force, accompanied, as always, by a justificatory ideology. In retrospect, the result is hardly surprising. The English colonists operated from a premise which has continued to have a strong impact on American thought: the Anglo-Saxon race is culturally and religiously superior; neither the validity nor the integrity of alien cultures can be recognized. (The Indian culture, though native to the land, was considered the alien one.) When it became clear that Indians could not be "saved," the settlers concluded that the race itself was inferior. This belief was strengthened by such racist theories as the Teutonic Theory of Origins, which pointed out the superiority of the Anglo-Saxons. The institution of slavery and its accompanying justification would seem to have been products of the same mentality.

It has, of course, been the white man's relationship with the black man which has led to the most powerful expressions of institutional racism in the society. This is a history which hardly needs retelling, although it might be instructive to consider how closely related was the justification of Indian extermination to that of black slavery. It was the heathenism or savagery, so-called, of the African, just as of the Indian, which became the early rationale for enslavement. A particularly ingenious version of the rationale is best known under the popular label "Social Darwinism."

The Social Darwinian theory of evolution greatly influenced social thought, hence social institutions, in nineteenth-century America. Social Darwinists extended the concept of biological evolution in the development of man to a concept of evolution in development of societies and civilizations. The nature of a society or nation or race was presumed to be the product of natural evolutionary forces. The evolutionary process was characterized by struggle and conflict in which the "stronger, more advanced, and more civilized" would naturally triumph over the "inferior, weaker, backward, and uncivilized" peoples.

> The idea of natural selection was translated to a struggle between individual members of a society; between members of classes of society, between different nations, and between different races. This conflict, far from being an evil thing, was nature's indispensable method of producing superior men, superior nations, and superior races.

Such phrases as "the struggle for existence" and "the survival of the fittest" became *lingua franca,* and white Americans had a full-blown ideology to explain their treatment of the "inferior race."

The contemporary expression of Social Darwinian thinking is less blatant but essentially the same as the arguments used in the nineteenth century. The poverty and degradation of the nonwhite races in the United States are thought to be the result of an innate lack of ability rather than anything white society has done. Thus a long line of argument reaches its most recent expression in the now famous "Moynihan Report": the focal point of the race problem is to be found in the pathology of black society.

Social Darwinism was buttressed with two other ideas widely accepted in nineteenth century America: manifest destiny and white man's burden. Briefly stated, manifest destiny was simply the idea that white Americans were destined, either by natural forces or by Divine Right, to control at least the North American continent and, in many versions of the theory, a much greater share of the earth's surface. Many churchmen supported the idea that such expansion was the will of God. The impact of this belief with respect to the Indians has already been noted. Let it suffice to say that manifest destiny helped provide the moral and theological justification for genocide. The belief that American expansion was a natural process was rooted in Social Darwinism. Expansionism was simply the natural growth process of a superior nation. This deterministic argument enjoyed wide popularity. Even those who were not comfortable with the overt racism of the expansionist argument were able to cooperate in policies of "liberation" in Cuba and the Philippines by emphasizing the evils of Spanish control. Many, however, felt no need to camouflage their racism. Albert J. Beveridge, Senator from Indiana, stated his position clearly:

> The American Republic is a part of the movement of a race-the most masterful race of history-and race movements are not to be stayed by the hand of man. They are mighty answers to Divine commands. Their leaders are not only statesmen of peoples-they are prophets of God. The inherent tendencies of a race are its highest law. They precede and survive all statutes, all constitutions. . . . The sovereign tendencies of our race are organization and government.

In any case, if racism was not invoked as a justification for imperialist expansion in the first place, it subsequently became a justification for continued American control of the newly "acquired" territories. This was particularly true in the Philippines. "The control of one country by another and the denial of rights or citizenship to the Filipinos were difficult ideas to reconcile with the Declaration of Independence and with American institutions. In order to make these opposing ideas of government compatible at all, the proponents of the acquisition of the Philippines were forced to rely heavily on race theories."

An argument commonly expressed was that the Filipinos were simply incapable of self-government. "'The Declaration of Independence,' stated Beveridge, 'applies only to peoples capable of self-government. Otherwise, how dared we administer the affairs of the Indians? How dare we continue to govern them today?' 'The decision, therefore, as to who was capable of self-government and who was not so capable was left to the United States Government. The criteria were usually explicitly racist, as it was simply assumed that whites, at least Anglo Saxons, had the "gift" of being able to govern themselves while the inferior nonwhite peoples were not so endowed.

The ideology of imperialist expansion had an easily foreseeable impact on the domestic race situation. As Ronald Segal points out in *The Race War,*

> Both North and South saw and accepted the implications. What was sauce for the Philippines, for Hawaii and Cuba, was sauce for the Southern Negro. If the stronger and cleverer race is free to impose its will upon "new-caught sullen peoples" on the other side of the glove, why not in South Carolina and Mississippi? asked the Atlantic Monthly. "No Republican leader, "proclaimed Senator Tillman of South Carolina,". . . will now dare to wave the bloody shirt and preach a crusade against the South's treatment of the Negro. The North has a bloody shirt of its own. Many thousands of them have been made into shrouds for murdered Filipinos, done to death because they were fighting for liberty. "Throughout the United States doctrines of racial superiority received the assent of influential politicians and noted academics. The very rationalizations

that had eased the conscience of the slave trade now provided the sanction for imperial expansion.

Another component of the ideology which has nurtured racist policies is that of "the white man's burden." This phrase comes from the title of a poem by Rudyard Kipling, which appeared in the United States in 1899. Whatever Kipling himself may have wished to convey, Americans soon popularized and adopted the concept as an encouragement for accepting the responsibility of looking after the affairs of the darker races. This notion of the "white man's burden" was that the white race, particularly Anglo-Saxons of Britain and America, should accept the (Christian) responsibility for helping the poor colored masses to find a better way of life.

It should be clear that this notion is no less racist than others previously mentioned. Behind the attitude lies the assumption of white supremacy. In exhorting Americans to follow British policy in this regard, the philosopher Josiah Royce stated the assumption clearly.

> The Englishman, in his official and governmental dealings with backward peoples, has a great way of being superior without very often publicly saying that he is superior. You well know that in dealing, as an individual, with other individuals, trouble is seldom made by the fact that you are actually superior to another man in any respect. The trouble comes when you tell the other man, too stridently, that you are his superior. Be my superior, quietly, simply showing your superiority in your deeds, and very likely I shall love you for the very fact of your superiority. For we all love our leaders. But tell me I am your inferior, and then perhaps I may grow boyish, and may throw stones. Well, it is so with the races. Grant then that yours is the superior race. Then you can say little about the subject in your public dealings with the backward race. Superiority is best shown by good deeds and by few boasts.

Both manifest destiny and the idea of a white man's burden, in disguised forms, continue to shape white America's values and policies. Manifest destiny has done much to stimulate the modern day myth that colored peoples are generally incapable of self-government. There are whites who continue to believe that black Afro-Americans are not ready to govern themselves. At best, blacks must first be "properly trained." Of course, this belief influences our relations with non-whites in other areas of the world as well.

The authors have found the concept of manifest destiny helpful in analyzing white response to "black power." Black power is based on the belief that black people in America are capable of governing and controlling their own communities. White rejection of black power reflects, in part, the widely accepted white myth that blacks are incapable of self-government and must be controlled and governed by whites. Many whites apparently still share with Albert Beveridge the belief that "organization and government" are among the "sovereign tendencies of our race."

The belief in a "white man's burden" also has its modern-day counterpart, particularly in the attitudes and practices of so-called "white liberals" busily trying to solve "the Negro problem." The liberal often bears a strong sense of responsibility for helping the Negro find a better life. He generally characterizes the Negro as "disadvantaged," "unfortunate," or "culturally deprived." The liberal generally feels superior to the black man, although he is less likely to publicly state his sense of superiority. He may not even recognize his own racist sentiments. In any case, much like Josiah Royce, he senses that "superiority is best shown by good deeds and by few boasts." Liberal paternalism is reflected not only in individual attitudes but in the procedures and policies of institutions such as the welfare system and most "war on poverty" efforts.

It is obvious that recent reports and action plans carry on a traditional, if diversionary, view that has long been acceptable to most white Americans: that it is not white institutions but a few bigots plus the deprived status of Negroes that cause racial tension. Such a view is mythical. . . . We are not content with "explanations" of white-black relations that are apolitical, that would reduce the causes of racial tension to the level of psychological and personal factors. Three hundred years of American history cannot be encapsulated so easily. To ignore the network of institutional controls through which social benefits are allocated may be reassuring, but it is also bad social history. America is and has long been a racist nation, because it has and has long had a racist policy. This policy is not to be understood by listening to the proclamations of intent by leading citizens and government officials; nor is it to be understood by reading off a list of compensatory programs in business, education, and welfare. The policy can be understood only when we are willing to take a hard look at the continuing and irrefutable racist consequences of the major institutions in American life. The policy will be changed when we are willing to start the difficult task of remaking our institutions.

STUDY QUESTION

How did social Darwinism influence nineteenth-century American institutions, according to Knowles and Prewitt?

Systemic Racism:
A Comprehensive Perspective

Joe R. Feagin

For over fourteen generations the exploitation of African Americans has redistributed income and wealth earned by them to generations of white Americans, leaving the former relatively impoverished as a group and the latter relatively privileged and affluent as a group.

The year is 1787, the place Philadelphia. Fifty-five men are meeting in summer's heat to write a constitution for what will be called the "first democratic nation." These founders create a document so radical in breaking from monarchy and feudal institutions that it will be condemned and attacked in numerous European countries. These radicals are men of European origin, and most are well-off by the standards of their day. Significantly, at least 40 percent have been or are slave owners, and a significant proportion of the others profit to some degree as merchants, shippers, lawyers, and bankers from the trade in slaves, commerce in slave-produced agricultural products, or supplying provisions to slave-holders and slavetraders. Moreover, the man who pressed hard for this convention and now chairs it, George Washington, is one of the richest men in the colonies because of the hundreds of black men, women, and children he has held in bondage. Washington and his colleagues create the first democratic nation, yet one for whites only. In the preamble to their bold document, the founders cite prominently "We the People," but this phrase does not encompass the fifth of the population that is enslaved.

LAYING A RACIST FOUNDATION

Many historical analysts have portrayed slavery as side matter at the 1787 Constitutional Convention. Slavery was central however, as a leading participant, James Madison, made clear in his important notes on the convention's debates. Madison accented how the convention was scissored across a north/south, slave/not-slave divide among the states. The southern and northern regions were gradually diverging in their politico-economic frameworks. Slavery had once been of some, albeit greatly varying, importance in all states, but the northern states were moving away from chattel slavery as a part of their local economies, and some were seeing a growing abolitionist sentiment. Even so, many northern merchants, shippers, and consumers still depended on products produced

Source: Joe R. Feagin, "Systemic Racism: A Comprehensive Perspective," in Racist America: Roots, Current Realities, and Future Aspirations (New York: Routledge, 2001): 6-36.

by southern slave plantations, and many merchants sold good the plantations. . . .

The trade in, and enslavement of, people of African descent was an important and divisive issue for the convention. Most of these prominent, generally well-educated men accepted the view that people of African descent could be the chattel property of others—and not human beings with citizens' rights. At the heart of the Constitution was protection of the property and wealth of the affluent bourgeoisie in the new nation, including property in those enslaved. There was near unanimity on the idea, as delegate Gouverneur Morris (New York) put it, that property is the "main object of Society." For the founders, freedom meant the protection of unequal accumulation of property, particularly property that could produce a profit in the emerging capitalist system. Certain political, economic, and racial interests were conjoined. This was not just a political gathering with the purpose of creating a major new bourgeois-democratic government; it was also a meeting to protect the racial and economic interests of men with substantial property and wealth in the colonies. . . .

The new nation formed by European Americans in the late eighteenth century was openly and officially viewed as a white republic. These founders sought to build a racially based republic in the face of monarchical opposition and against those people on the North American continent whom they defined as inferior and as problems. . . .

The U.S. Constitutional Convention, the first such in the democratic history of the modern world, laid a strong base for the new societal "house" called the United States. Yet from the beginning this house's foundation was fundamentally flawed. While most Americans have thought of this document and the sociopolitical structure it created as keeping the nation together, in fact, this structure was created to maintain separation and oppression at the time and for the foreseeable future. The framers reinforced and legitimated a system of racist oppression that they thought would ensure that whites, especially white men of means, would rule for centuries to come. . . .

Understanding the centrality and harsh realities of slavery leads to some tough questions for today: How are we to regard the "founding fathers"? They are our founding fathers, yet many were oppressors who made their living by killing, brutalizing, and exploiting other human beings. The combination of white freedom and black enslavement seems racially contradictory. However, William Wiecek notes that "the paradox dissolves when we recall that American slavery was racial. White freedom was entirely compatible with black enslavement. African Americans were, as the framers of Virginia's first Constitution determined, simply not part of the Lockean body politic." Indeed, the work of those enslaved brought the wealth and leisure that whites, especially those in the ruling class, could use to pursue their own liberty and freedom. . . .

Into the mid-nineteenth century, the majority of whites—in the elites and among ordinary folk—either participated directly in slavery or in the trade around slavery, or did not object to those who did so. The antihuman savagery called slavery was considered *normal* in what was then seen as a white republic. This point must be understood well if one is to probe deeply into the origins, maintenance, and persistence of racist patterns and institutions in North America. . . .

Frederick Douglass was one of the first U.S. analysts to develop a conceptual approach accenting *institutionalized* racism across many sectors of society. In 1881, speaking about the ubiquitous impact of racist prejudice and discrimination, he argued that "[i]n nearly every department of American life [black Americans] are confronted by this insidious influence. It fills the air. It meets them at the workshop and factory, when they apply for work. It meets them at the church, at the hotel, at the ballot-box, and worst of all, it meets in the jury-box. . . . [the black American] has ceased to be a *slave of an individual*, but has in some sense become *the slave of society*." . . .

Historically the social-science study of racial oppression has been identified by such terms as "intergroup relations" or "race relations." These somewhat ambiguous and euphemistic phrases are accented by many analysts who prefer to view an array of racial groups as more or less responsible for the U.S. "race problem." Such terminology, however, can allow the spotlight to be taken off the whites who have created and maintained the system of racism. Moreover, many white analysts have written about the "race problem" as "in" U.S. society. Yet, race relations—or, more accurately, *racist relations*—are no *in*, but rather *of* this society. In the American case systemic racism began with European colonists enriching themselves substantially at the expense of indigenous peoples and the Africans they imported for enslavement. This brutally executed enrichment was part of the new society's foundation, not something tacked onto and otherwise healthy and egalitarian system. . . .

Unjust enrichment is an old legal term associated with relationships between individuals. One legal dictionary defines the concept as "circumstances which give rise to the obligation of restitution, that is, the receiving and retention of property, money, or benefits which in justice and equity belong to another." This legal concept encompasses not only the receiving of benefits that justly belong to another but also the obligation to make restitution for that injustice. This idea can be extended beyond individual relationships envisioned in the traditional legal argument to the unjust theft of labor or resources by one group, such as white Americans, from another group, such as black Americans. I suggest here the parallel idea of unjust impoverishment to describe the conditions of those who suffer oppression. . . . For over fourteen generations the exploitation of

African Americans has redistributed income and wealth earned by them to generations of white Americans, leaving the former relatively impoverished as a group and the latter relatively privileged and affluent as a group.

RACIAL CLASSES WITH VESTED GROUP INTERESTS

Understanding how this underserved impoverishment and enrichment gets transmitted, reproduced, and institutionalized over generations of white and black Americans is an important step to developing an adequate conceptual framework. Black labor was used unjustly for building up the wealth of this white-dominated nation from the 1600s to at least the 1960s—the slavery and legal segregation periods. . . .

The racial-class system, initially created by the white ruling class, provided benefits to most white Americans. From the seventeenth century onward, the farms and plantations run with enslaved laborers brought significant income and wealth to many white Americans, and not just to their particular owners. These enterprises multiplied economic development for white Americans well outside the farms' and plantations' immediate geographical areas. . . . Ordinary whites for the most part brought into the identity of whiteness, thereby blinding themselves to the white racial class.

Slavery's impact extended well beyond the economy. Each institutional arena in the new nation was controlled by whites and was closely linked to other major arenas. As we have seen, the Constitution and its "democratic" political system were grounded in the racist thinking and practices of white men, many of whom had links to slavery. Those who dominated the economic system crafted the political system. Likewise the religious, legal, educational, and media systems were interlinked with the slavery economy and polity. Woven through each institutional area was a broad racist ideology—a set of principles and views—centered on rationalizing white-on-black domination and creating positive views of whiteness. . . .

Systemic racism is not just about the construction of racial images, attitudes, and identities. It is even more centrally about the creation, development, and maintenance of white privilege, economic wealth, and socio-political power over nearly four centuries. It is about hierarchical interaction. The past and present worlds of racism include not only racist relations at work but also the racist relations that black Americans and other Americans of color encounter in trying to secure adequate housing, consumer goods, and public accommodations for themselves and their families. Racism reaches deeply into family lives, shaping who has personal relations with whom, and who gets married to whom. Racism shapes which groups have the best health, get the best medical care, and live the longest lives. . . .

UNDERSERVED IMPOVERISHMENT AND UNDERSERVED ENRICHMENT

The Wealth of a White Nation

Not long ago, Bob Dole, onetime Senate Majority Leader and presidential candidate, spoke in a television interview of "displace" white men who must compete with black workers because of affirmative action. He said that he was not sure that "people in America" (presumably he meant whites) should now be paying a price for racial discrimination that occurred "before they were born." He was fairly candid about the past, saying, "We did discriminate. We did suppress people. It was wrong. Slavery was wrong." Yet Dole added that he was sure any compensation for this damage was now due. Similarly, Representative Henry Hyde (R-Illinois), who served as chair of the House

Judiciary Committee, has commented that the idea of collective guilt for slavery in the distant past "is an idea whose time has gone. I never owned a slave. I never oppressed anybody. I don't know that I should have to pay for someone who did generations before I was born." This questioning of the relevance of the racist past for the present is commonplace among white Americans.

SOURCES OF WHITE WEALTH: A VIGNETTE

Consider four young children coming into the American colonies in the late seventeenth century. An African brother and sister are ripped from their homes and imported in chains into Virginia, the largest slaveholding colony. Their African names being ignored, they are renamed "negro John" and "negro Mary" (no last name) by the white family that purchased them from a slave ship. This white (Smith) family has young twins, William and Priscilla. Their first and last names are those given to them by their parents, and they never wear chains. Then enslaved children are seen as "black" by the Smith family, while the twins will live as "white."

What do these children and their descendants have to look forward to? Their experiences will be very different as a result of they system of racist oppression. William's and Priscilla's lives may be hard because of the physical environment, but they and their descendants will likely build lives with an array of personal choices and the passing down of significant social resources. As a girl and later as a woman, Priscilla will not have the same privileges as William, but her life is more likely to be economically supported and protected than Mary's. Indeed, John and Mary face a stark, often violent existence, with most of their lives determined by the whims of the slaveholder, who has stolen not only their labor but their lives. They will never see their families or home societies again.

They can be radically separated at any time, a separation much less likely for William and Priscilla. From their and other slaves' labor some wealth will be generated for the Smith family and passed on to later generations. Unlike the white twins, John and Mary will not be allowed to read or write and will be forced to replace their African language with English. Where they eat and sleep will be largely determined by whites. As they grow older, major decisions about their personal and family relationships will be made by whites. Mary will face repeated sexual threats, coercion, and rape at the hands of male overseers and slaveholders, perhaps including William. Moreover, if John even looks at Priscilla the wrong way, he is likely to be punished severely.

If John and Mary are later allowed to have spouses and children, they will face a much greater infant mortality rate than whites. And their surviving children may well be taken from them, so that they and later generations may have great difficulty in keeping the full memory of their ancestors, a problem not face by William and Priscilla. If John or Mary resist their oppression, they are likely to be whipped, put in chains, or have an iron bit put in their mouths. If John is rebellious or runs away too much, he may face castration. John and Mary will have to struggle very hard to keep their families together because the slaveholders can destroy them at any moment. Still, together with other black Americans, they build a culture of resistance carried from generation to generation in oral tradition. Moreover, for many more generations John's and Mary's descendants will suffer similarly severe conditions as the property of white families. Few if any of their descendants will see freedom until the 1860s.

The end of slavery does not end the large-scale oppression face by John's and Mary's descendants. For four more generations after 1865 the near-slavery called legal or de facto segregation will confront them, but of course

will not affect the descendants of William and Priscilla Smith. The later black generations will also be unable to build up resources and wealth; they will have their lives substantially determined by the white enforcers of comprehensive segregation. Where they can get a job, where they can live, whether and where they can go to school, and how they can travel will still be significantly determined by whites. Some may face brutal beatings or lynching by whites, especially if they resist oppression. They will have inherited no wealth from many generations of enslaved ancestors, and they are unlikely to garner resources themselves to pass along to later generations. From the late 1600s to the 1960s, John and Mary and their descendants have been at an extreme economic, political, and social disadvantage compared to William and Priscilla Smith and their descendants. The lives of these black Americans have been shortened, their opportunities severely limited, the inherited resources all but nonexistent, and their families pressured by generations of well-organized racial oppression. . . .

From this vignette we can begin to see how racism is economically and systematically constructed. Unjust impoverishment for John and Mary and undeserved enrichment for William and Priscilla become bequeathed inheritances for many later generations. Undeserved impoverishment and enrichment are at the heart of the colonial land theft and the brutal slavery system. Over time this ill-gotten gain has been used and invested by white colonizers and their descendants to construct a prosperous white-dominated nation. Today there is a general denial in the white population that black Americans have contributed much to American (or Western) development and civilization. This denial is part of contemporary white racist misunderstandings of the reality of the history of the West. However, the facts are clear: The slavery system provided much stimulus for economic development and generated critical surplus capital for the new nation. . . . Without the enslaved labor of millions of black Americans, there might well not be a prosperous United States today.

STUDY QUESTION

What does Feagin mean by "unjust enrichment" and "unjust impoverishment" in "racist relations"?

Women of Color: Fighting Sexism and Racism

Nijole V. Benokraitis and Joe R. Feagin

Perhaps the saddest part of the current picture of gendered racism is that it reflects a 'slavery unwilling to die.' The current situation reveals a continuity with the past.

GENDERED RACISM

Social science theories of racial relations have for the most part ignored issues of gender roles and discrimination. However, several scholars, mostly women of color, have recently written about the situations of women within the racial stratification systems in the United States, Canada, and Europe. Their analyses assess the ways in which male dominance interacts with racial stratification. Asking whether racism or patriarchy has been the primary source of oppression, psychologist Philomena Essed interviewed black women in the United States and the Netherlands and found *racism and sexism* constantly interacting in their lives. Essed terms much oppression of black women a "gendered racism," where one type of oppression reinforces or interacts with the other. This gendered racism can be seen in a variety of settings, from the neighborhood, to the school, to the work place. In a recent study of the black middle class by Joe Feagin and Melvin Sikes, a black male executive in

New England argued that black women have suffered from double jeopardy:

> I think a black woman would have it really tough to get through because they have two obstacles to overcome, being a woman, trying to prove that they can do as good as a man, and then trying to prove that they can do as [good as] any white person, a white man in particular. So, that's a lot for a woman to overcome. And I think that's more stressful than what a black male would have to do, because he's just fighting against racism, as a woman is fighting against racism and sexism.

For black women, gendered racism means that those in power positions in institutions, usually white men, have two different ways to control or oppress them.

Gendered racism is deeply imbedded in the core culture of the United States. To take one important example, women of color suffer much from the dominant culture's image of female beauty. In advertising and the mass media, the white female, often thin or blond, is the standard. Black women models and actors have been relatively rare in the movies

---

Source: Nijole V. Benokraitis and Joe R. Feagin, "Women of Color: Fighting Sexism and Racism," in *Modern Sexism, Blatant, Subtle, and Covert Discrimination*, 2nd edition (New Jersey: Prentice Hall, 1995).

or advertising, and those who do appear are often light-skinned or white-looking. Other women of color are also victimized by this white European standard. They are even rarer in ads and the media. And they suffer in other ways as well. In the early 1990s, Japanese American skater Kristi Yamaguchi became the center of much public discussion after she won a gold medal at the 1991 Winter Olympics. Previous gold-medal winners, all European Americans, became household names as companies came to them for advertisements. Some corporate officials said that Yamaguchi's Japanese ancestry would stop her from getting as many lucrative endorsements as European-American skaters. Marketing people pointed to the strong anti-Japanese feeling among many non-Asian workers as a reason advertisers might not use someone who looked Japanese. Kristi Yamaguchi was forever stigmatized as a "skater with Japanese ancestry."

Gendered racism involves a range of negative evaluations of women of color. Patricia Hill Collins has critically analyzed the negative images of black women held by many white Americans. In her important and pioneering book *Black Feminist Thought,* Collins dissected the antiblack stereotypes of the "docile mammy," the "domineering matriarch," the "promiscuous whore," and the "irresponsible welfare mother." These severely negative portrayals of black women are common among many whites; they reinforce and flow out of whites' discrimination against black women. Other women of color have faced similar stereotypes. Native American women have long been stereotyped as inferior "squaws" or seductive "princesses," and Latinas, particularly Mexican American women, have been portrayed as "lazy" or "flirting señoritas." Looking at Latinas, Denise Segura has developed the concept of triple oppression, the mutually reinforcing and interactive set of race, class, and gender forces whose cumulative effects place women of color in reinforced

subordinate social and economic positions in U.S. society.

WORKING OUTSIDE THE HOME

For many years women of color have worked outside the home in much larger proportions than white women have. African American women have been holding down steady jobs outside the home for more than three centuries: first as slaves; then as poor farmers; then as maids, restaurant and laundry workers; and, most recently, as clerical and sales workers. African American women have long had to work for the survival of themselves and their families, and the proportion of black women in the labor force outside the home has long been higher than that for white women. In 1960, only 37 percent of white women were in the labor force, compared to 83 percent of black women. By the early 1990s, the white figure had grown to just over half, still much lower than the three quarters of black women working outside the home. Black women have long struggled in jobs outside the home, often serving as the chief breadwinners because of discrimination against black men, discrimination that results in low wages and unemployment. Nonetheless, most black women do not define themselves solely in terms of their work or their occupations, for they have long been used to balancing home, family, and work.

Black women have been subordinated and exploited in their jobs outside the home. The freedom to develop personally is sharply limited in the cold reality of daily work. Anthropologist John Gwaltney interviewed an older black woman from Tennessee who told him her father used to say that the "only two people who were really free was the white man and the black woman." Yet this woman went on to say that her father was wrong. Life had taught her that neither black men nor black women were truly free. By the time of the interview she had worked for 64 years "busting the white man's suds and mopping the white man's floors and minding the white man's kids." From her point of view the only people who are free in this world are "the people that can tell other people what to do and how they have to do it." Exploited labor outside the home does not make one free, just a different type of servant."

The Character of Outside Work

What type of work have women of color done outside the home? What sort of incomes do they have? Do they face high unemployment? During slavery, African American women in the South had a labor force participation rate near 100 percent. Whether girls or women, they worked as slaves in the field and in factories and homes of the white male slaveholding class. Jacqueline Jones has written about the lives of black women during and after slavery in vivid terms. The harsh nature of their lives is evident. Black female slaves had no choice in regard to back-breaking labor during slavery. One woman noted, "If you had something to do, you did it or got whipped." Slaveowner brutality was not lessened for black women: "Beat women! Why sure he [master] beat women. Beat women jes lak men. Beat women naked an' wash 'em down in brine." One woman recalled that "the things that my sister May and I suffered were so terrible . . . It is best not to have such things in our memory." After slavery, most black women remained in the fields of the South as farm workers, sharecroppers, and tenant farmers. Many also served as domestic workers, a group that grew in numbers as blacks left the fields for towns and cities from the 1910s to the 1960s.

With the black migration to the North came better working conditions for many. During a 1920 interview conducted by the Chicago Commission on Race Relations, a young black woman working in a factory showed her hatred of domestic work: "I'll never work in nobody's kitchen but my own any more. No indeed! That's the one thing that makes me stick to this job." Nonetheless, most of the work done by black women in the North took the form of domestic service, and conditions could be every bit as bad as in the South. One woman from Florida was reduced to near slavery in the 1920s by a white middle-class family in Chicago. She somehow managed to get away from the family but not before her employer "had kicked, beaten, and threatened her with a revolver if she attempted to leave."

By the 1960s, nearly four in ten black women workers were still employed as maids and servants. Yet by the mid-1980s, the percentage had dropped to only 6 percent, as black women finally moved into new job categories, including those traditionally occupied by white women. One recent analysis of the dramatic changes in racial segregation within traditional female jobs concluded that the biggest decline in segregation among women took place in the 1960s: "Clearly, the events of the 1960's—whether economic growth, the civil rights movement, or something else entirely—shook the longstanding structure of segregation of black women in the labor market. Segregation continued to diminish rapidly through the 1970s. Very little change was apparent in the 1980s." Bureau of Labor Statistics (BLS) data have shown occupational progress for black women, but still a less favorable job distribution than for white women. In 1990, there was still a larger proportion of black women than of white women in lower-paying, blue-collar jobs. And just under a fifth of black women were employed in managerial and professional jobs, compared with more than a quarter of white women. Note too that these government data can be misleading, for many women in professional-managerial occupations are in lower-paying jobs. This is particularly true for black women, who are often dieticians in school cafeterias, cafe and bar managers, and practical nurses. Although many are school teachers, few are lawyers, doctors, or corporate managers.

Elizabeth Higginbotham has pointed out that historically most black women professionals, such as teachers and nurses, have work-ed in more or less segregated settings. Even today, these professionals tend to be disproportionately "in agencies and hospitals located in Black communities and serving Blacks, Latinos and other people of color." To a substantial degree, this segregation signals the racial limitations on employment opportunities that black professionals still face in the United States.

A large proportion of black women are employed in clerical and sales jobs, many in lower-paying positions such as typists and retail clerks. In addition, many black women have labored outside the white-collar category. Like black men, black women are more likely than their white counterparts to be in jobs in the service, operative, transportation, and handler-laborer categories, altogether about 40 percent in BIS data, as compared with 25 percent for white women. In blue-collar job categories, black women serve disproportionately in jobs such as nurse's aides, cooks, janitors, and maids. As Cydney Shields, the author of a job guide for black women, recently put it, for a large number of black women the problem "isn't as much breaking through the glass ceiling as it is . . . getting off the sticky floor."

Other women of color have long labored in low-wage positions in order to enable their families and communities to survive. Mexican American women, for example, have worked in agriculture, as domestic servants, and in low-wage manufacturing jobs. And, regardless of the job, Mexican American women often earn less than comparable Anglos and are often assigned more physically demanding tasks. Like African American women, Mexican American women today are located primarily in clerical and sales positions and in service (e.g., maids) and operative (e.g., low-wage manufacturing) jobs. Some Latinas have played a central economic role in their communities. Most Cuban women who immigrated to the United States beginning in the late 1950s were not used to working outside the home, but such work was essential for family and group mobility. Today, Cuban American women, including those who are married and those with young children, are more likely than other Latinas to be in the paid labor force. This high level of labor-force participation is a major factor in the relative prosperity of Cuban American communities.

From the beginning of immigration, Asian American women have also been critical to the economic development of their communities. One researcher has reported that "from the moment they arrived, Japanese American women labored alongside the men; to secure their own and their families' livelihood." This work was frequently unpaid family labor on farms and in a variety of other businesses. Some women worked as domestic servants for whites. Until the 1950s, blatant discrimination against Asian American women precluded most from moving into white-collar work. Although many have moved into white-collar work in recent decades, discrimination has persisted. Research studies from the 1970s to the present have found significant occupational segregation and promotion restrictions for Japanese American and other Asian American workers, both male and female, when compared with white workers. One research examination of private employers in San Francisco found Asian American workers to be underrepresented in such employment areas as manufacturing, construction, and wholesale trade. Asian Americans were also underrepresented in better-paying jobs (such as managerial jobs) and overrepresented in lower-paying work (such as clerical jobs).

The Case of Domestic Workers

Many women of color, in the past and in the present, have labored in the homes of white men and women. Not only black women but also Mexican and other Latin American immigrants often work in low-wage domestic positions. These domestic household workers are sometimes said to be in an "obsolete" job category that is disappearing from U.S. society. Yet, the number of women in this category is still as large as it was a hundred years ago. Today, a disproportionate amount of this domestic work is being done, by women of color.

Domestic work is usually seen as "women's work" and is thus low-wage work. Numerous employers ignore the law passed in 1974 that requires a minimum wage for these household workers; and many employers also ignore the legal requirement (since 1951) to pay social security taxes for domestics. As we noted in an earlier chapter, in 1993 the failure to pay social security for domestic employees, who were illegal immigrants from Peru, forced Zoe Baird, one of President Bill Clinton's nominees for U.S. attorney general, to withdraw her name from consideration.

Domestic workers are often exploited, and those who are illegal have little recourse. As a recent report in *Newsweek* put it, "They feel powerless to complain in the face of outrageous demands—even sexual advances from employers." Still, they cope with exploitation and struggle hard to maintain their dignity. Some even fight exploitation. One woman from El Salvador worked as a domestic for one year for a white family "that made her sleep on the kitchen floor, piled chores on her, then fired her, still owing her much of the $100 a week they had agreed to pay." This case had a happier ending than most, however. The woman filed suit against her white employers and managed to win a $5,000 default judgment when they failed to show up in court.

A significant aspect of domestic work by women of color is that it is often done for white female employers. White middle- and upper-income women, Rollins notes, use the physical labor of women of color to free themselves for more enjoyable activities and thus to "provide ideological justification for the hierarchical social structure which affords them privilege." The domestics are exploited not only in material terms, in getting the most work for the lowest wage, but often in psychological terms as well. Rollins found that white women emphasize deference and treatment of domestics as "children" or "inferiors." From her own experience as a domestic and from interviews with domestics and employers, Rollins concludes that white women employers feed off "the low paid labor and the personhood of the domestic" in order to reduce their own repetitive domestic work and thus to make their own lives better. The exploitation of domestic workers also points up the larger issue of male domination of economic systems. In the case of domestics, some white women employers are "go-betweens," with their husbands controlling the purse strings and deciding how much domestic work is actually worth.

Unemployment and Low Incomes

Women of color tend to have high rates of unemployment. The black female unemployment rate has usually been double that of the white female and male rates for many decades. For example, in 1972 just under 6 percent of white women were unemployed, compared to almost 12 percent for black women. Two decades later, according to 1993 Labor Department figures, 7 percent of white men and 5 percent of white women were unemployed, compared to 13 percent for black men and 11 percent for black women. In addition, the *underemployment rate*, which includes those workers with very low wages and those who work part time but want full-time work, together with those so discouraged they have given up looking for work, is very high for women of color-at least a fifth of all these workers.

According to researchers Cunningham and Zalokar, historically about half the wage differential between black women and white women has resulted from black women's being forced to work in just a few occupations. Black women get a low return for their outside-the-home work efforts; they are at the bottom in terms of earnings. White men earn far more than black men or women. Recent BLS data showed that median weekly earnings for black women were just $323, compared to $374 for white women and $509 for white men. Black families with husband and wife working earned about 80 to 90 percent of similar white families; but for the many black families with just one earner, the proportion was about 60 percent. In addition, more than half of all black families headed by a woman fall below the government poverty level, compared to less than a third of comparable whites. The situation is similar for many Latinas. For example, the incomes of Mexican American women have been much lower on the average than those of Anglo women. Besides low earnings, women of color often get minimal employment benefits, and the majority do not have access to pensions or group health coverage because of unemployment or the type of low-wage jobs that they or their husbands hold.

There has been much recent discussion in the literature of the conditions and situations of the so-called "black underclass," the poorest 5 to 10 percent of black Americans. Looking at the situations of poor black women, sociologist William Julius Wilson has examined the "underclass" idea in a widely discussed policy book, *The Truly Disadvantaged*. In this book Wilson explores the fallacies in recent popular and scholarly analyses. As he explains, there are no real data that indicate welfare destroys the work effort or creates dependency among poor black Americans. Wilson also argues that the growing proportion of out-of-wedlock births among black women in recent years has nothing to do with their moral values or with poor welfare management. Instead, the growing proportion has to do with the *declining* birth rate among married women.

Wilson focuses on what he calls the problem of women finding "marriageable black men." The relative scarcity of young black men with decent-paying jobs is closely related to the problem of out-of-wedlock births. When young men cannot get jobs, they cannot afford to get married. Their girlfriends, as a result, establish their own households and often raise their children with the help of female relatives, sometimes relying on public assistance. The failure of the capitalistic economy and the federal government to provide decent-paying jobs for everyone who wants to work is the primary explanation for the problems of poor women, not some chapters how widespread this form of sex white stereotypical problem of "lazy black men" or "welfare queens." There are some weaknesses in Wilson's analysis. He does not deal with the gender and racial discrimination black women face today in many U.S. of workplaces; this gender-racial discrimination is a major reason why many black women cannot earn enough in wages to support their families. For them life remains constant struggle to survive.

Discrimination in the Workplace

As we have seen, there is a great range of work that is done by women of color. They work in low-wage blue-collar jobs as well as in management and professional positions. Yet in most job categories they face racial discrimination at the hands of whites and sex discrimination at the hands of (mostly white) men. If white women seeking promotions in white-collar settings often encounter a "glass ceiling" beyond which they cannot move, women of color face what has been called the "concrete wall." One management consultant has argued that "Women of color are ten years behind white women in terms of promotion and upward mobility." In the mid-1990s, less than 1 percent of those in top management positions are black women. In Bell and Nkomo's recent in-depth study of white and black women's experiences in management, black women reported receiving less support for career advancement from their bosses and less acceptance by colleagues, and felt that they had less control and authority in their jobs, than did their white counterparts. African American women also perceived greater gender discrimination compared with white women and were less optimistic about their company's commitment to improve the situation for women.

Black women, in both blue-collar and white-collar categories, experience much sexual harassment. We have seen in earlier chapters how widespread this form of sex discrimination really is. Some studies suggest that black women are twice as likely to be victims of sexual harassment as are white women. We note at the opening of this chapter that during slavery the raping black slave women was once a common practice of powerful white men. From the 1600s to the mid-1800s, many thousands of black female slaves, from 10 to 60 years of age, were rape by white men, including slaveholders and overseers, who considered black women to be property. Even after emancipation, and until recent times, white men have raped black women with impunity.

Court cases have documented the sexual harassment of black women in the contemporary United States. In a Michigan case, a recently separated black mother was hired as an assistance collections manager. She soon became a sexual target of her white male boss. On her first day she was propositioned by her boss, who asked if "she would make love to a white man." After refusing many suggestions that she have sexual intercourse with him, she was fired. Similarly, in a 1989 case a black woman who worked as a teleprocessor for Los Angeles County described how her superiors racially and sexually harassed her. An in another recent case, a black woman working in accounting at a Chicago firm reported that she was sexually harassed by white male employees. Sometimes when the men were playing cards at lunch, the black woman was referred to as a "slave" and told to serve them. Her white boss made racist jokes about the legs and walk of black women. This racist-sexist behavior is common in white-collar workplaces. Similar harassment is faced by women of color in blue-collar workplaces and as domestic servants.

White men are often the perpetrators of sexual harassment against black female employees in many business arenas because they are more likely than minority men to have the power to retaliate against women who reject their advances. Yet there are cases where men of color have harassed women as well. In a 1992 Alabama case, a white woman won a court suit on sexual harassment. The federal judge ruled that, while she was employed at a convenience store in Montgomery, she was sexually harassed by a black male employee so much that she eventually quit her job. Assessing the evidence, the judge found that three black female employees had suffered sexual harassment from the same male coworker.

The issue of sexual harassment in the black community came dramatically to national attention during and after the Anita Hill/Clarence Thomas hearings in 1991. Anita Hill, a conservative black law professor who had worked several years for President George Bush's Supreme Court nominee Clarence Thomas, also an African American, testified that Thomas had sexually harassed her numerous times. Hill testified about sexist joking and other sexual harassment at the hands of a black man, yet the hearing itself had overtones of racism. President Bush nominated Thomas, a black right-winger, as the "best qualified man" for the position, even though the American Bar Association rated Thomas as barely qualified. Bush chose the nominee to fit in with his own conservative political agenda, and he know white Democrats in Congress would have difficulty in voting against Thomas because he was a black candidate. Bush cared not at all that Thomas was out of touch with most African Americans.

Moreover, an all-white male Senate judiciary committee judged the testimony of Hill and Thomas. Entrenched white male power was quite evident in the makeup of that powerful committee and in the rejection (by the majority) of Hill's testimony about harassment.

The reactions of some black women, including MIT scholar Ella Bell, were strong and supportive of Hill: "I awoke from this dream crying, with an eerie sense of helplessness" and "Hatch [a key white Senator] was making me physically ill." In an article on the Hill/Thomas hearings, Bell has pointed out that Anita Hill was in a situation where she was sure to lose. By criticizing a black man for sexual harassment, Hill broke a taboo against black women speaking out on what some black men do to women. Bell speaks of a "Black Men's Club," which includes some of the black male civil rights leaders who supported the Thomas nomination. Not attending to the sexism of black men and viewing the black liberation struggle as mainly for "black manhood," Bell argues, makes no sense, for it is as much a struggle for black womanhood as for black manhood.

Like black women, Latinas and Asian American women are vulnerable to sexual harassment on the job. An Asian American employee at a U.S. military base reported sexual harassment, but suffered serious retaliation for her report. A U.S. Civil Rights Commission review noted that "because of the stereotypic expectation of compliance and docility, a formal complaint from an Asian American woman might have been considered as a personal affront or challenge. Her notification of the alleged retaliation to the base authorities was to no avail: it aggravated an already bad situation."

OTHER GENDERED DISCRIMINATION

Women of color face discrimination in many places and institutions, not just in the arena of employment.

Higher Education

When women of color move into educational settings, they often face racial and gender barriers. The impact of white male cultural dominance can be seen in our educational institutions, which are in the business of molding new students to fit established ways of doing things. For example, in an analysis of women of color in medical schools, Diana Kendall, has highlighted the cumulative impact of racial and gender discrimination on women in a number of oppressed groups. Many white men in medical school faculties and student bodies remain convinced that every medical school student should adapt to the white male mold. In Kendall's research, one Mexican American respondent defined the requirements of that mold:

> Not only do we have to fit the "Anglo mold," which sees medicine as curative rather than preventive, and which is impersonal and disease-oriented, we also have to fit the "male mold," which is aggressive, competitive, authoritative, a "take charge attitude," and a "little boys don't cry" bit. Furthermore, we have to try to think like they do culturally if we want good evaluations because you have to be aggressive in patient management, but not too aggressive; you have to ask questions and get involved with the patient, but not emotionally involved.

The fence that many female students straddle can be seen in the grades and evaluations given to these students during their clinical years in medical school. An example of how the white male mold shapes student evaluations is seen in these statements of health care workers evaluating the same Puerto Rican female medical student. The first evaluation is from a white male medical professor teaching at a hospital:

> This student consistently had difficulty in relating to . . . house staff and some patients. Her behavior, at times, was inappropriate and it was our feeling that she failed to appreciate her limitations as a student. She seemed to resent and

have difficulty coping with authoritative [sic] figures. Her manner, at times, was overbearing, demanding, and quite inappropriate. Unfortunately, her personality problems tend to overshadow her work as a student. . . . Although intellectually we feel she could make a physician, unless she is able to correct her personality deficiencies, her future as a physician remains questionable.

In this view the woman of color must change herself to fit the unconscious, or half-conscious. white male mold. In sharp contrast to this physician's comments are those of other health care workers with whom this same student had worked in neighborhood clinics in the city:

(I) She is clearly a bright, energetic and capable person and has demonstrated both independence and initiative in a situation where there is little supervision available. . . . Her relationship with other people was good, she was cooperative and flexible in situations requiring teamwork, and she accepted direction and criticism willingly. (2) She demonstrates a broad intelligence, a refreshing individuality, integrity, and most of all, courage in opposing pretense and rigidity.

The doctor's evaluation compared this Puerto Rican woman to the white-male subcultural mold and concluded that she had "personality deficiencies." The health care workers compared her to the sort of doctor needed for a more diverse set of minority patients and concluded that she was excellent. This minority student's career was nearly terminated by her white male professors because of her inability and unwillingness to fit the prescribed mold.

Recently, a black female medical student in a large southern city noted what her life was like inside and outside her historically white medical school:

When I first moved to New Orleans, I had my own preconceived ideas about white people, but I was encouraged by other blacks to give them a chance. . . However, I have been mistaken for a maid or a nurse and told that I'm in medical school because of a quota system, despite my high college average and my MCAT scores. I've been cussed out and called a stupid black bitch by several white males in Metairie while walking, driving or shopping. While eating in a restaurant, a white woman asked me to come and clean her house on my day off.

The Problem of Violence

Black women, like white women, are often the victims of gender-related violence, including wife beating and rape. As we noted earlier, sexual attacks on black women by white men are a major problem that has long been ignored. Historically, the rape of black women by white men has been far more commonplace than black men raping white women, the latter a common white-racist fantasy. Today, however, the main threat of sexual violence against black women comes from black men in their communities. In the United States, most rapes occur between members of the same racial group. Recently, a prominent black psychiatrist, Alvin F. Poussaint, has noted, "Unfortunately, some Black men tend to direct their destructive rage against Black women, employing violence. rape, battery and sexual harassment. Extremist rap musicians have even advocated sexual abuse and murder of 'the bitches.'" FBI data indicate that black women are twice as likely to be rape victims as white women, yet the rape of black women is less often reported in the media. More and more black women have begun to ask, as a woman writing in *Essence,* a magazine for black women, put it: "So why are there no protest marches in our communities, no impassioned speeches, no chest-pounding rhetoric from 'leadership' about that? When folks speak of Black-on-Black crime, shake their heads in shock, despair and sorrow, rarely is rape the crime that comes most to mind."

SLAVERY UNWILLING TO DIE?

Women of color face many obstacles in making their way in historically white worlds, whether that world is a white home, higher education, or the corporate work place. Black women in particular have a long history of racial and sexual discrimination, with these two types of discrimination often blending together to increase the disadvantage.

As we have seen, high achievement does not lessen the double-jeopardy discrimination that women of color encounter. Cheryl Harris, an assistant professor of law, recently commented that black female lawyers confront "the same barriers as other black women in the workplace, struggling against perceptions of race, gender, and class." In connection with a criminal case, she had confronted gendered racism that assumed she could not be a lawyer: "When I walked up with my white client, the clerk asked me for my bond slip. Obviously, I had to be the client and the white man the lawyer. The same thing happened in the courtroom when I went to sit at counsel's table." The oppression of women of color at the hands of white men is grounded in the belief that such women do not belong in historically white places and spaces, including the professional world.

Perhaps the saddest part of the current picture of gendered racism is that it reflects a "slavery unwilling to die." The current situation reveals a continuity with the past. Harris, commenting on the sexual harassment faced today by black women such as Anita Hill, noted that the bodies of black women "were the first workplace, where they as slaves were supposed to be sexually available to any man and the vehicle through which slaves were produced."

STUDY QUESTION

What are the institutional effects of *gendered racism* discussed by Benokraitis and Feagin?

CHAPTER 2

Inequality in American Education

INTRODUCTION

The American educational institution is a powerful instrument of racial oppression that limits the educational opportunity of persons of color in U.S. society. For most Americans, education is a vehicle for personal achievement and socioeconomic advancement. A fundamental premise of the so-called American dream, for example, is that the postponement of personal gratification in the pursuit of educational goals will result in social rewards attached to a prestigious occupational position. Yet for persons of color, the American dream amounts to nothing more than a dream—a dream that not only leaves unfulfilled the aspirations of people of color, but a dream that also silences them in the social fabric of U.S. society. In the end, the American dream is a barrier in public education for students of color: "black and Hispanic students in public education are significantly more likely to confront barriers to advancement than white students."[1]

Since its very inception, the American educational system has functioned systematically to exclude persons of color from full and equal educational opportunity. The educational system so dramatically limits opportunity through discriminatory practices that many persons of color never reach their full human potential. Nor do they acquire access to social opportunity. Throughout its history, U.S. public education has legitimated the unequal treatment of students of color by schooling them differently than white students. Gross disparities in school funding, for example, has ensured that white students have superior teachers, facilities, and more educational programs than what one finds in schools where nonwhite students are in the majority. A hidden curriculum, intelligence testing, and the selection and sorting of nonwhite students into remedial or developmental educational programs has resulted in the perpetuation of privilege for the dominant (white) group in society.

PUBLIC SCHOOL POPULATION CHANGES

Since the mid-1960s, the country's public school system has undergone a dramatic shift in minority student enrollments. Students of color accounted for about a fifth of public school enrollments four decades ago; today minority students have nearly doubled their number in school enrollments. National education statistics show that nearly 92,000 elementary and secondary public schools in the United States provide instruction to nearly 48 million students.[2] Of this population, students of color are 39 percent of national public school enrollments—black students are 17 percent of national enrollments, Latino students are slightly more than 16 percent, Asian and Pacific Islander students are about 4 percent, and American Indian students are slightly more than 1 percent of national enrollments. Some public school systems have considerably higher minority student enrollments. Black students have higher public school enrollments in southern regions of the country, Latino students constitute higher percentages of public school enrollments in the southwest, Asian American students populate more of California and Hawaii's public school systems, and American Indian students have higher public school enrollments in Alaska, Oklahoma, Montana, and South Dakota.[3] As the population of students of color has grown in public education, however, white student enrollments in public schools have decreased. White students were 70 percent of public school enrollments in 1986, but today they are 60 percent of enrollments. Such demographic changes in public school enrollments result from immigration, age structures, and fertility levels in the general population.[4]

Differential high school graduation rates by race are associated with racial segregation and poverty rates. Nationally, about 68 percent of all students who enter the ninth grade graduate on time in the twelfth grade. Although white and Asian American graduation rates exceed the national average (75 percent and 77 percent, respectively), roughly half of black (50 percent), Latino (53 percent), and American Indian (51 percent) students graduate from high school. Graduation rates are worse for high school districts located in central city neighborhoods with high concentrations of minority populations and poverty, with high percentages of disabled students, and with high percentages of English-language learners. Scholars suggest that the implications of low high school dropout rates are far reaching for individuals, communities, and the economic vitality of the United States generally. Unemployment rates, prison incarceration rates, and poverty rates are directly related to high school dropout rates.[5]

A wide racial gap remains for college enrollments and college completion rates as well. White students are about 68 percent of college enrollments, and college students of color are slightly more than 28 percent of college and university enrollments. Of minority college students, blacks are 11 percent of college enrollments, Latinos are 9 percent, Asian and Pacific Islanders are 6 percent, and American Indians are 1 percent of college enrollments.[6] Whites (68 percent) also comprise significant numbers of graduate students compared to blacks (8 percent), Latinos (5 percent), American Indians (0.6 percent), and Asian Americans and Pacific Islanders (5 percent).[7] But critical sociologist Edna Bonacich reminds us in *Racism in the Deep Structures of U.S. Higher Education* that even with affirmative action programs ostensibly promoting diversity on the campuses of colleges and universities, white administrators do not have the interests of students of color at heart. Bonacich argues that the goal of American education for people of color is to make them into "role models" for their people by succumbing to corporate capitalism and foregoing demands for social justice.[8]

Interestingly, although Asian and Pacific Islanders have much lower college enrollments than whites, they are more likely to complete college than whites—Asian American and Pacific Islanders (47 percent) are nearly twice as likely as whites (27 percent) to complete college. Blacks (17 percent) are less likely than whites to complete college. The latest government statistics on college graduation rates for persons 25 years old and over show disturbing levels of college completion among Latinos. Latinos (11 percent) have the lowest college completion rates compared to Asian Americans and Pacific Islanders and whites. Among Latino groups, Cubans (19 percent) have higher rates of college completion than Puerto Ricans (14 percent), who in turn have higher rates than persons of Mexican descent (8 percent).[9] One reason for lower minority student college completion rates is that educational institutions have yet to shift their focus from admission decisions to retention and completion. Educational researchers argue that institutions of higher learning must accompany access with tutoring, mentoring, and advising services to help students succeed. Unfortunately, these services are far too often unavailable to minority students, or they are understaffed and underfunded.[10]

PUBLIC SCHOOL *RESEGREGATION*

Even with noticeable growth in nonwhite enrollments in American schools, educational segregation persists. Fifty years after the U.S. Supreme Court ruled racial segregation in public schools unconstitutional in *Brown v. Board of Education* (1954) minority schoolchildren continue to attend schools where they are the majority of student enrollments. Social progress toward integration of public schools moved slowly because most school districts resisted integration ostensibly because of funding problems. Yet many states openly defied *Brown* and voided the decision, other states fought the Court's decision in court, and still other states used open violence to oppose school busing.[11] At the time of *Brown*, less than 1 percent of black schoolchildren attended white majority schools. This figure increased to more than 43 percent in 1988, and by 2001 the percentage of black schoolchildren enrolled in predominantly white schools fell to 30 percent. One reason for increased segregation in public schools is that the U.S. Supreme Court legitimated *resegregation* of public school districts nationwide by ending federal court oversight of school desegregation plans.[12] Today, white students attend schools where they are 79 percent of the student population, black and Latino students attend schools where they are 54 percent of student enrollments, Asian students are in schools where they are slightly more than 22 percent of school enrollments, and American Indians attend schools where American Indians are roughly a third of school enrollments.[13] New York, Illinois, Michigan, and California have more pronounced segregation of black students in public school enrollments than other states, and the effects of public school segregation are strongest for Latino students in New York, California, Texas, and New Mexico.

As one scholar puts it, "segregation is increasing, and it is leaving black and Hispanic children in impoverished apartheid schools."[14]

In *Success and Failure: How Systematic Racism Trumped the Brown v. Board of Education Decision*, sociologists Joe R. Feagin and Bernice McNair Barnett explore some of the reasons why desegregation of public schools is imperative to schoolchildren. These scholars explain that desegregation of public schools has proven extremely beneficial to all students by providing them greater access to educational and networking resources and greater opportunities to experience diversity. Conversely, racial segregation of public schools not only limits available resources and opportunities for minority schoolchildren, but it also has damaging effects on these children's psychological and emotional well-being. To Feagin and Barnett, no government educational policy implemented over the past several decades has addressed the substantive educational "realities" of millions of segregated and impoverished American schoolchildren. Undoubtedly, with significant proportions of persons of color in the United States living at or below a subsistence level, and the economic conditions of communities of color continuing to stagnate, the impact of concentrated poverty and school segregation on the social well-being of minority schoolchildren will worsen in the coming decades.[15]

INEQUALITY IN HIGHER EDUCATION

To James Blackwell, "institutional structures exist to meet the needs of individuals and groups who control inordinate power, authority, and resources within a social system and who simultaneously limit the access of others to the advantage of power."[16] This observation is particularly germane to the occupational structure of U.S. colleges and universities. Despite an understandable naïveté among some scholars that it is unimaginable racism exists among the educated elite, the entry of persons of color and women into the ranks of postsecondary educational institutions remains deliberately slow despite a generation of affirmative action.[17] The occupational structure of American education continues to use a racist organizational culture to establish and maintain parameters that regulate the entry of minority faculty. Many white faculty hold fast to the notion that the entry of minority faculty challenges the integrity of the academy.[18] One can see the effects of a constraining organizational culture, defined by a racial mindset among white faculty, on the small proportion of minority faculty in postsecondary educational institutions. Whites make up the vast majority of full-time faculty in postsecondary institutions; whites are 85 percent of instructional faculty and staff in higher education, and blacks are 5 percent, Asian and Pacific Islanders are 6 percent, Latinos are 3 percent, and American Indians are 1 percent. Females are 38 percent of instructional faculty in higher education, but they hold roughly half of the instructional positions in two-year institutions. The percentage of faculty of color holding instructional positions in two-year institutions is roughly equal to the percentage of positions they hold in four-year institutions. Similarly, most college athletes are black, but almost all head coaches in collegiate athletics are white: there are only five black head coaches in the 117 colleges and universities of the National Collegiate Athletic Association Division I-A.[19] Furthermore, white faculty members generally have higher salaries, are more likely to be tenured, and are more likely to be full professors than faculty of color.[20]

Not only are faculty of color and female faculty underrepresented as instructors in institutions of higher education, but minority faculty often encounter obstacles in their attempts to move up the academic ladder.[21] Faculty members of color often encounter overt and covert racism, tokenism, typecasting, and taboos. Academics often compel minority faculty to give up their ethnic identity. Other minority faculty members give in to racism and become so demoralized that they leave academia. Still, other minority faculty fight back and learn to play the so-called academic game. Often, faculty of color and female faculty find themselves as the sole minority professor within an academic department or division. Colleges and universities frequently relegate minority faculty to ethnic studies departments and in education and humanities programs, often regarded as the "academic dumping grounds" for minority faculty.[22] The racial and gender gap in higher education is particularly prominent on science and engineering faculties.[23] Rarely do minority faculty have access to sponsorship networks to aid in their academic mobility, and white faculty often marginalize minority faculty from the contexts of institutional decision making. As a result, Chicano sociology professor Adalberto Aguirre, Jr., tells us in "Academic Storytelling: A Critical Race Theory Story of Affirmative Action," minority faculty perceive their institutional role as peripheral to the operations of postsecondary educational institutions.[24] Clearly, given the context of minority faculty's presence and participation in higher education, the status of minority faculty in academe is a tenuous one: the manifestations of racism remain integral to minority faculty in educational institutions.[25]

One outcome of the dearth of minority faculty in American education is that the academic curriculum remains Anglocentric. Some scholars attest that most students learn little of the realities of American history regarding the mistreatment of African Americans, Native Americans, other minority Americans, and the poor, for example. One researcher candidly argues that "what has been taught and what our children have learned is an American lie—not American History." As Gwendolyn Zoharah Simmons explains,

> Sadly, most White American students have no real knowledge of slavery, the Middle Passage, or the millions lost in those hellish voyages. Nor have they ever been taught about the rigors, hardships, and dehumanization of the slavery experience—the deprivations, the brutal punishments, the rapes of women and children, the forced separation of families, the brutality of it all. Most White Americans, and sadly many racial minority students, know nothing of the true history of this country when they enter the university, and they will know nothing of it when they leave. They have never heard of Frederick Douglass, Harriet Tubman, Sojourner Truth, Ida Wells Barnett, the Grimke Sisters, Henry Lloyd Garrison, Nat Turner, Denmark Vesey, and on, and on, and on.[26]

The blatant manifestations of racism remain integral to student admissions in educational institutions. As President Lyndon Johnson explained in a 1965 speech on affirmative action to achieve equal opportunity: "You do not take a person, who for years has been hobbled by chains and liberate him, bring him up to the starting line of a race and then say 'you are free to compete with all the others,' and still believe that you have been completely fair."[27] But for the most part the U.S. educational institution has done exactly that. Beginning with *Regent of the University of California v. Bakke* in

1978, U.S. Supreme Court rulings have mostly disfavored affirmative action policies in colleges and universities.[28] The Court held in *Bakke* that college admission criteria can include race as one factor in determining qualified applicants, yet ruled that the medical school of UC Davis could not reserve admission spaces for minorities. The regents of the University of California voted to end affirmative actions programs in 1995 and held that admissions decisions could no longer use race, gender, ethnicity, or national origin in determining qualified applicants to any of its campuses. The effect of the regents' vote on affirmative action in its admission polices three years later caused minority enrollment to plummet by 61 percent at UC Berkeley and 36 percent at UC Los Angeles.[29] California voters rejected affirmative action in public education and state employment in Proposition 209 in 1996, and that same year the University of Texas won an appeal to the U.S. Courts of Appeals for the Fifth District prohibiting its law school from considering race in its admissions process that the U.S. Supreme Court let stand.[30] Florida and Washington voters have also affirmed bans on affirmative action in higher education, and several other states are threatening anti–affirmative action legislation within the near future.[31] Most recently, the Supreme Court the use of race among other factors in the University of Michigan law school admissions policy was constitutional, but the Court rejected an undergraduate admissions program that awarded admission evaluation points based on race and ethnicity.[32] Despite this disconcerting history of affirmative action in the U.S. educational institution, students of color have increased their college graduation rates even though their rates fall below those of Anglo students.[33] Affirmative action programs have been particularly helpful for Asian American students to realize equal access to higher education—the percentage of Asian Americans receiving bachelor's degrees doubled between 1990 and 2001. Yet, to some scholars, the model minority myth about Asian Americans in the United States has furthered an antiaffirmative action ideology against Filipino Americans at the Berkeley and Los Angeles campuses of the University of California.[34]

A Case Study in Inequality

The Educational Needs of American Indian Schoolchildren Unique to the American Indian educational experience is the legal relationship that the federal government established with Indian nations through hundreds of treaties providing specific government services to Indian people in exchange for access to tribal lands. Education was one such service. The history of American Indian access to formal education, however, is one of racial isolation. In the late 1800s, the federal government viewed education programs for American Indian children as a means to assimilate Indian children to its Anglo-dominated culture. This was the underlying philosophy of boarding schools for American Indian children. Often located great distances from the children's family and tribal ties, the boarding school essentially isolated Indian children and facilitated their indoctrination into mainstream American culture.[35] White officials considered American Indian culture (language, values, traditions, and customs) negative and hindering the educational process that created conflict between traditional American Indian culture and white culture. In *American Indians in Higher Education: A History of Cultural Conflict*, Bobby Wright and William G. Tierney suggest that the cultural conflict associated with American Indian education continues today. One outcome of the continued marginalization of American Indians is lower levels of educational attainment compared to non-Indians. Roughly 65 percent of all American Indians are high school graduates and 9 percent have bachelor's degrees or higher, but only about 3 percent of American Indians have been able to obtain graduate and professional degrees. The relative poor performance of American Indians to achieving noticeable levels of educational achievement means that large numbers of non-Indian professionals are involved in American Indian education—assuring still further a disturbing alliance of American Indian schools to cultural assimilation.

The learning environment provided by teachers can affect the quality of the educational experience of American Indian schoolchildren. About 1.2 million American Indian students are enrolled in K–12 schools in the United States. Of these students, about 90 percent attend public schools and about 10 percent attend Bureau of Indian Affairs (BIA)/tribal schools.[36] Educational researchers have identified the overwhelming importance of an American Indian teaching force to the academic success of American Indian schoolchildren: learning is enhanced when teacher and student share the same language and culture; American Indian teachers enhance the teacher–student relationship for Indian youth and increase the desire of students to remain in school; American Indian teachers are important role models; American Indian teachers provide connectivity to Indian students' community; and American Indian teachers are likely to be aware of Indian learning styles.[37] Yet non-Indian professionals are excessively involved in educating American Indian children. A recent study of schools, principals, and teachers serving American Indian schoolchildren shows that less than half of all principals and only 38 percent of the teachers in *tribal schools* are actually American Indian. The level of American Indians in administrative and teaching positions in *public schools* with high American Indian schoolchildren enrollments is worse: only 13 percent of the principals are American Indian and only 15 percent of the teachers are American Indian.[38]

Unfortunately, excessive involvement of non-Indian teachers in American Indian continues the use of historically based assimilationist policies in American Indian education. For example, Indian schools have played a significant role in carrying out early government language policies and to Christianize American Indians. In doing so, Indian schools have summarily destroyed the native language base among most American Indian schoolchildren by forbidding American Indian schoolchildren from using their native languages at school. As one Alaskan native researcher explains,

> The language base of my children and grandchildren is English. These two younger generations seldom, if ever, hear Tlingit spoken because they live in other parts of the country, seldom coming to Alaska where—to this day—they might hear my uncles and their generation speak the language to one another. I have lost the language, my children never learned the language, and my grandchildren have lost the opportunity to learn the language.[39]

The curriculum of American Indian education remains European centered.[40] The epitome of cultural chauvinism is illustrated by one researcher's visit to an elementary school on a Chippewa Indian reservation where he viewed students in a sixth-grade English class busily working on a composition for Thanksgiving entitled

"Why We Are Happy the Pilgrims Came."[41] Textbooks often portray American Indian culture as inferior to Anglo-European culture, or they ignore American Indian people altogether or reinforce negative stereotypes of American Indians as *savages*, *primitives*, *filthy*, *barely human*, *murderous*, *treacherous*, and *dumb*.[42] Clearly, the educational agenda of the United States for American Indians has been to make them less Indian; that is, to *Americanize* Indian students or, as some states (Louisiana, Mississippi, and North Carolina) have chosen to do, simply exclude American Indian children except on a segregated basis.[43] Not only has the assimilationist curricula of church schools, BIA/Indian schools, and public schools failed to meet the needs of American Indian schoolchildren, but the racist sentiments of non-American Indian teachers and students have furthered American Indian schoolchildren's alienation.[44]

SUMMARY

Decades of civil rights reform have *not* lessened the effects of institutional racism and ethnic chauvinism in American education for minority persons. For children of color, schools are segregated institutions with black, Latino, Asian American, and American Indian students educated separately and differently than Anglo students. The educational experience of students of color is unlike the educational experience of Anglo students: we treat students of color as inferior from the moment they enter the public school system and until they either drop out or are pushed out of the system. School curricula systematically devalue the cultural domain of students of color. Minority educators are absent from teaching and administrative positions in U.S. schools. White teachers are insensitive to the dynamics and consequences of racism in American society, and their actions further separate students of color from the mainstream of American education. One outcome of educational racism is that students of color are ill prepared as adults for equal participation in the occupational structure. Clearly, the only conclusion one can draw from the discussion presented in this chapter and its selected readings is that the design of American education is to promote and maintain a racially and ethnically stratified society.

ENDNOTES

1. Robert England, Kenneth J. Meier, and Luis Ricardo Fraga, "Barriers to Equal Opportunity: Educational Practices and Minority Students," *Urban Affairs Quarterly*, 23 (1988): 640.
2. Lee Hoffman, *Overview of Public Elementary and Secondary Schools and Districts: School Year 2001–02*, National Center for Educational Statistics (May 2003), http://nces.ed.gov/pubs2003/overview03/index.asp#4.
3. Digest of Educational Statistics, *Percentage Distribution of Enrollment in Public Elementary and Secondary Schools, by Race/Ethnicity and State: Fall 2000*, Table 42, 2002, http://nces.ed.gov/programs/digest/d02/tables/dt042.asp.
4. Hoffman, *Overview of Public Elementary and Secondary Schools and Districts*.
5. Gary Orfield, Daniel Losen, Johanna Wald, and Christopher B. Swanson, *Losing Our Future: How Minority Youth Are Being Left Behind by the Graduation Rate Crisis* (Cambridge, MA: The Civil Rights Project at Harvard University, 2004).
6. U.S. Census Bureau, *Statistical Abstracts of the United States: 2003*, Table 278, http://www.census.gov/prod/2004pubs/03statab/educ.pdf.
7. Ibid.

8. Edna Bonacich, "Racism in the Deep Structure of U.S. Higher Education: When Affirmative Action Is Not Enough," *International Perspectives on Education and Society* 1 (1998): 3–15.

9. U.S. Census Bureau, *Statistical Abstracts of the United States: 2003*, Table 227, http:// www .census.gov/prod/2004pubs/03statab/educ.pdf.

10. Robert H. Atwell, "The Long Road Ahead: Barriers to Minority Participation Persist," *Reflections on 20 Years of Minorities in Higher Education and the ACE Annual Status Report*, American Council on Education, Center for Advancement of Racial and Ethnic Equity (July 2004), pp. 1–3, http:// www.acenet.edu/bookstore.

11. Martin C. Evans, "Brown v. Board of Education," *Newsday*, May 16, 2004, p. A03.

12. Gary Orfield and Susan E. Eaton, *Dismantling Desegregation* (New York: New Press, 1996).

13. Orfield and Lee, *Brown at 50*.

14. *Supra* note 15.

15. Carmen DeNavas-Walt, Bernadette D. Proctor, and Robert J. Mills, *Income, Poverty, and Health Insurance Coverage in the United States: 2003*, U.S. Census Bureau (August 2004), http:// www .census.gov/prod/2004pubs/p60–226.pdf. See also David Walsh, "U.S. August Job Report Provides No Relief for Workers," *World Socialist Web Site* (September 4, 2004), http:// www.wsws.org/ articles/ 2004/sep2004/jobs-s04.shtml.

16. James Blackwell, "Current Issues Affecting Blacks and Latinos in the Educational Pipeline," in Gail E. Thomas, ed., *U.S. Race Relations in the 1980s and 1990s: Challenges and Alternatives* (New York: Hemisphere, 1990).

17. Maria de la Luz Reyes and John J. Halcon, "Racism in America: The Old Wolf Revisited," *Harvard Educational Review*, 58 (1988): 299–314.

18. Henry McComb, "The Dynamics and Impact of Minority Processes on Higher Education, The Curriculum, and Black Women," *Sex Roles*, 21 (1989): 127.

19. Black Players, White Coaches," *Journal of Blacks in Higher Education Weekly Bulletin* (September 9, 2004), http://www.jbhe.com/.

20. Michael T. Nettles, Laura W. Perna, and Ellen M. Bradburn, "Salary, Promotion, and Tenure Status of Minority and Women Faculty in U.S. Colleges and Universities," *Educational Statistics Quarterly*, http://nces.ed.gov/programs/quarterly/vol_2/2_2/q4–4.asp.

21. Manuel Avalos, "The Status of Latinos in the Profession: Problems of Recruitment and Retention," *Political Science and Politics* (June 1991): 241–246.

22. Denise Glover and Basmat Parsad, "The Gender and Racial/Ethnic Composition of Postsecondary Instructional Faculty and Staff: 1992–98," *Educational Statistics Quarterly*, http://nces.ed.gov/ programs/quarterly/vol_4/4_3/4_6.asp.

23. "Women, Minorities Race on Science, Engineering Faculties," *Black Issues in Higher Education*, http://www.blackissues.com.

24. Adalberto Aguirre Jr., "Academic Storytelling: A Critical Race Theory Story of Affirmative Action," *Sociological Perspectives*, 43 (2000): 319–339.

25. Maria de la Luz Reyes and John J. Halcon, "Racism in America: The Old Wolf Revisited," *Harvard Educational Review*, 58 (1988): 299–344.

26. Gwendolyn Zoharah Simmons, "Racism in Higher Education," *University of Florida Journal of Law and Public Policy*, 14 (2002): 29–43.

27. American for Fair Chance, *What Is Affirmative Action*, http://fairchance.civilrights.org/the_facts/ what_is_aa_new.html.

28. 438 U.S. 912 (1978).

29. Shirley J. Wilcher, *The History of Affirmative Action Policies*, Americans for Fair Chance (August 7, 2003), http://www.inmotionmagazine.com/aahist.html.

30. *Texas v. Hopwood*, 518 U.S. 1033 (1996).

31. Americans for a Fair Chance, *Anti-Affirmative Action Threats in the States: 1997–2004*, (June 2005), http://fairchance.civilrights.org/the_facts/reports/aa_state_2005.pdf.

32. *Grutter v. Bollinger* (539 U.S. 982, 2003) and *Gratz v. Bollinger* (539 U.S. 244, 2003).

33. Americans for a Fair Chance, *Facts on Affirmative Action in Higher Education* (January 2004), http://www.civilrights.org/issues/affirmative/AA_highereducation_2004.pdf.

34. See Annette B. Almazan, "Looking at Diversity and Affirmative Action Through the Lens of Pilipino/a American Students' Experience at UCLA and Berkeley," *Asian Pacific American Law Journal*, 9(2004): 44–82.

35. Mary Crow Dog and Richard Erdoes, "Civilize Them with a Stick," in Susan J. Ferguson, ed., *Mapping the Social Landscape: Readings in Sociology* (New York: McGraw-Hill, 2005), pp. 573–580.

36. Susan Faircloth and John W. Tippeconnic III, "Issues in the Education of American Indian and Alaska Native Students with Disabilities," *ERIC Digest* (December 2000), http://www.ael.org/page.htm? &pd=1&scope=ai&index=241&pub=x.

37. Kathryn D. Manuelito, "Building a Native Teaching Force: Important Considerations," *ERIC Digest* (December 2003), http://www.ael.org/page.htm?&pd=1&scope=ai&index=755&pub=x.

38.   D. Michael Pavel, "Schools Principals and Teachers Serving American Indian and Alaska Native Students," *ERIC Digest* (January 1999), http://www.ael.org/page.htm?&-pd=1&-scope=ai&-index=217&-pub=x.

39.   William Demmert, "Blueprints for Indian Education: Languages and Cultures," *ERIC Digest* (August 1994), http://www.ericfacility.net/ericdigests/ed372899.html.

40.   U.S. Department of Education, *Indian Nations at Risk: An Educational Strategy for Action*, October 1991.

41.   Richard Schaefer, *Race and Ethnic Groups* (New York: Prentice Hall, 2004), p. 191.

42.   Howard M. Bahr, Bruce A. Chadwick, and Robert C. Day, *Native Americans Today: Sociological Perspectives* (New York: Harper & Row, 1979); Jorge Noriega, "American Indian Education in the United States: Indoctrination for Subordination to Colonialism," in Michael Jones, ed., *The State of Native America: Genocide, Colonialization, and Resistance* (Boston: South End Press, 1992).

43.   U.S. Commission on Civil Disorders, *Racial Isolation in the Public Schools: Report of the U.S. Commission on Civil Rights*, 2 vols. Washington, DC: U.S. Government Printing Office, 1967.

44.   James S. Olson and Raymond Wilson, *Native Americans in the Twentieth Century* (Provo, UT: Brigham Young University Press, 1984).

Racism in the Deep Structure of U.S. Higher Education: When Affirmative Action Is Not Enough

Edna Bonacich

The goal of the educational system for people of color is to make the students into role models' for their people. See, if you shut up and give yourself up the White man and become like him, you can make lots of money like him. Do not struggle for social change. Do not demand justice.

I want to start by telling you a story. On our campus we have something called Chicano Student Programs. It was originally attached to our now defunct Chicano Studies Program. Its purpose was to support various Chicano student organizations, like Mecha, to organize cultural events, and to foster community outreach. Under its aegis, students would organize activities like running a tutorial program for poor Mexican-American children. Chicano Student Programs provided a small haven for the expression of the cultural and political concerns of Chicano students.

Today Chicano Student Programs is under attack by the campus administration. They want to change its orientation. The director is being told that her primary attention should be focused on enhancing the academic achievement of Chicago students on campus,

and on developing a career planning and placement program for them. She has been told to disassociate herself from student clubs like Mecha, and to curtail various community-oriented activities. Instead, her energies should be devoted to improving UCR's retention and graduation record for Chicanos.

The battle has been joined, at least to a certain degree. Some students are protesting the shift. They claim that their academic and career-oriented needs are being met by other agencies on campus, like the Learning and Study Skills Center or the Career Planning and Placement Center. Chicano Student Programs represented a different idea. But that idea is being squashed.

The head of the program is on probation. She was hired in this status because her predecessor showed some resistance to having the

---

Source: Edna Bonacich, "Racism in the Deep Structure of U.S. Higher Education: When Affirmative Action is Not Enough," International Perspectives on Education and Society, I (1998): 3–15.

program altered in this way. Indeed, he "permitted" a demonstration to occur that protested the abolition of Chicano Studies. He was fired and a legal case filed by him against the university is in progress. Meanwhile, the program is in a kind of receivership, with the new director having to work under the close scrutiny and constant directives of the administration.

Perhaps they hired a woman this time because they thought she would be more pliable. If so, they erred. The new director is responsive to the student concerns, which she believes she was hired to serve. Consequently, a battle is raging over her job. Her supervisors are giving her negative evaluations over her job performance and have extended her probation to the summer (when, presumably, if they fire her, no students will be around to object). She has challenged them point by point, and is trying to fight back—though the forces are hardly evenly matched.

What does all of this mean? I think it represents a lot more than just a minor personnel matter on an insignificant campus of the University of California. To me, it is symbolic of the relationship between the universities of this country and its minority peoples. It represents a conflict of values.

Before trying to explicate what these conflicting values are, I want briefly to consider the status of racial inequality in this country. It seems to me that many people believe that racial inequality is a thing of the past in the United States. They may recognize that pockets of prejudice still exist, and that discrimination occurs occasionally. But generally, there is a widespread belief that we are well on the way to solving this problem. Civil Rights legislation, coupled with affirmative action programs, has created a legal environment that fosters the upward mobility of minorities. If we just let these new legal arrangements work themselves out, equality will be achieved. Indeed, many Americans believe these laws have gone too far in pushing for racial equality, and that all that was required was the removal of active discrimination. After

that, each individual should compete on the basis of his or her own merits in a color-blind society. Affirmative action, by pushing more forcefully for racial equality, has been seen by some to be a form of reverse discrimination. Civil Rights legislation has gone far enough. We should stop there and let things gradually work themselves out.

I believe that the problem of racial inequality is far more intractable than this model supposes. I also believe that racial inequality is closely linked to the high degree of inequality that permeates this society in general, and that we cannot get rid of one without the other.

What I will do now is to describe, briefly, the degree of inequality, and especially racial inequality, that exists in our country today. Then I will consider how this inequality is deeply embedded in a particular ideology that dominates our nation, and that is at war with our democratic aspirations. I want to show how the university embodies that ideology, and thus contributes to racial inequality, even when its members speak out against it. And finally, I want very briefly to discuss alternative ideas and values, and what we might do to change this situation.

INEQUALITY

The United States is a vastly unequal society. Typically we like to evaluate our degree of inequality by looking at income or education statistics, and by these criteria we do not look so bad. True, we are among the more unequal of the Western democracies, but, compared to Third World countries, we look good. We have a fairly substantial middle class with reasonably high income and educational levels. That bulge in the middle makes us look pretty equalitarian.

But another measure of inequality concerns the ownership of property. And here the concentration is extreme. A recent study commissioned by a Congressional committee found that 1/2 of 1 percent of the nation's families own 35 percent of its wealth. If you include home ownership (which typically is not a means by which people make money) and only include items like stocks, bonds, rental real estate, and business ownership, the top 1/2 of 1 percent owns 45 percent of the nation's wealth. In other words, almost half of the wealth of this country is owned by a mere 420,000 families. And the study showed that the concentration of wealth has gone up over the past 20 years.

Within this elite group, who are worth an average of almost $9 million apiece, wealth is even more concentrated. Forbes Magazine did a survey of the wealthiest Americans and found that the richest individual owned $4.5 billion in assets. That is a ten digit number!

Another study, conducted by the Census Bureau, examined the median net worth of American households, that is, how much wealth or property they hold, subtracting out their debts. The average (i.e., median) American family held $32,667 worth of assets. The average White family held $39,135, while the average Black family held $3,395—less than 1/10 of what the average White family owns. The figure for Spanish-origin households was $4,913.

Female-headed households were worse off than the average. And the racial differences were even more marked here. White female-headed households held a median of $22,500 in assets. Black female-headed households only owned an average of $671, and Spanish-oriented, $478. The average Black or Hispanic female-headed household owns less than 2 percent of what the average White family owns.

I want to emphasize that these are averages. Not the poorest, but the average Black female-headed household commands only $671 in wealth, while some White man owns $4.5 billion. The vastness of these differences gives us a glimpse of the chasm that exists between rich and poor in this country. And poverty, while not limited to people of color, is heavily correlated with race.

Can anyone doubt that there exists in this society an impoverished sector of Blacks, Latinos and Native Americans, living in ghettos, barrios and on reservations? Can anyone doubt that these people lack adequate food, shelter and medical care? Can anyone question that they are locked out of the American Dream, and that, even if there exists a growing Black middle class, the lives of the impoverished remain unaffected? I think this nation is fooling itself when it claims that the race problem is solved, or well on the way to solution. We are purposefully blinding ourselves to an intractable social problem that will not go away by itself, no matter how much we hope it will.

UTILITARIANISM

Now I want to turn to the question of values, and try to show that the inequality that racial minorities suffer from is a direct product of some of the fundamental values of this society. Racism is not just a nasty blemish that has somehow attached itself to an otherwise healthy system. The existence of a racially-oppressed population is deeply tied to some of our most cherished ideas. I want to try to show this linkage, and to suggest that the university, no matter how liberal on the surface, represents this ideology in its deepest structures. Thus the university, like most other institutions, participates in the reproduction and maintenance of racial oppression.

The basic philosophy that I am talking about can be labelled utilitarianism. The idea is that every individual should pursue his or her enlightened self-interest. It is assumed that out of this pursuit will emerge the social welfare. The social welfare—the good of everyone—need not be attended to directly. The invisible hand of the marketplace will balance out all of the competing individual interests, so that the greatest good for the greatest number will emerge.

Another way to describe this value system is with the word meritocracy. American society is structured like a race. Everyone is supposed to line up at the same starting gate—we call this equality of opportunity—and run as fast as they can, and may the best man win. It is each person for himself in this race, each one pursuing his or her own self-interest. The winners of the race are given the big prize, their merit is rewarded, while the losers go home empty-handed. The basic idea is survival of the fittest.

According to the utilitarian-meritocratic ethic, however, the race does not just benefit the winners. It is supposed to benefit everyone. The winners become our leaders. They occupy positions of responsibility. They are our experts, our professionals. Having survived the competition, they have proven that they are the "best and brightest." Consequently we can count on getting the best from them. Their proven superiority will benefit us all. It will somehow "trickle down" to the rest of us.

Take the example of doctors. Surely we would not want a half competent individual to be our brain surgeon. We want the most qualified and capable person. Competition insures that only the most capable will survive medical school, and thus the rest of us can be sure that when we need brain surgery we will get someone who knows what he is doing.

The only small wrinkle in this model is that a lot of people cannot afford the high quality medical care so produced. Yes, our experts are able to create amazing technologies to save increasingly premature infants at great expense. But we still have a surprisingly high infant mortality rate, because many poor mothers get no prenatal care at all. Something does not work quite right. The invisible hand of the free market does not seem to have the mechanism to make sure that the benefits trickle down far enough.

The meritocratic ideology of winners and losers is deeply embedded in our schools and universities. Every student becomes a competitor in the race to get ahead. It is each per-

son for him or herself, striving to win, striving to be in first place so one can take the big prize. The teachers and professors are the judges of performance. They define who will win and lose. And they are themselves caught up in a race to win at their own level.

The allocation of prizes and booby prizes in this society is profoundly unequal. The ideology says that it has to be this way in order to motivate people to work their hardest. "Excellence," the buzzword of the 1980s, requires it. If you do not make big distinctions in terms of rewards, then no one will put out any effort to achieve, it is claimed.

The system of prizes for performance adds layers of inequality on top of each other. The good performer gets rewards which enhance his or her performance still further. The good student gets put into a gifted program, with greater attention and resources put into his or her development. At the university level, we provide honors programs for the "best and brightest," scholarships that enable the talented not to have to work while they are in school, and so forth. The winners accumulate rewards which add to their advantage in the race, until they are so far out ahead they are unreachable.

This structure of reward is shown in the 3-tiered system of higher education in California, where the most advantaged students go to the University of California, where much more money and resources are ploughed into their education than into the education of those who attend the factory-like, poorly supported, Community Colleges. State educators proclaim their disappointment that more students do not leap from the Community Colleges to UC, but the chasm between them is ever-widening, and the leap becomes more impossible with each passing year.

The point I want to emphasize is that the university is deeply enmeshed in this utilitarian social philosophy. It embodies it in every aspect of its daily functioning.

Now, the utilitarian ethic masks another, less charming reality. We all know, I am sure, how the rationale of free competition in the marketplace does not quite work the way it is supposed to. The public welfare is not necessarily well-protected. Indeed, pollution, the dumping of toxic chemicals, unsafe work conditions, excessive waste of resources, and a myriad of other social problems, arise out of the unrestrained workings of the "free market."

Worse, the "free market" ideology diverts our attention from an even uglier reality: exploitation. The truth of the matter is, American society is not a fair race in which everyone starts at the same starting line and runs like hell, and it never has been. Equal opportunity is a myth. It is a myth that justifies excesses of inequality. "The reason you are poor," it says, "is because you are lazy or stupid. You could not keep up in the race, that is why." The meritocratic ideology silences those people who are impoverished and cut out by the system, by teaching them that they deserve to be where they are. You dare not question the vicious inequality of the system because you will only draw attention to yourself and your own failure.

In fact, this myth stands reality on its head. The poor are not poor because they are lazy and stupid, but because they have been expropriated and are continually expropriated day after day. And the rich are not wealthy because they are the best and brightest, because they work hardest and show the most initiative. On the contrary, they are often the biggest crooks and speculators, or the laziest bums who just sit on mounds of property and milk it dry. Ownership is the key to wealth in this society—not merit. He who owns can keep collecting. He who owns nothing must keep forking over to the owners. The rental relationship shows this vividly. The owner need not lift a finger to have that old rent keep rolling in, while you work half your life away just to keep paying your rent. He is not better than you, or smarter. He just has what you need. He controls it and so can control you.

The owners of property rely on the impoverishment of everyone else, because otherwise their property would not be worth anything. The landlord, for example, requires a class of people who cannot afford to buy homes so that they will be forced to rent. The owner of property depends on poverty. But the myth of this society is that dependency runs in the opposite direction. The poor depend on the rich for the beneficence of giving them (out of the kindness of their hearts) jobs, apartments, loans, and the like. Are jobs an act of generosity on the part of employers? Is this not a ludicrous inversion of the true relationship?

Elites forever find ways of justifying their privileges because, if for one minute, people stepped back and looked at the whole picture, they would be so outraged at the patent injustices that they would tear the whole edifice down.

The schools, to repeat, are deeply implicated in the reproduction of inequality in American society, by teaching a meritocratic ideology and by implementing a utilitarian social ethic in their day-to-day practices.

This ethic, I believe, is profoundly racist. First of all, utilitarian social philosophy is a Western European invention. It is not the only way to organize society. Indeed, it is a highly questionable way. And yet it is placed at the center of the university's practice as the only way to do things.

There is a hidden belief that the utilitarian system is the best way of organizing human social life. Embedded in human nature, providing the maximum of individual free choice, utilitarianism is equated with democracy. And it is seen as the most advanced form that human civilization has yet attained.

Now there is tremendous arrogance implied in this world view. All other social systems are seen as backward, primitive, or else as totalitarian and dictatorial. Only the Western system is the pinnacle of social perfection, the system that has transcended history and will last forever.

Youngsters who derive from non-Western European cultures thus enter the schools with a heavy stigma upon them. They are "culturally deprived" because they do not belong to the culture of the master race. They have a lot of catching up to do. They come in with a badge of inferiority that haunts them throughout their schooling.

"But," says the bearers of the utilitarian ethic, "you can catch up if you want to. All you need to do is compete like the White man. Shed your past. Become like us and we will give you the rich rewards of our exalted civilization."

The minority person has every reason to view this message with suspicion. Not only is he asked to negate himself, to deny his family, to leave his loved ones behind and to never look back—actions of questionable human value, but he can also question the value of what he is being asked to join: "You do not look so happy to me" he can challenge. "You White folks look pretty sick and miserable. You are so caught up in your drive to be successful and to make money, that you have forgotten how to live. You rape and plunder Mother Earth. You build weapons of destruction that will probably blow all of us to pieces. Not only do you cheat and rob us, but you cheat and rob each other. Your whole civilization is based on trying to do each other in. Why on earth would I want to be like you? You look exceedingly ugly to me. I would prefer to retain my own being, thanks all the same. I like myself the way I am. I appreciate my own beauty—something you White sons of bitches cannot understand."

The point I am trying to make is that the university is essentially assimilationist. The minority person is required to alter him- or herself to fit into the university. The institution is not willing to change in any way, except the most superficial, to accommodate to these new entrants. Change is a one-way street. You become like the White man, period. Either you become like the White man, or you are out.

The minority person is forced to negate himself in order to be acceptable. Who he is, in reality, is not acceptable. He must become something else. He must learn to hate and reject who he is in order to become what the White man wants him to be. This does not add up to "equal access" or "equal opportunity." Minority individuals come in to the university with a special burden: the necessity of self-negation.

Now let us assume that the minority individual overcomes this handicap and decides that he will play the game by the White man's rules. Let us say he accepts the terms of the utilitarian promise, gives up any real vestiges of his heritage, and competes step for step with the White man. Will he then be allowed the big prize? Will he be accepted on equal terms, as an individual in a color-blind society?

In my experience, the promise of full acceptance is a phony one. The promise that—if one drops one's culture one will be fully accepted—is a hollow promise. It is not true. The person of color is always an outsider, always viewed with suspicion. He is only tolerated in positions of power. (I base this, in part, on my own experiences as a woman where, much as I would like to believe I am an "equal" member, I know I am not.)

Let me elaborate: The person of color (or the woman) is only allowed conditional acceptance. The acceptance is conditional on that individual's silencing himself or herself. So long as you do not say anything critical, so long as you retain a fairly low profile, you may be reasonably acceptable. But if you speak your mind, if you say what you think, you will no longer be welcome. The negation that is required is not just a denial of cultural heritage. It is a denial of your very right to think as an autonomous human being.

Ironically, minorities are "invited" into the university (after for so long having been denied their rightful place) in order to bring in new, previously excluded, perspectives, to broaden the basis of thought of the university. But if they should actually act on this premise, they will not last long. An original minority thinker, a person who thinks from a minority perspective, is not tolerated here. He is only allowed to survive if he retains an invisible profile, if he stands out in no way, if he shows no originality. He is, in other words, forced into mediocrity. In order to please and cajole the white establishment, he must cease to think for himself.

The utilitarian ethic preaches individualism, and in so doing, it strips minorities of their potential power. "Every man for himself," it says. "You get ahead on your own merits," which is the ultimate form of divide and rule. As everyone scrambles to get ahead on the narrowing ladder, they fail to look up and notice that the people in charge are highly-organized. They form disciplined hierarchies of corporate and bureaucratic power. But they want to ensure that those who might oppose them are fragmented, one from the other, trapped in their narrow ambition and struggle for survival.

Utilitarianism touts itself as beyond culture. It is the universal human form, free of content, each individual defining for himself who he will be. It is the ultimate in freedom. But, of course, this is sheer rhetoric. The truth is, this is the white man's way only. It is his culture that he is imposing, and the claim to its universality rests only on his power to assert it. He who has power can assert that he speaks for humanity.

To the minorities of the nation, the utilitarian free market is a hollow mockery of universal freedom. It was a market economy that led to the buying and selling of African slaves. It was the expanding free market that drove across the American plains, robbing and slaughtering American Indians and Mexicans. It was the imperialistic drive of capitalism that penetrated Asia and bolstered various forms of tyranny there.

So, in being asked to join the great color-blind American rat race, minorities are not only being asked to negate themselves, they are being asked to join the very system that has oppressed them and continues to oppress them. They are being asked to become sergeants for the army of occupation, policemen for their conquerors.

The goal of the educational system for people of color is to make the students into "role models" for their people. "See, if you shut up and give yourself up to the White man and become like him, you can make lots of money like him. Do not struggle for social change. Do not demand justice. Just look out for number one. Forget your community. They are just a bunch of deadbeats anyway— a heap of trash that deserves to be ploughed under. Leave them and never look back." The role model becomes the symbol for silencing protest. He is the stabilizer of the system, the proof that utilitarianism works and will lead to social progress.

This brings me back to my opening story. The battle at UCR over Chicano Student Programs is really a battle over utilitarianism. The university administration wants the Chicano students to become good utilitarians. It wants them to focus exclusively on their individualistic academic achievement and their careers. It wants them to forget about their culture, their community, and particularly to forget any identification they may feel for their community's oppression. It wants them to put all their energies into "making it."

The director's job is to implement this idea whether she and the students like it or not. The White administrators are determined to impose their vision. "We know what is good for you better than you do." It reeks with arrogance. The director is told in no uncertain terms: "Do what we want or you will lose your job. Your job is to get the students to accept what we say without protest." The administration has even used the term "role model" to define her task. "Role model" in this context means the teaching of passive acquiescence to a utilitarian ethic.

Note that the White administrators are pursuing their own self-interest in this game.

They want to increase minority enrollment and improve retention statistics because it makes them look good, brings the campus more money and enhances their status. Do they really have the interests of these minority students at heart? Worse still, do they give a damn about the decaying communities from which they recruit their "affirmative action" candidates? No—it is every man for himself in this system, and the highest level administrators are as corrupted by it as the poor person who has no choice in the matter.

All they want is the numbers that make the system look less oppressive. But they do not want any of the fresh ideas these people bring with them. They are only brought in to change the complexion of the university, but not in the least to change what it stands for. The basic structures of inequality in this society must not be challenged. If you dare to challenge them, you will lose your job.

WHAT IS TO BE DONE?

I cannot begin to do justice to this topic, so I just want to add a few words about it at two levels: the individual and the social levels. On the individual level we can ask: What can you and I do? What is our personal responsibility? It seems to me that each of us has a choice to make. The great irony of social reality is that it does not exist apart from what each of us does. Even though the social system can feel tremendously coercive upon us, it only exists in the activity of human beings, who make choices about whether they will joining the coercion or not. We either help to reproduce a given social order by joining it, even if we find it oppressive to ourselves and others, or we work to transform that system. Reproducers or transformers: we have to choose which we will be. Now in my view, the utilitarian ethic does not only hurt minorities, though its weight falls most heavily upon them. It hurts us all. We are all caught up in being forced to adhere to a narrow, self-serving,

careerism—a dedication of our lives to "making it"—that shrivels the heart and deadens the spirit. I believe that, if each of us looks deeply into his or her heart, we will find that we are not happy with the way we are made to live. Not only does utilitarianism constrict our most human aspirations to share, to love, to give, but it forces us to live in a society that is like an armed camp. Who among us in the university dares to walk in the inner cities of our nation? We live in a society that is bitterly divided. Hatred and violence seethe beneath the surface, ready to burst forth at any moment. Do we want to live like that? Can we afford to ignore this reality and continue with business as usual, as if there is nothing wrong?

The university embodies the value system of utilitarianism. These values are backed up by big business and the state which, in collaboration, what to insure that they are not challenged. Instead of the university fulfilling its mission to provide a sanctuary for a full and open debate about the major issues of our day, it is increasingly being forced into a mode of silent acquiescence. You do your job, get your grants, make your grades, and shut up. We are terrorized into silence by fear for our very survival. Survival in the rat race becomes the pre-eminent condition of our lives. We dare not involve ourselves in any important social questions for fear we will lose our position on the ladder.

I hope everyone will look into their hearts and ask: Can I say what I really think? And, more importantly, can I live by what I believe is right? Am I able to lead an authentic life? Has my life, and the lives of those around me, lost its authenticity? And when I look around at this society, can I honestly say justice is being achieved? And if not, what responsibility do I have as a social scientist, an intellectual, or a member of the university community, to do something about it? I want us to consider whether, when we behave as utilitarian individualists, we are not simply bystanders, but are actually part of the problem, deeply implicated in it, accomplices to the crime. I believe that right here, in the institution that is supposed to provide intellectual leadership to this nation, these issues must be debated and a plan of action developed.

This brings me to the social issue. It seems to me that the plan of action that we develop cannot be merely a modified form of utilitarianism, like affirmative action. Affirmative action only plucks the "best and brightest" out of minority communities and tries to make them into committed self-seekers, so that they can become good "role models" of assimilation and subordination to the dominant order. It changes the color inequality a bit, without changing the overarching fact of inequality one iota. An impoverished segment of the population remains untouched.

It seems to me that our plan has to involve a commitment—a full and complete commitment—to the idea of basic social, economic, and political equality for all peoples and groups. No one can be omitted. No one can be abandoned as beneath concern. Imagine what such a commitment would entail—what transformation would have to occur to achieve it! Instead of our leaders being caught up in their own self-aggrandizement, their priorities would have to center on the genuine advancement, the genuine and full democratic participation, of all peoples. Poverty would not be tolerated. Nor would lack of medical care or education or housing. These problems would not be handled in a halfhearted War on Poverty which too often served as a sinecure for a few middle class people, following a utilitarian ethic, to insure their own upward mobility. Nothing short of major reconstructuring would meet the challenge.

It is this idea, this vision, this commitment to full equality, that I believe captures what our responsibility is to the minorities of this nation. It certainly cannot be achieved by a trickle-down mechanism. You cannot expect those people who are trained for privileged positions, and who are encouraged to devote themselves solely to their careers, to become the leaders who will take on the problems of the poor. Nor is such a model morally tenable, suggesting as it does a kind of paternalistic charity, instead of genuine participation and power on the part of the poor.

The universities need to be called on to take action, to involve themselves in the affairs of the impoverished peoples in their region, to meet with the leaders of these communities, from all walks of life, and to draw up a plan of action. They need to ask: "How can we be of service to your people? How can we help to develop a plan that will alleviate your suffering? How can we contribute, under your leadership?"

Of course, I do not expect the universities to readily give up their elitist social philosophy. I simply aim to expose the degree to which they are committed to an inequalitarian ethic. They need to be fought on these issues, as the Director of Chicano Student Programs is fighting on my campus. We, who work and study in the university, need to decide on our own commitment to social change and social justice. If we decide that these issues are important enough, we do not have far to go to begin fighting for them. We can start right here in our own institution.

STUDY QUESTION

Explain how Edna Bonacich substantiates her claim that the American university embodies a racial inequality ideology. Do you agree with Bonacich's argument? Explain why. Can you think of any ways in which your university perpetuates racial equality?

Success and Failure: How Systemic Racism Trumped the Brown v. Board of Education Decision

Joe R. Feagin and Bernice McNair Barnett

Here we discuss numerous reasons why desegregated schooling is important for all children, including the provision of improved social and learning environments for all. Indeed, a key reason why school desegregation is important for segregated children of color is because, as is often said, "green follows white"—that is, schools with white student majorities typically get better educational resources from those (usually white) officials who have power to provide such socioeconomic resources.

U.S. school children have long pledged allegiance to a "nation . . . with liberty and justice for all," yet from the beginning this has been hypocritical rhetoric. When it comes to schools, African American children and many other children of color historically have rarely gotten justice. Never in U.S. history has there been a year when even half the country's black children attended schools where a majority of children were white. Today, even officially "desegregated" schools—which are decreasing in number—are intentionally divided internally into ability tracks that reflect racial, class, and gender stratification. Typically, a desegregated school facility is internally segregated with different educational experiences for most white and black children— "second-generation segregation." Despite supporting the ideal of a desegregated society in surveys, white leaders and citizens have been unwilling to implement the thorough-going desegregation of any major institution.

Today, in many larger cities there are relatively few white children left in public schools. Various factors, such as the rise of private academies, the increase in populations of color in cities, the flight of middle-class whites to predominately white school districts, the movement of middle-class blacks into predominantly white neighborhoods, and the acceptance of resegregation in neighborhood schools by federal courts, have greatly limited the possibilities for present and future school desegregation. As a result, the separation of white children from children of color is increasing. Indeed, recent government data indicate that segregation of black from white children in urban schools is high and has

Source: Joe R. Feagin and Bernice McNair Barnett, from "Success and Failure: How Systematic Racism Trumped the Brown v. Board of Education Decision," University of Illinois Law Review, 2004 (2005): 1099–1130.

increased a little over the last decade. Increased school segregation is particularly significant because residential segregation has decreased slightly during this same period.

Here we discuss numerous reasons why desegregated schooling is important for all children, including the provision of improved social and learning environments for all. Indeed, school desegregation is important for segregated children of color because, as is often said, "green follows white"—that is, schools with white student majorities typically get better educational resources from those (usually white) officials who have the power to provide such socioeconomic resources. . . .

THE RACIST FOUNDATION OF U.S. SOCIETY

This great and growing segregation of school children along racial lines is unsurprising for those familiar with U.S. history. Over centuries of colonial and U.S. development, whites created a system of systemic racism—initially in the enslavement of African Americans and genocidal land taking that targeted Native Americans. The fifty-five white men who drafted the U.S. Constitution, and then implemented it, built into the country's foundation certain mechanisms designed to maintain the enslavement of African Americans for the purpose of unjustly enriching many white Americans. These enslavement mechanisms were only removed eight decades later, and racial segregation was soon put in place. Legal segregation was a system of near-slavery for most African Americans; it was enshrined in state statutes and federal and state court decisions for nine decades. Whites have enforced various types of racial separation since the mid-seventeenth century, when the status of African Americans became that of enslavement for life. Today, school segregation is but part of a centuries-old system of racism.

Systemic racism involves the racialized exploitation and subordination of Americans

of color by white Americans. It encompasses the racial stereotyping, prejudices, and emotions of whites, as well as the discriminatory practices and racialized institutions engineered to produce the long-term domination of African Americans and other people of color. At the heart of systemic racism are discriminatory practices that generally deny Americans of color the dignity, opportunities, and privileges available to whites individually and collectively.

Some recognition of racism's systemic character is occasionally seen at the highest levels of national leadership. For example, Justice John Marshall Harlan, dissenting in the 1883 Civil Rights Cases, explained why anti-Black oppression persisted after slavery:

> That there are burdens and disabilities 'that' constitute badges of slavery and servitude, and that the power to enforce by appropriate legislation the Thirteenth Amendment may be exerted by legislation of a direct and primary character, for the eradication, not simply of the institution, but of its badges and incidents, are propositions which ought to be deemed indisputable.

In his minority view, the government had the right to eradicate racial badges, burdens, and the disability of slavery in the form of persisting discrimination. More recently, in the 1968 case of *Jones v. Alfred H. Mayer Co.*, the Supreme Court condemned housing discrimination, ruling that "when racial discrimination herds men into ghettos and makes their ability to buy property turn on the color of their skin, then it too is a relic of slavery." In his concurring opinion, Justice William O. Douglas added:

> Some badges of slavery remain today. While the institution has been outlawed, it has remained in the minds and hearts of many white men. Cases which have come to this Court depict a spectacle of slavery unwilling to die. . . . Negroes have been excluded over and again from juries. . . . They have been made to attend segregated and inferior schools. . . . They have been forced to live in segregated residential districts. . . .

Moreover, since the end of legal segregation, many whites have continued imposing the burdens of a "slavery unwilling to die" in a wide range of discriminatory practices.

The imposed segregation of racial groups, and the larger reality of systemic racism, are the normal condition of U.S. society. School segregation separates, on the basis of race, those defined by whites as different, and segregation is buttressed by an ideology that asserts that whites are superior. As one commentator noted:

> Black school children are not injured as much by a school board's placement of them in a school different from that in which it has placed white school children, so much as by the reality that the school exists within a larger system that defines it as the inferior school and its pupils as inferior persons.

Attempts at desegregation in the 1950s to 1970s were part of a brief period of progressive impulse. Such efforts need constant renewal, for established arrangements of centuries have a strong social inertia. Systemic racism stays in place so long as there is no counter pressure forcing change. Briefly, the civil rights movement—together with increased black political participation and international competition with the former Soviet Union for the allegiance of non-European peoples—pressed some white leaders to take notice of racial discrimination and move toward increased justice.

During the 1950s and 1960s, under pressure from black leaders, churches, and civil rights organizations, white liberals pressed for desegregation, especially in the South. By the 1970s, however, most white liberals were backtracking on commitments to substantial desegregation. Backtracking has been widespread since the 1980s due to the rise of presidential administrations and courts controlled by conservatives. White conservatives have been joined by a few conservatives of color, such as Justice Clarence Thomas and Ward Connerly, in blocking further progress in societal desegregation. The failure of school desegregation lies primarily in the hands of those with the greatest political, economic, and civic power, who have long been mostly white. White elites—including school board members, leaders of civic and business organizations, state and local legislators, and judges in state and federal courts—have made decisions that have reversed progress toward substantial school desegregation since the 1970s. . . .

THE *BROWN* DECISION: CONSTITUTIONAL, MORAL, AND POLITICAL SUCCESSES

Successful efforts by African Americans to end legal segregation showed how pervasive racism was in American society. The organized efforts of African Americans and their non-Black allies motivated elite whites to end apartheid, and thus enter the modern sociopolitical world. The *Brown* decision did not transpire because of the goodness of white hearts, but rather as the culmination of a long struggle by black children, men, and women. Without this enormous effort, the United States today might still be a backwater among the world's industrialized countries, indeed as a country trying to come to terms with apartheid institutions.

Finally, in 1954, nine white men were pressed by these efforts to see how unjust racial segregation was. At the heart of *Brown* was this broadly framed declaration:

> We conclude that in the field of public education the doctrine of "separate but equal" has no place. Separate educational facilities are inherently unequal. Therefore, we hold that the plaintiffs and others similarly situated for whom the actions have been brought are, by reason of the segregation complained of, deprived of the equal protection of the laws guaranteed by the Fourteenth Amendment.

With this statement, and with the rejection of previous court decisions upholding segregation, the Court rejected legal school segregation in the numerous states that still required or allowed it. With this broad framing, the Court asserted that the federal government has an obligation to extend full rights to African Americans, who were finally recognized by the Court as first-class citizens—a category to which they had been denied membership for centuries: "Segregation in the public schools is condemned for producing second-class citizenship for African Americans both because it imposed a stigma on them (as persons not fit to go to school with whites) and because it did not adequately prepare them to be effective citizens."

Brown had an important psychological impact on black Americans and others committed to desegregating U.S. society for it indicated that desegregation struggles were sanctioned by whites on the country's highest court. *Brown* provided moral encouragement for those active in accelerating the civil rights movement. As one commentator noted, "Civil rights leaders repeatedly invoked *Brown* in their political and moral arguments against segregation." They also cited the decision as moral authority for demonstrations. At the beginning of the 1955 Montgomery bus boycott, Dr. Martin Luther King, Jr., alluded to *Brown* in a speech: "If we are wrong, the Constitution of the United States is wrong." The success of that boycott was in turn facilitated by lawyers who filed suits against bus segregation.

Brown provided the moral and legal authority for ending segregation. The decision was interpreted by numerous judges as a mandate to dismantle state-created segregation. New discrimination cases came to courts in such areas as public accommodations and voting, and an end to discrimination was mandated in most cases, including interracial marriages. Official segregation in public facilities began to end, first in border states, then in most southern areas. *Brown* remains a beacon of liberty for many people in the United States and globally, including those seeking voting rights, gender equity in sports, freedom from harassment based on gender and sexual orientation, multicultural education, bilingual education, special education, and international human rights. As one commentator has noted:

> Many people take the Constitution to express the nation's deepest moral commitments. When the Supreme Court said that segregation could not be reconciled with the Constitution, it told the nation that segregation was wrong. . . . Even today Brown stands as the Court's deepest statement on the central issue in American history—how Americans of all races should treat one another. . . .

ADVANTAGES TO DESEGREGATION: ACCESS TO RESOURCES AND OPPORTUNITIES

When and where government officials have implemented substantial school desegregation with commitment, resources, and significant public support, it has generally worked to the benefit of all. Even where officials have only partially desegregated schools, we see substantial gains. In numerous ways, school desegregation has been successful, despite its limitations.

PROVIDING GREATER ACCESS TO EDUCATIONAL RESOURCES

From the beginning, black parents and community leaders sought desegregation primarily to secure greater access to educational and related socioeconomic resources. They did not seek desegregation because they felt that black children needed to sit with whites to be educated. The assumption has always been that better school resources come in racially desegregated schools, and this in turn usually means better learning environments and greater achievements for children of color.

In general, these assumptions have been correct. Research shows that attending desegregated schools usually facilitates achievement for black students. One major study found that "black third-graders in predominantly white schools read better than initially similar blacks who have attended predominantly black schools." Another extensive review found that most research studies of desegregation showed some positive effects on academic performance: "African American and Hispanic students learn somewhat more in schools that are majority White as compared to their academic performance in schools that are predominantly non-White." In addition, research on more than 1800 students in Charlotte-Mecklenburg schools found that black and white children did better in substantially desegregated schools than in segregated schools. Mickelson concludes from extensive data that "the more time both black and white students spend in desegregated elementary schools, the higher their standardized test scores in middle and high school, and the higher their track placements in secondary school." One major reason that desegregation in schools facilitates achievement for black students is that the most segregated schools (with children of color as the majority) get less in the way of socioeconomic and human resources.

PROVIDING GREATER ACCESS TO NETWORKING RESOURCES

School desegregation has brought African American, Latino, Native American, Asian American, and other students of color improved access to important job networks, most of which are controlled by white employers. Often greater in desegregated schools, networking resources help students later on in securing good jobs and advanced education. Black students from desegregated, substantially white schools typically are more successful in entering into the high-paying job and college networks than those students from traditionally segregated schools. Going to a substantially desegregated high school significantly increases the chance that a black or Latino student will attend college. Black students in desegregated schools are more likely to attend historically white colleges, work and live in desegregated environments, and have friends from other racial groups. Going to desegregated schools increases the "pool of contacts and informants from whom African Americans can obtain information about available jobs," thereby increasing opportunities. For children of color without much previous contact with whites, school desegregation may also help them develop coping strategies for dealing with racist whites in other settings.

Desegregation has often forced white officials to deal with insufficient resources in historically black schools. When schools are substantially desegregated, white officials typically spend more money on schools. When school systems resegregate with court approval, as many are now doing, per-student expenditure differentials again increase sharply. This is the lesson of big cities such as Milwaukee, where a recent report shows that the "separate but equal" notion increasingly accepted by courts fails. Per capita school expenditures for Milwaukee's children, mostly children of color, are now far lower than per capita expenditures for suburban children, who are mostly white. The differential is considerably more than one thousand dollars per child.

Half a century after the U.S. Supreme Court outlawed separate and unequal schools based on race, the Milwaukee area has firmly returned to both separate and unequal education . . . . As the percentage of African-American students and students of color has risen in the Milwaukee Public Schools (MPS), funding per pupil has plummeted compared to funding in over-whelmingly white suburban districts.

The report also notes the role of state government: "The state of Wisconsin is constitutionally responsible for providing public education. Yet the state not only toler-ates the funding gulf between Milwaukee and its suburban counterparts, it has instituted policies that allow the gap to widen. . . ." This increasing gap is one consequence of state-sanctioned resegregation now spreading across the United States. Such resegregation will, doubtlessly, result in sharply reduced access for many students of color to those critical college and job networks that deseg-regation provides.

While the school desegregation process stemming from the *Brown* decisions brought new opportunities and better access to resources for many children of color and their parents, at no point has a desegregated system equalized the array of educational resources. White officials and citizens are still unwilling to spend the money necessary to eradicate the long-term impact of racism in education. Interestingly, several studies of desegregation, including the famous Coleman report, downplayed school resources in explaining racial differentials. The Coleman report, for example, concluded that resources, such as per-pupil expenditures, were not greatly different between predomi-nantly black and predominantly white schools and had no significant correlations with achievement; the important correlations of achievement were with socioeconomic status and family characteristics. Many ana-lysts have interpreted those studies as mean-ing that significant differentials in school resources no longer exist—or that what dif-ferences remain are not critical for achieve-ment. However, even the Coleman report acknowledged that, while the differences in resources available to predominately white schools as compared to predominantly black schools are relatively small, those differences

can accumulate to a major difference in quality:

> The child experiences his environment as a whole, while the statistical measures necessar-ily fragment it. . . . The statistical examination of difference in school environments for minor-ity and majority children will give an impression of lesser differences than actually exist . . . so that the subsequent sections will probably tend to understate the actual disadvantage in school environment experienced by the average minority child compared to that experienced by the average majority child.

To assess whether critical resources are different in predominantly white and pre-dominantly black schools, one must consider the accumulation of small differences and an array of resources often neglected in com-parative assessments of schools. Even the best desegregation plans are unable to equalize historically black and historically white schools in fundamental ways. Researchers examining desegregated Charlotte-Mecklenburg schools have found many differences in the level of resources available to predominantly black schools as compared to predominantly white schools. Schools with more white children are more likely to have adequate media cen-ters, computers, and other technology, as well as newer buildings and more classes for advanced students. On the average, such schools have more teachers (regardless of race) with substantial teaching experience. Research indicates that other critical resources, such as the availability of small classes and college placement courses, are not equit-ably distributed. Today, de facto segregated schools are segregated not only by racial group, but also by income. Most black and Latino children remain in schools where low-income children are the majority, yet most white children attend schools where the majority of students are middle-class. Schools where the children's parents have higher incomes usually have an array of resource advantages, while those in low-income communities are likely to have fewer teachers, less adequate libraries, and fewer advanced courses. Again, the problem of racial segregation is inextricably linked to class stratification in U.S. society.

PROVIDING GREATER OPPORTUNITIES TO EXPERIENCE DIVERSITY

School desegregation has generated not only increased opportunities for black, Latino, and other children of color and their parents, but also new experiences for white children, parents, and teachers. Although since *Brown* many whites, in all regions, have chosen private schools and moved into higher-income communities where most children of color do not reside, the challenges of cooperatively living, learning, working, and participating democratically in a multiracial society and within a global economy are greater than ever before for all Americans. In the future, the U.S. public and policymakers will need to utilize the diverse ideas, knowledge, and talents of everyone even more than now.

Racial segregation exacts costs for whites in terms of fear, ignorance, conflict, and inhumanity. Population trends indicate that by 2050 the United States will likely have a population in which people of color will compose a majority. Increasingly, whites are pressed to understand the significance of racial-ethnic diversity in living, learning, and working cooperatively in communities, schools, government, businesses, and other arenas of society. Moral and practical reasons dictate building a country that expands socioeconomic and political participation in a multiracial-democracy framework. School desegregation provides opportunities for all, including whites, to dismantle historical barriers because students in truly desegregated schools gain opportunities to learn about, and associate with, those with whom they might not otherwise interact. For example, in a study of

young children in a multiracial preschool, researchers Van Ausdale and Feagin found that white children learn racial differences and how to discriminate at an early age, and that it is by experience, interaction, and education with children of color that they are able to reduce stereotypes and gain a significant opportunity to establish friendships and understanding of others. . . .

CONCLUSION: STRENGTHS OF BLACK CHILDREN, PARENTS, AND COMMUNITIES

We see significant successes and major failures following in the wake of *Brown*. Racial desegregation is a major break with apartheid, and desegregation works best when resources—economic, educational, legal, and political—are put into it wisely. The racial world of the United States is much different now than it was in the decade before *Brown*. We have documented important successes in desegregating educational institutions as well as in the larger society. Research shows that desegregated schooling has a positive impact on academic achievement for most students, typically with substantial gains for students of color. Research demonstrates, too, that black students attending desegregated schools tend to do better in job and educational attainments later in life. Those students who have attended desegregated schools are more likely to attend college, work in desegregated environments, and have diverse friends. Researchers have shown that many students in desegregated schools become less stereotypical in their thinking about other groups—which equips them better for life in this increasingly multiracial society. Clearly, *Brown's* impact is not limited to education, for, as Judge Robert Carter has underscored, *Brown* brought about "a radical social transformation in this country and whatever its limited impact on the educational community, its indirect consequences of altering the style, spirit, and stance of race relations will maintain its prominence for many years to come." *Brown*, together with other contemporaneous desegregation efforts, dismantled much of the legal architecture of antiblack oppression in the United States.

In spite of the substantial hostility African American students and other students of color face in desegregated schools, they have managed to achieve much. While historically and predominantly white school settings are social comfort zones for most whites, most black students integrated into these settings find themselves in difficult environments well outside their social comfort zones. There, as well as in the larger society, they face significant discrimination—for many, hundreds of discriminatory incidents each year. When black children face racism routinely, it is extraordinary that most do as well as they do in desegregated settings. The energy loss alone that results from dealing with hostility and discrimination may be enough to account for the remaining differences in school performance of white and black children. The extraordinary strength shown by black children in getting through a racialized day, as well as the academic achievements under these conditions, gets little discussion in most analyses of desegregation. These strengths deserve extensive research, as they are likely based in the collective values and knowledge that African Americans have accumulated over centuries of struggles against racism.

Indeed, we see evidence of the impact of successes in the civil rights struggle against racism and in the educational achievements of African Americans. Over the course of the 1950s and 1960s, black students made dramatic educational gains. By the mid-1960s, large numbers of black students were graduating from high school. The percentage graduating in the South increased from thirty-five percent in 1960, to seventy-one percent less than two decades later. Historically black colleges saw dramatic increases in black college graduates, as did formerly segregated white colleges.

Nonetheless, research documents the continuing significance of discrimination in majority white colleges, as well as the increasing disparity in the gender ratio among black students, especially because black males are more likely to drop out of college. Thus, current problems in education reveal the interrelatedness of racial, gender, and class factors in the pipeline to achievement—with some parents and educators of black children now supporting the idea of Africentric (often all-male) academies.

Today, African Americans, including students, place great emphasis on the importance of education in the larger society, despite historical relations of racial privilege that structure experiences of black students inside and outside of school classrooms. One recent analysis found that black students "have high educational aspirations, and they are more likely than whites to continue with their schooling at given test score levels." Black Americans with jobs are more likely to pursue education into adulthood than comparable whites. In surveys, African Americans show as much, or more, desire for education as whites, yet they are more likely than whites to understand the structural barriers African Americans face in attaining more education. Whites are more likely than blacks to view low socioeconomic status and lesser performance in school as indicators of personal failure, while blacks are more likely than whites to accent structural factors as barriers.

We should situate the great difficulties in desegregating schools in the context of structural barriers created in this racist and classist society. In our interviews, a middle-aged white teacher recently commented:

> I think what needs to be done nobody wants to do it. Like they talk about building one big giant school around here and everybody would go to it. . . . You can't have [names affluent school] —that's where all the money is at . . . . But [names poor school], they don't have a chance, and that's 80 percent, probably, minorities there.

We cannot bring profound change in one area of this racist society by dismantling discrimination in schooling alone, no matter how well done. Racism is systemic and reflected in all major U.S. institutions. Those Americans who are not white are generally at a huge disadvantage relative to whites. Because the privileged are resistant to significant change, successful progress against racial discrimination constantly faces the threat of backtracking. In American society constant organization for change is necessary.

The Declaration of Independence articulated the great American ideal that "all men are created equal," a doctrine the Founders meant to apply to white men with property. However, once this grand doctrine was articulated, subsequent generations have pressed for its application to ever-expanding groups of Americans. Thus, the Fourteenth Amendment was enacted to make newly freed African Americans into the full U.S. citizens they had not been before the Civil War:

All persons born or naturalized in the United States . . . are citizens of the United States and of the State wherein they reside. No State shall make or enforce any law which shall abridge the privileges or immunities of citizens of the United States; nor shall any State deprive any person of life, liberty, or property, without due process of law; nor deny to any person within its jurisdiction the equal protection of the laws.

All government actions that overtly or covertly create or sustain racial segregation in any area of society operate to subordinate and stigmatize African Americans and thereby blatantly violate the Fourteenth Amendment's promise of full citizenship "privileges and immunities" and the "equal protection" of the laws for African Americans. The authors of the *Brown* decision glimpsed the great promise of equality for all that is embedded in the Declaration of Independence and in the Fourteenth Amendment, yet neither they nor their official governmental descendants have been willing to turn this rhetorical promise into a social and political reality. That is now our task.

STUDY QUESTION

As outlined by Feagin and Barnett, discuss the various reasons why desegregated schooling is important for all children. Which of these reasons do you believe are the most important? Explain why.

READING 2. 3

American Indians in Higher Education: A History of Cultural Conflict

Bobby Wright and William G. Tierney

The earliest colonial efforts to provide Indians with higher education were designed to Christianize and civilize the Indians, saving them from the folly of their heathenish and savage ways.

Caleb Cheeshateaumuck, an Algonquian Indian from Martha's Vineyard, graduated from Harvard College, class of 1665. An outstanding scholar, Caleb could read, write, and speak Latin and Greek as well as English—not to mention his own native language. Although fully able to meet Harvard's rigorous academic demands, the young native scholar did not escape the dangers associated with life in an alien environment. He died within months of his college degree, victim of a foreign disease to which he had no immunity.

Caleb was among the first in a long line of American Indians who have attended colleges and universities during the past three centuries. He represents, too, the challenge and the triumph, as well as the failure and tragedy, that characterize the history of American Indian higher education. These conflicting outcomes reflect the clash of cul-

tures, the confrontation of lifestyles, that has ensured on college campuses since colonial days. Euro-Americans have persistently sought to remold Native Americans in the image of the white man—to "civilize" and assimilate the "savages"—but native peoples have steadfastly struggled to preserve their cultural integrity. The college campus has historically provided a stage for this cross-cultural drama.

Within a decade of the first European settlement in America, plans for an Indian college were already underway. The earliest colonial efforts to provide Indians with higher education were designed to Christianize and "civilize" the Indians, thus saving them from the folly of their "heathenish" and "savage" ways. The hope was that educated Indians, as schoolmasters and preachers, would become missionary agents among their own brethren.

Source: Bobby Wright and William G. Tierney, "American Indians in Higher Education: A History of Cultural Conflict," *Change*, 23 (1991): 11–18.

In 1617, King James I launched the initial design, when he enjoined the Anglican clergymen to collect charitable funds for "the erecting of some churches and schools for ye education of ye children of these [Virginia] Barbarians." The following year, the English set aside 1,000 acres at Henrico, Virginia, for construction of a "college for Children of the Infidels." However, the Virginia natives resisted such cultural intrusions. Their rebellion in 1622, an attempt to rid their lands of the English forever, was only partially and temporarily successful, but it abruptly ended the scheme for an Indian college in Virginia.

In New England, the 1650 charter of Harvard College heralded the next educational design. It provided for the "education of the English and Indian youth of this country in knowledge." Charitable contributions from England supported the construction of the Indian College building on Harvard's campus, completed in 1656. During the four decades of its existence, although it had a capacity for 20 students, the structure housed no more than six Indian scholars—Caleb Cheeshateaumuck among them. Most of that time, the "Indian college" housed English students and the college printing press.

In Virginia, the native rebellion of 1622 had ended the initial plans for an Indian college. Seven decades later, the 1693 charter of the College of William and Mary reaffirmed the English desire to educate and "civilize" the Indians. It established William and Mary, in part, so "that the Christian faith may be propagated amongst the Western Indians." Robert Boyle, an English scientist and philanthropist, inspired this divine mission when he willed a bequest for unspecified charitable and pious uses. The president of William and Mary obtained the lion's share of this charity, which he used to build the Brafferton building in 1723, purportedly to house resident native scholars. No Indian students were in residence for two decades following its completion, however, and only five or six attended during the life of the Brafferton school. Following feeble efforts and insignificant results, the American Revolution stopped the flow of missionary funds from England, and William and Mary has since ignored the pious mission on which it was founded.

In the mid-18th century, Eleazar Wheelock, a Congregational minister, passionately engaged in the academic training of Indian Youth. Wheelock founded Dartmouth College, chartered in 1769, for "the education & instruction of Youth of the Indian tribes in this Land in reading, wrighting [sic] and all parts of Learning which shall appear necessary and expedient for civilizing and Christianizing children of pagans . . . and also of English Youth." He built the College with charity collected by Samson Occum, Wheelock's most successful convert and a noted Indian scholar, who solicited a substantial endowment for native education. Nonetheless, by the time he established Dartmouth, Wheelock's interest in Indian schooling waned in favor of the education of "English youth." As a result, the College became increasingly inaccessible to potential Native American converts. While a total of 58 Indians attended from 1769 to 1893, Dartmouth produced only three Indian graduates in the 18th century and eight in the 19th.

The College of New Jersey (now Princeton University), although not specifically professing an Indian mission, admitted at least three Indian students. The first, a Delaware youth, attended the College in 1751 under the sponsorship of the Society in Scotland for the Propagation of Christian Knowledge, benefactors also of Dartmouth's Indian program. Although reportedly proficient in his learning and "much beloved by his classmates and the other scholars," the unfortunate young Delaware died of consumption a year later. Jacob Woolley, one of Wheelock's first students, enrolled in 1759, though he was expelled before completing his degree. Finally, Shawuskukhkung—also known by his English name, Bartholomew

Scott Calvin—attended the College in 1773. During his second year of residence, however, the charitable funds from Great Britain that supported his attendance ceased, as a consequence of the Revolutionary War, forcing Calvin to abandon his studies.

TRIBAL RESISTANCE

The colonial experiments in Indian higher education proved, for the most part, unsuccessful. Targeted tribal groups resisted missionary efforts and tenaciously clung to their traditional life ways. Among those who succumbed to education, their physical inability to survive the alien environment compounded the failure. Hugh Jones, an 18th-century historian of Virginia, admitted that, at the College of William and Mary

> hitherto but little good has been done, though abundance of money has been laid out. . . . [An] abundance of them used to die . . . Those of them that have escaped well, and been taught to read and write, have for the most part returned to their home, some with and some without baptism, where they follow their own savage customs and heathenish rites.

The general Indian sentiment is illustrated by the Six Nations' response to the treaty commissioners from Maryland and Virginia, who in 1744 invited the Indians to send their sons to the College of William and Mary. "We must let you know," the Iroquois leaders responded,

> We love our Children too well to send them so great a Way, and the Indians are not inclined to give their Children learning. We allow it to be good, and we thank you for your Invitation; but our customs differing from yours, you will be so good as to excuse us.

The colonial era ended and, with the birth of the new nation, Indian education increas-

ingly became a matter of federal policy. Influenced by the limited results of the colonial educational missions, George Washington voiced a shift in policy from an emphasis on higher learning to vocational training for American Indians. "I am fully of the opinion," he concluded,

> that his mode of education which has hitherto been pursued with respect to these young Indians who have been sent to our college is not such as can be productive of any good to their nations. It is perhaps productive of evil. Humanity and good policy must make it the wish of every good citizen of the United States that husbandry, and consequently, civilization, should be introduced among the Indians.

This educational philosophy unfolded in the 19th century and dominated until the 20th, even in the midst of tribal efforts to gain a foothold in higher education.

TRIBAL SUPPORT

While some tribes violently resisted attempts to "civilize" them through education, other Indian groups eagerly embraced higher learning. At the same time that Dartmouth was educating 12 members of the Five Civilized Tribes, the Cherokees and the Choctaws organized a system of higher education that had more than 200 schools, and sent numerous graduates to eastern colleges. The 1830 Treaty of Dancing Rabbit Creek set aside $10,000 for the education of Choctaw youth. The first official use of the funds provided under this treaty occurred in 1841, when the tribe authorized the education of Indian boys at Ohio University, Jefferson College, and Indiana University. The 1843 Report of the Commissioner of Indian Affairs mentioned the education of 20 Choctaw boys, 10 at Asbury University, and 10 at Lafayette College.

Choctaw graduates from tribally operated boarding schools were selected on the basis of their promise and allowed to continue their education until they had completed graduate and professional study at colleges in the states. Several members of the Five Civilized Tribes entered Dartmouth in 1838, and, in 1854, Joseph Folsom, a Choctaw, received a degree. In all, 12 Choctaw and Cherokee students received support to attend Dartmouth from the "Scottish Fund"—the legacy of their predecessor, Samson Occum. Ironically, the Choctaw academic system, responsible for a literacy rate exceeding that of their white neighbors, collapsed when the federal government became involved in the late 1800s.

The first university in which Indians were to play a significant role was proposed in 1862. As was the case at Harvard, however, the Ottawa Indian University was more a dream than a reality. The Ottawas never received the promised university, as they were removed by the federal government to Oklahoma in 1873.

Bacon College, founded by the Baptists in 1880s, also received Indian support, which came in the form of a land grant from the Creek tribe. Dedicated to training of Indian clergy, the college opened to three students. By the end of its fifth year, 56 students had enrolled. Bacon College still operates today with a strong (but not exclusive) commitment to educate American Indians.

EDUCATION AS ASSIMILATION

Indians who attended universities and colleges during the 17th, 18th, and 19th centuries, for the most part, studied the same subjects as did the white students. However, as the federal government began to dominate Indian education in the late 19th century, significantly reducing the role of missionary groups, private individuals, and the states, the result was a continual deemphasis on higher learning. Instead, the role of higher education changed to vocational training.

In 1870 Congress appropriated $100,000 for the operation of federal industrial schools. The first off-reservation boarding school was established at Carlisle, Pennsylvania in 1879. The boarding school, exemplified at Carlisle, dominated the federal approach to Indian education for half a century. Its methods included the removal of the students from their homes and tribal influences, strict military discipline, infusion of the Protestant work ethic, as well as an emphasis on the agricultural, industrial, and domestic arts— *not* higher academic study.

Most importantly, these institutions were designed to make their Indian charges in the image of the white man. Luther Standing Bear, a Sioux, attended Carlisle in 1879. He recalled the psychological assaults he and others encountered during the educational process.

> I remember when we children were on our way to Carlisle School, thinking that we were on our way to meet death at the hands of the white people, the older boys sang brave songs, so that we would meet death according to the code of the Lakota. Our first resentment was in having our hair cut. It has ever been the custom of Lakota men to wear long hair, and old tribal members still wear the hair in this manner. On first hearing the rule, some of the older boys talked of resisting, but realizing the uselessness of doing so, submitted. But for days after being shorn we felt strange and uncomfortable. . . . The fact is that we were to be transformed.

Fueled by a large congressional appropriation in 1882, 25 boarding schools opened by the turn of the century—among them, Santa Fe Indian School, which became the Institute of American Indian Arts, a two-year postsecondary school, and Haskell Institute (now Haskell Indian Junior College) in Lawrence, Kansas. These institutes, like the normal schools of the 19th century, were not true colleges. Their standards of training, at best, approximated only those of a good manual-training high school. The range of occupational futures envisioned for Indian students was limited to farmer, mechanic, and housewife.

By the turn of the century, only a few talented Indian youth went on for further training at American colleges and universities. Ohiyesa, a Sioux, was among them. Adopting the notion that "the Sioux should accept civilization before it was too late," Charles A. Eastman (his English name) graduated from Dartmouth College in 1887, and three years later received a degree in medicine at Boston University. Eastman was keenly aware that his academic success depended on his acceptance of American civilization and the rejection of his own traditional culture. "I renounced finally my bow and arrow for the spade and the pen," he wrote in his memoirs. "I took off my soft moccasins and put on the heavy and clumsy but durable shoes. Every day of my life I put into use every English word that I knew, and for the first time permitted myself to think and act as a white man."

Ohiyesa's accomplishments were rare in the 19th and early 20th centuries. The education of Native Americans—although still preserving the centuries-old purpose of civilizing the "savages"—seldom exceeded the high school level. The impact of this neglect on Indian educational attainment is reflected in enrollment figures. As late as 1932, only 385 Indians were enrolled in college and only 52 college graduates could be identified. At that time, too, American Indian scholarships were being offered at only five colleges and universities.

FEDERAL EFFORTS

Not until the New Deal era of the 1930s, a period of reform in federal Indian policy, did Indian higher education receive government support. The Indian Reorganization Act of 1934, among other sweeping reforms,

authorized $250,000 in loans for college expenses. By 1935, the Commissioner of Indian Affairs reported 515 Indians in college. Although the loan program was discontinued in 1952, the Bureau of Indian Affairs had established the higher education scholarship grant program in 1948, allocating $9,390 among 50 students. Indian veterans returning from World War II and eligible for GI Bill educational benefits added to the growing number of college students. According to estimates, some 2,000 Native Americans were enrolled in some form of post-secondary education during the last half of the 1950s. The enrollment grew to about 7,000 by 1965. Sixty-six Indians graduated from four-year institutions in 1961, and by 1968 this figure had almost tripled. Still, in 1966, only one percent of the Indian population was enrolled in college.

During the 1970s, a series of federal task force and U.S. General Accounting Office reports called attention to the academic, financial, social, and cultural problems that Indian students encountered in pursuing a college education. These reports fell on attentive Congressional ears. By 1979 the Bureau of Indian Affairs Higher Education Program was financing approximately 14,600 undergraduates and 700 graduate students. Of these, 1,639 received college degrees and 434 earned graduate degrees. In addition, federal legislation, including the Indian Self-Determination and Education Assistance Act of 1975 and the Tribally Controlled Community College Assistance Act of 1978, spawned striking new developments in Indian higher education.

Perhaps the most dramatic policy change reflected in the new legislation was the shift to Indian control of education. For the first time, Indian people—who had thus far been subjected to paternalistic and assimilationist policies—began to take control of their own affairs. Higher education was among the targets of the new Self-Determination programs, best illustrated by the development of tribally controlled community colleges.

TRIBAL COLLEGES

Tribal colleges evolved for the most part during the 1970s in response to the unsuccessful experience of Indian students on mainstream campuses. Today, there are 24 tribally controlled colleges in 11 western and midwestern states—from California to Michigan, and from Arizona to the Dakotas. These institutions serve about 10,000 American Indians and have a full-time equivalent enrollment of about 4,500 students.

Because Indian students most often live in economically poor communities, tuition is low and local tax dollars do not offer much assistance. Congress has authorized up to $6,000 per student, but, in reality, the amount released to the colleges decreased throughout the Reagan era so that by 1989 the amount generated for each student was only $1,900. Tribal leaders point out how odd it is that those students who are most at-risk receive the least assistance. One would think that if the government was serious about increasing opportunities for Indian youth, then colleges would be provided the funds necessary to aid those youth. Such has not been the case.

CURRENT DEMOGRAPHICS

By all accounts the Native American population of the United States is growing at a fast pace and becoming increasingly youthful. Current estimates place the total population of American Indians in the United States at slightly less than two million. Between 1970 and 1980, Indians between the ages of 18 and 24 increased from 96,000 to 234,000. The average age of this population is 16.

Although Native Americans live throughout the United States, over half live in the southwest. California, Oklahoma, Arizona, and New Mexico account for slightly less than 50 percent of the total Indian population. Native Americans are equally split between those who live in rural and urban areas. Los Angeles, Tulsa, Oklahoma City, Phoenix, and Albuquerque have the largest numbers of urban Indians. The largest reservations in the United States are the Navajo Reservation in what is now New Mexico and Arizona and the Pine Ridge Reservation in the present state of South Dakota.

American Indians are among the most economically disadvantaged groups in the United States. The unemployment rate for American Indians who live on reservations often approaches 80 percent, with the median family income hovering around $15,000. The percentage of Native Americans who live below the poverty line is three times the national average. About 50 percent of the Native American population over 30 years old has not completed high school.

Given the propensity for Native American students to leave one institution prior to an academic year's completion, valid estimates of how many high school graduates actually participate in a freshman year at a postsecondary institution are difficult to determine. A student, for example, may graduate from high school and decide to attend a particular college and he or she may leave relatively soon thereafter; a few months later the student may re-enroll at another institution. Meanwhile, the previous college may not even be aware the student has left. Consequently, a valid national percentage of Native American high school graduates who are college freshmen is unknown.

We do know that in 1980 there were 141,000 high school graduates, and 85,798 students were enrolled in postsecondary education. The general lesson to be learned here is that less than 60 percent of Native American high school students complete the 12th grade, and that less than 40 percent of those students go on to college. More simply, if 100 Indian students enter the 9th grade, only 60 will graduate from high school. Of these graduates, a mere 20 will enter academe, and only about three of these will receive a four-year degree.

Not surprisingly, more than half of those students who go on to college will enter a two-year institution, and over 70,000 of the students will attend public institutions. The proportion of American Indian students who enroll full-time is around 50 percent, and Native American women outnumber their male counterparts on college campuses by about 20 percent.

THE TASK AHEAD

What does this information tell us about American Indian participation in postsecondary education? The composite population of Native Americans is economically poorer, experiences more unemployment, and is less formally educated than the rest of the nation. A greater percentage of the population lives in rural areas, where access to postsecondary institutions is more limited. Although a majority of the population lives in the southwest, they attend post-secondary institutions throughout the country.

They have a population that is increasingly youthful, yet only three out of 100 9th-graders will eventually receive a baccalaureate. Those four-year institutions that have the largest percentage of Indian students are either in economically depressed states of the country such as Montana and South Dakota, and those colleges that have the highest proportion of Indian students—tribal colleges—receive only a fraction of what they should receive from the federal government to carry out their tasks.

This overview highlights the problems and challenges that American Indians have faced regarding higher education. One certainly is that the federal government must renew its support for at-risk college students. Society can no longer afford excluding populations simply because they are different from the mainstream or prefer to remain within their own cultural contexts. All evidence suggests that Indian students and their families want equal educational opportunities. They seek better guidance in high school, more culturally relevant academic programming and counseling, and more role models on campus. Indian students do not want to be excluded from a university's doors because they cannot afford the education, and they do not want to be lost on a campus that doesn't value and accommodate their differences.

Many of the same challenges that confronted Caleb Cheeshateaumuck at Harvard face Indian college students today. A Native American senior recently reflected on her four years at school and the dysfunction between the world of higher education and the world from which she had come. "When I was a child I was taught certain things," she recalled, "don't stand up to your elders, don't question authority, life is precious, the earth is precious, take it slowly, enjoy it. And then you go to college and you learn all these other things, and it never fits."

Now, more than three centuries after Caleb Cheeshateaumuck confronted the alien environment of Harvard, the time is long overdue for cultural conflict and assimilationist efforts to end. American Indians must have opportunities to enter the higher education arena on their own terms—to encounter challenge without tragedy and triumph without co-optation. Only then can higher education begin a celebration of diversity in earnest.

STUDY QUESTION

As explained by Wright and Tierney, in what ways was higher education used for assimilation of American Indians beginning in the late nineteenth century?

Academic Storytelling: A Critical Race Theory Story of Affirmative Action

Adalberto Aguirre, Jr.

The minority (nonwhite) can tell stories about institutional practices in academia that result in unintended benefits for the majority (white). One institutional practice in academia is affirmative action. This article presents a story about a minority applicant for a sociology position and his referral to an affirmative action program for recruiting minority faculty. One reason for telling the story is to illustrate how an affirmative action program can be implemented in a manner that marginalizes minority persons in the faculty recruitment process and results in benefits for majority persons. Another reason for telling the story to sound an alarm for majority and minority faculty who support affirmative action programs that the programs can fall short of their goals if their implementation is simply treated as a bureaucratic activity in academia.

This is a story about how affirmative action is practiced in academia. The story can be considered a *counterstory*, because it challenges the (while) majority's story, or stock story, about affirmative action in academia. The stock story justifies the world as it is by "perpetuating the distribution of rights, privileges, and opportunity established under a regime of uncontested white supremacy" (Crenshaw et al. 1995:xxix). Not surprisingly, the stock story disguises affirmative action as a vehicle for legitimating the majority's social reality (Delgado 1993). Delgado (1989) provides an example of how the majority tells the stock story in academia. This example focuses on a black lawyer who interviews for a teaching position at a major law school. Despite the law school's stated commitment to affirmative action and the recruitment of a minority law professor, the black lawyer is rejected. Had he been hired he would have become the first minority law professor at the school. In reaching the decision to reject him, the faculty felt that his interest in civil rights law was not compatible with their interests. They decided to wait another few years until the "crop of black and minority law students graduates and gets some experience" (Delgado 1989:2420) but felt that the black lawyer could be considered for a visiting teaching position while they continued their search.

Source: Adalberto Aguirre Jr., "Academic Storytelling: A Critical Race Theory Story of Affirmative Action," Sociological Perspectives, 43(2): 319–339. Copyright © 2000 by Pacific Sociological Association.

Delgado argues that his example shows how the majority tells the stock story about affirmative action in academia. First, the stock story "emphasizes the school's benevolent motivation ('look how hard we're trying') and good faith" (Delgado 1989:2421). The law school faculty did appear to give the black lawyer a "serious" look, perhaps even more serious than they would a similarly qualified white lawyer. Second, the stock story lessens the possibility that the black lawyer's "presence on the faculty might have altered the institution's character, helped introduce a different prism and different criteria for selecting future candidates" (Delgado 1989:2421). The law school faculty would rather continue to promote the belief that there are very few black lawyers available than assume responsibility for hiring one and altering the complexion of the faculty. Third, the stock story is neutral; "it avoids issues of blame or responsibility" (Delgado 1989:2422). You cannot blame the law school for not trying to hire a minority person. In the end, the stock story justifies the majority's view—"there are very few black lawyers out there so let's not rush into something, let's wait a while longer." The *wait* is an excuse for not doing anything.

WHY TELL THE STORY?

My Story is nested in my experiences during the past twenty-two years as a Chicano professor of sociology in institutional settings dominated by the majority. During my tenure as a faculty member in academia, I have served on numerous committees, especially *the* affirmative action committee, and participated in activities that have focused on faculty recruitment. As a result, I have had the opportunity to listen to majority faculty stories of minority faculty *recruitment* and their stories of *attracting* majority faculty. I suspect that the stories are told by the majority to justify their competing outcomes. The story in this article is gleaned from my participation in

those committees and activities. It is representative of what Richardson (1997:32) calls a *collective story:* "The collective story displays an individual's story by narrating the experiences of the social category to which the individual belongs, rather than by telling the particular individual's story or simply retelling the cultural story." My story is about real experience, an experience that is as real as my social reality. It is an experience that is representative of the practices, rules, and customs that minority persons like myself encounter inside and outside of academia (Austin 1995; Essed 1992; Feagin 1991). I tell my story to bring to light an alternative interpretation of institutional practices in academia that support the majority's stock story.

I assume the role of *sociologist as narrator* in my story. Implicit in this role is the premise that sociological work consist of stories. Stories are social events that instruct us about social processes, social structures, and social situations (Maines and Bridger 1992). Stories also "comprise a series of remembered events in the field in which the author was usually a participant" (Van Maanen 1998:102). As a result, sociologists as narrators are "storytellers in producing accounts of social life" (Ewick and Silbey 1995:203). My story is, thus, a social event because it gives meaning to an experience nested in a complex arrangement of social relations that is known as *academia*.

In the role of sociologist as narrator I have also decided what kind of story to tell (Maines 1993). I have decided to tell a story of how an organizational process, affirmative action, is implemented in academia to reflect the unequal power relations between the majority and the minority. I use the terms *minority* (nonwhite) and *majority* (white) to reinforce the perception that the difference in social relations experienced by white and nonwhite faculty in academia is rooted in structure. That is, the difference in social relations is not simply the outcome of racial or ethnic differences, it is an outcome of social position in the organizational structure of academia (Aguirre, Martinez, and Hernandez 1993). In particular, my story becomes a *critical tale* because it attempts to make "it clear who . . . owns and operates the tools of reality production" in academia (Van Maanen 1998:128). As a result, I have taken a side in my story. It is very difficult not to take a side. Unfortunately, it is often "whose side" the storyteller takes that determines if the story is legitimate (Baron 1998; Morris, Woodward, and Peters 1998). Taking the minority's side has often resulted in the storyteller being accused of bias. According to Becker (1967:243), "We accuse ourselves of bias only when we take the side of the subordinate. . . . [W]e join responsible officials and the man in the street in an unthinking acceptance of the hierarchy of credibility. We assume with them that the man at the top knows best. We do not realize that there are sides to be taken and that we are taking one of them." As a story about the minority, my story can be heard and given the credibility associated with the majority's stories.

CRITICAL RACE THEORY AND TELLING STORIES

The story in this article is grounded in critical race theory (CRT) (for a comprehensive review, see Crenshaw et al. 1995; Delgado 1995; Delgado and Stefancic 1993, 1994, 1997; Ladson-Billings and Tate 1995; Matsuda et al. 1993; Russell 1999; Valdes 1997). CRT became noticeable in the mid-1970s when scholars of color realized that the civil rights movement of the 1960s had stalled and that there was a need for alternative and critical explanations for the continuing presence of racism in American society. According to Crenshaw et al. (1995:xiii), "Critical Race Theory embraces a movement of left scholars, most of them scholars of color, situated in law schools, whose work challenges the ways in which race and racial power are constructed and represented in American legal culture and, more generally, in American society as whole." While rooted in legal scholarship, CRT also examines topics of sociological interest such as the social construction of race (Haney-Lopez 1994; Scales-Trent 1990), the discriminating effects of immigration law on social identity (Fan 1997; Olivas 1995), and the intersectionality of gender and race (Caldwell 1991; Hernandez-Truyol 1997).

The most distinguishing feature of CRT writings is the use of stories or firstperson accounts. According to Bell (1995a:899), critical race theory writings are "characterized by frequent use of the first person, storytelling, narrative, allegory, interdisciplinary treatment of law, and the unapologetic use of creativity." Critical race theorists use storytelling as a methodological tool for giving *voice* to marginalized persons and their communities. They tell stories that challenge the majority's stories in which it constructs for itself "a form of shared reality in which its own superior position is seen as natural" (Delgado 1989:2412). As a result, critical race theorists focus on giving *voice* to marginalized persons and communities because they are suppressed in the majority's stories.

According to Litowitz (1997:520), the majority of CRT stories are "drawn from the experiences of minority law professors, detailing not only negative experiences such as name calling and ostracism, but also positive aspects of their heritage, such as racial solidarity, the importance of tradition and honor, and the struggle against oppression." CRT stories are written by minority persons to humanize their experiences in their own eyes and in the eyes of majority (Delgado 1989). They can "stir our imaginations, and let us begin to see life through the eyes of the outsider," and they can bring to "light the abuses and petty and major tyrannies that minority communities suffer . . . that might otherwise remain invisible" (Delgado 1990:109). They can cleanse the minority's soul and allow the majority to examine its practices that marginalize the minority

(Brown 1995; Delgado 1995). CRT stories thus offer both the minority and the majority the opportunity to "enrich their own reality" and acquire the "ability to see the world through other's eyes" (Delgado 1989:2439).

CRT stories are not simple anecdotal accounts. They organize the minority's "experiences into temporally meaningful episodes" (Richardson 1990:118). For the sociologist, CRT stories are significant social events because they transform the minority into a self-narrating organism that exhibits spatial and temporal features; it has a past, present, and future. Further, CRT stories instruct sociologists about the minority's social reality, especially such issues as oppression and victimization, that is often ignored in traditional sociological research. Last, CRT stories introduce competing interpretations into sociological practice. In short, they are instructive. For example, they can instruct sociologists on how federal Indian laws have been implemented by the majority to subordinate Indians (Williams 1989, 1990); on how federal immigration laws deprive Latinos in the United States of fundamental social and political rights (Murray 1998; Olivas 1990); and on how the political state, when offered the opportunity, deprives black persons of their personal freedom (see "The Space Traders" narrative in Bell 1992:158–94; see also Delgado and Stefancic 1991). In sociology, CRT stories are a communicative form for the minority that frees it from silence by giving it voice.

A caveat about storytelling in sociology: In a discipline that often defines its relationship to persons, objects, and events as empirical statements about social phenomena, storytelling may be suspect. Storytelling, or narrative, however, has been present in sociological research—from case histories and personal interviews to content analysis (Maines 1993). Storytelling can even be found in unexpected corners of sociological research, such as empirical studies that examine narrative events as underlying structures for social and historical contexts of social action (see Gotham and Staples 1996; Griffin 1993; Kiser 1996; Somers 1992). Storytelling is also used as a primary means of gathering and interpreting data in ethnographic work (Van Maanen 1988), as a research strategy in social science research (Ewick and Silbey 1995), and as an interpretive tool for defining sociological concepts, such as *identity* and *community* (Maines and Bridger 1992; Somers 1994, 1995). Richardson (1990), however, suggests that storytelling, or narrative, has been suppressed in sociological research by a *scientific frame* that dominates sociological thinking. Supporters of the scientific frame argue that storytelling is illegitimate scholarship because it "violates reason's mandates in two ways: first, it substitutes passion for reason and emotion for logic; and second, in its celebration of partiality and 'voice,' it substitutes perspective for truth" (Hayman 1998:10).

A Contentious Topic

The story in this article focuses on affirmative action. Very few topics are as pregnant with controversy. The majority's storytelling about affirmative action focuses on issues of *preferential treatment* and *reverse discrimination*—on "who benefits and who doesn't." According to Wellman (1997:322), the stories majority males tell about affirmative action "articulate the experience and sentiment of white men in both senses of the word: they link and express their aggrieved sentiments. That is why so many men tell the same story about the job they lost to an 'unqualified' woman or person of color. That is how 'all things being equal' came to mean 'reverse discrimination.'" Members of the majority usually ask questions regarding the appropriateness of using a remedy that seeks to alter the unequal distribution of social opportunity in a society that is heavily weighted in their favor. In the eyes of the majority, access to social opportunity is earned on merit; those with "more" access to opportunity have earned it and those with "less" have not. The attempt to alter the distribution of social opportunity through affirmative action results in the majority's observation that the minority seeks to gain opportunity at their expense (Brest and Oshige 1995; Saphir 1996; Wilkins and Gulati 1996). The majority's story reaches the conclusion that society "would have a meritocracy were it not for affirmative action" (Wasserstrom 1977:619).

In its stories about affirmative action, or about related strategies that seek to redress the inequalities experienced by the minority, the majority portrays itself as *innocent victim*. The majority asks in its stories, Are we not innocent victims of affirmative action? Because of the power of the majority's stories, "most of the successful constitutional discrimination cases in the last decade or so have been won by white male plaintiffs" (Kairys 1992:42). To illustrate the power of the majority's story over the minority's story, Hayman and Levit (1996) review three decisions that favored the majority from the 1994–95 term of the United States Supreme Court: Missouri v. Jenkins, 115 S. Ct. 2038 (1995); Adarand Constructors, Inc. v. Peña, 115 S. Ct. 2097 (1995); and Miller v. Johnson, 115 S. Ct. 2475 (1995).

In *Jenkins*, the majority argued that a desegregation initiative to reduce racial inequality between white and black students in the Kansas City, Missouri, School District would result in making black students "feel" superior to white students. The majority argued that desegregation efforts, coupled with affirmative action initiatives, would victimize white students. According to Justice Thomas, "Making blacks feel superior to whites sent to lesser schools—would violate the Fourteenth Amendment, whether or not the white students felt stigmatized, just as do school systems in which the positions of the races are reversed" (quoted in Hayman and Levit 1996:387).

In short, the stigmatization of white students outweighed reducing inequality for black students. After all, racial stigmatization is "new" for white students but not for black students. So why should one expect white students to become victims of racial stigmatization?

In *Peña*, the majority argued that a federal affirmative action law designed to increase the participation of minorities in federal contracting created a system of paternalism in which minorities expected to be given preferential treatment. The majority argued that the law was premised on an invalid assumption that minority contractors are disadvantaged in a manner that white contractors are not. The majority's story argued that using "minority status" to overcome disadvantages in federal contracting resulted in a system of "intentional discrimination" against the majority. That is, the majority depicted itself as victim. Interestingly, after "centuries of discrimination against 'individuals' because of their 'race,'" it seemed almost absurd to insist that 'individuals' were not entitled to redress because of their 'race'" (Hayman and Levit 1996:392). The Supreme Court thus supported the majority's argument that while minority status (race) could be the target of discriminatory actions that result in disadvantage, it could not be used to seek redress for its disadvantages if such redress victimized the majority. (Ironically, it was estimated that Adarand received more than 90 percent of state roadway construction money in Colorado, while Peña's bid would have amounted to less than 5 percent of that money.)

In *Johnson*, the federal government required the state of Georgia to create three congressional districts, each with a majority of black persons, before approving its congressional redistricting plan. White voters in one of the majority black districts, the 11th district, sued "perhaps because they did not like being in the minority" (Hayman and Levit 1996:393). The majority's story in this case argued that using "race" to create political communities violated the democratic ideal of racial neutrality in governmental decision making. It stressed that "race" could not be a factor in redistricting because political decisions are made in race-neutral contexts. White persons thus became "victims" when "race" was used to redress political inequalities that diluted minority access to a voting process designed to be race-neutral. Perhaps what is buried in the subtext of the majority's story is the majority's awareness that creating voting districts with a majority of black voters would expose the dependence of its privileged position on a political process that deprived black voters of their rights.

The majority's story in the three decisions is also interesting for what it does not tell. In *Jenkins*, the majority's story does not tell about the historical and social outcomes for black students of racial inequality in schools. It does not tell how disparities in educational funding and quality of school facilities result in black students' unequal access to the opportunity structure in U.S. society. In *Peña*, the majority's story fails to tell about uneven playing fields encountered by minority contractors, uneven playing fields that have historically favored the majority. It does not tell how racism and discrimination in trade associations harms minority contractors but benefits the majority. In *Johnson*, the majority's story does not tell how redistricting has been used historically by the majority to disenfranchise the minority in the political process. It does not tell that its use of redistricting to silence minority voters is a signal that the political process is not race-neutral.

The minority is thus portrayed as the oppressor and the majority as the oppressed in the majority's stories. The majority's storytelling about affirmative action does not tell that for more than two hundred years the majority has "benefited from their own program of affirmative action, through unjustified preferences in jobs and education resulting from old-boy networks and official laws that lessened the competition" (Delgado 1991:1225). I believe that a central purpose of the majority's storytelling about affirmative action is to manufacture the perception that its benefits and privileges are under attack from the minority. According to Quindlan (1992:A21), "The worried young white men I've met on college campuses . . . have internalized the newest myth of American race relations, and it has made them bitter. It is called affirmative action, a.k.a. the systematic oppression of white men." The majority's stories about affirmative action argue that it is under attack because affirmative action uses "racial discrimination as an ever-ready excuse for demanding preferences while disdaining performance" (Bell 1997a:1454). The majority portrays affirmative action a vehicle that benefits the minority at the majority's expense. Thus the majority portrays itself as *innocent victim* of reverse discrimination in its stories of affirmative action.

AN AFFIRMATIVE ACTION STORY

Setting: A professor and a student are talking in the professor's office. The professor and the student are both white. Stephen Narrows is a tenured full professor and chair of the sociology department. The student, Beverly Owens, is a fourth-year prelaw honors student and editor of the campus student newspaper. The student is interviewing Professor Narrows about minority faculty recruitment in his department.

Beverly Owens (BO): Professor Narrows, your department just completed a search for a senior faculty position in the areas of race/ethnic relations and social inequality. How many minorities were in the applicant pool?

Stephan Narrows (SN): I believe there were three minorities in the applicant pool. A Latino, an African-American male, and an Asian-American female.

BO: How large was the applicant pool?

SN: There were sixty-seven applicants in the pool

BO: How many of the minority applicants made it to the short list?

SN: From the initial applicant pool of sixty-seven, a short list of five applicants was derived. The Latino applicant made it to the short list.

BO: Who were the other applicants on the short list?

SN: Three white males and a white female.

BO: Did the Latino applicant meet the requirements for the position?

SN: Yes. He was a senior faculty member at an Ivy League school, and he had an impressive publication and research record and excellent teaching evaluations. The recruitment committee was quite pleased when it received his application. The department has been trying to recruit a qualified minority faculty member for quite a while. He appeared to be an excellent choice for this department. Given the lack of minority faculty, the department was really overjoyed with his application.

BO: I understand he would have been the first minority faculty member in your department.

SN: Yes, and it was quite a disappointment when we lost him.

BO: How exactly did you lose him? Did he remove his application from consideration? Did he go to another institution?

SN: It's a rather complicated story. The university has a DOT, Diversity Opportunity Targets, program for recruiting minority faculty.

BO: I'm not familiar with the DOT program. What does it do?

SN: The DOT program is an affirmative action initiative developed by the university to increase the representation of minority faculty on campus. The campus administration has set aside a certain number of faculty positions for the DOT program. Departments identify potential candidates for the program from the applicants that respond to a job announcement. The DOT candidate's name is forwarded to the campus administration for their review. The campus administration reviews the candidate's qualifications, along with the department's needs, and makes a decision whether to provide the department with a faculty position for the minority candidate or decline to consider the candidate for a DOT appointment.

BO: So, how did you lose the Latino applicant? I believe his name is Dr. Adrian Dia.

SN: The department felt that Dr. Dia was an excellent candidate for the DOT program and forwarded his name to the campus administration. After about six weeks the department was notified by the campus administration that all of the DOT appoinments had been made. By then it was too late for the department to consider Dr. Dia for the faculty position in sociology.

BO: Why was it too late?

SN: By the time we were notified by the campus administration about its decision regarding Dr. Dia, the department had already made an offer to one of the other applicants, Dr. Tom Smith.

BO: Did the department consider suspending the recruitment process until the campus administration made a decision regarding Dr. Dia?

SN: Not really. You see we didn't want to lose any of the other applicants.

BO: Why didn't the department keep Dr. Dia's application active while the campus administration reviewed his file?

SN: Because the department felt that it would be unfair to the other applicants. You see, Dr. Dia would have had two chances for a faculty position, the DOT program and ours, whereas the other applicants would have had only one chance. The department felt that the other applicants could accuse it of reverse discrimination.

BO: But wasn't it worth the risk to recruit Dr. Dia for a faculty appointment? After all, you did admit that minority faculty are hard to find, and that you've been trying to recruit one for a while now.

SN: I suppose it would have been worth the risk. However, the department was concerned with the issue of reverse discrimination.

BO: But couldn't Dr. Dia argue that he was the victim of discrimination by being removed from the applicant pool, especially since his name was on the short list?

SN: I suppose he could. However, in the department's view he was being considered for a faculty position in the DOT program. Remember the campus administration declined the DOT appointment for Dr. Dia. As a department we do not control the administration's decision-making process regarding the DOT program.

BO: SO the department believes that it lost Dr. Dia because of the campus administration's decision?

SN: Yes.

BO: Is the department still interested in recruiting minority faculty?

SN: Most certainly. We will continue to use the recruitment process, especially the DOT program, to increase the representation of minorities on the faculty.

[The conversation comes to an end.]

WHAT DOES THE STORY TELL US?

What does the story tell us about affirmative action? First, affirmative action initiatives, such as the DOT program, can be implemented in a manner that results in unintended benefits for the majority. By referring minority applicants to the DOT program, the university administration and the department increase the risk that minority applicants will be suppressed in the hiring process. According to Mickelson and Oliver (1991:161), this is not surprising if one considers that "greater numbers of minority faculty per se are not their [affirmative action programs'] direct goal." Accordingly, Delgado (1991:1224) observes that affirmative action protects the majority by limiting the number of minority persons that are "hired or promoted. Not too many, for that would be terrifying, nor too few, for that would be destabilizing." Similarly, Steele and Green (1976) have observed that an outcome of pursuing affirmative action goals in academia is a decreased effort to *actually* recruit minority faculty. In this sense, affirmative action *cools* minorities in the recruitment process while the majority pursues its own interests.

For example, Professor Narrows suggests that his department's options are limited when it comes to recruiting minority faculty. In his eyes, and the department's, there is really only one viable option, to refer the minority applicant to the DOT program. As an outcome of the referral, however, the minority applicant is removed from consideration for the position advertised by the sociology department. By referring Dr. Dia to the DOT program the sociology department shifts responsibility for recruiting minority faculty from itself onto the campus administration, a much larger bureaucratic structure that serves as a burying ground for institutional accountability: If you must blame someone, blame the administration. Moreover, the department increases the chances that he will be lost in a bureaucratic context designed to deal with campuswide needs and not necessarily departmental needs. The department may have believed that it was increasing its chances of recruiting Dr. Dia through the DOT program. However, the university administration may not have shared its interest in recruiting Dr. Dia.

In particular, the sociology department may not have done an adequate job of communicating its interest in recruiting Dr. Dia to the campus administration.

The ability to shift responsibility for recruiting minority faculty between organizational units shields institutions of higher education from its critics, especially minority critics. How can one be critical of an institution for not recruiting minority faculty if the institution defends itself by showcasing its affirmative action plan for recruiting minority faculty? All too often affirmative action plans for recruiting minority faculty are touted for their "promise" in promoting institutional diversity. However, they are not evaluated for their ability to increase the number of minority faculty: "Affirmative action has made a marked difference in the initial stage of the search process, but unfortunately not in the results" (Mickelson and Oliver 1991:153). The institution's ability to shift its responsibility for recruiting minority faculty thus makes it difficult for critics to "blame" someone for not implementing an affirmative action plan that increases the number of minority faculty. In Dr. Dia's case, the sociology department made an adequate effort to recruit him. The university's DOT program also communicated an institutional commitment to recruiting minority faculty. So who does one blame for not recruiting Dr. Dia? Who does one blame for not implementing a DOT program that benefits minority applicants?

By referring Dr. Dia to the DOT program, the sociology department decreased his chances for a faculty appointment by excluding him from competing with the other four applicants on the short list. One must not ignore the fact that the other four applicants were white and that excluding Dr. Dia allowed four white persons to compete among themselves for the faculty position. The DOT program appears to have benefited the white applicants more than it did Dr. Dia, because his referral to the program reduced the competitive context for the white applicants. While the DOT program may not be intended to increase opportunity for members of the majority, its implementation may reflect academia's interest in protecting majority interests. That is, the DOT program is implemented by the administration to protect the majority from minority competition, thereby protecting an institutional culture and environment that promotes majority interests.

Professor Narrows makes the observation that Dr. Dia's consideration for both the DOT program and a sociology position would be unfair to the other applicants on the short list. He implies that Dr. Dia is being considered for two faculty positions. The issue of "fairness" is often used by the majority to avoid drawing attention to the real issue involved—exclusion (Roithmayr 1997; Sturm and Guinier 1996). Professor Narrows raises the question of *reverse discrimination* in his observation. Is reverse discrimination really an issue if one considers that the only applicants remaining for the sociology position are white? Can the issue of reverse discrimination serve as a device for the majority to avoid questions about an all-white applicant pool? Dr. Dia responded to a job announcement for a sociology position. He did not respond to an announcement requesting minority faculty to submit their credentials for review by the DOT program. While the DOT program is allocated faculty slots (FTE) by the administration for recruiting minority faculty, the DOT program is not an academic unit or department. The DOT program can operate only as a recruitment vehicle, and it is only effective if an FTE is available and an academic unit identifies a qualified minority person it wants to recruit. As a result, contrary to Professor Narrows's observation, Dr. Dia can be considered for one faculty position only, the one in sociology, because he cannot be appointed to the DOT program. Who then is the victim of reverse discrimination?

One also needs to consider that the sociology department did not ask Dr. Dia if he would like his application to be forwarded to the DOT program. Perhaps a reasonable approach would have been to inform Dr. Dia about the DOT program and to offer him the option. The sociology department, however, referred his application to the DOT program because it felt that he was an excellent candidate for the DOT program. Also, before referring his application, the sociology department could have asked the administration if there were any FTEs available in the DOT program. In a sense, Dr. Dia's minority status rendered him *powerless* in the recruitment process; the majority faculty in sociology made a decision for him based on the "paternalistic attitudes of the decision-makers" (Reyes and Halcon 1991:176–77). The majority reasoned that it "knew best" for Dr. Dia by referring him to the DOT program. However, assuming "what's best" for Dr. Dia resulted in an unintended benefit for the white applicants. The lack of consultation between the sociology department and Dr. Dia is, I believe, a reflection of an implicit institutional belief that favors the majority: the powerless position of minority persons constrains them in questioning institutional decisions made for them by the majority. After all, the sociology department appears to have done "its best" to recruit Dr. Dia.

For the sake of discussion, let us assume that the sociology department asked Dr. Dia if he wanted his application to be forwarded to the DOT program. If Dr. Dia refuses, does this mean that he will not be considered for the sociology position? If Dr. Dia agrees, does this mean that the DOT program is his only opportunity for being considered for a sociology position? Regardless of whether he agrees or refuses, Dr. Dia is involved in a "nonchoice" situation. That is, either response decreases his chances for a sociology position. For example, by refusing to have his application forwarded to the DOT program, Dr. Dia's application may no longer

look "attractive" to the sociology department. In particular, Dr. Dia's application looks less attractive if one considers that the sociology department views his application as a vehicle for obtaining an "extra" faculty position for the department. That is, the sociology department perceives itself as having access to two faculty positions, the FTE available from the DOT program and the one it advertised. Dr. Dia's application is thus a benefit rather than a liability for the sociology department.

In contrast, by agreeing to have his application forwarded to the DOT program, Dr. Dia is removed from consideration for the position advertised by the sociology department because his opportunity for a sociology position depends on the availability of an FTE in the DOT program. Thus, Dr. Dia does not have a *choice* he controls. Where then is the "preferential" issue that could lead to charges of reverse discrimination? What "choice" does Dr. Dia control that gives him "preference" over the white applicants on the short list? Dr. Dia's condition of powerlessness has robbed him of choice and the ability to control his own fate. How then can he control the fate of others, especially the fate of those who can charge him with "reverse discrimination"?

Finally, the recruitment event described in the story suggests that affirmative action can be a device for the application of exclusionary practices in academia. Majority faculty often lament that minority faculty are so hard to find. Olivas (1988) refers to their lament as a "high-demand/low-supply" myth promoted by majority faculty to camouflage their lack of responsibility for recruiting minority faculty. However, one does not hear, Now that we've found a minority faculty person, let's hire them. In contrast, majority faculty, especially males, are often found without anyone looking for them—Professor Tom Smith has expressed interest in joining the department, let's ask the dean for an FTE for him. The recruitment of

majority academics by other majority academics for, in most cases, faculty positions
that are created for them is attributed to
networking in academia, never referred to as
affirmative action. Or, borrowing from
Scheff (1995), similar to membership in a
gang, majority faculty recruit each other for
positions they create for themselves in order
to maintain their territorial control in academia. In many ways, majority persons have
always had a DOT program in academia that
serves their interests (Bell 1995b; Delgado
1991; Lamb 1993; Wilson 1995).

An emphasis on recruiting minority faculty
requires that academia alter its practices for
including minority faculty in its environment.
It requires that academia use affirmative
action initiatives, such as the DOT program,
to enhance the inclusion of minority faculty
rather than their exclusion from faculty
recruitment practices (Montero-Sieburth
1996; Verdugo 1995). Despite the implementation of affirmative action programs to
recruit minority faculty, especially during the
past two decades minority faculty are rarely
found in academia (Aguirre 1995a; Cortese
1992; Johnson 1997; Rai and Critzer 2000).
For example, between 1980 and 1993 the
representation of white persons in the U.S.
professorate increased from 87 to 88 percent. In contrast, the representation of black
persons and Latino persons in the professorate remained unchanged at 5 percent
and 2 percent, respectively, between 1980
and 1993 (National Center for Education
Statistics 1986, 1997). Accordingly, a survey
of the thirty-four top-ranked sociology
departments in the Unites States documents
the relative absence of minority faculty:
"Fewer than 15% of the departments have
more than one full-time, tenure track African
American faculty member and more than
one full-time, tenure track Latino faculty
member" (Bonilla-Silva and Herring 1999:7).
It would appear that the inclusion of minority
faculty in the professorate remains an elusive
goal.

CONCLUDING REMARKS

Is the story just another story? I suspect that
most majority academics, and perhaps even
some minority academics, will regard my
story as just another story, an imaginative
one but certainly not real. That may happen
in the outside world, but not in academia, the
majority academic might say. I believe that
majority academics prefer to ignore the story,
because not to do so requires that they
examine themselves and their control of
academia. It especially requires majority faculty to consider their role in promoting
unequal power relations for the minority in
academia. The story in this article argues that
affirmative action can be implemented in a
manner that results in unintended benefits
for the majority. Affirmative action programs, such as the DOT program, are usually
not the problem; rather, it is their implementation that often turns a technical issue into
a moral argument. Their implementation
becomes even more problematic if one considers that the institutional environment in
academia is designed to enhance the majority's presence, not the minority's pursuit of
opportunity.

The affirmative action program described
in the story is representative of affirmative
action initiatives in academia that are
designed to increase the representation of
minorities in the professorate (Johnson et al.
1998; Justus 1987; Moore 1996; Moore
1997; Morgan 1996; Myers and Wilkins
1995; Solorzano 1993; Young 1984). These
initiatives have been around since the late
1960s, and they have been funded in a variety of ways, from private foundations to
challenge grants from corporate sponsors.
However, the emergence of broad-based
conservative political interests during the
1980s in U.S. society, especially the structur-
ing of conservative political interest in the
Supreme Court, seriously constrained the
use of affirmative action initiatives (Gamson
and Modigliani 1987; Pratt 1999; Sidanius,

Pratto, and Bobo 1996). Affirmative action initiatives in academia may have become more susceptible to attack because they appear to have increased the *representativeness* of minority students and minority faculty in academia (Aguirre 1995b; Bowen and Bok 1998; Gose 1998). However, the initiatives have fallen short of reducing the obstacles faced by minorities in academia. For example, minority faculty encounter obstacles rooted in prejudice and discrimination in their pursuit of professional goals, such as tenure and promotion (Aguirre 1981, forthcoming; Kulis, Chong, and Shaw 1999). Also, minority faculty are often expected to alter their professional goals in an institutional environment defined by the professional goals of majority faculty (Aguirre, Martinez, and Hernandez 1993; Bonilla-Silva and Herring 1999). While affirmative action has opened the door to academia for minorities, it has not extended very far beyond the doorway to help them navigate their way in an institutional environment that is often not receptive to their presence (Johnson 1997).

The story presented here argues that affirmative action can be implemented so as not to benefit the minority. It must be understood that while affirmative action programs, such as the DOT, target minorities, they do so not to discriminate against the majority but to combat the discrimination experienced by the minority. Proposition 209, for example, was voted into law in California because it depicted affirmative action as a threat to the majority's access to opportunity in the state (Bell 1997b). The debate over Proposition 209 questioned the need for affirmative action in academia; its passage increased the chances that minorities would be turned away by academia (Karabel 1997; Tierney 1996). Ironically, one of the outcomes of the passage of Proposition 209 was a decrease in the numbers of minority students applying for admission and the recruitment of minority faculty in institutions of higher education in California (Schneider 1998). Is the decrease in numbers of minority students and minority faculty a signal that affirmative action programs were improving access for minorities? Or are the decreasing numbers a response from an institutional environment that has become less receptive to the minority's presence? I prefer to believe that affirmative action was working to increase the *representativeness* of minorities in academia.

It is because I prefer to believe that affirmative action is necessary for academia to become an inclusive and multicultural institution that I tell the story in this article. But while we may dream about how affirmative action can shape academia into an inclusive and multicultural institution, we should not be deluded about how affirmative action is implemented. A social fact about academia is that it is controlled by the majority; its numerical representation alone convinces the casual observer that it is the dominant group. Another social fact about academia is that most of its activity is designed to promote the majority's interests; even affirmative action was created by the majority (Law 1999). Not surprisingly, the majority practices affirmative action by itself and on itself in academia. In a few cases, the minority derives some benefit from these practices.

My story urges majority and minority faculty members who support affirmative action to examine the implementation of affirmative action programs. One must not lose sight of the fact that affirmative action in academia is implemented in an institutional environment that often has difficulty responding to minority concerns. Affirmative action must be used by majority faculty as a device for pursuing the inclusion of minorities in academia. Perhaps one way in which majority faculty can examine the implementation of affirmative action is by asking themselves if they receive any unintended benefits from the manner in which academia practices affirmative action.

Finally, some stories are difficult to tell, especially if they address uncomfortable topics. The story here is one of those. The storyteller may be accused of addressing a topic, affirmative action, regarded by the majority as benefiting only the minority. Majority persons may ask, Why is he biting the hand that feeds him? As the storyteller, I am aware of the benefits and obstacles that affirmative action places in the path of an academic career. However, after so many years in academia, listening to conversations between majority faculty in mailrooms or in faculty meetings in which I am often invisible to them, I have come to realize that they have their own faculty recruitment system that only benefits their presence in academia. I regard their system as *affirmative action*. It would appear then that both majority and minority faculty benefit from affirmative action in academia. The question is, Who benefits more from affirmative action in academia? That is another story in need of telling.

Acknowledgments

A version of this article was presented at the annual meeting of the Sociology of Education Association, February 21–23, 1997, in Monterey, California. The comments and suggestions I received from people in the audiences have been very helpful in framing the story in this article. The anonymous reviewers for *Sociological Perspectives* played a critical role in expanding the scope of using critical race theory to examine affirmative action in academia. My thanks to Chuck Hohm for helping me, in his own way, to pursue this project, to Michael Olivas for his insights on how stories become stories, and to my graduate students for their patient listening to my tales. I assume responsibility for any shortcomings.

STUDY QUESTION

In Aguirre's article on Academic Storytelling, he uses the term "counterstory" to accent his comments on how affirmative action is practiced in academia. What does Aguirre mean by the term "counterstory"? Give examples from his article that illustrate why Aguirre is adopting the term counterstory to reflect his thesis.

CHAPTER 3

Inequality in American Criminal Justice

INTRODUCTION

Most Americans fail to recognize the U.S. legal system as an institution preventing persons of color from competing with the white population for favorable positions and valued resources in society. Put another way, most Americans are unaware that white society uses the legal system to shield its social, political, and economic interests from minority group infringement. Societal interests of marginalized groups are not the concern of the legal system: the official and often callous tasks of law enforcement, prosecutors, judges, juries, correctional officers, and even state executioners is to protect dominant group interests. One report on the adverse impact of crime and criminal justice on Americans of color explains that the "laws and public policies in the United States reflect the contradiction of a society attempting to act within an egalitarian ideological posture while treating minorities with direct, blunt and flagrant inequality."[1] One explanation for this racial and ethnic double standard of the American legal system is that U.S. society has yet to attach real meaning to fundamental rights and constitutional freedoms and to support these civil liberties with powerful institutions.[2]

SELECTIVE LAW ENFORCEMENT

Law enforcement has aimed its violent methods of control mostly a persons of color.[3] One scholar notes that the history of policing in the United States "reflects the evolution of a socially approved armed institution whose role has frequently been at odds with the freedom and the very lives of minority peoples."[4] One only needs to review the accounts of mistreatment targeted against Latinos by the Texas Rangers, the Border Patrol, state and city police, county sheriffs, and the U.S. Immigration and Naturalization Service (INS) to get a sense of this history.[5] Texas Rangers, for example, were often involved in the beating, lynching, and summary execution and even dismemberment of Mexican Americans.[6] Yet today we glamorize the Texas Rangers in a television program—*Walker, Texas Ranger*—with actor Chuck Norris playing the title role. In *State Violence and the Social and Legal Construction of Latino Criminality: From El Bandido to Gang Member*, sociologist Mary Romero explains much about the troubled 150-year history of police violence and misconduct in the Latino community as an artifact of law enforcement's image of the Latino as a criminal.[7]

Police violence is pervasive and widespread.[8] Unjustified shootings, severe beatings, fatal choking, and unnecessarily rough treatment of detainees occur in police departments throughout the country.[9] Race is central to police brutality because police consider persons of color more dangerous than white persons. But such high-profile cases as the police violence surrounding Los Angeles police officers and black motorist Rodney King in 1991, the vicious attack on Abner Louima by New York police officers in 1997, the punching of sixteen-year-old Donovan Jackson by Inglewood police officer Jeremy Morse in 2002, the police-involved killing of Nathaniel Jones by the Cincinnati police in 2003, and the atrocities associated with the antigang unit based in the Los Angeles Police Department's (LAPD) Rampart Division tend to limit our societal notion of police lawlessness to out-of-control rogue city cops. Yet considerable evidence indicates that police misconduct is highly institutionalized in large metropolitan police departments and that police aim their wrongdoing particularly at persons of color.[10] In its most recent investigations of the LAPD, the Special Litigation Section of the U.S. Department of Justice revealed that LAPD officers regularly engage in practices of excessive force, false arrests, and unconstitutional searches and seizures including making police stops not based on reasonable suspicion.[11] In addition, these are the same police practices identified by earlier investigations that apparently remain unresolved.[12] Black women are the victims of police violence: in 1978 two white Los Angeles police officers shot and killed Eula Love, a black woman with intellectual disabilities, and in 1998 four white Riverside (California) police officers shot and killed Tyisha Miller, an unconscious black woman. Black women often encounter institutionalized racism when white police officers show little interest and take no action when black women are rape victims. Police often fail to support black female rape victims. At an April 2000 conference in Santa Cruz, California, professor and social critic Angela Y. Davis told a horrific story of black female victimization by a white police officer:

> Many years ago when I was a student in San Diego, I was driving down the freeway with a friend when we encountered a black woman wandering along the shoulder. Her story was extremely disturbing. Despite her uncontrollable weeping, we were able to surmise that she had been raped and dumped along the side of the road. After a while, she was able to wave down a police car, thinking that they would help her. However, when the white policeman picked her up, he did not comfort her, but rather seized upon the opportunity to rape her once more.[13]

Police brutality against Americans of color often results from the nativist and anti-immigrant sentiments associated with political campaigns. The hateful rhetoric and negative portrayal of Mexican Americans during California's debate on Proposition 187 (barred undocumented immigrants from access to benefits and public services) and Proposition 227 (outlawed bilingual education in public instruction), for example, may instill some distorted sense of moral justification for police misconduct. One analyst argues that police behavior may be rooted in a political history of racism in which whites perceive Mexican Americans essentially as violent or criminal.[14] Another observer finds that the shock white Americans profess concerning police misconduct "illustrates the pattern of denial about the pervasiveness of racism in law enforcement. Police racism is a perversion of justice that undermines confidence in the rule of law."[15] A review of several hundred complaints of Mexican immigrants found that state and federal agents patrolling the U.S.-Mexico border incessantly violate their civil rights. These violations include illegal searches of persons and private property, verbal, psychological, and physical abuse, child abuse, deprivation of food, water, and medical attention, torture, theft, excessive force, assault and battery, and murder.[16] The victims lodged complaints against the U.S. Border Patrol, the INS, U.S. Customs, the U.S. Port Authority, the sheriff's departments of San Diego, Vista, San Marcos, Fallbrook, and Riverside, the San Diego Police Department, the California Highway Patrol, and the California National Guard.

SENTENCING DISPARITY

The criminology literature is replete with empirical evidence that whites are dealt with far more leniently than nonwhite minorities in the criminal justice system. One illustration of the oppressive relationship between America's minority nonwhite populations and justice administration is the overrepresentation of racial and ethnic minorities in the criminal justice system. Moreover, the overrepresentation of a population in the criminal justice system permits researchers to examine the operation of extralegal factors, such as biased attitudes and perceptions, in the processing of the population by the criminal justice system. Several studies have examined the extent to which Latinos suffer ethnic discrimination in criminal court processes.[17] Latinos tend to receive harsher prison sentences from courts and serve more time in prison than whites convicted of similar crimes. Latinos are also less able to make bail than whites, and they are more likely to have court-appointed counsel. A study of two southwestern cities found that Latinos tried for a crime and found guilty, rather than simply entering a guilty plea as part of a plea bargaining agreement, received harsher sentences.[18] Another study of Latinos convicted of felonies in California found that a Latino's prior criminal record was a significant predictor of their sentence length, but that prior criminal record accounted for little or no variation in sentence length among other racial and ethnic groups.[19] In California, then, Latino defendants with prior records are processed differently by authorities than defendants without prior records, and the use of sentence enhancements is essentially restricted to Latinos. A similar study found that Latinos have higher conviction rates and are more likely to be sentenced to prison than Anglos.[20] Even in states that do not have significant Latino populations, Latinos are subjected to inequitable treatment by the criminal justice system. A study in Nebraska found that authorities arrest and charge Latinos with misdemeanor offenses at considerably higher rates than Anglos. Authorities also charged Latinos with more counts, they received higher fines, and they were sentenced to more probation time than Anglos. In effect, a higher conviction rate for misdemeanor offenses ensures that Latinos will have a higher rate of prior offenses—which courts consider a valid predictor of future convictions, thereby setting the stage for future disparate encounters with the criminal justice system. As a result, higher fines and more probation become practical and lawful methods of controlling the Latino population economically and socially without jeopardizing their labor power.[21]

To the National Minority Advisory Council on Criminal Justice, the displacement of American Indian sovereignty by the encroaching Anglo-European system of laws and values has had pernicious, debilitating effects on the American Indian community. The council noted that "the discriminatory law enforcement experienced by American Indians is perpetuated in the US judicial system, where it assumes the more subtle form of institutionalized discrimination and racism."[22] A compilation and analysis of data on American Indians by the U.S. Department of Justice supports this contention by revealing an extremely disturbing portrait of American Indians as offenders of violent crime in the United States.[23] The incarceration rate of American Indians is about 38 percent higher than the national rate, with some 4 percent of the American Indian population in custody or otherwise under the control of the American criminal justice system. Although American Indians constitute less than 1 percent of the U.S. population, nearly 2 percent of all federal cases filed in U.S. District Courts in 1997 were against American Indians, with roughly half of these cases for such violent crimes as murder and rape. The correctional system subjects American Indians to more abuse than any other minority group, particularly when indigenous inmates attempt to identify with their native cultures—such as "wearing head-bands, using native languages, maintaining long, braided hair, enjoying native music, or securing cultural-related leisure and educational materials."[24] American Indian prisoners serve more of their sentences than do non-American Indian prisoners. It is not surprising that the *ethnic identifiability* of American Indian prisoners exerts such a strong and independent effect on the proportion of time American Indian prisoner are incarcerated before release.[25] Much of the criminality attributed to American Indians results from the social disorganization and economic deprivation plaguing their communities.[26] Yet these social problems in American Indian communities appear beyond the concern of America's national leadership.

The federal prison population has increased dramatically over the last thirty years, and it has become an increasingly a population of color. Whites are underrepresented in federal prison populations, and persons of color are overrepresented. Some 57 percent of the nearly 178,000 federal prisoners are white, 40 percent are black and Asian Americans, and American Indian prisoners are about 1.6 percent of the federal prison population, respectively. According to Federal Bureau of Prisons classification of ethnicity, Latinos can be of any race and are slightly more than 32 percent of the federal prison population. Most federal prisoners have been sentenced to between five and ten years, and slightly more than 54 percent of them are imprisoned for nonviolent drug offenses. Analyses of federal correctional facilities inmate survey data shows that blacks and Latinos are discriminated against in the judicial system and that this differential treatment results in larger incarceration rates for blacks and Latinos than for whites. Socioeconomics, language barriers, child-rearing practices, and family structure account for higher nonwhite incarceration rates in federal prisons.

In response to concerns over increasing crack cocaine use in inner cities, in 1986 Congress enacted disproportionately harsher penalties for possessing crack cocaine than for possessing powder cocaine because crack cocaine was perceived as more potent and socially disruptive than powder cocaine. The minimum sentence for possession of 5 grams of *crack* cocaine is five years in prison for first-time offenders, and a ten-year-to-life minimum prison sentence for persons arrested with more than 10 grams. But the same minimum five-year sentence is not given to defendants in possession of *powder* cocaine unless they are arrested with at least 500 grams. Federal sentencing guidelines, then, require a hundred times more powder cocaine for the minimum five-year sentence than what is needed to invoke the minimum sentence for crack cocaine. Consequently, the average sentence for possession in federal convictions is 3.2 months for powder cocaine and 30.6 months for crack cocaine. Yet, in a special report to the Congress, the U.S. Sentencing Commission denied that these statistical variations are indicative of racial bias in the use of this federal sentencing law:

> One of the issues of greatest concern surrounding federal cocaine sentencing policy is the perception of disparate and unfair treatment for defendants convicted of either possession or distribution of crack cocaine. Critics argue that the 100-to-1 quantity ratio is not consistent with the policy, goal, and mission of federal sentencing—that is to be effective, uniform, and just. While there is no evidence of racial bias behind the promulgation of this federal sentencing law, nearly 90 percent of the offenders convicted in federal court for crack cocaine distribution are African-American while the majority of crack cocaine users is white. Thus, sentences appear to be harsher and more severe for racial minorities than others because of this law. The current penalty structure results in a perception of unfairness and inconsistency.[27]

To law professor Kenneth B. Nunn in *Race, Crime and the Pool of Surplus Criminality: Or Why the "War on Drugs" Was a "War on Blacks,"* government efforts to control drugs has been one way in which dominant groups can express racial power—"the drug war is simply a prominent example of the central role both race and the definition of crime play in the maintenance and legitimization of white supremacy." Indeed, minority defendants receive much harsher sentences for crack cocaine violations than white defendants because crack cocaine cases involving nonwhite defendants are prosecuted more often in federal courts than in state courts where penalties for drug possession are far more severe. As a result, blacks and Latinos account for 97 percent of all defendants prosecuted in federal courts for crack cocaine violations, whereas whites are only 3 percent of crack cocaine defendants prosecuted in federal courts. In fact, no whites were federally prosecuted for crack cocaine offenses from 1988 through 1994 in seventeen states. Federal arrests for powder cocaine violations are also disproportionately made by race and ethnicity. White persons account for 32 percent of all federal arrests for powder cocaine violations; blacks account for 27 percent and Latinos account for 39 percent.[28] Although the federal sentencing guidelines may appear facially neutral with no racist intention, Michael Tonry argues that the racially disparate effect of the government's war on drugs (evidenced by the statistics just noted) was foreseeable by "the architects" of the campaign against drug trafficking and drug use. For one, urban police departments have found it far easier to focus the drug war on disadvantaged minority neighborhoods than in suburban white neighborhoods.

GENDER AND CRIMINAL JUSTICE

The etiology of female criminality, criminal justice outcomes and female offenders, and whether police, judges, correctional officers, and other criminal justice professionals victimize female prisoners remain ambiguous to social scientists because criminologists, legal scholars, and social scientists have simply ignored female criminality.[29] Although the representation of women in the U.S. criminal justice system as both offenders and victims has increased significantly over the last several decades, the academic literature addressing inequalities in the administration of criminal justice has remained primarily focused on the male offender. In her analysis of the relationship between gender, race, and class in the justice system, law professor Jennifer Ward in *Snapshots: Holistic Images of Female Offenders in the Criminal Justice System* concludes that the connection between a history of physical and/or sexual abuse and subsequent drug use are important factors in a woman's incarceration. Ward's research gives credence to the notion that the conventional theoretical perspectives are inadequate to explain the peculiarity of female criminality. Schulhofer has analyzed the male-dominated nature of the criminal law and the administration of criminal justice and addresses the complexities of applying existing criminal justice theory and practice to female victimization and offending. He advances the proposition that a feminist theory must be constructed to make clear the particularistic nature of female criminality and victimization. To combat gender inequality in the criminal justice system effectively, the theory must guide its practice away from the male-dominated ideologies of inequality toward a gender-specific, or gender-sensitive, structure of policy and practice.[30]

RACE AND CAPITAL PUNISHMENT

The United States has increased dramatically its pace of executions over the last several decades. Death penalty authorities executed 11 prisoners between 1976 and 1983, but since then state and federal jurisdictions have executed another 917 prisoners. Black defendants constitute a disproportionate segment of the executed prisoner population. Capital sentencing researchers find that the "race of the victim" and the "race of the defendant" are powerful predictors of how state prosecutors decide to seek the death penalty, and that there are clear patterns of racial discrimination in capital sentencing. Death penalty jurisdictions sentence black defendants to death at significantly higher rates than white defendants, and black defendants are particularly at risk of capital sentencing and actual execution when their victims are white. A comprehensive review of capital sentencing research by the U.S. General Accounting Office (GAO) reveals that in 82 percent of the studies, the race of the victim was found to influence the likelihood of a defendant being charged with capital murder or receiving the death penalty.[31] That is, persons who murdered whites were found more likely to be sentenced to death than persons who murdered blacks. In a more recent report expanding on the GAO's review, researchers found that in almost all capital punishment states, the race of the victim correlated with whether the jurisdiction sentenced the defendant to death.[32] The report also indicated that in nearly half of all states the race of the defendant is a predictor of who received death sentences.

One study found that prosecutors seek the death penalty in 70 percent of all cases involving a black defendant and a white victim, but do so in only 15 percent of all cases involving a white defendant and a black victim.[33] Other studies find that prosecutorial discretion in capital cases accounts for why prosecutors are far more likely to charge black defendants with aggravated murder and try them as capital offenders when their victims are white.[34] To these researchers, prosecutorial discretion amounts to *intentional discrimination* against black defendants with white victims. North Carolina researchers found that jurisdictional authorities are nearly four times more likely to give death sentences to defendants whose victims are white than defendants whose victims are nonwhite.[35] Finally, in a report by the Justice Department, researchers found that federal prosecutors are nearly twice as likely to recommend death for a black defendant when the victim is nonblack as when the victim is black.[36]

Escalating execution rates have also increased the possibility that authorities may execute an innocent defendant. That possibility has become so disconcerting to the legal community that the American Bar Association has called for death penalty jurisdictions to halt executions until authorities can ensure fairness and impartiality in their administration.[37] One of the more troubling studies on wrongful executions has identified some 350 cases in which U.S. jurisdictions have wrongfully convicted a defendant of a capital crime.[38] Of these cases, authorities sentenced 159 defendants to death: they actually executed 23 prisoners and 22 others came within seventy-two hours of executions before defense lawyers established their innocence.[39] Predictably, defendants of color constitute a significant proportion of the hundreds of cases of wrongfully convicted defendants. In fact, 53 of the 115 capital defendants released from death rows across the country since 1971 have been black defendants. This number suggests a strong probability that jurisdictions erroneously convict black defendants more than white defendants. Black defendants also spend more years in prison between conviction and exoneration than white defendants; innocent black defendants spend an average of 8.8 years in prison, whereas innocent white defendants spend an average of 6.9 years in prison. Undoubtedly, the procedural safeguards established to diminish racism in capital sentencing will prove evermore meaningless and ineffectual when the United States continues to execute innocent black men at such an unreasonably fast rate that the defense lawyers cannot establish defendants' innocence until it is too late. In *The Race Effect on Wrongful Convictions*, law professor Arthur L. Rizer recommends various criminal justice reforms to diminish the influence of race on wrongful convictions, including videotaping of police interrogations, requiring that juries comprise some persons of the defendant's race, and holding prosecutors civilly or criminally accountable for blatant prosecutorial racism.[40] Interesting, prosecutors engage in some form of misconduct in roughly 40 percent of wrongful convictions.[41]

Summary

The representation of persons of color, poor people, and women subjected to criminal justice processes in the United States results from disparate social control of these populations. That is, racial and ethnic oppression and subjugation result in higher rates of crime and criminal sanctions for minority persons and illustrates the selectivity used by justice professionals. This chapter reviewed criminal justice research showing the differential treatment of persons of color, poor people, and women by criminal justice professionals in most facets of American criminal justice. As the principal vehicle for defining deviance in society, the criminal justice system uses selectivity to process persons for deviant labels. To legitimate its presence in American society, criminal justice professionals use a process of selectivity to reinforce the differential position of persons of color, poor people, and women in the structure of opportunity in the U.S. society. Moreover, this process of selectivity is inversely associated with minority group members' position in the structure of opportunity. Consequently, the restricted access of minority persons to the U.S. opportunity structure increases their selective treatment by the criminal justice system.

ENDNOTES

1. Raymond S. Blanks, *The Inequality of Justice: A Report on Crime and the Administration of Justice in the Minority Community*, National Minority Advisory Council on Criminal Justice, Washington, DC (January 1982).
2. Arnold S. Trebach, *The Rationing of Justice: Constitutional Rights and the Criminal Process* (New Brunswick, NJ: Rutgers University Press, 1964), p. 205.
3. Alison L. Patton, "The Endless Cycle of Abuse: Why 42 U.S.C. Sec 1983 Is Ineffective in Deterring Police Brutality," *Hastings Law Journal*, 44 (1993): 753–808; William J. Stuntz, "Terrorism, Federalism, and Police Misconduct," *Harvard Journal of Law and Public Policy*, 25 (2002): 665–679; Jennifer E. Koepke, "Note: The Failure to Breach the Blue Wall of Silence: The Circling of the Wagons to Protect Policy Perjury," *Washburn Law Journal*, 39 (2000): 211–242.
4. National Minority Advisory Council on Criminal Justice, *The Inequality of Justice: A Report on Crime and the Administration of Justice in the Minority Community* (1982), p. 225.
5. Michael Huspek, Roberto Martinez, and Leticia Jimenez, "Violations of Human and Civil Rights on the U.S.-Mexico Boarder, 1995 to 1997: A Report," *Social Justice*, 25 (1998): 110–130; Rodolfo Acuña, *Occupied America: A History of Chicanos* (New York: Longman, 2000).
6. Adalberto Aguirre and Jonathan Turner, *American Ethnicity: The Dynamics and Consequences of Discrimination* (New York: McGraw-Hill, 1995), p. 133.
7. See also Mary Romero and Marwah Serag, "Violation of Latino Civil Rights Resulting from INS and Local Police's Use of Race, Culture and Class Profiling: The Case of the Chandler Roundup in Arizona," *Cleveland State Law Review*, 52 (2005): 75–96.
8. See, generally, William A. Geller and Han Toch, eds., *Police Violence: Understanding and Controlling Police Abuse of Force* (New Haven: Yale University Press, 1996). See also Jennifer E. Koepke, "Note: The Failure to Breach the Blue Wall of Silence: The Circling of the Wagons to Protect Policy Perjury," *Washburn Law Journal*, 39 (2000): 211–242; Susan Bandes, "Patterns of Injustice: Police Brutality in the Courts," *Buffalo Law Review*, 47 (1999): 1275–1341; David S. Cohen, "Official Oppression: A Historical Analysis of Low-Level Police Abuse and a Modern Attempt at Reform," *Columbia Human Rights Law Review*, 28 (1996): 165–199; David Dante Troutt, "Screws, Koon, and Routine Aberrations: The Use of Fictional Narratives in Federal Police Brutality Prosecutions," *New York University Law Review*, 74 (1999): 18–122.
9. Human Rights Watch, *Shielded from Justice: Police Brutality and Accountability in the United States* (1998), http://www.hrw.org/reports98/police/index.htm.
10. Ibid.
11. U.S. Department of Justice, *Conduct of Law Enforcement Agencies Investigations. Los Angeles Police Department*. Washington, DC: U.S. Government Printing Office, March 2000.
12. Christopher Commission Report, Report of the *Independent Commission on the Los Angeles Police Department* (1991); Los Angeles Police Commission, *Five Years Later* (1991); Los Angeles Police Department, *Board of Inquiry into the Rampart Area Corruption Incident: A Public Report* (2000).
13. Angela Y. Davis, "Color of Violence: Violence Against Women of Color," conference, Santa Cruz, California (April 2000), http://www.colorlines.com/article.php?ID=72.
14. Roberto Rodriguez, "Beyond Brutality," *Black Issues in Higher Education*, 13 (May 2, 1996), p. 22.
15. Jack E. White, "Fuhrman Is No Surprise. Police Racism Is Common in the U.S.," *Time*, September 11, 1995, http://www.time.com/time/magazine/article/0,9171,983416,00.html.

16. Michael Huspek, Roberto Martinez, and Leticia Jimenez, "Violations of Human and Civil Rights on the U.S.-Mexico Boarder, 1995 to 1997: A Report," *Social Justice*, 25 (1998): 110–130.

17. U.S. Commission on Civil Rights, *Mexican Americans and the Administration of Justice in the Southwest* (1970); Juanita Diaz-Cotto, *Gender, Ethnicity, and the State: Latina and Latino Prison Politics* (Albany: State University of New York Press, 1996); Malcolm D. Holmes and Howard C. Daudistel, "Ethnicity and Justice in the Southwest: The Sentencing of Anglo, Black, and Mexican American Defendants," *Social Science Quarterly*, 64 (1984): 265–277; Terrance D. Miethe and Charles A. Moore, "Racial Differences in Criminal Processing: The Consequences of Model Selection on Conclusions About Differential Treatment," *Sociological Quarterly*, 27 (1986): 217–237; Ruth Peterson and John Hagan, "Changing Conceptions of Race: Toward an Account of Anomalous Findings of Sentencing Research," *American Sociological Review*, 49 (1984): 56–70; Charles Pruitt and James Wilson, "A Longitudinal Study of the Effect of Race on Sentencing," *Law and Society Review*, 17 (1983): 613–635; Cassia Spohn, John Gruhl, and Susan Welch, "The Effect of Race on Sentencing: A Reexamination of an Unsettled Question," *Law and Society Review*, 16 (1981): 71–88; James Unnever, Charles Frazier, and John Henretta, "Racial Differences in Criminal Sentencing," *Sociological Quarterly*, 30 (1980): 197.

18. Gary LaFree, "Official Reactions to Latino Defendants in the Southwest," *Journal of Research in Crime and Delinquency*, 22 (1985): 213–237.

19. Margorie Zatz, *Differential Treatment in the Criminal Justice System by Race/Ethnicity*, paper presented at the annual meeting of the American Sociological Association, Toronto, Canada (August 1981).

20. Susan Welch, John Gruhl, and Cassia Spohn, "Dismissal, Conviction, and Incarceration of Latino Defendants: A Comparison with Anglos and Blacks," *Social Science Quarterly*, 65 (1984): 257–264.

21. Ed A. Muñoz, David A. Lopez, and Eric Stewart, "Misdemeanor Sentencing Decisions: The Cumulative Disadvantage Effect of 'Gringo Justice,'" *Hispanic Journal of Behavioral Sciences*, 20 (1998): 298–319.

22. National Minority Advisory Council on Criminal Justice, *The Inequality of Justice: A Report on Crime and the Administration of Justice in the Minority Community* (1982).

23. U.S. Department of Justice, *American Indians and Crime* (1999). For a review of the criminological literature on American Indians, see Donald E. Green, "The Contextual Nature of American Indian Criminality," *American Indian Culture and Research Journal*, 17 (1993): 99.

24. Coramae Richey Mann, *Unequal Justice: A Question of Color* (Bloomington: Indiana University Press, 1993), p. 235.

25. Steve Feimer, Frank Pommerstein, and Steve Wise, "Marking Time: Does Race Make a Difference? A Study of Disparate Sentencing in South Dakota," *Journal of Crime and Justice*, 13 (1990): 86–102.

26. Ronet Bachman, "An Analysis of American Indian Homicide: A Test of Social Disorganization and Economic Deprivation at the Reservation County Level," *Journal of Research in Crime and Delinquency*, 28 (1991): 456–471; Ronet Bachman, "The Social Causes of American Indian Homicide as Revealed by the Life Experiences of Thirty Offenders," *American Indian Quarterly*, 15 (1991): 469.

27. U.S. Sentencing Commission, *Cocaine and Federal Sentencing Policy* (1997).

28. Dan Weikel, "War on Crack Targets Minorities over Whites," *Los Angeles Times*, May 21, 1995, p. A1; Vanessa Gallman, "Cocaine Sentencing High on List of Racial Issues," *Riverside Press-Enterprise*, November 2, 1995, p. A3.

29. Harry E. Allen and Clifford E. Simonsen, *Corrections in America* (New York: Macmillan, 1992), p. 350; Imogene L. Moyer, "Academic Criminology: A Need for Change," *American Journal of Criminal Justice*, 9 (1985): 197.

30. Stephen J. Schulhofer, "The Feminist Challenge in Criminal Law," *University of Pennsylvania Law Review*, 143 (1995): 2151–2207, 2184.

31. U.S. General Accounting Office; *supra* note 79.

32. David Baldus and Gary Woodworth, *Race Discrimination in America's Capital Punishment System Since Furman v. Georgia: The Evidence of Race Disparities and the Record of Our Courts and Legislatures in Addressing This Issue*, report prepared for the American Bar Association(1997), cited in Richard Dieter, *The Death Penalty in Black and White: Who Lives, Who Dies, Who Decides*, Death Penalty Information Center (June 1998), http://www.deathpenaltyinfo.org/racerpt.html.

33. David C. Baldus, George Woodworth, David Zuckerman, Neil A. Weiner, and Barbara Broffitt, "Racial Discrimination and the Death Penalty in the Post-Furman Era: An Empirical and Legal Overview, with Recent Findings from Philadelphia," *Cornell Law Review*, 83 (1998): 1638; see also Thomas J. Keil and Gennaro F. Vito, "Race, Homicide Severity, and Application of the Death Penalty: A Consideration of the Barnett Scale," *Criminology*, 27 (1989): 511.

34. Jon Sorensen and Donald H. Wallace, "Prosecutorial Discretion in Seeking Death: An Analysis of Racial Disparity in the Pretrial Stage of Case Processing in a Midwestern County," *Justice Quarterly*, 16 (1999): 559; U.S. Department of Justice, *The Federal Death Penalty System: Supplementary Data, Analysis and Revised Protocols for Capital Case Review* (2001), http://www.usdoj.gov/dag/pubdoc/deathpenaltystudy.htm.

35. Isaac Unah and John Boger, *Race and the Death Penalty in North Carolina: An Empirical Analysis, 1993–1997* (2001), http.//www.deathpenaltyinfo.org/NCRaceRpt.html.

36. Raymond Paternoster and Robert Brame, *An Empirical Analysis of Maryland's Death Sentencing System with Respect to the Influence of Race and Legal Jurisdiction* (February 20, 2003), http.//www.urhome,umd.edu/newsdesk/pdf/finalrep.pdf.

37. *Supra* note 4.

38. Hugo Adam Bedau and Michael L. Radelet, "Miscarriages of Justice in Potentially Capital Cases," *Stanford Law Review*, 40 (1987): 21; see also Michael L. Radelet, William Lofquist, and Hugo Bedau, "Prisoners Released from Death Rows Since 1970 Because of Doubts About Their Guilt," *Thomas M. Colley Law Review*, 13 (1996): 907. See, generally, Barry Scheck, Peter Neufeld, and Jim Dwyer, *Actual Innocence: Five Days to Execution and Other Dispatches from the Wrongly Convicted* (New York: Doubleday, 2000); Stanley Cohen, *The Wrong Men: America's Epidemic of Wrongful Death Row Convictions* (New York: Carroll and Graf, 2003).

39. The Death Penalty Information Center identifies twelve other defendants that authorities have released from death row because of evidence of their innocence even though authorities have not completely exonerated these defendants of their crimes. The center also identifies five other capital defendants whom authorities have commuted their sentences to life in prison because of doubts about their guilt. Still further, the center identifies five defendants that state jurisdictions have executed despite doubts about their guilt. See The Death Penalty Information Center, *Additional Innocence Information*, http.//www.deathpenaltyinfo.org/article.php?scid=6&=did=111#Released.

40. N. Jeremi Duru, "The Central Park Five, the Scottsboro Boys, and the Myth of the Bestial Black Man," *Cardozo Law Review*, 25 (2004): 1315, 1364–1365.

41. Arthur L. Rizer III, "The Race Effect of Wrongful Convictions," *William Mitchell Law Review*, 29 (2003): 845, 861.

State Violence, and the Social and Legal Construction of Latino Criminality: From El Bandido to Gang Member

Mary Romero

In this article, . . . I examine the construction of Latino criminality that is enacted and mediated textually in the everyday organization in the police bureaucracy.

HISTORY AND DEVELOPMENT OF THE LATINO CRIMINAL STEREOTYPE

Taco Bell's use of "dinky," the heavily accented Chihuahua imitating the popular pose of Che Guevara, is an updated version of the Latino male as a revolutionary bandit. Unlike the Frito Bandido used to advertise Frito Corn chips in the late 60s, corporations no longer construct racist caricatures by dressing the human body of the "other" but rather rely on their audiences understanding the symbols. The power of the Latino and African American criminal narrative is so dominant in American society that its use can be accomplished through images not embodied by Latinos or African Americans. In the same way that we were able to read the racialized text presented in the "California Raisins" commercial, Taco Bell is able to rely upon the Latino criminal trope without using the Latino physical bodily image. The Chihuahua stands in for the Mexican, the beret replaces the sombrero, and the cigar replaces the weapon. The trope works because after decades of presenting specific stereotypes on the silver screen, the popular racist narrative is easily called forth without calling the image a "bandido." Taco Bell does not have to mention a hot-blooded, violent tempered, treacherous, knife-wielding gang-banger, or drug-selling vato. While based on images of the Mexican struggle for social change and equality, the narrative is constructed by reducing history to individual characters that become a generic revolutionary social bandit. American culture has reduced the Mexican American War and the history of resistance and struggle against dispossession and oppression to the image of a

Source: Mary Romero, "State Violence, and the Social and Legal Construction of Latino Criminality: From El Bandido to Gang Member," Denver University Law Review, 78 (2001): 1081–1118.

violent, barbarous, and ferocious Latino bandido. Film portrayal of Latino males is saturated with images of gangs, prisoners, drug dealers, wife abusers and other violent characters. Even contemporary writers trying to gain from the interest in the Latinization of American culture have exploited the racist bandido icon to sell books.

The lasting image of the bandido strongly points to the success of American popular culture in wiping collective memory of the history of conquest and the extensive use of armed force to subordinate Mexicans and Mexican Americans in the Southwest. Reference to the southwestern U.S. as "Occupied America" captures the essence of the history from which the Latino criminal stereotype originated. Latino entrance into the U.S. legal and judicial system began as conquered subjects of the violent Mexican-American War. Fueled by the white supremacy ideology of a Manifest Destiny, the U.S. carried out acts that General Winfield Scott characterized as, "atrocities to make Heaven weep and every American of Christian morals blush for his country. Murder, robbery and rape of mothers and daughters in the presence of tied-up males of the families have been common all along the Rio Grande." In regions that did not experience a massive demographic change, such as the California Gold Rush, economic circumstances or control through economic and political means, a reign of terror followed the war and the signing of the Treaty of Guadalupe-Hidalgo. As an occupying force, the U.S. government had to be ready for possible uprisings; however, the primary interest of state repression was the dispossession of land and other resources. The history of conquest in the Southwest, and the extensive use of armed forces to subordinate Mexicans and Mexican Americans became subliminally grafted in the American psyche as a "foreigner," even though the land had once belonged to Mexico. While economic and

political repression were extremely successful in dispossession and subordination of Mexicans living in occupied territory, state sanctioned violence, which in the early 1900s took the form of lynching, has never entirely been replaced. Resistance against the state violence carried out by the police, military, Border Patrol, and the Arizona and Texas Rangers has included insurgent movements, riots, and other forms of armed protest. The armed resistance against the privatization of communal salt beds by Mexicans and Mexican Americans became known as the El Paso Salt War. In Las Gorras Blancas, an insurgent movement against the privatization and fencing of communal lands in New Mexico united poor white farmers and Native Americans against Anglo carpetbaggers and the Hispano rico. The list of social rebels that emerged after the Mexican American War are numerous and include Tiburcio Vasquez, Juan Cortina, Joaquin Murietta, Juan Flores, Francisco "Chico" Barela, Juan and Pablo Herrera, and Gregorio Cortez. The Mexican American War, the Treaty of Guadalupe-Hidalgo, Las Gorras Blancas, El Paso Salt War, Zoot Suit Riots, and struggles up to the 1960's high school walkouts all get depoliticized and the mythology of the Latino banditry masks protests and resistance to social and economic injustices. And thus, Che Guevara becomes one more image of "El Bandido." The media, politicians and law enforcement frequently used aspects of the bandido stereotype to frame demonstrations, protests, and other political activity during the Chicano Movement.

Civil rights leaders and labor activists were frequently characterized as criminal and violent and state violence was sanctioned by the press and local officials. Civil rights activities carried out by Corky Gonzales and the Crusade for Justice, Reies Lopez Tijerina and La Alianza Federal de Mercedes (The Federal Alliance of Land Grants), and the union organizing activities by Cesar Chavez and the United Farm Workers were frequently construed as Mexican and Chicano criminality.

Since WWII, Latino youth have been constructed as inherently criminal. Although most of the time the construction of youth as criminal has fallen under the gang rubric, political activity in the late 60s and 70s was also treated as criminal activity. The specific focus on Mexican and Mexican American youth as embodying the bandido violent and treacherous character is well documented in the 1943 Zoot-Suit Riots. The demonization of the youth by the press and police in Los Angeles occurred within days of the removal of the last Japanese to internment camps. Mexican crime, Mexican juvenile delinquency and Mexican gangs became the new scapegoat group. National and international attention of the targeting of Latino youth in Los Angeles occurred during the trial known as the Case of Sleepy Lagoon and from the work of the Sleepy Lagoon Defense Committee who continued two years after the trial to gain the freedom of the youth convicted. Latinos in the US military stationed throughout the world serving their country in the war effort donated money. In response to political pressure, the press replaced the reference to Mexican and replaced it with "Zoot-Suit" and "Pachuco." However, authorities (military and police) continued to treat Mexican youth as inherently criminal.

State violence against Latino youth received public attention during the Chicano Movement. "Between January 1, 1965, and March 31, 1969, the United States Justice Department received 256 complaints of police abuse against Hispanics in the Southwest. Over a two-year span, the American Civil Liberties Union of Southern California filed 174 complaints of serious police brutality against Chicanos." In 1970 the U.S. Commission on Civil Rights report concluded: "Mexican American citizens are subject to unduly harsh treatment by law enforcement

officers . . . they are often arrested on insufficient grounds, receive physical and verbal abuse, and penalties which are disproportionately severe." Given the continuous history of state violence against the Mexican American communities, the study was long overdue. The Congress of Mexican American Unity and the Chicano Moratorium Committee requested UCLA Professor Armando Morales to "make an inquiry into the duration, depth and nature of the problem, and develop recommendations that would have the effect of reducing the conflict." The study followed the 1970–71 East Los Angeles riots. Examining police deployment practices in Los Angeles, Morales found a disproportionate number of police deployed in the predominately Mexican American community of Hollenbeck Division even though the incident of crime was greater in the middle-class community of Wilshire Division. Comparing the findings from the U.S. Riot Commission Report to the 1970–71 East Los Angeles riots, Morales argued that "Chicano" could easily be substituted for "Black" and "barrio" for " ghetto." Community-police conflict was not restricted to Los Angeles. Studies conducted by researchers and civil rights organizations, such as the Mexican-American Legal Defense and Education Fund, documented the number of Latinos who died while in police custody and were physically abused. Research on the Brown Beret, student movement, and other Chicano youth activities have suggested that law enforcement targeted this population for surveillance and harassment.

The most widely distributed representation of Latino youth today is as a gang member. Although the existence of gangs can be traced back to the Middle Ages in Europe and found throughout the world, the War on Gangs launched over the last few decades by U.S. local police departments has targeted Black and Latino youth. While there is a lack of consistency in defining gangs and gang members, the public's acceptance of racialized versions has resulted in an over identification of gangs in low-income communities of color and has rejuvenated the bandido image. The link between immigration, poverty and urban life that social scientists highlight in theorizing about gangs, appears in the popular racialized definitions acted upon by the media and public officials. In the case of Latino youth, primary importance is placed on Chicano culture.

Next to the image of gangs, Latino criminality appears in the American psyche as the "illegal alien" and has become analogous to the "immigration problem." Criminalization of Mexican immigrants stigmatizes the Latino community in the US and reinforces the bandito stereotype. In his 1948 book, *American Me*, B. Griffiths writes:

> In police and sheriffs' stations throughout the state today, picture displays show Mexican "criminals" and "bandits" of the early (19th century) days of California, and there are showcases with guns and other souvenirs that were used in the fights. Occasionally, too, you see a block-framed picture of a police officer killed by a Mexican in line of duty. Such facts and folklore become a real part of the rookie officer's indoctrination. Policeman and sheriff's deputies add stories of their personal experiences with "those sneaky greasers—who knife you as soon as look at you." False arrests, unjustifiable beatings, and sometimes the tragic deaths of Mexican youths at the hands of officers who shoot first and think later are the natural consequences of the usual prejudice intensified by such training.

If we consider the videotape beating of two undocumented immigrants that occurred in April 1997, Griffiths' description appears to capture contemporary experiences. The meaning of the Justice Department's decision not to prosecute the two Riverside County sheriff's deputies in this case provides a significant training message to law enforcement officers. While Proposition 187 has fueled anti- immigration sentiment in California, images of criminality embodied in Latino immigrants is not limited to law enforcement

in Los Angeles. In their April 1995 report, "Crossing the Line," Human Rights Watch described INS agents as employing "'Wild West' behavior entirely inappropriate for a professional, federal law enforcement agency." The use of excessive force and racial profiling involves constructing Latino criminality to the immigrant profile and applied to INS policing practices.

TEXTS, FACTS, AND LATINO CRIMINALITY

Power relations following the Mexican American War to the present have certainly included violence, coercion, and armed forces in the form of the Texas Rangers, the Arizona Rangers, the Border Patrol, as well as the military, and the local police. The textual practices that constructed Latino criminality can be traced back to military and police reports to Washington, and later used by historians, to document official accounts of events occurring in the newly acquired territory. Consequently, community perspectives are frequently discarded in public documents and are left to oral history. These textual practices are most evident in the treatment of insurgent movements in the Southwest. Frequently Chicano resistance is attributed to the interference of outside agitators or manipulative leaders. This characterization is accomplished by distorting the actual function of leadership roles in community mobilization and implying that Latino fatalism and ignorance demands outside leadership as a catalyst for action. Embedded in early academic writings is reference to inherent weakness for domination as a dominant cultural feature of New Mexican life.

The first group of historians engaged in documenting accounts of the transformation from communal to private ownership were primarily Anglo lawyers and politicians writing memoirs. The next major writings on land documentation occurred after the depression. At this time, social scientists focused on the aftermath of drought and land loss. Again, attention to value orientations resulted in defining the land grant issue as a consequence of cultural conflict between Chicanos and Anglos. The third major group of studies were written in response to Reis L. Tijerina's activities in northern New Mexico. Sociological notions of cultural pluralism and assimilation had little political meaning to people struggling to retain their land. Having constructed insurgents movements as riots and void of political consciousness, the construction of the lawless bandido became the primary character in historical accounts as well as a common feature in popular culture.

The process of constructing Latino criminality became an ongoing function of policing. Investigations of the use of excessive force produced textual documentation of a violent Mexican character. Returning to the Zoot- Suit Riots, we find a report about the problem of Mexican youth written by Captain E. Duran Ayres, chief of the "Foreign Relations Bureau" of the LA sheriff's office. Characterization Latino youth as violent is presented in the following passage of the report:

> When the Spaniards conquered Mexico they found an organized society composed of many tribes of Indians rules over by the Aztecs who were given over to human sacrifice. Historians record that as many as 30,000 Indians were sacrificed on their heathen altars in one day, their bodies being opened by stone knives and their hearts torn out while still beating. This total disregard for human life has always been universal throughout the Americas among the Indian population, which of course is well known to everyone. The Caucasian, especially the Anglo-Saxon, when engaged in fighting, particularly among youths, resort to fisticuffs and may at times kick each other, which is considered unsportive, but this Mexican element considers all that to be a sign of weakness, and all he knows and feels is a desire to use a knife . . . to kill, or at least let blood. That is why it is difficult for the Anglo-Saxon to understand the psychology of the Indian and for the Latin to understand the psychology of the Anglo-Saxon or those from Northern Europe.

Over the next decade, racist statements by state officials continue to be made by high officials in law enforcement and judges.

Contemporary cases of police violence conducted under the military language of the War Against Gangs and War Against Drugs are mediated through texts that rationalize and objectify the use of excessive and lethal force. Police violence is thus a reasonable response to criminality encapsulated under the category of Latino gang member. Military language if further warranted as conspiratorial qualities of gangs are added to the description by characterizing gangs as secretive, spreading to new neighborhoods, dealing in drugs, violence and other crime, organized and structured around a "secretive culture of colors, gang signs, and initiation rites." Conspiracies call for "gang intelligence units," in addition to "the dissemination of workshops and educational materials designed to help adult recognize and interpret the gesture, clothing, graffiti, and other secret symbols of gang involvement."

SUMMARY

Having constructed the Latino criminal as an inner-city super-predator, the only "rational" solution to the Valerio shooting becomes purchasing stun guns. Rather than proposing Spanish language and communication skills, the requirement for stun guns becomes part of the police bureaucracy. The purchase of new weapons, or the addition of training to use the new weapons, still does not address the original questions posed by community members: How is it that six armed police officers (all taller and bigger than the suspect) accompanied with four additional officers in a well lighted area feared for their lives or the life of their fellow officer? What did they see that night? Only a paramilitary framework that defines Latino youth as the enemy and reconstructs victims of color into one of criminality explains Julio's death.

At a meeting at one of the community colleges, a Chicana mother expressed fear for her twelve-year-old son's safety. She described the clothing and hair cuts that many of our youth wear and he is six feet tall and two hundred pounds—a big kid—but a kid nevertheless. The fear I heard expressed stemmed from the recognition that Chicano youth have been demonized as super- predators. How could any Latino family ever turn to the police again to assist them in a family crisis; in a time that an adolescent child is in trouble? The motto, "(t)o serve and protect" becomes a farce.

The question remains: What was it that the police saw through their racially saturated field of visibility that solicited their deadly response? How was a cornered sixteen-year-old with a butcher knife seen as a deadly threat by six armed officers?

The incredible outpour of support for the police demonstrated in the blue ribbon rally confirms that the racially saturated field of visibility or the kind of "seeing" that the police acted upon that night is shared with members of the larger community. The editorials and cartoons printed in the local newspaper demonstrated the degree to which Mexican youth are demonized. While the image of the Mexican male has shifted over the last 150 years from the bandit to the gang member, the image remains one of a criminal.

STUDY QUESTION

Summarize the history and development of the Latino criminal stereotype as presented by Mary Romero.

Snapshots: Holistic Images of Female Offenders in the Criminal Justice System

Jennifer Ward

This essay attempts to pull together the various threads of thought regarding the relationships between gender, race, and class within the justice system, and suggests possible patterns that could be used to create holistic images of female offenders.

This essay attempts to pull together the various threads of thought regarding the relationships between gender, race, and class within the justice system, and suggests possible patterns that could be used to create holistic images of female offenders. Hopefully, a clearer understanding will foster more effective programs or policies to lower the number of women processed through the criminal justice system. Part I provides a brief overview of the various explanations used over time to account for criminal behavior by women. Part II details the ways in which gender can affect the processes of the criminal justice system. Part III discusses the impact that race can have on the female offender's experience in the system. Part IV briefly overviews the types of influences that class status produces. Part V concludes that while some research has been done combining these factors, additional research, using all of these factors, is required in order to achieve a more accurate picture of female offenders in America.

OVERVIEW OF FEMALE CRIMINALITY THEORIES

Theories regarding the causes of female offending have varied greatly over time. Yet, even with these temporal differences, the majority of these theories can usually be grouped into one of three categories—biological, psychological, or socioeconomic theories. Nonetheless, far from being distinctly separate categories, these three theories often overlap.

Attempts to explain criminal behavior by women began as early as the turn of twentieth century. The first scientific study of female offenders came in 1894, with the

Source: Jennifer Ward, "Snapshots: Holistic Images of Female Offenders in the Criminal Justice System," Fordham Urban Law Journal, 30 (2003): 723–749.

publication of The Female Offender. In this study, the authors, Caesar Lombroso and William Ferrero, examined both the skeletal remains of female offenders and the bodies of living female prisoners. Lombroso and Ferrero concluded that the number and types of physical abnormalities in female offenders indicated the extent to which women were predisposed to criminal acts; the authors even attempted to determine which particular criminal acts women were more likely to commit. Due to its methodological deficiencies, however, this study was quickly rejected. Nevertheless, attempts to correlate female criminality with biological factors have continued into the present.

Psychological theories began appearing soon after early biological theories, and often relied on biological assumptions regarding women. The work of W.I. Thomas was considered a "departure from biological Social-Darwinian theories to complex analyses of the interaction between society and the individual." Yet, at the same time, Thomas used biological differences as the basis for his work. Additionally, Thomas characterized female criminal behavior as a "normal" response to specific social conditions, and believed that such behavior could be controlled by changing the woman's attitude towards those specific social conditions or by imposing "beneficial" conditions.

Freud's analysis of female offenders assumed the existence of biological inferiority in women. Freud connected a woman's lack of male genitalia with her inability to resolve her Oedipal complex. He argued that this unresolved conflict led to an inability of women to control their impulses, therefore making women more likely to commit criminal acts. Under Freud's framework, deviant acts, criminal or otherwise, were part of a woman's frustration with her gender, and an "expression of her longing for a penis." As with Thomas, the solution was to help the woman adjust to her lack of masculinity.

While Thomas's and Freud's theories on the causes of female criminal behavior are no longer in use, some of their conclusions can still be seen in modern psychological theories regarding female offending. For example, a study done by Gisela Konopka showed four factors associated with female offending: the onset of puberty, the process of identification with the mother, changes in the position of women in society, and an indistinctive authority resulting in low self-esteem and loneliness. These findings are a restatement of earlier theories that blatantly ignore the effects of economic and social factors; these theories also describe female criminal behavior as an emotional response to being deprived of the opportunity to play out a traditional gender role.

The third category of theories are those which can be loosely considered as socioeconomic theories. One of the first studies of female offenders that can be considered an example of socioeconomic theory was conducted by Eleanor and Sheldon Glueck, who followed five hundred female offenders from childhood to life after parole. The Gluecks studied such factors as ethnicity, religion, parental jobs, educational background, offender's employment, substance abuse, and whether the subject exhibited an obviously unstable. personality. The Gluecks found that environmental and biological conditions affected a woman's chances of rehabilitating. Unlike earlier studies, the Gluecks focused on criticizing the criminal justice system, rather than merely adjusting the female offender to society.

Later studies in this area focused on the relationship between a woman's delinquent behavior and the "blocked," or lack of, opportunities a woman has during her life. Other studies in this area have focused on criminal behavior as a reflection of economic necessity. These studies show that the majority of female offenders are economically disadvantaged, self-supporting, and often have children. Such factors have led various researchers to comment that this economic reality may make criminal behavior necessary for women to provide for themselves and their families.

Other variants of socioeconomic theories that focus on different environmental or external influences include the following: differential association, labeling, social control theories, and even the women's liberation movement.

Current Trends in the Incarceration Process

Female Offenders and Their Criminal Offenses

Female offenders differ from their male counterparts in many respects. Women tend to commit less serious offenses, have a longer history of physical and/or sexual abuse, are more often the parent or guardian of minor children, are more likely to have inferior economic situations, and have a higher rate of substance abuse. A significant majority of female offenders are convicted on non-violent offenses, such as property, drug, and public order offenses. According to the 1998 statistics compiled by the Bureau of Justice Statistics ("BJS"), about sixty percent of women in state prisons have had a prior history of physical and/or sexual abuse. In about one-third of the cases in which women reported prior abuse, the abuse started at a young age, and continued into adulthood. Such abuse often leads to drug use as a coping mechanism to numb and survive both emotional and physical pain.

Those few women incarcerated for violent offenses usually victimized other women, and often had a prior relationship with the victim. In cases where women were convicted of murder or manslaughter, the victim tended to be either a husband or boyfriend, who had "repeatedly and violently" abused the offender. Drug use also plays a significant role in violent crime by women. For example, in a study of women arrested for violent crimes in New York City and Washington, D.C., over fifty percent had been using at least one or more illegal drugs before their arrest.

In general, drugs play a major role in the incarceration of women. In 1998, approximately eighty-two percent of federal cases involving female offenders included at least one drug offense. Male offenders in federal cases have comparable rates of drug charges. Yet women offenders in state prisons report significantly higher overall drug usage than their male counterparts. Forty percent of convicted women in state prison were under the influence of drugs when they committed their offense, and one-third reported that the reason they committed their crime was to obtain the money necessary to support their drug habits.

The majority of incarcerated female offenders are the mothers of minor children. Prior to their offense, sixty-four percent of state and eighty-four percent of federal female inmates lived with their minor children. Unlike their male counterparts, the children of female inmates are more likely to be placed in the care of persons outside the nuclear family group, usually with an immediate family member. These placements can create a variety of problems both for the individuals in the family unit and the general community. The separation of an incarcerated mother from her child strains the mother-child relationship, and often causes emotional and/or behavioral problems for the children. Additionally, the general community suffers when a child's future is jeopardized by a mother's incarceration, and becomes responsible for directly and indirectly providing a variety of resources towards the basic needs of some of those children.

Female offenders are most likely to be economically inferior and poorly educated. Less than half of female inmates in state prisons held a full-time job prior to their arrest. Additionally, before their arrest, about thirty-seven percent of the women had an income of less than six hundred dollars a month, and thirty percent received government welfare as a primary source of income. Surprisingly, however, the majority of women in both state and federal prisons, fifty-six and seventy-three percent, respectively, graduated high school. Of those women who graduated high school, thirty to forty percent attended various kinds of higher or continuing education.

Generally, these characteristics support the idea that female offenders' needs require programs that address the issues mentioned above to prevent female offending and recidivism. The prevalence of long-term physical, emotional, and/or sexual abuse, and widespread drug use suggests that the issues surrounding these characteristics must be addressed before a decline in female offending occurs. Due to the mostly non-violent nature of the crimes committed by women, the possibility of switching the emphasis from traditional incarceration, to programs modeled on outpatient services is feasible. Programs of this nature may also allow women who have children to remain with, or in relatively greater contact with, their children, thus lowering the harm done by forced separation and isolation.

Gender as a Factor in the Incarceration Process

Even though the rate of female incarceration is at an historic high, women are still significantly less likely to be imprisoned than men. Once arrested and placed into the criminal justice system, gender plays a variety of roles in the treatment of individual offenders. The most prevalent argument is that female offenders are granted more leniency than men because of the traditional view of women as the more vulnerable gender, in greater need of protection. The other two major arguments regarding gender as a factor in the incarceration process are that: 1) the criminal justice system treats female and male offenders equally, and uses the same factors in the decision-making process; and 2) women are treated more harshly than men who have committed the same crime, because the female offender has broken not only a law, but a code of gender behavior. Which argument prevails depends on the phase of the process the female offender is dealing with at the time, for example, pretrial decisions or sentencing.

At the arrest or police decision-making stage, these three arguments are equally plausible and are each supported by different studies. The results of these studies are problematic, however, because they fail to take into account certain factors regarding these interactions, such as people who are less willing to report women perpetrators or the female offenders police chose not to arrest.

At the sentencing stage of the process, women tend to receive treatment equal to that of their male counterparts. The evidence in some studies lends strength to the argument that before the enactment of the Federal Sentencing Guidelines, federal courts were more likely to give female offenders either probation or lesser sentences than their male counterparts. Additionally, the disparity in sentencing practices between state and federal courts demonstrates the harsh effects of mandatory minimum sentences on female offenders. Due to the enactment of the Federal Sentencing Guidelines, and comparable state sentencing schemes, however, this leniency towards women seems to have disappeared.

Under Congressional orders to produce sex-neutral sentencing guidelines, the United States Sentencing Commission created guidelines that "explicitly mandate that sex is not relevant in the determination of a sentence." Despite the good intention to eliminate invidious discrimination in sentencing, the Federal Sentencing Guidelines appear to play a significant role in the increase of both the incarceration of, and longer sentences for, female offenders.

African-American Women in the Incarceration Process

African-Americans in the United States, both female and male, possess a long documented history of discrimination by the criminal justice system. Currently, African-American women make up a majority of those incarcerated in both state and federal prisons. In general, African-American female offenders demonstrate many of the same characteristics as the overall female offender population. The majority of offenses committed by African-American women are nonviolent offenses; these crimes mainly consist of property, drug, and public disorder crimes. In contrast to the total female offender population, however, African-American female offenders commonly have less formal education, and are more likely to: 1) come from a single parent family; 2) head a single mother household; 3) have lived with their minor children; 4) be on welfare; and 5) are less likely to have ever held a job.

Among African-American female prisoners and female prisoners of other races, the contrast in education, jobs, and the number of welfare recipients appears to be a reflection of the generally lower economic position of African-Americans in the United States. These contrasts, however, can also be attributed to the focus that government places on drug enforcement in minority communities. The War on Drugs has not only contributed to the increase of African-American women in prison, but also has placed a significant number of young African-American men in jail as well.

In the short term, the imprisonment of these men can increase the number of single mother households, the number of children

with an incarcerated parent, the number of women on welfare, and the number of unemployed women. In the long term, a man's history of incarceration contributes to unemployment rates and low wage jobs. Together, these factors contribute to the low income of African-American families and to the number of children who live below the poverty line. Research has consistently demonstrated a connection between a history of youth poverty and crime, whereby a significant number of African-American children living below the poverty line perpetuates the circle of criminal arrests and incarceration.

Programs instituted for rehabilitative purposes, as well as those designed to prevent first-time offending and recidivism, will need to address the fact that the majority of African-American female offenders have slightly different needs than the general pool of female offenders. For African-American women already incarcerated, creating ways in which there can be greater and more consistent contact between parents and children are especially important, given the higher rate of single mother households. Allowing such a program to place women outside the prison, for example, in a halfway house, poses little threat to the community, as a majority of the women placed in this type of program would be non-violent offenders. These programs could be available in conjunction with opportunities to provide such women with education and/or job skills that would allow access to jobs with higher wages.

Much like gender, the effects of race on an individual's treatment at various stages of the incarceration process vary depending upon the stage. African-American women are likely to encounter racial bias in the criminal justice system even before arrest. The government's policy of focusing enforcement measures—particularly of drug laws—in minority communities, makes African-American women more likely to be arrested than white women. If the processes subsequent to arrest were free of racial bias, the arrest statistics would roughly parallel that of the prison population.

As compared to white Americans, approximately three times as many African-Americans are arrested for non-violent offenses. African-Americans, however, are seven times more likely than white Americans to be imprisoned. Yet, no study appears to point directly to any one stage in the incarceration process as either the sole or even primary cause of this disparity. It appears that the disparity between arrest and incarceration rates is a product of the total process between arrest and incarceration. For example, bail decisions, the decision to incarcerate before trial, and plea-bargaining, are all stages that evidence a racial disparity which cannot be explained by the differences between individual crimes and the offenders' histories.

The evidence of discrimination in sentencing is generally inconclusive regarding the effect race has on the outcome. At the sentencing stage, however, all the discrimination involved in prior stages, particularly arrest and charging decisions, can easily affect sentencing, even in cases where no racial bias exists in the sentencing body. For example, African-Americans are more likely than white Americans to be arrested due to the decision to focus drug enforcement efforts on minority communities. The resulting arrests, whether founded or unfounded, will give most African-Americans longer criminal records than their white counterparts, which is a significant factor in deciding sentences for the offender.

Hispanic Women in the Incarceration Process

Statistical data on Hispanic women in the criminal justice system is severely lacking. In 1997, the total number of Hispanic prisoners being held by state and federal authorities was 198,673. Of this total, seventeen percent of prisoners in the state prison system, and twenty-seven percent in the federal sys-

tem, were female. According to the sparse information available, it appears that the trends surrounding Hispanic female offenders do not appear to vary significantly from the trends found in the general female offender population, as a high rate of drug use, and conditions of poverty, also exist among Hispanic offenders.

Much more statistical information needs to be gathered regarding Hispanic female offenders before any other conclusions are drawn. Without more specific information, making suggestions for programs directed at Hispanic female offenders is problematic. It is likely that once comprehensive data has been gathered, a visible pattern will exist specific to the Hispanic female offender population. This assertion is based on the fact that white, African-American, and Native American Indian female offenders have all shown patterns deviating from the picture created by the aggregate female offender pool.

One of the major intersections between race and gender can be seen in the treatment of Hispanic female offenders. Anecdotal evidence suggests that the stereotype of Hispanic women as "ultra-feminine" can affect the treatment of Hispanic female offenders. This stereotype may help some Hispanic female offenders avoid some of the harshness of the Federal Sentencing Guidelines and/or the penalties imposed by the Anti-Drug Abuse Act of 1986, as judges sometimes rely on theories based on cultural stereotypes. The "uses of gender and culture," however, "place Latina defendants in a double bind. They can choose to accept the harsh statutorily mandated sentences, or they can embrace stereotype and play to a court's sympathy by presenting themselves as pawns of their husbands, naive and lacking in self-determination." Creating this type of identity conflict is part of the disparate treatment that Hispanic female offenders face. This particular type of conflict, however, does not appear to be a significant factor for white, African-American, or Native

American Indian women. Nonetheless, additional research might reveal that other female offenders, such as Asian or Middle-Eastern women, whom the American justice system perceives as coming from a culture with a similar stereotype, will often face the same decision.

Native American Indian Women in the Incarceration Process

Although Native American Indians represent a small fraction of all criminals charged in the United States, they represent a disproportionately large number of those incarcerated in the criminal justice system. Information regarding Native American Indian female offenders is scarce, but the statistics gathered on Native American Indian offenders of both sexes may provide some insight.

Of those Native American Indian offenders incarcerated, a majority was held in local jails. As of June 1999, Native American Indian female offenders accounted for sixteen percent of the population in jails of Indian country. Generally, Native American Indian offenders are less likely than any other race to have been incarcerated for either a violent offense or drug offense. Yet, the majority of studies do not indicate that drug use is less prevalent among Native American Indians as opposed to any other racial or ethnic group. Native American Indian offenders are typically younger than the average incarcerated offender. Furthermore, as to the living conditions surrounding Native American Indians, many who live on reservations live in near third-world conditions, although these conditions vary depending on the particular reservation. Additionally, conditions are likely to vary between Native American Indians who live on reservations, and those who do not.

The most significant trends that differentiate Native American Indian offenders from those of other races are the greater percentage of alcohol-related charges and the greater likelihood of a history of childhood abuse among them. Native American Indians have traditionally and consistently had the highest arrest rate of any racial or ethnic group for alcohol-related offenses. Yet the chances of a Native American Indian being arrested for such offenses may depend on their location, as approximately seventy-five percent of these arrests occurred in cities between 1976–1985. Although no statistics have been collected regarding the percentage of Native American Indian offenders with a history of abuse, it is likely to be a fairly high percentage, because Native American Indian children are reported as abuse victims at twice the rate of their population.

Obviously, a considerable amount of statistical research needs to be conducted in this field, especially research that considers gender as a separate category. Whether the offender lives on or off a reservation is another major factor that warrants consideration. If possible, the research should also differentiate between reservations based on each individual reservation's average income level, and its proximity to the closest major city. The current research indicates an even stronger need for providing alcohol treatment programs and addressing the history of abuse in appropriate cases. Due to the unique nature of Native American Indian reservations, traditional job and educational programs will most likely be inadequate, given the lack of employment opportunities on or near reservations. Economic improvement programs targeted at the reservation community as a whole are needed to help offenders gain skills while incarcerated to ensure that they have employment upon release.

The lack of statistics makes it hard to track the treatment of female Native American Indians through the criminal justice system and uncover the points at which their race and gender affect their treatment. Moreover, unlike all other groups of female offenders, Native American Indian women are subject to the vagaries of multiple jurisdictions because they are caught between federal and/or state law. Native American Indian offenders on reservations can be subject to tribal court jurisdiction; furthermore, it is possible that several states can also claim jurisdiction over one reservation, depending on where the crime occurred within the reservation and the identity of the victim. For example, on the Navajo Reservation, a Native American Indian offender can be prosecuted for an offense against a non-Native American Indian under Arizona, New Mexico, or Utah law. These states have different required elements and punishments for the same crime, making criminal justice for Indians on the Navajo Reservation a matter of location.

The way courts resolve jurisdictional issues often place Native American Indians who commit offenses on a reservation at a greater disadvantage than Native American Indians who commit an offense off the reservation, and non-Native American Indians who commit an offense on the reservation. Congress can amend the Major Crimes Act to include any offense, and can thus determine which traditional state crimes will be ceded to federal jurisdiction when both the offender and victim are Indian and the crime occurs on the reservation. The same crimes committed by non-Indians fall under state jurisdiction, unless Congress has specified it as a federal crime. This dichotomy means that Native American Indian offenders are often subjected to the harsher penalties of the Federal Sentencing Guidelines.

Class as a Factor in the Incarceration Process

Class affects the treatment of female offenders in a variety of ways. One of the most significant aspects of an offender's class within the criminal justice system is that the law offers no equal protection based on income. In other words, a female offender can object to treatment based on gender and race, but not on class status.

Without this type of protection, the criminal justice system may operate in a manner that discriminates on the basis of an offender's class. Examples of this type of class bias during the enforcement phase of the incarceration process are the search and seizure of buses, decisions to target low-income neighborhoods for drug enforcement, laws that have a disproportionate effect on inner city residents, "three strikes" sentencing laws, the standards used in consent to search cases, and Terry stops.

Once a low-income female offender is in the criminal justice system, class discrimination persists. The most visible and important area in which this can be seen is in both the Supreme Court's interpretation of the right to counsel, and the actual performance of attorneys assigned to low-income offenders. Three areas exist in which the Supreme Court's Sixth Amendment interpretations greatly limit the effectiveness of counsel for the poor: 1) the right to counsel prior to indictment; 2) the right to counsel on appeal; and 3) the adoption of a low standard for determining effective assistance of counsel.

Despite these limitations on the right to counsel, however, the actual performance of public counsel differs slightly from that of private counsel. In 1998, only a one percent difference existed between the conviction rate for federal offenders with public counsel, and federal offenders with private counsel. Federal defendants with public counsel, however, were more likely to be incarcerated. In large state courts, conviction rates were approximately the same, but defendants with public counsel were less likely to gain pretrial release than those with private counsel. As in federal courts, defendants represented by public counsel in state court were more often incarcerated, however, these defendants faced shorter sentences than those represented by private counsel. Consistent with the Supreme Court's decision that the right to counsel only attaches after indictment, incarcerated offenders with public counsel spoke with their attorneys later and less often than offenders with private counsel.

CONCLUSION

The research summarized in this essay reveals that trends exist within the female offender population that should influence the types of programs offered to reduce female offending and recidivism. Regardless of race or class, the connection between a history of physical and/or sexual abuse and subsequent drug use appears to be the most important factor in a woman's incarceration. The predisposition to incarceration by abused women indicates that programs to prevent abuse, particularly abuse that starts in childhood and becomes long term, is essential to reduce the number of female offenders. Additionally, programs designed to provide treatment to sexually and/or physically abused female offenders, as well as female offenders with substance abuse problems, are important in reducing recidivism.

Job training skills and education would ensure the success of these programs. Women with the means to be financially independent are less likely to stay in abusive relationships, less likely to feel the need to turn to crime for money, and in some cases, less likely to turn to drug use as a coping mechanism. In addition, for those low-income, mostly minority female offenders who do use their new skills to obtain

a job that pays a living wage, the possibility of removing themselves from neighborhoods targeted by law enforcement exists.

Beyond these broad suggestions, detailed research is necessary to discover all the facets of female offenders in America. When we have a more fully formed picture of female offenders, it will reveal that the criminal justice system does have flaws, particularly in regards to police and prosecutorial discretion. Based on the scant research currently available, however, this picture will reveal that many of the disparities in our justice system are merely reflections of the disparities, inequalities, and discriminations within our civil society. Reforms within the justice system may provide greater equality for those women already in the system. Nevertheless, to truly address the issue of female offending, we as a society must take responsibility for the consequences of our decisions to allocate resources in places other than where those resources would be most effective in fighting female offending.

STUDY QUESTION

Discuss the trends identified by Jennifer Ward that exist within the female offender population that should influence the types of programs offered to reduce female offending and recidivism.

The Race Effect on Wrongful Convictions

Arthur L. Rizer III

Regardless of how social scientists label it, it is agreed that a shift has occurred in the way racists express their racist attitudes. This attitude is spilling over into the criminal justice system at the expense of innocent people of color.

HISTORICAL VIEW AND EFFECTS OF RACE IN THE CRIMINAL JUSTICE SYSTEM

In order to truly understand why race is such a major factor when it comes to wrongful convictions, one must discuss the broader historical context of race in the criminal justice system and the development of certain laws. Also, one must recognize that criminal statutes targeting race existed for most of the twentieth century. The administration of punishment, or the lack thereof, has direct ties to both the race of the offender and the race of the victim. For instance, North Carolina had mandatory capital crime statutes for those cases where a black man was convicted of raping a white woman. In contrast, a white man convicted of the same crime would receive a maximum of one year in prison. Throughout the legal history of the United States the criminal code illustrates these types of disparities.

THE SCOTTSBORO EFFECT

The issue on racial disparity in the system went un-addressed for many years. Then, in 1931 the Court decided *Powell v. Alabama*, better known as the "Scottsboro Boys Case." In this notorious case, nine black men were charged with raping two white girls on a freight train while traveling near Scottsboro, Alabama. On the day of each trial there was not a definitive defense attorney in place, and in four one-day trials, eight of the nine were found guilty and received the death penalty. As a consequence of this injustice, organizations like the American Civil Liberties Union and the Communist Party became involved in the campaign to vindicate the men or to mitigate their penalties. Publicity generated by this case prompted an exploration of the effect of race in the judicial system. The exploration made it clear that race was one of the major obstacles to a fair and just proceeding.

The Justice Department began collecting statistics in 1930 regarding how sentences and criminal prosecutions were being conducted. Their data reinforces the notion that race was a factor in criminal prosecution and punishment. For instance, in Alabama less than 5 percent of murders involved black perpetrators and white victims. Most people

Source: Arthur L. Rizer III, Esquire, *The Race Effect on Wrongful Convictions*, 29 William Mitchell U. Law Review 845–867 (2003) (citations omitted). Reprinted by permission of the Author and the William Mitchell Law Review. I would like to thank my wife, Monique Rizer, for her help in editing this article.

are astonished to hear this; they expect the number to be much higher. The death rows in Alabama perpetuate the misconception. "Although 67 percent of all murder victims in the State of Alabama are black, 84 percent of all people who have been sentenced to death in that state have been sentenced to death for crimes committed against people who are white." Furthermore, approximately three-quarters of those who have been executed in Alabama were black. The trend is not changing; a higher percentage of black people were executed in Alabama between 1972 and 1997 than between 1930 and 1972.

The Justice Department was also able to establish that between 1930 and 1972, 89 percent of the people who were executed for the crime of rape in America were black men convicted of raping white women. In addition, 100 percent of the people executed for a rape conviction perpetrated their crime on a white victim. This statistic is even more disturbing when one considers that black women are much more likely to be victims of sexual assault, yet the punishments for their perpetrators are conspicuously less severe. These racial disparities give a historical backdrop to the race factor and its influence on the criminal justice system.

In the 1960s there was incredible activism to combat certain aspects of racism ("Jim Crow" laws, racial bias, segregation laws, voting challenges, etc.); however, little of this energy has been directed toward the undercurrent of racism still flowing in the courts. Today, if one had to find an area of public administration where the remnants of slavery still survive, it would be in the criminal justice system. The courts have been reluctant to examine this issue. The lack of judicial attention to racial injustice can be seen in its most insidious form with the inequitable administration of the death penalty.

Three cases highlight this point. First, in *Furman v. Georgia*, opponents of the death

penalty argued that the use of the death penalty was a violation of the Eighth and Fourteenth Amendments because it was arbitrary, unpredictable, and racially discriminatory. To support their argument, they presented the same type of data provided above, arguing that the respective races of the victim and the offender was the primary variable regarding administration of the death penalty. The Court accepted this data and held that the death penalty was being administered unfairly.

After the *Furman* decision, states scrambled to pass new death penalty statutes that conformed to the new decision. However, opponents of the death penalty persisted, which brought about the second case, *Gregg v. Georgia*. Here death penalty opponents argued that as long as racial bias is evident in society, bias would exist in criminal justice. Furthermore, they asserted that the new death penalty statutes did not protect against a racially biased application of the death penalty. The Court held that they were not going to presume racism simply because it was a death penalty case. This gave rise to the third case, *McCleskey v. Kemp*, which embraces the critical issues of race consciousness in criminal law.

THE *MCCLESKEY* EFFECT

In *McCleskey*, opponents of the death penalty went back to the Supreme Court with data that examined every homicide in Georgia that occurred in a seven-year period and came up with extremely powerful data demonstrating that a black perpetrator is eleven times more likely to get the death penalty than a white criminal charged with the same crime. Moreover, a black defendant is twenty-two times more likely to get the death penalty if the victim is white.

The data shows that race was the greatest predictor of who received the death penalty in the state of Georgia. In addition, it is important to point out that the Court accepted the data as presented; it did not challenge the numbers and accepted the fact that there was sufficient evidence proving race played a factor in the administration of the death penalty. However, the Court refused to order a stay on the execution on two grounds. First, the Court reasoned that a stay on executions would open a Pandora's box. Clever lawyers would respond to a stay with evidence of disparity in other crimes and disrupt many areas of the justice system other than capital cases. Justice Brennan responded to this notion by saying that the Court has a "fear of too much justice." Second, the Court reasoned that a certain amount of racial bias is "inevitable."

THE IMPACT OF *MCCLESKEY*

When one thinks about *McCleskey*, one thinks about abdication—a concession to racial bias. In *Brown v. Board of Education* the Court was faced with a situation where it could have said that a certain amount of racial bias is "inevitable," and that the problem is too big for the Court. Instead, the Court said that depriving a child of an equal opportunity to an education because of the color of his or her skin was unconstitutional and wrong. Thus, because it was unconstitutional it was not inevitable. Although these cases address substantially different factual situations and sought different outcomes, they contain the same core questions of equality and fairness. Yet, in one case the Court was willing to stay for the long fight in the interest of justice and fairness while in the other case the Court retreated from a commitment to equal justice and equal opportunity.

The most important impact of *McCleskey* is the attitude it sets. The case established the basis for how race continues to undermine the hope of minorities who are brought before the criminal courts. By tolerating a presumption of criminality that is assigned to minority defendants, the indifference the criminal justice system creates an atmosphere where the innocent have an increased likelihood of wrongful conviction.

EYEWITNESS TESTIMONY AND CROSS-RACIAL IDENTIFICATION

Few studies have focused on the ability of Hispanic, Native American, or Asian individuals to accurately identify other races or be accurately identified. Thus, this section will primarily focus on cross-racial identification between white witnesses and black suspects. "There has been a growing body of social science research that reveals the important role in which race plays in assessing the reliability of a witness identification when the witness and the person identified are of the same or of different races." As a result of this research, it is conclusive that race influences the accuracy of witness identification.

WRONGFUL CONVICTIONS DUE TO FAULTY EYEWITNESS TESTIMONY

Eyewitness testimony is the most influential evidence for juries. Ironically, this same testimony is extremely unreliable. There is "no clear method for estimating the frequency of wrongful accusations based [solely] on faulty eyewitness testimony." However, the evidence shows that eyewitness testimony is unreliable. Because juries rely heavily on unreliable eyewitness testimony as a basis for conviction, the role it plays in wrongful convictions is clear. In fact, 74 percent of wrongful convictions that were vindicated due to DNA testing had the element of a bad eyewitness.

The problem with eyewitness identification is embedded in psychology. For example: When a witness to a crime must later identify the person who was seen before, various psychological factors can play an important role: the retention interval or period of time between the crime and the identification; the exposure time and amount of time that the witness has had to look at the essential subject; prior knowledge; expectations; misleading suggestions; and stress . . . . [T]hese factors will operate to reduce the accuracy of an identification, just as they affect the accuracy of any kind of testimony.

The inherent unreliability of this kind of testimony makes the admission of this evidence in criminal trials problematic; this problem is enhanced in situations involving cross-racial identifications.

FAULTY EYEWITNESS TESTIMONY IN CROSS-RACIAL IDENTIFICATION INCREASES WRONGFUL CONVICTIONS AMONG MINORITIES

William Jackson spent five years in an Ohio penitentiary on a spurious rape charge before being released. The real rapist did not particularly look like Mr. Jackson. Nevertheless, two white women swore under oath that Mr. Jackson was the man who raped them. They were wrong. Despite Mr. Jackson's several alibi witnesses, the (all white) jury convicted him. These types of misidentifications are neither unique nor rare. "Legal observers have long recognized that cross-racial identifications by witnesses are disproportionately responsible for wrongful convictions."

People make identifications by recognizing facial features. Those of one race have a harder time recognizing faces of people from different races. It is not totally understood if this is due to prejudices or from having fewer experiences with members of other races. It is not clear why one person can more easily identify someone from the same race. Psychologists believe two reasonable explanations exist: "[1] different races often have distinctive features in common; and [2] people make more mistakes in cross-racial

identification" situations due to a decrease in attention to people of other races.

What is clear is that there are discrepancies in cross-racial identification, and those discrepancies have crept into our criminal justice system in the form of eyewitness testimony.

SOLUTIONS AND SAFEGUARDS

One suggestion towards alleviating the problem is to help, not hinder, jury education. First, permit the defense to "present psychological testimony about the factors that affect the reliability of eyewitness accounts," particularly the problems associated with cross-racial identification. Second, allow for jury instructions that inform the jury of this problematic evidence and that they should weigh the evidence accordingly.

In addition, steps should be taken to ensure that the police conduct correct line-ups (both actual and photo). There is no point in compounding the problem with unfair lineups that increase the defendant's chances of being erroneously identified.

Courts have already applied procedural safeguards to prevent erroneous identifications. One such safeguard is the defendant's right to counsel at post-indictment line-ups. Another is the due process fairness requirement in all identification proceedings, including uncounseled photo arrays and pre-indictment line-ups. If these safeguards are breached, the evidence will be deemed inadmissible at a suppression hearing. In order to further eliminate racial bias, these safeguards should be enforced more rigorously.

Finally, some argue that there should be an outright exclusion of inherently untrustworthy identification evidence. At the very least, there should be required collaboration for the admission of eyewitness testimony. However, neither remedy is likely to be universally adopted and both are inappropriate for selective application to cross-racial identifications.

IT IS BETTER TO BE RICH AND GUILTY THAN POOR, INNOCENT, AND A MINORITY

By some accounts the title of Jeffrey Reiman's book, *The Rich Get Richer and the Poor Get Prison*, gives a good prelude to justice in America. One fact that puts this into perspective is that 51 percent of the people executed in America were executed in the state of Mississippi and its fellow southern states. Compensation for lawyers appointed to try capital cases in Mississippi is capped at $3,500. In Alabama, lawyers representing post-conviction death row inmates cannot be paid more than $1000. For states that report how much they spend on capital punishment trials, the average cost is $40,750 almost $40,000 over the post-conviction cap in Alabama.

This section will show that people in poverty are at a much greater risk to be wrongfully convicted. Further, it is well documented that minorities are disproportionately poor. Thus, if the dots are connected from the lack of justice for the poor to poverty rampant in minority communities, coupled with the fact that minorities warm a lot of beds in prison, it can be deduced that minorities are at a higher risk of being wrongfully convicted.

WRONGFUL CONVICTIONS AND THE IMPOVERISHED IN AMERICA

There are many factors that account for the wrongful convictions of poor people. The most prevalent are the lack of competent counsel, the lack of resources, police misconduct, the focus of law enforcement, and a general lack of credibility given the impoverished by society.

Many people clutch their pocketbooks or keep an eye over their shoulder when a street person is walking close by. Why is this? This author believes that people in poverty have an automatic lack of credibility in this society. The general public harbors a chauvinism that criminals are usually poor. Thus, poor people get treated like criminals.

With the lack of credibility comes a host of other problems, such as police misconduct in the gathering of confessions. Based on what has been learned from DNA exonerations, 44 percent of wrongful convictions involved false confessions obtained through police misconduct.

There is a considerable amount of evidence to indicate that the criminal justice system benefits the rich, not the poor, because: the wealthy benefit from a criminal justice system that sends the message that it is the poor, not the rich, who commit crimes and whom the middle class should fear. As a result of the criminal justice system's focus on street crime and not "white collar" or environmental crime, it is the poor who seem a threat to the social order, not the rich; and this view reinforces the familiar American association between wealth and virtue, poverty and moral bankruptcy . . . . "If we can convince [society] that the poor are poor because of their own shortcomings, particularly moral shortcomings like incontinence and indolence, then we need acknowledge no . . . responsibility to the poor." [The result is that] "the ultimate sanctions of criminal justice dramatically sanctify the present social and economic order, and the poverty of criminals makes poverty itself an individual moral crime!"

Perhaps the major deterrent to obtaining justice for indigent defendants is the lack of competent lawyers to represent them. Since most people who are charged with crimes are poor, most lawyers who represent them are public defenders. The public defender system has many problems in itself. For instance, the National Association of Criminal Defense Lawyers issued a warning in 1997 that "such low-bid contracting, designed to 'process the maximum number of defendants at the lowest cost-without regard to truth, justice, or innocence' was violating citizens' rights and leading to wrongful convictions." It is estimated that 28 percent of wrongful convictions are in part or directly a result of shoddy defense work.

Another factor that compounds the lack of competent counsel is the limit put on resources to support a meaningful defense. All defendants are entitled to a forceful defense, and it is practically impossible to assemble a compelling defense without access to some of the multitude of assets that are accessible to the state. This problem is exponentially amplified in the case of poor defendants.

MINORITIES AND POVERTY IN AMERICA

As stated, the poor are predominantly represented by public criminal defense lawyers. "The clients of [these] criminal defense lawyers are not only predominantly poor, but they are also disproportionately nonwhite." This is not surprising in view of the composition of American cities. The result of this poverty and other elements discussed is that minorities experience an increased likelihood of being wrongfully convicted because they are more likely to be poor.

SUGGESTIONS AND SOLUTIONS

This is an embedded social issue, one that needs to be addressed on the most basic levels of fundamental fairness and respect for fellow humans. While this country has come a long way with issues of racism through education and a public focus on diversity, there needs to be an equally strong focus on understanding those who are poor. We also should enact zero-tolerance policies for police misconduct (the extraction of false confessions in particular). This can be accomplished by legislating civil remedies, by firing rogue police officers, and, in some cases, by criminal prosecution for the worst offenders. Attracting

public defenders who care about the system by increasing their pay and "prestige" in society would also begin to address this problem. We should ban, or at least modify, caps on the monetary resources allowed public defenders. After all, access to justice comes at a price. Finally, we should search for ways to help public prosecutors to seek justice, rather than rewarding only the highest conviction rates.

CONGRESS/LEGISLATURE

Lawmakers of this country have been on a crusade to criminalize some varieties of behavior, most notably with the drug laws. The issues relating to the war on drugs will be addressed in this section because they are legislative-based movements.

The drug laws are discriminatorily designed in their very basis. As public knowledge grew about crack and its effects on criminal behavior in the 1980s, so did legislative concern. The public wanted action against the crack epidemic, and Congress responded with laws mandating much stiffer penalties against crack cocaine than its powder counterpart.

These harsher penalties had a disparate effect on the black community. The Federal Sentencing Guidelines mandate a minimum five-year and maximum twenty-year imprisonment term for simple possession of five grams or more of crack cocaine. Thus, the sentence for possession of one gram of crack cocaine is equal to the sentence for possession of 100 grams of powder cocaine. This particularly impacts the black community because 91 percent of those who are charged with crack-related offenses are black. Conversely, those charged with possession of powder cocaine are predominately white.

Another example that exhibits this disparity is the "meth war." By some accounts, Methamphetamine, or crystal meth, is considered one of the most devastating drugs available to users. Yet the sentencing related to this drug is minimal, even though its presence is considered an epidemic. Is it any coincidence that its users are predominantly white?

Partly due to these guidelines, incarceration is at a historic high, particularly among blacks. This fuels the perception and presumption that minorities are mostly criminals. Thus, the current crack laws have created an environment with a substantially greater risk of wrongful conviction based upon race-biased suspicions for people of color.

An easy solution to this quandary is to simply standardize the punishment. Although this would not prevent blacks from going to jail, it would make their powder cocaine counterpart users equally culpable.

THE PROSECUTOR

Another fact that has been learned from DNA exonerations is that 40 percent of wrongful convictions contain an element of prosecutorial misconduct. The obvious case where this happens is where the prosecutor himself is racist and prosecutes because of the defendant's race and not the likelihood of guilt. The more subtle and harmful problem is the prosecutor's discriminatory use of peremptory strikes in jury selection. In *Batson v. Kentucky*, the Supreme Court said that the discriminatory use of preemptory strikes was unconstitutional. The *Batson* decision laid out a three-step test to determine whether the state's employment of peremptory challenges is a violation of the Fourteenth Amendment. First, the defense must show intentional racial discrimination. Second, once the defense has made this showing, the burden then shifts to the prosecution to offer a race-neutral reason for the challenge. Lastly, the court determines if the explanation is race-neutral or racial discrimination.

Prosecutors, however, can get around this mandate by stating racially-neutral reasons for excusing prospective jurors. A problem with this is that many courts consider almost anything other than an overt statement such as "I want him off because he is black" as a race-neutral reason. As a result, many black defendants are tried by a panel of all white jurors. A perfect illustration of this can be seen in the 1996 motion picture, *A Time to Kill*, when the defendant, a black man, looks at his all white jury and asks, "This is a jury of my peers?"

In *Booker v. Jabe*, the prosecutor exercised twenty-six of his allotted thirty peremptory challenges; twenty-two of those challenges were used against black jurors. The end result was an all white jury.

Prosecutorial misconduct also results in wrongful convictions when race is injected in a trial in a prejudicial manner. For instance, in *Russell v. Collins* the prosecutor said in his closing arguments, "Can you imagine the fear that [the victim] went through . . . with three blacks[?]" This was asked to an all white jury when referring to a white victim. These comments are especially exasperating to defendants because appellate courts refuse to remedy the situation, instead employing the harmless error doctrine and not reversing the conviction. In *Russell*, the Fifth Circuit deemed the comments "regrettable" in a footnote giving a cursory glance at its impact.

Blatant prosecutorial racism that leads to wrongful convictions can be addressed by eliminating prosecutors' shields from civil and criminal liability. Simple misconduct can be somewhat thwarted with other disciplinary actions, including termination. Courts could also prevent such misconduct leading to wrongful convictions by being willing to prevent the use of peremptory strikes when they appear to be racially based. This author believes a common sense approach would be sufficient. Further, courts could use the same common sense approach to stop prosecutors from using racially charged language in order to exaggerate jurors' fears and reservations by judicial intervention at the moment the comment is made and even calling a mistrial if the misconduct is severe. In addition, appellate courts could give due weight to the issue and refrain from automatically deeming such conduct harmless.

THE COURT/JUDGES

It has been said that, as a minority, you should be more concerned with people wearing black robes than those wearing white ones. The judicial system has shown an indifference to certain levels of racism through the "inevitable" doctrine and, in accepting race as a legitimate category for suspicion, by tolerating racial profiling.

These indifferences show up in ways that are disempowering to minorities. For example, in *Peek v. State* the judge, who was sitting over a capital case said, "Since the nigger mom and dad are here anyway, why don't we go ahead and do the penalty phase today instead of having to subpoena them back at cost to the state." If the judge had been a businessman for a major corporation, he would have been fired, but in a system where racial bias is "inevitable," biased people can continue to preside over our courts.

Some solutions to this particular problem may be unrealistic because of their side effects. One suggestion is to limit the liability shield of judges. Another is to remove judges who show a tendency for racial bias. Further, there is an argument to mandate a reversal where the judge makes racially motivated comments during the proceeding.

THE JURY

"Many jurors harbor racial prejudices. Although these prejudices are often subtle," and other times overt, they contaminate the jury behind the curtain of jury deliberation. Thus, it is imperative that attorneys eliminate

prospective jurors before they are shielded by the deliberation room door.

Juries are more likely to convict a person of another race than of their own. "Because most juries are predominantly white, even when only marginal evidence is provided," black defendants are acquitted less often than white ones. Furthermore, if the victim is white, a black defendant's chances of an acquittal are even less.

The races of the defendant and the victim play a major role in wrongful convictions. A study done in 1978 by Marina Miller and Jay Hewitt demonstrates this phenomenon. The study was of 133 college students. They were told to pretend they were jurors and then were shown a videotape of a case involving a black man charged with the rape of a thirteen-year-old girl. Half of the study participants were told that the girl was black and the other half were told she was white.

Miller and Hewitt found that both [b]lack and [w]hite students tended to convict more often when they shared racial affinity with the victim. Sixty-five percent of the [w]hite students voted for conviction when they thought the victim was [w]hite, but only 32 percent voted for conviction when they thought the victim was [b]lack. Eighty percent of the [b]lack students voted for conviction when they thought the victim was [b]lack, but only 48 percent voted for conviction when they thought the victim was [w]hite.

To help alleviate this problem, the court should strive to maintain a jury pool whose makeup reflects the community at large. Further, the system should take on the responsibility of obtaining participation from minorities in the trial process. Attorneys should use voir dire to examine prospective jurors with regard to racial biases, because jurors will usually give only slight inferences to such biases in their examination. Also, attorneys should attempt to create a comfort zone so that jurors feel free to talk about race. Moreover, attorneys should not be too narrow-minded about who they believe could be a racist. Prospective jurors are not likely to come in with white robes or with swastika tattooed on their foreheads.

CONCLUSION

" 'Symbolic racists' do not express blatantly racist attitudes because it is no longer socially acceptable to do so, while 'aversive racists' believe that they are not racist even while holding racist beliefs." Regardless of how social scientists label it, it is agreed that a shift has occurred in the way racists express their racist attitudes. This attitude is spilling over into the criminal justice system at the expense of innocent people of color. It is affecting people like Walther McMillan, who spent six years on death row even though he had thirty-five alibi witnesses to prove his innocence.

Avoiding wrongful convictions is not just about the innocent souls who are trapped by it. It is also a law-and-order issue: when innocent people go to jail, the real killers or rapists are still on the loose and free to break the law anew. In the *McMillan* case, the real killer had six years to commit other crimes. Avoiding wrongful convictions also is essential to the social contract that we all have with our government. If we lose faith in the belief that the criminal system is attempting to represent "justice," how many will embrace radical, even revolutionary, methods to obtain the justice they feel eludes them?

This concern is especially relevant in the aftermath of September 11. There is a high potential for arbitrary and capricious convictions based on emotion and fear, rather than justice and due process. While protecting against terrorism is paramount to this nation, faith in a fair system is equally imperative.

STUDY QUESTION

Discuss how specific aspects of the criminal justice system contribute to racial disparities in wrongful convictions as explained by Arthur Rizer.

Race, Crime and the Pool of Surplus Criminality: Or Why the "War on Drugs" Was a "War on Blacks"

Kenneth B. Nunn

What made the War on Drugs become, for all practical purposes, a war on Blacks? In this article, I argue that the drug war's focus on the African American community was neither an accident nor a conspiracy. Rather, the drug war is simply a prominent example of the central role both race and the definition of crime play in the maintenance and legitimization of white supremacy. Race and crime, as two significant social phenomena, are linked in an endless cycle of oppression.

HOW THE DRUG WAR TARGETED BLACK COMMUNITIES

By almost any measure, the drug war's impact on African American communities has been devastating. Millions of African Americans have been imprisoned, many have been unfairly treated by the criminal justice system, the rights of both legitimate suspects and average citizens have been violated and the quality of life of many millions more has been adversely affected. These effects are the consequences of deliberate decisions; first, to fight a "war" on drugs, and second, to fight that war against low-level street dealers in communities populated by people of color. In this section, I consider the impact of the War on Drugs specifically on the African American community.

MASS INCARCERATION AND DISPROPORTIONATE ARRESTS

As a result of the War on Drugs, African American communities suffer from a phenomenon I call "mass incarceration." Not only are large numbers of African Americans incarcerated, African Americans are incarcerated at percentages that exceed any legitimate law enforcement interest and which negatively impact the African American community. While African Americans only comprise twelve percent of the U.S. population, they

Source: Kenneth B. Nunn, "Race, Crime and the Pool of Surplus Criminality: Or Why the 'War on Drugs' Was a 'War on Blacks,'" Journal of Gender, Race and Justice, 6 (2002): 381–445.

are forty-six percent of those incarcerated in state and federal prisons. At the end of 1999, over half a million African American men and women were held in state and federal prisons. A disparity this great appears inexcusable on its face. However, the inequity is even worse when one considers the rate of incarceration and the proportion of the African American population that is incarcerated.

The rate of incarceration measures the likelihood that any African American male will be sentenced to prison. In 2000, the rate of incarceration for African American males nationwide was 3457 per 100,000. In comparison, the rate of incarceration for white males was 449 per 100,000. This means, on average, African American males were 7.7 times more likely to be incarcerated than white males. For some age groups, the racial disparities are even worse. For young men between the ages of 25 and 29, African Americans are 8.7 times more likely to be incarcerated than whites. For 18 and 19 year olds, African American men are 8.8 times more likely to be incarcerated than whites.

Another way to measure the extent of mass incarceration is to examine the proportion of the African American population that is serving time in prison. In some jurisdictions, as many as one third of the adult African American male population may be incarcerated at any given time. Nationwide, 1.6 percent of the African American population is in prison. However, nearly 10 percent of African American males ages 25–29 are in prison. Nearly 8 percent of African American males between the ages of 18 and 39 are in prison.

The mass incarceration of African Americans is a direct consequence of the War on Drugs. As one commentator states, "Drug arrests are a principal reason that the proportions of [B]lacks in prison and more generally under criminal justice system control have risen rapidly in recent years." Since the declaration of the War on Drugs in 1982, prison populations have more than tripled.

The rapid growth in prison populations is particularly clear in federal institutions. Although the overall federal prison population was only 24,000 in 1980, by 1996, it had reached 106,000. The federal prison population continued to grow in the 1990s. In 2000, the federal prison population exceeded 145,000. Fifty-seven percent of the federal prisoners in 2000 were incarcerated for drug offenses. In 1982 there were approximately 400,000 incarcerated persons. By 1992, that number had more than doubled to 850,000. In 2000, there were over 1.3 million persons in prison. From 1979 to 1989, the percentage of African Americans arrested for drug offenses almost doubled from 22 percent to 42 percent of the total. During that same period, the total number of African American arrests for drug abuse violations skyrocketed from 112,748 to 452,574, an increase of over 300 percent.

Jerome Miller analyzed arrest statistics from several American cities to determine the impact of the War on Drugs on policing. He found striking racial disparities in how drug arrests were made. In many jurisdictions, African American men account for over eighty percent of total drug arrests. In Baltimore, for example, African American men were eighty-six percent of those arrested for drug offenses in 1991. The fact that African Americans are incarcerated in such large percentages and are arrested and incarcerated at such disproportionate rates is shocking. It is obscene in the absence of a strong showing that African Americans are responsible for a comparable percentage of crime in the United States.

The claim that African Americans violate the drug laws at a greater rate, and that this justifies the great disparities in rates of arrest and incarceration, seems unlikely. Most drug arrests are made for the crime of possession. Possession is a crime that every drug user must commit and, in the United States, most drug users are white. The U.S. Public Health Service Substance Abuse and Mental Health Services

Administration reported in 1992 that 76 percent of drug users in the United States were white, 14 percent were African American, and 8 percent were Hispanic. Cocaine users were estimated to be 66 percent white, 17.6 percent Black, and 15.9 percent Hispanic. Rather than demonstrating patterns of use that approach arrest disparities, African Americans "are less likely to . . . [use] drugs than whites are, for all major drugs of abuse except heroin."

There also seems to be insufficient evidence to conclude that African Americans are more likely to deal drugs, and thus more likely to be arrested. Most drug users purchase drugs from persons of the same race and socio-economic background. So, the large numbers of white users would suggest an equally large number of white dealers, as well. On the other hand, there are logical reasons to conclude that the number of African American dealers may be disproportionately large. Still, it is unlikely that drug use and offense are so out of balance that Blacks constitute the vast majority of drug offenders given that they are such a small minority of drug users.

Disproportionate enforcement is a more likely cause of racial disparities in the criminal justice system than is disproportionate offending. Differences in the way that Black dealers and white dealers market drugs may encourage law enforcement officers to concentrate efforts against African Americans. Michael Tonry argues that it is easier for police to make arrests in "socially disorganized neighborhoods" because drug dealing is more likely to occur on the streets and transient drug buyers are less likely to draw attention to themselves.

In addition, disproportionate arrests may simply be a function of discriminatory exercise of discretion by police officers. Police officers may decide to arrest African Americans under circumstances when they would not arrest white suspects, and they may be in a position to do so more frequently than with whites because they are more likely to stop and detain African Americans.

CRACK COCAINE AND SENTENCING DISPARITIES

Perhaps no aspect of the drug war has contributed to the rapid increase of African American prisoners in federal prisons more than the federal cocaine sentencing scheme. Federal sentencing rules for the possession and sale of cocaine distinguish between cocaine in powder form and cocaine prepared as crack. A person sentenced for possession with intent to distribute a given amount of crack cocaine receives the same sentence as someone who possessed one hundred times as much powder cocaine. This difference in sentencing exists notwithstanding the fact that cocaine is cocaine, and there are no physiological differences in effect between the powder and the crack form of the drug.

The difference in crack/powder cocaine sentencing is significant because African Americans are more likely to use crack, while white drug users are more likely to use powder cocaine. Since the passage of the Anti-Drug Abuse Act of 1986, which first enacted the crack/powder sentencing disparity, virtually all federal cocaine prosecutions have been against African Americans charged with the possession or sale of crack cocaine. Although, the disproportionate racial impact of the Anti-Drug Abuse Act of 1986 has been noted by the U.S. Sentencing Commission, neither Congress nor the executive branch has moved to rectify the disparities in the law.

The disparity in cocaine sentencing is obvious and may be traced to the language of the underlying statute. Even in the absence of such a manifest cause of discrimination, African Americans have traditionally received more severe sentences than similarly situated whites. Although it is by no means conclusive, there is substantial evidence that racial discrimination within the criminal justice system is the cause of the sentencing disparities that exist between Blacks and whites. Numerous surveys have found racial disparities in the sentencing process and attributed those disparities to racial discrimination. For example, a study by Miethe and Moore in 1984 found that African Americans received longer sentences than whites and that African Americans were less likely to benefit from lower sentences as a result of plea-bargaining. Likewise, Welch, Spohn, and Gruhl reviewed convictions and sentences in six cities nationwide in 1985. They found that African Americans were substantially more likely to be sentenced to prison than whites and that the disparity in incarceration rates is due to "discrimination in the sentencing process itself." In 1983, Baldus, Pulaski, and Woodworth subjected death sentences in Georgia to painstaking review. Using multiple regression analysis to control for over 230 nonracial factors, the researchers found that the race of the victim was the determining factor in whether a defendant received the death penalty. They found defendants who killed white victims were over four times more likely to receive a death sentence than defendants whose victims were not white. In addition, African American defendants who killed whites were eleven times more likely to receive a death sentence than white defendants who killed Blacks.

Racial discrimination in sentencing can only be worsened by efforts to make sentences tougher and harsher. The War on Drugs has spawned a panoply of "get tough on crime" measures such as "three strikes and you're out" and habitual offender provisions, as well as enhancements for possession of weapons and for selling drugs near schools or public housing. The cumulative effect of these sentencing policies has been to increase the proportion of convicted drug dealers sentenced to prison and increase the length of their sentences. A substantial increase in length of sentence for drug offenders is precisely what Marc Mauer found when he analyzed the impact of mandatory sentences in the federal court system. Mauer observed: Drug offenders released from prison in 1990, many of whom had not been sentenced under mandatory provisions, had

served an average of 30 months in prison. But offenders sentenced to prison in 1990—most of whom were subject to mandatory penalties—were expected to serve more than twice that term, or an average of 66 months.

Guideline sentencing has also contributed to the increase in African Americans incarcerated as a result of the drug war. The Federal Sentencing Guidelines, by depriving judges of discretion, have resulted in many more defendants serving substantially longer sentences. This combined with the fact that African Americans in general usually get longer sentences than comparably situated whites, means that drug war sentencing has been particularly unkind to African Americans.

DRIVING WHILE BLACK, DRUG SWEEPS AND THE OVERPOLICING OF THE AFRICAN AMERICAN COMMUNITY

The gross disparities that exist in the criminal justice system may be traced to the differential treatment that African Americans and other people of color receive from the police. A growing body of evidence suggests that Blacks are investigated and detained by the police more frequently than are other persons in the community. This unwarranted attention from the police is a result of the longstanding racism that pervades American culture. Like all who are socialized in American culture, police officers are more suspicious of African Americans and believe they are more likely to engage in crime. Consequently, police concentrate their efforts in areas frequented by African Americans and detain African Americans at a greater rate.

In part, this concentration of effort may be designed to uncover specific illegal activity. Certain police activity, such as undercover drug buys, may be more frequent in African American communities than in other areas of a city. As a consequence, a disproportionate number of African American drug dealers may be arrested, leading to racial disparities in drug prosecutions and sentencing. To the extent that the concentration of investigation and arrests in African American communities exceeds that in white communities, without reason to believe that African Americans offend at a greater rate than whites, then such practices amount to unjustified "over-policing." Over-policing may also occur when the police concentrate their efforts not on illegal activity, but on legitimate citizen behavior with the hope that in the process of investigation some evidence of crime may be uncovered. This kind of over-policing is what occurs when police conduct drug sweeps in Black neighborhoods and detain African American motorists for "driving while Black."

"Driving while Black" refers to the police practice of using the traffic laws to routinely stop and detain Black motorists for the investigation of crime in the absence of probable cause or reasonable suspicion for the stop. There is reason to believe that this is a widespread practice performed by police officers throughout the nation. Many prominent African Americans have reported being victimized by these stops. Although they have unfortunately become routine, "[s]uch stops and detentions are by their very nature invasive and intrusive."

The intrusive and invasive practice of detaining African American motorists without cause has occurred in other contexts as well. "Driving while Black" is essentially a type of racial profiling. People have claimed to be the victims of racial profiling while walking on the street, shopping or strolling through department stores and malls, seeking entry into buildings, traveling through airports, or passing through immigration checkpoints. In all of these situations, African Americans are subjected to police harassment and denied the freedom of movement to which other citizens are entitled.

Perhaps the most egregious intrusion into the rights of African Americans occurs during so-called "drug sweeps." "Drug sweeps" or "street sweeps" occur when the police simply close off a neighborhood and indiscriminately detain or arrest large numbers of people without lawful justification. Police conduct street sweeps in order to subject those caught in the dragnet to questioning and searches in the absence of probable cause or reasonable suspicion. One such drug sweep, which occurred in New York City, was described in the following account: In a publicized sweep on July 19, 1989, the Chief of the Organized Crime Control Bureau (OCCB), led 150 officers to a block in upper Manhattan's Washington Heights. Police sealed off the block and detained virtually all of the 100 people who were present there for up to two hours, during which time the police taped numbers on the chests of those arrested, took their pictures and had them viewed by undercover officers. By the end of the operation, police made only 24 felony and two misdemeanor arrests . . . which strongly suggests there was no probable cause to seize those who were arrested.

African Americans have long had to suffer police harassment and disregard for their rights. However, the drug war made the types of police harassment described above more likely to occur. One of the key consequences of the War on Drugs is that courts have relaxed their oversight of the police. In a series of decisions written since the declaration of war on drugs, the Supreme Court has made it easier for the police to establish grounds to stop and detain motorists and pedestrians on the street. In particular, two recent decisions have made it virtually impossible for African Americans to move freely on the streets without police intervention and harassment.

In *Whren v. United States*, the Supreme Court held that an officer's subjective motivations for a stop were irrelevant to Fourth Amendment analysis, and that the legitimacy of the stop should solely be determined by an objective analysis of the totality of the circumstances. Under Whren, so long as an officer can offer an "objective" reason for a detention or arrest, it does not matter whether the officer's "real" reason for the stop was racist. In *Illinois v. Wardlow*, the Supreme Court ruled that the flight of a middle-aged Black man from a caravan of Chicago police officers provided reasonable suspicion for his detention and search. In the majority's view, African Americans have no legitimate reason to flee the police. Thus, the Court, in essence, established a per se rule that flight equals reasonable suspicion. As Professor Ronner has remarked, this perspective takes "an apartheid approach to the Fourth Amendment and actively condones police harassment of minorities."

NO-KNOCK WARRANTS, SWAT TEAMS AND MILITARY-STYLE POLICE TACTICS

The War on Drugs has led to the militarization of police departments across the nation. More specifically, it has led to the increased deployment of military-style tactics for crime control in African American communities, with a correspondently greater potential for death and destruction of property. As these new tactics have become commonplace, the role of police has changed, altering the character of many police departments from law enforcement agencies to military occupation forces.

The militarization of local police forces can be traced to the proliferation of paramilitary police units, often referred to as Special Weapons and Tactics (SWAT) teams. Los Angeles established the first SWAT team in the 1960s. Originally, paramilitary police units were intended for use in special circumstances, such as hostage situations and terrorist attacks. In the 1960s and 70s, there were few SWAT units; those that existed were typically found in large metropolitan areas. However, the policies and practices of the drug war encouraged the use of SWAT teams to expand rapidly into small and medium sized cities throughout the country. As a consequence, "most SWAT teams have been created in the 1980s and 1990s." A study by Peter Kraska and Victor

Kappeler showed that by 1997, in cities with populations over 50,000, SWAT teams were operated by nearly ninety percent of police departments surveyed. Surprisingly, the survey also disclosed that seventy percent of the police departments in cities under 50,000 had paramilitary units, as well.

SWAT units have provided a conduit for the transfer of military techniques and materials into the hands of ordinary police departments. As a result of a 1994 Memorandum of Understanding between the Justice Department and the Department of Defense, civilian police departments have access to "an array of high-tech military items previously reserved for use during wartime." Between 1995 and 1997, the U.S. military donated 1.2 million pieces of military hardware to domestic police departments, including 73 grenade launchers and 112 armored personnel carriers. Other sophisticated equipment provided to police departments includes the following: "automatic weapons with laser sights and sound suppressors, surveillance equipment such as Laser Bugs that can detect sounds within a building by bouncing a laser beam off a window, pinhole cameras, flash and noise grenades, rubber bullets, bullet-proof apparel, battering rams, and more."

Although originally intended for extreme and dangerous situations that were beyond the response capability of regular police patrols, the ubiquity of SWAT teams means that police departments often use their paramilitary units for routine law enforcement activities. The main use of a SWAT team in departments throughout the country appears to be to support the drug war. According to Kraska and Kappeler, the respondents to their survey "reported that the majority of call-outs were to conduct what the police call "high risk warrant work," mostly "drug raids." Less than twenty percent of paramilitary police unit calls were for situations understood as typically amenable to SWAT team intervention. Particularly in so-called "high crime areas," police departments are likely to use SWAT teams as proactive units to seek out criminal activity, as opposed to using them solely to respond to a crisis situation. Kraska and Kappeler found 107 departments that used paramilitary police units as a proactive patrol in high crime areas. According to some of the SWAT team commanders that Kraska and Kappeler interviewed, "[T]his type of proactive policing—instigated not by an existing high risk situation but one generated by the police themselves—is highly dangerous for both PPU [police paramilitary unit] members and citizens."

Warrant work conducted by SWAT teams "consists almost exclusively of what police call 'no-knock entries.'" The potential danger of allowing police officers to enter homes and businesses without announcing their identity and purpose has been well-known since colonial times. Officers may startle residents who may seek to defend their homes. Officers may inadvertently harm residents or innocent bystanders by the use of force necessary to effect the sudden entry of targeted buildings. Breaking into buildings through surprise and stealth seems like a tactic better suited to an occupying army, then to civilian peace officers. However, the drug war has worn down the traditional resistance to the no-knock warrant. Since the onset of the drug war, courts have been willing to legalize no-knock warrants and issue them to the police. Thus, African American communities are now subject to this potentially dangerous and intimidating police technique.

The extension of paramilitary police units into everyday policing not only escalates the degree of force and violence that may be interposed between citizens and the state, it also escalates the likelihood that more forceful methods will actually be used. In the context of a war on drugs, the identification of drug users and dealers as an enemy upon whom force may be used, is not surprising. The very use of the metaphor of "war," as a conceptual matter, implies the use of force.

As Kraska and Kappeler state: [I]t takes little acumen to recognize how the metaphor of "war"—with its emphasis on occupation, suppression through force, and restoration of territory—coincides naturally with the "new science" of the police targeting and taking control, indeed ownership, of politically defined social spaces, aggregate populations, and social problems with military-style teams and tactics.

Thus, the growing collaboration between the police and the military can be expected to have ideological consequences, as well as technological ones. As police paramilitary units train with military organizations, they may be encouraged to develop what amounts to a "warrior mentality." While training "may seem to be a purely technical exercise, it actually plays a central role in paramilitary subculture," as several scholars of police behavior have observed. The inoculation of a "warrior mentality" in police officers, however, is inappropriate because police and military have different social functions: The job of a police officer is to keep the peace, but not by just any means. Police officers are expected to apprehend suspected law-breakers while adhering to constitutional procedures. They are expected to use minimum force and to deliver suspects to a court of law. The soldier on the other hand, is an instrument of war. In boot camp, recruits are trained to inflict maximum damage on enemy personnel. Confusing the police function with the military function can have dangerous consequences. As Albuquerque police chief Jerry Glavin has noted, "If [cops] have a mind-set that the goal is to take out a citizen, it will happen."

The danger that SWAT teams pose to inner-city communities has been exposed by several incidents in which citizens have been unnecessarily harmed as a result of paramilitary police activity. In Dinuba, California, a man was wrongly killed when a SWAT team stormed his house looking for one of the man's sons. The man was shot fifteen times before he or his wife could determine who was breaking into their house and why. Albuquerque, New Mexico has experienced several controversial SWAT team killings. Professor Samuel Walker of the University of Nebraska was hired by the City of Albuquerque to evaluate police department policies and procedures. According to Walker, "The rate of killings by the police was just off the charts. . . . They had an organizational culture that led them to escalate situations upward rather than de-escalating. . . . [T]he mindset of the warrior is simply not appropriate for the civilian officer charged with enforcing the law."

As a consequence of the War on Drugs, the use of military-style weapons and tactics by police departments throughout the nation has become routine. Police departments are locked in a race to see who can arm themselves with the most powerful weaponry available for civilian use. Yet, the easy manner in which military technology can be obtained, and the militaristic attitudes that police officers using this technology also acquire, pose potential dangers to citizens who are unfortunate enough to encounter paramilitary police units, especially those African Americans who live in the areas where these units regularly patrol.

TONRY'S THESIS: DID DRUG POLICY MAKERS INTENTIONALLY TARGET THE BLACK COMMUNITY?

In 1995, Michael Tonry, a criminologist and law professor at the University of Minnesota, wrote a book published by the Oxford University Press entitled "Malign Neglect: Race, Crime and Punishment in America." In his book, Tonry proffered a thesis, which generated a significant amount of controversy. Tonry charged that the racial disparities in the criminal justice system were not merely happenstance, but the result of a "calculated effort foreordained to increase [the] percentages [of Blacks in prison]." According to Tonry, the planners of the drug war knew

that the War on Drugs was unnecessary, and that the policies they selected to fight the War on Drugs would not work. More critically, Tonry charged that the drug war's planners were aware that the ineffective policies they proposed to implement would adversely affect African American males.

The War on Drugs was unnecessary, according to Tonry, because drug use was already declining in the United States, and had been doing so for several years. If less and less Americans were using drugs, then a costly war to reduce drug usage would not seem to make sense. More importantly, Tonry charged, even if the drug war was necessary to address a burgeoning problem with illegal drugs in the United States, the policies the drug warriors selected to deal with that problem were not likely to work. Tonry argues that changes in drug usage are best effected through a combination of supply reduction and demand reduction strategies. The anti-drug policies of the Reagan and Bush administrations were skewed too far in favor of supply reduction approaches to be effective. The drug policy strategists who planned the drug war, Tonry asserts, knew this.

Tonry's most explosive charges addressed the racial imbalance in drug war motivated arrests, prosecutions, and convictions. According to Tonry, "The War on Drugs foreseeably and unnecessarily blighted the lives of hundreds of thousands of young disadvantaged [B]lack Americans." Tonry believes the planners of the drug war knew their decision to increase penalties for drug possession and sale would adversely and disproportionately affect African Americans because while white middle-class drug use was declining, other data showed that drug use among poor, urban African Americans and Hispanics remained steady. In Tonry's words: The white-shirted-and-suspendered officials of the Office of National Drug Control Policy understood the arcane intricacies of NIDA surveys, DUF, and DAWN better than anyone else in the United States. They knew that drug abuse was falling among the vast majority of the population. They knew that drug use was not declining among disadvantaged members of the urban underclass. They knew that the War on Drugs would be fought mainly in the minority areas of American cities and that those arrested and imprisoned would disproportionately be young blacks and Hispanics.

Thus, the adverse impact of the drug war could not be accidental. The architects of the drug war had to know who would be most affected by their policies. They had to understand what Daniel Patrick Moynihan pointed out in 1993 when he said "[B]y choosing prohibition [of drugs] we are choosing to have an intense crime problem concentrated among minorities." At best, according to Tonry, the explosion in the Black prison population was "a foreseen but not an intended consequence" of the War on Drugs. At worst, Tonry says, it was "the product of malign neglect"—a consequence that was malicious and evil.

If the architects of the drug war knew their plans would have devastating impact on the African American community, then they apparently did not care. What could provide the motive for such an assault on African Americans? According to Tonry, the motive was two-fold. First, Tonry claims that to the extent the Reagan and Bush administrations attempted to craft an actual drug policy, they intended to use the criminalization of behaviors disproportionately found in the African American and Hispanic community to shape and encourage anti-drug values and beliefs in the white community. Thus, the drug war was "an exercise in moral education" that inflicted great damage on young African Americans and Hispanics "primarily for the benefit of the great mass of, mostly white, non-disadvantaged Americans." But Tonry suggests there is another, more sinister, reason for the sacrifice of the young African American victims of the drug war. According

to Tonry, the drug war was "launched to achieve political, not policy objectives." Reagan's advisors wanted to reap the political benefits of appearing tough on drugs at a time when drug use had fallen into disfavor with the American public. The drug war, then, was a cynical way to "use. . . disadvantaged [B]lack Americans as a means to the achievement of politician's electoral ends."

DRUGS, MYTHS, AND RACE

Blacks and Cocaine

The identification of African Americans with cocaine predates the recent panic over crack cocaine and the current War on Drugs. African Americans were associated with cocaine use as early as the 1890s. At that time, cocaine was widely available in the United States, particularly in the South, in the form of patent medicines and soft drinks. While cocaine use was then acceptable for whites, it was considered dangerous to allow African Americans access to the drug. Around the turn of the century, as racism against African Americans solidified, whites viewed African Americans as threatening in new ways. White society viewed Africans as docile and childlike during slavery, but following the Reconstruction, whites came to view Blacks as a threat to white property, interests, and lives. African Americans were thought to be untrustworthy scoundrels, who if left uncontrolled, would rob and steal. From the Reconstruction on, propaganda in the North and South portraying the vulnerability of white families, particularly white women, to Black scoundrels was common.

It was thought Blacks used cocaine to fortify themselves for criminal activities. Whites believed cocaine would make Blacks bolder, more aggressive, and oblivious to pain. Rumors stated that Blacks under the influence of cocaine were more inclined toward crime and harder to catch. Most importantly, "[s]outhern whites believed that cocaine use by [B]lacks would cause them to 'forget their place' and lead to violence against whites, particularly the dreaded rape of white women." The belief that cocaine made African Americans impervious to pain led police departments all across the South to switch from .32 caliber revolvers to the more lethal .38 caliber revolvers.

DRUGS AS A THREAT TO WHITE SOCIAL CONTROL

The use of drugs threatens white control of non-European communities and individuals. It threatens the present social and political order in three ways. First, social control is ultimately maintained by coercion. African Americans, and other people of color who know they are oppressed, submit to the oppression predominantly because of their fear of the consequences should they not. Drug intoxication may prevent people of color from recognizing the extent of the threat posed by white institutions of social control, thereby undermining the coercive power of the white power structure. Secondly, people of color who use drugs are by this very act rebelling against the authority of the white power structure. Their disobedience may cause them to lose respect for white authority or may cause others to lose respect for white authority. Finally, and perhaps most significantly, drug use may tie users to cultural institutions and cultural practices that are not dominated by whites and are competitive to white institutions. Different cultures have different ways of relating to mind altering substances. One culture may use a substance for recreational purposes, while another culture may use the drug for religious purposes. In either case, the social practice of "drug use" requires the establishment of a network of social institutions that "support" the use (or abuse) of the substance in question. For example, in the United States, the

cultural interpretation of cocaine use has required the establishment of social institutions of ostracization, punishment and purification (e.g. jails, prisons, drug abuse treatment programs, etc). But this constellation of social institutions is culturally specific. That is, cocaine use does not necessarily have to result in the same set of social institutions. This is most readily seen in cases such as the use of peyote by Native Americans, or ganja by Rastafarians, but in any case, the principle is the same. The suppression of the drug is also the suppression of a particular cultural point of view.

Every society uses natural and artificial substances to alter moods and change psychology. The substances used for such purposes in a given culture are familiar. Their effects are well known and understood. Substances used for such purposes by other cultures, on the other hand, are unknown, and their use is viewed as strange and unnatural. According to historian John F. Richards: Generally each society and culture has drugs of choice that have been assimilated to its cultural practices. The pleasures of these familiar drugs are known; their dangers minimized by taboos and social rituals of consumption, and their damage contained [or] ignored. Similar adaptations in other cultures are invisible, or, if seen, grotesque. The use of unknown drugs produces fear precisely because they are unknown, and because what is perceived of as "other" is not controlled. . . .

THE SYMBIOTIC RELATIONSHIP OF RACE AND CRIME

Even with an understanding of the multiple ways in which crime can be used and with the recognition that the definition of crime is politically contested, our theory of race and crime is not yet complete. For within this interactive network of meaning, race plays a particularly important role. Race forms a special relationship with crime, which enhances the ideological function of both of these socially constructed categories. In this relationship, race helps to define crime, and crime helps to define race.

Crime as a Definer of Race

In addition to establishing the boundaries of the consensus, crime functions as a means of defining race. Once conduct is defined as criminal, it is then excluded from the consensus. It is behavior in which law-abiding citizens, who are within the cultural mainstream do not engage. But, this conceptual distinction does not apply to persons who are part of the racialized "other." The "other" is impressed with the negative characteristics that those who occupy the center, or who are within the consensus, wish to exclude. That is, race and crime share the same conceptual space within the discourse of social formation. They are both outside of the center, and the demarcation of one lends itself to the social construction of the other.

Crime, then, is intimately associated with race. Crime sets the borders of race and crime is language that constitutes the definition of race. African Americans, in particular, have been defined by their proclivity to commit certain criminal acts. Theft, rape, and drug use have all been associated with African Americans. Floyd Weatherspoon describes the white culture's view of African American males succinctly: "Generally, stereotypical attitudes and feelings from white Americans and foreigners are that black males are overly aggressive, violent, involved in drugs, dishonest, shiftless and lazy, desirous of white women, lacking in work ethics, and are often rapists and criminals." Without crime it would be difficult to describe African Americans other than in physical terms. Crime gives content to the image of African Americans produced in western cultures. In fact, the very notion of race is determined by socially constructed notions of crime.

Race as a Definer of Crime

While crime is a definer of race, at the same time, race is a definer of crime. That is, those acts that are conceived of as criminal, as being outside of the consensus, are often the very acts that are associated with African people and other people of color. According to Dorothy Roberts, a leading criminal law theorist, the very meaning of crime is racially determined: Not only is race used in identifying criminals, it is also used in defining crime. In other words, race does more than predict a person's propensity for committing neutrally defined offenses. Race is built into the normative foundation of the criminal law. Race becomes part of society's determination of what conduct to define as criminal. Crime is actually constructed according to race.

Consequently, conduct can become criminalized simply because African people engage in that conduct—either because negative connotations are supplied to the conduct through its association with African people, or because controlling the conduct is desirable as a means to control Africans. Nowhere is this more apparent than in connection with drugs. The previously described association of the Chinese with opium, Chicanos with marijuana, and Africans with cocaine led to the criminalization of these substances. Furthermore, when the same substances (at least in the case of marijuana and cocaine) began being used by white youths in the 1960s and 70s, then there was a movement to decriminalize them and provide drug treatment programs.

Consequences from the Combination of Race and Crime

The fact that race defines crime, and crime defines race, produces three consequences that are worth examining. The first is the production of racism from the intersection of race and crime. The second is the criminogenic effect of racism, and the third is the obscuration and legitimation of racist oppression.

Crime and the Production of Racism

Crime as a social phenomenon creates racism. When crime occurs, whites generally associate Blacks and certain other people of color with criminal activity. This association creates animus in the white community towards people of color. This is observable in every public opinion survey about racism. Substantial portions of the white majority have repeatedly admitted that they dislike or are suspicious of Blacks and Hispanics because they believe these groups cause crime.

Crime causes fear and fear is the chief ingredient in racism. This is true whether the criminal behavior feared by the white majority is behavior that is indigenous to the African American community or something that was imposed on that community by the policies and practices of the white majority. It is the prevalence of crime in communities of color and, more specifically, the representation of crime as the unique province of communities of color that has fostered and encouraged racism in American society.

Racism and the Creation of Crime

Racism produces crime in ways that go beyond that definitional sense we have already discussed. White racism—that is animus toward African Americans and other people of color—leads to racist oppression. Racist oppression is made up of those social practices that are designed to subjugate and punish a disfavored group, to enable those who hold racist sentiments to experience the pleasure of superiority. The history of the United States is replete with examples of the use of the criminal justice system as an instrument of racist oppression. These include the imposition of the death penalty, police brutality, the denial of the right to

counsel, and the long and protracted struggle to get African Americans on juries. Indeed, in a social landscape where the occurrence of racism is, at least openly, discouraged, the criminal justice system may be one of the few venues where racist practices can continue.

Consequently, racism leads to the creation of crime in order to produce opportunities for racist oppression. The corollary in interpersonal relations would be for a tormentor to invent transgressions so that he or she could inflict more pain on his or her target. In the criminal justice system, racism calls for more and more criminal offences, particularly offences of the character that persons of color are likely to commit, and harsher and harsher criminal punishments.

Crime and the Legitimation of Racist Oppression

Crime produces racism and racism produces crime. But crime does more than simply produce racial animus toward disfavored groups. Crime plays a unique role in the whole structure of racist oppression. This is because crime actually legitimates and masks the very racism it creates. Crime provides an easy and convenient excuse for racist attitudes and behaviors. As a result of the working and reworking of the consensus as political ideas compete for acceptance, racism is currently a disfavored political ideology. Racism still holds tremendous sway as a persuasive force and even more as a subterranean cause of conduct, either unrecognized or not admitted. But this residual power of racist ideology must remain hidden and crime provides the perfect hiding place. Crime generates race hatred and focuses it on its target, while claiming all along that it is not so.

Open racial animus toward a member of a non-white group is not acceptable in most mainstream social circles, but animus toward a criminal is not only acceptable, it is encouraged. Even the most elite gentleman is free to hate criminals and even slavery is all right, under the Constitution, if it is imposed as a punishment for crime. It matters not, in this analysis, whether the ranks of criminals are disproportionately Black, or whether racial discrimination contributed to the numbers of Africans entrapped in the system. The fact that they can be called criminals justifies the hatred directed toward them.

Thus, cycling through a semiotic system of articulation, crime produces racism, racism produces crime, and crime produces again more racism. At the same time, crime also legitimizes the very racism it produces. Consequently, the criminal justice system can easily be called the most significant source of racism today, and its greatest protector. The criminal justice system is therefore the weak link in any serious effort to rid American society of racism. Social equality cannot be had unless the criminal justice system as refuge for racist ideology is eliminated.

CONCLUSION

Because of their historic connection to drugs in the American public consciousness, African Americans provide a ready and available target for the nation's war on drugs. Socially constructed as an "other" which is both lascivious and violent, African Americans provide the perfect source when white policy makers seek out both drug users and drug dealers for punishment and ostracization. The close connection of race and

crime in American culture helped lead to the identification of drugs as the preeminent threat facing the nation as Ronald Reagan assumed the presidency. Once drugs were identified as a threat, African Americans were sure to be identified as the source of that threat.

But the culpability of African people in the Euro-American mind is not limited to drugs. Since race actually defines crime and crime produces racism, African Americans will constitute "the usual suspects" no matter what the social concern. The drug war is just a specific instance of this general problem. To address the general problem, and thereby drain the pool of surplus criminality, American culture has to be reshaped. The deep and sometimes hidden attraction to racism in American culture must be confronted head on. In particular, the way racism is both invoked and sheltered within the criminal justice system must be addressed and eliminated. The criminal justice system, I have argued, provides the foundation for racist attitudes and behaviors throughout society. When the criminal justice foundation of racial prejudice is shattered, the entire racist edifice will fall.

STUDY QUESTION

What evidence does Kenneth Nunn put forward to support his argument that the war on drugs has targeted black communities?

CHAPTER 4

Inequality in the American Family

INTRODUCTION

Two family tragedies occurring at opposite sides of the country put family violence back in the public spotlight. The catastrophes surrounding O. J. Simpson and the brutal murder of his estranged wife Nicole Brown Simpson in Los Angeles, California, and Susan Smith who murdered her two young boys in Union, South Carolina, assaulted the public's consciousness about intimate relationships that often languish in vicious maltreatment. One could also consider the killing of six-year-old JonBenet Ramsey in the basement of her parent's Colorado home and the murder of Bonnie Lee Bakley and the subsequent prosecution and acquittal of Robert Blake. Prosecutors in the Simpson case specifically portrayed the murder of Nicole Simpson as the additive outcome of years of abuse by her ex-husband. Following O. J. Simpson's arrest for the murder of his ex-wife, the American public learned from media reports that Simpson pleaded no contest to criminal charges of spousal battery against Nicole Simpson. O. J. Simpson's sentence was incredibly light; he served no jail time, paid $200 in fines, contributed $4,500 to a shelter for battered women, performed 120 hours of community service, and the court placed him on two years' probation. The court also permitted a psychiatrist to treat Simpson over the telephone between public appearances. To many commentators, Simpson's unusually light sentence illustrates the cavalier attitude of justice professionals toward cases of wife abuse. [1] Indeed, scholars have addressed the severe inadequacy of state justice systems to deal effectively with domestic violence.

> [I]n the incidents of violence against women, at every step of the way, the criminal justice system poses significant hurdles for victims. The gender biases within state law enforcement and the state judicial systems prevent the existing laws from being adequately and

evenly enforced, especially those concerning domestic violence. . . . [I]n many incidents of domestic violence police may refuse to take reports; prosecutors may encourage defendants to plead to minor offenses; judges may rule against victims on evidentiary matters. This response to domestic violence cases commonly stems from the misperception of the victim's situation and the belief that the woman should simply leave her abuser. In the rare case where a domestic violence victim's attacker is brought to justice, it is important to recognize that the criminal system's remedies and the battered women's needs may not correspond.[2]

Susan Smith rolled her car into a lake near her home, drowning her two young sons—three-year-old Michael and fourteen-month-old Alex. Smith initially claimed that a black man had kidnapped her sons in a car jacking. For nine days, fear of the fate of Susan Smith's two young children gripped the nation. The public's overwhelming interest and the incessant media coverage eventually resulted in Smith's confession that she had murdered her children. Smith claimed she had been suffering from extreme depression over a failed love affair and that she was suicidal. In the Susan Smith case, the public could not understand why a supposedly loving mother would kill her innocent children. The public could not understand why Susan Smith fabricated a story in which a black man had kidnapped her children.[3]

These are horrifying cases. Yet they epitomize our conventional notions about family violence in U.S. society. Contrary to popular belief, we cannot limit domestic violence to crimes of husbands against wives, or adult children to aging parents, or mothers to adolescent children. The dimensions of family violence far exceed our stereotypical imagery. Women are regularly the aggressors in domestic violence, elderly abuse is frequently committed by an elder spouse, and often teenage children beat and kill their parents.[4] Some scholars explain that *facts* about domestic violence *contradict* our fixed notions about the problem:

> Half of spousal murders are committed by wives, a statistic that has been stable over time. The 1985 National Family Violence Survey, funded by the National Institute of Mental Health and supported by many other surveys, revealed that women and men were physically abusing one another in roughly equal numbers. Wives reported that they were more often the aggressors. Using weapons to make up for physical disadvantage, they were not just fighting back. The *Journal for the National Association of Social Workers* found in 1986 that among teenagers who date, young women were violent more frequently than boys. Mothers abuse their children at a rate approaching twice that of fathers, according to state child-protective service agencies surveyed by the Children's Rights Coalition. Because men have been taught to "take it like a man" and are ridiculed when they reveal they have been battered by women, women are nine times more likely to report their abusers to the authorities.[5]

Recent data show that nearly 112,000 men are violently victimized by intimates in the Untied States.[6] In *Recognizing Domestic Violence Directed Towards Men*, Alexander Detschelt explains that domestic violence against men is a severe problem in America and that we must overcome gender stereotypes about domestic violence, conduct accurate studies, and enact responsible legislation if U.S. society is going to address legitimately the problem of male victimization in domestic situations.[7]

DIMENSIONS OF FAMILY VIOLENCE

Law enforcement agencies across the country arrest some 141,000 persons for offenses against family and children annually. Of these arrests, 75.5 percent are male offenders and 24.5 percent are female offenders.[8] Arrest figures for offenses against family and children reveal that the percentage of females less than eighteen years old arrested for these offenses has increased by 0.4 percent over recent years while the percentage of males less than eighteen years of age for these offenses decreased by 10.0 percent.[9] For persons over eighteen years of age arrested for offenses against family and children, the number of males arrested increased by 1.3 percent and the number of females increased by 5.7 percent.[10] The problem with these figures, however, is that they tell only part of the story. We do not know, for example, if the arrests over this two-year period were for offenses involving sibling-to-sibling or child-to-parent violence, or if the arrests were primarily for the abuse of infant children by teenage parents.

Justice statistics reveal racial disparities in arrest data regarding family violence. Law enforcement personnel arrest more white persons for offenses against family and children than persons belonging to other racial or ethnic groups. White persons account for slightly more than 68 percent of all arrests for offenses against family and children, black offenders are nearly 29 percent, 1.3 percent are American Indians or Alaskan Natives, and 1.5 percent are Asian or Pacific Islanders.[11] Justice statistics do not include arrests for offenses against family and children for the Latino population. In any event, police arrest whites and Asian Americans for offenses against family and children proportionate to their representation in the U.S. population, whereas blacks and American Indians are overrepresented in arrests for offenses against family and children relative to their numbers in the U.S. population.

National victimization data show that current or formal spouses, boyfriends, or girlfriends commit nearly 700,000 nonfatal violent victimizations against intimates annually, and that 85 percent of these intimate partner victimizations are committed against women. Acts of violent victimization include rape, sexual assault, robbery, aggravated assault, and simple assault. Despite these striking statistics, the rates of nonfatal intimate violence appear to have dropped significantly over the last decade. Since 1993, the rate of nonfatal intimate violence against men fell 42 percent and the rate of intimate violence against women declined by 49 percent.[12]

An intimate kills about 33 percent of all female murder victims and 4 percent of all male murder victims—intimate partners killed some 1,247 women and 440 men in 2000. Fatal intimate partner violence appears to have decreased over the past three decades, although the rate of decrease is more significant for men than women. Between 1976 and 2000, the numbers of men murdered by intimates decreased by 68 percent while the number of women killed by an intimate declined by 22 percent over the same period. While the number of homicide victims killed by intimate partners decreased for black males, black females, and white males, the number of white females killed by intimates actually increased over the period by 15 percent. Since 1993, the percentage of all male murder victims killed by an intimate remains relatively stable at 3.7 percent, and the percentage of all female murder victims killed by an intimate increased from 18.5 percent to 33.5 percent. White women experienced most of the fatal victimization increase among domestic partners over this period.

Black intimate partners victimize one another at higher rates than other racial or ethnic groups. Black females are 35 percent more likely than white females to suffer intimate partner violence, and black males are 62 percent more likely than white males to suffer intimate partner violence. Compared to men of races other than whites, black males are more than twice as likely to suffer intimate partner violence. For Latinos, the rate of intimate partner violence is no different from the rate of intimate partner violence for non-Latinos.[13] In *Violence Toward Black Women in a Nationally Representative Sample of Black Families*, Robert Hampton and Richard J. Gelles examine the incidence of violence toward women in black families among a nationally representative sample of nearly six hundred families and found a higher incidence of husband-to-wife and wife-to-husband physical violence among black families.[14] Moreover, young black husbands of a lower socioeconomic status, who have resided in their neighborhoods for a short period and are either unemployed or work part time, are most likely to victimize their wives.

To some researchers the prevalence of violence in American black families results from their status as a colonized people.[15] Indeed, characteristics of intimate partner violence reveal that among black women, being divorced or separated, earning lower incomes, living in rental housing, and living in urban areas are all associated with higher rates of intimate partner victimization.[16] To Robert Staples, the emphasis on violence in the mass media is associated with acts of violence among black youth. One only needs to look at the movies produced by Hollywood—*Boys in the Hood, Strapped*—to observe how violence among black youth is portrayed as part of black culture. The music industry has also capitalized on rap and the *gangster* image of young black men. Violence among black youth, as portrayed in the media and entertainment industries, serves as a tool for white society to colonize black persons. That is, the media and entertainment industries portray violence as an expressive outcome of black social and cultural values. In turn, black persons incorporate violence into their social behavior. Thus blacks replicate violence into their social lives. One can make the same argument for Latino youth whose cultural image in white America is often associated by researchers with that of young black men.

GAY MARRIAGES AND PARENTHOOD

For over thirty years, gay and lesbian couples have sought societal recognition of their families, but American society has reacted with extreme homophobia. The federal government and many state governments define marriage as a legal union *only* between a man and a woman. By barring homosexual couples from marriage, jurisdictions deny gay and lesbian couples marital privileges and benefits including joint property ownership rights, joint income tax returns, and survivorship rights. Yet the legal and political landscape of gay marriages and civil unions is changing rapidly. Although no state recognizes same-sex marriages, the Massachusetts Supreme Court did raise the possibility of a successful challenge to the ban on same-sex marriages when it held that denying marriage licenses to gay couples is unconstitutional. The court argued that denying gay couples the right to marry is incompatible with the constitutional principles of respect for individual autonomy and equality under law.[17] Vermont's Supreme Court ruled that gay couples are entitled to the benefits of marriage—including the use of family law (annulment, divorce, child custody, child support, alimony, domestic violence, adoption, property division), the right to use tort law related to spousal relationships (wrongful death, loss of consortium), medical rights (hospital visitation, notification, power of attorney), family leave benefits, joint state tax filing, and intestate property inheritance. San Francisco's mayor challenged California's prohibition against gay marriages by issuing marriage licenses, claiming that state governments cannot prohibit marriages without a legally valid reason. In August 2004, however, the California Supreme Court voided all same-sex marriages authorized by San Francisco's mayor. In any event, same-sex marriage lawsuits are under way in New Jersey, Oregon, Washington, California, Connecticut, Indiana, Florida, Maryland, and New York.[18]

In responses to challenges to long-standing prohibitions against gay marriages, President George W. Bush called for a constitutional amendment prohibiting homosexual couples from same-sex marriages. Missouri, Louisiana, Hawaii, Alaska, Nebraska, and Nevada have amended their constitutions to prohibit same-sex marriages, and ten other states are considering similar amendments. Some legal commentators have argued that courts should apply the legal rationale established in *Loving v. Virginia* to same-sex marriages.[19] In *Loving*, the high court held that state laws prohibiting interracial marriages are unconstitutional. The *Loving* case involved the 1958 marriage of Richard and Mildred Loving in the District of Columbia. Although the Lovings were residents of Caroline County, Virginia, state antimiscegenation laws prohibited their interracial marriage. After returning to Virginia, state prosecutors convicted the Lovings for violating the prohibition against their interracial marriage, and the court sentenced each of them to one year in jail. The county court suspended their criminal sentences because the Lovings were willing to leave Virginia and not return for twenty-five years. The Lovings returned to Washington, D.C., and in 1963 they filed suit in Virginia challenging the constitutionality of the antimiscegenation law. The Virginia Supreme Court upheld the law, but the U.S. Supreme Court unanimously ruled Virginia and sixteen other states' antimiscegenation laws unconstitutional in 1967.

About 4 million gay and lesbian couples are rearing some 10 million children in the United States. Research shows that homosexual parents do not differ in their parenting behaviors from heterosexual parents. As a result, children raised by homosexual parents have no distinguishable differences in self-esteem, gender identity, sexual orientation, and adolescent development than children raised by heterosexual parents.[20] Despite predictable outcomes of *normality* in homosexual child-rearing practices, law professor Erica Gesing explains in *The Fight to Be a Parent* that many state child welfare agencies still prohibit gay and lesbian couples from participating in foster care and adoption because of their sexual orientation. Gesing notes that without attitudinal changes of Americans toward gay and lesbian people parenting skills, the "best interests of the child" standard will continue to mask the institutional discrimination against homosexuals as foster and adoptive parents.

CHILD VICTIMIZATION

The prevalence of child sexual abuse by Catholic priests and the failure of state child welfare agencies to safeguard children placed in foster care have again focused national attention on child victimization in the United States. One study revealed that

4,692 priests and deacons committed 10,667 incidents of serious sexual offenses against mostly male postpubescent minor children between 1950 and 2002.[21] The compensatory costs associated with the Catholic Church scandal are approaching $600 billion, and there are still about a thousand unsettled cases. Additionally, disclosures of foster care abuses and missing foster children in several states are calling for dramatic reforms in child welfare services in the United States. Inspection reports of state child welfare agencies are showing that thousands of children around the country are lost in state systems and that far too many cases of child abuse and neglect go uninvestigated by state agencies.[22] Florida's child welfare agency, for example, came under attack when authorities discovered that five hundred children in the state's foster care system were missing. Included among them was five-year-old Rilya Wilson whom authorities did not realize had been missing for fifteen months. Caseworkers have yet to find Rilya.[23]

Child protection agencies receive concerns about the welfare of an estimated 4.5 million children throughout the United States. Of these, child protection agencies accept for investigation and assessment roughly 1.8 million cases. About half (56.5 percent) of the reports alleging child abuse or neglect are made by educators, law enforcement and legal personnel, social services personnel, medical personnel, mental health professions, and child day-care and foster care providers. Friends, neighbors, and relatives also make about half (43.6 percent) of all reports of child victimization. Authorities substantiate about 30 percent of reported cases of child abuse.[24] Research shows that the physical, psychological, behavioral, and societal consequences of child abuse and neglect are detrimental, the effects of which can disable children for a lifetime.[25] Yet, in many states, child protection services fail to investigate adequately the complaints of child abuse and neglect. For example, state investigators never substantiated most of the complaints against Houston's Child and Adolescent Development Center concerning child abuse and neglect.[26] In other cases, state agency continue to send foster care children to private child placement agencies despite learning that the agencies had hired managers suspected of endangering children in the past.[27]

Child protective services place about 20 percent of child victims in foster care and remove about 4 percent of nonvictims to short-term placements during investigations for child abuse and neglect. Yet, as Andrea Charlow explains in *Race, Poverty, and Neglect*, child welfare systems remove poor children from their families more often than nonpoor children. Because child abuse is more prevalent among poor families than nonpoor families, there is a disparate impact of removing children from families of color since minorities are overrepresented among the poor. One result is that the percentage of African American and Native American children in the child welfare system is greater than the percentage of each group in the U.S. population.[28]

Even so, nearly a million children in the United States annually are victims of child abuse or neglect. Although child victimization rates have decreased since 1990, the rate of victimization is still high at 12.3 children per 1,000 children in the U.S. population. Most child victimization involves neglect, but 20 percent of victimized children are physically abused, 10 percent are sexually abused, and 7 percent suffer emotional maltreatment. Perpetrators victimize younger children more often than older children, with children younger than three years having the highest rates of victimization at

16.0 per 1,000 children. In addition, young girls suffer maltreatment slightly more often than young boys.[29]

Child victimization is most common among white families. More than half of all cases of child abuse and neglect occur in white families, about 26 percent of all child abuse cases are in black families, about 0.8 percent occur in Asian American families, about 1.4 percent are in American Indian families, and nearly 10 percent of all child abuse cases take place in Latino families. Compared to their percentages in the U.S. population, however, child victimization is overrepresented in minority families and underrepresented in white families. The highest rates of child victimization occur in American Indian and Alaskan Native families (21.7 percent) and African American families (20.2 percent). The child victimization rate in white families is 10.7 percent per 1,000 children.[30]

Perpetrators of child victimization are most often parents. Parents are 80 percent of the perpetrators of violence against children, 7 percent are other relatives, and 3 percent of child victimizers are unmarried partners of parents. Interestingly, roughly 10 percent of the perpetrators of child abuse and neglect are other persons including camp counselors, school employees, and unknown persons. Women (58 percent) perpetrate child victimization more than men (42 percent). Of child sexual predators, 29 percent are relatives other than parents (3 percent), and nearly 25 percent are other persons in nonrelative or non-child-care roles.[31] Moreover, about 1,400 children die each year from abuse and neglect, and three quarters of them are children younger than four years. Researchers attribute a third of child fatalities to neglect; physical and sexual abuse also contribute to child fatalities.[32]

SUMMARY

The O. J. Simpson case opened America's eyes to the plight of women often silenced by a judicial system that seeks to protect them. The Simpson trial instructed American society about how difficult it is for the justice system to hear women that are the victims of spousal abuse. In contrast, the Susan Smith case showed American society the fragility of the family. In particular, the Smith case showed how easy it is for children to become victims. Researchers and practitioners can misperceive family violence. Cultural variation in parenting techniques, for example, often result in physical punishment—such as spanking with a belt or paddle—being perceived as physical abuse. Poverty also plays a role in shaping perceptions of abuse; thus poor children are more likely to be perceived as the victims of abuse than middle-class children are. Researchers and practitioners can also summarily ignore victimization—as in the case of elder victimization.

The political and legal landscape of the American family is changing. Traditional notions of family have focused on heterosexual parents and their children, but changing demographics are challenging our customary ideas about family and its organization and character. The varieties of American families include nuclear families, extended families, spouse-only families, single-parent families, and combined families from divorced couples. Americans must wake up to the idea that large numbers of gay and lesbian couples are bringing children into their families from previous heterosexual relationships, artificial insemination, or surrogate motherhood even if foster parent-hood and adoption are problematic avenues in many states.

ENDNOTES

1. Devon W. Carbado, "The Construction of O. J. Simpson as a Racial Victim," *Harvard Civil Rights—Civil Liberties Law Review*, 32 (1997): 49.
2. Jennifer R. Hagan, "Can We Lose the Battle and Still Win the War?: The Fight Against Domestic Violence After the Death of Title III of the Violence Against Women Act," *DePaul Law Review*, 50 (2001): 919, 933–934.
3. For a discussion on racial hoaxes, see Katheryn K. Russell, *The Color of Crime: Racial Hoaxes, White Fear, Black Protectionism, Police Harassment, and Other Macroaggressions* (New York: New York University Press, 1998); Katheryn K. Russell, "The Racial Hoax as Crime: The Law as Affirmation," *Indiana Law Journal*, 71 (1996): 593.
4. K. Pillemer and D. Finkehor, "Prevalence of Elder Abuse: A Random Sample Survey," *The Gerontologist*, 28 (1988): 51; M. Paulson, R. Coombs, and J. Landsverk, "Youth Who Physically Assault Their Parents," *Journal of Family Violence*, 5 (1990): 121.
5. R. L. McNeely and Gloria Robinson-Simpson, "The Truth About Domestic Violence: A Falsely Framed Issue," *Social Work*, 32 (1984): 485.
6. Shannon M. Catalano, *Criminal Victimization*, 2004, Department of Justice, Bureau of Justice Statistics, National Crime Victimization Survey (September 2005), http://www.ojp.usdoj.gov/bjs/pub/pdf/cv04.pdf.
7. Alexander Detschelt, "Recognizing Domestic Violence Directed Towards Men: Overcoming Societal Perceptions, Conducting Accurate Studies, and Enacting Responsible Legislation," *Kansas Journal of Law and Public Policy*, 12 (2003): 249.
8. U.S. Department of Justice, *Sourcebook of Criminal Justice Statistics Online*, http:// www.albany.edu/sourcebook/pdf/t48.pdf.
9. Ibid.
10. Ibid.
11. Ibid.
12. Callie Marie Rennison, *Intimate Partner Violence, 1993–2001*, U.S. Department of Justice, Bureau of Justice Statistics (February 2003), http://www.ojp.usdoj.gov/bjs/pub/pdf/ipv01.pdf.
13. Callie Marie Rennison and Sarah Welchans, *Intimate Partner Violence*, U.S. Department of Justice, Bureau of Justice Statistics (May 2000), http://www.ojp.usdoj.gov/bjs/pub/pdf/ipv.pdf.
14. Robert L. Hampton and Richard J. Gelles, "Violence Toward Black Women in a Nationally Representative Sample of Black Families," *Journal of Comparative Family Studies*, 25 (1994): 105.
15. Robert Staples, "Race and Family Violence: The Internal Colonial Perspective," *Journal of Black Studies*, 38 (1987): 85.
16. Callie Marie Rennison and Sarah Welchans, *Intimate Partner Violence*, U.S. Department of Justice, Bureau of Justice Statistics (May 2000), http://www.ojp.usdoj.gov/bjs/pub/pdf/ipv.pdf.
17. *Goodridge et al. v. Department of Public Health*, 440 Mass. 309 (2004).
18. Cheryl Wetzstein, "Nine States Vying in Gay Marriage Legalization Race," *The Washington Times*, p. A06. September 27, 2004.
19. *Loving v. Virginia*, 388 U.S. 1 (1967).
20. Dolores W. Maney and Richard E. Cain, "Preservice Elementary Teachers' Attitudes Toward Gay and Lesbian Parents," *Journal of School Health*, 67 (1997): 236.
21. *The Nature and Scope of the Sexual Abuse of Minors by Catholic Priests and Deacons in the United States*, A Research Study Conducted by the John Jay College of Criminal Justice, United States Conference of Catholic Bishops (April 16, 2004), http://www.nccbuscc.org/nrb/johnjaystudy/ index.htm.
22. Heather Grier, "America Must Do More to Protect Vulnerable Children," *The Columbus Dispatch*, May 17, 2003, p. 11A.
23. Jack Kresnak, "Across the Country, Concerns Mount About Child Welfare Agencies Cases of the Missing Prompt Call for Reform," *Boston Globe*, August 31, 2002, p. A3.
24. National Clearinghouse on Child Abuse and Neglect, *Child Maltreatment 2002: Summary of Findings*, http://nccanch.acf.hhs.gov/pubs/factsheets/canstats.pdf.
25. National Clearinghouse on Child Abuse and Neglect, *The Long Term Consequences of Child Abuse and Neglect* (March 2004), http://nccanch.acf.hhs.gov/pubs/factsheets/long_term_consequences.cfm.
26. Polly Ross Hughes, "Strayhorn Blasts Child Abuse Probe," *Houston Chronicle*, August 18, 2004, p. B1.

27. Polly Ross Hughes, "Foster Children Sent to Agencies Despite Violations," *Houston Chronicle*, September 11, 2004, p. A1.
28. Andrea Charlow, "Race, Poverty, and Neglect," *William Mitchell Law Review*, 28 (2001): 763.
29. National Clearinghouse on Child Abuse and Neglect, *Child Maltreatment 2002: Summary of Findings*, http://nccanch.acf.hhs.gov/pubs/factsheets/canstats.pdf.
30. Ibid.
31. Ibid.
32. Ibid.

Recognizing Domestic Violence Directed Towards Men: Overcoming Societal Perceptions, Conducting Accurate Studies, and Enacting Responsible Legislation

Alexander Detschelt

This note takes the position that domestic violence against men is in fact a serious social issue that must be fully addressed by overcoming societal perceptions, conducting accurate studies, and enacting responsible legislation.

THE HIDDEN SIDE OF DOMESTIC VIOLENCE

It should be obvious why society assumes that men are almost never victims of domestic violence—such abuse "has been minimized, justified, and ignored for a very long time."

Popular culture has had a great impact on minimizing the problem of domestic violence against men. Upon hearing about the topic of battered men, the public's first reaction is usually that of incredulity and amusement. Historically, battered husbands have been ignored, ridiculed, and chastised. Print media has also made battered men a topic for jokes, a common example being the stereotypical cartoon image of a woman chasing her husband while wielding a rolling pin above her head.

A researcher has also noted that women are depicted as the perpetrators in seventy-three percent of newspaper comics addressing domestic violence situations. Furthermore, surveys regarding public attitudes about slapping have changed dramatically for men, but not for women. Movies and television have continually presented scenes in which women who, upon being subjected to emotionally upsetting circumstances, immediately slap the man who is the cause of them. The audience's reaction can range from that of laughter and cheer to even applause; however, were a man to do the same things, the reaction would be quite the opposite.

The media is also instrumental in perpetuating this stereotype, and in effect is detrimental to the recognition of domestic

Source: Alexander Detschelt, "Recognizing Domestic Violence Directed Towards Men: Overcoming Societal Perceptions, Conducting Accurate Studies, and Enacting Responsible Legislation," Kansas Journal of Law and Public Policy, 12 (2003): 249–261.

violence against men. News headlines regarding domestic violence against men have been phrased in such a way as to be sensational and evoke humor. Even more recently and on a national level, the issue of domestic violence against women has received significantly increased attention since the murder of Nicole Brown Simpson. Unfortunately, the media has not presented similar incidents of domestic violence against men with equal fervor, as evidenced by the Phil Hartman tragedy. These societal reactions and media perceptions are in keeping with the unfortunate, stereotypical view society holds of men as being sturdy and women being the weaker, more helpless sex.

Feminists view domestic abuse as an "essential element of the vast male conspiracy to suppress and subordinate women," not through the individual male, but rather through patriarchy. Furthermore, Gloria Steinem has asserted that "patriarchy requires violence or the subliminal threat of violence in order to maintain itself." Therefore, one would believe that a patriarchal society is directly responsible for domestic violence against women. While no one doubts the existence of a patriarchal society, it is incorrect to hold that domestic violence is a gender issue. The patriarchal model of domestic violence fails when one examines domestic violence in same-sex relationships. For example, lesbians batter each other at about the same rate as couples in heterosexual relationships. Some studies have found even higher figures, finding that abuse and violence occur in more than fifty percent of lesbian relationships as compared to approximately ten percent in other types of relationships. These figures could not exist if domestic violence were in any way related to a patriarchal society. Therefore, society must recognize that domestic violence is not a gender issue, but rather a power issue, stemming from the dominance and control structure that can be found in any relationship.

This gender-neutral view is not reflected in the social programs addressing domestic violence. In literature distributed to victims and perpetrators, gender-neutral language is usually absent and the perpetrators are described as "he," with the victim always being referred to as "her." Some domestic violence counselors honestly believe that continuing such practices is beneficial to combating domestic violence. Similar beliefs are prevalent in domestic violence treatment programs, as evidenced by the widely used Duluth Model. Its creators have conceptualized domestic violence into a "Power and Control Wheel" diagram that "depicts the primary abusive behaviors experienced by women living with men who batter." The authors state that the Duluth Model is meant for battering men and battered women and that it can't work for the treatment of battering women. Treatment programs across the country for batterers are based on the gender-polarizing Duluth Model, and therefore reject other effective methodologies such as couples counseling, family systems theory, and anger management, "in favor of a gender-polarizing view that battering is a conscious strategy by men to assert male dominance over women." The lack of gender-neutrality not only perpetuates the belief that domestic violence only affects women, but also results in direct harm to men, in that "a man seeking help would feel he is not wanted, and cannot be a victim, if the language does not acknowledge his existence."

Due to gender stereotypes regarding domestic violence against men, social ridicule is the fear that confronts male spousal abuse victims. Men perceive society as expecting them to be the strong, dominant party in their intimate relationships, and therefore are less willing to report incidents of domestic violence. Men are less likely to call law enforcement, even when there is an injury, because they feel shame about disclosing family violence, especially since the police adhere to traditional gender role expectations. Hence, the stereotypical male feels shame and inadequacy when he realizes that he cannot keep his wife under control. The impact of domestic violence is also less apparent and less likely to come to the attention of others outside of law enforcement when a man is abused. For example, it is assumed that a man with a bruised or black eye was involved in a fight with another man, he was injured during employment, or was playing a contact sport. Society's disbelief and the humiliation directed towards abused men makes disclosure even more difficult. Since the general public refuses to confront the issue of domestic violence against men, one would assume that in the professional realm of shelters and counseling, there would be more recognition of this problem unfortunately, this is not the case.

In 1999, the National Coalition Against Domestic Violence reported that the number of agencies providing services to battered women in the United States surpassed 2,000. In Ohio, there are neither any battered men's shelters, nor any resources dedicated specifically to helping abused men. These facts clearly indicate that there is no direct support for male victims of domestic violence. The domestic violence movement argues that women's shelters do in fact work with men, when in actuality what they mean is that "they may work with male victims if they [men] happen to show up at their door." As for domestic violence crisis lines, most men would not call such lines because of the assumption that such crisis lines existed only for women. This statement does not take into account the underlying social stereotypes mentioned earlier, which would have the greater effect of further discouraging men from calling such crisis lines.

Another reason for abuse against men not being recognized in the area of domestic violence is that unlike the numerous support groups available for women, there are hardly any men's groups, or more importantly, movements, representing the issues affecting such men. Also, many therapists and clinicians are resistant in believing that women are abusers, and hence rarely ask questions of their male clients about the possibility of domestic violence. For almost thirty years, the "battered women's movement has worked to provide services while, at the same time, advocating for change in laws and institutions . . . [and] . . . since the eighties, there have been . . . programs offering direct services for survivors of domestic violence." While abused women are fortunate to have such resources available to them, the domestic violence movement has neglected to address the problem of abused men in its entirety. This leads to another critical factor that has great influence on whether domestic violence against men will ever be acknowledged.

Advocates against domestic violence continually point out that silence regarding domestic violence only increases the probability that this social problem will intensify, yet these same advocates have acted to ensure that there will not be equal recognition for all victims. According to David L. Fontes, this is due to "any discussion of the problem of "battered men [being] considered politically incorrect." Gender feminists, compared to equity feminists, "are primarily, if not exclusively interested in showcasing the maltreatment of females by males in society and are not particularly interested in showcasing the maltreatment of males by females, especially in the area of spousal abuse and child abuse," says Fontes. These same gender feminists were involved in establishing and operating domestic violence shelters around the country. Without feminists, there might not be the shelters and support available to women today, but it should also be recognized that many shelters across the country have "become havens for feminists to gather and promulgate their beliefs," says Fontes.

Erin Pizzey, founder of the first battered women's shelter in 1972, believes that the shelter movement has been "hijacked" by feminists. Because gender feminists focus their attention on the oppression and victimization of women, it is very difficult for them to acknowledge domestic violence against men, especially since the importance of providing services to abused women would possibly be de-emphasized. This could threaten the budgets allocated for women's shelters and services. The troubling aspect of the domestic violence movement, Fontes says, is that it has "become a feminist political movement more than an agency for helping all victims of domestic violence equally and with the same concern. Although feminists have indeed helped many women, they have done so at the expense of men who are also victims of abuse."

Even within the realm of legal academia, there appears to be a lack of recognition of the problem of domestic violence against men. While there is an astronomical amount of scholarly legal information regarding domestic violence against women, legal writings addressing domestic violence against men is scarce, almost non-existent. Interestingly, the stereotypical notion of equating domestic violence with abused women is prevalent even in legal databases. Of the few legal writings that do mention this paper's topic, the majority criticize the validity of domestic violence against men, and therefore do not analyze their own topic as it pertains to abused men. It is very difficult to address domestic violence against men if one must overcome barriers that hinder the flow and discussion of this topic even in the realm of legal academia.

STATISTICAL DATA AND INTERPRETATION

Although social stereotypes and popular culture affect the way society thinks about domestic violence, statistical data impose the greatest obstacle in having society acknowledge the seriousness of domestic violence directed towards men.

According to the latest National Crime Victimization Survey by the U.S. Department of Justice, in 1998, there were approximately one million non-lethal domestic violence offenses, and 876,340 of them were directed against women. On a local level, of the 2,125 domestic violence cases filed in Summit County, Ohio in 2000, 1,782 were female victims and 343 were male victims. Both national and local statistics emphasize the widely accepted 85/15, female/male domestic violence victimization rates. This ratio is affirmed by various health and medical organizations' startling facts regarding the high degree of domestic violence encountered by females. Therefore, it is very difficult to believe that in fact men and women engage in domestic abuse at almost the same rate as each other.

But how can one honestly make such an assertion, when the majority of other sources indicate to the contrary? The answer obviously lies in the statistical process of gathering and interpreting the data. For example, studies have presented the number of women abused in the United States each year by male partners, ranging from just below one million to almost six million. This should indicate that by employing poor research methodologies, studies can misrepresent the true ratio of male to female abusers.

Current government sponsored policy research has focused exclusively on the risks that women face from domestic violence. For example, of all the domestic violence research projects conducted by the National Institute of Justice, none mentions domestic violence by women directed against men. Several other explanations have been offered to explain the true disparity in the ratio of male to female batterers. For example, each study uses varied definitions for what constitutes domestic violence; some studies only consider serious assault, while others also include slapping, pushing, and kicking. Feminists have stretched the definition of abuse to also include "acts of lying, humiliation, withholding information, and refusing to help with child care or housework." Furthermore, a general pattern of underreporting by men can also contribute to skewed statistics. Abused men fail to complain to authorities at even greater rates than women due to the negative gender stereotypes that result from men admitting that they have been beaten by a woman. Conversely, women are more likely to report their victimization than men. Underreporting is also prevalent in injuries sustained during domestic violence episodes. Two-thirds of the injuries reported as part of a domestic violence-related physical assault are scratches, bruises, or welts. Most men would not consider such inflictions of injury as an assault and therefore would not report it as such. Even if victims of domestic violence do seek medical attention, hospital staffs usually fail to identify domestic violence as the cause of the injuries, especially because men are less inclined to report such injuries due to social stereotypes.

Critics argue that even if the studies did indicate an equal assault rate, the figures should be ignored because they include women acting in self-defense. This is not true in the majority of cases, because mutual abuse is the custom in violent households. Some research suggests that fifty to eighty-three percent of spousal abuse is either bi-directional or mutual assault, and that only ten to twenty percent of assaults by women are clearly for self-defense reasons.

In order to understand that men face similar spousal abuse rates as women, more accurate studies need to be conducted. The result will be undeniable evidence supporting the argument for recognizing domestic violence against men. In the interim, while social scientists and academics debate the statistics, it is imperative that appropriate legislation be enacted to address the legal inequities facing male victims of domestic violence.

THE NEED FOR RESPONSIBLE LEGISLATION

Neither federal nor state legislative bodies have enacted explicit statutes and provisions dealing with domestic violence against men.

Even those domestic violence laws that purport to be gender-neutral do not fully address the concerns of battered men.

The Violence Against Women Act (VAWA) is a primary example of what is wrong with the current state of domestic violence legislation. The very title of the VAWA and the congressional findings underlying its enactment indicate that it encompasses male offenders and female victims. Although it has been argued that the VAWA uses gender-neutral language when referring to substantive legal provisions, it would be intellectually dishonest to state that male victims of domestic violence were even remotely considered as the rationale used for enacting the VAWA. In fact, the VAWA is discriminatory as applied, in that it excludes men from some of the services and support offered to women by the Act. For example, The Safe Homes for Women Act of 1994, which was incorporated into the VAWA, requires "establish[ing] and operat[ing], a national toll-free telephone hotline to provide . . . information on the availability of shelters [throughout the United States] that serve battered women." In terms of financial expenditures, the VAWA mandated the issuance of grants for objectives such as "strengthen[ing] effective law enforcement and prosecution strategies to combat violent crimes against women, and . . . develop[ing] and strengthen[ing] victim services in cases involving violent crimes against women." Funding was also allocated to "develop a research agenda to increase the understanding and control of violence against women," and to overcome gender stereotypes against women. Through the VAWA, a government-sponsored office has been established to deal with domestic violence against women, resulting in service and support initiatives targeted specifically towards women.

States must also be concerned with enacting responsible legislation that adequately addresses men within the domestic violence context. Although society approves of the admission of the battered woman syndrome self-defense into court, it excludes men from claiming such a defense. Of the five states that explicitly admit battered syndrome self-defense into court, three of those states have gender-specific statutes, in that they allow only the battered woman syndrome evidence to be admitted.

One of those states, Ohio, debated in its House whether its battered syndrome statute should be gender-neutral, thereby reading "battered person" or "battered spouse" syndrome, instead of "battered woman" syndrome. The Ohio Senate Judiciary Committee eventually decided against it, thereby passing a gender-specific version of the bill to the Senate, which was then later enacted into law. The committee limited the syndrome to women because it determined that the battered person or spouse syndrome was not an established syndrome. This results in an unfortunate situation for any battered man in Ohio who retaliates due to the abuse he has endured, in that he is precluded from defending himself using legal self-defense instruments that are otherwise readily available to any females accused of retaliating against their aggressors. Furthermore, enacting gender-specific legislation perpetuates the stereotype that only women are capable of being abused, and hence, are the only victims who would have a need for such a defense.

Not only do such gender-specific statutes create a disparity in the protections afforded to male victims of domestic abuse as compared to female victims, but they also invoke constitutional issues of equal protection. The Equal Protection Clause of the Fourteenth Amendment provides in relevant part that "no State shall make or enforce any law which shall . . . deny to any person within its jurisdiction the equal protection of the laws." The United States Supreme Court has interpreted this clause to mean that persons who are similarly situated must be treated alike. Therefore, male victims of domestic violence,

who suffered the same forms of abuse as women and wish to introduce battering syndrome self-defense evidence into court are being denied their constitutional rights.

Although it is true that a few states, such as Pennsylvania, Arizona, and Washington, have appellate or state supreme court decisions allowing battering syndrome self-defense evidence to apply to battered men, by not having explicit gender-neutral statutes, it is more difficult for legal and law enforcement professionals to understand that legislative protections are offered to both genders. Furthermore, by not codifying gender-neutral statutes, male victims of domestic violence are victimized twice; first by their abusers, and second by the judicial system. Now men must fight to convince the judge to overcome social stereotypes, and allow them to introduce battering syndrome self-defense evidence.

It is obvious that gender-specific legislation only perpetuates the stereotype that men are immune from domestic violence, yet changing the scope of the language is not sufficient to overcome all domestic problems. Therefore, new approaches to reducing overall domestic violence must be considered. As Dr. Sally L. Satel says, the "dogma that women never provoke, incite, or aggravate domestic conflict, further, has led to some startling departures in domestic law." Many jurisdictions such as Ohio, have enacted "must-arrest" or "preferred-arrest" laws which mandate that where a "peace officer has reasonable grounds to believe that the offense of domestic violence . . . has been committed . . . it is the preferred course of action in this state that the officer arrest [the offender]." The noticeable advantage is that the offender is immediately removed and any actual abuse or threats of domestic violence cease. Unfortunately, there are also negative aspects to enacting such legislation.

The first disadvantage to "must-arrest" or "preferred-arrest" laws is that the officer at the scene has significant discretion in deciding which party to arrest. As previously mentioned, law enforcement personnel still hold certain stereotypes about the aggressor and will therefore more willingly arrest the male, when in fact, the preferred result would be an arrest of the prime perpetrator. Secondly, "preferred-arrest" policies usually create more tension in an already strained relationship. What would have been considered a minor, non-physical altercation that would not need police intervention, could now result in one of the parties being arrested, thereby creating even greater animosity between the spouses or partners. Finally, because "preferred-arrest" policies result in more arrests, jails become more overcrowded in a shorter amount of time, and the spousal offender may be prematurely released. These adverse consequences are not impossible to overcome, and even with its associated problems, a "preferred-arrest" policy can provide an objective, fair, and vigorous means of dealing with domestic violence for both female and male victims.

PREVENTING HARM TO OTHERS

Domestic violence is "damaging in a number of ways, not just in terms of physical injury," says Philip W. Cook. This damage is compounded by perpetuating the stereotype that males are the perpetrators and females are the victims. Victims of domestic violence suffer blows to their self-esteem, which could result in drug and alcohol abuse, mental illness, attempted suicide, and depression. These consequences not only reduce the victim's ability to be a productive citizen, but also create a burden on the state in terms of providing resources to effectively deal with such problems. Furthermore, not recognizing domestic violence against men will disadvantage other groups as well, including children, women, and sexual minorities.

It must be recognized that violence in the home is a social problem, regardless of whether it is committed by men or women.

Additionally, it is imperative to have assaults by women be a focus of social policy, in order to fully understand the implications and harm to children growing up in a violent household. Children who grow up with domestic violence are more likely to become perpetrators themselves. Murray A. Straus, Richard J. Gelles, and Suzanne Steinmetz state the following statistics in their book on domestic violence:

> Men who had seen parents physically attack each other were almost three times more likely to hit their own wives. . . . Women whose parents were violent had a much higher rate of hitting their own husbands . . . as compared to the daughters of non-violent parents. . . . In fact, the sons of the most violent parents have a rate of wife-beating 1000 percent greater than that of the sons of non-violent parents. . . . The daughters of violent parents have a husband-beating rate that is 600 percent greater than the daughters who grew up in non-violent households. . . .

When a woman engages in violence against a man, by pushing, shoving, or hitting, even if no physical harm results to the man, a message is sent to children that violence is an accepted behavior.

Another significant reason why advocates for female victims of domestic abuse should be concerned about female perpetrators is that when a woman strikes her male partner, her chances of becoming a victim increase as well.

By not recognizing that women can be as abusive as men, the "substantial numbers of women who physically attack their mates do not get the kind of official sanctions and social service help that is commonly available to men," says Philip W. Cook. Pioneering sociologist Suzanne Steinmetz argues that when a man physically assaults a woman, "right away he's put in a program for batterers. . . . He's helped to deal with his problems. He's also sometimes sent to jail. But when a woman does it, it's passed off as [no big deal]. . . . No one says, 'Gosh if you're acting this way, you might be troubled [and need help]. . . .'" For example, as previously mentioned, the Duluth Model is tailored to only aid male perpetrators in terms of counseling and treatment. This effectually denies women the services that they need to deal with their problems.

Additionally, some feminists argue that women have fought very hard to be taken seriously and treated as equals, but by not recognizing their potential to also be abusive, women are again finding themselves portrayed as weak and helpless. These are exactly the same stereotypes that have been traditionally used to justify discriminating against them.

Because society wants to reduce domestic violence with each successive generation, it must be concerned with abuse and violence from both genders. Recognizing that domestic violence is gender-neutral is not enough, for abuse transcends gender and also affects a broad class of society, namely the gay and lesbian population. Since the prevailing societal assumption is that domestic violence involves a man who beats his wife, abuse in same sex relationships is significantly overlooked in social responses to domestic violence. In the early 1990s, studies estimated that approximately five percent of gay men and twenty-six percent of lesbians in relationships experience partner violence and abuse. Does society want to deny this segment of the population the resources, counseling and treatments that are currently available to heterosexual female victims of domestic abuse?

Gay men seeking protection may encounter law enforcement that is unwilling to take same-sex abuse seriously, and therefore not address the true problem. For example, it is common for police officers to believe that a man can defend himself in a dispute, therefore not classifying the assault in terms of domestic violence. Many officers also lack the sensitivity training and pressure from victim advocate groups to take action, because most of the education efforts focus on women.

The argument that same-sex couples are adversely affected because society thinks that only males can be abusers is even more applicable to the lesbian community. Due to the high rate of abuse in lesbian relationships, one can no longer afford to view violence as purely a male phenomenon.

Generally, many lesbians feel that violence in a relationship is a trait inherent only in men, which leaves lesbian battered women outside of feminists' theories that attempt to explain domestic violence as a form of male oppression and patriarchy. Due to a lesbian's feelings of shame and the fact that the lesbian relationship was supposed to free her from male oppression, she is less likely to admit the abuse than a heterosexual woman. Additionally, reporting the domestic violence does not fall into the template that the legal system uses to contextualize the victim's experience: the gendered story. As Krisana M. Hodges explains:

> [The gendered story] allows police officers, attorneys, judges, and juries to hear the story and fill in the gaps of heterosexual women's experiences of abuse. The gendered story of abuse gives credibility to heterosexual women's claims of abuse from their male partners. Additionally, when heterosexual women tell stories which fit into the gendered story of domestic violence, police and judges may use these models as a substitute to fact finding because under this model, heterosexual women's claims of abuse carry a presumption of truth. The story provides that men abuse and that women experience abuse. Heterosexual women need only fill in the details of their own experience. Lesbian battered women must tell a new story—a story of dominance and control, absent the endorsement of gender norms.

Even after overcoming cultural assumptions, if domestic violence laws are found to encompass lesbian battered women, Hodges suspects that they will not "shield [lesbians] against the persistent misunderstandings of same-sex domestic violence infecting the legal process." Given the gendered discourse of domestic violence, judges and juries have difficulty in conceptualizing women as batterers, and therefore may respond to lesbian battery with confusion or denial, in effect blocking protection to lesbian victims.

By continuing to hold gender stereotypes regarding domestic violence, not only men, but children, women, and sexual minorities will suffer, thus creating a greater social problem than already exists. It is imperative that society challenge the heterosexual model of domestic violence, by forcing domestic violence advocates to re-examine the roles of the male batterer and the female victim.

CONCLUSION

"Domestic violence against men is just not a social problem."

This statement was made by Ellen Pence, founder of the nationally acclaimed Domestic Abuse Intervention Project in Duluth, Minnesota, and a leader in the battered women's movement. Such statements are disheartening but are in a sense a wake-up call to how much more needs to be accomplished in order for society to fully realize and deal with the problem of domestic violence against men. Fortunately there are signs of optimism, evident in the fact that an increasing number of women each year are being arrested for domestic assaults. Even in Summit County, Ohio, there has been a visible increase in the past four to five years in the number of arrests of women for domestic violence. Neither social scientists nor law enforcement agencies can explain this increase in arrests, although some theories that have been posited are: (1) that women

are being more aggressive, (2) that women are beating other women, (3) that with the increase in female police officers, gender stereotypes are lessened, and (even more probable) (4) that male victims are increasingly likely to come forward and be believed by both law enforcement officers and the courts. Regardless of the reasons, these statistics give hope that the hidden side of domestic violence is finally beginning to be recognized and presented in a fair manner to enhance social awareness.

Murray A. Straus, co-developer of the National Family Violence Survey, believes that the most important reason for recognizing domestic violence against men is for morality, in that violence of any kind should not be tolerated. The ultimate question, says one commentator, is whether society's perceptions of "masculinity will become more humane and less judgmental," allowing society to acknowledge that women can be as abusive of their partners, as men can. Only by overcoming societal perceptions, conducting accurate studies, and enacting responsible legislation, will equal resources and protections be allocated and made available to all victims of domestic violence, women and men alike.

STUDY QUESTION

What evidence does Alexander Detschelt present to support the position that domestic violence against men is a serious social issue that must be addressed by (1) overcoming societal perceptions, (2) conducting accurate studies, and (3) enacting responsible legislation?

Violence Toward Black Women in a Nationality Representative Sample of Black Families

Robert L. Hampton and Richard J. Gelles

Interpersonal conflicts arise between black males and black females because many black males are aware of their role failures and are inclined to counterattack any perceived challenge to their manhood with violence.

Despite the growth of research on family violence, our knowledge about family violence in families of color or minority families is limited. One reason for this is because there have been few systematic studies of family violence based on representative samples of a single city, state, or the entire country that include a sample of minority families of sufficient size for analysis. A second reason is the perception that such research would lead to more negative assumptions about minority families, especially African-American families. Studies of violence could be perceived by some as de-emphasizing the positive features of black family life while emphasizing the negative features. A third reason is that many researchers are not interested in studying any aspect of non-majority family life. The present study examines spousal violence in a large national survey on family violence and presents its findings concerning prevalence and risk factors for violence in a representative sample of African-American families. The study was designed to examine the incidence, patterns, and causes of husband-to-wife, wife-to-husband, and parent-to-child violence in American families.

STUDYING MARITAL VIOLENCE IN BLACK FAMILIES

In their review of spouse abuse research during the period 1977–1987, Odell Uzell and Wilma Peebles-Wilkins found 13 publications that included a reference to black spouse abuse. Among these articles, two specifically dealt with black subsamples, one with a non-white sample, and one that focused on

Source: Robert L. Hampton and Richard J. Gelles, "Violence Toward Black Women in a Nationally Representative Sample of Black Families," Journal of Comparative Family, 25 (1994): 105–120.

"causes" of black spouse abuse. These 13 articles represented a very small fraction of the articles on marital violence.

The battered women's literature often ignores the experiences of non-majority women. The battered-wife literature typically addresses the issue of ethnicity and abuse in one of three ways: (1) by failing to mention the race of the women studied; (2) by acknowledging that only majority women are included; or (3) by including some women of color but not in proportions comparable to their number in the population. Because there are no official reporting statistics on wife battering, most studies of battered women are based on small, nonrepresentative samples drawn from shelters, clinical populations, social service agencies, or in response to advertisements. Researchers have yet to investigate whether there are issues unique to black women in violent relationships, and if so, what they are and how they can be addressed.

The First National Family Violence Survey is generally cited as the primary (and sole) source of data on the prevalence and incidence of spousal violence in black families. Straus and his colleagues reported that black husbands had higher rates of overall and severe violence toward their wives than white husbands. The rate of severe violence toward wives, or wife abuse, in black families was 113 per 1,000, while the rate was 3 over 1,000 in white household, Black wives were almost twice as likely to engage in acts of severe violence against their husbands (76 per 1,000) compared with white wives (41 per 1,000).

Cazenave and Straus found that when income is controlled, black respondents were less likely to report instances of spousal slapping at every income range except the $6–11,999 level. Black respondents at both the lowest and highest income categories were less likely to report engaging in these behaviors than white respondents with comparable incomes. Cazenave and Straus note that the persistence of higher rates of spousal violence for the large income group containing the black working class, and for blacks in both blue collar and white collar occupational groups, suggests that even aside from income differentials, black spousal violence is notably high.

Cazenave and Straus also found that embeddedness in primary networks is closely associated with lower rates of spousal slapping for black couples than for white couples. For black couples, the number of year, in the neighborhood, the number of children, and the number of non-nuclear family members in the households were all associated with lower levels of spousal violence. In spite of the small sample size (N=147 black families) these data provided some important insights concerning violence in black families. The study revealed that a number of variables must be examined in order to do a thorough comparison. It also revealed that rates of violence among blacks vary by family income, social class, and degree of social network embeddedness.

To assess the effects of race on spousal violence, Lockhart and White and Lockhart found that a larger proportion of middle class African-American women than of middle-class European-American women reported that they were victims of violence by their marital partners. Using data gathered through a purposive sample in a large major southeastern metropolitan city, Lockhart argues that her data support Staples's conclusions that African-American couples are not inherently more violent than European-American couples. Higher levels of violence, when they do exist, may be due in part to the particular social predicament of African-Americans in American society. By this reasoning, many blacks have achieved middle-class positions only recently as a result of relatively recent changes in their lives and may have retained the norms, values, and role expectations of their lower-SES developmental experiences. Aggressive and violent problem solving strategies may be partially related to this background. Many African-Americans also are subject to additional stress because of the uncertainty and tenuousness of their newly acquired position; this situation may influence their use of violence.

The limited research on black spouse abuse reveals several relevant variables. These include occupation, income, embeddedness in social networks, unemployment, and violence in one's family of orientation. Although statistics suggest that black families represent a significant portion of violent families identified and served by agencies, this may in part reflect the actions of gatekeepers and not racial differences in the type, nature, or severity of family violence. Cazenave and Straus's analysis of data from the First National Family Violence Survey seems to suggest that there is a need to examine further factors associated with spouse abuse among blacks.

The Second National Family Violence Survey was designed to address many of the shortcomings of previous research. A comparison of data from the two surveys revealed that overall husband-to-wife violence was unchanged between 1975 and 1985. Severe violence, or "wife beating" declined by 21.8 percent. Furthermore, these data revealed an increase in the rate of overall and severe wife-to-husband violence.

The present study extends the examination of spousal violence in black families and examines the incidence of spousal violence and risk factors for abusive violence in a representative sample of black families.

METHOD

Sample and Administration

A national probability sample of 6,002 households comprised the Second National Family Violence Survey. The sample was drawn using a Random Digit Dial procedure. The sample was composed of four parts. First, 4,032 households were selected in proportion to the distribution of households in the 50 states. Then 958 households were oversampled in 25 states. This was done to assure that there would be 36 states with at least 100 completed interviews per state. Finally, two additional oversamples were drawn— 508 black and 516 Hispanic households. The procedure for identifying the black and Hispanic oversamples was identical to the procedure for developing the main sample. The data analyzed for this paper are based on responses from black respondents selected through both the main sample and black oversample.

To be eligible for inclusion in the sample, a household had to include adults 18 years of age or older who were (a) presently married, or (b) presently living as a male-female couple, or (c) divorced or separated within the last two years, or (d) a single parent with a child under 18 years of age and living in the household. When more than one eligible adult was in the household, a procedure was used to randomly select the gender and marital status of the respondent

Telephone interviews were conducted by trained interviewers employed by Louis Harris and Associates. When telephones were busy or not answered, three call-backs were made before substituting a new household. If contact was made and the subject refused to be screened or to participate, trained "refusal conversion" interviewers were assigned to the household. The response rate, calculated as "completes as a proportion of eligibles," was 84 percent. Interviews lasted an average of 35 minutes.

Defining and Measuring Violence

For the purpose of this research, violence was nominally defined as "an act carried out with the intention, or perceived intention of causing physical pain or injury to another person." The injury could range from slight pain, as in a slap, to murder. The motivation might range from a concern for a person's safety (as when a child is spanked for going into the street) to hostility so intense that the death of the person is desired. Abuse was defined as those acts of violence that had a high probability of causing injury to the person (an injury did not actually have to occur).

The Conflict Tactics Scales (CTS) was used to measure the incidence and frequency of violence. The CTS starts by asking respondents to think of the times when they had a conflict with their child or Spouse or just got angry with them. Respondents are then given a list of tactics that they might have used in these situations of conflict or anger. The tactics range from calm discussion to attacks with a knife or a gun. The 1985 version of the CTS (used for this paper) consisted of 19 tactics, 9 of which refer to acts of violence. The violent acts are: throwing something at the other; pushing grabbing or shoving; slapping or spanking; kicking, biting or hitting with a fist; hitting or trying to hit with something; beating up the other; choking; threatening with knife or gun; or using a knife or firing a gun.

There are various scoring methods for the Conflict Tactics Scales. This study used two indices. The first is, "Most severe form of violence experienced in the last 12 months." This ordinal scoring method has three values: no violence experienced; minor violence (threw something at other; pushed grabbed, or shoved other; slapped or spanked other); and severe violence (kicked, bit, hit with fist; hit or tried to hit other with an object; beat up the other; choked other; threatened with knife or gun; used knife or fire a guy.) The second index is a measure of overall violence. This dichotomous index indicates whether any form of violence occurred at least once in the previous 12 months.

The items of the Conflict Tactics Scales are presented to subjects. The subjects are asked how often they used each technique when they had a disagreement or were angry

with a family member, both in the previous year and in the course of the relationship with the family member.

The reliability and validity of the Conflict Tactics Scales have been assessed over the 18-year period of their development. A full discussion of their reliability and validity can be found in Straus and Gelles. There is evidence of adequate internal consistency, reliability, concurrent validity, and construct validity.

RESULTS

Incidence

Seventeen percent of the wives in our study had at least one violent episode during the survey year (1985). Seven percent of the wives experienced severe violence. A projection of these rates to the number of black couples in the United States in 1985 suggests that more than 603,006 black women were victims of husband-to-wife violence and more than 244,000 black women were victims of extreme violence.

Comparing Black and White Couples

Comparing the rates of husband-to-wife violence in black and white families, we find that black wives were 1.23 times more likely to experience minor violence, and more than twice (2.36) as more likely to experience severe violence. This difference is statistically significant.

Previous investigations have shown that black-white income differences appear to be a major factor contributing to black-white differences in family violence norms and behavior. . . . Even when income is controlled, the rates for wife abuse are higher among black couples. Although the difference in the rate of husband-to-wife violence for black families with incomes below $10,000, compared to whites in the same income bracket, barely missed achieving statistical significance, the difference was in the predicted direction. For families with income greater than $10,000, wife battering was twice as common among blacks than among whites.

Social Factors

Previous research suggests, that there is a gender difference in reporting violence. This research suggests that men underreport their violence when compared to women's reports of men's violence. Men who batter may deny their vise of violence.

Our data reveal that male respondents reported higher rate of minor violence than female respondents. The rate of severe husband-to-wife violence reported, however, is almost twice as great when the respondents are women than when they are men. This gender difference is similar to the pattern reported by Stets and Straus.

In addition to gender differences in reporting violence, men were more likely to have been hit by their fathers and mothers as teens than women were, and men were more likely to have witnessed their mothers hitting their fathers. There were also significant gender differences in rates of approval of husband slapping in some situations. Mates were more likely to approve of this concept than females. Much to our surprise there were no gender difference in attitudes toward wife slapping.

Marital violence can occur among any age group, Previous studies revealed that couples under age 30 have higher rates of violence. Similarly, studies based on women who seek help from agencies or shelters also show that the mean age is 30 or younger. The rates of violence in our sample were significantly higher in younger couples than in older couples. The rates of severe violence were more than three times greater in couples under 30 than in families over 40.

Families that frequently move or who have been in a community for a short period are at greater risk for several negative outcomes. Couples who have been in a community for a short period are more likely to be isolated from their kin and other supportive social networks. We see among the couples in our sample that those who have been in the community for less than two years reported nearly twice the rate of minor violence. The rates for wife assault were comparable for couples who lived in the community for less than two years and those who have lived in the community for two or more years.

Several studies have shown that family violence is inversely related to family socioeconomic status . . . Lower income families have higher rates . . . of wife-battery than upper income families.

If having a lower sums and lower-paying job is more likely to increase the rates of family violence, then not having a full time job or not having a job at all would dramatically raise the likelihood of violence in the home. This was the case for the black families in our sample. Households in which the husband was unemployed had the highest rates of husband-to-wife violence.

Intergenerational Transmission

There is abundant evidence from both clinical observations and survey research that individuals who have experienced or witnessed violence in their family of orientation have a higher probability of using violence as adults than those who have not. Black respondents who were |hit as a teen' by their mothers or who observed parental violence had statistically significant higher rates of husband-to-wife violence. Respondents |hit as a teen' by either parent were twice as likely to be in households where there was severe violence in the past year.

When we control for gender of the respondent we see that for females there is no relationship between witnessing or experiencing violence in the family of orientation and the highest level of husband-to-wife violence in the past year. The relationship found between these variables appear to be less relevant for victims than for perpetrators. . . .

Psychological Distress and Violence Toward Women

The literature on abused women reports negative psychological and emotional well-being among battered women who have sought help or refuge in a shelter or agency. These studies have shown that battered women frequently lack self-esteem, suffer from feelings of loss and inadequacy, depression and learned helplessness.

Several psychological distress items were included in the Second National Family Violence Survey with the intent of measuring the three aspects of mental health that have been mentioned as being related to experiencing violence: depression, stress, and somatic symptoms. Items were derived from the Psychiatric Evaluation Research Interview (PERI) and the Perceived Stress Scales developed by Cohen, Kamarck, and Mermelstein. As reported by Gelles and Harrop, the study developed two composite measures of distress: . . . moderate distress and severe distress. Because this study used a cross-sectional design, it is impossible to determine whether the reported psychological distress of the respondents preceded their experience with violence and abuse or was a consequence of their victimization.

Except for "cold sweats" and "felt difficulties were piling up," women who experienced severe violence reported higher levels of psychological distress. Note that the percentages presented are for respondents who reported that they experienced the form of distress either "fairly often" or "very often." There was a statistically significant relationship between the highest level of violence reported in the last year and nine of the ten psychological distress items.

Multivariate Relationships Among Variables

To aid in the interpretation of differences between households where husband-to-wife violence occurred and households where it did not, we performed a stepwise multiple discriminant analysis. The goals of this analysis were to provide a measure by which the relative importance of several variables could be assessed and to determine which variables were more strongly related to household differences. We chose to conduct this analysis using highest level of violence as the dependent variable and the other variables discussed above as predictor variables.

This analysis revealed that "age of the respondent," "respondent's mother hit father," and " |respondent could approve of wife slapping in some situations" were the three variables with the most discriminating power. These variables were followed in order by "health of the respondent," "family income," "sex of respondent," and "respondent hit as teen by father."

Because socioeconomic status and sex of respondent have an important bivariate relationship to the highest level of violence reported in the last 12 months, we conducted separate analyses controlling for each. Among upper income respondents, "witnessing maternal violence as a child" was the variable with the most discriminating power. The respondent's attitude toward wife slapping was the variable with the most discriminating power among lower income respondents. The age and health of the respondent entered the discriminant analyses for both income categories. "Sex of respondent," "being hit as a teen by father," and "years lived in community" were also important factors for upper income families. "Husband's education" and "observing the father hit mother" were important factors among lower income families.

When we analyze the data controlling for the sex of the respondent we find that among males, "age," "witnessing maternal violence toward father," and "attitude toward husband slapping" were the three most important discriminators. "Health," "experience being hit by father," and "observing the father hit mother" contributed to differences in levels of violence. It should be noted that "attitude toward wife slapping" was not an important discriminator.

The results of the discriminant analysis for female respondents revealed "family income" and "attitude toward wife slapping" as the most powerful discriminators.

Although many of the same variables continually emerged as the primary factors differentiating households by level of violence the order in which the variables entered the discriminant function equations differed slightly when we controlled for either income or gender.

DISCUSSION AND CONCLUSIONS

The present study addressed the issue of spousal violence in black families. We first examined the prevalence of violence among this group and compared the rates of violence among African-American couples with the rates of violence among white couples. The results suggest that there is a higher incidence of husband-to-wife and wife-to-husband physical violence among blacks. We then focused on violence toward black women and tried to assess which variables separated black households where violence occurred from those where it did not.

The findings of this study were consistent with previous research that demonstrates a significant association between family violence and age, socioeconomic status, length of time in the community, and employment status of the husband. We note that when we controlled for gender of the respondent, there was no relationship between witnessing or experiencing violence in the family of orientation and highest level of violence in the

past year for females. The relationship did exist, however, for male respondents. This was important in that it suggests that the intergenerational transmission of violence may have a greater impact on black perpetrators than victims.

When we examined the differences between female victims and non-victims in the incidence of psychological distress we see that associated are highly associated with psychological injury. It is important to note that the psychological consequences of violence and battering may be as serious as the physical consequences. These consequences pose worrisome challenges for the woman who, in spite of her distress, must continue to care for dependent children. They pose additional challenges to professionals involved in treatment and intervention programs.

Black-on-black violence is a serious social problem confronting American society. Blacks are overrepresented among violent crime perpetrators and victims. Little consensus exists regarding the causes of this violence. Although few studies have attempted to link family violence and other forms of violence in the black community, there is reason to believe that they share a common etiology.

In general, the literature argues for a social-structural theory of violence as well as a structural-cultural theory of violence. The latter perspective suggests that black-on-black violence, including male-to-female violence, is produced by structural pressures and dysfunctional cultural adaptations to those pressures. It looks at structurally induced economic problems, for example unemployment or underemployment, as an important variable affecting black men's ability to enact traditional male roles in the family. These structural factors prevent many black males from successfully enacting the traditional male roles and thereby contribute to the emergence of several alternative role prescriptions. Interpersonal conflicts arise between black males and black females because many black males are aware of their role failures and are inclined to counterattack any perceived challenge to their manhood with violence.

Additional research is needed to explore fully the structural-cultural perspective. This research would allow us to better account for the high rates of interspousal violence. It would permit us to determine the extent to which the structural denigration of blacks is experienced differently by those who have a history of assaultive violence and those who do not. It also would allow us to examine alternative approaches to prevention and treatment that address intrafamilial and community violence.

STUDY QUESTION

What are the risk factors identified by Hampton and Gelles of violence in black families?

The Fight to Be a Parent: How Courts Have Restricted the Constitutionally-Based Challenges Available to Homosexuals

Erica Gesing

This Note analyzes the current legal trends pertaining to homosexual adoption and foster parenting in the United States and the avenues available to challenge these laws.

COMBATING THE REALITIES AND MYTHS OF THE HOMOSEXUAL'S PARENTAL FITNESS

Are Homosexuals Immoral?

Some of society's concerns about homosexuality stem from ancient Judeo-Christian beliefs that sodomy, a part of the same-sex relationship, is sinful. The implementation of state laws criminalizing sodomy, reflect this abhorrent view of this sexual activity which has resulted in many people viewing homosexuals as immoral criminals. The distastefulness associated with homosexuals attributed to these sodomy laws continues to be reflected in other forms of discrimination of homosexuals, such as prohibiting them from becoming adoptive or foster parents because of their alleged immorality. However, it is suggested by some that the religious or moral justification of condemning sodomy is used by some people as "a smokescreen for what is actually a secular ideology of homophobia and heterosexism" and may have little to do with actual moral conflicts. Additionally, since so many people in today's culture have differing views on morality, by eliminating a group of people from being adoptive or foster parents according to any characteristic that some people find immoral, such as being an atheist or a gambler, "we would have almost no parents left to adopt and provide foster care." American society has surely evolved to the point where ten percent of the population should not be prohibited outright from adopting or becoming foster parents based solely on a morality argument.

Source: Erica Gesing, "The Fight To Be A Parent: How Courts Have Restricted the Constitutionally-Based Challenges Available to Homosexuals, New England Law Review, 38 (2004): 841–896.

Are Children of Homosexuals More Likely to "Become Gay"?

The same argument that has been used to advocate placing homosexual children in the homes of gays and lesbians has been used to discourage placement of heterosexual children in homosexual homes. Some agencies hesitate to place children and teenagers in homosexual homes "for fear the lesbian or gay parent will 'contaminate' " the child's developing sexuality. However, in reviewing twelve studies—testing more than 300 children—that compared children of divorced lesbians or gays with children of divorced heterosexual couples and other studies that compared children of homosexual parents with children of heterosexual parents, "[n]ot one study provide[d] any evidence for concern." The proportion of children living in homosexual homes who become bisexual or homosexual is equivalent to the amount of children growing up in heterosexual homes who become same-sex orientated. In addition, because "[m]ost adolescents . . . have some concern about being gay or lesbian . . . there is no basis for restrictive rules based on concerns about development of sexuality" for those children living in homosexual homes. The American Academy of Pediatrics confirmed this fact in a policy statement released in February, 2002, which cited two decades of study on the effects of living with homosexual parents, both biological and adoptive, on their children. The findings revealed that:

> [N]one of the more than 300 children [raised by lesbian mothers] studied to date have shown evidence of gender identity confusion, wished to be the other sex, or consistently engaged in cross-gender behavior. No differences have been found in the toy, game, activity, dress, or friendship preferences of boys and girls who had lesbian mothers, compared with those who had heterosexual mothers.

Although young adults who were raised by lesbian mothers were reported to be "slightly more likely to consider the possibility of," and experiment with a same-sex relationship, adult men and women who were raised in lesbian homes and later identified themselves as homosexual were of the same proportion as those adults who were raised in heterosexual homes reporting themselves as gay or lesbian. Therefore, the belief that children living in homosexual homes are more likely to become homosexual or bisexual themselves is also unfounded, and should not be used as an excuse to refuse a homosexual to become an adoptive or foster parent.

Are Homosexuals More Likely to Molest Children Than Heterosexuals?

Another concern raised by opponents of homosexuals as adoptive parents is that parents involved in same-sex relationships are more likely to molest their children than heterosexual parents. This is also unsupported since "[n]inety percent of child abuse is committed by heterosexual men." One study that examined 269 cases of sexual abuse revealed that only two of the abusers were homosexual. Additionally, in seventy-four percent of the cases where a male sexually abused a boy, the offender had been or was currently involved, in a heterosexual relationship with the child's mother or a relative. Although experts routinely testify to these statistics in an effort to convince the courts that these myths are unfounded, the stereotypical labeling of homosexuals as pedophiles sometimes remains. One Missouri judge stated that "[e]very trial judge . . . knows that the molestation of minor boys by adult males is not as uncommon as the psychological experts' testimony indicated." This supports the fact that despite the numerous studies that have confirmed that homosexuals are not more likely to molest their children, stereotypes still remain in the court system.

Are Children Living in Homosexual Homes at a Social Disadvantage?

The final common concern is that children living in homosexual homes will face more ridicule and harassment than children raised in heterosexual homes. Some courts have concluded that the stigma of homosexuality and risk of harassment associated with homosexuality is too great to warrant placing a child in a same-sex home. Admittedly, homosexuals are often subject to discrimination, political opposition, and are sometimes targets of violence, based on their sexual orientation. However, even though some homosexuals experience varying degrees of harassment, it is not necessarily true that their children will suffer because of it; therefore, this potential risk should not be the sole basis for denying homosexual individuals or couples from adopting, becoming foster parents, or having custody of a child. The Alaska Supreme Court followed this logic in a case involving an attempt by a father to gain custody of a child who had been living with his mother since the child's birth. The father argued that circumstances had changed since their initial custody agreement and the mother, a lesbian, was too politically radical and emotionally unstable to be raising their son. The court disagreed with the father's argument that the child should not be raised in a lesbian home simply because of "any real or imagined stigma attaching to mother's [sic] status as a lesbian." Children are often subject to teasing and ridicule on the basis of a number of characteristics, "for being too short or too tall, for being too thin or too fat, for being of a different race or religion or speaking a different language. [The fact is] children show remarkable resiliency, especially if they are provided with a stable and loving home environment." Foster children in particular can feel unwanted and are often already teased because they lack a permanent family. A New Jersey court refused to allow the threat of teasing to result in the removal of two girls from their lesbian mother's home to live with their father on the theory that her homosexuality would cause them embarrassment and lead to teasing by their peers. The judge believed "the child would probably grow up to be a more tolerant person, more understanding of differences in our society." If a homosexual individual or couple is willing to give a child a permanent home, the courts should not preclude this opportunity simply because the child may experience difficulties in the new home. It has been argued that this, like many other excuses offered by courts for denying the placement of a child in a homosexual home, is a mere misuse of the "best interests of the child" standard masking discrimination.

A Summary of the Findings of Children Living in Homosexual Homes

Most of the research that has been conducted on this subject points to the same conclusion—children raised in lesbian homes seem to "develop normally" when compared with children raised in heterosexual homes and share many of the same experiences through adolescence and adulthood. These children with homosexual mothers have "been described as more tolerant of diversity and more nurturing toward younger children" and one recent study revealed that children of lesbian parents "reported their self-esteem to be similar to that of children of heterosexual parents and saw themselves as similar in aggressiveness and sociability." There is also no evidence to support the assertion that homosexuals are, as a class, poor at parenting. In fact, the Iowa Foster and Adopted Parents Association named a gay couple foster parents of the year in 1996. Since experts in psychology and other social sciences have not revealed any real disadvantages in the way that children raised in homosexual homes mature and become adults, and "[l]esbian and gay adults choose to become parents for many of the same reasons heterosexual adults do"—to nurture, protect, and love their children, as well as to pass their family history to a new generation—the law should not prevent homosexuals from becoming parents because of fear and conservative beliefs disguised as a "best interest of the child" argument

THE SUPREME COURT'S EXAMINATION OF STATUTES ADVERSELY AFFECTING HOMOSEXUALS

Laws affecting homosexuals in a different way than others have traditionally been challenged under the Due Process or the Equal Protection Clauses of the Fourteenth Amendment of the United States Constitution. The Court examines the State's purpose behind a law and scrutinizes the means employed to achieve this purpose to determine whether the law should be struck down as unconstitutional. The level of scrutiny used by the Court depends on the statutes' provisions; if a statute threatens a fundamental right or suspect class then a "strict scrutiny" analysis should be employed.

SUBSTANTIVE DUE PROCESS RIGHTS UNDER THE FOURTEENTH AMENDMENT

The Due Process Clause of the Fourteenth Amendment prohibits any state from "depriv[ing] any person of life, liberty, or property, without due process of law." *Griswold v. Connecticut* established the fundamental right of marital privacy under the Due Process Clause in a case involving a Connecticut statute prohibiting the use of contraception that punished not only birth control users but also anyone who helped or instructed another person to use contraception. The Supreme Court majority held that the Constitution did not specifically refer to privacy as a fundamental right, as it referred to other fundamental rights, such as freedom

of speech and freedom of religion. However, the Court determined that "specific guarantees in the Bill of Rights have penumbras," broader connotations that include a "zone of privacy" as a fundamental right, and, therefore, warrant a strict scrutiny analysis. The Court stated that the protection of the intimacy of marriage was included in this zone of privacy and that interfering with "the sacred precincts of marital bedrooms . . . is repulsive to the notions of privacy surrounding the marriage relationship." As such, the statute could not stand as applying to married persons and the Supreme Court struck it down.

Subsequent cases expanded this fundamental zone of privacy beyond protection of infringement into the lives of married couples. However, the Supreme Court has not extended the zone of privacy rights to include the fundamental right to engage in homosexual activity. The first time this issue was presented to the Supreme Court was in a 1986 case involving the challenge of a Georgia statute prohibiting consensual sodomy, which resulted in a 5–4 decision upholding the statute. The challenge arose after "police in Georgia, acting on a tip regarding an unrelated crime, entered the bedroom of Michael Hardwick's home and discovered him in bed with another man." After the District Attorney charged him with the crime, Hardwick filed a claim challenging the constitutionality of the statute.

The *Bowers* Court examined three issues in assessing the statute's constitutionality: 1) whether privacy cases "spanning the education of one's children to abortion rights" extended to homosexual rights; 2) whether there was a fundamental right to homosexual activity; and 3) whether infringement on privacy was more pronounced in analyzing statutes when the violation generally occurs within one's own home. The Court answered in the negative for all these questions and upheld the statute, stating:

> it [is] evident that none of the rights announced in those cases [discussing the protected zone of

privacy] bears any resemblance to the claimed constitutional right of homosexuals to engage in acts of sodomy that is asserted in this case. No connection between family, marriage, or procreation . . . and homosexual activity . . . has been demonstrated. . . . Moreover, any claim that these cases nevertheless stand for the proposition that any kind of private sexual conduct between consenting adults is constitutionally insulated from state proscription is unsupportable.

The Court also stated that they were "quite unwilling" to determine that engaging in homosexual sodomy was a fundamental right deserving heightened protection mainly because of the "ancient roots" and history of prohibition of sodomy in the United States. The majority further determined that since other criminal activities such as illegal drug use were prohibited even if they occurred in one's own home, Hardwick's request to strike down the statute on these grounds was also inadequate.

Justice Blackmun's dissent vehemently questioned the Court's holding arguing that homosexual activity was related to other cases within the zone of privacy aspect of substantive due process because it involved "the right to define oneself through the relationships that one forms." He considered this issue an accurate extension of the protection of family, children and other personal matters already covered under the Due Process Clause. Justice Blackmun also could not justify the Court's use of the history of prohibition of sodomy in reaching their decision, quoting the words of Justice Holmes that "[it] is revolting to have no better reason for a rule of law than that so it was laid down in the time of Henry IV." Justice Blackmun continued his dissent by stating "[n]o matter how uncomfortable a certain group may make the majority of this Court . . . [prior cases have determined] that 'mere public intolerance or animosity cannot constitutionally justify the deprivation of a person's physical liberty.'"

The *Bowers* decision had a pronounced impact on claims challenging the constitutionality of statutes impacting gays and lesbians and the level of scrutiny employed for their analysis. The *Bowers* Court's clear unwillingness to establish homosexuality as a fundamental right has made homosexual claimants challenging laws restricting their rights "chary of seeking Supreme Court review of the lower court decisions" and has surely contributed to the upholding of many laws affecting a homosexual's right to adopt or have foster children. The Bowers opinion "made it clear that five Justices of the highest court in the land have a significant distaste for homosexuality." In the words of one contemporary writer commenting on Bowers the ruling was a "benediction of homophobia [which] will reinforce the prejudices of lower court judges and encourage lay persons to use homosexuality as a legitimate tool in litigation with gay persons."

However, in June 2003, the Supreme Court overruled Bowers, suggesting that the highest court may have more support for homosexuals than was thought for the near two decades following the Bowers decision. *Lawrence v. Texas* arose out of facts similar to *Bowers*. Police were called to a Houston, Texas apartment after receiving word of a weapons disturbance. After lawfully entering the home, the police discovered the occupant, John Geddes Lawrence, "engaging in a sexual act" with another man. The two men were arrested for violating the Texas statute making it a crime to engage in "deviate sexual intercourse, namely anal sex, with a member of the same sex." The men later pleaded no contest and challenged the statute on the grounds that it violated the Equal Protection Clause. The trial court convicted the defendants who appealed to the Court of Appeals for the Texas Fourteenth District to consider whether the statute violated the Equal Protection Clause and the Due Process Clause of the Fourteenth Amendment. Relying on Bowers, the Court of Appeals upheld the convictions and declared the statute constitutional.

The Supreme Court granted certiorari to answer three questions: 1) whether the Texas statute, treating homosexual sodomy differently from heterosexual sodomy, violated the Equal Protection clause; 2) whether the defendants' convictions were in violation of their liberty and privacy guaranteed by the Due Process Clause of the Fourteenth Amendment, and 3) whether Bowers should be overruled. However, the majority of the Court decided to only consider "whether the petitioners were free as adults to engage in the private conduct [of sodomy] in the exercise of their liberty under the Due Process Clause" and in doing so, looked at the cases extending liberty under the Due Process Clause through Bowers.

The Court considered their prior decisions in *Griswold*, *Eisenstadt*, and *Roe v. Wade*—which had held that a woman's decision to have an abortion, although not absolute, was protected under the Due Process Clause because of its "substantive dimension of fundamental significance in defining the rights of the person"—and *Carey v. Population Services International*, which confirmed that not only married adults should benefit under the protection of the Due Process Clause. The Court then criticized the majority in the *Bowers* opinion which had failed to: appreciate the extent of the liberty at stake. To say that the issue in *Bowers* was simply the right to engage in certain sexual conduct demeans the claim the individual put forward, just as it would demean a married couple were it to be said marriage is simply about the right to have sexual intercourse . . . [sodomy statutes and the fact that they exist as punishable crimes] have more far-reaching consequences, touching upon the most private human conduct, sexual behavior, and in the most private of places, the home. . . . It suffices for us to acknowledge that adults may choose to enter upon [a sexual] relationship in the confines of their homes and their own private lives and

still retain their dignity as free persons. When sexuality finds overt expression in intimate conduct with another person, the conduct can be but one element in a personal bond that is more enduring. The liberty protected by the Constitution allows homosexual persons the right to make this choice. The Court continued with its disagreement of *Bowers* stating that the "ancient roots" of distaste for homosexual sodomy, which the Court had relied on in allowing the Georgia sodomy statute to remain in place, were not as ancient, nor as rooted as the *Bowers* majority had portrayed them. While sodomy laws had existed in England, and later America, for centuries, they were not targeting sexual acts between members of the same sex specifically, but were enacted to "prohibit nonprocreative sexual activity more generally" and not usually enforced against "consenting adults acting in private." Rather, these statutes were primarily used for punishing adult men for engaging in nonconsensual sodomy with minor boys or girls. The *Lawrence* Court further stated that laws specifically against homosexual sodomy had not even emerged until the twentieth century, and concluded that the *Bowers* Court had oversimplified and even misrepresented the "historical premises" for upholding sodomy laws. This is especially true since both the American Law Institute and British Parliament had recommended in the 1950s that prohibiting sodomy between two consenting adults in their own home violated the privacy rights of individuals. This suggested that society's attitudes about morality had shifted away from the ancient Judeo-Christian beliefs that had sought to criminalize sodomy in the first place.

The *Lawrence* Court then reviewed two post-*Bowers* decisions that further shed doubt on the Bowers holding. *Planned Parenthood of Southeastern Pennsylvania v. Casey* had "again confirmed that our laws and tradition afford constitutional protection to personal decisions relating to marriage, procreation, contraception, family relationships, child rearing, and education" under the Due Process Clause. Also, *Romer v. Evans* had stood for the premise that homosexuals were a class of people that deserved to be treated as equal to all other groups, and could not be denied protection by a Colorado anti-discrimination statute because of their sexual preference. *Romer* resulted in the striking down of a statute as violating the Equal Protection Clause of the Fourteenth Amendment. These two decisions, made subsequent to *Bowers*, suggested that society and the law had moved forward to a point where the privacy of sexual acts, between all consenting adults, was accepted as a right guaranteed by the Constitution, and should no longer be criminalized, which only "demean [s] [homosexuals] existence" without any legitimate state purpose.

The Court finished its opinion by commenting on the importance of stare decisis, while recognizing the need to change the law in certain situations. The *Lawrence* Court recognized that this was one of those times that stare decisis should be abrogated. The Court then looked towards Justice Stevens' dissenting opinion in *Bowers* that stated sodomy laws should not be upheld because of traditions of morality, and perhaps more importantly, since unmarried persons were already extended privacy protections of their intimate relationships, then this right should be extended to homosexuals. Agreeing with this reasoning, the Court stated "Justice Stevens' analysis, . . . should have been controlling in *Bowers* and should control here." The Court then concluded, even more emphatically, by stating: "Bowers was not correct when it was decided, and it is not correct today. It ought not to remain binding precedent. *Bowers v. Hardwick* should be and is now overruled."

Not surprisingly, Justice Scalia wrote a vigorous dissenting opinion in Lawrence. Justice Scalia was quick to point out that although the majority had overruled *Bowers*, the Court had not "declare[d] that homosexual sodomy is a 'fundamental right' under the Due Process Clause; nor [did the majority's opinion] subject the Texas law to the standard of review that would be appropriate (strict scrutiny) if homosexual sodomy were a 'fundamental right.'" He then pointed out that even though the result of Bowers had been overruled by declaring sodomy statutes unconstitutional, "the Court [left] strangely untouched . . . [*Bowers'*] legal conclusion" and only stated that the defendants' sexual acts were protected as a liberty interest using an "unheard-of form of rational-basis review that will have far-reaching implications."

Justice Scalia first questioned the Court's choice to overrule *Bowers*, stating that despite the fact the opinion had been eroded by subsequent Supreme Court cases, *Bowers* had encouraged consistency in law by allowing "[s]tate laws against bigamy, same-sex marriage, adult incest, prostitution, masturbation, adultery, fornication, bestiality, and obscenity" to continue. By overruling Bowers, the Court had removed the "validation of laws based on moral choices" which would result in confusion within society and "a massive disruption of the current social order." The *Bowers* opinion had cautioned against repealing laws based on moral choices for this very reason.

Justice Scalia also did not adhere to the belief that the Fourteenth Amendment prevents the state from violating an individual's privacy in all situations. It only requires that these liberties cannot be taken away without due process of law, and only fundamental rights should be protected under a substantive reading of the Due Process Clause. Since the Court had neither determined that sodomy was a fundamental right, nor held that it was "deeply rooted" in American tradition and history—thereby warranting a heightened form of scrutiny—there was no reason to strike down the sodomy statute under the rational-basis analysis.

Justice Scalia concluded his dissent by stating that the Court had bowed down to pressure from the outside, namely homosexual activists, by ruling the way it did in *Lawrence*. He believed that "the Court has taken sides in the culture war, departing from its role of assuring, as neutral observer, that the democratic rules of engagement are observed" by siding with this "homosexual agenda." He characterized this Court action as dangerous and stated that this type of issue should be left to the legislature; if society is really so opposed to existing laws which are related to moral decisions—an idea that he is more than skeptical of—then they will act accordingly. Justice Scalia concluded by stating that he does not "have [anything] against homosexuals, or any other group, promoting their agenda through normal democratic means"; he is simply opposed to the Court intervening where it has no business doing so, especially when its decision is not supported by anything other than the whims of the public and a misreading of history and legal precedent.

Gay advocates have applauded the *Lawrence* decision as an important victory in their quest for equal rights. However, it is too soon to know the long-standing implications of this decision. Although the Court has determined that consensual homosexual activity is permitted in private, it has still not declared that there is a fundamental right to engage in homosexual behavior or that homosexuals are members of a suspect class, warranting heightened protection. While this decision will likely bring more success to homosexuals in some jurisdictions in their quest to have a legally recognized family, the progress in other states—namely those who still have legislation banning homosexuals from adopting and/or becoming foster parents—may be nonexistent in the short-term. However, *Lawrence* does send a clear message that the unwillingness of former members of the Supreme Court to expand rights for homosexuals has been replaced by the recognition by some justices that the law needs to evolve with society's changing ideals of morality.

EQUAL PROTECTION CHALLENGES

Constitutional claims that a law violates the Equal Protection Clause are a way for the Court to strike down statutes that are facially discriminatory. This is especially true if the person or group of people targeted by the statute is a member of a "discrete and insular minorit[y]" in danger of being exploited by the tyranny of the majority. Individuals who are members of a group that is a "suspect classification" trigger a strict scrutiny analysis of the statute, often resulting in the law being overturned. If the Court determines that the statute is simply threatening an individual's economic or welfare rights, or the individual is not a member of a suspect class, then a far less rigorous standard of scrutiny, the rational relationship scrutiny test, will be applied.

One of the most significant cases argued under the Equal Protection Clause challenged a statute prohibiting whites from marrying anyone outside of their race. *Loving* re-emphasized that racial-based classifications trigger a more rigid scrutiny than other types of classifications. The Court employed the strict scrutiny analysis of the statute because the Equal Protection Clause had been added to the Constitution precisely "to eliminate all official state sources of invidious racial discrimination in the States." The statutory purpose—established in a prior Virginia Supreme Court of Appeals case on this issue—was "'to preserve the racial integrity of . . . [the state's] citizens,' and to prevent 'the corruption of blood,' 'a mongrel breed of citizens,' and 'the obliteration of racial pride.'" The *Loving* Court determined that this purpose was not even legitimate, let alone compelling, and held that a statute enacted only "to maintain White Supremacy," could not stand.

Subsequent Supreme Court cases have emphasized the use of a strict scrutiny analysis when reviewing laws that make status-based classifications and, as a result, many statutes have been overturned. However, it is not clear what exactly determines a suspect class. The Supreme Court first faced the issue of whether laws affecting homosexuals on the basis of their sexual orientation should trigger a strict scrutiny analysis in 1996. *Romer* involved the challenge of an amendment to the Colorado Constitution that prohibited any governmental branch from affording special protection to homosexuals filing discrimination claims on the basis of their sexual orientation. The Court held that Colorado's explicit reason for the amendment—placing "gays and lesbians in the same position as all other persons . . . [that would result in] no more than deny[ing] homosexuals special rights"—was "implausible" and not sufficiently legitimate to survive a rational basis analysis. The Supreme Court declared the amendment unconstitutional because its broad language effectively took basic rights—afforded to all citizens by the Equal Protection Clause—away from homosexuals solely based on their sexual orientation, a concept that was "obnoxious" to the purpose of the Equal Protection Clause itself.

Despite this apparent victory for homosexuals, *Romer* declined to implement a heightened scrutiny analysis to laws affecting homosexuals and failed to refer to the fundamental right question of homosexuality raised in *Bowers*—an issue addressed by Justice Scalia in his dissenting opinion. Justice Scalia argued that the decision reached by the majority ignored the Court's prior ruling in *Bowers* and had the Court properly looked to this precedent in its analysis, the holding should reflect that "if it is constitutionally permissible for a State to make homosexual conduct criminal, surely it is constitutionally permissible for a State to enact other laws merely disfavoring homosexual conduct." As such, Justice Scalia argued that the

amendment should stand, since under the *Bowers* rationale the legislature has the authority to pass laws based on society's view of morality.

Like the *Bowers* decision reached beforehand, the Supreme Court's decision in Romer has been criticized for its failure to adequately address the question of whether homosexuals should receive heightened protection because of their membership in a suspect class. However, some advocates of homosexual rights consider Romer a necessary stepping stone and victory because it suggests that the Supreme Court has recognized that homosexuals are on a somewhat "level playing field" when it comes to challenging statutes on constitutional grounds. The attorney who represented Michael Hardwick in *Bowers* stated that *Romer* gives homosexuals "cautious optimism" in initiating claims of discrimination. Yet, despite this victory, the exact type of behavior that would be considered unlawful discrimination by the Supreme Court in the area of homosexual rights in the future still remains unclear. However, *Lawrence v. Texas* is a clear example that the Court has used the analysis and holding in Romer to move forward toward increased protection for homosexuals, which may ultimately result in the establishment of homosexuals as a suspect class, entitled to heightened protection under the Equal Protection Clause.

How the Supreme Court Has Classified the Foster Family Relationship

The Supreme Court first recognized that parents have a substantive due process liberty interest in the rearing of their own children in 1923. In *Meyer v. Nebraska*, a statute prohibiting teachers from leading classes in foreign languages to children who had not yet passed the eighth grade was struck down partly on the basis that the statute infringed on parents' rights to determine how they wanted their children to be educated. The *Meyer* Court determined that this notion of familial privacy was derived from the Due Process Clause of the Fourteenth Amendment that guaranteed a right "to acquire useful knowledge, to marry, [to] establish a home, and [to] bring up children."

This idea of familial privacy was expanded in subsequent years. In 1977, the Court determined that an extended family also warranted this Fourteenth Amendment protection in a suit involving an ordinance that required individuals living together in a dwelling unit to be members of the same nuclear family. Moore, a grandmother living with two grandsons, who were cousins rather than brothers, challenged the ordinance, which was struck down by the Court because of its arbitrary method of infringing upon an individual's familial right to privacy. However, subsequent Supreme Court cases have declined to grant this extended family right to other non-traditional families, preventing individuals from using a substantive due process argument to either become a foster parent or adopt their own foster child.

The Supreme Court has recognized a procedural right under the Due Process Clause of the non-traditional family in at least one context, an avenue that several foster parents have used to clarify their role in their relationship with foster children. In 1972, the Court determined that an unwed father had a right under the Due Process Clause to contest the placement of his children into the custody of the State after their biological mother had died. The Court determined that the nature of the father's relationship established a fundamental right to be heard on the issue of the custody of his children, despite the fact that an Illinois statute did not recognize an unwed father's interest in his child's ultimate custody. The Illinois statute was overturned and an unwed father's right to a hearing under the Due Process Clause was established.

In 1977, the same year *Moore* established the notion of a non-traditional family warranting substantive due process privacy

protection, the Supreme Court considered the issue of a foster parent's procedural due process rights in *Smith v. Organization of Foster Families for Equality & Reform*. Smith involved a Fourteenth Amendment challenge initiated by several foster parents objecting to the New York administrative and statutory procedures under which authorized placement agencies have discretion to remove foster children from foster homes. The foster parents challenged the procedures on the ground that they did not provide an ample opportunity to foster parents and other interested parties to be heard on the issue of the foster children's ultimate placement when they are removed from their current foster home. The plaintiff's further argued that foster parents have a liberty interest in their right to preserve their foster family. Instead of establishing whether foster parents have a protected liberty interest under the Due Process Clause, the Court focused on the New York procedure itself, and reversed the lower court's decision, upholding the procedure as constitutional.

In reaching this conclusion, the Court examined the goal of the foster care system in New York and recognized that it was a method of providing children with a temporary home until they could either return to their natural parents' home or be adopted. Since the goal was to ultimately return foster children to their parents' home, "[t]he New York system divides parental roles among [the foster] agency, foster parents, and natural parents, and the definitions of the respective roles are often complex and often unclear." The Court acknowledged the appellees' argument that because of these blurry roles and the fact that children often end up staying in foster homes for an extended period of time, foster children often develop a strong emotional attachment to their foster parents. However, this alone could not justify affording members of foster families the same rights from government intrusion as biological families, because even though the importance of family "stems from the emotional attachments that derive from the intimacy of daily association" and from raising the children, there are two important differences between biological families and foster families.

First, the Court emphasized that the foster family is created through a contractual relationship between the State and the foster parent, thus, it is not based on the "intrinsic human right" to have a family of one's own. The contractual relationship between the state and foster parents has established "expectations and entitlements of the parties" that do not support a heightened due process guarantee for foster parents. Second, the Court raised concern that increasing the procedural rights of the foster parent would "inevitably conflict with [the] absolute [substantive] right of the natural parents." The Court went on to conclude that the current procedure was "constitutionally sufficient regardless" of whether foster parents had any substantive due process guarantees, and if the people of New York wanted to increase the role and guaranteed rights of the foster parent then they could amend the procedure through the legislature.

Based on its analysis, the Court seemed hesitant to determine that the foster family is protected under the familial liberty interest of the Due Process Clause, as the appellees argued. Instead of directly addressing this issue, the Court stated that it did not have to determine whether a liberty interest existed under the Due Process Clause because its only role was to analyze whether New York provided foster parents with proper notice and an opportunity to be heard satisfying procedural due process guarantees. Thus, whether foster parents have substantive rights is still unresolved, and state courts have returned mixed opinions on this issue. Until the Supreme Court chooses to definitively determine the rights of foster parents there is still hope that foster parents can increase their guaranteed rights in the foster family relationship, including establishing a right to adopt the foster child should they desire to do so.

Lower Court Decisions in the Area of Homosexuality, Foster Parenting and Adopting

Although the Supreme Court has only recently allowed substantive Due Process protection to engage in homosexual conduct, the Court still has not declared that there is a fundamental right to sodomy or that homosexuals are members of a suspect class. Furthermore, the Court has held that foster parents do not have any heightened protection to preserve their foster family. Litigants have nevertheless challenged these issues in several states with varying results. Although Smith seemed to conclude that foster parents have "no expectation or entitlement that a child will remain permanently in their home" and are not entitled to Due Process protection under the Fifth or Fourteenth Amendments for their liberty and property interests when it comes to former or current foster children, some states have passed legislation allowing foster parents to be part of judicial proceedings regarding the adoption of the foster child. Other courts have given the foster family preference over other potential adoptive parents should the child become available for adoption; and some courts have determined that foster children do have a constitutional right to keep a relationship with the foster parent should the relationship through the foster system end. These state actions suggest that the guaranteed rights of foster parents may be higher than what the Supreme Court discussed in *Smith* and can give persons, homosexual or otherwise, wanting to become foster parents or to adopt their foster children a glimmer of hope. . . .

Summary of Lower Court Decisions in the Area of Foster Parents' Rights

While courts in some states have determined that there are certain guaranteed rights of foster parents to preserve their family, these heightened rights only apply in specific situations. The *Smith* decision effectively limits granting foster parents rights under the Fourteenth Amendment. Those courts that have extended foster parents substantive due process protection have done so mainly because of a biological relationship or where the foster parent-child relationship has developed because of a direct request from the biological parent, especially if there is little chance that the parent will be able to care for the child again. Until the Supreme Court faces this issue again, it is unlikely that courts will extend these foster parents' rights further. However, following the reasoning in *Webster*, it is possible that foster children may be able to increase the rights of their foster parents indirectly by relying on their fundamental rights to maintain their relationship with them. If this can eventually evolve into a right of foster children to choose to be adopted by their current foster parents, rather than any other prospective adoptive parents, this could increase the rights of the foster parents to turn their temporary family relationship into a permanent one. This should certainly be possible in situations where the child has developed a long-term and emotional relationship with his foster family and there is little or no chance that the goal of the foster care system—to reunite the child with his biological parents as soon as possible—will be met.

THE FUTURE OF LAWS REGARDING HOMOSEXUALS AND THEIR ATTEMPTS TO BECOME FOSTER AND ADOPTIVE PARENTS

Since foster care is an issue that is rooted in state law, the only way that the system could change uniformly would be through a decision by the Supreme Court or federal legislative reform. In 1980, "the federal government took on a revolutionary role in the foster care system by enacting the Adoption Assistance and Child Welfare Act." The purpose of this statute was to minimize the need for foster care by encouraging biological families to stay intact. More important though, was the Act's attempt to emphasize that foster children need a "permanency plan" for their future. This involved not only improving the relations of the child with his natural parents, but also requires making an early determination as to the child's future when it appears that it is unlikely the child will be returned to his natural parents. However, the Act's effects have been limited, emphasizing the need for more changes on the federal level in order to mainstream the system.

An appeal in the *Lofton* case may provide a step towards establishing changes for homosexuals, not only in the world of adoption and foster care, but in more guaranteed rights to foster parents in general. Should the *Lofton* decision be appealed to the Supreme Court, Smith and Romer will have to be reconsidered, as the Florida Federal District Court and the Eleventh Circuit Court of Appeals has relied on both of these cases in upholding the Florida statute that prevents homosexuals from adopting. Additionally, the Supreme Court would have to determine how Lawrence, and its extension of privacy and liberty rights under the Due Process Clause, factor into the area of homosexuals' rights to create and maintain a family. Unfortunately, it is unlikely that the extension of *Lawrence* will translate immediately into additional protections for homosexuals under the Due Process Clause, although it has almost certainly opened the door for more legal arguments in this area. Decisions in lower courts have increased the rights of foster children and have allowed homosexuals to legally become parents, even in the absence of a biological relationship. While these decisions may eventually increase the chances that foster parents and homosexuals can increase their rights under the Fourteenth Amendment, this may not have as widespread effect as supporters of these causes would like.

CONCLUSION

While the foster care system has expanded its pool of potential foster parents and some courts have recognized the changing American family, other states continue to bar homosexuals from participating in the areas of foster care and adoption based on their sexual orientation alone. Although lower courts will no longer be able to rely on *Bowers*, it is still difficult to predict how the *Lawrence* decision will impact the rights of homosexuals, especially in their quest to become foster and adoptive parents. Homosexuals still do not have a fundamental right to engage in sodomy, nor have they been declared a suspect class, so they are still not receiving heightened Fourteenth Amendment protection. Additionally, it is too early to know how *Goodridge* and court proceedings and legislation in other states regarding same-sex marriage will ultimately impact this issue. The fact is, despite the recent victories of homosexual rights' activists throughout the United States, stereotypes against homosexuals and their ability to function as supportive, loving, and fit parents remain. Until this mentality changes and the *Smith* classification of the foster family relationship is reconsidered, homosexuals desiring to adopt their foster children in states that prohibit them from doing so, will likely continue to be barred under the "best interests of the child" standard masking discrimination.

STUDY QUESTION

What are the current legal trends pertaining to homosexual adoption and foster parenting in the United States as identified by Erica Gesing? Also, what avenues does she see available to challenge these laws?

Race, Poverty, and Neglect

Andrea Charlow

We need to understand better the correlation between poverty and maltreatment if we are to improve the system and truly protect minority and poor children.

Although a majority of families charged with maltreatment are white, a disproportionate number are minority. In 1997, 1,054,000 children (fifteen of every one thousand children) were confirmed victims of child abuse or neglect. The percentage of African-American and Native-American children who were purportedly maltreated was nearly twice the proportion of those children in the general population. Despite the disproportion of minority children deemed maltreated by the child welfare system, the Third National Incidence Study of Child Abuse and Neglect (NIS-3), commissioned by the U.S. Congress, found that all races had the same maltreatment rates. Not only is the rate of initial maltreatment the same, but the rate of repeat abuse appears to be the same as well. More recent studies confirm the NIS-3 finding that the rate of maltreatment is the same for all races. A 1999 study found no significant difference in the incidence of neglect, physical abuse, sexual abuse or emotional abuse between Caucasian and African-American families. Similarly, a narrower

study of shaken baby syndrome found no statistically significant difference in the rate of white and non-white victims.

Many studies conducted by different groups have repeatedly confirmed a connection between poverty and child maltreatment rates. Although the NIS-3 found no statistically significant difference in the rates of fatal injury or emotional neglect among income groups, significant differences were found in all other categories of maltreatment. Total maltreatment rates for families earning less than $15,000 per year were forty-seven out of every one thousand children (nearly one in twenty-one low income children) compared to only 2.1 of every one thousand children living in families earning more than $30,000 per year. The rate differences are staggering, and the prognosis for poor children appears bleak.

When the poverty rate for minority children is added to the rate of maltreatment by poor families, the impact on the minority community becomes clear. In 1999, about seventeen percent of American children lived

---

Source: Andrea Charlow, "Race, Poverty, and Neglect, William Mitchell Law Review, 28 (2001): 763–790.

in families with incomes below the federal poverty level. Broken down by race, approximately thirty-three percent of African-American children and thirty percent of Latino children live in poverty compared to only nine percent of white children. Thus, the high numbers of maltreated minority children may be due to the high levels of poverty in minority families. One may also argue that racial prejudice results in increased numbers of minorities accused of maltreatment, which then skews the maltreatment rates of the poor, but studies have not borne out this latter theory.

The correlation between poverty and child maltreatment is more revealing when it is broken down by case type. Although the media focuses attention on sensational cases of severe physical abuse, and legislation treats abuse and neglect identically, most maltreatment cases—fifty-four percent—involve neglect. Only twenty-two percent of cases consist of physical abuse and only eight percent involve sexual abuse. Further, although all maltreatment rises with poverty, the increase in the rate of neglect that accompanies poverty is twice the increase in the rate of physical abuse attributed to poverty. The import of the abundance of neglect cases becomes clear when we note that despite the fact that removal is more readily justifiable in abuse cases (definitions are more clear and harm more obvious), most removals involve neglect. In other words, it appears that the system, true to its origins, is removing children simply because they are poor, and because minority children are more likely to be poor, an inordinate number of them are being separated from their families without sufficient reason.

The problem for minority children does not end with their disproportionate classification as maltreated. In addition to being removed from their homes more often than white children, removal of African-American children is more likely to become permanent. Recent statistics show that although both Caucasian

and African-American children enter foster care at approximately the same rate they leave foster care, instead of being returned home, a higher percentage of African-Americans were adopted out of foster care than Caucasians. In addition, a disproportionate number of African-American children were waiting for adoption and/or had parents whose rights were terminated.

In a 1997 article, Richard Barth reported on the effects of age and race on adoption for children in foster care. Barth's study spanned six years and covered all children who entered out-of-home care in California after 1988, including a group of nearly 4,000 African-American and Hispanic children. During that period, only forty-one percent of African-American children were reunited with their families, although fifty-eight percent of their white counterparts and fifty-seven percent of the Hispanic children were sent home. At six years after placement, twenty-four percent of the Caucasian children were adopted, but only sixteen percent of African-American children and seventeen percent of Hispanic children were adopted. Not only were African-Americans returned home less often, but they were also more likely to languish in foster care waiting for a family to adopt them after the system terminated the rights of the only parents they were ever likely to have.

The loss of family for African-Americans is more likely to become permanent than for whites or even other minorities. If we are to help these children, we must understand more than statistical correlations of race, poverty and maltreatment. We need to establish causation and to identify factors that can counteract the ill effects of poverty and maltreatment.

Current research on child maltreatment can be criticized for a number of reasons. Most studies on the effects of child abuse and neglect consist of children in the clinical setting—those children who have suffered most severely from maltreatment. They therefore may not represent the majority of children who are maltreated. Study populations culled from government agencies may skew data because they tend to consist primarily of lower socioeconomic groups and single mothers with little education. Neglect and abuse at different periods of a child's development may have different effects, yet most studies do not control for timing of maltreatment. Chronicity may also play a part in the effect of abuse and neglect, yet most studies do not test for that factor either. Lack of control groups and small sample sizes also present problems in some studies. Nonetheless, this research provides us with the only clues we have about the effects of race, poverty and neglect on children. The following sections examine some of these studies.

RESEARCH ON RACE

If the rate of child maltreatment is the same for all races, why, then, is a disproportion of minority children involved in the child protection system? Several explanations have been proffered. One is that the system and workers are racist and therefore more willing to charge minority families and remove their children. Minority families are not seen as valuable, and minority parents are presumed incompetent. Another theory posits that minority families are more likely to be reported and investigated because they are more likely to be poor and therefore under the scrutiny of government welfare officials. In other words, the problem arises because of increased government intrusion into the lives of poor families. A third possibility is that the phenomenon is merely a corollary to poverty. Poverty increases the likelihood of child maltreatment. Because more minorities are poor, more will mistreat their children. Finally, the problem may be one of class bias rather than race bias. The vague definition of neglect allows middle-class child care professionals to impose their standards on the poor. In essence, bias against the poor, or at least a lack of understanding of poverty and the "culture" of poverty together with a vague definition of neglect, leads to charges of maltreatment where there is none. This last theory is hard to test.

The argument that racism is a factor in the large numbers of minorities in the child protection system appears to be supported by the latest NIS report (NIS-3). The NIS-3 concluded that different races receive differential attention at some point in the process of referral, investigation, and service allocation despite the fact that there is no difference in the rate of abuse by race. The NIS-3 also concluded that a re-analysis of the NIS-2 study data indicated young minority children were more likely to be investigated than white children. Although analysis of the statistics alone would indicate differential treatment on the basis of race, other explanations like differential treatment of the poor and higher scrutinization of poor families may also explain the data.

NIS-3 discounts the explanation of lower income family scrutinization by governmental agencies as a reason for the disproportionate rates of minority children in the system. It states that fifty-nine percent of their sample was reported by public school officials who see children from all income levels. Hospital personnel also accounted for a large part of child maltreatment reports. Despite the NIS-3 conclusion, it is possible that hospital and school officials are more willing to report abuse or neglect in lower socio-economic families. Early studies on mandatory reporting of child abuse found that doctors were less likely to report suspected abuse in middle-class families than in poor families. Thus, the differential attention the NIS-3 observed may be due to poverty and not race.

Bias in filing initial child abuse reports has been posited as a cause of the large number of minority children in the system. If minorities are reported for maltreatment more often than whites, it might be because of racism, it might occur because of other factors that bring minorities to the attention of authorities, or it might result from the fact that poor people are more likely to be reported and minorities are more likely to be poor. Studies on this phenomenon do not provide clear answers.

Some studies have noted differential reporting rates for blacks and whites. In a 1990 Florida study, African-American women were reported for substance abuse during pregnancy at approximately ten times the rate of white women although the rate of substance abuse in those two groups was approximately the same. Another study confirmed that although the use of drugs by pregnant women was similar for black and white women, nearly twice as many pregnant black women were reported. Although one study found differential reporting rates between African-American and Caucasian pregnant women, all of the reported women in that study were of lower socio-economic status. Thus, the reports may have been based on poverty status rather than race. Early studies of abuse and neglect reporting patterns and recognition showed that children of lower socio-economic parents were more likely to be reported as being abused even when they suffered the same injuries as children in better economic circumstances. Again, because minorities are disproportionately poor they may be more likely to be reported for child maltreatment.

Other studies did not find differential reporting or treatment of minorities. A 1996 study in western New York state showed all children were slightly more likely to be reported by mandatory reporters—doctors, social workers, teachers and other professionals required to report by law—than by permissive reporters. However, African-Americans were most likely to be reported by non-parent relatives (twenty-four percent for blacks and thirteen percent for whites), while Caucasians were most likely to be

reported by law enforcement, a friend or neighbor (seventeen percent for whites, eight percent and six percent respectively for blacks). If there was racial bias in reporting, it would more likely come from non-relatives, but that group reported most often on Caucasians, not African-Americans. Analyzing data on mandatory reporters, the author noted about twice as many reports on African-American families originated from medical sources, but twice as many reports on Caucasian families were made by law enforcement personnel. Most medical reports came from hospitals or clinics which the authors posit would be used more frequently by poor African-Americans. Again, poverty may play a part in reporting, and it does not appear that race bias accounts for the overly large proportion of African-American families in the system.

Another study measuring substantiation and provision of services, rather than reporting rates, found no difference in the rate between African-Americans and Caucasians of unsubstantiated, substantiated and closed (maltreatment occurred but nothing more needed to be done), and substantiated and open (further supervision by child protection officials was needed) cases. In addition, a prior substantiated report of maltreatment was more likely to lead to substantiation of a present report in Caucasian children than in African-American children. The opposite would be expected if racial bias was involved in the substantiation decision. Services were offered with the same frequency to both races, although Caucasians were more likely to be referred for counseling. Overall, the investigators found that African-American families were not handled differently than Caucasians.

Contrary to the NIS-3 conclusion, a number of studies conducted to measure racial prejudice by child welfare professionals reached the conclusion that racial bias was not the cause of increased numbers of minorities in the child welfare system. In a study conducted in Pittsburgh between 1986 and 1989, researchers found that there was no significant difference in the likelihood that a case of neglect would be confirmed for African-American as compared to Caucasian families. Although the rate of neglect was the same for African-Americans and Caucasians in that study, African-Americans were disproportionately represented in cases referred to the county for neglect (twelve to thirteen percent of the county population but forty-three percent of the neglect cases). Thus, the study sample was consistent with NIS-3 data in that there was a disproportion of minorities in the system, but the study disproves bias on the part of child welfare workers who determined whether a case was confirmed. If child welfare workers had been biased, the rate of confirmed cases for minorities would have been higher than that for Caucasians.

Other studies have gone beyond examining statistics to test racial bias through hypothetical cases presented to child welfare professionals. A 1995 Canadian study presented police officers and social workers with a removal decision on a hypothetical case that included unsubstantiated vague accusations of neglect. Age, race and socioeconomic status were changed to test the effect of those factors on removal decisions. The authors found that when the child was older and lived in a predominantly black lower-class neighborhood, police and social workers were less likely to agree with removal. If the social workers were biased against blacks, the opposite would have been found. One can argue about whether this result shows reverse prejudice is involved (less is expected from black families), that social workers are actually more aware of the daily realities and problems of being poor (sometimes poor parents have no choice but to leave a child unattended), or that social workers believe poor black children are more capable of taking care of themselves. In any event, the attitude of the social workers in this study does not support the

bias theory. When read together, these studies seem to negate the theory of race bias to explain the disproportion of minorities in the child welfare system.

On the other hand, a number of studies appear to support the theory that the cause of the minority over-representation in the system is the disproportionate number of poor minorities. In other words, neglect is related to poverty, not minority status. When comparing the ratio of racial minorities living in poverty in a particular county with the proportion of minority children in the child welfare population in that county, one study found consistency. African-American children were disproportionately represented in maltreatment cases when compared to their proportion of the general population, but their representation in these cases was proportionate to their ratio of the poor population of the county studied. In addition to the NIS-3 statistics cited above, one study, comparing black families whose children entered the hospital because of accidents with those who were hospitalized for abuse, concluded that abusing parents were poor, of lower occupational status, socially isolated and depressed. Thus, even within the black community, poverty is associated with maltreatment.

RESEARCH ON POVERTY

Recent studies seem to point to poverty as a more likely cause of the disproportionate numbers of maltreated minority children than biased reporters and child protective service workers. NIS-3 statistics and those of other studies repeatedly link poverty with child abuse and neglect. Severe violence toward children is more common in families with income below the poverty level. Over the past decade, rates of persistent poverty and child abuse have both increased. However, statistical tests merely demonstrate a connection between poverty and child maltreatment. They do not prove cause and effect. Given that most poor parents do not abuse or neglect their children, poverty status alone does not explain child maltreatment. Although minorities do not abuse their children at a higher rate than whites, because minorities are disproportionately poor, the answer to why more poor parents than wealthy parents abuse is crucial to the well-being of the minority community.

Several theories may explain the increased rate of maltreatment among the poor. One may argue that the greater stress of poverty, the dangerous neighborhoods in which poor people generally reside, and the lack of money for adequate child care, food, medical care, and housing, all contribute to the likelihood that a poor parent will not have the energy or time to properly care for her children or will be more likely to lose her temper and inappropriately discipline her children. On the other hand, it is possible that some of the problems that cause poverty such as drug abuse, poor interpersonal skills, and criminal or violent behavior also cause child maltreatment. For example, a parent with a substance abuse problem will be poor and not likely to properly care for her children while she is high. Similarly, a parent who lacks interpersonal skills would be unable to get or keep a decent job and is likely to have the same problem relating to her child as she does relating to other people. Thus, the parent is both poor and neglectful without poverty directly causing the neglect. The NIS-3 report concedes that poverty is associated with other factors, including substance abuse, which may cause maltreatment. A third possibility is that poverty acts along with other problems such as lack of an adequate support system to cause an increased likelihood of maltreatment. A final argument is that many children are in the system because of cultural or middle-class bias that results in inappropriate findings of neglect. In other words, children are being removed because they are poor, not because they have

been maltreated. All of these theories appear to be partially correct.

If the connection between neglect and poverty is higher than that between other types of abuse and poverty, it may mean that the lack of resources (money for basic needs, medical care, child care, etc.) connected with poverty causes neglect, or it may point to middle-class bias. As it happens, the correlation between poverty and neglect is greater than that between poverty and other types of maltreatment. Increases in substantiated neglect have occurred primarily in poor areas while abuse increases occurred across all socio-economic levels. Although substantiated cases of abuse were about three times as frequent in poor communities, substantiated neglect cases in poor communities were nearly six times more frequent than in more affluent communities. African-Americans had higher rates of substantiated neglect, which is consistent with the correlation between poverty and neglect and the high proportion of African-Americans living in poverty.

In one study, reports of maltreatment were compared with census data for poor areas in Missouri. Increased poverty correlated not only with higher numbers of reports but also with higher substantiation rates for physical abuse and neglect. Substantiation rates of sexual abuse were relatively level for all income groups, but substantiation rates sorted by income varied widely for physical abuse and neglect. Neglect was more highly correlated to poverty than other types of maltreatment. There is no way to test whether this data is the result of middle-class bias or poverty, but it tends to support the "lack of resources" theory.

The fact that most poor people do not abuse their children might point to the fallacy of the theory that the stress of poverty causes maltreatment. However, if the poorest people have higher rates of abuse or neglect, it might mean that poverty is a strong contributing factor to maltreatment and, at the deepest levels of poverty where stress is highest, it leads to abuse. In one study of chronic neglect, researchers found that although the income of chronically neglecting families was not significantly different from that of newly neglecting families, the chronic families supported more members on that income so that they were effectively poorer, "considerably poorer than the average for their neighborhoods." For example, while about eighty-six percent of the chronically neglecting families had enough money to pay rent and eighty-four percent had enough to pay for food, seventy-one percent could not afford a babysitter, forty-three percent could not pay utility bills, and thirty-one percent could not afford medical treatment. To put this in perspective, statistics for the locale (Pittsburgh) at the time of the study indicated that an average family of 3.1 people had income of $20,971 per year and the federal poverty level for a family of four was $11,650, but the families in the study averaged 3.8 people on income of $7,476. Chronically neglecting families were also less educated and more likely to be unemployed. Overall, newly neglecting families could be distinguished from chronically neglecting families in that the new neglect involved parents who were facing a crisis and were isolated from family and friends.

It can be argued that this study supports the theory that poverty causes maltreatment given that families with the highest levels of poverty would suffer the most stress and, indeed, those families chronically maltreated their children. It can also be argued that the fact that these families could not provide basic necessities to their children caused child protective services personnel to find that they neglected their children. Finally, the study does not rule out the possibility that intractable problems (lack of education and poor job skills) that cause extreme poverty contribute to maltreatment. The lack of a support network for newly neglecting families may also indicate that poverty in

conjunction with other problems causes child maltreatment.

Several studies have attempted to further refine the correlation between poverty and child maltreatment by comparing persistent poverty with temporary poverty. An understanding of the effects of chronic poverty on child maltreatment is especially important to minorities given that African-American children are more likely to be poor for multiple years than white children.

In one study of child fatalities in Philadelphia designed to measure the effects of prolonged poverty versus short-term economic stress on physical child abuse, researchers found that poor children are nearly twice as likely to suffer severe abuse as children who do not live in poverty. Sixty-four percent of the sample who repeatedly abused their children were of extremely low socioeconomic status. The study suggests that long term poverty is related to the risk of recurrent abuse more than poverty at the time of the maltreatment. However, once parental criminality and domestic violence were factored, the relationship between recurrent abuse and chronic poverty was not clear. Specifically, it was not clear whether parental violence caused poverty and child abuse or whether the stress of parental poverty caused violent behavior. Again, the correlation of maltreatment to poverty is clear, but causation is not.

A number of studies have focused on the effect of a lack of social support for maltreating parents. Hashima and Amato studied the effects of poverty and social support on negative parenting. They defined "unsupportive parenting" as self-reported frequency of hitting, yelling, lack of praise, and lack of hugging. In a random national sample, they found that the perception of inadequate social support was associated with unsupportive parenting in low income families but not in middle-class families. However actual help with baby-sitting and child care resulted in lower levels of unsupportive parental behavior regardless of income level. This result may be supported as well by another study in which low income single mothers with low levels of social support and high levels of crises were more likely to be reported for child maltreatment. The study shows the effect of poverty in that the lack of social support in middle-class families did not have the same negative effect on parenting as it did in poor families. In addition, child care assistance helped families at all income levels. Thus, the lack of a social support system and the lack of child care may explain why some poor parents maltreat their children while others do not.

It appears that no study proves definitively which, if any, of the above theories is correct. In all likelihood, each theory is somewhat true. Clearly more research needs to be done to better understand the connection between poverty and child maltreatment.

EFFECTS OF NEGLECT, POVERTY, AND REMOVAL

Despite the possible contributing factor of poverty, children who are being physically or sexually abused need to be removed from their families for their own safety. However, the case for removal of neglected children is less clear. Although neglected children can suffer serious physical injury or death, for example, when a young child is left unattended, serious physical injury rarely occurs as a result of neglect. Given the high rate of poverty associated with neglect, the lack of studies on neglected children (as opposed to maltreated children in general), and the lack of a clear consistent definition of neglect, it is difficult to determine exactly what functions are impaired by poverty as opposed to neglect. If there are no serious long-term negative effects of neglect separate from those of poverty, it can be argued that removal of children from their families for neglect is not appropriate except in the most

compelling circumstances. Thus, we need to examine the effects of neglect, poverty and removal to evaluate current child protection policies.

Neglected children "may suffer significant short-term and longer-term cognitive, emotional, and social problems." Poor school performance is closely associated with neglect. Studies suggest that neglected children may suffer from intellectual and language delays, but the lack of matched samples in most of these studies make "it difficult to discern any independent effects attributable to child neglect." Findings on the effect of neglect on behavior problems including aggression are mixed. Neglected children appear to have increased coping difficulties. Nonetheless, there is no clear link between neglect and criminality. Less than twenty percent of neglected children are arrested for juvenile or adult crimes and most neglect does not appear to be transmitted from generation to generation.

Poverty affects children in ways similar to neglect. Poverty negatively affects cognitive functioning, academic achievement, self-esteem, social development, and self-control. Poor children are more likely to have learning disabilities and emotional and behavioral problems. Verbal ability is more likely to be affected by poverty than problem behavior or mental health. Chronic poverty appears to have a stronger negative impact than temporary poverty. Children raised in persistent poverty exhibited lower intelligence test scores than those who were not poor for long periods of time.

Depth of poverty is important as well. Those who are poorest fare the worst in terms of intellectual and educational achievement. As discussed above, chronic poverty and depth of poverty are associated with chronic neglect as well as negative cognitive effects on children. In sum, the effects of poverty are strikingly similar to the effects of neglect, although some authors claim the negative effects of neglect are greater than those of poverty alone.

Removal has negative effects on children as well. Children in foster care exhibit high rates of emotional, behavioral and developmental problems. Attachment theory points to the need for children to bond with their adult care-givers in order for them to develop self-esteem. Multiple placements are common in foster care. These disruptions in bonding have negative emotional consequences for the children in foster care. Further, children who "age out of the system" (reach the age of majority while in foster care) are "over-represented among welfare recipients, prison inmates and the homeless." On some occasions, children are maltreated in foster care. Reports on how children fare in foster care are not helpful in determining what effect foster care has on neglected children because these reports do not separate out neglected children from abused children. Even if neglected children experience improved educational performance after they are removed from their homes, the negative effect of removal likely outweighs any intellectual impairment that may have been caused by neglect.

Although it is often claimed that neglect is just as harmful to children as abuse, studies have not confirmed these claims. Neglected children do not fare as well as non-maltreated children in a number of ways, most of which relate to intellect and educational achievement. Poor children in general exhibit similar intellectual and educational problems. Even if neglect increases the negative effects of poverty, if it does not do so appreciably or if those effects are not as damaging as problems caused by removal, one may argue that removal is inappropriate in most neglect cases.

Factors Affecting Removal

Given that most children in the child welfare system are victims of neglect, that neglect is closely associated with poverty, that the negative effects of neglect are difficult to prove, that poverty alone may cause some of the ill effects associated with child neglect, and that removal has serious negative consequences for the child, removal of children from poor parents for neglect should be heavily scrutinized and generally not permitted. Statutes require that children be in imminent danger of harm before they can be removed and that reasonable efforts should be expended to avoid removal.

If children are being removed from their homes to protect them from imminent harm, one would expect that children who have already suffered a serious physical injury would be more likely to be removed than children who have not suffered an obvious injury. Surprisingly, that is not the case. A number of studies have found that family income, not severity of maltreatment, was the most predictive factor of child placement in foster care. In one study examining several factors in placement decisions, the fact that a child was sent to an emergency treatment center for physical or sexual abuse was the weakest predictor of later placement in foster care. In other words, children who were physically or sexually abused were not more likely to be removed from their homes. Another study of children, referring to a hospital child abuse team, found that severity of the injury was not related to placement and that physical injury decreased the likelihood of an out-of-home placement. Overall, children with non-physical injuries were more likely to be removed from their homes. One study found that "only 25 percent of children classified as neglected by a protective services agency suffered immediate physical harm." If children are not being consistently removed to protect them from physical abuse, it is hard to justify removing most neglected children for their own protection when the negative effects of neglect are not as certain as those of abuse that leads to a hospital visit.

If children fare better when they are removed from their homes, one may argue that removal is a positive event for neglected children. However, the negative effects of removal must be weighed against any positive effect on school performance or other behavior. A child who has been adjudicated neglected will, in all likelihood, miss her family and feel a sense of loss when separated, no matter how much better conditions may be in a foster home. Even physically abused children miss their families. In addition, neglected children will suffer permanent loss if their parents' rights are terminated, especially the large number of black children who will never be adopted. Finally, if any positive effects of foster care are due solely to the removal of poverty, removal cannot be justified solely on the basis of poverty even if it has some positive effect on the child.

Treatment

One can argue that poverty will always exist, but if we do not try to alleviate some of the problems caused by poverty, how can we justify removing children from their families? Many critics of the child welfare system argue that, in addition to doing little about the problem of poverty, and despite federal requirements that "reasonable efforts" be expended to keep a family together before a child is removed and before parental rights are terminated, we are not doing enough to help the families whose children we remove. Statistics appear to substantiate these claims.

Foster care placement as a "treatment" for child maltreatment has risen dramatically from thirty percent of children in the system in 1977 to fifty percent in 1997. However, the number of children receiving services has dropped substantially since 1977, when 1.8 million children received services, to approximately 1 million children in 1994. This occurred despite the fact that nearly the same number of children were in foster care in both years.

One study found that, although the most frequent reason for referral for neglect was inadequate supervision of preschool children, a little under eleven percent of the families received day care assistance. Despite the large percentage of child welfare cases involving substance abuse, less than five percent of the families received substance abuse treatment. Thus, service is falling at the same time that the number of families in the system is increasing.

Intervention strategies and treatment programs to alleviate child maltreatment have had mixed results. If we don't know what will be effective and if not much has been effective to date, it may be argued that criticism about state efforts is misplaced. In one project aimed at increasing family reunification, although intensive efforts were helpful, reunification was impossible despite serious efforts in a significant percentage of cases. Factors that indicated a small likelihood of success were severe abuse, school problems, and few socio-economic resources, in that order. It seems that severe poverty plays an important role in who can benefit from therapy as well as who is likely to maltreat, although the question arises once again of whether intractable parental problems result in poverty and difficulty in treatment or whether the depth of poverty causes the decreased likelihood of treatment success.

It is possible that the lack of treatment success might be reversed by trying different intervention tactics. For example, when therapy was aimed at children instead of parents, more than seventy percent of neglected and abused children in one sample showed improvement in all areas of functioning measured by the studies. In other studies aimed at correcting specific behaviors, positive results were obtained and maintained for forty-two weeks after the program ended.

One study found that the negative effects of poverty can be mediated by other factors such as cognitive stimulation and parenting style. However, another study found that good parenting has less beneficial effects on poor children than on those from higher economic families. The authors of the latter study admit to problems with their research model.

Clearly, more work needs to be done to determine to what extent negative outcomes for children are caused by poverty and neglect and how and to what extent government programs can combat those negative effects and protect and nurture children. To the extent we can aim child protection programs at children to remedy the negative effects of neglect and poverty and towards giving poor parents access to mediating conditions that would lower the likelihood of maltreatment, we need to change the focus of child protection efforts. It can be argued that removal in all but the most severe neglect cases (such as failure to thrive or abandonment) is not good for children and that removal without more is not helpful to the children the system aims to protect. Certainly, a sizeable portion of the large proportion of child welfare money that now goes to foster care would be better spent in other ways if the government truly wants to protect children.

CONCLUSION

The United States has a history of separating poor children from their families under the guise of child welfare. Have we rationalized and institutionalized that separation in the name of neglect to the point where we can no longer see it for what it is? Worse yet, have we added to the already heavy burden of the minority community by doing so?

Statistics tell us that poor parents maltreat their children more often than middle class and wealthy parents. The disproportionate numbers of minority parents charged with maltreating their children is not due to any increased maltreatment by minorities, nor does racial bias adequately explain this phenomenon. Minority children are disproportionately poor and, consequently, they are over-represented in the child welfare population.

Many authors have argued, on the basis of the correlation between poverty and maltreatment, that alleviation of poverty would greatly decrease the problem of child maltreatment. It is entirely possible, and likely, that some maltreatment could be averted through financial programs for the poor, especially for the chronically poor and those in the most dire financial straits. The provision of reliable child care and adequate housing and medical care would likely eliminate some potential maltreatment cases. However, most poor parents do not maltreat their children, and it is likely that factors in addition to or other than poverty may cause child maltreatment. What then should be done about neglected children?

Child welfare laws treat abuse and neglect the same. Abuse and neglect are not the same. They result from different causes, respond to different treatments and require different action on the part of the state. Although maltreatment rates increase with poverty, the connection between poverty and neglect is much stronger than that between poverty and abuse. Although there are some problems with defining physical abuse—such as delineating between permissible corporal punishment and impermissible abuse—physical abuse is generally easier to discern than neglect. The definition of harmful neglect is neither clear nor uniformly accepted. Definitional vagaries and the frequent use of a threat of harm instead of proof of definitive past harm make neglect more readily susceptible to bias—racial bias or "middle-class bias"—that *789 reflects cultural differences rather than actual harmful situations. Thus, removal of poor children for neglect should be heavily scrutinized to avoid its disparate impact on minorities.

The most common intervention in child welfare cases is removal of children to foster care. Children are separated from their parents ostensibly to protect those children from abuse, but removal is not based on severity of injury or proven physical injuries. Instead, removal appears to be related to poverty. In fact, despite similar maltreatment rates, different states remove children with differing frequency. Nobody would dispute that a child who has been severely physically injured should be removed from his parents for his protection. If a child is beaten, the damage is clear. Although neglect can cause physical harm (a child left unattended can hurt herself), most children are not removed for physical harm that has already occurred. In addition, otherwise good parents can momentarily neglect their children and not pose a future threat that would require removal.

It is possible that psychological injuries may be worse than physical injuries, but the psychological effects of neglect are not readily distinguishable from those of poverty. Poor children in general have learning and self-esteem problems. Even if some allegedly neglected children fare better in school when they are moved to foster homes, we need to ask if better performance is the result of improved socio-economic conditions or services provided in foster homes that were not available in biological homes. Perhaps everyone would reach their full potential more readily if they could reap the educational benefits that money can buy, but we would not send children to the most affluent families simply for that reason. Additionally, if the removal causes more negative effects than the original neglect, by exacerbating or causing attachment disorders, removal is not for the child's benefit. The need to remove a neglected child to protect him or her is therefore not as clear as for other types of maltreatment.

Much more work needs to be done to understand the causes and effects of poverty and neglect and how to obviate the negative effects of each on children. In the meantime, because the effects of neglect absent poverty are not yet clear, because minorities are disproportionately being removed from their families for what may be poverty without proof they are being critically harmed by their families, serious thought should be given to curbing the practice of removal of neglected children from their homes. It is hard to believe such a policy would cause more harm than the current policy of removal and termination.

STUDY QUESTION

What evidence does Andrea Charlow put forth to support her conclusion of a relationship between *poverty* and *maltreatment*?

CHAPTER 5

Inequality in the Economic Institution

INTRODUCTION

The U.S. economy is an institutionalized system for the production, distribution, and consumption of goods and services. Besides consumerism, *work* is the principal mechanism by which people are involved in the economy. Social scientists are concerned with the unequal distribution of work in the occupational structure. That is, not all racial and ethnic groups and women participate fully and equally in the occupational structure. Rigid patterns of occupational segmentation are pervasive among the nearly 148 million American workers. [1] The U.S. occupational structure is segmented into a primary labor market and a secondary labor market—often called *the dual labor market*. Occupations in the primary labor market provide extensive benefits to workers such as high income, prestige, and job security. These occupations are personally challenging and intrinsically rewarding, they require higher levels of educational attainment, they offer considerable opportunity for advancement, and workers in these positions have significant autonomy and independence from immediate supervision. Primary labor market jobs are traditional white-collar professions such as physicians, lawyers, college and university professors, and corporate and government upper-level management positions. In contrast, occupations in the secondary labor market provide minimal benefits to workers. Attached to secondary labor market occupations are lower incomes, longer workweeks, less job security, less opportunity for advancement, and often the use of harsh and arbitrary discipline. Compared to primary labor jobs, secondary labor market jobs are volatile and vulnerable to economic fluctuations adversely affecting employment rates. [2]

OCCUPATIONAL SEGREGATION

The quest for equal employment opportunity in the United States began in the early 1940s. President Franklin D. Roosevelt decreed that because defense contractors were racially discriminating against badly needed wartime black workers, the federal government required contractors doing business with the federal government to pledge nondiscrimination in the employment of black workers. Not until the 1960s, however, did the federal government require contractors to employ female and black workers. Title VII of the 1964 Civil Rights Act, for example, makes it unlawful for public or private employers to discriminate against persons of color and women, and the 1963 Equal Pay Act makes it illegal for employers to pay unequal wages to women who do the same work as men.[3] Moreover, Congress has used its plenary power over interstate commerce to require American industries to reduce employment discrimination.

Even with prohibitions against employment discrimination, persons of color and women continue to suffer workplace discrimination, resulting in white men continuing to enjoy more affluence and wider participation in the occupational structure than do persons of color and women.[4] White male workers disproportionately occupy positions in the primary labor market, whereas workers of color and women are overrepresented in the secondary labor market. For example, white men are far more likely than persons of color and women to hold positions in managerial and professional specialties and technical, sales, and administrative support. White men occupy approximately 97 percent of the senior management positions in most industrial firms in the United States. Persons of color are disproportionately found in government jobs, elementary and secondary schools, and health and social welfare agencies, but not at the helms of American industries. Although Asian Americans have twice the level of educational attainment as the general population, they are less likely than whites to occupy managerial and executive positions in corporate America. Disproportionate concentrations of Asian American workers are in low- and mid-level jobs with little opportunity for advancement into the managerial ranks of private industry.[5] In contrast, blacks, Latinos, and American Indians are more likely to have such occupations as operators, fabricators, and laborers. Latinos are overrepresented in agricultural production compared to other groups.[6]

Women are similarly situated in the occupational structure. Women are concentrated in such occupational categories as teachers, counselors, and librarians in elementary and secondary schools; in the health and medical field as registered nurses, dietitians, and therapists; in retail sales as cashiers; in administrative support staff as secretaries, typists, and clerks; and in such service occupations as private household workers, health aides, house cleaners, and hairdressers. Men generally hold more prestigious and higher paying positions as executives, managers, and administrators; in such professional specialties as engineers, mathematicians, computer scientists, and lawyers and judges; and in such health care professions as physicians, dentists, and pharmacists; and as college and university professors.[7]

Women of color are not situated similarly to white women in the U.S. occupational structure. Although one can find women of color throughout the occupational structure, the majority of these women remain relegated to low-wage labor positions. Female workers of color have a much lower socioeconomic standing in U.S. society than white female workers despite higher occupational participation rates, primarily because female workers of color have far lower levels of educational attainment. As a result, the annual incomes of women of color are far less than the annual incomes of white women.[8]

Much of the occupational segregation in the United States results from what social scientists term *the glass ceiling,* an invisible barrier preventing workers of color and women from advancing upward in corporate organizations above middle management and into higher-level executive positions. The glass ceiling presents major obstacles to workers of color and women in obtaining higher status occupations in both the private and public sectors.[9] The federal government established a panel of experts commissioned to study the glass-ceiling phenomenon in the American occupational structure. The commission focused primarily on eliminating barriers to the advancement of workers of color and women and to promote workforce diversity. In its first major report, the commission identified several barriers preventing the advancement of workers of color and women to elevated positions in the U.S. occupational structure. One of the most important findings of the commission is that persistent stereotyping creates formidable barriers to occupational advancement for women and workers of color. In *Many Paths to Justice: The Glass Ceiling, The Looking Glass, and Strategies for Getting to the Other Side,* M. Neil Browne and Andrea Giampetro-Meyer suggest legal and nonlegal strategies for women to sever the obstacles created by the "glass ceiling" and "looking glass" to their advancement in the workplace.

An outcome of occupational discrimination is that persons of color are less effective than white persons in transferring higher levels of educational attainment into economic prosperity. For example, white persons earn higher yearly incomes than do blacks, Latinos, Asian Americans, and American Indians with the same educational level. That is, an increase in educational attainment levels for persons of color does not reduce the earnings gap between them and white persons. U.S. census data show that women earn lower incomes than men within all major occupational categories regardless of educational attainment levels. The median earnings of men who worked full time, year round was $40,668 in 2003 and the median earnings of women was $30,724—reflecting a female-to-male earning ratio of 0.76.[10] The wage gap between men and women results from the continued occupational segregation of women into traditional low-wage female-dominated jobs. In California, for example, state civil service jobs pay female workers less than they pay white male workers. There is about a $12,000 difference in the annual salaries between men and women holding civil service jobs in California. Men are generally three times more likely than women to hold state jobs with annual salaries above $70,000. Black and Latino males earn lower annual salaries than white males.[11] There is an exorbitant cost of unequal pay practices resulting from sex discrimination in the workplace. One estimate is that women lose more than $130 billion annually to pay inequity. Unequal pay practices account for an estimated loss of about $420,000 over a lifetime for the average woman.[12]

The earnings ratio between women and men changes dramatically when one considers the race of the women and their earnings measured against white men. The female-to-male earning ratio is 0.75 for Asian American women and white men, but the ratio is 0.70 for white women, 0.62 for black women, 0.58 for American Indian women, and 0.52 for Latinas.[13] Asian American women earn more than white women. In turn, white women earn significantly more than other women of color. The median annual earnings for full-time, year-round employed women is about $33,100 for Asian American women, $30,900 for white women, $27,600 for black women, $25,500 for American Indian women, and $23,200 for Latinas.[14] Women of color have lower annual earnings than white and Asian American women in part because women of color generally have much lower occupational positions and much lower levels of educational attainment.[15] Earning disparities across race, ethnicity, and gender result from the discriminatory practices that produce a segmented labor market, family responsibilities, and direct institutional sex discrimination.[16]

UNEMPLOYMENT

One problem facing American workers is finding meaningful employment. Official statistics show that nearly 8.4 million persons are unemployed in the United States.[17] This figure constitutes 5.8 percent of the labor force. The statistics, however, are misleading because the unemployment rate in the United States is a measure of those persons receiving benefits for unemployment. The national unemployment rate, then, does not account for the hundreds of thousands of workers who have become so discouraged that they have given up looking for a job. The official unemployment rate also does not include the nearly 1.6 million persons that are actively searching for a job. Still other workers are working part time because they cannot find full-time work. Inclusion of discouraged workers, persons that cannot find work, and under-employed workers would surely more than double the unemployment rate in the United States. Similarly, not all racial and ethnic groups are equally represented in unemployment statistics. For example, blacks workers (10.3) are twice as likely to be unemployed than white workers (5.1). Latino workers generally have an unemploy-ment rate of 7.5, but the unemployment rate of Puerto Rican workers is higher at 9.4 and lower for Cuban workers at 6.7. The unemployment rate for Mexican American workers is 7.5, and the unemployment rate for Asian American workers is well below the national average at 4.3. Female workers (5.6) of all races have a lower unemploy-ment rate than male workers (5.9). These unemployment ratios between racial and ethnic groups and among gender groups have remained largely consistent since the 1970s, meaning that the rates endure during recessionary periods as well as during periods of economic growth and expansion. The continued concentration—*ghettoization*—of persons of color into low-wage and low-skilled jobs in manufactur-ing and production will ensure continued race and ethnic disparity in unemployment rates.[18] The American Indian unemployment rate is sometimes *twenty times* higher than what government officials report. George Tinker and Loring Bush explain in *Native American Unemployment: Statistical Games and Coverup* that institutional racism in the national economy, as exemplified by the misrepresentation of unem-ployment rates, prevents American Indians from securing economic well-being.

In a related context, U.S. Census Bureau data show that a significant associa-tion between levels of educational attainment and race and family size. U.S. Census Bureau data documents educational attainment by race and the *size* of the family. For blacks, there is little fluctuation in the rate of family heads who have earned a college degree when the family has between one and five members. But for black families with six or more members, the head of the household is considerably less likely to hold a college degree than black families generally. For whites, four- and five-person families are significantly more likely than smaller families to have a head with a college education. Presumably, the economic success of these families with an educated householder allows them to support more children. But as is the case with black families, once the family size reaches six or more persons, the likelihood that the householder has a college degree goes down sharply.[19]

EXPLOITED CHILD LABOR: AMERICA'S SHAMEFUL SECRET

The events surrounding Kathie Lee Gifford and the Wal-Mart stores that carried her line of clothes labeled Global Fashion paint a deceptive national image of the child labor issue in the United States—young teenage Honduran girls working under armed guard for fifteen-hour-shifts for thirty-one cents an hour produced garments with Gifford earning $9 million and Wal-Mart stores earning $300 million. Gifford is not alone, however. President George W. Bush recently sought approval of the U.S. Congress for the Central American Free Trade Agreement (CAFTA), creating an international free-trade zone between the United States and the Central American countries of Costa Rica, Guatemala, Honduras, Panama, and El Salvador. CAFTA essentially amends trade agreements between these countries for manufactured goods and agricultural products to cross the U.S. borders duty free. Human rights investigators have found that the working conditions of laborers working in factories in Central American countries subject to CAFTA are deplorable and in blatant contradiction to U.S. labor standards. Factories throughout the free-trade zone manufacture clothing for JCPenney, Kohl's, Kmart, Wal-Mart, Sears, Nike, Adidas, Hanes, Fruit of the Loom, Gloria Vanderbilt, Bugle Boy, Old Navy/Gap, Tommy Hilfiger, Polo Jeans, and OshKosh. Under other trade agreements, workers in Haitian sweatshops earn twelve cents an hour manufacturing Mickey Mouse and Pocahontas pajamas for Walt Disney Corporation.[20] In El Salvador, some five thousand boys and girls as young as eight years use machetes to cut sugarcane for nine hours a day in the scorching sun for suppliers to the Coca-Cola Company.[21]

Yet our societal belief of exploitative child labor as primarily a problem in developing nations is far from accurate because millions of children are working in deplorable conditions throughout the United States.[22] More than 4 million American children work in U.S. industries, and most them work in agriculture, manufacturing, and food service.[23] Take thirteen-year-old Damaris, for example, who picks broccoli and lettuce in Arizona where she works fourteen hours a day in 100-degree temperatures. Human Rights Watch investigators explain that Damaris suffers from nosebleeds and has fainting spells related not only to the unbearable physical condition of farm labor but from illnesses caused by exposure from dangerous pesticides as well. Like Damaris, many of these children work to contribute to their family's income. They estimate that between 300,000 and 800,000 children from five to fifteen years of age work as hired laborers in commercial agriculture where work-related fatality rates for child workers are *five times higher* than for children working in nonagricultural jobs.[24] The life expectancy of child agricultural workers is forty-nine years.[25]

About 100,000 farm worker children suffer injuries annually in the United States. Moreover, farm labor contractors subject many young female agricultural workers to sexual advances with impunity out of the children's fear of reporting such abuses to officials. There is no societal commitment to protect American children from abusive labor in the United States, although the federal government has acted boldly to protect child labor in foreign nations. Human Rights Watch put it this way:

> This shameful tolerance for abusive child labor in American fields stands in stark contrast to U.S. leadership in combating child labor overseas. The U.S. devotes $30 million a year to international programs to end abusive child labor—a tenfold increase from just two years ago. Last year, the U.S. became one of the first countries to ratify a new international convention to eliminate the worst forms of child labor, including practices such as child slavery, debt bondage, sexual exploitation and forced labor. Congress recently acted to deny trade preferences to countries that fail to meet their legal obligations to end such abusive child abuse.
>
> This commitment to abolish inappropriate child labor abroad must be matched by a commitment to protect children from abusive labor here in the Untied States.
>
> Child labor in U.S. agriculture is America's shameful secret. Our laudable efforts to protect children from exploitative labor overseas appear deeply hypocritical unless matched by efforts . . . to protect children here at home.[26]

Agriculture involves extremely hazardous work for children, but it provides the least protection to child labor. The impact of working long hours under dangerous physical conditions poses long-lasting and severely negative consequences for children who are still developing physically, mentally, and emotionally. The long hours of work deprive child farm workers of education, which perpetuates poverty already afflicting farm worker families. Forty-five percent of farm worker children drop out of school, and because of their poverty children of farm worker families must work, which in turn denies them the "joys of childhood" and "robs them of a future in which fully realize their potentials as human beings."[27]

But the federal government simply ignores the problem of child farm workers.[28] Congress has yet to revise the child labor provisions under the 1938 Fair Labor Standards Act (FLSA) that allows children as young as twelve years to labor in agriculture (although the most common ages at which children begin agricultural work are between thirteen and fifteen), provides no limits to the number of hours per day a child can work, and makes no provisions for overtime pay to child workers. Moreover, Congress exempts all farms with fewer than eleven employees from enforcement of the Occupational Safety and Health Administration regulations.[29] As a result, farm owners refuse to give child workers access to adequate drinking water and rest room facilities, which, in turn, contributes to the children's dehydration, pesticide poisoning, and susceptibility to bacterial infections.[30] One study found Mexican American children working in farm fields still wet with pesticides, and interviews with child farm workers discovered a sixteen-year-old boy mixing and spraying pesticides several times a week without wearing protective gear "because his employer told him he had nothing to worry about." As law professor Maria L. Ontiveros explains in *Lessons from the Field: Female Farmworkers and the Law*, exposure to toxic chemicals in the fields of California is one reason the farm worker infant mortality rate exceeds twice the infant mortality rate for the greater U.S. population.[31] She explains further that the mortality rates among young California farm worker children are 50 percent higher than that.

Moreover, the rates of diabetes, parasitic and infectious diseases, and chronic disease are well above the national average for the farm worker population.

Large farming operations circumvent workers' rights by claiming that farm labor contractors bringing children across the border are the children's actual employer. The laws governing child labor in agriculture are completely inadequate, and government officials are extremely lax in enforcing child labor laws. Although more than a million child labor violations occur in U.S. agriculture every year, only a small fraction are actually uncovered by the Department of Labor—officials cited only 104 child labor violations in agriculture in 1998. Penalties for child labor law violations are also weak (less than $1,000 per violation) so farmers are not at all deterred from using illegal child labor.[32] Some legislators have unsuccessfully urged the Department of Labor aggressively to pursue and punish agricultural employers who illegally employ children.[33]

Hundreds of thousands other children work in equally dangerous nonagricultural jobs that government agencies do not count because they work in jobs that are largely not reported. Unfortunately, official statistics never recognize the thousands of children suffering from ruthless exploitation, disabling injuries, and fatalities in the workplace. Hospital emergency rooms treat some 64,000 teenagers annually for job-related injuries. Industrial machinery, electrocution, and falls primarily contribute to work-related fatalities of teenagers. Hundreds of children die every year from work-related injuries. Many of these deaths occur in direct violation of federal and state labor laws. In Los Angeles, for example, half of all working teenagers are working in violation of laws barring employers from working youngsters past 7 P.M. during the school year. Fifteen percent of these children are working in violation of laws barring companies from employing children in construction jobs. Another 5 percent of working children are employed in violation of laws barring children from working with meat slicers, dough-making equipment, and in occupations involving driving. Many companies prefer to hire teenagers because they can work teenagers part time without paying benefits. Illegal child labor is particularly rampant in sweatshops in the garment industry. Investigators in New York have found children working in sweatshops who had lost fingers while operating machines.

POVERTY

Many social commentators are concerned that the persistence of poverty in U.S. society may be generating a permanent underclass consisting mostly of minorities and nontraditional families. In 2003 nearly 36 million people in the United States, or 12.5 percent of the overall population, lived in poverty.[34] Over the last several decades, the nation's poor have become increasingly black and Latino and increasingly concentrated in inner-city ghettos. Although 15.9 million poor white people account for 44.4 percent of impoverished persons in the United States, blacks and Latinos are *three times* more likely than whites to be poor. While 8.2 percent of the white population is poor, 24.4 percent of blacks and 22.5 percent of Latinos are poor. The poverty rate for Asian Americans is 11.8 percent. About a fifth of all American children under the age of eighteen are poor, and roughly two fifths of these children are children of color. The poor continue to live in mostly female-headed households (28.0 percent) where the head of the household has a very low level of educational attainment and skill development and is often functionally illiterate. About a third of all white families and nearly half of all families of color are female-headed families living in poverty.

Policymakers have implemented reforms to encourage poor people to leave public assistance programs and enter the workforce. For example, Congress passed the Personal Responsibility and Work Opportunity Reconciliation Act in 1996 intending to transform public assistance in the United States by moving recipients from welfare to work. Such reforms are based on the notion that most indigent single mothers could move out of poverty if they would get jobs. The fact is most poor women are active participants in the labor force but they are concentrated in low-skilled, low-wage jobs that provide them little hope of escaping poverty. Our national image of a welfare mother is that "she's poor, deceptive and slovenly . . . neglects her children and spends taxpayers' hard earned wages on drugs or booze . . . [and] the color of her skin is dark."[35] Essentially, welfare mothers have become a convenient scapegoat for a nation concerned with gross economic uncertainty. We blame welfare mothers for the exorbitant cost of entitlement programs, and we often portray these women as "unwed mothers." To many Americans, an unwed mother is "any mom without a male breadwinner, whether she is separated, divorced, abused, abandoned or widowed, and 'illegitimate child' is the label for any kid not claimed by a male breadwinner."[36]

In enacting the Personal Responsibility and Work Opportunity Reconciliation Act (PRWORA) in 1996, Congress repealed the program of Aid to Families with Dependent Children (AFDC) and instead created the block grant program of Temporary Assistance for Needy Families (TANF). The act entitles states to fixed block grants and to operate their own programs if the programs impose work-trigger time limits, lifetime benefit cutoff time limits, and minimum work participation rates. The act also expanded funding for childcare. Despite these reforms, our conventional notion of welfare mothers remains inaccurate. Consider the following facts about welfare mothers.[37] First, in 2003, the annual maximum combined TANF, food stamps, and earned income benefit for a single parent family with two children, working part time at minimum wage, ranges from a high of $19,686 (103 percent of poverty) in Alaska to a low of $12,219 (69.9 percent of poverty) in Tennessee. Given the official poverty level for a family of four is $18,660 a year, Alaska's assistance to needy families is 103 percent of poverty and Tennessee's is 69.9 percent of poverty.[38] States benefits fall far below the money necessary to maintain even a subsistence level of existence for families with children. Often families must defer some of the basic living requirements. Interestingly, roughly 3 million female-headed families have the highest rates of hunger in America, and more than 13 million children live in families with severe food shortages.[39] The cash money received from state assistance would make it difficult for even some mothers to support drug or alcohol habits. Second, welfare mothers do not have additional children to increase their monthly welfare allotments. The average size of welfare families is actually smaller than the typical size of American families. Welfare families usually consist of a single mother and two children. Third, government cash subsidies (including food stamps) to welfare mothers are about 3 percent of the federal budget. Entitlements to other welfare recipients are far more costly to the federal government than welfare families. Fourth, black females are not most of the welfare mothers. Black welfare mothers are 39 percent of the families that qualify for assistance, whites are slightly more than 32 percent, Latinos are nearly 24 percent, Asians Americans and Pacific Islanders are

2.5 percent, and American Indians are 1.4 percent.[40] Additionally, because of federal grant minimum work participation rules and sixty-month limits on eligibility (excluding family violence and other hardship waivers), most welfare mothers receive aid for the short term. Fifth, welfare mothers often work outside the home at jobs that pay minimal wages and provide no health benefits or child-care facilities (although state programs provide for Medicaid and child care). Nevertheless, "when they stay at home to care for their children, they are condemned as lazy. When affluent married homemakers do the same, they are praised for their maternal devotion."[41] In her article in *Women, Welfare, Reform, and the Preservation of a Myth*, Susan L. Thomas examines how traditional poverty myths influence the sociopolitical discourse on contemporary welfare reform. She argues that the "prevailing 'culture of single motherhood' myth engendered current reforms and that the result welfare reforms strengthen the basis for the myth."

Moreover, substantial evidence indicates that this distorted image of welfare mothers is often the justification for disparities in access to and receipt of services for mothers of color on welfare. A recent statement of the U.S. Commission on Civil Rights revealed disturbing facts about the experiences of women of color and welfare assistance: welfare officials require people of color more often than white persons to perform "workfare" (working for a welfare check rather than actual wages); one out of six female welfare recipients experience sexual harassment in the workplace; more than a third of women experience invasive behavior from welfare officials regarding their sexual activities; 62 percent of recipients with English-speaking difficulties experience language barriers; welfare officials are more likely to sanction black and American Indian recipients than members of other racial groups for noncompliance with the regulations governing welfare; whites are more likely to receive child-care subsidies (70 percent) than other groups, with Americans Indians being least likely (42 percent) to receive similar subsidies; and in many cases, white women are more likely to receive TANF benefits for unborn children than women of color. Based on these and other findings, the commission has recommended that the federal government promote policies to alleviate the disparities in welfare entitlement and advance the underlying societal objectives of welfare reform in America.[42]

SUMMARY

This chapter provides compelling evidence that occupational segregation and segmentation, unemployment and underemployment, workplace divisiveness and dangerousness, exploitation and endangerment of child workers, housing segregation, and impoverishment drastically hamper American workers. Workers of color and women are highly segmented in the occupational structure because of institutional discrimination. Relatedly, unemployment and underemployment disproportionately affect workers of color and women more than white workers. Occupational segregation creates a divisive work environment where persons of color and women perceive their workplaces as unfair and repressive. Labor statistics further show that because of occupational segregation, some workers are more susceptible to workplace dangers than other workers. At first glance, we may not relate housing discrimination to the workplace; many scholars have argued that where one lives affects employment opportunities. Limiting employment opportunities also has an effect on poverty rates. We have also questioned the profit motivation of corporate America and its systemic oppression of child labor in the agricultural and manufacturing industries both inside and outside of the United States. The exploitation of child workers by U.S. corporations creates inherent dangers to the safety and welfare primarily of children of color. Moreover, children laboring in sweatshops, farm fields, and restaurants at the cost of lost educational opportunities perpetuates the cycle of poverty for these children.

ENDNOTES

1. U.S. Department of Labor, Bureau of Labor Statistics, *The Employment Situation: August 2004*, http://stats.bls.gov/news.release/pdf/empsit.pdf.
2. Arne Kalleberg, Barbara F. Reskin, and Ken Hudson, "Bad Jobs in America: Standard and Nonstandard Employment Relations and Job Quality in the United States," *American Sociological Review*, 65 (2000): 256.
3. For a comprehensive discussion on Title VII of the 1964 Civil Rights Act and the Equal Pay Act of 1963 pertaining to female workers, see Leo Kanowitz, *Women and the Law: The Unfinished Revolution* (Albuquerque: University of New Mexico Press, 1969), pp. 100–148.
4. Reynolds Farley, "Blacks, Hispanics, and White Ethnic Groups: Are Blacks Uniquely Disadvantaged? *American Economic Review*, 80 (1980): 2.
5. Nancy Rivera Brooks, "Study of Asians in U.S. Finds Many Struggling," *Los Angeles Times*, May 19, 1994, p. A1.
6. U.S. Census Bureau, *Statistical Abstracts of the United States: 2003*, http://www.census.gov/prod/2004pubs/03statab/labor.pdf.
7. Ibid.
8. Amy Caiazza, April Shaw, and Misha Werschkul, *Women's Economic Status in the States: Wide Disparities by Race, Ethnicity, and Region*, Institute for Women's Policy Research (2004), http://www.iwpr.org/pdf/R260.pdf.
9. Nijole Benokraitis and Joe R. Feagin, *Modern Sexism: Blatant, Subtle, and Overt Discrimination* (Englewood Cliffs, NJ: Prentice Hall, 1995).
10. Carmen DeNavas-Walt, Bernadette D. Proctor, and Robert J. Mills, *Income, Poverty, and Health Insurance Coverage in the United States: 2003*, Current Population Reports, U.S. Census Bureau (August 2004), http://www.census.gov/prod/2004pubs/p60–226.pdf.
11. "State's Female Workers Paid Less Than Men, Study Finds," *Los Angeles Times*, April 25, 1995, p. A1.
12. WIN News, "Face the Facts: Wage Discrimination and Equal Pay in the U.S.," 23 *Women International Network*, 77 (1997).
13. Caiazza et al., *Women's Economic Status in the States*.
14. Caiazza et al., *Women's Economic Status in the States.*.
15. Gloria Bonilla-Santiago, "A Portrait of Hispanic Women in the United States," in S. Rix, ed., *The American Woman 1990–1991: A Status Report* (New York: W.W. Norton, 1990).
16. *Supra* note 9; R. Fuller and R. Schoenberger, "The Gender Salary Gap: Do Academic Achievement, Intern Experience, and College Major Make a Difference?" *Social Science Quarterly*, 72 (1991): 715.
17. U.S. Census Bureau, *Statistical Abstracts of the United States, 2003*, http://www.census.gov/prod/www/statistical-abstract-03.html.
18. Matt L. Huffman and Philip N. Cohen, "Racial Wage Inequality: Job Segregation and Devaluation Across U.S. Labor Markets," *American Journal of Sociology*, 109 (2004): 902.
19. The Journal of Blacks in Higher Education, *Census Bureau Reports on Educational Attainment by Race and Family Size* (October 14, 2004), http://www.jbhe.com/.
20. National Labor Committee, *Gildan Production in El Salvador*, April 2004, http://www.nlcnet.org/campaigns/copatex/copatex.opt.pdf; Elizabeth Becker, "Central American Deal Ignites a Trade Debate," *New York Times* (April 6, 2004), http://www.nlcnet.org/campaigns/copatex/NYT040604.pdf; National Labor Committee, *AAA Honduras* (ret. May 19, 2004), http:// www.nlcnet.org/campaigns/ca03/AAA/aaa.pdf; National Labor Committee, *Sweating for Kohl's* (ret. May 19, 2004), http://www.nlcnet.org/campaigns/archive/sweatingforkohls/thefacts.shtml; National Labor Committee, *KB Manufacturing* (October 2003), http://www.nlcnet.org/campaigns/ca03/ kb/kb.report.pdf; National Labor Committee, *Industrial Embroidery* (ret. May 19, 2004), http://www.nlcnet.org/campaigns/ca03/industrial/industrial.pdf; U.S. Department of State, "Trafficking in Persons Report," June 11, 2003, http://www.state.gov/g/tip/rls/tiprpt/2003/21262.htm.

21. Human Rights Watch, *Turning a Blind Eye: Hazardous Child Labor in El Salvador's Sugarcane Cultivation* (2004), http://hrw.org/reports/2004/elsalvador0604/.

22. Philip Landrigan and Jane McCammon, "Child Labor: Still with Us After All These Years," *Public Health Report*, 112 (1997): 466.

23. U.S. Department of Health and Human Services, "Worker Related Injuries and Illnesses Associated with Child Labor," *Morbidity and Mortality Weekly Report*, 45 (1996): 464.

24. Guadalupe T. Luna, "An Infinite Distance?: Agricultural Exceptionalism and Agricultural Labor, *University of Pennsylvania Journal of Labor and Employment Law*, 1 (1998): 487, 498; Human Rights Watch, *Fingers to the Bone: United States Failure to Protect Child Farmworkers* (June 2000), http://www .hrw.org/reports/2000/frmwrkr/.

25. Jeanne M. Glader, "A Harvest of Shame: The Imposition of Independent Contractor Status on Migrant Farmworkers and Its Ramifications for Migrant Children," *Hastings Law Journal*, 42 (1991): 1455, 1460.

26. Victoria Riskin and Mike Farrell, *Profiting on the Backs of Child Laborers*, Human Rights Watch (October 12, 2000), http://www.hrw.org/editorials/2000/farmwrk1012.htm. See also Human Rights Watch, *Fingers to the Bone: United States Failure to Protect Child Farmworkers* (June 2000), http://www.hrw.org/reports/2000/frmwrkr/.

27. National Council of Churches USA, "Farm Worker Conditions," http://www.ncccusa.org/ publicwitness/mtolive/conditions.html; Human Rights Watch, *Fingers to the Bone: United States Failure to Protect Child Farmworkers* (June 2000), http://www.hrw.org/reports/2000/frmwrkr/ ; Darlene Adkins, "Health, Education, Labor and the Convention on the Rights of the Child," *Georgetown Journal on Fighting Poverty*, 5 (1998): 295; Judy Wiseman, "Barriers to Education for Children of Migrant Farm Workers," *San Joaquin Agricultural Law Review*, 1 (2003): 49.

28. For a discussion on the history of the legislative oversight of child labor in agriculture discussing obstacles such as the potential costs to the industry, the pervasive myths, and the balance of political power that have opposed the limiting or prohibiting of child labor in agriculture, see Davin C. Curtiss, "The Fair Labor Standards Act and Child Labor in Agriculture," *Journal of Corporation Law*, 20 (1995): 303.

29. National Council of Churches USA, "Farm Worker Conditions," http://www.ncccusa.org/ publicwitness/mtolive/conditions.html.

30. Nate Albee, "Protecting Child Farmers," http://www.consistentlife.org/Protecting%20child% 20farmers.htm.

31. Maria L. Ontiveros, "Lessons from the Field: Female Farmworkers and the Law," *Maine Law Review*, 55 (2003): 157, 170.

32. Human Rights Watch, "Failure to Protect Child Farmworkers," http://www.hrw.org/campaigns/ crp/farmchild/failure.htm.

33. "Tougher Regulation Urged for Child Farm Labor," *Omaha World Herald*, June 12, 1998, p. 11.

34. Carmen DeNavas-Walt, Bernadette D. Proctor, and Robert J. Mills, *Income, Poverty, and Health Insurance Coverage in the United States: 2003*, U.S. Census Bureau, Current Population Reports (August 2004), http://www.census.gov/prod/2004pubs/p60–226.pdf.

35. "Which of Us Isn't Taking Welfare," *Los Angeles Times*, December 27, 1994, p. A1.

36. U.S. Commission on Civil Rights, *Disadvantaged Women and Their Children* (Washington, DC: U.S. Government Printing Office, 1983).

37. The *official* purposes for welfare reform under PRWORA provide assistance to needy families so that children may be cared for in their own homes or in the homes of relatives; to end the dependence of needy parents on government benefits by promoting job preparation, work, and marriage; to prevent and reduce the incidence of out-of-wedlock pregnancies and establish annual numerical goals for preventing and reducing the incidence of these pregnancies; and to encourage the formation and maintenance of two-parent families. See U.S. Department of Health and Human Services, House Ways and Means Committee Prints: 108–6, 2004 Green Book, Section 7: Temporary Assistance to Needy Families (TANF), http://frwebgate.access.gpo.gov/cgi-bin/getdoc.cgi?dbname=108_green_book& docid=f:wm006_07.pdf.

38. U.S. Department of Health and Human Services, House Ways and Means Committee Prints: 108–6, 2004 Green Book, Section 7: Temporary Assistance to Needy Families (TANF), http://frwebgate .access.gpo.gov/cgi-bin/getdoc.cgi?dbname=108_green_book& docid=f:wm006_07.pdf.

39. Mark Nord, Margaret Andrews, and Seven Carlson, U.S. Department of Agriculture, *Household Food Insecurity in the U.S., 2002* (October 2003), http://www.ers.usda.gov/publications/fanrr35/.

40. U.S. Department of Health and Human Services, House Ways and Means Committee Prints: 108–6, 2004 Green Book, Section 7: Temporary Assistance to Needy Families (TANF), http://frwebgate. access.gpo.gov/cgi-bin/getdoc.cgi?dbname=108_green_book& docid=f:wm006_07.pdf.

41. *Supra* note 81.

42. U.S. Commission on Civil Rights, *A New Paradigm for Welfare Reform: The Need for Civil Rights Enforcement*, A Statement by the U.S. Commission on Civil Rights (August 2002), http:// www.usccr.gov/.

Many Paths to Justice: The Glass Ceiling, the Looking Glass, and Strategies for Getting to the Other Side

M. Neil Browne and Andrea Giampetro-Meyer

Whether an employee or group of employees is trying to shatter a glass ceiling, or tumble through a looking glass with the blessing of powerful people on the other side, they must recognize the many paths to justice, and the overriding importance of their relationship with their employer as a determinant of their strategy.

THE MESSY REALITY OF THE GLASS CEILING

Putting the Issues in Context

Factors that hold workers back fall into two general categories. First, some factors that hold workers back relate to the individual worker. For example, a particular individual may lack the right background or experience to be eligible for promotion. However, the individual worker has control over some factors; he or she can strive to attain the experience necessary to be eligible for promotion. The second category of factors includes those that are external to the individual worker. The employer, who shapes and defines the ways workers advance, enacts formal or informal policies that may hold individual employees back. In some organizations, informal and formal policies hold back entire groups of workers. When writers describe the glass ceiling, they often make assumptions about the extent to which employees or employers hold the tools necessary to shatter the glass ceiling.

As this section describes the many factors that hold managers back, envision a pie with slices of different sizes each representing a factor that impedes promotion. Legal scholars, organizational behavior experts, and others who write about glass ceiling issues using this approach envision different sized slices for each factor. For example, some writers assume that choices individual workers make account for almost the entire glass ceiling phenomenon, while others assume an employer's

---

Source: M. Neil Browne and Andrea Giampetro-Meyer, "Many Paths To Justice: The Glass Ceiling, The Looking Glass, and Strategies for Getting to the Other Side," *Hofstra Labor and Employment Law Journal.*

discriminatory practices constitute the largest portion of the pie. Additionally, writers might look at the same facts and categorize them differently. One writer might see a particular employment practice as a glass wall, while another writer might look at the same facts and interpret them as raising an issue of individual choices.

It is also important to point out that when writers think about the glass ceiling, they are likely to envision competing versions of the "stock story." The introduction to this Article presented the stock story of the glass ceiling defined as a white woman who believes her lack of advancement is related to the sexist attitudes of the white men in superior positions. In this scenario, the white men in positions of power are bewildered and believe their rationale for holding a particular woman back is rooted in factors that are gender neutral. This stock story is so often acted out in media portrayals of the glass ceiling that many Americans assume the glass ceiling issue is a gender issue, and nothing more.

Some writers, however, either offer competing stories or assume the stock story focuses on the particular glass ceiling issue they face. The glass ceiling story could highlight the experience of a black man whose employers hold him back because they continually underestimate his potential and assume he is bound for failure. Alternatively, a gay man might wish the stock story focused on the glass ceiling issue that his ability to discuss his personal life at work is impaired. When he cannot discuss his personal life, he cannot befriend those in positions of power as readily as workers whose personal lives are more socially acceptable. This lack of collegiality affects his ability to rise in the organization. Consider also the story of an African American woman who sees issues of race as far more important than issues of gender. This woman may see the unfair assumptions executives make about her because of her gender, but these assumptions are far less troubling than blatantly racist comments

employers make about her. The point of these examples is to add another layer of complexity to the glass ceiling picture. It is likely that several groups of employees wish the stock story of the glass ceiling showed an awareness of their particular circumstances.

As the following paragraphs describe the many barriers that hold workers back, note that these descriptions take place in the context of differing opinions about whether the primary focus should be on the individual worker, a group of workers, or the employer. Also note the different perceptions about the magnitude of each factor as a barrier and competing stock stories about the glass ceiling.

THE MANY FACTORS THAT HOLD MANAGERS BACK

Choice

Scholars who write about glass ceiling issues generally agree that the personal choices workers make affect the likelihood they will rise to a high-level position in a company. For example, most people would agree that employees use their time differently, and different choices about the use of time affect the likelihood of job promotion. Employees who value leisure more than spending time at work cannot expect this choice to be rewarded with promotions. Also, individuals make different investments in human capital. General human capital consists of investments people make to increase their productivity, such as education, on-the-job training or experience. Assuming equal opportunity in access to an employer's programs that allow investment in human capital, an employee who seeks additional education, training, and experience would reasonably expect promotions, while one who does not make similar investments could not reasonably expect rewards.

In addition to personal choices with a clear link to productivity, other personal choices may also affect whether upper-level executives perceive a particular manager as having the potential to become an upper-level executive. For example, a book that gives guidance to women who want to shatter the "last glass ceiling," the American presidency, provides a "how to" guide that includes tips about looking good and getting a haircut. These tips are two of thirteen "how to" points. Another author devotes a book to telling managers how to create an executive image. This book covers everything from the facial expressions a person should choose to display, to the kinds of clothing most consistent with creating an executive image.

Informal Barriers

Sometimes employees point out informal barriers that prevent them from attaining promotions in corporations. For example, some employees point out that employers who call meetings after standard working hours (e.g., 5 or 6 P.M.) create an informal barrier for employees with child care responsibilities. The employees who complain are often women. This policy is informal when meetings arise somewhat spontaneously, or when an employee accepts a job not knowing bosses will expect flexibility in scheduling meetings. Another informal barrier is that some employers assume women will not want to travel abroad because of work/life balance issues. This policy is informal when it is an unstated assumption that guides an executive's unwritten policy. In reality, this assumption is a myth that harms women's upward mobility, especially if job promotion requires evidence of international experience.

Glass Walls

The metaphor of a glass wall relates to the concept of occupational segregation. The metaphor refers to lateral barriers that prevent employees from seeking the kinds of jobs that lead to promotions. Occupational segregation refers to the fact that women and some minorities (e.g., African Americans) pursue or are forced into certain kinds of jobs. For example, women may choose, or employers may force them into occupations that require the ability to smooth disagreements. Specifically, women are more likely than men to end up in jobs in the human resources department. Some employers are likely to steer African American and Hispanic employees away from visible, strategically important jobs and into supportive, less powerful positions, such as positions in communications departments. Sometimes, employers refuse to believe women and African Americans can expand their skills into other areas, such as jobs that require intense data analysis or an understanding of complex finance issues. When employers refuse to offer a range of job opportunities to women and minority employees, these employees are likely to say they are experiencing a glass wall.

Stereotypes

Sometimes, employers rely on stereotypes when they decide whom to advance in a particular organization. A stereotype is a probabilistic belief people use to categorize people. Stereotypes often generate erroneous generalizations about women and people of color. Examples of common stereotypes that affect managers are the view that women should be deferential rather than assertive, African American workers are lazy or incompetent, and employees of certain national origins might be untrustworthy. If an employer acts based upon stereotypical beliefs about a particular employee or a group of employees, many people would describe this form of action as discriminatory.

Discrimination

One form of discrimination is individual discrimination. This type of discrimination is what we typically think of when we say we believe someone is treating someone else less favorably due to a particular trait, such as race or gender. Individual discrimination is a result of "isolated prejudiced individuals" who make inappropriate decisions about who gets the organization's rewards (e.g., the job, the promotion, the admission into a particular program). For instance, if a particular corporate vice-president fails to promote an assertive African American woman because he sees her as "uppity," that would be an example of individual discrimination. Those who care about individual discrimination want to remove prejudiced individuals from decision-making roles. The organization should fire or discipline the vice-president who fails to promote the female executive based upon uninformed or irrational beliefs about others. There is no need for broad remedies for discrimination if the cause of discrimination is individual prejudice. We blame the "bad actor," implement an individual consequence, and move on.

A second form of discrimination is institutionalized discrimination. This form of discrimination "is not only historical, but also pervasive and ongoing." This view assumes that no individual prejudice or hostility is necessary to show discrimination. Rather, when discrimination is institutionalized, it becomes part of the shared expectations about who deserves the organization's rewards. These shared expectations are eventually built into the way things are done. "Institutional inequity is often hard to see in everyday interactions." An example of institutionalized discrimination would be an employer who uses a performance evaluation system as a barrier to advancement for a group of employees, such as African American employees.

Legal Responses to Obstacles

Although several federal statutes prohibit employment discrimination, the most important statute is Title VII of the Civil Rights Act

of 1964. This law prohibits discrimination on the basis of race, color, national origin, religion, and gender at any stage of employment, including promotion. In particular, Title VII prohibits discrimination against protected classes "with respect to compensation, terms, conditions, or privileges of employment. . . ." Title VII also makes it illegal for an employer "to limit, segregate, or classify his employees . . . in any way which would deprive or tend to deprive any individual of employment opportunities or otherwise adversely affect his status as an employee. . . ." Under Title VII, plaintiffs have two tests they can assert to prove their claims—the disparate treatment and disparate impact tests.

The disparate treatment test is relevant when an employer has engaged in intentional discrimination. The disparate treatment test has several steps. First, the plaintiff must prove by a preponderance of the evidence that she is a member of one of the protected classes (in this case sex), and that she was not treated as well as a similarly situated employee who is not a member of the protected class. If the plaintiff succeeds in proving the first step of the test, the court presumes the employer engaged in unlawful discrimination. At all times, the burden of proof remains with the plaintiff. However, once the presumption has been made, the burden of production shifts to the defendant. The defendant must articulate a legitimate, nondiscriminatory reason for the alleged discrimination. If the defendant meets its burden of production, the burden shifts to the plaintiff, who must prove that the employer's legitimate reason was a mere pretext for an illegal motive. Employees often show pretext by proving that the employer applied its legitimate employment practice unevenly. Also, the plaintiff may show that the employer was motivated by discrimination. Although courts are allowed to infer a discriminatory motive, the United States Supreme Court has made it clear the plaintiff must allege and prove intentional discrimination.

The disparate impact test is relevant when the plaintiff wants to focus on an employer's facially neutral practice that has a disparate impact on a protected group and cannot be justified by a business necessity. To prove a prima facie case of disparate impact discrimination, a plaintiff must identify a specific employment practice that created the disparate impact. Next, the plaintiff uses statistical evidence to show that "the practice in question has caused the exclusion of applicants for jobs or promotions because of their membership in a protected group." If the plaintiff succeeds in proving these two elements of the prima facie case, the burden of production and persuasion shifts to the defendant, who must show that the challenged practice is job related for the position in question and consistent with business necessity.

MANY PATHS TO JUSTICE: ALTERNATIVE STRATEGIES FOR RESPONDING TO LOOKISM

Putting the Issue in Context

As the introduction pointed out, lookism is the belief that appearance is an indicator of a person's value. It refers to society's construction of a standard for beauty or attractiveness, and the resulting oppression that occurs through stereotypes and generalizations about those who do and do not meet society's standards. In the context of hidden barriers to advancement, lookism is important because employers may be judging the worth of particular managers based upon superficial characteristics rather than merit. Employers may be comparing good-looking managers to managers with below-average looks, and rewarding attractiveness.

When putting the issue of lookism in context, it is also important to note that the metaphor of a glass ceiling is off-track. Instead of a glass ceiling, imagine a looking glass. Women step up to the looking glass and see

their own image reflected back. Like Alice stepping through her looking glass, all that women must do is step through the mirror to join the corporate world. The factor that allows some women to step through and forces others to stay behind is the actual image reflected in the mirror. Women who are more attractive can step through the looking glass and tumble into the world of business, while women who are not as attractive are left to gaze at their reflections on the other side of the mirror.

As revealing as that metaphorical jaunt may be, it has things more than a little wrong. A mirror ordinarily provides a visual copy of what it reflects. But in the case of a woman who stares into the mirror, the relevant image is not the one bouncing back to the woman, but rather what a typical man sees when he views an image such as the one ricocheting back to the woman in the mirror. The significance of this external interpreter of the image is that, unlike the woman in the looking glass illustration above, women cannot just step through the glass; they must be permitted to enter the corporate hierarchy. Power relations thereby mediate between how women look and how they will be treated in labor markets. It is possible that a variety of factors, including race and sexual orientation, also affect power relations.

Some good-looking managers have the additional advantage of good looks as granting sexual power. For example, an attractive white woman may be the most promotable employee if the men above her in a corporate hierarchy factor in sexual attraction in addition to good looks. If heterosexual white men are the decision-makers about who will and will not get promoted, and attractiveness defined in sexual terms is an unstated part of the decision-making process, some groups are at a disadvantage, even if they are relatively attractive. For example, gay men and African American women may be out of the running for upper-level positions, even if they are especially attractive. It is possible that some white men are willing to allow women to break out of their traditional roles as helpers into positions of equality. Some men may prefer to pass this power to white women over other groups, as they may feel an affinity to white women. In addition, white men may feel some need to protect the white women who tumble through the looking glass, especially if they perceive these women as potential mates and/or similar to their own working wives and mothers of their children.

APPEARANCE AS ONE OF THE MANY FACTORS THAT HOLD MANAGERS BACK

Choice

For some managers, choices they make with regard to their appearance affect the likelihood they will rise to high-level positions within a company. "How-to" books on the glass ceiling include numerous tips about how to create an executive image. Writers who suggest that employees' choices hold them back would point out that employees have a great deal of control over their attractiveness, and hence their promotability. Below-average looking managers are free to choose whether to become more attractive. Employees make choices about whether to purchase high-quality clothing, take steps to reach an attractive body size and shape, undergo plastic surgery to improve facial features, fix imperfect smiles, and wear the right shoes to achieve an appealing pealing height.

Informal Barriers

Informal barriers are unstated assumptions that guide an employer's unwritten policies. For example, suppose an employer develops a highly competitive leadership development program. The program seeks applicants with the most leadership potential. Presumably, leadership potential would be defined and

measured by upper-level management. Selection criteria would include standard measures of merit, such as the manager's ability to use resources efficiently, and his or her ability to motivate subordinates. Now, suppose a review of photographs of past participants in the program suggests that decision-makers have demonstrated a preference for good-looking managers. It is possible, perhaps likely, that below-average appearance presents an unstated barrier to entry into a program that is likely to enhance a manager's future promotions.

Glass Walls

It is possible that a manager's appearance is linked to occupational segregation. The question here is whether upper-level managers channel employees into particular jobs based upon their perceptions of an employee's attractiveness, and whether this channeling puts some workers at a disadvantage. It is important to note the link between promotability and access to line or revenue generating jobs. Here, the issue of attractiveness may be tricky. It is likely that upper-level executives will urge relatively attractive employees to take positions that allow them to use their appearance to gain favor with those outside the company. For instance, one might imagine an attractive woman working in the public relations department, presenting a positive image of the company to outsiders. Public relations jobs are not linked to generating revenue, so managers who take this kind of position may eventually experience a glass wall. On the other hand, imagine the attractive person in a sales position, a job that is obviously linked to revenue generation. This attractive manager is setting the stage for upward mobility. Managers who are below-average in terms of appearance might face subtle bias that will prevent them from generating the kind of revenue employers associate with "high potential" employees.

Stereotypes

People have been reluctant to talk about the bias toward more attractive people, which this article refers to as 'lookism.' Admitting this bias reveals an unpleasant side of humans. Favoring people because they are attractive implies that we are more concerned with superficial features than we are with performance variables. Some people simply refuse to believe that lookism persists and that it might be a factor in women's success. People are also reluctant to discuss 'lookism' because it is difficult to determine whether people are exhibiting a bias for the beautiful. Unlike racism or sexism, where the subject of the discrimination is more easily distinguishable, determining whether a person is attractive is subjective, or so we say.

Despite our aversion to talking about the prevalence of 'lookism,' research indicates that attractiveness benefits both men and women in most forums. For purposes of this article, we will focus on how attractiveness affects women in business situations. A survey of 700 managers illustrates the importance of appearance in the business forum. The managers were asked to rank what factors help a person survive and succeed in organizations. Based on the 662 returned surveys, personal appearance was ranked the eighth most important factor out of twenty. The results reflect a belief among managers that attractiveness helps a person succeed in business.

Attractive women can gain an advantage from the earliest stages of employment through the later ones. For instance, when photographs are attached to resumes, research indicates that attractive women will be favored over unattractive women. These results are consistent even when the attractive women are rated as less competent in terms of experience and education. Studies have shown that managers are likely to recommend higher starting salaries for more attractive people. Attractive women are evaluated higher than unattractive women in terms of task performance. When making decisions about promotions, attractive persons in general even tend to be favored over people with a better work record.

A woman's beauty can also influence her earnings over time. Economists Jeff Biddle and David Hamermesh are leading researchers in the area of attractiveness bias. Biddle and Hamermesh's research indicates that attractive women earn five percent more, even when controlling for education. Their research also revealed that women whose looks are rated "below-average" are three percent less likely to even enter the work force. The results of the American studies were recently confirmed by the work of British economist, Barry Harper. Harper discovered that unattractive British women suffered an earnings penalty of negative 10.9 percent. The evidence presented in these studies support the proposition that, on average, more attractive women receive higher salaries than their unattractive colleagues.

The previous research focused on the influence of general attractiveness. Other research has narrowed this field of general beauty by focusing on the effects height and weight have on employment. Harper's study indicates that very short females are paid less than their colleagues of average height. Shorter women are seen as less powerful and more susceptible to traditional stereotypes, making the women appear less fit for managerial and upper-level employment positions. Stereotypically, taller women are seen as more masculine, which usually means they appear to be more demanding, decisive, and powerful. Such perceptions translate into an advantage for taller women in the workplace. Women above average height were found to enjoy higher pay even beyond those of average height. Blending in with the male-dominated business world might be more feasible for taller women.

Just as height has been found to influence women's wages, so too has weight. Women who are significantly overweight or obese tend to incur negative ramifications in the workplace. For example, women considered "fat" earn twenty percent less in hourly wages than women of average weight. Harper also found pay penalties for overweight women in the UK. These research findings support the hypothesis that unattractive women are earning less than attractive women, if we assume that being overweight is considered unattractive.

Assuming that the previously discussed research is valid and reliable, we can conclude that beauty is playing a role in determining which women succeed in business. The next logical question to ask is why do beautiful people enjoy an advantage in business. One possible answer to this question is the tendency to assign positive characteristics to attractive people. This tendency to associate what is good with what is beautiful is known as the "beauty myth."

The positive traits that attractive people are often assumed to possess are traits that businesspersons value. For instance, attractiveness has been shown to contribute to high self-esteem. Studies have demonstrated that attractiveness is equated with creativity, intelligence, and general competence. Beautiful people have been shown to experience less stress and are less at risk for mental illness. People are more likely to offer help to those who are more attractive. Studies indicate that persons rated as attractive have a higher internal locus of control than unattractive persons. Highly attractive women have a tendency to be more assertive than their less attractive female colleagues. The business community views traits such as assertiveness, self-control, intelligence, self-esteem, and creativity favorably. When employers assume that more attractive women have such traits, the assumption translates into various rewards for the women.

The assumption that beautiful women have desirable traits may not be completely invalid. Attractive individuals are treated differently from a very young age. In the classroom, attractive students reap numerous benefits from the teachers. Teachers give attractive students more attention, more information, and more opportunities to perform than they do less attractive students. This preferential treatment by parents, teachers, and peers helps to develop feelings of self-worth, confidence, and self-reliance. A subtle message is sent to the watchful eye when beautiful females are treated preferentially. The message is that attractiveness is a source of power for women. The researcher R.J. Freedman refers to this type of power as hedonic, or the ability to indirectly acquire influence "by virtue of one's appearance, charm, or political savvy." Freedman asserts that hedonic power is "a woman's primary source of social power." Women learn that beauty can work in their favor and they aim to use it that way. Such behaviors can manifest into qualities that make attractive women more successful in the business world.

Discrimination

While beauty can be an asset to women, it can also be a detriment to women's advancement. Some researchers as well as some female executives argue that attractive women are more likely to be subject to traditional stereotypes than unattractive women. Businesspersons assume that attractive women will get married, or in the event that they are already married they will have children. Beautiful women can also be seen as potential targets for harassment, an issue no employer wants to ignite. One executive pointed out that beautiful women cannot blend in as easily as average-looking women can. An inability to blend in can increase the amount of scrutiny and evaluation one receives. While this evidence indicates the potential pitfalls of beauty, it is not as convincing as the evidence that attractive women are more easily breaking through the glass ceiling.

Regardless of whether women incur negative or positive ramifications because of their appearance, basing employment decisions on attractiveness has potentially deleterious effects for society. Many women view the emphasis on appearance as a form of discrimination, primarily because "females suffer disproportionately from this evaluation device."

Legal Responses to Lookism

As more women entered the workforce, the issue of appearance discrimination became more prevalent. Soon women began bringing lawsuits against employers on grounds of appearance discrimination. These lawsuits generally fall into one of two broad categories. The first type includes instances of discrimination against a person's physical characteristics, such as height and weight. The second type of appearance discrimination suits are those related to a person's grooming habits and attire.

Women seeking legal remedies for appearance discrimination have limited options for redress. A few states or municipalities have laws that prohibit appearance discrimination, but these are in the minority. Most women must evoke federal legislation by tying their appearance to an already protected category, such as disability, race, color, religion, sex, national origin, or age. These are the protected categories as defined by the Americans with Disabilities Act ("ADA"), Title VII of the 1964 Civil Rights Act ("Title VII"), and the Age Discrimination in Employment Act ("ADEA"). Each piece of legislation requires different elements to prove discrimination.

Appearance discrimination presents a unique problem under the ADA. Before an individual can argue that her unattractiveness contributed to discrimination, she has to prove that she is considered unattractive.

Unlike other disabilities protected under the ADA, ugliness is a considerably subjective determination. If an individual can prove that an attribute is considered unattractive, then she must show that the attribute is also an impairment. Under the ADA, an individual's impairment must be shown to substantially limit a major life activity before it can be considered a disability. For example, the court ruled that missing teeth substantially limited the life activity of working. Cases of missing teeth, facial disfigurement, or missing limbs, are not as common as the claims that obesity should be considered a disability.

Many people have tried to argue that obesity is a physical impairment and therefore deserving of protection under the ADA. Generally, obese persons are found to not have a disability unless they suffer from a physiological disorder or are perceived as disabled. The court assumes that persons who do not have a physiological disorder can control their own weight. Control is an important issue in terms of considering appearance as an impairment. If appearance can be controlled, then it's protection under the ADA is limited even more than it is currently.

Another avenue of redress for appearance discrimination victims is the ADEA, which protects people over forty from age discrimination. If an older woman wishes to use the ADEA, then she must argue that older women are disproportionately impacted by attractiveness policies. This argument unites the ban on age discrimination with appearance discrimination. Cases brought under the ADEA are not usually based on appearance, but "they may implicitly involve an applicant's or employee's 'old' or 'older' appearance and the stereotypical assumptions derived from that visual perception."

The final and most common avenue of redress for appearance discrimination is Title VII. Plaintiffs must prove that the employer's policy results in either disparate treatment or disparate impact of protected classes. Under Title VII, the plaintiff can invoke the "sex plus" theory. This theory allows the plaintiff to demonstrate that she was discriminated against because of her sex plus another characteristic, such as race, marriage, or appearance. In general the courts have held that attractiveness, appearance, attire, and grooming requirements are not legally permitted if they impose different standards based on gender, are a result of sexual stereotypes, or raise the risk of harassment. Courts have upheld attractiveness requirements when the policies were found to be gender-neutral. When appearance discrimination can be linked to judgmental treatment of a protected class, then Title VII does afford some legal protections.

However, legal protections are beneficial only when the victims are aware that they need to be protected. Lookism is such a subtle form of discrimination that most do not actually realize it is happening. While the evidence suggests that beauty is helping some women to step through the looking glass, the women left on the other side are not likely to realize that attractiveness can be so influential. Because lookism is covert and subjective, the likelihood of quelling its impact is slight.

CONCLUSION

The reality of the glass ceiling is messy. In fact, for some, the glass ceiling is the wrong metaphor. This article has suggested that the looking glass presents a more appropriate metaphor. Once an individual or group of managers recognizes the complicated nature of the obvious and hidden barriers to advancement in organizations, he or she must assess the extent to which legal and non-legal strategies for change hold promise. Whether an employee or group of employees is trying to shatter a glass ceiling, or tumble through a looking glass with the blessing of powerful people on the other side, they must recognize the many paths to justice, and the overriding importance of their relationship with their employer as a determinant of their strategy.

STUDY QUESTION

Why do M. Neil Browne and Andrea Giampetro-Meyer suggest that the *looking glass* is a more appropriate metaphor than the *glass ceiling* in analyzing barriers preventing individuals from advancing in organizations?

Lessons from the Fields: Female Farmworkers and the Law

Maria L. Ontiveros

This Article explores the lived experiences of one particular group of workers—immigrant farmworking women in California. From their experience, there are many lessons we can draw to make the law more responsive for all workers, but especially for all female immigrant workers.

LIFE IN THE FIELD

California produces about 44 percent of the nation's labor intensive fruit and nut crops, vegetables and melons, and flowers and nursery products. For most of this century, workers have immigrated from Mexico, the Philippines, and Central America to harvest these crops. The number of farmworkers has grown steadily over the last twenty-five years. California witnessed a 25 percent growth in total hired farmworker employment between 1975 and 1999. In 1997, there were approximately 550,000 farmworkers in California. This increase in employment corresponds with an increase in the cash receipts from farm marketings, which has tripled from $8.6 to $27 billion, and a doubling in tons produced. Most of the increase has taken place in the production of wine grapes, almonds, strawberries,

greenhouse crops, bagged salad mixes, and dairy. Although some of these crops are seasonal, many are grown or tended year-round.

Currently 90–95 percent of California's farmworkers are foreign-born, with almost all having been born in Mexico. Most farmworkers (60–70 percent) are "undocumented," meaning they do not have legal authorization to work in the United States. Since 1989, the percentage of undocumented workers has increased steadily, about 3–4 percent a year. In 1989, only 8 percent of U.S. crop workers were undocumented, primarily because most agricultural workers at that time received the legal right to work in 1986 under the Special Agricultural Worker provision of the Immigration and Reform Control Act of 1986. After receiving the right to work in the United States, most workers left the field and took other types of jobs.

Source: Maria L. Ontiveros, "Lessons from the Fields: Female Farmworkers and the Law," *Maine Law Review.*

About 80 percent of farmworkers are men, with a median age of thirty (63 percent are less than thirty-four years old). About 61 percent are married, and among those who are married, they have an average of three children. Most farmworkers (60 percent) have their children with them, while a significant minority (40 percent) leave their family in Mexico. Most do not speak English, and only 15 percent are considered more than "marginally literate," in terms of reading and writing in their own language. The statistics for female farmworkers are very similar, except female farmworkers are even less likely to speak English.

STRUCTURAL COMPONENT: UNDOCUMENTED WORKFORCE

Two unique structural components of the agricultural industry create and maintain the snapshot of the industry presented above: the employment of undocumented workers and the use of farm labor contractors. Simply put, growers need undocumented workers to harvest their crops. Most workers with documentation find other employment. An undocumented worker, on the other hand, will work in the fields because she does not have as many other options. There are several important realities faced by all undocumented workers. First, undocumented workers live with the constant risk of being deported. Deportation means loss of a job, separation from family, and the specter of an illegal border crossing to return to the United States. Second, undocumented workers hazard illegal border crossings to visit Mexico and return to the United States. These border crossings are extremely hazardous for at least two reasons: the United States policy known as Operation Gatekeeper and the smugglers (or coyotes) who often arrange the crossings. Third, undocumented workers do not have the right to recover the same remedies for labor abuses as do documented workers.

One alternative to an undocumented workforce that has been repeatedly suggested and tried is the development, through an immigration visa program, of a special class of agricultural workers who are allowed to legally work here for a short period of time. These workers are called "guest workers" or "nonimmigrant workers" because there is no expectation that they will settle in the United States and become permanent residents or citizens. The historic version of this program was the Bracero program, created during World War II to help growers deal with the labor shortages caused by the war. The program, under which the United States government contracted with the Mexican government for agricultural laborers, led to such widespread abuse that Lee G. Williams, a United States Department of Labor official who helped supervise the program, called it "legalized slavery." The abuses included wages depressed by an oversupply of workers, the inability of workers to leave or change employers, too few hours to earn subsistence wages, low wages coupled with huge deductions for room and board, illegal payroll deductions for nonexistent services, and substandard housing. In addition, the federal government withheld 10 percent of their paychecks, which was supposed to be paid upon the worker's return to Mexico as an incentive for the workers to return home. The workers never recovered this money, and a movement has begun to recover that money, in partial reparation for the harms caused to the Braceros.

The more recent version of this alternative is the H-2A visa program, dubbed by many as the New Bracero Program. The program is designed to allow growers to bring in nonimmigrant, temporary foreign agricultural labor when domestic workers are not available. In 1996, approximately 15,000 workers were hired under this program. Although growers like the concept of the program because it helps guarantee a supply of agricultural workers, many growers perceive the existing program as being unworkable. Within the last two years, a variety of different H-2A visa legislation has been proposed.

Many farmworkers and farmworker advocates, on the other hand, oppose this alternative because of the problems it causes for farmworkers. First, they argue that there is no shortage of agricultural workers. Without an agricultural labor shortage, an increase in workers will depress wages and harm domestic farmworkers. Second, many workers do not see their contracts until they arrive in the United States. Third, such workers are easily exploited because they are only authorized to work for a single employer. If they are abused or cheated, they must either put up with the conditions or quit and go home. Finally, since they immigrate temporarily without family or kinship ties, they are left without a social support system and must rely on their employer who thereby possesses undue control over their lives. In short, they end up very much like modern day.

BRACEROS STRUCTURAL COMPONENT: FARM LABOR CONTRACTORS

Farmworkers can be employed in one of two ways: as a direct-hire employee or as a contract employee. A direct-hire employee is one who is hired by and works directly for the grower. A contract employee is a person employed by a farm labor contractor. The farm labor contractor has an agreement with the grower to provide labor. The grower negotiates a lump sum that is paid to the farm labor contractor for a certain number of workers. The grower does not negotiate with or pay the farmworkers individually. Any individual negotiation is done between the farm labor contractor and the farmworker. Currently, about two-thirds of farmworkers are direct hires and one-third are employed through a contractor. Most contract work is seasonal—either tending seasonal crops or performing seasonal or short-term work

for growers with year-round crops. The situation was summed up by Don Villarejo as follows:

> One of the most dramatic shifts in farm employment in California has been the sharp reduction in direct-hire seasonal workers, even though there has been a substantial increase in the number of regular direct-hire workers. . . . [C]ontract jobs now outnumber direct-hire "seasonal" jobs on California farms.

This is a remarkable finding. It shows that California farmers have found it important to hire significantly more year-round workers today as compared to the pre-ALRA period [before 1975], and, at the same time, now primarily rely on farm labor contractors for short-term or seasonal workers.

Not only are more contract workers utilized for seasonal jobs, more California farms than ever are turning to labor contractors to furnish laborers.

The farm labor contractor system has grown substantially since 1986. According to a survey of California growers, they use contractors because they are a reliable source of labor, because they view them as a good way to handle short-term needs, because they have had trouble finding employees themselves, and because they can reduce the burden of paper work. When a farmworker is hired, the law requires a variety of records be kept (i.e., employment taxes, income tax withholding, workers' compensation insurance). Since 1986, all employers must also complete an I-9 form, which certifies that the employer has verified that an employee has the legal right to work in the United States. When a farmworker is employed through a farm labor contractor, the contractor, not the grower, is the legal employer. The grower does not have to keep this paperwork. In addition, the legal obligation to pay minimum wage, provide workers compensation insurance, etc., belongs to the farm labor contractor and not the employer. By securing labor through a farm labor contractor, the grower insulates himself from the legal (and, perhaps in his mind, moral) responsibility for the workers.

Farmworkers prefer direct-hire work for several reasons. First, this work tends to be year-round, rather than seasonal or short-term. The pay is usually more and somewhat guaranteed. The pay is usually hourly, as opposed to piece rate. Growers often see their regular workers more as people with whom they have a connection and treat them better. Finally, a grower tends to be more stable and have some resources, so that workers have the possibility of recovering compensation for legal violations.

Employment with a labor contractor, on the other hand, is less desirable. At the very least, farmworkers have fewer hours, have less stable employment, and make less money. From a structural standpoint, contractors, who are in competition with one another, often make a bid with a grower at a very low price in order to get the contract. If they cannot win the bid, they will go out of business. Once they have a low-ball contract, the only way for the contractor to make a profit is to pay the workers at substandard rates or engage in some other illegal activity. A common practice among contractors is to keep a part of the payroll off of their records. When a worker is kept off the payroll records, they contractor does not have to pay their taxes or social security deductions. They pay those workers out of their pockets and keep the taxes. Few contractors, most of whom are former farmworkers, get rich. Many feel paternalistic towards their employees and are simply glad to be out of the fields. In addition, farmworkers find it harder to effectively assert their legal rights against contractors because they disappear and do not have the resources from which to collect an award.

The problems of working for a farm labor contractor can be much worse, though, than low pay and uncertain employment. Less scrupulous contractors make false promises when recruiting workers, provide substandard housing, transport workers in dangerous vehicles, refuse to pay wages, and loan money at exorbitantly high interest rates. Penalties for these types of abuses, even if they can be collected, are not sufficient to outweigh the "years of cheap labor" from which they profited. Further, the paternalism can turn to cruelty when a contractor controls all aspects of the workers lives. As one interviewer described the situation:

> Contractors often wield enormous authority over their workers, sometimes running their crews like small fiefdoms, hiring and firing at will, and displaying constant favoritism. They commonly play off of farmworkers' basic vulnerabilities—their poverty and limited options, their lack of working papers, their inability to speak English, their minority status, and their addictions.

Overall, from an employee's perspective, then, there is a two-tier system of employment, with direct-hire being preferred and contract employment being seen as marginal. Growers can be selective in their regular hiring and fill in with workers from a farm labor contractor. Those employees who are seen as undesirable or trouble makers because they complain, because they are undocumented, or because they seek to organize are least likely to be directly hired by a grower and must find employment, if at all, with farm labor contractors. As a result, as Marcos Camacho of the United Farm Workers wrote, "it is in this atmosphere that workers much choose whether to risk their jobs if they exercise their rights. . . ."

CONDITIONS OF WORK, HOURS, AND COMPENSATION

A farmworker's day starts early, often around 3:00 A.M. The exact time depends on whether the worker has a regular job to report to or whether he needs to try to find work with a labor contractor. If he arrives too late, the contractors will fill their spots with other workers. Distance to the job site and the availability of transportation also affect the time he gets up. Many farmworkers walk, bicycle, or take buses to jobs or to meet with contractors. These commutes routinely take several hours. A female farmworker also has to allow time to get her family ready for the day. In most households, the woman is still expected to perform all the household chores and prepare meals for the family. Farmworkers are then transported to their worksite for the day, often in overcrowded, unsafe vans.

Once at the worksite, work begins. The work can be harvesting lettuce or strawberries, either requiring hours of crawling through muddy rows. Alternately, a farmworker might be climbing ladders, while carrying a large bag over her shoulder to pick nectarines or apples. In addition to harvesting, farmworkers weed, cultivate, and tie vines. Although women perform most all the same jobs as men, there is some segregation between "men's jobs" and "women's jobs," with the "men's jobs" paying more. All of the jobs are physically demanding, dangerous work. The workday is long, and breaks are discouraged. The rate of work is regulated, either by foremen or "crew pushers," constantly walking among the workers and urging them on or by field-packing vehicles which lead the workers up the rows. As the produce is picked, it is put onto the conveyor belt to be processed so that the speed of the machine controls the pace of the work.

A farmworker must work fast to retain her job. The compensation structure ensures this. Originally, agricultural employees were excluded entirely from the provisions of the Fair Labor Standards Act (FLSA), including the payment of minimum wage. Currently, the overtime provisions of the FLSA do not apply to agriculture, and small farms are excepted from the minimum wage requirement. Instead, many workers are paid a piece-rate, which varies by how much they are able to pick. Although the piece-rate at large farms must comply with the minimum wage, growers still determine how fast they want workers to harvest and then set how much they will pay per piece based on that speed and the minimum wage. Philip Martin explained it this way:

> After minimum wage laws were applied to agriculture, farmers were required to keep records of the hours each employee worked and how many units of work each employee accomplished. . . . Most farm employers terminated workers who did not work fast enough to earn the minimum wage at the piece rate offered, establishing an "iron triangle" between minimum wages, piece rates, and minimum productivity standards. For example, if the minimum wage is $5 an hour, and the employer is paying a piece rate of $10 a bin, then workers must pick an average one-half bin an hour to earn the minimum wage; slower workers may lawfully be terminated.

Those hired by farm labor contractors are paid by the contractors, with the compensation problems discussed above.

The result is a group of extremely hardworking, very poor people. In California, farmworkers average an annual farm income of $5500, with 55 percent earning less than $7500. Nationwide, over three-fifths of farmworker households fall below the poverty line. Farmworking women earn even less than their male counterparts because they are given fewer hours and are paid less per hour.

METHODS OF WORKPLACE CONTROL

Most employers use hiring and retention as a way to motivate workers. Just as work rate and pay, as traditional methods of workplace control are different for farmworkers, so is the area of retention. For farmworkers, the retention decision is affected by three things: the threat of deportation; the possibility of losing a direct-hire job and becoming a contractor; and the H-2A guest worker program. An employer who employs an undocumented worker possesses the incredibly powerful threat of contacting immigration officials to try to have a worker deported. This threat is used to prevent employees from complaining about wages that are too low or conditions that are unjust. Farmworkers fear deportation because of the hardships involved in the deportation process (including detention and transport), the separation from their family, and the specter of a dangerous bordering crossing to return to the Untied States. Growers and contractors realize this and use the threat to their advantage.

A less significant, though still powerful threat, is the loss of a direct hire job. This loss means that the workers must look for less desirable work with a farm labor contractor. As Marcus Camacho, General Counsel for the United Farm Workers of America, commented,

> Many times the loss of a seasonal [direct-hire] job can mean no work for the rest of the year, or finding intermittent work through farm labor contractors that many times pay much lower wages and provide worse working conditions than their usual job. In addition farm labor contractors give little hope of continued employment. It is in this atmosphere that workers must choose whether to risk their jobs if they exercise their rights under the [Agricultural Labor Relations Act].

By firing a direct-hire worker and hiring a contract worker, the grower can retain the benefits of having an employee while still punishing the employee for asserting his or her rights. Many women do not report discrimination because they fear such negative economic repercussions.

A different issue is unique to employment through Guest Worker programs. Under these programs, workers come to the United States to work with a specific employer. If that employer no longer wants the employee's services, either because of poor performance or because of an assertion of rights, the employer can simply terminate the employment and terminate the visa. Although the programs theoretically have provisions to protect workers, workers do not have access to courts to enforce any of these provisions. Finally, the "unwritten rules" for H-2A workers that they should keep silent, be productive, not complain, and not organize has led to the anomalous result in North Carolina that no H-2A worker has ever made a complaint with a government agency.

Female farmworkers are particularly subject to two other methods of workplace control: harassment and commodification. Ninety percent of female farmworkers report that sexual harassment is a major problem. Female farmworkers are constantly badgered for dates and sexual favors. If they reject these requests, they are fired or find themselves with lower pay and inferior job assignments. They are routinely touched, groped, and assaulted. If they complain or resist, their work assignments suffer. While investigating harassment of farmworker women California, EEOC staff discovered that hundreds, if not thousands, of women had to have sex with supervisors to get or keep jobs and/or put up with a constant barrage of grabbing and touching and propositions for sex by supervisors. A worker from Salinas, California eventually told us that farm workers referred to one company's field as the field de calzon, or "field of panties," because so many supervisors raped women there.

These women are targeted because of a combination of their sex, national origin, class, and immigration status. All these factors are used to control how women behave in the workplace.

Growers and contractors also control female farmworkers, using their sex, national origin, class, and immigration status, in a process I have previously labeled commodifiction, but can also be understood as a form of identity-based exploitation. Under this theory, growers and contractors treat female farmworkers differently than others because they do not view them as human beings. They view them as something less—a commodity to be utilized or exploited. Labeling immigrants as "illegals" or "aliens" constructs them as a less-than-human other. Because of our socially held view of racial and gender hierarchies, certain types of exploitation and control are uniquely acceptable when applied to certain workers, especially women, immigrants, and workers of color. Therefore, growers and contractors feel free to provide housing and sanitation facilities that would better fit animals than people. In addition, in order to increase productivity, female farmworkers are bullied, threatened, and abused in ways that draw upon the hierarchies that have their roots in the paternalism of Latino culture and anti-immigrant sentiment.

HEALTH & SAFETY, CHILD LABOR, AND OTHER WORKPLACE CONDITIONS

Conditions in the field are rough, at best. Farmworkers are exposed to pesticides, either by handling the produce that has been sprayed, by applying the pesticide themselves, or, in particularly egregious situations, by being directly sprayed along with the crops. As a result, "farmworkers suffer the highest rates of chemical-related illnesses." Female farmworkers face additional risks because of their smaller relative size and because the harmful effects of pesticides may be passed onto the fetus of a pregnant woman or to her baby through nursing. The children of farmworkers, who are exposed either by their presence in the fields or through residue which their parents bring home with them, are particularly susceptible because of their immature immune system, smaller physical size, and lack of protective clothing.

Although required by law, fields often lack basic sanitation such as hand-washing facilities or bathrooms. The lack of facilities particularly hurts female farmworkers because they are at an increased risk for urinary infections if they are unable to use a bathroom. A pregnant woman with a urinary infection has an increased likelihood of miscarriage, premature labor, and neonatal death.

Where there are farmworkers, there are children. In California, there is roughly one child for every adult farmworker. The education available for these children is sporadic and, often times, ineffective. Often, the children work in the fields under the same conditions as their parents. Children as young as twelve are allowed to work in the fields, and much younger children often accompany their parents if they lack childcare. As eleven-year-old Luisa Cervantes said, "We go to the fields and weed and pick. It's hard because we don't eat until we get home. Sometimes I like for school vacation to be over so we don't have to go to the fields."

The health of farmworkers and their children is tragic. In 1991, the average life expectancy in the United States was seventy-three years. A migrant farmworker could expect to die before he or she was fifty. In the California farmworker population, 30 out of every 1000 infants die—more than twice the infant mortality rate for the overall United States population, and mortality rates among young California farmworking children was 50 percent higher than that. The rates of diabetes, parasitic and infectious diseases, as well as chronic disease for the farmworker population are also substantially above the national average.

Work-Family Issues

At the end of a long day, the farmworker returns to her house. Her house may consist of a cardboard, plywood, or tin shack, which may be part of a camp nestled in the hills. She most likely does not have a telephone or other access to the world. If she lacks housing, she will make a home in the fields. After her long day at work, she is now expected to cook, clean, and take care of the children. Like so many women, she must perform double-duty.

At home, her behavior and future may be controlled by her husband or the other men in her household. Due to the cultural values of machisimo, many female farmworkers subordinate their own desires, interests, and needs to the will of their husbands or fathers. Approximately one-third of female farmworkers are victims of domestic abuse. Because of their cultural upbringing these women may not even recognize the treatment as domestic abuse. Once they do, these women face enormous obstacles to ending this abuse, including the lack of money, having nowhere to go, and not speaking English. In addition, lack of culturally-sensitive resources presents a problem. For those women who are undocumented, fear of being reported to immigration also prevents them from escaping the abuse.

Finally, for female farmworkers, especially, the concerns of her children also affect her. She may be concerned about the tangible problem of lack of childcare, or she may be plagued by the intangible worry that affects women when they see their children suffering from illness, toiling in the fields, and going without education. Rafael Guerra, a migrant educator and former migrant worker summarized it as follows:

> Let me give you an idea of how it was. You're getting ready to go up North. The father would make a decision with his compadre. We are going to go to Plainview, we are going to go to California. But as soon as the decision was made, the mother was the one that started putting things together, whatever we were going to take up North.

It was the mother that would cook the pinole or whatever she could take on the road. The mother was worried all the time.

What do you do when you're in the truck and you're together with thirty or forty other people, and sometimes you don't even know the people. It was the mother who had to worry all day—I hope my son won't have diarrhea. And if he has diarrhea, how do you take care of it in the truck when the truck is driving and the crew leader is not going to stop.

And then we got to the place. It was the mother who was hoping for the best living area, which was not much, maybe a 12-by-12 little shack or together with everybody else. Sometimes they'd put three or four families in one long barrack, but she had to find a little corner where she was going to put her stove which was made out of kerosene.

But comes day to work, the mother would get up an hour before anybody else. She was the one who had to get the food ready. Cook the breakfast okay. Cook the breakfast early, so you could see that little burner, and you could see that kerosene, and you were under the covers because it was cold and you were hoping it wasn't time to get up. But it was time.

A Response From the Fields

Female farmworkers, confronted with the conditions described above, have not sat idly by. Instead, they have actively challenged these conditions. In reviewing their response, two things stand out. First, the law, as it was interpreted before their challenges, was not ideally suited to address their problems. The "fit" between the problems that they experience as immigrant women workers and the solutions offered by the existing law was not very close. Second, the workers and their representatives created new ways to challenge the problems that did reflect their unique identities. In many ways, their response drew upon the strengths of these unique characteristics to forge a successful response. Each of the following responses will highlight a specific farmworker response, the limitations with the preexisting law, and how these responses worked around the existing law.

LESSONS FROM THE FIELDS

The Importance of Identity-Based Organizing

The first thing we learn when looking at the lives of female farmworkers and their effective responses is that in order to be effective, labor policy must take into account both the workplace (or class) identities of these workers, as well as the nonworkplace or personal identity factors, such as race, gender, ethnicity, national origin, citizenship status, community, sexual orientation, and religion.

The United Farm Workers, as a union, was and is effective when it uses identity-based organizing. They provide services outside the workplace that the community needs. They meet with people at home and within the community. They utilize religious symbols and holidays to energize their campaigns. They base their call for workplace rights within a call for dignity and civil rights for immigrants and Latinos. They use bilingual, bicultural organizers. They negotiate the dynamics of farm labor contractors and first versus second-generation immigrants.

California's Agricultural Labor Relations Act is most effective when it recognizes how the unique characteristics of farmworkers and the agricultural industry affect the collective bargaining model. Access in the fields is necessary and effective because of the uncertain housing of employees, their long commutes, and their lengthy work hours. Quick elections take into account the short growing season and migrant nature of the workforce. Utilizing a definition of employer that includes both growers and farm labor contractors, as well as the definition of a wall-to-wall bargaining unit, prevents the grower from using contractors to avoid liability. The statutorily created, but unenforced,

provisions allowing for make-whole remedies and secondary boycotts would help the workers balance their real inequality of power and the ability of growers to stall through the short work season and would allow them to create a political, civil rights issue rather than a strictly workplace issue.

The Equal Employment Opportunity Commission's recent sexual harassment cases were successful because they gained the trust of the community, used bilingual counselors, and undertook training in cultural and gender aspects of credibility. They also addressed the immigration concerns by refusing to inquire about immigration status and began to recognize discrimination beyond a black-white paradigm. Most importantly, they recognized that this type of workplace harassment, even though it involved sex, was also based on race, national origin, and citizenship status. Thus, the solution had to take into account all these factors.

Community groups, such as the Citizenship Project and Lideres Campesinas, draw on the transnational nature of farmworkers' lives to improve their conditions. They help farmworkers to realize that, even if they are not naturalized, they still have rights to participate in our society—at the workplace, in schools, in unions, and in social service offices. They utilize the strength of the communities formed in their home countries and the cultural values of caring and community to organize and help each other. These activities, which often take place in the home or community, are connected to their ability to have better workplace lives.

Finally, the international law challenges are working with the notion that workers rights, human rights, and civil rights are intertwined. These challenges all rest on the argument that the denial of basic rights in the workplace because of a person's status as a migrant worker is a violation of international norms. Such an argument looks to both the workplace identity and the personal identity of workers because it recognizes the special oppression that has often been visited upon those least powerful because of their immigration status and ethnic origin.

This lesson can be extended to all workers, especially all women workers because all workers have both workplace and personal identities that affect them. Women workers, even those who are not immigrants or people of color, face treatment in the workplace that is influenced by their gender. Male workers also face a variety of constraints because of the gender roles they face. For example, men who choose to take parental leave from work are acting against their dominant gender role and are often penalized for their actions. In order to craft effective labor policy, these identities must be taken into account.

Labor unions, for their part, are beginning to realize this and are crafting effective organizing campaigns among women workers, immigrant workers, and other workers of color. Women clerical workers in universities, female nurses in hospitals, and women of color home-care and domestic workers are building models of workplace organization that take into account both the unique structure of their industries and their personal identities. Immigrant janitors organized through the Justice for Janitors campaign, followed in the footsteps of successful organizing at the Camagua waterbed facility, and foreshadowed successful organizing in the yard maintenance sector. Each of these successful campaigns, as well as others involving immigrant workers, drew upon the personal identity of the workers and dealt explicitly with the unique characteristics of the workplace. Paul Johnston has argued that, in this regard, the United Farm Workers and their model of unionization chart a course for labor's future, as opposed to simply being a part of labor history.

The Fragmentation Inherent in Current Labor Policy

The current approach to labor policy is not well suited to help female farmworkers or other marginalized workers for several reasons.

First, the law continues to fragment and compartmentalize claims into various pigeonholes. We turn to labor law to address class-based, economic issues involving unions and collective bargaining. Employment discrimination examines claims of discrimination based on race or sex or national origin or religion or color. Employment law covers the various contract and tort claims of individual employees, as well as their wage and hour problems. Immigration law looks at problems affecting those coming from other countries. Environmental law focuses on the problems of pesticides. Workers Compensation and OSHA law cover issues involving occupational safety and health. Issues of domestic violence and childcare fall into the vast fields of criminal law or women and the law. By fragmenting these areas, the reality of a marginalized worker whose oppression is affected by all these different issues can never be adequately addressed.

Second, each of the fields within the labor and employment law canon privilege certain workers, leaving those at the intersection or margin unprotected. Besides excluding certain marginalized workers entirely, traditional labor law focuses on a white, male manufacturing based model, to the detriment of women, people of color, and especially women of color. Labor law also has a narrow, wage-based, workplace focus that prohibits workers from organizing around community or political issues that would recognize the exploitation they experience based on their personal identity factors.

Employment discrimination law, by focusing on protected classes separately, cannot adequately address the problems of those whose oppression is defined by more than one category, such as women of color or older women. A powerful metaphor for considering this problem is whether oppression is seen as a wall created by one factor, such as class or race or sex, or whether it is a cage, in which each of these factors is one of the bars in the cage. If oppression is caused by only one factor (if the one factor acts as a wall), than removing that problem will clear the path. For example, a white woman, who is only confronting a problem of sex discrimination, can move forward when the problem of sex discrimination is corrected. If, on the other hand, the oppression is caused by many factors (and each factor acts as one of many bars in a cage), then removal of one bar from a cage will not allow the occupant to escape. So, even if the sex discrimination problems facing a female farmworker are corrected, she still must battle the problems facing her as a working class, undocumented, Latina. Employment discrimination law also misses the unique problems caused by the intersection of more than one protected class.

The portion of employment law that deals with wrongful discharge focuses on workers as individuals, trying to address individual rights, generally through torts or contracts. This individualized approach misses the complexity of workers as a class addressing workplace problems as a group. It also focuses only on a privileged group of workers—those who earn enough money that a contract claim is worth litigating and those few employees who have an implied or written contract. Unfortunately, the courts have recently begun to bring the individual contract model into the other fields of employment (labor law and employment discrimination), allowing employers and employees to agree to arbitrate statutory disputes. This works to decontextualize these other areas of the labor and employment law canon. Finally, the portion of employment law that deals with wages, hours, and the use of independent contractors misses the key issues of farmworkers' lives by not fully recognizing the problems associated with these institutions or the huge costs to an undocumented worker who is deported.

Third, the law as written and generally interpreted offers no guarantee of a nuanced, identity-based approach to labor policy. The policy successes described in this Article were innovative interpretations of the law or new legislation passed during politically liberal times. If the Equal Employment Opportunity Commission did not have a lead attorney with a background in immigrant rights, the Alfara case would not have been approached in such a sensitive manner. The fate of California's Agricultural Labor Relations Act during Republican administrations shows that many gains may be transitory. Currently, anti-immigrant sentiment continues to be a huge problem for these workers, as evidenced by the continuation of Operation Gatekeeper.

With the political will, there are several important legislative changes that could be made to ensure more identity-based organizing. Law affecting union organization must help immigrant workers in general and female immigrant workers in particular to be able to organize. Organization efforts could be facilitated by allowing workers to discuss unionization on company property during the workday; protecting the rights of all workers to organize, including agricultural workers and domestic workers; and allowing workers to organize around broader issues than the narrowly construed "wages, hours and terms and conditions of employment."

Immigration laws must no longer be designed to create a surplus of workers, battling over a limited number of jobs. These same laws must allow for empowered immigrant workers, by allowing immigrants to bring their families so they form the type of supportive communities and networks necessary to fully participate in society and that give them the human capital or capacity to participate. The legality of immigration status must not be tied to the decision of a single employer to continue their employment; otherwise, the employer simply retains too much control over the worker's life. Finally, the government's policy of pushing illegal immigration to the most dangerous regions, simply to keep the immigrants out of visible areas, must be stopped.

Employment discrimination laws, especially in the area of sexual harassment, job assignments, pay, hiring, and firing, must be stringently enforced, and those enforcing the laws must be bilingual and bicultural. The employment standards laws, dealing with minimum wage, overtime, health and safety, and child labor must be enforced without regard to immigration status. The laws that define employers as contractors or subcontractors, rather than the large identifiable business entities gaining from the exploitation of immigrant workers, need to be revised. Finally, some way must be found to value the work that women perform at home.

CONCLUSION

All workers, including female farmworkers, are people. As such, they must be afforded basic human rights in their communities and at their workplaces. Female farmworkers are workers. As such, they must be accorded the full rights and benefits of work, including a decent wage, the right to organize, and statutory protection against discriminatory treatment. We must strive to build a labor policy that acknowledges and guarantees these two simple principles. Such a policy will help all workers and the communities in which they live.

STUDY QUESTION

Explain what Maria L. Ontiveros means by *identity-based organizing*. How does she use this construct to describe the plight of California female farmworkers?

Native American Unemployment: Statistical Games and Coverups

George E. Tinker and Loring Bush

American social structures must recognize their culpability in the codependent relationship in which subtle racist institutional structures use statistical devices in order to conceal massive social deficiencies in Indian communities.

Unemployment is a tragedy for any American citizen old enough to work, but this tragedy is compounded for Native Americans by (1) a dramatic difference between Indian and non-Indian unemployment figures reported for any particular locale in the United States, and (2) what appears to be a severe undercount of Native American unemployment rates reported by federal and state government agencies. In part, this chapter tries to find some explanation of the discrepancy between these government statistics and the figures reported unofficially by many tribes themselves. These undercounts mask the reality of Native American unemployment rates that are apparently, in some cases, almost twenty times higher than what is reported by government agencies. Furthermore, such undercounts result in less funding for government programs that attempt to alleviate

these high rates of unemployment. Most important, the undercounts point to the continuation of the corporate and institutional racism entrenched in a system that prevents Native Americans from improving their situation and procuring there sources necessary to ensure their well-being, both as individuals and as culturally discrete communities of people.

The chronic nature of Native American unemployment is well known in Indian circles. Although the reports referred to here were published in various years, it is precisely the chronic problem of Native American unemployment that allows us to validly compare these figures. Despite chronological gaps in the reporting of rates, it seems a virtual certainty that the high rate of unemployment has remained relatively constant. While overall unemployment statistics in the United

Source: George E. Tinker and Loring Bush, "Native American Unemployment: Statistical Games and Coverups," in George W. Shepherd, Jr., and David Penna (eds.) Racism and the Underclass: State Policy and Discrimination Against Minorities (Westport, CT: Greenwood Publishing Group, 1991).

States are relatively volatile, depending on general and/or local economic factors, Native American unemployment statistics have been relatively static and at an extraordinarily high level for an extended period of time. In this chapter, both published and unpublished reports are compared and used for a survey of three states with high populations of Native Americans and high rates of Native American unemployment.

NATIVE AMERICAN UNEMPLOYMENT STATISTICS

Definitions

Before beginning our analysis, the issue of the definitions used for determining members of the labor force and calculating unemployment rates must be addressed. Indeed, the fact that different government agencies use different definitions for unemployment has particular implications for unemployed Native Americans. These implications are addressed after surveying the data. But even before terms such as labor force and unemployment are defined, it must be noted that there is confusion over the definition of *Indian or Native American* on the part of government agencies. The Bureau of Indian Affairs (BIA), for instance, bases its Native American statistics on persons,

> who are members of Indian tribes, or who are one-fourth degree or more blood quantum descendants of a member of any Indian tribe, band, nation, rancheria, colony, pueblo, or community, including Alaska Native Villages or regional village corporations defined in or established pursuant to the Alaska Native Claims Settlement Act.

On the other hand, the U.S. Department of Labor (DOL) defines Native Americans as those who classified themselves as such on 1980 census forms.

The DOL uses what is called the Local Area Unemployment Statistics (LAUS) methodology to measure unemployment. The data for this methodology are derived from a Current Population Survey (CPS), which is performed by the Bureau of the Census under a contract with the DOL. The CPS combines monthly surveys of approximately 60,000 households nationwide with unemployment claims activity to provide a statistical reflection of what is actually happening in the labor market.

Characteristic data, such as race and age, are collected with the CPS. However, the data by race are collected only for white, black, and Hispanic populations and exclude Native Americans. Thus, DOL does not track unemployment statistics for Native Americans. Some state labor divisions, particularly in areas with high Native American populations, do calculate Native American unemployment. These states use a census methodology of "sharing out" CPS figures by making future labor force projections for racial/ethnic groups based on proportions from the most recent national census data. It must be noted that individuals are not actually counted in this census methodology of sharing out data among racial/ethnic groups. Rather, a cumulative figure derived from the CPS is proportionally divided among racial/ethnic groups, including Native Americans, based on the racial/ethnic proportions from 1980 census information. It seems that assignment of numbers to categories that are over a decade old would result in arbitrary conclusions about the reality of Native American unemployment.

The DOL defines the *civilian labor force* as "All persons, 16 years of age and over, who are not in institutions or in the Armed Forces and are either 'employed' or 'unemployed.'"

DOL defines *those not in the labor force* as "Persons, 16 years old and over, who are not employed and not seeking employment or are unable or unavailable to work regardless of the reason, such as homemakers, students, retirees, disabled persons, or institutionalized persons."

The *unemployed*, according to DOL, are

Individuals, 16 years of age and older, who are not working, but are looking for work and are available to work. Looking for work requires specific efforts such as sending resumes or canvassing employers. Discouraged workers (those who have given up looking for work because they feel there are no jobs available) are not counted as unemployed.

Clearly implied, but never baldly stated instate labor reports, is that in addition to not counting as unemployed, *discouraged workers* are not included as part of the labor force in DOL unemployment statistics. According to Richard Pottinger, one reason for this exclusion of discouraged workers from the state labor force counts is that the LAUS methodology is structured with a "logical contradiction" between being trained and unemployed. In the LAUS methodology, it is assumed that those who have training and are unemployed will secure work again within the time limit set by DOL (four weeks). Pottinger explains DOL actions toward those who do not fall within the parameters established by the Department:

If these unemployed stop actively looking for jobs, through disillusionment or despair in confrontation with a lack of opportunity, they are actually dropped from the statistical tabulation of the "labor force"! Irrespective of the actual availability of jobs, they are no longer considered part of the labor force and are therefore no longer statistically "unemployed."

This exclusion of discouraged workers from the parameters of DOL's official labor force definition has particular implications for Native Americans. The experience of the Native American work force consists primarily of isolation from job opportunities. Hence, a great many unemployed Native Americans

do not have access to employers whom they can canvass for employment. As a result, we would argue that most unemployed Native Americans fall under DOL's definition of discouraged workers and are consequently dropped from calculations of Native American unemployment.

In addition to its methodological oversight of discouraged workers, DOL masks Native Americans unemployment statistics by calculating overall unemployment rates with figures for all races. When very low unemployment rates for whites are figured in with very high unemployment rates for racial/ethnic groups, and especially the high rates for Native Americans, the overall figure becomes diluted to the point where Native American rates are calculated out of the picture.

It would be expected that the Bureau of Indian Affairs (BIA) would account for this oversight. In its biannual *Indian Service Population and Labor Force Estimates*, the BIA gives an indication that Native American unemployment statistics are consistently higher than figures for the rest of the population. A breakdown of BIA methodology does reveal the percentage of the labor force who are discouraged workers, and the BIA publishes statistics that account for Native American discouraged workers. In order to understand more fully the distinction of the BIA and DOL reports, it is necessary to look at the entire BIA unemployment statistic methodology.

According to its *Population and Labor Force Estimates*, local BIA agencies gather data from the tribes themselves—actual house-to-house surveys conducted by tribal programs and contracts, school and employment records, tribal election statistics, tribal membership rolls maintained by the tribes, and BIA program services records. . . .

The BIA differs from the DOL in that the BIA only counts Native Americans, so its official unemployment rate comes somewhat closer to the reality of Native American unemployment than does the DOL. But this provides only minimally greater accuracy that does not yet reflect the true magnitude of Indian unemployment.

Data Comparisons

The 1985 "First Friday Report," *American Indian Unemployment: Confronting a Distressing Reality*, contrasts BIA unemployment figures. The "First Friday Report" uses BIA figures but not those officially reported as Indian unemployment. It uses statistics tucked away in the BIA report that do indeed include discouraged workers. By contrasting these figures with the figures derived from DOL methodology, the "First Friday Report" publicly articulates for the first time the severity of Native American unemployment and the nature of the undercounts in official government reporting.

The problem is best illustrated with actual data. According to the 1980 census, Arizona had the third highest population of Native Americans in the United States. The "First Friday Report" contrasts BIA Native Americans unemployment rates for Arizona with DOL figures for that state. While DOL reported overall unemployment in the state to be 11.2 percent in 1985, BIA reported Indian unemployment in the state at 41 percent. Using BIA estimates, the "First Friday Report" puts Navajo unemployment as high as 75 percent.

The Navajo Nation is the most populated reservation in the United States, with a population of 94,451 in its Arizona sector in 1989(the tribe also has some land holdings in Utah and extensive holdings in New Mexico). Of these residents, 88,739 (93.8 percent) are Native Americans, which is certainly to be expected on tribal lands. Further, Native Americans comprise 88 percent of the labor force on Navajo lands in Arizona. The overall 1989 Navajo reservation unemployment rate, which includes all races, is reported by the Arizona Labor Market Information (ALMI) report as 17.8 percent.

A 1985 study of Navajo unemployment, however, estimates a reservation ratio of about 1 job for every 100 people. . . . [M]any of the scarce jobs on reservations are being filled by non-Indians. Given this information, the ALMI 1989 report records a surprisingly low Native American unemployment rate of 19.8 percent on the Navajo reservation. This is in stark contrast to the 75 percent estimate of the "First Friday Report." Because Native American unemployment has been a chronic problem, it is appropriate to assume that their community's unemployment rate has not fluctuated by 55 percent over a 4-year period. This discrepancy demands some explanation.

The ALMI report does break down statistics with reference to racial/ethnic heritage, and the statistics reported are consistent with the already noted general tendency of a much higher unemployment figure for Native Americans than for the general population and other racial/ethnic groups. In 1985, there were between 6,000 and 7,000 jobs held by non-Navajos on the reservation. Of the 188 Hispanics who were in the reservation work force, none were unemployed. Of the 2,396 whites in that particular labor force, 2.2 percent were unemployed.

The discrepancy between Indian and non-Indian unemployment on the Navajo reservation and indeed on every reservation has its explanation in differences in Indian and non-Indian inculturation and in psychological factors related to the self-image of the people as aggressive, independent, and "in control" or as conquered and dependent. Non-Indians on a reservation typically are agriculturalists who lease Indian lands, small business traders who have the capital or access to the capital to run successful businesses targeting Indian people as their primary market, and management-level specialists brought in by the federal government or corporate business structures to provide administrative or technical expertise that the Indians are assumed unable to provide. Hence non-Indian unemployment figures are always character-istically low in any reservation context . . . .

The complexities at the heart of conflict-ing statistics and government undercounts of Native American unemployment are issues of the psychology of Indian versus white, his-torical factors, and structures of power in this country. The complexities involve decisions that were made by the federal government, such as the 1887 Dawes Severalty Act, the 1934 Indian Reorganization Act, the disas-trous relocation policy initiated by the Eisenhower administration, and a multiplicity of other federal government attempts to "solve" the Indian "problem."

One important factor that has not been considered among these complexities is the perspective of the Indian people themselves. What do Native Americans see as the root of these problems, particularly concerning issues of unemployment?

Karen Thorne, Job Training and Partnership Administration (JTPA) director of the Phoenix Indian Center, and Charlee Hoyt, of the Pascua Yaqui Tribal Job Training and Placement Program, point to some of the major reasons that Native Americans not only have high rates of unemployment but also why they are discouraged workers and thus uncounted in the DOL methodology. Thorne states that the high level of migration between the reservation and the urban area of Phoenix is a major factor in analyzing Native American unemployment. According to Thorne, Native Americans come to Phoenix because the job opportunities seem relatively better, yet most do not find jobs. As a result, many return to the reservation, to what is at least a marginally better support system, in part because of the continuing role of kinship systems and extended family and the comfort provided by cultural placement in some continuing traditional structure. This forces families to make difficult choices because the urban areas afford more employ-ment opportunities. Families become sepa-rated so that one member can work in the

city while the others stay on the reservation. Hoyt concurs on this point. She states that apart from the unavailability of jobs on the reservation, transportation problems invari-ably pose another major obstacle to Native American unemployment.

Both Thorne and Hoyt refer to cultural differences as another important barrier to full Indian employment. Thorne states that on the reservation, the pace of life is not as fast as in the urban centers. Punctuality and new technology are difficult for more tradi-tional people. Furthermore, tribal cultures tend to teach cooperation rather than individ-ual competition. By rising above the rest, an individual violates the culture.

Again, Hoyt offers a similar view. She gives the example of job interview techniques to illustrate the divergent cultural values of Native Americans and the dominant white culture. According to Hoyt, the Pascua Yaqui people are not as aggressive as those in the white culture, and thus they do not extol their virtues or talk about their talents during employment interviews. They do not main-tain direct eye contact when they are speak-ing. These actions are often taken by majority culture employers as signs of passivity or lack of accomplishment on the part of Native Americans. Therefore, people such as Thorne and Hoyt, from job training programs, edu-cate potential Native American employees in interview techniques and "front-run" through contact with personnel officers to answer cul-tural questions that they may have. Because of the realities in training Native Americans to function in a labor market driven by the majority culture, Thorne says that Native Americans must wear multiple hats. She notes that this causes difficulties in adjusting.

The issues raised by these two women are, for the most part, common concerns among members of the Native American community as they address their unemployment crisis. These issues must be kept in mind as we turn to a sample of unemployment statistics for Minnesota.

The Native American community of Minnesota resides largely on reservations that are much more distant from major metropolitan centers than in the case of reservations in Arizona. The Minnesota urban centers are found in Minneapolis and St. Paul, where the "First Friday Report" indicates a 1985 unemployment rate of 49 percent. Because of the chronic nature of Native American unemployment rates, it is assumed that this statistic remains roughly the same today.

As was the case in Arizona, the unemployment figures derived from DOL methodology that pertain directly to the Native American community are misleading because they show, with few exceptions, single-digit unemployment rates in areas where much higher unemployment rates can be expected due to the higher numbers of Native Americans in those particular populations. For the counties that intersect the Minneapolis/St. Paul area, however, the December 1989 state unemployment figures do not reflect the large numbers of unemployed Native Americans in the area . . . .

[I]t is appropriate to question the validity of the Department of Labor LAUS methodology of counting the unemployed as it applies to Native Americans. In October of 1988, this challenge was taken up jointly by Job Service North Dakota, the South Dakota Department of Labor, and the Standing Rock Sioux Tribe, whose reservation straddles both North and South Dakota. In response to "longstanding and substantial controversy" over the unemployment rates for counties containing Indian reservations, these three parties collaborated to contract with the Bureau of the Census for a special census of the Standing Rock reservation. . . . Standing Rock has a very high unemployment rate as reported by the "First Friday Report." According to the Standing Rock study, the collaboration among these three entities to conduct a special census amounts to a

governmental recognition of flaws in counting unemployed Native Americans. The study states, "There is concern that the official unemployment rates are not adequately reflecting the worsening economic situation nor the human capital available on Indian reservations, and are in turn impeding job development."

In conducting the special census, the Standing Rock study located what was believed to be the major factor, overlooked in standard LAUS methodology, which could account for the consistent undercount and might provide a corrective to reflect more accurately Native American unemployment.

> Employment opportunities are closely related to the availability of federal and tribal funds and to the starting and ending of programs administered by the federal and tribal governments. People enter the labor market as employment opportunities expand. For many workers on reservations, however, it is not possible to work long enough or earn enough wage credits to qualify for unemployment insurance and be counted in the claims data. The results of the special census indicate that the major difference between the estimates derived from the LAUS methodology and those shown by the special census occur in the area of labor force entrants and reentrants. . . . [T]his makes perfect sense for a geographic area where the timing of work search is determined by news of job openings for short-term tribal or federal government programs or other short-term, seasonal work.

Table I summarizes the major statistical findings of the study. In comparing these figures with the respective state labor department figures for Corson and Sioux counties, we can see that the Standing Rock study numbers are significantly higher.

Figures I and 2 graph our analysis of the breakdowns of the Standing Rock study statistics. Our purpose in representing the statistics in this way is to illustrate that although the Standing Rock study produces figures

Table 1.   Standing Rock Special Census Highlights

Population

Total	Stndg. Rock Ind.	Other	Total	Sioux Cty. Ind.	Other	Total	Cor. Cty. Ind.	Other
8,019	4,799	3,220	3,817	2,833	984	4,202	1,966	2,236

Labor Force Participation

	Civilian Non-Institutional Population (16 and older)	Labor Force	Participation Rate
Total Reserv.	4,688	2,624	56.0%
Indian	2,402	1,136	47.3
Non-Indian	2,286	1,488	65.1

Joblessness

	Official Unemployment Rate	Alternative Measure of Econ. Hardship Joblessness Including "Discouraged"	Alternative Measure of Econ. Hardship Joblessness Including "Discouraged" and "Underemployed"
Total Reserv.	14.1%	20.3%	24.4%
Indian	28.7	38.6	43.0
Non-Indian	3.0	4.3	8.2

Source: South Dakota Department of Labor, Press Release, Pierre, S.D., May 8, 1989, p. 4.

that are a more accurate reflection of Native American unemployment on the reservation, the new methodology has apparently been ignored. The DOL methodology was still used for the December 1989 report and consequently showed very low 1989 unemployment rates for the counties that constitute Standing Rock reservation. It should be acknowledged that the methodology variance was granted only in October 1989, and there may be a significant delay before the results in state unemployment reports can be seen. However, if Corson County is taken as an example, the Labor Market Information Center reports an unemployment rate of 2.8 percent for December 1989. Figure 2 shows that this statistic, according to the Standing Rock study, represents only a fraction of the

unemployed population in Corson County. Since the vast majority of unemployed in Corson County are Native Americans, the statistic functions to conceal Indian unemployment. Even if the variance does begin to rectify these severe undercounts on Standing Rock reservation in the future, it must be noted that Standing Rock is the only reservation in the country that has been granted this variance. It is not at all certain that such a methodology variance will be implemented for any other reservation in the United States.

If the Standing Rock study methodology is implemented for other reservations, there is still the problem of unemployment undercounts of Native Americans in urban centers. They face many of the same difficulties as the Indians on the reservations, and we have shown that they also suffer high unemployment rates. We can expect that the undercount problem will continue.

Figures 1 and 2 illustrate another point that was considered when looking at the statistics from the Navajo Nation. In Standing Rock, as on the Navajo reservation, the white sector of the work force has the lowest rate of unemployment, while the Native American sector of the work force has the highest rate. This fact begins to make explicit the complex

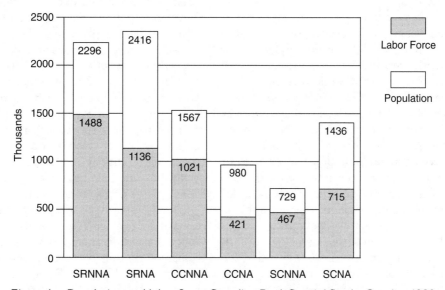

Figure 1.   Population and labor force, Standing Rock Special Study, October 1988.

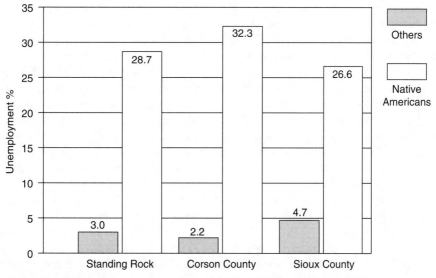

Figure 2.   Unemployment rates, Standing Rock Study, October 1988

economic, political, and social issues that have resulted in not only the high rates of Indian unemployment but also the subsequent oversight of this information in DOL methodologies. . . .

CONCLUSION

Indeed, American social structures must recognize their culpability in the codependent relationship in which subtle racist institutional structures use statistical devices in order to conceal massive social deficiencies in Indian communities. The political reality moves even further in blaming racial/ethnic peoples themselves for any social dysfunctionalities in their communities without attempting to put those dysfunctionalities into a broader context of oppression and social or cultural dislocation. It is an example of the victim being blamed for his or her own victimization.

The explanation of the unemployment crisis for Native Americans is found within the larger issue of corporate and institutional racism. Private enterprise alone—even if it is initiated from Native American rather than white capital—will not remove the obstacles to full Indian participation in the U.S. economy because a tribal economy will always, for the foreseeable future, be dependent on the national economy of the United States. It is at that level that institutional racism always functions implicitly and, often enough, naively to create new obstacles. If Native Americans were really welcomed into the political and economic life of the United States, they would demonstrate unemployment rates on par with that of the white population. There would be no "grants economy" to keep Indian communities dependent on the U.S. government. The future of Indian lands would be determined by the people who live on those lands.

That is not the reality today. The reality that determines public policy toward Native Americans may best be illustrated through the analogies used by two racial/ethnic individuals, one black and one Native American. The contrast between these two people—both based on similar images—explains how Native Americans perceive themselves as more excluded from mainstream American society than other racial/ethnic groups. When recently asked about white antagonism toward affirmative action, a black university student replied that the dominant culture of this society does not see affirmative action as racial/ethnic people see it. For this black citizen, affirmative action represented another trip to the rich master's "big house"—which is now the White House—in order to find opportunity in American society. In other words, not much has changed since the days of slavery. Racism still drives the American government even in its liberal policies of affirmative action.

In testimony at hearings on Pine Ridge reservation regarding the Guaranteed Job Opportunity Program, Sandra Frazier, chairwoman of the Employment Services Department of the Cheyenne River Sioux Tribe, illustrated the overall situation of Native Americans in contemporary American society. Frazier repeated a story told by Felix Cohen, an expert on Indian law. As a rich man enjoyed a plentiful banquet at a table groaning under the weight of food and drink, he looked out the window and saw an old woman, half starved and weeping. The rich man's heart was touched with pity. Because the old woman was breaking his heart, he told his servant to chase her away. The same characterizes the treatment of Native Americans by the U.S. government. Frazier used this story to illustrate that "Many things in Indian country are like nothing else in America."

Unlike the perception of the black student, who at least felt he could go to the "big house" to address his grievances, Native Americans have been consistently "chased away" by the U.S. government and American society as a whole. While we could argue that blacks and other racial/ethnic peoples have been (grudgingly) invited to share a room in the "big house" through affirmative action, Native Americans remain uninvited, despite affirmative action provisions that include Indian communities. All racial/ethnic peoples know who still owns this "big house." They are reminded every time unemployment rates are published for their minority group. For Native Americans, there is a double insult because their unemployment rates surpass those of other racial/ethnic groups and yet remain masked by governmental jargon and methodology. Today, after more than two decades of civil rights reforms in this country, racial/ethnic peoples can only imagine no longer being shutout of the American "big house" or being relegated to the status of a guest in that house. For North American racial/ethnic peoples, and particularly for Native Americans, having their own house remains a distant hope.

STUDY QUESTION

How do George Tinker and Loring Bush account for the discrepancy between government statistics on unemployment and the figures reported by many American Indian tribes?

Women, Welfare, Reform and the Preservation of a Myth

Susan L. Thomas

The solution to the poverty problem is perceived to be birth control and reduction in welfare benefits. The implicit assumption is that one poor women are properly coerced to stop bearing children their poverty will be alleviated and society will return to its healthy state.

Welfare mothers are promiscuous. Most of them are morally weak and undeserving. If women do not want to be poor they should make different choices, and change their behavior. This is the myth of the "culture of single motherhood"

THE MYTHS OF POVERTY

We live in a society of culturally constructed myths. We are their architects and their adherents, their advocates and opponents. These myths defy simple description: they inform and deceive, disclose and conceal reality, mirror and model unacknowledged assumptions and biases—and that is precisely why they are effective. Myths are distinguished by a "high degree of constancy" across generations and by an "equally pronounced capacity for evolution," adapting to changes in knowledge and social circumstances. Social attitudes about myths shape the meanings assigned to the myths and the purposes to which they are put.

When legislators devise public policy and make arguments on its behalf, they rely on myths shared by their colleagues and constituents. Lawmakers depend on these myths both because they give their arguments power and the potential for influence, and because the legislators, as members of the society, are likely to believe them. The myth of the moral weakness of the poor has been around in various forms throughout history. Likewise, the argument that the poor must change their behavior has a long lineage in public discourse in the

---

Source: Susan L. Thomas, "Women, Welfare, Reform and the Preservation of the Myth," *The Social Science Journal*, 34 (1997): 351–368.

United States. Consequently, the premise of individual immorality has been a part of public policy aimed at alleviating the problem of poverty. Similarly, because the dominant cultural myth today sees poverty as a product of women trapped in a culture of single motherhood, it is not surprising that the legislative remedy to this problem is the prevention of motherhood. To understand the meaning and power of these myths requires some understanding of the history, evolution, and significance of their basic premises.

THE CULTURE OF POVERTY

They myth that poverty is a moral condition has a very old history. Throughout the nineteenth century political elites and public officials attempted to distinguish between the "deserving" and the "undeserving" poor, or the worthy and the unworthy poor. Early reformers claimed that inadequately conceived and administered poor laws harmed paupers by increasing poverty and its costs to the taxpayers. Others unambiguously linked weak moral character to lack of industry as a cause of poverty. The 1860 Annual Report of the New York Association For Improving the Conditions of the Poor concluded that, "one of the primal and principal causes of poverty and crime is the want of early mental and moral culture." According to the report, much of the misery of the poor derived from the moral weakness of the poor—their laziness, debauchery, drunkenness, and lack of foresight. Reformers understood that preservation of the social order required some assistance to the poor, but only to the deserving poor—the orphans, the aged, the senile, and the genuinely infirm. They opposed indiscriminate almsgiving, because the donor did not know the exact use to which the recipient put the aid or if he was deserving. The solution to poverty instead was patient and systematic efforts at

moral uplift that "inculcated" poor persons with ideas of "temperance, frugality, and industry" which would raise the poor from the "idleness and sensuality" of their "low and groveling life" and guide them toward "higher hopes and nobler principles."

The myth of poverty as a moral condition carries over into our own day, as the popularity of cultural theories of poverty bears abundant witness. Developed in the mid-nineteenth century, named in the 1950s by the anthropologist Oscar Lewis, and popularized in the 1960s by Riessman, Harrington and others, the culture of poverty myth locates the sources of poverty in the intractable habits and attributes of poor persons who are committed to a set of "subcultural" values and behaviors which impede their chances of stable employment and upward mobility. Opportunity is there, proponents believe, but the culture of poverty prevents the poor from grasping it. The cure rests in providing a moral education for the poor and their children, one which resocializes them in terms of the way they think, value and act.

The subtext of the culture of poverty is a male-centered conception of poverty: Poverty is a male phenomenon and men are the transmitters of deficiency-based poverty. Because the financial dependency of women within marriage has long been assumed to protect them against poverty, their economic vulnerability and circumstances have been obscured by assumptions about their dependence on men. Women's poverty, if it was noticed, was assumed to follow from men's poverty, hence men's pathology. Through the filter of the culture of poverty myth, it is men who are condemned for failing to live decent and productive lives: It is men who "dislike regular work," "avoid every social responsibility" and "yield themselves to every animal passion;" and it is men who are exhorted to develop "habits of thrift and ambitious industry" as well as "sobriety and cleanliness." It is men whose morality needs reform.

THE CULTURE OF SINGLE MOTHERHOOD

At the beginning of the twentieth century, culture of poverty images reflected the dominant view of poverty as a male-centered phenomenon. By the middle of the century cultural myths about poverty embodied the new focus on women's role in causing poverty and the view of indigent women as not so much innocent victims of irresponsible men as immoral. The change in attitudes resulted, in part, from the creation of Aid to Dependent Children—known as Aid to Families With Dependent Children since 1962, rising nonmarital fertility and marital disruption rates, and the growing number of Black women in need of public assistance.

The 1935 Social Security Act included a program—Aid to Dependent Children—which, for the first time, provided public money to substantial numbers of unmarried mothers and their dependent children. In the beginning years of the program, most who received this aid were deserving White widows. By mid-century, however, normal population growth along with rising rates of divorce, desertion, fertility, and births outside marriage enlarged the ADC caseload and the number of undeserving recipients-unwed mothers and women of color. For example, by 1961, widowed families comprised just 7.7 percent of the ADC caseload, down from 61 percent in 1939. The majority of ADC mothers were now separated, divorced or single. Black women also became overrepresented in the ADC caseload in the postwar years, although the absolute number of Whites remained larger. According to one estimate, Black families accounted for two-thirds of the increase in ADC rolls between 1948 and 1961, rising from 31 percent of the caseload in 1950, to 48 percent in 1961.

Consternation over this shifting caseload helped to transform political discourse about poverty and heightened concerns about non-marital sexuality and maternity. Lawmakers now used a language more focused on the personal characteristics of poor women on welfare, criticizing their morality and behavior, particularly their increased willingness to bear children outside marriage. A perceived "illegitimacy crisis" triggered the alarm about women's sexuality and provided politicians an opportunity to blame women's behavioral pathology for rising levels of poverty, illegitimacy and welfare dependence. The alleged promiscuity and immorality, the resulting children, the spiraling cost of welfare were all traceable to a growing culture of single motherhood: out-of-control sexuality, expressed in nonmarital pregnancy and childbirth; changing family patterns, represented by woman-headed families; and welfare dependence, incorrectly believed to encourage illegitimacy and family breakdown. Shifting attention to women's behavior and morality helped transform a male-centered culture of poverty into a female-centered culture of single motherhood.

In many respects the culture of single motherhood resembles its culture of poverty predecessor. It is informed by the same assumptions and myths about behavioral pathology that were evident in evaluations of men's poverty in earlier decades. Like its predecessor, the culture of single motherhood treats poverty as a product of individual failure; poverty is not seen as a symptom of a malfunctioning society or economic system, but as a pathological condition affecting the individual poor person. Indeed, poor persons are thought to perpetuate the condition of poverty through their adherence to unhealthy or dysfunctional values and by their own inability or unwillingness to defer gratification of their immediate material or sexual desires in order to plan for the future. Yet, inherent in the premise of the culture of single motherhood is a reversal of the relationship between poverty and immorality assumed by the culture of poverty. Rather than women's poverty as a residuum of male pathology, the culture of single motherhood presumes that poverty is a female-based phenomenon brought about by a breakdown in women's moral virtue which has resulted in rising illegitimacy rates, declining marriage rates, and growing numbers of poor woman-headed families. Assumptions about whose poverty derives from whose pathology have been transformed; under the culture of poverty women's poverty is assumed to follow from men's poverty. In the revised version causality is reversed so that the welfare mother is the root of greater poverty and pathology. The resulting revised culture of single motherhood marks a turning point in the evolution of culturally constructed images of poverty.

LEGISLATIVE ENLISTMENT OF THE CULTURE OF SINGLE MOTHERHOOD

Beginning in mid-century in several welfare reform bills, lawm7akers encapsulated the emerging culture of single motherhood myth. In 1951, Georgia lawmakers launched a campaign of resistance against "unwed Negro mothers on aid" becoming the first state to legislate the custom of denying public assistance grants to more than one illegitimate child of a single mother. Georgia Governor Talmadge's speech before the state legislature in January, 1951, endorsing the legislation, foreshadowed the shifting connotations of poverty as a pathology that most seriously afflicted women. Governor Talmadge pleaded with state lawmakers to pass legislation denying welfare to "promiscuous" women with "loose morals" who were bearing children in order to collect welfare money as a "business venture." The governor acknowledged that state taxpayers were "willing to tolerate an unwed mother who makes one mistake but not when the mistake is repeated two, three, four or five times." His proposal to limit welfare to children born to single mothers passed both houses of the state legislature and was signed into law on February 21,1951, to become effective immediately.

During that same decade efforts were made in at least 18 other states to enact laws or introduce administrative policies to require sterilization of welfare mothers or deny benefits to reproductively active single mothers whom lawmakers characterized as immoral and amoral, willing to trade on their reproductive function. This was possible because the Social Security Act of 1935, which created Aid to Dependent Children, left states free to determine the nature and size of their welfare programs: No national standard of need was established nor were states obliged to provide sufficient assistance to meet minimum standards of health and decency. Congress, in other words, allowed states to define welfare eligibility in any way they desired so long as they did not contravene federal statute, and in its early reports Congress clarified that the "moral character" of the woman seeking assistance could be taken into consideration in determining her or her child s eligibility. Without explicit federal guidelines, states became remarkably creative in devising reforms that, by the 1950s and 1960s, targeted single women of color and their children.

In 1958, for example, Representative David Glass introduced a bill into the Mississippi House of Representatives providing for the sterilization of single mothers on welfare which he titled "An Act to Discourage Immorality of Unmarried Females by Providing for Sterilization of the Unwed Mother Under Conditions of this Act; And for Related Purposes." Representative Glass explained that the law was necessary because "[t]he Negro woman, because of child welfare assistance, [is] making it a business, in some cases of giving birth to illegitimate children . . . The purpose of my bill was to try to stop, or slow down, such traffic at its source." In 1957 the Arkansas legislature passed legislation which allowed denial of public assistance to children whose mothers "continued to have illegitimate children" while AFDC eligible. Governor Faubus bragged in 1960 that the law had resulted in "8,000 illegitimate children being taken off the welfare rolls during my term of office" as a result of the 1957 action. Shortly before this statement he condemned welfare for rewarding "sin." Similarly, the Texas legislature passed a bill which allowed exclusion from welfare rolls any woman who "subjects her children to immoral surroundings." "Subjection to immoral surroundings" included "birth of an illegitimate child," "lack of sexual discipline," "rowdiness, late parties," and "the intimate and intermittent presence of various men in and out of the household." Altogether lawmakers in states across the nation considered and, in some cases passed, legislation designed to "clean up" the welfare caseload by eliminating benefits for women who were "promiscuous" . . . have illegitimate children . . . and lack moral and ethical standards." Lawmakers claimed that they were "not trying to be punitive" but rather were "only interested in providing an incentive for conforming behavior." "Get right," it was declared, "and the grants will be resumed."

These bills linking women's (reproductive) behavior and welfare epitomize the shift to a culture of single motherhood myth. They draw on cultural rhetoric, linking poverty and escalating welfare costs to women's allegedly immoral behavior: It is the woman who has loose morals and does not practice birth control; it is the woman who is sexually enticing the men; and it is the woman who bears full responsibility for the pregnancy and the children. It is the woman whose morality needs reform. In recasting the discourse, defining poverty in terms of women's uncontrolled reproductive behavior, lawmakers gave shape to a culture of single motherhood image of poor women whose poverty is inextricably linked with concepts of morality. Through the filter of the culture of single motherhood myth, such women were no longer the innocent victims of men trapped in a culture of poverty; rather, they appeared as victims of a

fault in which there was no one more culpable than they.

These bills also demonstrate that by the early 1950s the problem of women's morality had become racialized. Prior to the 1950s, out-of-wedlock births and poverty rates were higher in African American communities, yet an image racializing women's morality and sexuality as a causal feature of poverty had not yet emerged. This is because until then, the oppression of African American women was so total that their subjugation was maintained without having to use what Patricia Hill Collins refers to as "controlling images of Black womanhood." As African American women gained economic and political clout beginning in the 1940s and 1950s, however, morality and "cultural pathology" were racialized. At the same time that White women's illegitimacy was perceived as a treatable individual psychological phenomenon, African American unwed mothers were mythologized as innately biologically flawed by hypersexuality. Such racialized assumptions, used to mark African American women as the least deserving of dependent populations, profoundly influenced attitudes toward indigent women and conditioned the treatment of poor mothers receiving public assistance.

THE REFORMS

By the 1990s, the fusion of race, gender and poverty implicit in culture of single motherhood images became the tacitly accepted starting point for making dramatic changes in their welfare programs. An usually broad spectrum of political elites drew on the culture of single motherhood to explain women's impoverishment and to justify harsh policy initiatives to address their concerns. Starting in New Jersey and Wisconsin and spreading to over three dozen states, lawmakers relied on the specter of a spreading culture of single motherhood to justify legislation designed to curb welfare mothers' fecundity, and thus the transmission of a pathological culture. Two of the most popular legislative measures to emerge in the 1990s which link public assistance benefits and fertility regulation are benefit cap plans and temporary sterilization measures.

Benefit Caps

On April 10, 1992, President George Bush announced at a White House press conference that the state of Wisconsin had been granted federal approval to implement the "Parental and Family Responsibility Initiative" which, for the first time in the nation's history, imposes a stringent one-child-per-family cap on AFDC benefits. The goal is to prevent births among women on welfare by imposing harsh monetary penalties on women who bear children while AFDC eligible. The new law differs radically from current federal law; under existing law every state provides incremental AFDC grant increases as a family's size increases from 2 to 3, from 3 to 4, etc. The benefit cap plan signed into law by Wisconsin Governor Tommy Thompson provides that a woman who has another child while receiving welfare will receive only half the current grant increment for that child and no additional increment for another subsequent child. It does not provide for an exception for the birth of twins, rape, incest, or pregnancy where the father is perpetrating domestic violence on the woman and forcing her to go on with the pregnancy.

Eager to capitalize on the success of Wisconsin's effort to win federal approval for its benefit cap plan, coupled with clear signals from the Bush and later Clinton administrations that states would be given much greater latitude to "experiment" with their welfare programs, thirteen states followed in quick succession. (Another 60 benefit cap bills in 28 states, all introduced in the first quarter of 1995, remain pending). The statutes enacted were quite similar throughout the nation, for example, lawmakers in Arizona, Arkansas, California, Delaware, Georgia, Indiana, Kansas, Maryland, Massachusetts, Mississippi, Nebraska, New Jersey, and Virginia each passed legislation providing that a mother receiving AFDC will no longer receive a grant increase if she bears a child while her family is AFDC-eligible. The plans differ with respect to the age of the mother, the timing of compliance, and the breadth of the cap. The Georgia "Personal Accountability and Responsibility Act," for example, excludes from the AFDC grant additional children born 24 months or more after initial receipt of welfare whereas the Arizona "Employing and Moving People Off Welfare and Encouraging Responsibility Act," the Delaware "A Better Chance," the Maryland "Family Investment System," the New Jersey "Family Development Initiative," and the Arkansas "Reduction in Birthrates Project" deny financial assistance to children born to women more than ten months after the AFDC application. Twelve state plans exempt a child born as a result of incest or rape; Wisconsin and New Jersey do not. Only California amended its benefit cap law to include exceptions for cases where children were conceived as a result of contraceptive failure.

The arguments for benefit caps stressed the need to contain illegitimacy and its apparent associated "depravation of morality" especially among women. Wisconsin Governor Thompson, like state legislators, solicited legislative support for his benefit cap plan as necessary to halt women's "irresponsible poverty behavior." Rather than rewarding women by allowing them to collect money for their promiscuous behavior, the Governor demanded that state laws should strive toward changing the "poverty behavior" of women mired in poverty. A Wisconsin lawmaker registered her support of benefit caps legislation because, she said, it was time to shut off the welfare "irrigation system" nurturing many of the defects of the poor—their laziness, debauchery, promiscuity—that led to poverty. Georgia Representative Tom Bordeaux, Jr. remarked that accepting benefit caps in order to lower women's birthrate while on AFDC would "restore public confidence" and prevent the ascendancy of more extreme measures "such as mandatory sterilization for women who get welfare benefits."

The implicit premise of the benefit cap concept is that increased grants for additional children encourage promiscuous behavior, lead to more illegitimate children and make women indifferent to their fault. Legislative debates encouraged this interpretation. Consider, for example, the analysis of the problems of poor women and the recommendations emanating from New Jersey Assembly member Wayne Bryant, author of his state's benefit cap legislation:

> It is simply stupid to pretend that poverty isn't caused by poor folks—who have no values—having more babies than they should. The question is, why should we who live in good suburbia, who do not have children we cannot afford, continue to support folks who . . . don't seem willing to make the same kinds of choices by themselves? Why can't poor folks make those same kinds of decisions? If there is an unplanned pregnancy, you have the right to get an abortion in our state . . . my bill will make mothers think before they have a baby.

Assembly member Bryant identifies the problem as one of poor folks—welfare mothers—whose behavior and values are a threat to society, producing too many unwanted newborns. The proof of the welfare mother's irresponsibility is that fact that she hasn't prevented or terminated her pregnancy. Predictably, keeping indigent women from reproducing is Bryant's primary and almost exclusive concern. Rhetoric about the state's determination to make indigent women think before they get pregnant not only scores points with voters, it reinforces the myth that poor mothers are out-of-control reproducers who should be punished

for thoughtlessly having babies they cannot afford. Denying relief to undeserving mothers and their children is justified if it will lower fertility rates among poor women, even though women and children will be hurt in the process.

Opponents of benefit cap plans cited the growing body of academic evidence demonstrating that there is no empirical evidence to support the proposition that an AFDC recipient would have an additional child solely for the purpose of receiving an incremental increase in AFDC cash benefits. The National Organization for Women, for example, cited leading national authorities, for example, Jodie Levin-Epstein and Mark Greenberg of the Center of Law and Social Policy, to support the basic proposition that there is no empirical support for the supposition that increased grants for additional children encourage the conception of additional children. On the contrary, Levin-Epstein and Greenberg pointed out that nationwide, 72.5 percent of welfare families have only one or two children; that fertility rates for welfare mothers are lower than the rates for the general population, and the longer a woman remains on welfare, the less likely she is to give birth; that families receiving welfare are not bigger in states with larger welfare grants; and that most babies born to welfare mothers in a recent study were conceived prior to welfare receipt. Although the evidence contradicts the culture of single motherhood postulates, this was not enough to overcome the support of legislators in states across the nation, however, as they moved to pass benefit cap legislation and send the bills to their respective governors for signature.

Norplant

In addition to benefits caps, many state legislatures have considered bills, none of which has yet been approved, designed to force poor women to use contraceptives as a condition of welfare receipt. Unlike benefit caps, which use economic coercion to force women to delay childbirth, these bills use economic coercion to curtail fertility a priori. The most common proposal has related to Norplant, the female contraceptive implant effective for up to five years.

Norplant, approved for use in the U.S. in 1990, is a contraceptive device which comes in the form of six match-stick sized silicone rubber capsules that are implanted by a physician under the skin of a woman's upper arm during a minor surgical procedure. The capsules contain a synthetic female hormone, levonorgestrel, which is released in minute amounts into the body. The device is 99 percent effective in preventing pregnancy for up to five years. After five years the levonorgestrel runs low and the capsules must be removed. Unlike other forms of birth control, once implanted, a woman can render Norplant ineffective only by having it surgically removed. In short, the technology is a safe, effective means of temporarily sterilizing women.

Less than two months after the Food and Drug Administration approved Norplant, Kansas Representative Kerry Patrick introduced a bill to authorize free Norplant implants and $500 "insertion bonuses" to women on welfare. An additional "bonus" would have been paid to women for each year they kept the device in their arm. At roughly the same time, Louisiana State Representative David Duke, a former Grand Wizard in the Ku Klux Klan and current gubernatorial candidate, introduced legislation that offered $100 per year to welfare mothers who agreed to Norplant implantation. By mid-1995, 70 bills in 35 states had been proposed on Norplant's availability, most which offer financial inducements to women on welfare to use Norplant or which make Norplant use a condition of welfare receipt. For example, Florida Representative George Albright introduced a bill that would have provided a number of financial rewards to AFDC recipients who agreed to be

implanted with Norplant, including a $50.00 bonus check per quarter for up to 10 years, a dental voucher, in the amount of $200 per year for up to ten years, and an education tuition and books voucher for postsecondary education, in the amount of $200 per year for up to 10 years. Connecticut Representative Robert Farr's proposed bill was designed to pay welfare women who agree to Norplant implantation an immediate $700 bonus and $200 a year for as long as they remain "on the device." Colorado, Maryland, Ohio, Tennessee, Washington, West Virginia among others have also considered bills designed to encourage voluntary implantation by women on welfare.

Several states, however, have considered legislation mandating Norplant implants as a condition of welfare receipt. South Carolina's "Responsible Parenting Act" would mandate that all welfare mothers "must consent to and have a birth control device surgically implanted." Women who refuse implantation would lose all public assistance benefits. Tennessee Senator Steve McDaniel also introduced legislation that would have required all fertile women on AFDC to receive Norplant implants. Women who rejected implantation and became pregnant while AFDC-eligible would have lost additional welfare benefits for themselves and their newborn infant, including Medicaid benefits. And Mississippi State Senator Walter Graham proposed that his state require Norplant for women with at least four children who wanted any kind of government assistance. Florida, North Carolina and Washington have considered similar legislation.

Like the campaign for benefit caps legislation, the legislative movement to promote temporary sterilization of poor mothers on welfare drew on culture of single motherhood images of poor women as indiscriminate breeders of unwanted children, lacking in self control and passing on their bad values and welfare dependence to their offspring.

One way to see the premise of the culture of single motherhood in these bills is to imagine the public response to a similar effort directed against middle class women's fertility. If lawmakers chose to put a cap on the number of dependents that could be claimed for tax purposes, and lawmakers defended that law's rationality as providing "incentives for fertility reduction," the public protests would be widespread and intense. People would argue that determining the size of the family is a personal choice, beyond lawmakers' interest. People would be outraged by the assumptions of the government's argument, that it has any interest in the matter or that middle class women have acted in an irresponsible fashion. Although the children of families in the middle class are subsidized by the government through tax deductions, public school financing, and other publicly funded services, middle class taxpayers usually see the two cases as different in part because they do not make the same assumptions about the two sets of mothers. However furious many middle class families would be at the use of governmental power to make them plan their family size, they see little problem in doing just that to poor women because they assume that welfare mothers are immoral and more likely to act irresponsibly

MAPPING THE MYTH

Much of the discussion of the birth control and benefit cap legislation illustrates the process by which cultural myths are inscribed in legislation: legislators state the assumptions explicitly, and they implicitly incorporate the assumptions by making arguments that encourage the public to supply them. For example, New Jersey Assembly member Bryant made explicit assumptions of the behavioral pathology among welfare mothers. Most notable were his claims that much of the state's poverty derived from the imprudence of the poor: women did not restrain

their sexuality, bore children whom they could not support, or often did not marry. He denounced the appalling "lack of control" among women in poverty, condemned calculating recipients for bearing children "for the money," and urged women, rather than bearing more unwanted children, to "choose abortion." The analysis Bryant offered of the causes of poverty created an image that supported the construction of women's cultural pathology as the culprit; one cannot tackle the problems of poverty without first reforming the poor.

Implicitly, the discussions surrounding the Norplant and benefit cap legislation embody the premise of the culture of single motherhood several ways. Representative Kerry Patrick, who proposed the Kansas Norplant legislation for welfare recipients, asserted:

> The real question is, do we, as a society, since we're paying welfare to these people, taking care of people who can't take care of themselves—is our obligation in the reproductive area unlimited? And just like anything, there's got to be some sort of limits. Why do we have an obligation as a taxpayer for her to have two, three, four, or five children, when we can provide an incentive that would limit it? I mean, the taxpayers have rights.

Representative Patrick locates the problem of poverty and welfare in women's reckless reproductive behavior; the evidence of the AFDC recipient's recklessness is found in her repeated pregnancies. His proposed solution, Norplant legislation, says nothing explicit about women's immorality or promiscuity. Yet, the legislation draws its power from the implicit premise that welfare mothers are bearing children irresponsibly, often for the purpose of supplementing a welfare check. Representative Patrick has drawn conclusions about women's morality (nonmarital births) from facts he interprets as illustrating women's inability or unwillingness to control their own bodies. The assumptions is that poor women are not competent to control their own reproduction, and that the state must regulate their fertility for them. Because lawmakers are so used to the idea that welfare mothers are out-of-control they advance the idea without hesitation, and assume that their constituents will agree.

The explicit and implicit identification of poverty, nonmarital births, and welfare dependence as a product of the cultural pathology of welfare mothers creates a dimension to welfare opposition that many lawmakers find appealing. Locating the etiology of poverty in poor women's behavior—chronic pregnancy, welfare dependence—allows lawmakers to cite and give weight to the attributes considered part of the myth of women's poverty, thus promoting popular assumptions about idle, promiscuous welfare mothers constrainable only by coercive, economic sanctions. Under these assumptions, lawmakers' arguments are a coherent explanation for benefit cap and Norplant legislation. By capping benefits, for example, any mother who is receiving AFDC has an incentive to avoid incurring the financial burden of another child because she will receive no additional financial benefits. The decision to have another child then becomes a decision to put her entire family, already in desperate financial straits, in a worse position. Presented this way legislative efforts to control poor women's decisions about procreation are justified; the solution seems perfectly to fit the problem.

CRITICAL ASSESSMENT OF THE MYTH

Advocates of fertility regulation legislation for welfare recipients argue that it will cut the public assistance rolls and end poverty by lowering the birth rate among women in the poverty class. Unfortunately for women, however, rather than alleviating their poverty, fertility regulation legislation helps preserve the poverty status of women in the welfare system. Most obviously, these reforms

contribute to women's pauperization because they reinforce the myth that poverty is an individual woman's problem (unbridled sexuality) in need of redress (fertility regulation). By substituting women's behavioral pathology for labor market discrimination, sexual harassment, unemployment and underemployment, poor schooling, lack of access to birth control and abortion services, and other institutional forces in our society which help perpetuate deprivation, cultural myths of poverty divert attention from the socioeconomic inequities affecting poor women and their children and suggest that poverty could be alleviated if only women would change their behavior, and make different choices. Moreover, the attempt to use economic coercion to create changed behavior in welfare mothers leads to solutions that are contrary to empirical evidence and thus cannot solve the problems for which they are ostensibly designed. This is true for several reasons, not least that the underlying assumptions—that AFDC mothers have many children, that they have free access to medical options for family planning, that they get pregnant in order to receive additional benefits—are wrong.

The sexism, racism and classism embedded in these policies is also troubling. Forced temporary sterilization by Norplant and benefit cap plans place all the blame for poverty and welfare dependence on women and their mistakes in controlling their own behavior. Only women risk having their welfare benefits conditioned on the implantation of a contraceptive device—vasectomies are not proposed as a condition of eligibility for initial or increased public assistance for men. Fertility regulation legislation thus makes women unequal citizens because of a biological makeup that allows them to have babies despite men's equal importance in the reproductive process.

Moreover, a higher standard of conduct is imposed upon women in the poverty class than upon nonpoor women. Political elites claim the fertility regulation legislation is for the "recipient's own good." The culture of single motherhood model of poverty sees lawmakers as the functional equivalent of social workers, curing and rehabilitating women through the behavioral reforms that they force upon them through the manipulation of benefits. Poor women are coerced economically to change their behavior, and lead less deviant and more socially approved forms of lives. In the process, a higher standard of behavior is forced upon on poor women than women in the public at large. It is not wrong (anyway, not illegal) to engage in pre-or extra-marital sexual relations; it is not wrong (anyway, not illegal) to bear children outside of marriage. It is only wrong (anyway, legally discouraged) to do so if you are poor. The conditions that lawmakers impose upon welfare mothers discourage such behavior. If society wants to discourage nonmarital births and sexual relations, it should do so across classes. It should not take advantage of poor women's plight to enforce standards upon them that are not enforced upon the rest of society.

It could be argued, of course, that women who are poor would still have the freedom to have children by going off welfare. However, the choice between sustenance and children does not seem much of a choice. Five hundred dollars to a woman poor enough to be on welfare is a fortune. If she couldn't see her way through the financial fog and someone offered her $500.00, how free would she feel to say no? In short, desperate economic circumstances can force women to submit to notionally voluntary conditions attached to welfare services; most would feel forced to choose sustenance and therefore would have Norplant inserted, or postpone childbirth. Lawmakers are laying down conditions (birth control) in circumstances (poverty) wherein welfare recipients have "no reasonable choice" but to comply.

Finally, benefit cap and Norplant bills have unmistakable racial overtones. The public perception is that welfare mothers are single and Black. Therefore, the legislation may draw support from prejudice and racist stereotypes. Racism certainly provides a motivation for some politicians who seek to prevent women of color from reproducing. Although the official justification for the fertility reduction legislation is that it will reduce poverty rates by lowering fertility rates among women in the poverty class, government sponsored plans which use economic coercion to force low income women not to procreate in a society where the proportion of African American women who earn low incomes and receive welfare support (34.6 percent) is highly disproportionate to their representation in the population (6.35 percent) is troubling, to say the least. Combined with the history of racism, sterilization abuse and the devaluation of African American motherhood, it does not seem unreasonable to conclude that benefit cap and Norplant policies perpetuate the eugenic goals of historical sterilization abuse of women of color. That single, poor women of color are most affected by this legislation again reveals that the myth of the reproductively out-of-control welfare mother, implicitly or explicitly Black, engenders and enables the reproductive control of women.

CONCLUSION

Although culture of poverty myths have historical origins, they continue to be played out in public policies and reemerge in modern interpretations, i.e. the culture of single motherhood. The myths about women in poverty that permeate our culture shape the development of welfare policy, for example, the racist and sexist myth of the hyper-sexual Black welfare mother bearing children for financial gain supports repression of Black women's fertility. In addition, myths drive assessments that poor women on welfare are likely to be sexually active in the future and unlikely to use contraceptives, and that a contraceptive such as Norplant that removes control from the woman herself is the only effective and appropriate solution. Lawmakers may use these myths to make normative judgments about which women deserve to be mothers and which therefore deserve public support and sustenance. By limiting women's control of their reproductive bodies, however, laws regulating poor women's fertility sustain the myth that welfare mothers are out-of-control reproducers in need of external supervision. The myth in turn legitimizes degrading, restrictive welfare plans which condition material assistance on poor women's submission to state supervision of their sexual practices and fertility.

These reforms seem to have very little to do with the fundamental goal of providing for women's welfare. Instead they are designed to penalize their alleged moral shortcomings, saving money for the deserving poor rather than just giving it to women strictly on account of their poverty, which is what welfare is supposed to require. It seems reasonable to conclude that by attempting to force indigent welfare mothers into childlessness or delayed childbearing without taking steps to remedy social inequities, benefit caps and Norplant laws both perpetuate discriminatory structures and subject women who are poor to their abuse.

STUDY QUESTION

How have the myths about women in poverty shaped the development of welfare policy as discussed by Susan Thomas?

CHAPTER 6

Inequality in the Political Institution

INTRODUCTION

Unauthorized immigration, reparations, felony disenfranchisement laws, human trafficking, and *America's brutal imperialism* are contemporary social problems directly challenging the veracity of America's federal government and political establishment. The prevailing social myths surrounding unauthorized immigration to the United States, for example, contradict the reality of immigrants as hardworking, industrious, and enterprising people. Americans presume that undocumented immigrants come to the United States to live at public expense, and they blame undocumented immigrants for their social and economic troubles. What many Americans overlook, however, is that U.S. industries actively recruit undocumented immigrants to fill low-wage laboring positions.[1] Similarly, Americans tend to misunderstand the issues associated with reparations. The United States has committed severe atrocities against black Americans, American Indians, Latinos, and Asian Americans for which the country has been unjustly enriched. America continues the systemic racism underlying these historically based atrocities with felony disenfranchisement laws designed to deny political participation to millions of Americans. Moreover, people in the United States have turned a deaf ear to the continued atrocities of human trafficking of mostly women and children of color forced into prostitution and domestic servitude. Lastly, we must take a look at the brutal imperialism undermining America's international credibility as a nation dedicated to "peace."

UNAUTHORIZED IMMIGRATION

U.S. industries satisfy their labor needs by employing native-born workers, foreign guest workers, and *undocumented* immigrant workers. Of the nearly 140 million workers in the United States, native workers are about 85 percent and about 15 percent are foreign born.[2] Undocumented immigrant workers, mostly from Mexico and Latin American countries, are roughly 30 percent of foreign workers.[3] Contrary to popular belief, however, undocumented migrant workers do not displace native workers in the United States. Overwhelming, job losses in the United States to native workers stem from foreign guest workers and U.S. industries subcontracting and outsourcing work to overseas labor markets in India, other Asian countries, and Latin America. Documented foreign guest workers displace large numbers of native workers in high-tech industries because of a general unwillingness of U.S. industries to train and employ native workers. For example, many U.S. industries regard black Americans as residual laborers drawn on only when undocumented workers are unavailable. As one economist explains it, "Today, as manufacturing and industrial jobs continue to decline, the competition for the remaining blue-collar jobs intensifies, and when this happens black Americans lose for a variety of reasons ranging from racial stereotypes to employer preference for vulnerable workers fearing deportation."[4] Moreover, subcontracting and outsourcing by U.S. industries will cost the United States some 3 million jobs over the next decade.[5]

Besides a misunderstanding that undocumented immigrants displace native workers, central to the debate on illegal immigration is that undocumented immigrants burden already economically strapped health, education, and social services. Those critical of illegal immigration clearly overstate much about the costs of undocumented immigration to public programs. Providing medical care to undocumented immigrants is exorbitant, but considerable evidence indicates that undocumented immigrants do not use public health services carelessly. Two recent studies, for example, found that immigrants from Mexico receive substantially fewer health care services than U.S. citizens, and immigrant Mexicans are half as likely as native-born whites to use emergency rooms.[6] Undocumented immigrants are disinclined to use public health facilities because they fear being identified as an illegal immigrant and deported. As a result, undocumented immigrants often postpone medical attention to health conditions until they become life threatening. Health officials warn that delaying medical attention escalates health care costs because it is far more expensive to treat an aggravated medical condition.

Most undocumented immigrant workers are in low-paying agricultural operations where they are critical to U.S. food production. Many economists concede that agriculture would prosper in the United States even without undocumented workers. What is more, the average American family's food costs would increase insignificantly if agriculture employers provided farm workers with decent wages and working conditions. Despite the *illegality* of hiring undocumented migrant workers, there is a very low risk of government action against employers of illegal immigrants. In fact, employers hire illegal immigrants with virtual impunity nationwide.[7] Over the last ten years the number of employers fined for hiring illegal workers dropped from 944 to 124, and the number of undocumented workers arrested at work sites fell from 7,630 to 445. One reason for the dramatic decrease in sanctioning employers is the lack of Immigration and Customs Enforcement (ICE) agents. In Los Angeles, for example, some four hundred ICE agents are responsible for investigating cases in involving narcotics, gangs, port security, criminal immigrants, computer crimes, smuggling, and customs violations in seven Southern California counties and parts of Nevada. Still, federal authorities have held some large employers liable for violation of laws prohibiting employers from hiring undocumented workers. Wal-Mart Stores, for example, recently paid $11 million in fines to settle charges that it employed hundreds of undocumented workers as janitors.

Unauthorized immigrants depend on work and not on welfare services for their livelihoods. Granted, illegal immigrants have high poverty rates, high rates of participation in public assistance programs, and high rates of uninsured persons, but data also show that proportionate representations of undocumented immigrants on poor sociodemographic measures is far less than native persons. This is not to argue that significant fiscal outlays by local and state governments are not attributable to illegal aliens. In one of the few studies to estimate the total impact of illegal immigration on the federal budget, the Center for Immigration Studies found that "when all taxes paid (direct and indirect) and all costs are considered, illegal households created a net fiscal deficit at the federal level of more than $10 billion in 2002. We also estimate that, if there was an *amnesty* for undocumented workers, the net fiscal deficit would grow to nearly $29 billion."[8] The report points out that much of the cost associated with the illegal alien population is attributed to their American-born children. Among the largest costs identified with illegal immigrants are medical treatment for the uninsured; food assistance programs including food stamps, Women, Infants and Children (WIC), free school lunches; and federal aid to schools. Medicaid costs and those associated with the federal prison and court system are substantial. Still, the report is clear that the fiscal deficit for the federal government created by illegal immigrants does not result from a disinclination to work. "Although many Americans are upset about their use of public services, there is little evidence that illegals come to America to take advantage of public benefits. Most illegal aliens come for jobs, and the vast majority are in fact employed. But low levels of education mean they unavoidably create large costs for taxpayers." As a result, low levels of educational attainment contribute dramatically to the fiscal impact of illegal alien workers because most are unskilled low-wage workers for whom employers provide little health and welfare benefits. As explained by the Center for Immigration Studies, demographics on illegal aliens in the United States reflect a population with extremely low levels of educational attainment and predictably much smaller incomes than other households. Illegal households paid $16 billion in taxes to the federal government in 2002, less than 1 percent of all taxes collected; unfortunately, their tax payments are less than their use of public services. But this fiscal deficit would not change with a change in aliens' legal status in the United States. Even so, the attributed costs to illegal aliens is far less than other populations.

Public opinion on illegal immigration has fostered extreme public dissension toward Mexican immigrants. Voters in southwestern states, most notably in California and Arizona, have passed referendums preventing undocumented immigrants from receiving educational, health, and social welfare services even though courts have found these measures mostly unconstitutional. Illegal immigration has become the new scapegoat for the federal government's inability to stabilize its international borders in light of President Bush's so-called war on terrorism and establishment of the U.S. Department of Homeland Security. As Kevin Johnson explains in *September 11 and Mexican Immigrants: Collateral Damage Comes Home*, Mexican immigrants will be adversely affected by changes in post-911 enforcement of immigration law. For example, although the federal government enforces laws prohibiting the hiring of undocumented workers in the United States, a 2005 National Public Radio report reveals that undocumented Mexican nationals apprehended by the U.S. Border Patrol are immediately shuttled back across the U.S.-Mexico border, but law enforcement officials permit non-Mexican illegal immigrants to stay in the United States after promising to appear before an immigration judge, even though some 98 percent of them never appear before the court.[9]

FELONY DISENFRANCHISEMENT LAWS

Prison is far more costly than just the loss of physical freedom. One troubling aspect of the gross disparity of persons of color in the inmate population is that while these people sit warehoused in prisons and jails they are not actively participating in society's other social institutions, such as education, employment, and politics. U.S. society imprisons more young black men than it enrolls in its colleges and universities: nearly 20 percent of the black male population eighteen to twenty-four years old are under correctional supervision, and only 8 percent of black men attend college.[10] *Felon disenfranchisement laws* deny felons in prison and ex-felons their fundamental right to vote and the opportunity to participate in the political process. Scholars have traced disenfranchisement policies to the nation's founders, who carried over the medieval European concept of "civil death," the deprivation of all rights to people convicted of a felony. There is some confusion as to when disenfranchisement statutes actually appeared in the United States, but Virginia's constitution prohibited felons from voting as early as 1776,[11] and other provisions appeared in the 1810s.[12] A majority of states had no felon disenfranchisement laws as late as the 1850s, but by the 1860s two thirds of the states had such provisions. Today only Maine and Vermont have no disenfranchising provision.[13] In the post-Reconstruction period, southern states used disenfranchisement statutes to exclude black voters in the same way that state legislatures used poll taxes and literacy tests.[14] But as Monique Dixon explains in *Minority Disenfranchisement During the 2000 General Election: A Blast from the Past or a Blueprint for Reform,* officials continue to turn away blacks from the polls because their voter registration applications were not processed in a timely manner or they were wrongfully removed from the voter rolls as a result of aggressive "list-cleansing procedures" that are tantamount to modern-day literacy tests and poll taxes.

All states and the District of Columbia prohibit felons from voting while in prison, thirty-two states prohibit felons from voting while on parole, and twenty-nine states prohibit felons from voting during probation. Some jurisdictions take voting rights away from felons for life. The result of these laws is that 3.9 million felons are disenfranchised from political participation. Denying felons voting rights has had a pernicious effect on black communities because states bar *one in eight* of the 10.4 million black men of voting age from voting because of a prior felony conviction.[15] In the 2000 presidential election, previous felony convictions disenfranchised 25 percent of black voters in Iowa, 17 percent of black voters in Nevada, and 25 percent of black voters in New Mexico.[16] Several southern states permanently disenfranchise *over 30 percent* of the black male vote, and in other regions, *one in four* black men are permanently disenfranchised from voting.[17] Felon disenfranchisement laws passed by mostly white male legislators nationwide are also silencing the political voice of black women. Such draconian measures deny nearly a quarter million black women from participating in local, state, and national elections; the black female disenfranchisement rate is *three times* the national average for women, resulting in a disparity ratio of 4.3 given that the disenfranchisement rate is 0.45 for nonblack women and 1.92 for black women.[18]

HUMAN TRAFFICKING AND SEXUAL SLAVERY

Political activists consider human trafficking to be one of the most serious human rights violations facing the United States today. A comprehensive report by the Center for the Study of Intelligence estimates that criminal operatives traffic some 700,000 to 2 million women and children worldwide every year—a $6 to $12 billion a year industry. Of these, 45,000 to 50,000 are forced into "sexual servitude, domestic servitude, bonded sweatshop labor and other debt bondage" in the United States annually.[19] Most are trafficked to New York, California, and Florida from Southeast Asia, Latin America, and Eastern Europe.[20] One report calculates that traffickers have sent some 750,000 foreign women into the United States within the past decade.[21] Human trafficking into the United States has gained the attention of President George W. Bush who, in a speech before the United Nations General Assembly on human trafficking in September 2003, exclaimed that "governments that tolerate this trade are tolerating a form of slavery." Yet President Bush failed to mention in his speech that most advocates recognize that the growth of human trafficking is more dramatic "in countries where traditional economies have collapsed as a result of neo-liberal economic policies imposed by U.S.-backed international financial institutions such as the International Monetary Fund."[22] Nevertheless, U.S. law enforcement agencies have not adequately addressed human trafficking into the United States. Carolyn Seugling points out in *Toward a Comprehensive Response to the Transnational Migration of Unaccompanied Minors in the United States,* for example, that immigrant children are often abused and neglected by the very law enforcement agencies designated to care for their safety and welfare. Some critics also explain that children forced into prosecution are not receiving the protection and support from government agencies that is warranted for their situations.[23] Strangely enough, evidence indicates that federal law enforcement officers may be complicit in the illegal activities of human traffickers as patrons of child sex slavery. A particularly horrid case of law enforcement indifference to sex trafficking in the United States took place in the now infamous "open-air child rape camps" of San Diego County in Southern California. For more than *ten years,* law enforcement agencies knew that adult men were raping Mexican young girls (seven to eighteen years old) trafficked to the region and forced into prostitution. After learning of the camps ten years earlier, federal and local law enforcement agencies finally made raids and made more than forty arrests of people involved in the trafficking ring, but state prosecutors failed to win convictions. The forty-seven young Latinas who had been forced into sexual slavery at the camps apparently refused to talk to police because their kidnappers had threatened them and their families with physical harm should they aid law enforcement. *LibertadLatina,* a nonprofit organization working to end the sexual exploitation of women and children in the Americas, claims that San Diego County is a "zone of impunity" where notoriously violent gangs continue to kidnap and enslave young Mexican girls with legal impunity because U.S. law enforcement are not shutting down the child rape camps. In a series of newspaper articles on the camps, *El Universal* (*The Universal Newspaper*) explains how a social worker witnessed federal immigration agents having sex with the young Mexican girls in exchange for legal protection.[24] Such atrocities to innocent children continue to plague U.S. society.

AMERICA'S BRUTAL IMPERIALISM

Critical commentator James Cogan refers to the trial of former Iraqi president Saddam Hussein and Baathist party leader as a "legal travesty."[25] The Supreme Iraqi Criminal Tribunal and the Iraqi government are trying Hussein for crimes committed against the Iraqi people. But Cogan claims that the trial is nothing more than a show "designed to have the former dictator quickly sentenced to death and executed." Apparently, the tribunal is only prosecuting Hussein for nineteen charges relating to the massacre of 150 people in Dujail in 1982 following a failed attempt on Hussein's life. But to Cogan, the tribunal has purposefully chosen the Dujail incident. Cogan writes,

> The Dujail massacre has been carefully chosen, instead of other Baathist crimes that were encouraged or sanctioned by the major powers. These include the slaughter of Iraqi Communist Party members in 1979; the murder of thousands of Shiites in the lead-up to the 1980 U.S.-backed Iraqi invasion of Iran; the use of Western-supplied chemical weapons against Iranian troops and civilians during the 1980–88 Iran-Iraq war; the pogroms against the Kurdish population in the late 1980s; and the butchery of tens of thousands of Shiites and Kurds following the 1991 Gulf War.

Since the Iraqi invasion, President George W. Bush has consistently described democratic and free societies as peaceful societies, describing the United States as a peaceful society fighting global aggression to bring democracy and freedom to otherwise oppressive nations. Nothing could be further from the truth. The United States unilaterally invaded Iraq causing the deaths of at least 100,000 dead Iraqi men and women, but mostly children in "American air strikes, helicopter gunship assaults and shelling in densely populated urban areas such as Fallujah [that] have caused the greatest number of violent deaths."[26] President Bush gained national consensus for the Iraqi invasion with deception and fabrications concerning weapons of mass destruction and claims that Iraq was training and harboring al-Qaeda operatives responsible for the September 11, 2001, attacks.[27] Yet later, Americans were horrified by photographs depicting Washington's use of torture and abuse of Iraqi prisoners in the Abu Ghraib prison in Iraq and at Guantanomo Bay in Cuba. But by rejecting legislation barring the Central Intelligence Agency from torturing foreign prisoners outside the United States, Congress sanctioned the Bush administration's vicious violence toward Muslim people while publicly condemning the atrocities at Abu Ghraib and Guantanomo Bay. Through deception the United States is spreading its tentacles into most parts of the world. The deception of the federal government to morally justify its unique form of brutal imperialist expansion throughout the world is not new.

In *Sixty Years Since the Hiroshima and Nagasaki Bombings*, Joseph Kay claims that although most Americans believed the Second World War was fought to eliminate the worldwide threat of "Hitlerite fascism and Japanese militarism," Washington's motivation was altogether different. He writes,

> The American ruling class entered the Second World War in order to secure its global interests. While the political character of the bourgeois democratic regime in the United States was vastly different than that of its fascist adversaries, the nature of the war aims of the United States were no less imperialistic. In the final analysis, the utter ruthlessness with which the United States sought to secure its objectives—including the use of the atomic bomb—flowed from this essential fact.

SUMMARY

This chapter challenges some of the more troubling issues confronting America's political establishment. Unfortunately, the question of undocumented immigration, recognizing reparations for past social injustices, continued voter disenfranchisement, human trafficking of women and children of color, and the brutality associated with American imperialism have long-reaching ramifications for marginalized groups in the United States. The readings adopted for this chapter reveal the perverted effects of the U.S. government's war on terrorism on the Mexican community, and they describe how today's political establishment has essentially implemented voting policies reminiscent of Jim Crow voting right schemes. Other readings find that the continued institutionalization of racial discrimination against black Americans may stand at odds with the U.S. government's failure to afford adequate group compensation for past injustices resulting from legal segregation. Moreover, the U.S. government continues to do preciously little to protect the human rights of unaccompanied children of color migrating to the United States. And a continued campaign of political, social, and economic dominance over the Middle East will undoubtedly raise the numbers of dead and wounded in an attempt to secure those interests of the U.S. government.

ENDNOTES

1. Kevin F. McCarthy and R. Burciaga Valdez, *Current and Future Effects of Mexican Immigration in California* (Santa Monica, CA: Rand Corporation, 1986).
2. U.S. Department of Labor, Bureau of Labor Statistics. *Labor Force Characteristics of Foreign-Born Workers in 2004* (May 15, 2005), http://www.bls.gov/news.release/pdf/forbrn.pdf.
3. Jeffrey S. Passel, *Unauthorized Migrants: Numbers and Characteristics*, The Pew Hispanic Center (June 14, 2005), http://pewhispanic.org/files/reports/46.pdf.
4. John Schmitt, *Recent Job Loss Hits the African-American Middle Class Hard*, Center for Economic and Policy Research (October 7, 2004), www.cepr.net/publications/job_tenure_report.htm.
5. Cable News Network (CNN), *Lou Dobbs Tonight* (November 16, 2004), Transcript Number 111601CN.V19; Employment Policy Foundation, *National Security and the Economy: The Numbers Behind Foreign Guest Workers* (January 9, 2002), www.epf.org/pubs/newsletters/2002/pb20020109.pdf.
6. Rong-Gong Lin II, "Mexican Immigrants Not Burdening Ers, Study Says," *Los Angeles Times*, October 14, 2005, B3.
7. Anna Gorman, "Employers of Illegal Immigrants Face Little Risk of Penalty," *Los Angeles Times*, May 29, 2005, pp. A1, A34, A35.

8. Steven A. Camarota, *The High Cost of Cheap Labor: Illegal Immigration and the Federal Budget* (August 2004), Center for Immigration Studies, www.cis.org/articles/2004/fiscal.pdf.

9. John Burnett, *Non-Mexican Immigrants Who Are Detained Allowed to Stay in United States*, Morning Edition, National Public Radio (July 11, 2005).

10. Samuel Walker, Cassia Spohn, and Miriam DeLone, *The Color of Justice: Race, Ethnicity, and Crime in America* (Belmont, CA: Wadsworth, 2004), p. 297.

11. Douglas R. Tims, "Note: The Disenfranchisement of Ex-Felons: A Cruelly Excessive Punishment," *Southwest University Law Review*, 7 (1975): 124.

12. Christopher Uggen and Jeff Manza, "Democratic Contraction? Felon Disfranchisement and American Democracy," *American Sociological Review*, 67 (2002): 777–803, 788.

13. Alexander Keyssar, *The Right to Vote: The Contested History of Democracy in the United States* (New York: Basic Books, 2000).

14. Marc Mauer, "Felon Disenfranchisement: A Policy Whose Time Has Passed?," *Human Rights*, 31 (Winter 2004): 16–17, http://www.sentencingproject.org/pdfs/mauer-aba-winter2004.pdf

15. Rebecca Perl, "The Last Disenfranchised Class," *The Nation* (November 6, 2003), http://www.thenation.com/doc.mhtml?i=20031124&c=1&s=perl.

16. Common Dreams News Center, *Million Blocked from Voting in U.S. Election* (September 22, 2004), http://www.commondreams.org/headlines04/0922-03.htm.

17. R. A. Lenhardt, "Understanding the Mark: Race, Stigma, and Equality in Context," *New York University Law Review*, 79 (2004): 803–932, at 917–918.

18. The Sentencing Project, *Felony Disenfranchisement Rates for Women* (August 2004), http://www.sentencingproject.org/pdfs/fvr-women.pdf.

19. Anita L. Botti, "The Trade in Human Beings Is a Worldwide Scourge," *Common Dreams* (June 1, 2000), http://www.commondreams.org.views/060100–103.htm.

20. Amy O'Neil Richard, *International Trafficking in Women to the United States: A Contemporary Manifestation of Slavery and Organized Crime*, Center for the Study of Intelligence (April 2000), http://www.cia.gov/csi/monograph/women/trafficking.pdf. See also U.S. Department of Justice, National Conference on Human Trafficking, *Human Trafficking in the United States: Rescuing Women and Children from Slavery* (2002), http://www.ojp.usdoj.gov/humantraffickingconf/docs/766474unat.pdf.

21. Mark Arner, "Task Force to Prosecute Sex-Trade, Slavery Cases," SignOnSanDiego.com (March 3, 2005).

22. Stephen Zunes, "An Annotated Refutation of President George W. Bush's September 2003 Address Before the United Nations," *Common Dreams* (September 24, 2003), http://www.commondreams.org/views03/0924–02.htm.

23. Jim Lobe, "Exploited Girls in U.S. Seek Same Protection Afforded Foreign Women," *Common Dreams* (March 5, 2005), http://www.commondreams.org/headlines04/0305–07.htm.

24. The Sex Trafficking of Children in San Diego, California," *El Universal* (January 9, 10, 11, 2003), http://www.libertadlatina.org/US_Sex_Trafficking_San_Diego_Case_01122003_English.htm.

25. James Cogan, "Legal Lynching of Saddam Hussein Begins in Iraq," *World Socialist Web Site* (October 19, 2005), http://www.wsws.org/articles/2005/oct2005/huss-o19_prn.shtml.

26. James Cogan, "Study Estimates 100,000 Additional Iraqi Deaths Since the Invasion," *World Socialist Web Site* (October 30, 2004), http://www.wsws.org/articles/2004/oct2004/iraq-o30.shtml; James Cogan, "More Killings of Civilians by U.S. Led Forces in Iraq," *World Socialist Web Site* (July 14, 2004), http://www.wsws.org/articles/2005/jul2005/iraq-j14.shtml.

27. Patrick Martin, "The Twenty Lies of George W. Bush," *World Socialist Web Site* (March 20, 2003), http://www.wsws.org/articles/2003/mar2003/bush-m20.shtml.

September 11 and Mexican Immigrants: Collateral Damage Comes Home

Kevin R. Johnson

This Article analyzes important collateral damage of the "war on terrorism," specifically the impact of the government's response to September 11 on the Mexican immigrant community in the United States, as well as on prospective Mexican immigrants and temporary visitors.

The federal government responded swiftly to the mass destruction and horrible loss of life on September 11, 2001. Quickly initiating a war on terror, the U.S. government pursued military action in Afghanistan. The violation of the civil rights of Arab and Muslim noncitizens in the United States followed as well. In the months immediately after September 11, the federal government arrested, interrogated, and detained more than one thousand Arab and Muslim "material witnesses" without charging them with crimes. Congress swiftly passed the Uniting and Strengthening America by Proving Appropriate Tools Required to Intercept and Obstruct Terrorism Act (USA PATRIOT Act), which, among other things amended the immigration laws in important ways. Although Arab and Muslim noncitizens felt the brunt of the civil rights deprivations in the immediate aftermath of September 11, immigrants in general will suffer the long-term consequences of the many measures taken by the federal government in the name of fighting terrorism.

The U.S. government directed drastic measures at noncitizens, in part because the law affords great deference to the executive branch in immigration and national security matters. This Article analyzes important collateral damage of the "war on terrorism," specifically the impact of the government's response to September 11 on the Mexican immigrant community in the United States, as well as on prospective Mexican immigrants and temporary visitors. More than 200,000 immigrants from Mexico came to the United States in 2001 alone, the largest contingent of migrants from any nation and almost 20 percent of all immigrants to this

Source: Kevin R. Johnson, "September 11 and Mexican Immigrants: Collateral Damage Comes Home," *DePaul Law Review*, 52 (2003): 849–870.

country. In addition, the Immigration and Naturalization Service (INS) has estimated that, at least as of 1996, more than 2.7 million undocumented immigrants from Mexico, over half of the total undocumented population, live in the United States. In sum, Mexican citizens comprise the largest group of immigrants, legal and undocumented, in the United States.

As we will see, past immigration reforms in response to terrorism fears offer sobering lessons for immigrants. The history of ideological regulation, including severe steps in the name of fighting the communist threat such as ideological exclusion and deportation, indefinite detention, and similar extreme measures, shows the extremes that U.S. immigration laws have gone to protect the nation's security. Recent events fit in well with the historical pattern. In 1996, Congress enacted immigration reform legislation, motivated in no small part by a desire to fight terrorism, which adversely impacted the immigrant community as a whole. The reforms resulted in record levels of deportations, including the removal of thousands of Mexican nationals. Similarly, post-September 11 immigration restrictions, enforcement measures, and citizenship requirements will likely have a disparate impact on immigrants, particularly those from Mexico. To this point, little attention has been paid to the general impacts on the immigrant community of the U.S. government's response to the tragedy of September 11, 2001. As with immigration measures generally, the new enforcement measures will predominately impact people of color.

This Article focuses on concrete immigration law and policies affected by the events of September 11. The federal government's reaction, however, may well have stirred the nativist pot, thereby triggering a general antipathy for immigrants. The nasty efforts of one member of the U.S. Congress in the summer of 2002 to deport an undocumented

honor student and his family to Mexico suggests the resurgence of a generalized anti-immigrant sentiment not limited to Arabs and Muslims. Nativism historically has proven difficult to limit to certain immigrant groups. For example, public concern with the use of public benefits by undocumented immigrants, exemplified by California's Proposition 187, culminated in the denial of most benefits to legal immigrants in the 1996 welfare reform. In a similar vein, the attacks on immigrants may effectively amount to thinly veiled attacks on racial minorities, with U.S. citizens sharing the ancestry of certain immigrant groups stereotyped as "foreigners." Consequently, the legal damage to the immigrant community outlined in this Article is only part of the entire picture.

Part II of this Article considers the possible immigration reforms that may come on the heels of September 11 and identifies how they might well have broad negative impacts on the immigrant community, including on many immigrants having nothing remotely to do with terrorism. Part III analyzes how September 11 put the brakes on reform efforts that would have benefited immigrants immensely and has encouraged law enforcement conduct that will likely have adverse effects on immigrant and minority communities. Ultimately, persons of Mexican ancestry—citizens and noncitizens—will be disparately affected by the legal changes triggered by September 11.

PAST IMMIGRATION REFORM AS PRELUDE? CHANGING IMMIGRATION AND IMMIGRANT LAW AFTER SEPTEMBER 11

The leeway afforded the federal government in immigration matters allows the political branches to swiftly take aggressive actions, thereby appearing to respond to complex problems. Such actions historically have injured immigrant communities. A concrete example is the effort to seal the U.S./Mexico border as part of the "war on drugs" and halting undocumented immigration, which has had a limited impact in achieving those goals. However, heightened border enforcement has resulted in increased race-based law enforcement and hundreds of deaths of Mexican citizens along the border.

In the wake of the 1995 Oklahoma City bombing, Congress passed two pieces of tough immigration legislation. As Professor Peter Schuck succinctly observed, the 1996 immigration reforms constituted "the most radical reform of immigration law in decades—or perhaps ever." Congress tightened the U.S. immigration laws despite the fact that a natural born U.S. citizen masterminded the Oklahoma City bombing, and there was absolutely no evidence of any involvement of foreign citizens. This recent history sheds valuable light on the downside potential of immigrant reforms in response to fears of terrorism spawned by the events of September 11.

Antiterrorism and Immigration Reform in 1996: Lessons About Reform in the Name of Terrorism

In the end, the Antiterrorism and Effective Death Penalty Act of 1996 (AEDPA) arguably did little to quell the threat of terrorism in the United States. However, AEDPA and Illegal Immigration Reform and Immigrant Responsibility Act (IIRIRA), passed just months later, denied judicial review of many deportation and related orders of the immigration bureaucracy. Not until 2001 did the Supreme Court resolve a conflict among the circuits and ensure that habeas corpus review of removal orders remained intact, a result that the executive branch strongly opposed at every step. Terrorism fears also fueled passage of a new summary exclusion procedure in 1996 by which a noncitizen could be barred admission

into the country at the port of entry by an INS officer without judicial review. In signing AEDPA into law, President Bill Clinton candidly admitted the collateral damage of the new law, which "makes a number of major, ill-advised changes in our immigration laws having nothing to do with fighting terrorism."

Besides limiting judicial review of a variety of immigration decisions, the 1996 reforms vastly expanded the definition of "aggravated felony," which subjects an immigrant to deportation (without judicial review) and mandatory detention. As Professor Nancy Morawetz aptly summarized, the expanded definition of "aggravated felony" has an

> Alice-in Wonderland-like [quality]. . . . As the term is defined, a crime need not be either aggravated or a felony. For example, a conviction for simple battery or for shoplifting with a one-year suspended sentence—either of which would be a misdemeanor . . . violation in most states—can be deemed an aggravated felony.

To exacerbate matters for noncitizens, until the Supreme Court corrected the practice in 2001, the INS retroactively applied the new deportation grounds in the 1996 reforms to criminal convictions before passage of the law.

With the prodding of Congress, the INS made deportation of criminal aliens its highest priority. The 1996 immigration reforms resulted in record levels of deportations of "criminal aliens," with by far the largest number to Mexico. In fiscal year 1999, for example, the INS removed more than 48,000 (of a total of 62,359, or over 77 percent) Mexican nationals on criminal grounds. In fiscal year 1998, the INS removed over 170,000 noncitizens from the United States, with over 139,000 (over 80 percent) from Mexico on all grounds. Removals increased from 42,469 in fiscal year 1993 (with over 27,000, about 64 percent, from Mexico) to over 170,000 in fiscal year 1998, with over 147,000 (about 83 percent) from Mexico.

In sum, although AEDPA ostensibly was focused on terrorism, it and IIRIRA went well beyond that concern. Immigrants, especially those from Mexico, suffered.

THE USA PATRIOT ACT, VISA MONITORING, AND OTHER IMMIGRATION REFORMS

As suggested by the aftermath of the Oklahoma City bombing, a congressional response to September 11 likely will include immigration reforms. Congress has already taken some initial steps in this direction; more are on the horizon.

The USA PATRIOT Act expands the definition of "terrorist activity" for purposes of the immigration laws in ways that may result in an additional removal ground for noncitizens convicted of assault and similar crimes. "Terrorist activity" thus has gone the way of "aggravated felony" for immigration purposes, expanded well beyond what one normally would consider to be truly "terrorist" in nature. The USA PATRIOT Act further provides that a spouse or child of a "terrorist" generally is inadmissible. A noncitizen also may be deemed inadmissible for being "associated with a terrorist organization," broad terms reminiscent of the principle of guilt by association, a discredited law enforcement technique popular during the dark days of the McCarthy era. Fears also have been expressed that the expanded definition of "terrorist activity" in the USA PATRIOT Act will adversely affect bona fide asylum-seekers fleeing persecution in their native lands.

Although there is no evidence that the terrorists involved in the September 11 hijackings evaded border inspection, the USA PATRIOT Act appropriated funds for increased enforcement of the U.S./Canada border. The new funding responded to fears that terrorists might seek to enter the United States from Canada; on the eve of the new millennium, the federal government arrested an Algerian man with bomb-making materials seeking to enter at the Canadian border who was plotting to bomb Los Angeles International Airport. Because the INS often utilizes race in border enforcement, one can expect an expansion of race-based immigration enforcement. One potential benefit, however, is that the USA PATRIOT Act may help shift the myopic focus from the southern border with Mexico, which saw a dramatic escalation in border enforcement in the 1990s resulting in hundreds, perhaps thousands, of deaths of undocumented Mexican citizens seeking to cross the border in desolate, inclement locations.

In sum, the USA PATRIOT Act expanded the definition of "terrorist activity" in ways that will offer the INS expanded powers to deport noncitizens having only the most attenuated connection to "terrorist activity." Border enforcement also will be bolstered. In light of the current national mood, the federal government can be expected to aggressively exercise such powers against noncitizens.

Visa Processing and Monitoring

Most of the September 11 airplane hijackers apparently entered the country on student visas, which understandably provoked concern. Concern erupted into a national furor when the INS sent visa renewals to two suspected hijackers many months after their deaths. Efforts by the INS to improve the monitoring of temporary visitors on student and other visas became a high priority.

Immediately after September 11, the State Department began to slow the processing of visa applications, especially in nations believed to harbor terrorists. In December 2001, the INS announced the arrests of noncitizens who had violated the terms of their student visas from nations with alleged terrorist links. Shortly after, the Justice Department announced that its "Operation Absconder" would focus deportation efforts on six thousand young Arab and Muslim men from the same nations.

The federal government followed nation-specific monitoring of student visas with across-the-board efforts. In May 2002, Congress passed the Enhanced Border Security and Visa Reform Act to improve the monitoring of noncitizens in the United States on student and other visas. Attorney General John Ashcroft later proposed a new National Security Entry-Exit Registration System that imposed special registration requirements on noncitizens who, as determined by the federal government, posed "national security risks." Despite concerns that the proposed regulation would allow discrimination on the basis of race and religion, the final regulation was almost identical to the proposal.

In fiscal year 1998, Mexico was the third leading nation of origin of nonimmigrants (generally speaking, temporary visitors), sending over 65,000 nonimmigrants to the United States. As a consequence, even if tightened visa monitoring is not aimed directly at Mexican noncitizens, it will negatively impact them. Mexican students already have faced difficulties in entering the United States. More generally, tighter enforcement at the border has slowed trade and migration within North America, with economic and related consequences for Canada, the United States, and especially for Mexico.

In essence, increased visa monitoring, and more general concerns with the verification of the identity of noncitizens, have had ripple effects that have negatively affected the immigrant community. For example, the California governor vetoed a law that would have made certain groups of undocumented immigrants in California eligible for driver's licenses—and would have given them access to a certain degree of security in U.S. society—because of concerns about identity fraud by terrorists after September 11. Efforts of the Social Security Administration to verify the social security numbers of employees have resulted in many undocumented immigrants losing their jobs.

As with immigration reform generally, increased monitoring of nonimmigrants will adversely affect noncitizens from many countries. Mexican citizens will be disproportionately affected by increased efforts at visa monitoring.

INCREASED IMMIGRATION ENFORCEMENT

As part of efforts at fighting terrorism, the U.S. government likely will pursue immigration enforcement policies that will adversely affect immigrants generally, not simply Arab or Muslim noncitizens. The Justice Department already has announced its intention to enforce the requirement that noncitizens report changes of address within ten days of moving or be subject to deportation. Enforcement of this reporting requirement likely will result in many more possible removal cases based on a technical, relatively minor violation of the law. Given Attorney General Ashcroft's stated willingness to use the immigration laws, or, for that matter, any law, necessary to remove suspected "terrorists" from the country, it is troubling to see any expansion of the grounds for removal.

The most dramatic change in immigration enforcement may be the incorporation of the INS into the new Department on Homeland Security, the proposal of which stemmed directly from the events of September 11. The INS long has over-emphasized enforcement to the neglect of its service mission, which includes adjudication of visa and naturalization petitions. The reorganization may well result in an even greater over-emphasis on immigration enforcement in the name of "homeland security." Consequently, the reorganization likely will exacerbate the enforcement priority of the INS and adversely affect noncitizens.

CITIZENSHIP REQUIREMENTS

The Supreme Court has permitted state governments to impose citizenship requirements on state jobs that perform a "political function." By executive order, the federal government has barred noncitizens from federal civil service jobs. As a result of the tragedy of September 11, the nation may well see a new round of citizenship requirements for a variety of jobs to ensure loyalty to the United States. The Aviation and Transportation Security Act, which placed airport security in the hands of the federal government, made U.S. citizenship a qualification for airport security personnel. The citizenship requirement injures many lawful immigrants who had held these low-wage jobs in airports across the country.

It was reported that over eighty percent of the security screeners at San Francisco International Airport and about forty percent of those at Los Angeles International Airport were lawful immigrants. Although immigrants can be conscripted into the military and stationed at airports, they no longer can work in airport security positions.

Immigration checks of airport employees have led to the arrests of undocumented persons. Few were of Arab or Muslim ancestry, and many almost invariably were from Asia and Latin America. Moreover, the INS enforcement focus on airports has generated fear and heightened insecurity in immigrant communities.

Discrimination based on alienage can have disparate impacts on particular national origin groups. For example, in *Cabell v. Chavez-Salido*, the Supreme Court in 1982 rejected an equal protection challenge to a California law interpreted to require that probation officers be citizens. For that reason, Los Angeles County did not hire Jose Chavez-Salido, a lawful permanent resident for twenty-six years who had been born in Mexico and had received all of his formal education, including a Bachelor of Arts degree, in the United States. After reviewing the history of the California law, Justice Harry A. Blackmun wrote in dissent that, "I can only conclude that California's exclusion of these appellees from the position of deputy probation officer stems solely from state parochialism and hostility toward foreigners who have come to this country lawfully."

Justice Blackmun's hint has gone largely unexplored. The scholarship analyzing the alienage discrimination decisions of the Supreme Court focuses on the constitutionality of the states' imposition of citizenship requirements, without considering their racial impacts. A few commentators, however, suggest the need for strict scrutiny of alienage classifications in part because they can mask racial animus. This argument finds historical support. At various times in U.S. history, alienage discrimination, with state "alien land" laws targeting Japanese Americans, a notorious example, has served as a device to discriminate on the basis of race.

The federal government's movement toward citizenship requirements can be expected to encourage state and local governments, as well as private employers to do the same. Even before September 11, immigrants often found it difficult to avoid discrimination by employers in the workplace. The most potent bar to employment discrimination—Title VII of the Civil Rights Act of 1964—does not prohibit discrimination based on immigration status. Although the immigration laws prohibit discrimination against noncitizens eligible to work, evidence suggests that discrimination by employers against persons of Latina/o and Asian ancestry continues to be a problem. New citizenship requirements will likely increase discrimination against Latina/os and Asian Americans, who are stereotyped as "foreign" even if they are U.S. citizens.

Large numbers of lawful permanent residents from Mexico reside in the United States. Although Mexican naturalization rates have increased in recent years, many legal immigrants from Mexico live in the country and will be affected by the imposition of citizenship requirements.

INCREASED LOCAL INVOLVEMENT IN IMMIGRATION ENFORCEMENT AS A THREAT TO CIVIL RIGHTS

The "war on terrorism" has caused the federal government to reconsider its exclusive domain over immigration enforcement and show a new willingness to delegate power to state and local law enforcement agencies to enforce the immigration laws. In the summer of 2002, for example, the Justice Department entered an agreement with Florida to train a group of police officers to assist in the enforcement of the immigration laws. This devolution-to-the-states movement ultimately could change the entire balance of immigration law enforcement power, which until relatively recently was almost exclusively in the hands of the federal government.

State and local involvement in immigration enforcement warrants concern because of the many civil rights violations of immigrants by local authorities, even though not officially in the business of immigration enforcement. When given the opportunity, local governments have fallen prey to the popular stereotype of Latina/os as foreigners. A videotape captured local police in Riverside County, California in 1996 brutally beating two undocumented Mexican immigrants who tried to evade the Border Patrol. In an effort to rid the community of undocumented immigrants, police in a Phoenix, Arizona suburb violated the constitutional rights of U.S. citizens and lawful immigrants of Mexican ancestry by stopping persons because of their skin color or use of the Spanish language. The Los Angeles Police Department's Ramparts Division reportedly engaged in a pattern and practice of violating the rights of immigrants over many years. One can expect additional civil rights violations when local law enforcement authorities, who generally are not well versed in the immigration laws, seek to enforce those laws.

A shift in immigration enforcement from the federal to local level would have a dramatic impact on the immigrant community in the United States, perhaps the most significant of all the responses to September 11, 2001. It would open the door to further civil rights abuses of Latina/os. Moreover, it may also be bad for law enforcement, as immigrant communities would be afraid to cooperate with the police in reporting crime and participating in criminal investigations. That is precisely why so many police agencies prohibit their officers from inquiring about the immigration status of victims, suspects, and witnesses.

More immigration reform may be coming in the future, with likely negative impacts on immigrant communities having nothing to do with terrorism. In dealing with noncitizens, the political branches of government can act with relatively few constraints, at least in the short run. Consequently, security measures in the immigration laws can be overbroad to the detriment of noncitizens. In times of crisis, politicians and policymakers are reluctant to resist laws, such as the Antiterrorist Act and the USA PATRIOT Act, because of the possible claim that they are "soft" on the terrorist threat. Despite the relative lack of legal constraints, several courts have intervened to halt the excesses of the federal government's war on terrorism. Nonetheless, efforts at persuading the political branches of the federal government—Congress and the President—to soften the "war on terrorism" will no doubt also be necessary in attempts to fully protect the rights of noncitizens.

INDIRECT LEGAL IMPACTS OF SEPTEMBER 11 ON IMMIGRANT AND MINORITY COMMUNITIES

The events of September 11 likely will have more general legal consequences than simple reform of the immigration laws. Two major immigration reform measures in the works on that date—both which would have particularly benefited Mexican citizens—fell by the wayside. More ominously, after years of national consciousness-raising about its evils, racial profiling enjoyed a comeback in popularity as efforts to locate Arab and Muslim terrorists were the number one priority of the federal government. This development threatens not simply immigrants but minority communities generally in the United States.

THE END OF POSITIVE IMMIGRATION REFORM

Before the tragedy of September 11, immigrant rights advocates believed it possible that Congress would ameliorate the harshest edges of the 1996 immigration reform legislation. Over several years, immigration rights activists had built broad support for a series of immigration reforms to "Fix 96." All such legislative proposals appear to have died a quick death on September 11. Immigrant advocacy groups currently marshal scarce political resources to attempt to thwart aggressive pieces of restrictionist legislative and regulatory measures that would adversely impact the immigrant community.

The demise of immigration reform legislation will allow the harsh 1996 immigration laws to continue to injure immigrants. As discussed previously, immigrants from Mexico have been adversely affected by the 1996 immigration reforms, with record levels of deportations. Consequently, Mexican immigrants who stood to gain the most from immigration reform are now the big losers with the failure to "Fix 96."

A more far-reaching immigration reform possibility also was moved to the back burner on September 11. A short-lived historical moment appeared in 2001 that promised to fundamentally transform migration to the United States from Mexico. Only days before September 11, the highest levels of the U.S. and Mexican governments discussed dramatically changing the migration relationship between the two nations; both U.S. President George W. Bush and Mexican President Vicente Fox expressed optimism about the possibility of a historic bilateral agreement addressing migration. The Mexican government supported a program that would allow for greater labor migration and the "regularization" of the status of many undocumented Mexican migrants in the United States, while members of the Bush administration hoped for a revamped guest-worker program. Although difficult issues remained to be resolved, compromise appeared possible. After September 11, discussions virtually stopped in their tracks. A U.S./Mexico migration agreement restructuring migration between the United States and Mexico was apparently another casualty of the catastrophic events of that day. The immigration talk of the day became about closing, not opening, the borders.

The end of serious discussions of a migration pact means that undocumented Mexican immigrants, the largest group of undocumented immigrants in the United States, will not have the opportunity to legalize and enjoy some modicum of security in their daily lives. Undocumented immigrants live on the periphery of U.S. social life, always subject to possible removal and often subject to economic exploitation in the workplace. They also are more likely to experience the ripple effects of heightened border enforcement accompanying the overall enforcement crackdown after September 11. Only time will tell whether the historic opportunity to fundamentally change the migration relations between the United States and Mexico was destroyed with the World Trade Center.

SEPTEMBER 11 AND THE COMEBACK OF RACIAL PROFILING

Over the last few years, scholars and policy-makers have been critically scrutinizing the use of racial profiling in criminal law enforcement, which in its most extreme form finds manifestation in police stops of African Americans, Latina/os, and other racial minorities on account of their perceived group propensities for criminal conduct. Not long before September 11, the highest levels of the federal government publicly condemned racial profiling of African Americans by state and local government's law enforcement on the nation's highways. Public support appeared to coalesce around efforts to end racial profiling. Similarly, race-based enforcement of the immigration laws also was being re-examined. Although the Supreme Court condoned the practice in 1975, one court of appeals in 2000 held that the Border Patrol could not consider a person's "Hispanic appearance" in making an immigration stop. Similarly, sustained public criticism of racial profiling in national security matters came in the wake of the Wen Ho Lee case in which trumped-up espionage charges evaporated when exposed to the light of day. Presumptively disloyal because of long-held stereotypes about persons of Asian ancestry, Lee stood falsely accused of crimes against national security.

The core argument against racial profiling is that law enforcement measures based on alleged group propensities for criminal conduct run afoul of the U.S. Constitution, which is generally premised on the view that individualized suspicion is necessary for police action. Unfortunately, governmental reliance on statistical probabilities at the core of racial profiling has been resurrected by the September 11 terrorist attacks and has been met with broad public support.

After September 11, persons of apparent Arab ancestry and Muslims were questioned for possible links to terrorism, removed from airplanes, and generally subject to scrutiny at every turn. Many commentators proclaimed that the reconsideration of the use of race in law enforcement made perfect sense. Public opinion moved to favor racial profiling, which will not affect the vast majority of U.S. citizens, in the "war on terrorism." The Wall Street Journal proclaimed that racial profiling in fighting terrorism "isn't discrimination; given the threat, it is common sense." A Case for Profiling, The Case for Using Racial Profiling at the Airports, and Americans Give in to Racial Profiling were titles of articles found in the popular press that offer a clear indication of the direction that the post-September 11 political winds are blowing on the issue.

The federal government's profiling of Arabs and Muslims in the terrorist dragnet promoted the legitimacy of racial profiling. It also undermined federal efforts to pressure state and local law enforcement agencies to end the practice in criminal law enforcement. Ironically, a handful of local law enforcement agencies refused the Attorney General's request to interview Arabs and Muslims on the grounds that this constituted impermissible racial profiling.

Racial profiling in the "war on terrorism" poses serious risks to all minority communities in the United States, not just Arab- and Muslim-appearing people who may be subject to profiling given the current fears. Once the government embraces the use of race-based statistical probabilities as a law enforcement tool, the argument logically follows that probabilities may justify similar law enforcement techniques across the board, from terrorism to fighting crime on the streets to apprehending undocumented immigrants. As they were for many years, statistical probabilities can also be employed to justify focusing police action on African Americans, Asian Americans, and Latina/os in cities across the United States. Besides ordinary criminal law enforcement, the reliance on statistics, which justified internment of persons of Japanese ancestry during World War II, could be used to justify racial profiling in immigration and national security matters.

CONCLUSION

The federal government's multifaceted response to the horrible loss of life on September 11 has had, and will continue to have, a devastating impact on Arabs and Muslims in the United States. Although the harms to Mexican immigrants, as well as other immigrant communities, are less visible, these communities also will be adversely affected by the changes to the immigration laws and their enforcement. As the largest single group of lawful and undocumented immigrants in the United States, Mexican noncitizens are particularly sensitive to immigration regulation and stand to be the group most affected by immigration reform. Similarly, Mexican-American families who have immigrant members, or seek to bring family members to the United States from Mexico, will be affected as well. Unfortunately, however, little attention has been paid to the impacts of the "war on terrorism" on persons of Mexican ancestry. To avoid the negative impacts on Mexican immigrants that followed the 1996 immigration reforms designed to address concerns with terrorism, attention must be given to the post–September 11 immigration reforms allegedly directed toward terrorism.

The lessons of the immigration reforms triggered by the events of September 11, 2001 reinforce broader teachings about immigration law and policy. Immigration law can be reformed in overbroad ways to the detriment of immigrant communities, with much political support and little political resistance. Those adversely affected—immigrants of color in modern times—have limited political power, which is easily overcome in times of national crisis. This latest chapter simply reinforces what we have seen time and again in U.S. history.

STUDY QUESTION

Discuss the evidence proffered by Kevin Johnson that post–September 11, 2001, immigration reforms in the United States will have negative impacts on immigrant communities.

Minority Disenfranchisement During the 2000 General Election: A Blast from the Past or a Blueprint for Reform

Monique L. Dixon

Disenfranchisement in Florida and across the nation went beyond antiquated voting machines and butterfly ballots. Many voters were turned away from the polls because their voter registration applications were not processed in a timely manner, or they were wrongfully removed from the voter rolls as a result of aggressive "list cleansing procedures" that are tantamount to modern-day literacy tests and poll taxes.

"This is America, Count Every Vote" was the chant that was heard all over the country as the hotly contested presidential race in the November 2000 general election unfolded in Florida. On November 7, and the days that followed, reports of the antiquated voting machines that caused many ballots cast by voters in Florida to be rejected were repeated in the media. The discussion about hanging, pregnant, and dimpled chads of voters who were able to cast a ballot, however, muted the cries of many voters who were not even allowed to vote on that fateful day. Disenfranchisement in Florida and across the nation went beyond antiquated voting machines and butterfly ballots. Many voters were turned away from the polls because their voter registration applications were not processed in a timely manner, or they were wrongfully removed from the voter rolls as a result of aggressive "list cleansing procedures" that are tantamount to modern-day literacy tests and poll taxes.

This article will argue that the 2000 presidential election has uncovered two realities: the problems states are experiencing as they implement the provisions of the National Voter Registration Act ("NVRA") of 1993 and the extent to which racial minorities and the poor are systemically being denied the benefits of the Act's provisions. It will argue further that as states strive to implement reform initiatives to correct some of the problems that occurred on Election Day 2000, state legislators, civil rights advocates and community activists should work collectively to implement reforms that will complement the NVRA and not compromise it.

Source: Monique L. Dixon, "Minority Disenfranchisement During the 2000 General Election: A Black from the Past or a Blueprint for Reform," Temple Political and Civil Rights Law Review, 11 (2002): 311–325.

First, the article will discuss the history of racial minorities' struggle to exercise the right to vote and will capture the widespread disenfranchisement of minority voters that occurred in Florida during the November 2000 presidential election. Second, the article will discuss the NVRA and problems with its implementation.

Third, the article will discuss how several election reform measures currently being discussed, including same day registration, computerized central voter registration files, and provisional ballots, will affect access to the franchise.

Finally, drawing on Advancement Project's model of partnerships between organized communities and civil rights lawyers, the article will highlight an innovative grassroots strategy designed to monitor election reform efforts so that the administration of elections is conducted in a uniform and nondiscriminatory manner.

HISTORY OF MINORITY DISENFRANCHISEMENT NATIONALLY AND IN FLORIDA, PAST AND PRESENT

> There were people with voter registration cards who were told they couldn't vote.
>
> I thought it'd be a happy day. . . . I was telling my mom and dad, "We're a voting family, but I would never want to vote again." It is a hassle. If you have all your stuff and ID and you're registered and everything is right, why go through that if you still can't vote.

On first blush, one would think these quotes are excerpts from the pages of history books from a time when Jim Crow laws or the Black Codes disenfranchised entire populations of African Americans and other racial minorities in spite of the clear mandates of the Thirteenth, Fourteenth, and Fifteenth Amendments. Sadly, these quotes are all too recent. In fact, these examples of minority disenfranchisement occurred just two years

ago during the 2000 presidential election in the State of Florida and across the country, and will likely be repeated in the coming years without adequate election reform.

Students of American history should not be surprised by these discriminatory practices, as they are direct descendants of an unbroken line of systemic obstacles that have ensured that racial and ethnic minorities do not have equal access to democracy. Any effort to understand or address the concerns of minority voters today must begin with a clear view of how last November's election fits into historical patterns of exclusion nationally, particularly in the State of Florida. The fact that the African-American community reacted to the 2000 presidential election with outrage is in part because the experiences of black voters at the polls in November 2000 seemed to mirror those of earlier generations.

MINORITY ACCESS TO THE FRANCHISE AND VOTER REGISTRATION—THE PAST

Prior to the 19th Century, white men in this country were not subjected to voter registration. Shortly after the Civil War, however, there were several movements by federal troops to disenfranchise all white men who supported the Confederate army and enfranchise all freedmen. As a result, by the end of 1867, "Black registration rates in seven of the eleven former Confederate states equaled or exceeded that of whites." This trend, however, was short lived.

In 1877, federal troops withdrew from the South signaling the end of Reconstruction and the beginning of government-assisted campaigns to disenfranchise blacks and other minority voters. Between 1890 and 1910, all southern states rewrote their state constitutions previously enacted by a strong black Reconstruction electorate. These new constitutions incorporated a plethora of restrictions designed to disenfranchise black voters across the South. With Mississippi taking the lead, followed by South Carolina and Louisiana, many southern states created laws that imposed residency requirements against voters, poll taxes, literacy or understanding requirements and, in many instances, outright voter intimidation. While these laws were neutral on their face, they were discriminatory in their impact. White election officials often exempted white voters from these requirements. Not surprisingly, these restrictions resulted in extremely low black registration rates. For example, between 1898 and 1990, black voters in Louisiana decreased from 85.2 percent to four percent.

Florida's history is similarly disturbing. At the time of the Civil War, almost half the state was African-American, and through the time of Reconstruction, which ended in 1876, black political participation was actually high. Adult black males voted in significant numbers and were elected to local, state, and federal offices. In fact, 19 of the 76 legislators elected to the legislature after Florida adopted its new constitution in 1868 were black. Josiah Walls, a former slave, was Florida's first black member of Congress and was elected three times, in 1870, 1872, and 1874. It would be another 118 years, however, before Florida sent its next black representative to Congress.

This incredible reversal of progress in black voter participation was the direct result of Florida's passage of a series of election laws that effectively shut blacks out of the political process. Florida was the first southern state to adopt the poll tax, and it also took other steps to disenfranchise blacks. One such step was multiple ballot boxes, which required voters to place eight separate ballots in corresponding ballot boxes. With only a 60 percent literacy rate in the black population, voters were unable to place the correct ballot in the proper ballot box and did not have their votes counted. From 1888 to 1892, black male turnout dropped from 62 percent to 11 percent.

One stark example of minority voter suppression in Florida's history, memorialized by the author Zora Neale Hurston, occurred in the farming town of Ocoee in 1920. There, a prosperous black community consisting of landowners, homeowners, automobile owners, merchants, and farmers was destroyed in one night by white rioters and the Ku Klux Klan angry over black citizens' attempts to vote. On Election Day, November 2, 1920, the black population of the town numbered several hundred; the next day, it was down to two. The Sunday before the election, the Ku Klux Klan held a silent march, as the Republican Party conducted registration drives of black citizens in order to involve them in the political process. A prominent black citizen of Ocoee, Mose Norman, who had paid his poll tax and complied with registration requirements, was told he was not registered and was not allowed to vote when he went to the polls. Later when another prominent black citizen, July Perry, properly registered and attempted to vote, a fight broke out. The white community erupted, and by night's end, lynchings and arson changed the town forever. In 1921, the city directory had 17 black citizens; the 1925 directory had no blacks; and in 1978, Ocoee had one black voter.

RENEWING ACCESS TO THE FRANCHISE FOR MINORITY VOTERS—THE PRESENT

The landmark Voting Rights Act of 1965 ("the Act") put an end to literacy tests and poll taxes, and offered hope that the incidents described above would become relics of the past. Federal registrars implementing the Act added thousands of minority voters to the rolls. In 1975, Congress strengthened the Act by adding minority language provisions recognizing that large numbers of non-English speaking citizens had been effectively excluded from the democratic process.

Despite these efforts, almost two decades after the enactment of the original Voting Rights Act, registration barriers remained. In 1982, black voter registration rates in Georgia, for example, continued to lag behind that of white voters. Federal registrars believed that this low rate among black voters was due in part to the fact that voter registration was allowed only at the county courthouse. According to these registrars, "the lack of continuing, reasonable opportunities for registration in the country has contributed to the low registration rate for blacks."

As a result of the sustained resistance to expanding the franchise to minorities, in 1984, civil rights organizations brought a series of cases in several states, including Arkansas, Georgia, Louisiana and Mississippi, that led to court decrees that made voter registration more accessible. Then, in 1993, the NVRA, commonly referred to as "Motor Voter," was enacted.

National Voter Registration Act of 1993 ("NVRA")

The provisions of the NVRA were drafted based on recognition by the U.S. Congress that voters who participated in federal elections had declined substantially in the late 1980s (only about one half of the voting age population went to the polls during the 1988 presidential election). As a result, Congress conducted national research of state election laws, and heard hours of oral and written testimony from civil rights advocates, election law experts and community activists to determine the cause of the low voter turnout and develop remedies for the problem. Finding that discriminatory and unfair registration laws continued to have a "direct and damaging effect on voter participation in elections for federal office and disproportionately harm voter participation by various groups, including racial minorities," the NVRA was enacted and required states to pass laws that would achieve three main

goals: 1) increase the number of eligible citizens who register to vote in federal elections; 2) protect the integrity of the electoral process by ensuring that accurate and current voter registration rolls are maintained in a uniform nondiscriminatory manner; and 3) enhance the participation of eligible citizens as voters in federal election.

This section will review the key provisions of the NVRA that were designed to achieve these three goals and how states have fared in the implementation of NVRA. The 2000 general election in Florida will be used as an example of how the failure to effectively implement the NVRA allegedly resulted in the disenfranchisement of minority voters.

Voter Registration Provisions: Increasing the Number of Eligible Citizens Who Register to Vote

The NVRA significantly liberalized voter registration practices by expanding the locations and opportunities for eligible citizens to apply for voter registration. Under the NVRA, states must provide citizens with an opportunity to simultaneously register to vote when they apply for or renew a driver's license, when they apply for services at certain public agencies, and by mail.

Driver's license offices were selected based on the fact that approximately 87 percent of the voting age population (eighteen years and older) secures driver's licenses or identification cards through these offices. Public assistance, state-funded disability pro-grams, and other public agencies, places where application forms are similarly required, were selected in order to ensure that the poor and persons with disabilities who do not have driver's licenses would have equal access to voter registration. Mail-in registration had been successfully implemented by states prior to the NVRA and was believed to effectively reach racial minorities and other groups who were underrepresented on the registration rolls.

While voter registration has increased since the passage of the NVRA, many states are struggling with the effective implementation of this provision of the Act. According to a 2001 survey conducted by the Federal Elections Commission, 23 of the 45 states covered by the NVRA reported having "significant problems with motor voter registration programs during the last election cycle." Eighteen states reported problems with driver's license agencies which failed to deliver completed voter registration applications within five days after the applications are accepted as required by the NVRA. Additionally, several states reported receiving complaints from "a significant number of individuals" who stated that they had completed voter registrations at motor vehicles offices which had never been received by elections offices. Identical reports of unprocessed voter registration application emerged from black voters in Florida during the presidential election, and were the subject of litigation.

Ensuring the Accuracy and Integrity of Voter Registration Rolls—The Search for List Maintenance Procedures That Are Uniform and Nondiscriminatory

The tradeoff for liberalized registration was the addition of several provisions to ensure that "once a citizen is registered to vote, he or she . . . remain[s] on the list so long as he or she remains eligible to vote . . ." NVRA list maintenance provisions prohibit states from removing names from the voter rolls for failure to vote or for a change of address to another location within the voter's jurisdiction—usually within the same county. The law requires election officials who receive notice that a voter has moved within the jurisdiction to automatically update the person's voting address.

Additionally, the NVRA permits states to conduct a "uniform and non-discriminatory" general program to remove the names of eligible voters who are deceased, provide written confirmation that their address has changed to a location outside of the jurisdiction, or fail to respond to certain address confirmation mailings and do not appear to vote in two federal elections following the confirmation mailings. Finally, the NVRA permits states to remove the names of voters by reason of mental incapacity or criminal conviction as provided by state law.

These list maintenance procedures, however, leave states a great deal of discretion in the way they implement the list maintenance provisions. Some states are more aggressive than others and this has resulted in the disenfranchisement of many voters, particularly racial minorities, during the 2000 general election.

States have reported numerous problems with implementing their list maintenance programs. For example, Kansas, Ohio, and West Virginia have reported "inaccurate change of address information used to identify potential movers." Virginia and Ohio have complained of faulty felony conviction notifications or death notices that resulted in the erroneous removal of persons from the voter rolls. Indeed, Florida had its own share of broad purges of alleged felons who were later found not to be felons and voters removed from the roll who were reportedly dead, but showed up at the polls to vote on election day.

Fail-Safe Voting Programs—Striving to Enhance Participation of Eligible Voters

Civil rights organizations predicted that lower levels of functional literacy, bad mail delivery and higher mobility meant that the address confirmation mailing procedures would disproportionately disenfranchise poor and minority voters who were fully qualified to vote. They argued that voters who had not moved would be purged erroneously and complained that voters who move only a short distance should not have to re-register.

At the urging of these groups, protections were added to the NVRA to ameliorate the impact of the list cleansing mechanisms. These "fail-safe" provisions require states to ensure the franchise to voters who did not respond to certain notices sent to confirm their address or who moved within the jurisdiction but did not update their voter registration address. These voters are marked as questionable and some states, including Florida, transfer them to a separate "inactive" list. The "inactive" registrants have two federal general elections to appear at the polls, vote, update their registration information and return to the active list. If the voter has not moved at all, the law requires that she simply sign an affirmation to that effect. If the voter has moved within the jurisdiction, the NVRA allows states to choose where these voters can appear to vote and update their status. Florida has chosen to allow such voters to vote at their new polling place.

Like other provisions, many states have reported challenges in implementing the "fail safe" provisions of the NVRA. Indiana, for example, revealed problems with poll worker mistakes and Rhode Island reported difficulties with polling officials who had trouble "grasping the concept of fail-safe voting." Similar poll worker errors allegedly occurred in Florida.

Implementation of NVRA in Florida—A Case Study

The various challenges in complying with the NVRA that are faced by states across the country were found in Florida during the 2000 general election. In the months prior to the November election, Florida officials aggressively implemented the purge provisions of NVRA. Yet, on election day, there appears to have been widespread failure to comply with the voter protections in the Act, such as allowing inactive-list voters to vote after signing an affidavit, allowing voters who moved within a county to vote, and helping voters identify their new polling place.

Additionally, the impact on black voters of the "list cleaning" mechanisms in the NVRA is only beginning to be felt. Florida for example did not pass legislation fully implementing the "list cleaning" provisions of the NVRA until 1998, making the 2000 Election the first election in which the impact of these provisions was felt. The removal of voters may be greater in the 2002 election when those on the inactive list are removed altogether unless reform efforts are undertaken and realized.

The irregularities in voter registration and purge practices of Florida were a major part of NAACP v. Smith, a suit filed in Florida in January 2001 by six civil rights organizations on behalf of the NAACP and a class of black voters in Florida. The law suit alleged, among other things, that the State of Florida and seven county supervisors of elections violated the NVRA by failing to properly and timely process voter registration applications and changes of address, appropriately carry out purges and transfers to inactive lists in a uniform and nondiscriminatory manner, and failing to uniformly permit voters who moved within their county to vote or update their registration at their polling place.

In response to this lawsuit, federal investigations, and public pressure, the Florida Legislature passed the Florida Election Reform Act of 2001 ("FERA"), which seeks to correct several problems faced by voters on election day. For example, the law decertifies punch card machines—the nemesis to voters, particularly black voters, whose hanging, dimpled, and pregnant chads were not counted. FERA does not, however, propose improvements in the way the State implements the NVRA. Smith seeks to fill in the gaps of FERA by seeking remedies that include: a requirement that all voter registration applications be processed and the voter notified within a stated number of days; adopting and implementing procedures that will ensure that voters who appear at the polls are permitted to vote even where their status cannot be verified (provisional ballots created by FERA, discussed below, only partially address this concern); restoring to the rolls all persons wrongfully purged; discontinuing all purges until purge procedures are uniform; and requiring independent verification of identity and ineligibility before removal of a voter from the rolls.

REFORM EFFORTS—A BLUEPRINT

In the wake of the 2000 election, a nationwide movement for election reform began. Responding to widespread discomfort with the state of the nation's election system, many state legislatures have considered and passed election reform measures. Several election reform task reports have issued hosts of recommended reforms, and many groups have issued analyses of what happened in the 2000 election with prescriptions for avoiding the debacle in the future.

The civil rights community has forcefully argued that states and localities must comply with existing NVRA provisions, and furthermore, that any provisions enacted by Congress in the field of electoral reform should preserve and strengthen the NVRA. Discussed here are some of the leading ideas and reform proposals to address the tremendous burden voter registration and purge systems place on voters.

Same-Day Registration

Same-day registration is widely viewed by voting rights experts to be a highly desirable reform. Yet, progress toward this policy has stalled, with only six states currently having no registration or same-day registration. Recent improvements in voter registration and voting list technology, e.g., centralized computerized voter databases, mean that same-day registration is no longer as vulnerable as in the past to arguments that it is impossible to administer in large states with high mobility. Improved technology also can

help overcome concerns that same-day registration will result in fraud.

Interim Steps Toward Same-Day Registration

If same-day registration is not politically viable at the current time in some states or in Congress, there are interim steps that could be taken in this direction. These include shortening the registration cutoff, for example, from 29 to 5 days prior to the election, or allowing same-day change-of-address for persons already registered in the State. Another interim step is allowing voters whose registration application is incomplete to be provisionally placed on the rolls, subject to providing the missing information at the polling place. These and other reforms stop short of universal same-day registration. Yet, they expand the opportunity to participate in elections and could lead to a gradual transition to same-day registration.

Provisional or Challenge Ballots

Almost all election reform reports have endorsed the provisional ballot. Provisional ballots are referred to by many names, such as challenge ballots, affidavit ballots, and escrow ballots, but the basic premise is the same—if the eligibility status of a voter cannot be confirmed on election day, she is given a provisional ballot that she can cast; if after the election, her registration is verified, her ballot must be counted. Last year, Maryland and Florida passed provisional ballot statutes.

As states implement provisional ballot provisions, standards as to when these ballots can be cast and counted are critical to their value. FERA, for example, does not include standards to determine when such ballots must be counted. Also, FERA extends provisional ballots only to voters who appear at the correct polling place to vote. This was problematic during the 2000 general election because many voters were misdirected to polling places by poll workers. Another concern is implementation; in some states, even if provisional ballots are available, local election officials may not uniformly offer them to voters.

Automatic Address Updates for Voters Who Move Within the State

The average American moves once every five years. Under NVRA and the laws of most states, voters who move across a county line must re-register in the new county of residence, but those who move within county are not required to re-register. States must comply with these provisions of the NVRA to ensure that eligible voters remain on the rolls.

Central Voter Databases

Several states, including Florida, have enacted laws creating statewide computerized database systems. These systems offer the potential of shortening voter registration deadlines, eliminating re-registration for cross-county moves, and making registration easier. And, when integrated into polling place management, poll workers could dial into such systems to help voters whose names are not on precinct voter list to locate their correct polling place.

However, it does not now seem likely that such systems will be used in a way that will realize this potential. Indeed, it appears that legislatures and election officials primarily view these databases as a better vehicle to purge voters. While these systems, with safeguards against errors, may improve the purge process and produce more accurate registration rolls, the larger potential benefits should not be ignored.

Monitoring the uses of statewide databases is critical to ensuring that states comply with the NVRA list maintenance provisions. Voting rights advocates should be mindful that the NVRA prohibits removing voters for

non-voting. Additionally, the Act prohibits purges based on address changes in the ninety days prior to an election. Florida's new law develops computerized databases that may be updated daily. Implementation of this and similar database systems should be monitored to ensure compliance with the NVRA.

Tightening Accuracy Requirements for Voter Purges and Address Verification Programs

Voter roll purges by state and county election officials can be very damaging to minority voting rights, as the potential for abuse is high. The errors that occurred during the purging of names from voter rolls in Florida two years ago illustrate the potential problems. The State of Florida conducted an unprecedented collaboration between Florida election officials and a database company which resulted in the production of an error-plagued "scrub list" distributed to all Florida counties in order to purge felons from the voter rolls. This list cast a net so broad that it included persons who committed a felony in a state other than Florida, served their time, and had their voting rights restored in that state. These voters, mostly racial minorities, should have been permitted to vote in Florida during the 2000 election, but were purged from the list. Additionally, the "scrub list" included people who committed only misdemeanors, not felonies; people who had never committed any sort of crime; and people whose names did not even match names on county voting rolls. Some Florida counties used the list without verification and without notifying the very people whose voting rights might have erroneously been taken away.

Whether such purge lists are prepared inside the state government or by a private contractor, more legal safeguards against errors are needed. One such safeguard included in the NVRA prohibits change of address purges within ninety days of an election. The NVRA and state laws should be revised to extend the ninety-day limitation to all purges, thus giving voters sufficient time to correct any errors.

Community Organizing Efforts

Grassroots efforts are central to reclaiming American democracy for people of color. The pro-democracy movement that is currently underway will succeed if community groups actively monitor the actions of elections officials and ensure the election process is as transparent as possible. Harvard Law Professor Lani Guinier describes the possibilities of community organizing around these issues: A pro-democracy movement would need to build on the experience of Florida . . . Such mobilization would seek to recapture the passion in evidence immediately after the election as union leaders, civil rights activists, black elected officials, ministers, rabbis, and the president of the Haitian women's organization came together at a black church in Miami . . . "It felt like Birmingham last night," Maria Castellanos, a Latina activist in Miami, wrote in an e-mail describing the mammoth rally . . . The sanctuary was standing room only. So were the overflow rooms and the school hall, where congregants connected via large TV screens . . . The people sang and prayed and listened. Story after story was told of voters being turned away at the polls, of ballots being allegedly destroyed, of NAACP election literature being allegedly discarded at the main post office, of Spanish-speaking poll workers being sent to Creole precincts and vice-versa. Following the 2000 election, many groups began spearheading voting rights campaigns designed to monitor elections and increase voter participation. A very important effort undertaken by People For the American Way Foundation ("PFAWF") will likely prevent many instances of voter disenfranchisement, and serves as a useful model for organizations nationwide. The "Election Protection" program of PFAWF functions on many levels by

working in coalition with grassroots election organizations, attorneys, and community groups to make sure Florida's experience in the 2000 election is not repeated. "Election Protection" provides voter education so that voters know their rights when they enter the polls, and training to lawyers who serve as volunteers to monitor elections.

On voter education, PFAWF is reaching voters by translating election law protections into a "bill of rights" that is provided on palm cards and fliers. They are also organizing community groups to recruit poll workers, register voters, and take voters to the polls. When a voter for example is told she is not on the registration rolls, Election Protection information will prove useful in prompting that voter to request a provisional ballot, if it is available, or verify the accuracy of the rolls. As to lawyer training, the initiative has trained many attorneys to volunteer on election day. These lawyers will go to the polling place or to the courthouse to make sure voters are able to cast ballots and that the ballots are counted. Polling place monitors in "Election Protection" t-shirts will be able to call lawyers by cell phone, or individual voters can call a toll-free number.

The Election Protection program has already proven successful. In the special congressional election of June 2001 in the 4th congressional district in Virginia, stories of voter disenfranchisement were sharply reduced, due in large part to the presence of Election Protection volunteers. In fact, there is evidence that the program spurred the poll workers themselves to be more vigilant and professional in their work. Election Protection will be extended statewide in November 2001 to the states of New Jersey and Virginia, and will focus on communities in those States most at risk of voter disenfranchisement.

This on-the-ground work involves bridging the resources of many organizations, including but not limited to, the NAACP Legal Defense Fund, Voices of the Electorate, Lawyers Committee for Civil Rights, the

State Baptist Convention (Virginia), the League of Women Voters (New Jersey), Citizens Action (New Jersey), and the A. Phillip Randolph Institute (New Jersey and Virginia).

During the recent September 2002 primary election in Florida, attorneys from PFAWF, the Advancement Project and the Lawyers Committee for Civil Rights Under Law trained volunteers on voters' rights in light of the new laws passed by the Florida legislature. These volunteers were dispersed to precincts in Duval, Broward, Palm Beach and Miami-Dade Counties to assist voters with any problems faced at the polls. The biggest challenge confronted by voters during the primary election in Miami-Dade County, for example, were new voting machines that were not operating properly. Almost immediately after the polls were scheduled to opened, monitors documented and reported that polling places were not open because the voting machines were not working. The volunteer monitors and lawyers collected hundreds of complaints that day, and was able to persuade Governor Bush to keep polling places open for two additional hours so that voters would have an opportunity to cast their ballots. Community groups and lawyers are now reviewing the complaints and will take steps to ensure that the same errors will not occur during the November 2002 general election.

CONCLUSION

The right to vote is one of the most fundamental rights of citizenship. Unfortunately, that right has historically not been fully extended to racial minorities. Although many of the most perverse legal restrictions have been lifted, their progeny are still with us and constitute systemic hurdles to democratic participation. These hurdles include harsh registration list maintenance requirements, purging techniques, and poorly implemented legal provisions.

As we mark the two-year anniversary of the 2000 Election, state legislators are called upon to pass comprehensive, nondiscriminatory reform laws and community activists should carefully monitor the implementation of these laws. Without this, we will allow the failures of the 2000 presidential election, which flowed directly from two centuries of discrimination, to be repeated for elections well into this new century.

STUDY QUESTION

Why does Monique Dixon argue that several proposed election reform measures (same-day registration, computerized central voter registration files, provisional ballots) will affect access to the "franchise"?

Toward a Comprehensive Response to the Transnational Migration of Unaccompanied Minors in the United States

Carolyn J. Seugling

Children may begin their migration on their own initiative most likely fleeing war and civil unrest, forced recruitment as soldiers, child labor, prostitution, or life as a street child. Some become separated from their parents in transit, as the family flees oppressive conditions. Others could be shipped by their parents to the United States. Others are forcibly separated from their families and countries of origin in trafficking or smuggling schemes.

CARE, CUSTODY, AND CONTROL OF UNACCOMPANIED MINORS IN THE UNITED STATES

History of Custody and Control

Before January 2003, when the INS apprehended unaccompanied minors in the United States, they retained sole custody and corresponding responsibility for their well-being. The INS also initiated removal proceedings in the Executive Office for Immigration Review (EOIR). This puts the INS in an awkward situation because it is both an unaccompanied minor's caretaker and their prosecutor. This situation creates an inherent conflict of interest and prohibited the INS from making decisions regarding care and custody issues that served the best interest of the child.

Unaccompanied minors are detained in a national network administered by the INS. Individual children could be transported to facilities wherever and whenever a bed became available, regardless of the distance from extended family or advocates assisting them. Many children were held in detention for over three months and some have remained for as long as three years. As a result, unaccompanied minors remained unfairly detained in harsh correctional facilities until their immigration status became resolved.

The United States is one of a very few countries that detains children. Most other countries adhere to the UNHCR guidelines which suggest alternatives to detention, such as placing unaccompanied minors in a

Source: Carolyn J. Seugling, "Toward a Comprehensive Response to the Transnational Migration of Unaccompanied Minors in the United States," *Vanderbilt Journal of Transnational Law*, 37 (2004): 861–895.

country's child welfare programs and granting unaccompanied minors equivalent services to those provided its citizens. Moreover, because the INS does not provide information about detained children, outside agencies have difficulty monitoring detention conditions. Language barriers and the general lack of knowledge about U.S. immigration law compounds these difficulties in the detention facing unaccompanied minors.

The inadequacy of facilities and procedures for the care and custody of unaccompanied minors was supposed to be resolved after *Reno v. Flores*. At issue in *Flores* was the INS policy of releasing children only to a legal guardian or parent except in "unusual and extraordinary cases." Since unaccompanied minors have neither parents nor guardians, prior to *Flores*, they were often housed for long periods in juvenile detention facilities, or in facilities intended for adult criminals. Unlike traditional procedures typically followed in the treatment of domestic children, the INS did not determine if placement in less restrictive facilities was an option. The INS agreed to settle the dispute at issue in *Flores* after the Court handed down this decision. The settlement instituted nationwide procedures allowing unaccompanied minors to be released "to any adult who executes an agreement to care for the child and ensures his or her presence at immigration proceedings." The *Flores* settlement also allowed the INS to hold children in detention for only seventy-two hours, except in emergencies.

The INS has asserted that it is in substantial compliance with *Flores* settlement. An INS spokesperson stated that "the priority is to put [unaccompanied children] in the least restrictive facility, where we have space. When a juvenile is placed in juvenile hall, it is because it is the absolute only location left." Unfortunately, over one third of these children are held in juvenile jails. The settlement illustrated one of the ways the INS has sought through structural reorganization and not substantive reforms to improve an unaccompanied minor's condition. "In 2000, the INS transferred all of its children's programs to its Detention and Removal office." This change has made it forty percent less likely that a child will be reunited with family. Critics argue that "while such efforts might be well-meaning, they cannot work because the federal government's bias toward incarceration and deportation will always trump its responsibility to look out for a child's best interest." Several hundred unaccompanied minors still remain in long-term detention. Although the INS has maintained it was in substantial compliance with the *Flores* settlement, four years later in 2001 Human Rights Watch found that this has not prevented an "institutional bias" favoring law enforcement over the best interest of the child. A 2001 Justice Department Report from the Inspector General criticized the INS for similar reasons. Most recently, Amnesty International's national report confirmed that the detention of children in the United States violates standards of care for refugees and is "unconscionable."

Experiences of Children While in INS Detention Facilities

Problems in the INS policies relating to unaccompanied minors are illustrated in the stories of those who have faced INS detention. For instance, Mekabou fled Liberia after his father was murdered. Unfortunately, he encountered more violence in the United States. He was apprehended by the immigration police who beat him. Mekabou was then sent to adult prisons and only won asylum after a year and a half in detention. Similarly, Malik Jarno was in detention for over three years. Though the INS claims he is an adult, Jarno asserts he is a minor. In custody, he has been housed with adults and allegedly severely beaten by immigration officials. Jarno filed a civil rights claim against the INS and the Piedmont Regional Jail for his claimed "abuse and neglect." Alfredo Lopez Sanchez spent eighteen months in detention and was transferred between eleven shelters, a jail, and a hotel before he was released. n66 Immigration officials thought he had an undocumented relative in the United States and refused to release him to an acceptable sponsor. After being neglected and abused by his father in Guatemala, his time in INS custody made him, in his own words, "just want . . . to die." Edwin Larios Munoz fled Honduras after being abandoned, and feared that if he was homeless and living on the streets he would be killed. Edwin told his story at Senate hearings on the Unaccompanied Alien Child Protection Act. He discussed being locked up, beaten with sticks, crying, and having to reside next to criminals for almost six months while in INS custody.

RECENT DEVELOPMENTS: CHANGE OF CUSTODY AND CONTROL

Advocates claim the INS violated "hundreds, perhaps thousands" of other unaccompanied minors' rights. Developing a consistent, coherent approach for these children's care and custody is essential. In the words of U.S. Senator Dianne Feinstein, "The INS has not done what it should have done up to this point. Therefore, my view is that the only way to handle this is to put it in legislation." In January 2001, Feinstein introduced the Kids Act. The Kids Act sought to find solutions to the procedural and substantive issues facing unaccompanied minors. The Kids Act's primary focus was to insure respect of unaccompanied minors' human rights while they are in detention.

The Kids Act would have addressed both procedural and substantive issues. It would have created a Special Office of Children's Services within the Department of Justice that "would [have been] responsible for ensuring that the children's needs are met and that their best interests are held paramount in all

proceedings and actions involving them." It would also have established minimum standards of custody, and have provided trained guardians ad litem to children so that their needs in custody were met. This guardian ad litem would also have made recommendations regarding their custody, detention, release, and removal based on the best interests of each child. The Kids Act would also have assured legal representation, first through pro bono programs and then at the expense of the government, if other representation was not available. Finally, the Act would have sought to ensure that INS adjudicators, immigration judges, and other personnel would have been trained on how to address children's needs in asylum claims.

Essential parts of the Kids Act aimed at protecting children from abuse within the INS detention system were passed via incorporation into the Homeland Security Act of 2002 (HSA). The HSA authorized "the largest reorganization of the U.S. government in over fifty years." Among other things, the Homeland Security Act transferred the care and custody of unaccompanied minors to the Office of Refugee Resettlement (ORR) within the Department of Health and Human Services when it was signed into law on November 25, 2002.

The ORR has extensive experience in the child welfare area because it has resettled vulnerable and traumatized children for years. Since 1975, ORR has resettled over 2.2 million refugees (adults and children). ORR has resettled approximately 12,000 juveniles since 1980. Advocates hope the ORR will improve conditions of detention, and hasten unaccompanied minors release to appropriate caregivers. Alfred P. Carlton, Jr., president of the American Bar Association, referred positively to this change stating that "children who arrive at our borders alone and unprotected will no longer have their prosecutor serve as their caretaker." Transferring unaccompanied minors' care to the ORR also eliminated some advocates' fear that the Department of

Homeland Security, responsible for adult immigration enforcement, might over time "treat these [unaccompanied minors] as potential terrorists, regardless of the need to do so." As such, it has removed the possibility of there being any conflict of interest on the part of one agency.

Additionally, the HSA recommended that ORR use the refugee child foster care system as a means to place unaccompanied minors until their status is resolved. Refugee children have been placed through foster care, group care, independent living, or residential treatment. Nguyen Van Hannah, head of ORR, said, "Our direction is to look into foster care as a major way to handle the children." Lastly, the HSA required tracking unaccompanied minors so that advocates and attorneys could be informed of their status upon arrival.

Several substantive rights and improvements in asylum proceedings that the Kids Act would have guaranteed were omitted from the HSA. Senator Feinstein, sponsor of the Kids Act, spoke negatively about choosing reorganization over reform when she said, "the provisions to provide them the critical help they need were left out." These provisions included the right to a guardian ad litem to make a determination as to what was in the best interests of the child, government funded attorneys to represent those interests, the requirement that the best interest of an unaccompanied minor be paramount in the decision making process, as well as increased strength for special immigrant juvenile visas. Training for judges and personnel administering unaccompanied minors' asylum claims was also omitted from the HSA. In response, Feinstein introduced a bill including many of the provisions omitted from the HSA.

By not adopting any of the substantive provisions of the Kids Act, Congress chose to take its traditional "path of least resistance" by reorganizing rather than addressing substantive issues regarding the rights of unaccompanied minor children. Since the HSA

requires a study to facilitate the best way attorneys may be appointed, the substantive issues remain to be addressed.

SYSTEMIC CHALLENGES: OBTAINING LAWFUL PERMANENT RESIDENCE

Lawful Permanent Residence

An unaccompanied minor may obtain lawful residence in the United States depending on why they left their country of origin. Unaccompanied minors may apply for lawful permanent residence if they qualify as (1) a special immigrant juvenile, (2) a victim of trafficking under the Violence Protection Act of 2000, or (3) because they have been granted asylum. The first two legal remedies take into account unique circumstances that children might encounter in which they played no active role. The third applies the same standard to children as applied to adults seeking asylum and remains the only remedy for a children who have played an active role in their transnational migration into the United States.

Victims of Trafficking

Under the Victims of Trafficking and Violence Protection act of 2000, if a child has been a victim of trafficking and suffered physical or mental abuse they would qualify for a U-visa and be allowed to remain in the United States. If a child has suffered a "severe form of trafficking in persons," and can demonstrate that they would suffer "unusual and severe harm if they were removed from the United States" the child would qualify for a T-Visa. This legislation offers protection to the estimated 45,000 to 50,000 women and children illegally trafficked into the United States. After successfully applying for a T-visa, a child would obtain a nonimmigrant visa valid for three years and could later apply for permanent residency status.

Special Immigrant Juveniles

Unaccompanied minors, in the custody of a state's juvenile system, who have been abused or neglected while in the custody of another country, can petition the Attorney General to allow an application for special immigrant status. If an application is made, the state court must then find that the child has been abused and neglected, and that it is in the child's best interest to remain in the United States. If so determined, the unaccompanied minor will be placed in the foster care system and may eventually become a lawful permanent resident.

Children Seeking Asylum

Children fleeing persecution in their country of origin, or who are abused, can bring a claim for asylum if they have a "well founded fear of persecution based on race, religion, nationality, political opinion or membership of a particular social group." "When an alien is seeking withholding of deportation, he bears the burden of demonstrating that it is "more likely than not' that he will be persecuted or tortured upon his return to the country in question." This standard is both objective and subjective. Applicants must prove both the objective reasonableness of their fear of persecution as well as that they have subjectively experienced this fear. A ten percent possibility of persecution is sufficient to establish a well-founded fear.

Systemic Challenges

Even if unaccompanied minors would satisfy these legal requirements, they often face difficulties that prevent them from obtaining lawful residency. The first challenge in meeting all of the above legal tests is that counsel is not appointed at the expense of the government, as it is in domestic criminal proceedings for children. About eighty percent of unaccompanied minors wade through the complex process of obtaining lawful residency, outlined

above, without representation. Unaccompanied minors

> encounter a stressful situation in which they are forced to make critical decisions. Their interrogators are foreign and authoritarian. The environment is new and the culture completely different. The law is complex. . . . In short, it is obvious to the Court that the situation faced by unaccompanied minors is inherently coercive.

Even if a child has a viable claim under the current standards, without representation it is likely the children will be deported to their country of origin. Unaccompanied minors are fifty percent more likely to win their claims and get protection if they have an attorney. Rud Luubers, U.N. High Commissioner for Refugees, said that a "renewed commitment from countries around the world was needed, to ensure that children had access to asylum procedures and that they were assisted by legal representatives."

Responding to this "coercive" environment in 1998, the United States developed guidelines that provide advice on interviewing and processing an unaccompanied minor's claim for asylum. Although the guidelines do not alter or provide substantive rights, they do recognize that during the asylum process a child may not be able to respond as an adult would and may need special interviewing procedures tailored to the child's developmental capacity. However, as guidelines, they neither guarantee nor mandate judicial compliance with or training on the guidelines.

The second challenge for unaccompanied minors is that if their claims are appealed to Article III courts, Article III courts do not uniformly apply or adhere to the guidelines implemented for the purpose of assisting unaccompanied minors in asylum proceedings. The guidelines specifically establish that an unaccompanied minor should be interviewed in a child sensitive manner and their testimony given sufficient credibility even if a child has some gaps of recollection.

Interviewing remains a recommendation and not a requirement. For example, in Elian Gonzalez's highly publicized case, no interview was conducted and the Eleventh Circuit held that an interview was not required.

Additionally, "the guidelines recognize that children under the age of 18 may experience persecution differently from adults and may not present testimony with the same degree of precision as adults." The guidelines, however, have not persuaded immigration judges to reevaluate their conceptions of children's testimony or of children as rights holders. Immigration judges continue to deny asylum because of credibility issues as well as disbelief that minors can hold political ideas for which they could be persecuted. Applying the same asylum standard to children as to adults, without factoring in whether or not children have the developmental and psychological ability to prove they have been subjectively and objectively persecuted leads to denial of otherwise viable claims made by unaccompanied minors.

The third challenge that unaccompanied minors face is that immigration judges have a demanding docket requiring fast processing creating an almost insurmountable barrier for an unrepresented, unaccompanied minor to obtain asylum. EOIR has not systematically incorporated the guidelines into its adjudication, and the reviewing body, the Board of Immigration Appeals (BIA) consists of nineteen judges responsible for processing 32,000 cases a year. One immigration judge, speaking to the Human Rights Watch Child's Rights Project, stated:

All the INS people in Washington care about are the numbers, so we're under a lot of pressure just to move things along faster. . . . That's a problem for kids, who can't get counsel. There are ways to get around rules and it's in the judge's discretion to decide who's a "responsible person." In other judges' courtrooms, I just don't know what happens to these kids. There aren't enough lawyers for them. . . . The kids are scared. . . . Generally they don't know what the hell is going on.

Recognizing that these guidelines have not been implemented across the board, on February 1, 2002, then-INS Commissioner Ziglar outlined reforms at the National Immigration Forum as part of a new initiative to "revise the 1998 guidelines on children's asylum claims to reflect recent development in law and policy; and providing supplemental training following publication of the guidelines." A year later, nothing has been accomplished regarding this, despite the dire need, and Ziglar has been replaced by an acting Commissioner.

Compounding the Challenges: The Homeland Security Act

The HSA abolished the INS and transferred all of the INS's service functions to the Bureau of Citizenship and Immigration Services (BCIS), a department within the HSA. EOIR remained within the Department of Justice. The EOIR is the only immigration body remaining under the Department of Justice supervised by the Attorney General. The effect of this transfer raises many concerns for advocates. Locating immigration services within the DHHS along with five other divisions raises three primary concerns: (1) that there will be competition for resources and resulting decrease of asylum seekers in the country; (2) that the mission of the new department aimed at keeping out terrorists will create a "paramilitary culture" at odds with assisting valid immigration services; and (3) that the nation's ability to both enforce immigration laws and prevent terrorist attacks would be diminished.

SUBSTANTIVE CHALLENGES: OBTAINING ASYLUM

Unaccompanied Minors Experience Persecution Differently Than Adults

Understanding how unaccompanied minors experience persecution is essential to adjudicating their asylum claims. Notably left out of the Homeland Security Act was a proposal in the original Senate version that would have required a report on the "worldwide situation faced by unaccompanied refugee children." An assessment of the problems faced by unaccompanied minors is needed to create understanding that these children are persecuted around the world because of their status as children without a protective guardian. The following is a brief and incomplete description of the persecution of unaccompanied minors and their increased likelihood of persecution. Human rights research should be continued to document the continued persecution of unaccompanied minors.

Displaced Unaccompanied Minors

The general hardships minors face are compounded because they face them without legally responsible caregivers. Rud Luubers, U.N. High Commissioner for Refugees, has said that refugee children "are often exposed to armed conflict, and lack of access to food, water, shelter and basic health care. They are vulnerable to manipulation and forced military recruitment and they are often exposed to HIV/AIDS." Study findings show that unaccompanied children are vulnerable specifically because they are not protected by an adult responsible for their care. The U.N. General Assembly has said that unaccompanied refugee minors to be "among the most vulnerable refugees and the most at risk of neglect, violence, forced military recruitment and sexual assault and therefore require special assistance and care." A recent study aimed at assessing the refugee child's concerns identified that separated children or unaccompanied children face: "a greater risk of sexual exploitation and abuse . . . ; a greater risk of military recruitment; a greater risk of child labor. . . ."

Refugees "defy easy categorization because some face abuse and neglect at home, others face abuse and neglect in their own country while separated, yet others face persecution after they have become a refugee." Children are displaced for reasons specific to their status as children: forced abduction in times of unrest, forced military recruitment, sexual abuse, and forced labor are examples of forms of refugee-producing phenomena which are either peculiarly meted out to children or which take on a dimension that can only be experienced by child refugees.

Children have also been increasingly used as soldiers in the developing world. The study explains that military recruits may be as young as ten years old. Boys are generally used in military activities, while girls are "recruited" for purposes of sexual slavery and forced labor. In one instance, approximately one hundred boys were conscripted from a refugee camp into the Sudan People's Liberation Movement/Army which had a base near a UNHCR refugee camp.

Young females are used for sexual slavery. Scholars have noted that girls are taken from refugee camps and "sold for sex to highly organized networks operating transnationally." "Unaccompanied minors . . . face a particular risk of sexual exploitation, abuse and violence since they may not have a trusted adult to protect and assist them." Fourteen-year-old Vietnamese girls were trafficked into Cambodia for sex and arrested for illegally entering Cambodia by the same officers who freed them from being sexual slaves. Minors are specifically targeted for sexual exploitation because it is believed that they are "less likely to be infected with HIV."

Unaccompanied minor refugee children also experience persecution different from that which adults suffer within newly formed care networks within refugee camps. For example, while in refugee camps, unaccompanied children band together to form groups usually headed by an older child. In the newly formed unit the children are forced to work and are denied educational opportunities. Many times an unaccompanied minor might be taken in by a stranger and suffer abuse, neglect, and exploitation by this caregiver. Many caregivers are not related to the unaccompanied minors and are struggling economically. These caretakers force the unaccompanied minors to work as cooks, in other forms of domestic labor, or in the marketplace, while their own children do not. The unaccompanied minor is discriminated against in favor of the child for whom the foster parent is legally responsible. Unaccompanied minors in a foster family unit complain of being given little food or eating only once a day while the other members of the new social unit eat twice. Unaccompanied minors are often also physically and emotionally abused while the biological children of caretakers do not suffer similar abuses. These unaccompanied minors suffer, "a kind of slavery . . . the child thinks she has to obey, that she can't go anywhere." Although these children would likely qualify for special immigrant status, they should also be able to qualify for asylum because of their persecution based on being a child without anyone legally responsible for their care.

According to the Convention on the Rights of the Child which secures "children separated from their parents . . . the same rights as other children," the UNHCR or the government where the refugee camp is located is responsible for their protection and assistance. UNHCR is responsible for identifying separated children, monitoring their care, intervening if they are being abused or their needs are not being met. . . . [However] it may be very difficult to obtain reliable information about what goes on within families or communities . . . . When social workers do detect mistreatment . . . [they] have few resources at their disposal and have seldom been able to do more than provide occasional assistance to the child or the family.

Unaccompanied Minor Street Children

Street children are also unaccompanied minors. Interestingly, many street children feel that other children within their street child group are "like a family." In Spain, Moroccan migrant children are abused by Spanish police officers and then expelled to Morocco, where they are reported to be beaten again by the Moroccan police force and abandoned on the street. Human Rights Watch published a report that details Spanish officials' abuse of unaccompanied minor children in an effort to force them to return to Morocco so that they will not drain welfare services which are guaranteed to them under Spanish law. The Spanish government admits to failing to monitor the situation or remedy these abuses. The children are in effect persecuted because of their very status as unaccompanied minors.

Street children also endure hardship in other countries. Guatemalan street children often experience violence including beatings and sexual assault by private security guards who report to the Interior Ministry. These children are persecuted for their homeless status under the auspices of what the police deem to be "creating a public scandal." "In December 1999, the Inter American Court of Human Rights ruled that two police officers were responsible for the 1990 deaths of five street youths and that the Guatemalan government had failed to protect the rights of the victims." In Albania, children are exploited rather than protected by the police. "There are approximately 800 street children in Tirana. Trafficking in children for sex and, to a lesser degree, for begging rings was a serious problem. . . . Albania is a country of origin and a transit country for trafficking. Police corruption and involvement in trafficking was a problem." Reports have been made of abuse of Brazilian, Colombian, Indian, Kenyan, Egyptian, and Sudanese street children. Human Rights Watch notes in some countries the "notion of social cleansing" is applied to street children even when they are not distinguished as members of a particular racial, ethnic, or religious group. Branded as "antisocial" or demonstrating "anti-social behavior," street children are viewed with suspicion and fear by many who would simply like to see street children disappear.

Proposals For Change: Old and New

Create New Visa Status for Unaccompanied Minors

One solution for unaccompanied minors, not just unaccompanied minor refugee children, is to have Congress create a new non-immigrant visa based on their status as unaccompanied minors. This solution may result in negative consequences such as separation of families over the long term. For example, if parents feel it is in their child's best interest to send him or her to the United States, upon arrival the child could be granted a non-immigrant visa. The United States should not encourage this separation and harm to the child by granting universal visas. Children who are given visas for humanitarian reasons may still end up involved in smuggling, living as prostitutes, involved in crime, or murdered. Abuse of a system aimed at assisting unaccompanied minors but not narrowly tailored could cause the idea of refugee protection to fall into disfavor. Moreover, family reunification and unity has been a longstanding goal of immigration policy, and statutory provisions should not be created that would thwart this policy which is in the best interest of the child.

Expand the Interpretation of Refugee to Include Unaccompanied Displaced Minors as a Specific Social Group

Congress adopted the 1980 amendment to the definition of refugee without providing any meaningful guidance on interpreting or defining its terms. A refugee, as noted above, is someone who has a "well founded fear of persecution based on race, religion, nationality, political opinion, membership of a particular social group." Race, religion, and nationality

are relatively determinate. Defining what constitutes persecution and membership in a particular social group has posed significant challenges for courts. There is no universal definition of social group or persecution.

No court has ruled that unaccompanied displaced minors constitute a particular social group capable of experiencing persecution because of their membership in this group. The guidelines do not mention the possibility that unaccompanied displaced minors could constitute a particular social group. Rather, the guidelines stipulate that age and generally harsh conditions suffered by many cannot define a particular social group. However, unaccompanied minors experience persecution unique to their circumstances which the definition of refugee should be expanded to recognize.

Displaced Unaccompanied Minors Meet the Current Standard and Should Therefore Be Recognized as a Persecuted Social Group

Persecution must be due to one of the five enumerated grounds to be granted asylum, the last of which is membership in a particular social group. Courts have defined the term "social group" because it is not defined in the Act. The First, Third, and Seventh Circuits follow a standard based on a BIA decision, *Matter of Acosta*, which suggests that a social group must be based on a shared characteristic that might be an innate one such as sex, color, or kinship ties. . . . The particular kind of group characteristic that will qualify under this construction remains to be determined on a case-by-case basis. . . . whatever the common characteristic that defines the group, it must be one that the members of the group either cannot change, or should not be required to change because it is fundamental to their individual identities or consciences.

The Ninth Circuit allows for a social group to be comprised of a "voluntary associational relationship or by an innate characteristic that is so fundamental to the identities or conscience of its members that members either cannot or should not be required to change it." This standard parallels the UNHCR's definition of a social group. The UNHCR defines social group as "persons of similar background, habits or social status." The Second Circuit defines a particular social group as one "comprised of individuals who possess some fundamental characteristic in common which serves to distinguish them in the eyes of the persecutor or in the eyes of the outside world in general."

As the INS guidelines illustrate, membership in a particular social group cannot be based on broad characteristics such as youth and gender. Furthermore, the guidelines also state that, "the type of harm a child may suffer cannot serve to define the particular social group on account of which that particular harm is suffered." The reason that these children are persecuted or targeted for military service is because they lack parents to protect them. Their vulnerability is a product of their lack of a primary caregiver. This characteristic distinguishes them from other youth and can serve to define them as a group. Unaccompanied minors largely lack the ability to change their circumstances. Although unaccompanied minors suffer similar types of harms, under either the voluntary association or innate characteristic standards, unaccompanied minors should be recognized as a social group capable of experiencing persecution.

Unaccompanied minors suffer persecution on account of their membership in a social group of children without primary caregivers to look out for their interests. The BIA has defined persecution to include "threats to life, confinement, torture, and economic restrictions so severe that they constitute threat to life or freedom, . . . physical or mental harm . . . [and] discriminatory practices [that] can accumulate over time or increase in intensity so that they may rise to the level of persecution."

Persecution must be proved by objective facts that show that past persecution can be inferred or that there is a risk of future persecution. After persecution has been objectively proven, the applicant must prove that they have actually been persecuted or fear persecution. Persecution need not consist of "country-wide civil strife and anarchy." The BIA has stated that "Congress specifically rejected a definition of "refugee". . . that would have included "displaced persons," i.e., individuals who flee widespread conditions of indiscriminate violence resulting from civil war or military strife in a country."

Unaccompanied minors in refugee camps generally become separated from their parents and displaced as a direct result of civil conflict. This said, the guidelines for unaccompanied minors point out that "generally harsh conditions shared by many other persons do not amount to persecution." Consequently, the grave experience and existence of unaccompanied minors under their "generally harsh conditions" do not prove they have been either objectively or subjectively persecuted. However, individual unaccompanied minors suffer physical and mental abuse as well as receiving so little food that it could constitute a threat to their lives. The discrimination against unaccompanied minors as compared with the biological children of the caretakers rises to the level of persecution when they are denied educational opportunities and forced into domestic labor. Unaccompanied minors are also specifically targeted for military conscription because they are more malleable than adults and have no adult to protect them.

Street Children Recognized as a Specific Social Group of Unaccompanied Minors

Support for expanding the definition of refugee to encompass unaccompanied minors comes from a recent decision that a street child, if returned to his country of origin, would suffer persecution based on membership in a particular social group of street children. In November 2001, an unaccompanied minor street child was considered for the first time to be part of a particular social group of other unaccompanied minors and granted asylum. The immigration judge relied on the UNHCR Handbook on Procedures and Criteria for Determining Refugee Status, not the U.S. government guidelines, to determine that "sensitivity to the age of the child might affect the analysis of his or her refugee status." In this case, a sixteen-year-old native of Guatemala would become part of a group of "street children" if returned to Guatemala. The immigration judge relied on Acosta's definition of a social group: a group which shares a "protected characteristic [of which] the prosecutor could become aware, and that the persecutor has the means and inclination to persecute . . . to be defined on a case by case basis." The judge concurrently applied the Sanchez-Trujillo definition of social group as "a collection of people closely affiliated with each other, who are actuated by some common impulse or interest."

Displaced Unaccompanied Minors Are Similar to Unaccompanied Minor Street Children

Unaccompanied minors in refugee camps share characteristics and experience similar persecution to that of street children. Often times, unaccompanied minor refugee children band together to form new care groups in refugee camps led by an elder girl child for their protection and survival. The "characteristic" that unaccompanied minors share is their unaccompanied status in their home country which leaves them open to persecution. They face similar persecution to that of street children, such as physical and sexual abuse from which neither their government nor the UNHCR protects them. All these children should be considered a social group.

The definition of refugee should be explicitly expanded to include unaccompanied minor refugee children who suffer persecution, and have a well-founded fear of persecution at the hands of the new caretaker or an outside group that preys on children living together. Membership in a particular social group was last expanded when the BIA recognized gender as a possible reason for persecution. Expanding the interpretation to include unaccompanied minors would promote the purpose of the Refugee Convention.

Ratify the Convention on the Rights of the Child

One last possibility that would grant unaccompanied minors more extensive rights within the refugee context is if the United States ratified the Convention on the Rights of the Child. One hundred and ninety state parties have explicitly recognized children's vulnerability by adopting the Convention on the Rights of the Child. The United States has signed but has not ratified the convention, and until it becomes ratified it does not have the force of law. The United States remains one of only three member states that have not ratified the Convention. At the U.N. General Assembly Special Session on Children, supporters of the Convention, accused the United States of trying to marginalize the Convention and prevent it from becoming the "global standard" that the rest of the world recognizes for children's rights.

If the United States does not ratify the Convention, it could theoretically be bound under the CRC if it has "acquired the status of customary international law" not contrary to domestic laws. However, because so many non-optional provisions are contrary to domestic law, it is unlikely that the CRC would ever bind the United States if it does not ratify the convention itself.

The United States is unlikely to ratify the CRC because of numerous articles that face

U.S. opposition. Moreover, "contrasting obligations" within the CRC make it unlikely that even if ratified it would have the force to give children new substantive rights within the refugee convention. Additionally, the committee who reviews compliance with the CRC criticizes many of the countries that have adopted it for failure to meet its standards.

CONCLUSION

Everyone wants to help children. No one ever answers the question of why so many children still suffer. Advocates and politicians have taken the first steps towards alleviating unaccompanied minors' suffering in U.S. custody by changing their custodians. However, "reform lies in politicians" recognition that "restructuring alone is not going to solve all the problems, [but rather] just begins the effort" of reexamining the assumptions, goals, and approaches of immigration policy." It is important to reexamine the assumptions, approaches, and goals of immigration policy for unaccompanied minors. At the very least, unaccompanied minors deserve legal counsel and help with the research necessary to document their claims. Unaccompanied minors should be considered as children who experience different forms of persecution because of their unaccompanied status and not under the same standards applied to adult asylum seekers. Expanding the definition to include recognition of unaccompanied minors as a social group would protect their interests and align U.S. immigration law with international norms.

STUDY QUESTION

Briefly outline Carolyn Seugling's overview of how unaccompanied minors reach the United States and the recent changes in custody procedures aimed at ameliorating the harsh detention conditions faced by these children.

Sixty Years Since the Hiroshima and Nagasaki Bombings

Joseph Kay

There is no part of the world in which the United States does not have an interest. It has sought to progressively expand its influence in Central Asia and the former Soviet Union through the war in Afghanistan and political intervention in countries such as Ukraine. It is seeking to dominate the Middle East through the war in Iraq and the threat of war in Iran. It is expanding its activities in Africa and has made repeated threats against North Korea and China as part of its efforts to secure its influence in East Asia.

PROMPT AND UTTER DESTRUCTION

In the early morning hours of August 6, 1945, an American B-29 warplane, named the *Enola Gay*, rolled down the runway of an American airbase on the Pacific island of Tinian. It flew for almost six hours, encountering no resistance from the ground.

At 8:15 a.m. local time, the plane dropped its payload over the clear skies of Hiroshima, a Japanese city with an estimated population of 255,000. The atomic bomb that the plane was carrying, "Little Boy," detonated some 600 meters above the city center, killing 80,000 people—30 percent of the population—immediately or within hours of the explosion.

Three days layer, on August 9, a similar plane carrying a more powerful weapon left Tinian but had more difficulty reaching its intended destination. After encountering fire from the ground, and finding its target city Kokura covered in clouds, it flew on to its second target, Nagasaki, a heavily industrialized city of about 270,000. Due to the specific topological features of Nagasaki, and to the fact that the bomb missed the city center, the effects were slightly less devastating. An estimated 40,000 people were killed outright.

Over the next several months, tens of thousands more died from their injuries, including radiation sickness caused by the nuclear devices. While exact figures involving such magnitudes are inherently difficult to

Source: Joseph Kay, "Sixty Years Since the Hiroshima and Nagasaki Bombings," World Socialist Web Site, Three-Part Series, August 6–9, 2005, available at http://www.wsws.org/articles/2005/aug2005/hiro-a06.shtml; http://www.wsws.org/articles/2005/aug2005/hiro-a08.shtml; http://www.wsws.org/articles/2005/aug2005/hiro-a09.shtml.

come by, estimates of the total number of men, women and children killed within four months of the two blasts range from 200,000 to 350,000. Never before had such devastation been wrought so quickly.

The bombs, combined with a Soviet invasion of Japanese-controlled Manchuria on August 8, led quickly to the end of the war in the Pacific. On September 2, the government of Japan signed a treaty with the allied powers that essentially ceded complete control of the country to the American military.

Japan's surrender, coming four months after the surrender of Germany, brought the Second World War to an end. At the same time, it marked a new stage in the increasingly antagonistic relationship between the United States and the Soviet Union, which had been military allies in the war. Within four years, the Soviet Union acquired its own nuclear weapon, initiating a nuclear arms race that continued for four decades.

The official rationale given by the US government for its use of nuclear weapons in the war has always been that it was necessary to save American lives by avoiding the necessity of an invasion of Japan. After the war, government officials, facing criticism for their decision to use the bomb, suggested that between 500,000 and 1 million Americans, and several million Japanese, were saved by dropping the bombs that completely destroyed Hiroshima and Nagasaki.

This rationale has always been highly suspect, and in subsequent years much evidence emerged demonstrating that not only were the estimated casualty figures from an invasion highly exaggerated, but that the war could have been quickly ended even without an invasion.

While the reasons for the use of the bombs are complex, they center around two interrelated geopolitical aims of the American ruling elite at the end of the war: (1) the desire to limit the influence of the Soviet Union in East Asia by bringing the war to an end before the Soviet forces advanced far into China toward Japan, and (2) the wish to have a physical demonstration of the unrivaled power of the American military, and its willingness to use this power to advance its interests.

The motives behind the decision to use the atom bomb will be examined in detail in the second part of this series. The contemporary significance of this most terrible anniversary—including the recent explosion of American militarism and the push to develop new types of nuclear weapons—will be the subject of the third article.

A New Type of Bomb

The Potsdam declaration, issued by the Allied powers on July 26, 1945, pledged the "prompt and utter destruction" of Japan if it did not agree to unconditional surrender. For the cities of Nagasaki and Hiroshima, this is certainly what the atomic bombs brought.

By the time of the bombing of Hiroshima, many of Japan's large cities had been attacked severely by American air power. After the US military had gained control of Japanese airspace, the Air Force began to systematically bomb metropolitan areas, including the devastating firebombing of Tokyo earlier in the year, which killed an estimated 87,000 people. The fact that Hiroshima had so far not been targeted was considered something of an anomaly by its residents, since, in addition to civilian production facilities, the city housed an important military headquarters.

Nevertheless, the bomb caught the people of Hiroshima unprepared. A weather scouting plane had triggered sirens earlier in the morning, but an all-clear signal had been given once it departed. The *Enola Gay* and two planes that were accompanying it were assumed to be more scouting planes, and therefore the alarms were not sounded when they flew over the city.

The blast of the uranium bomb dropped on Hiroshima had the explosive equivalent of about 13,000 tons of TNT. The nuclear reaction in the bomb generated temperatures of several million degrees Centigrade. At the hypocenter, the point on the ground 600 meters below the explosion, temperatures reached 3,000 to 4,000 degrees Centigrade, two times the melting point of iron. The intense flash of heat and light, which incinerated everything within a kilometer-and-a-half of the hypocenter, was followed by an enormous shock wave that destroyed most buildings within two kilometers.

The Hiroshima bomb was targeted at the Aioi Bridge, which it missed by about 250 meters. According to one account, the bomb exploded instead directly above a hospital headed by a Dr. Shima: "The Shima hospital and all its patients were vaporized. . . . Eighty-eight percent of the people within a radius of 1,500 feet died instantly or later on that day. Most others within the circle perished in the following weeks or months."

Those close to the hypocenter were instantly incinerated without leaving behind a trace, except for perhaps a shadow on a wall or street where their bodies had partially protected the surface from the initial flash of heat. One author notes that those closest to the blast "passed from being to nothingness faster than any human physiology can register."

Those slightly farther from the center of the explosion did not die immediately, but suffered from severe third-degree burns all over their bodies, in particular to any areas that were exposed directly to the heat. They suffered a period of intense pain before dying of their injuries. Those who witnessed the explosion and survived invariably describe these victims in the most horrific terms.

A doctor who had been on the outskirts of the city when the explosion occurred wrote about what he saw as he rushed in to help the victims. He explained how, as he approached the city center, a "strange figure came up to me little by little, unsteady on its feet. It surely seemed like the form of a man but it was completely naked, bloody and covered with mud. The body was completely swollen. Rags hung from its bare breast and waist. The hands were held before the breasts with palms turned down. Water dripped from the rags. Indeed, what I took to be rags were in fact pieces of human skin and the water drops were human blood. . . . I looked at the road before me. Denuded, burnt and bloody, numberless survivors stood in my path. They were massed together, some crawling on their knees or on all fours, some stood with difficulty or leaned on another's shoulder."

The description of disfigured people with "skin hanging down like rags" is common among those who survived to tell what they saw. Many saw people roaming the streets, in intense pain, often blind from the burns or deaf from the explosion, with their arms stretched out in front of them, "with forearms and hands dangling . . . to prevent the painful friction of raw surfaces rubbing together," some "staggering like sleepwalkers."

Perhaps thousands died in this way. A doctor named Tabuchi described how, "all through the night," hundreds of injured people "went past our house, but this morning [August 7] they had stopped. I found them lying on both sides of the road so thick that it was impossible to pass without stepping on them." One survivor wrote how he witnessed "Hundreds of those still alive . . . wandering around vacantly. Some were half-dead, writhing in their misery . . . . They were no more than living corpses."

Many of those who did not die immediately sought to find their way to the rivers or reservoirs to seek relief from the burning pain. A survivor describes how he "saw that the long bank of the river at Choju-En was filled with a large number of burned human beings. They occupied the bank as far as the eye could see. The greatest number lay in the water rolling slowly at the mercy of the waves," having drowned or died at the bank's edge. Another doctor, Hanoka, described how he "saw fire reservoirs filled to the brim with dead people who looked as though they had been boiled alive."

Much of the city within several kilometers of the blast's center was completely destroyed. Buildings that were not flattened by the explosion itself were consumed in the ensuing fire that engulfed the largely wooden homes. Many who were trapped when their homes collapsed over them died in this fire.

Dr. Hachiya writes, "Hiroshima was no longer a city, but a burnt-over prairie. To the east and to the west everything was flattened. The distant mountains seemed nearer than I could ever remember. The hills of Ushita and the woods of Nigitsu loomed out of the haze and smoke like the nose and eyes of a face. How small Hiroshima was with its houses gone."

Within a week of the explosions in both Hiroshima and Nagasaki, most of those who had been severely injured had either died or were beginning to recover. However, it was at this point that thousands of patients unexpectedly began to experience "sudden attacks of high fever which had risen above forty degrees Celsius. . . . And then they began to bleed from their mucous membranes and soon spat up quantities of blood. . . . It was also at this time that an uncanny form of depilation, or hair loss, began among the survivors. When patients raised their hands to their heads while struggling with pain, their hair would fall out with a mere touch of the fingers."

This was radiation disease caused by the nuclear reaction, which emitted enormous quantities of gamma rays. At the time, however, doctors in the city had not yet learned about the peculiar nature of the bomb dropped over the city, and speculated that the population was suffering from a wave of dysentery, or perhaps chemical poisoning from something released by the bomb.

A British medical report explained that the radiation released from the explosion did not destroy the cells in the bloodstream, but attacked "the primitive cells in the bone marrow, from which most of the different types of cells in the blood are formed. Therefore serious effects begin to appear only as the fully-formed cells already in the blood die off gradually and are not replaced as they would normally by new cells formed in the bone marrow. . . . As red cell formation ceased, the patient began to suffer from progressive anemia. As platelet formation ceased, the thin blood seeped in small and large hemorrhages into the skin and the retina of the eye, and sometimes into the intestines and the kidneys. The fall in the number of white cells . . . in severe cases lowered resistance, so that the patient inevitably fell prey to some infection, usually spreading from the mouth and accompanied by gangrene of the lips, the tongue, and sometimes the throat. . . . Deaths probably began in about a week after the explosion, reached a peak in about three weeks and had for the most part ceased after six to eight weeks."

The radiation disease affected those nearest the blast most severely. However, it left profound psychological scars on many of those who survived, constantly tormented by the thought that, though healthy today, they too could succumb tomorrow.

The above description is derived primarily from testimony of survivors of the Hiroshima bomb. However, the effects in Nagasaki were similar. The Nagasaki bomb was dropped before the full devastation of the Hiroshima bomb had become widely known. The day of the bombing was pushed up to August 9 from August 11, because of poor weather forecasts for the latter date.

Nagasaki had long been a principal port and one of the most beautiful cities on the Japanese island of Kyushu. Its main industry was shipbuilding, which made it a target for the second bomb. The bomb exploded over the suburb of Urakami, home to what was then the largest cathedral in East Asia.

While there were many atrocities committed during the Second World War, the bombings of Hiroshima and Nagasaki were undoubtedly two of the greatest single acts of wanton destruction, in which the lives of hundreds of thousands of people, mainly civilians, were wiped out. They are events that should not be allowed to slip from the memory of working people around the world—a testament to the ruthlessness and destructive capacity of American militarism.

AMERICAN IMPERIALISM AND THE ATOM BOMB

The destruction wreaked upon the populations of Hiroshima and Nagasaki has long been justified by the American government on the grounds that it was necessary "to save American lives." This rationale has not ceased to be the officially sanctioned historical truth even though it has been thoroughly debunked by evidence that has come out over the past sixty years.

To cite one example, the editorial page of the *Wall Street Journal* wrote on August 5, 2005 that the bombs averted an invasion of the Japanese mainland, "for which the Truman Administration anticipated casualties of between 200,000 and one million." Moreover, "a mainland invasion could have resulted in millions of Japanese deaths." According to this calculus, the hundreds of thousands of Japanese citizens, mainly civilians, who suffered an inexpressible agony and death from the atom bomb were sacrificed in the interest of preserving as many lives as possible.

Even if one were to accept the premises of this argument, it would not mitigate the fundamental criminality—legal and moral—involved in the annihilation of these urban centers. However, the premises are entirely mythical. Not only have the estimated casualty figures been exaggerated, but the main reasons for the US government's decision to drop the bombs had nothing to do with avoiding an American invasion of Japan.

As with any great historical question, there were a number of different factors that went into the decision to drop the bomb, and it will be impossible to deal with all of them here. We will confine ourselves to touching on some of the basic issues and documents.

It is first of all necessary to note that the dropping of the atomic bombs on largely defenseless cities—which, while they held military headquarters or military-related industries, were predominantly civilian in character—had a certain continuity with the manner in which the United States was carrying out the war in the Pacific.

Once it had gained control of Japanese airspace, the American military increasingly turned to what can only be described as terrorist methods—indiscriminate attacks on civilian populations for the purpose of spreading fear and panic. Before Hiroshima and Nagasaki, the most devastating example of these methods was the firebombing of Tokyo on March 9, 1945, which killed some 87,000 people. This followed by less than a month the infamous firebombing of the German city of Dresden, on February 13–14, 1945.

Despite its humanitarian pretenses, the American military was demonstrating in these actions that it was capable of acting just as brutally as Germany or Japan in the conduct of war. There was an interesting exchange, during a discussion between President Harry Truman and Secretary of War Henry Stimson on June 6, 1945 that gives a sense of the manner in which the American government considered the question of the mass annihilation of Japanese civilians.

Stimson records in a memorandum that he raised certain pragmatic concerns with the area bombing of Japanese cities being carried out by the US Air Force: "I told [Truman] I was anxious about this feature of the war for two reasons: first, because I did not want to have the United States get the reputation of outdoing Hitler in atrocities; and second, I was a little fearful that before we could get ready the Air Force might have Japan so thoroughly bombed out that the new weapon [the atom bomb] would not have a fair background to show its strength. He laughed and said he understood." Stimson was concerned that the wanton destruction of Japanese cities would disrupt plans for the use of the atom bomb because there would be no "fair background," that is, a suitably populated and intact urban center. The conversation also demonstrates that at this point the United States completely dominated Japan militarily, able to destroy its cities virtually at will.

The use of the bomb as a terrorist weapon—that is, as a means of instilling mass terror among the Japanese population—was underscored in a meeting of the Interim Committee on May 31, 1945. The Interim Committee consisted of those directly involved in the Manhattan Project, such as Robert Oppenheimer and other scientists, as well as Truman administration officials, including Secretary of State James Byrnes and Secretary of War Stimson. It was set up to discuss the use of the atomic bomb, propose targets and consider related issues. According to a transcript of that meeting, "After much discussion concerning various types of targets and the effects to be produced, the Secretary [of War Stimson] expressed the conclusion, on which there was general agreement, that we could not give the Japanese any warning; that we could not concentrate on a civilian area; but that we should seek to make a profound *psychological impression* on as many of the inhabitants as possible. At the suggestion of Dr. [James] Conant, the Secretary agreed that the most desirable target would be a vital war plant employing a large number of workers and *closely surrounded by workers' houses*" (emphasis added).

Despite the reference to not concentrating on a civilian area, the committee explicitly rejected the use of the bomb first on a purely military or uninhabited region, as some of the scientists who had worked with the panel recommended.

Many of the scientists who worked or supported the Manhattan Project did so because of their intense hatred of Hitler and the Nazi regime. The project was originally justified on the grounds that if Hitler were to acquire the bomb first the consequences would be absolutely devastating. But by the time the United States had perfected the technology, Germany had been defeated. Nevertheless, the Truman administration not only decided to use the bomb, but did so with evident glee. Truman famously declared that he did not lose a night's sleep over the decision. According to one account, when he heard the news about Hiroshima while crossing the Atlantic, he declared, "This is the greatest thing in history," and then "raced about the ship to spread the news, insisting that he had never made a happier announcement. 'We have won the gamble,' he told the assembled and cheering crew."

Commenting on this phenomenon, the historian Gabriel Jackson remarked, "In the specific circumstances of August 1945, the use of the atom bomb showed that a psychologically very normal and democratically elected chief executive could use the weapon just as the Nazi dictator would have used it. In this way, the United States—for anyone concerned with moral distinctions in the different types of government—blurred the difference between fascism and democracy."

The Atomic Bomb and the Drive for American Hegemony

Prior to World War II, it would have been taken for granted that any civilized society could use a weapon such as the atomic bomb only under the most desperate conditions. The idea that such a weapon could be used against a civilian population would have been considered incomprehensible unless done by a society thoroughly debased and morally corrupted. And yet the United States has the singular distinction of being the only country ever to use an atomic bomb. Moreover, it used it not out of military necessity, but for political and strategic reasons, above all, as a tool in its conflict with the Soviet Union. To understand the broader interests involved, it is necessary to place the events of August 6 and August 9, 1945 in their historical context.

By early 1945, the war in Europe, begun in 1939, was coming to an end, though Germany's final surrender did not take place until May. The turning point of the war had been the German defeat at the Battle of Stalingrad in February 1943, followed by the American-British invasion of Europe in the spring of 1944.

While the Soviet Union was allied with the United States and Britain, there were enormous divisions within the Allied camp. In spite of the Stalinist degeneration of the USSR, the Soviet bureaucracy still based itself on the property relations established in the October revolution of 1917. And in spite of Stalin's best efforts to accommodate the imperialist powers, neither the British nor the American ruling elite ever reconciled themselves to the existence of these property relations.

But at the time, the United States and Britain required the help of the Soviet Union in the war against both Germany and Japan. The leading role of the Red Army in defeating Germany meant that the other powers were forced to grant it concessions, particularly in Eastern Europe. At the conference at Yalta in February 1945, the "Big Three" essentially agreed to the division of Europe between them, including the joint control of Germany. Moreover, the administration of US President Franklin Delano Roosevelt felt that it was critical to gain Soviet participation in the war against Japan in order to bring it to a quick conclusion. Since 1941, the Soviet Union and Japan had maintained what has been called a "strange neutrality": while the Soviet Union was at war with Japan's ally Germany and Japan was at war with the Soviet Union's ally the United States, the two countries had agreed to a neutrality pact in 1941, which stipulated that they not engage in war with each other.

At Yalta, in return for an agreement that the Soviet Union would join the war against Japan "in two or three months" after Germany's surrender, Roosevelt and Churchill accepted several territorial and commercial concessions, including Soviet control of much of Mongolia and several islands and ports near Japan that were considered crucial to Soviet interests.

By the spring of 1945, the Truman administration—Roosevelt died on April 12— was looking to the possession of the atomic bomb as a way to alter the equation and shift the balance of forces toward the US. In his diary of May 14, 1945, Secretary of War Stimson reported a conversation with General George Marshall, the President's chief of staff, in which Stimson warned against getting in a confrontation with the Soviet Union before possession of the atom bomb was certain. Stimson writes that he told Marshall "that my own opinion was that the time now and the method now to deal with Russia was to keep our mouths shut and let our actions speak for words . . . It is a case where we have got to regain the lead and perhaps do it in a pretty rough and realistic way. They have rather taken it away from us because we have talked too much and have been too lavish with our beneficences to them. I told him this was a place where we really held all the cards. I called it a royal straight flush and we mustn't be a fool about the way we play it. They can't get along without our help and industries and we have coming into action a weapon which will be unique."

The next day, Stimson expressed concerns that an upcoming meeting between Truman, Stalin and Churchill at Potsdam would take place before the first atomic test. "It may be necessary," Stimson wrote, "to have it out with Russia on her relations to Manchuria and Port Arthur and various other parts of North China, and also the relations of China to us. Over any such tangled wave of problems the S-1 [code name for atomic bomb] secret would be dominant and yet we will not know until after that time probably, until after that meeting, whether this is a weapon in our hands or not. We think it will be shortly afterwards, but it seems a terrible thing to gamble with such big stakes in diplomacy without having your master card in your hand."

In the end, Truman had the Potsdam conference postponed for several weeks in order to give the Manhattan Project more time. On May 21, Joseph Davies, the former ambassador to the Soviet Union, reported on a meeting with Truman in which Truman said he "did not want to meet [at Potsdam] until July. He had his budget (*) on his hands. The test was set for June, but had been postponed until July." At the bottom of the page, Davies added later an explanation of what he meant by "budget": "Footnote (*): the atomic bomb. He told me then of the atomic bomb experiment in Nevada. Charged me with the utmost secrecy."

Thus officials in the Truman administration quite consciously saw the atomic bomb as the "master card" in its dealings with the Soviet Union. Because of uncertainty that the test would succeed, Truman went to Potsdam with his Secretary of State James Byrnes with the aim of again gaining a promise from the Soviet Union that it would enter the war against Japan. Truman wrote in his diary, "If the test [of the atomic bomb] should fail, then it would be even more important to us to bring about a surrender [through a Soviet invasion] before we had to make a physical conquest of Japan."

The successful test of the atom bomb on July 16, shortly before the formal opening of the Potsdam Conference, gave Truman what he later called "a hammer on those boys." Truman's demeanor at Potsdam completely changed, and he became much more aggressive and arrogant in negotiations with Stalin. During the initial days of the Potsdam Conference, Truman was still seeking to get assurance from the Soviet Union that it would join the war with Japan. However over the next several weeks, it is clear that administration officials hoped that use of the bomb would bring a quick end to the war before the Soviet invasion progressed very far and before Japan made a separate deal with Stalin.

This was certainly the position of Secretary of State Byrnes. Responding to a statement by Secretary of Navy James Forrestal that Truman had said "his principal objective at Potsdam would be to get Russia in the war," Byrnes declared that "it was most probable that the President's views changed; certainly that was not my view."

Truman and Byrnes became worried that Japan would try to reach a deal with the Soviet Union and sue for peace through the Sovie Union rather than through a neutral power or through the United States. These concerns were amplified by communications from Japan that were intercepted by the Americans. For example, the diplomatic summary of one intercepted Japanese message notes, "On 11 July [Japanese] Foreign Minister Togo sent the following 'extremely urgent' message to Ambassador [to the Soviet Union] Sato: "We are now secretly giving consideration to the termination of the war because of the pressing situation which confronts Japan both at home and abroad. Therefore, when you have your interview with [Soviet Foreign Minister] Molotov in accordance with previous instructions you should not confine yourself to the objective of a rapprochement between Russia and Japan but should also sound him out on the extent to which it is possible to make use of Russia in ending the war." The message went on to indicate that Japan was willing to give large concessions to Russia in order to prevent a Russian invasion. At this point Japan still hoped that it could forestall a Soviet invasion.

A significant July 24 diary entry of Walter Brown, assistant to Secretary of State James

Byrnes, records that, "JFB [Byrnes] still hoping for time, believing after atomic bomb Japan will surrender and Russia will not get in so much on the kill, thereby being in a position to press for claims against China." Later, on August 3, three days before Hiroshima, Brown writes, "Aboard Agusta/President, Leahy, JFB [Byrnes] agrred [sic] Japas [sic] looking for peace . . . President afraid they will sue for peace through Russia instead of some country like Sweden."

What these and other documents make clear is that not only were American leaders concerned that the war would end in a way favorable to the Soviet Union, but also that they knew Japan was very close to suing for peace. In his book *The Decision to Use the Atom Bomb*, Gar Alperovitz makes a convincing case for a "two-step" theory of Japanese surrender. According to Alperovitz, the combination of the Soviet invasion, which eventually took place on August 8, and a guarantee to the Japanese state that the position of the emperor would not be threatened, would have put an end to the war without an invasion and without the use of the atom bomb.

This indeed was the conclusion of a Joint Intelligence Committee report to the Joint Chiefs of Staff on April 29, 1945: "The increasing effects of air-sea blockade, the progressive and cumulative devastation wrought by strategic bombing, and the collapse of Germany (with its implications regarding redeployment) should make this realization [that absolute defeat is inevitable] widespread within the year . . . The entry of the USSR into the war, would, together with the foregoing factors, convince most Japanese at once of the inevitability of complete defeat . . . If . . . the Japanese people, as well as their leaders, were persuaded both that absolute defeat was inevitable and that unconditional surrender did not imply national annihilation [that is, the removal of the emperor], surrender might follow fairly quickly."

Under the direction of Byrnes, the Potsdam Proclamation—an ultimatum to Japan demanding unconditional surrender—was worded in such a way that the guarantee to the emperor was not given. Moreover the US and Britain decided not to invite the Soviet Union to sign the proclamation. On the one hand, this made it clear that the US and Britain were taking their own route to a Japanese surrender. On the other hand, it made the threat of a Soviet invasion ambiguous, thus sustaining Japanese hopes of an eventual Soviet mediation. This made Japanese rejection of the proclamation a certainty, opening the way for the use of the bomb.

Furthermore, the invasion of Japan by American troops was scheduled for November. If the American government used the bomb primarily to avoid the necessity of an invasion, it is impossible to explain why Truman did not wait longer before making the decision, particularly given the mountain of intelligence indicating the desperate position of Japan at the time.

Another question that emerges is why the second bomb was dropped so quickly, before the Japanese had a chance to understand what had happened in Hiroshima and to respond. Again, the question of the Soviet invasion is central. The bombing of Nagasaki occurred one day after this invasion began. Moreover, Alperovitz notes, "Truman declared that Rumania, Bulgaria, and Hungary were 'not to be spheres of influence of any one power' on August 9—the day of the Nagasaki bombing."

Bound up with the immediate interests of the United States in curtailing Soviet influence in Eastern Europe and East Asia was the general aim of the Truman administration to establish America's hegemonic position following the end of the war. Historian Thomas McCormick summed it up well when he wrote, "In two blinding glares—a horrible end to a war waged horribly by all parties—the United States finally found the combination that would unlock the door to American hegemony."

To achieve this hegemonic aim, it was necessary to sacrifice the cities of Hiroshima and Nagasaki. McCormick notes, "A prearranged demonstration of the atomic bomb on a non-inhabited target, as some scientists had recommended, would not do. That could demonstrate the power of the bomb, but it could not demonstrate the American will to use the awful power. One reason, therefore, for American unwillingness to pursue Japanese peace feelers in mid-summer 1945 was that the United States did not want the war to end before it had had a chance to use the atomic bomb."

There is a certain naïveté on the part of the American people with regard to the utter ruthlessness of the American ruling class, particularly in relation to the Second World War. That war has long been presented by the American media and political establishment as a great war for democracy, against fascism and tyranny. In fact, the principal reason that the United States entered the war—and the underlying motivation behind all its actions in prosecuting the war—was to establish itself as the dominant and unchallenged world power. In pursuit of this aim the lives of hundreds of thousands of Japanese were of little consequence.

AMERICAN MILITARISM AND THE NUCLEAR THREAT TODAY

The decision by the administration of President Harry Truman to use atomic weapons against Japan was motivated by political and strategic considerations. Above all, the use of the bomb was meant to establish the undisputed hegemonic position of the United States in the post-war period.

These motivations were also the basic driving force behind the American intervention in the war itself. The Second World War has long been presented to the American people

as a "Good War," a war for democracy against fascism and tyranny. While it was no doubt true that millions of Americans saw the war in terms of a fight against Hitlerite fascism and Japanese militarism, the aims of those who led them to war were altogether different. The American ruling class entered the Second World War in order to secure its global interests. While the political character of the bourgeois democratic regime in the United States was vastly different than that of its fascist adversaries, the nature of the war aims of the United States were no less imperialistic. In the final analysis, the utter ruthlessness with which the United States sought to secure its objectives—including the use of the atomic bomb—flowed from this essential fact.

The American government hoped that by using the bomb it would shift the balance of forces in its growing conflict with the Soviet Union. However, the American monopoly of the bomb was short-lived. The Soviet Union responded to the bombing of Hiroshima on August 6, 1945 by rapidly increasing the amount of resources devoted to its own atomic bomb project. In 1949, the Soviet Union carried out its first atomic weapon test.

Sections of the US ruling elite and military establishment still hoped that they might be able to use the bomb in actual military situations. In 1950, Truman threatened to use nuclear weapons against the Chinese during the Korean War, and General Douglas McArthur urged the government to authorize the military to drop a number of bombs along the Korean border with Manchuria. These proposals were eventually rejected for fear that the use of the bomb might provoke a nuclear exchange with the Soviet Union.

With the development of the much more powerful hydrogen bomb, first tested in late 1952, the US hoped to renew its nuclear advantage. The Republican Eisenhower administration came into office in 1953 pledging a more aggressive policy against the

Soviet Union, including the "rollback" of Soviet control over Eastern Europe. In January 1954, Secretary of State John Foster Dulles gave a speech in which he stated that the US would "deter aggression" by depending "primarily upon a great capacity to retaliate, instantly, by means and at places of our own choosing." This pledge of "massive retaliation" was generally interpreted as a threat to use nuclear weapons in response to a local war such as the Korean War or the war that later developed in Vietnam.

However, this nuclear advantage was again eliminated in August 1953, when the USSR tested its first hydrogen bomb. The two countries rapidly developed a capacity that created conditions of "mutually assured destruction" in the event of a nuclear war.

Throughout this period and the following decades, a battle raged within the political establishment over policy in relation to the Soviet Union and the atom bomb. Even with the threat of nuclear war, there continued to exist a substantial section of the American ruling class that was unwilling to tolerate any constraints on American military power.

The option of engaging in nuclear war was never off the table for any post-Hiroshima/Nagasaki administration, Democratic or Republican. What Truman's Secretary of War Henry Stimson called the "master card" was always there in the background ready to be pulled out if need be. In 1962, the Kennedy administration nearly initiated a nuclear war with the Soviet Union over the Cuban missile crisis.

As the economic situation deteriorated in the 1970s, those who advocated a more aggressive orientation toward the Soviet Union began to gain in prominence. This started under the Democratic Party administration of Jimmy Carter and received a boost during the Reagan administration in the 1980s. Reagan oversaw a renewed arms buildup and also sought to gain an offensive

nuclear superiority by developing a defensive missile shield (the so-called "Star Wars" program), something that the Anti-Ballistic Missile (ABM) Treaty of 1972 had been designed to prevent. A successful defensive shield would allow the US to strike with nuclear weapons first, since it could shoot down any retaliatory action.

Since the self-destruction of the Soviet Union in 1991, the American ruling class has reached a new consensus based upon pre-emptive war and the unilateral assertion of American interests through military force.

Fewer Treaties, More Bombs

The post-Soviet eruption of American militarism has assumed an especially malignant form during the presidency of George W. Bush. Since coming into power, the Bush administration has developed a two-pronged strategy to expand American military capacity. On the one hand, it has rejected or undermined any international agreement or treaty that places boundaries on what the United States can or cannot do militarily. On the other hand, it has taken steps to develop its military technology, including its nuclear technology, to prepare the way for the use of this technology in future wars.

In 1999, the Republican-dominated US Senate went out of its way to reject the Comprehensive Test Ban Treaty (CTBT), which had previously been signed by the Clinton administration. In 2001, Bush announced that he would not seek Senate approval again, and instead would look for a way to "bury" the treaty. The treaty would ban the testing of new nuclear weapons, which the Bush administration opposes because it is planning on developing new nuclear weapons that it will need to test.

In December 2001, Bush announced that the US would unilaterally withdraw from the ABM Treaty in order to allow it to renew the "Star Wars" project, now called National Missile Defense. The development of a NMD system is still a priority of the administration, and is part of its drive to achieve military domination of space. Like the Reagan administration program, a missile defense system would open up the way for offensive nuclear strikes against countries such as China or Russia.

During an international review of the Nuclear Non-Proliferation Treaty (NPT) earlier this year, the Bush administration announced a position that was aimed at undermining the foundation of the agreement. In exchange for a promise not to acquire nuclear weapons, the treaty guarantees non-nuclear powers the right to develop non-military nuclear technology. The treaty also includes a pledge from the nuclear powers to gradually eliminate their nuclear stockpiles. The new Bush administration position, however, is to deny states that the US determines to be "rogue states," such as Iran, the right to develop nuclear energy programs. At the same time, far from eliminating its own nuclear stockpiles, the US has taken steps to modernize its existing weapons and develop new weapons for offensive use. Indeed, in the run-up to the conference, which ended without an agreement, the Bush administration explicitly insisted on its right to use nuclear weapons against a non-nuclear power.

Over the past decade, the US government has developed a policy of offensive nuclear weapon use, rejecting the Cold War conception that nuclear weapons would be intended primarily as a deterrent. A Nuclear Posture Review in 1997 during the Clinton administration reportedly took the first steps toward targeting countries such as North Korea, China and Iran.

This policy was made explicit in another review, leaked to the press in 2002, in which the Pentagon announced that "the old process [of nuclear arms control] is incompatible with the flexibility US planning and forces now require." It explicitly threatened a host of countries by targeting them for potential nuclear attack. It also provided very general guidelines for the future use of nuclear

weapons, declaring that these weapons may be used "against targets able to withstand nonnuclear attack" or "in the event of surprising military developments."

Last summer, Defense Secretary Donald Rumsfeld issued an "Interim Global Strike Order" that reportedly includes a first strike nuclear option against a country such as Iran or North Korea. There were also nuclear weapons options in the planning guidelines for the wars in Iraq and Afghanistan.

The Bush administration has taken steps toward the development of new "bunker-busting" nuclear weapons specifically designed for use in combat situations. Existing stockpiles have been modernized, and according to a *New York Times* article from February 7, 2005, "American scientists have begun designing a new generation of nuclear arms meant to be sturdier and more reliable and to have longer lives" than the old weapon stockpiles.

The US repeatedly issues threats against countries over their alleged development of nuclear weapons and other "weapons of mass destruction." The most recent target has been Iran, which the US has threatened with military attack if it does not abandon its nuclear energy program. All these threats are meant to justify future US invasions, in which the use of nuclear weapons by the United States is by no means excluded.

Through the policy of preemptive war, the US has arrogated for itself the right to attack any country that it deems to be a threat, or declares might be a threat sometime in the future. There is no part of the world in which the United States does not have an interest. It has sought to progressively expand its influence in Central Asia and the former Soviet Union through the war in Afghanistan and political intervention in countries such as Ukraine. It is seeking to dominate the Middle East through the war in Iraq and the threat of war in Iran. It is expanding its activities in Africa and has made repeated threats against North Korea and China as part of its efforts to secure its influence in East Asia.

Under these conditions, there are innumerable potential scenarios in which a war will erupt leading to the use of nuclear weapons. This includes not only invasions of countries such as Iran; an American war against a smaller power could easily spark a broader conflict—with China, Russia or even the powers of Europe, all of which have nuclear weapons themselves.

The catastrophe that befell Hiroshima and Nagasaki will never be forgotten. Their fate will stand forever as testimony to the bestiality of imperialism. Against the backdrop of the renewed eruption of American militarism, the events of August 1945 remind us of the alternatives that confront mankind—world revolution or world war, socialism or barbarism.

STUDY QUESTION

How does Joseph Kay debunk the official justification of why the United States dropped atomic bombs on Hiroshima and Nagasaki?

CHAPTER 7

Inequality in the Health and Medicine Institution

INTRODUCTION

The institution of health and medicine perpetuates social inequality in the United States by rationing health care according to a person's ability to pay, by providing inadequate and inferior health care to poor people and persons of color, and by failing to establish structures that can meet the health needs of Americans. The health care industry manifests inequality with its enormous costs of health care in the United States, the large numbers of uninsured Americans, institutional neglect of women's health issues, medical experimentation and forced sterilization of women of color, the AIDS epidemic in the United States, and criminalization of the mentally ill.

Many commentators expressed uneasiness at Senator John Kerry selecting Senator John Edwards as the vice-presidential running mate in 2004 presidential election because Edwards was a medical malpractice plaintiff's attorney who had earned millions of dollars in damage awards to injured clients: one case involved a $25 million products liability verdict for a five-year-old girl who survived disembowelment after being suctioned by a wading pool's defective drain manufacturer.[1] Essentially, Edwards epitomized wealthy attorneys responsible for significant increases in medical malpractice insurance premiums and fostering President George Bush's claim that limiting damages in medical malpractice suits would drastically cut health care costs for Americans because such limits would lower medical malpractice insurance premiums.[2] Considerable evidence shows that medical malpractice awards have little effect on the overall cost of health care in the United States; medical malpractice insurance costs accounts for less than 2 percent of all spending on health care in the United States. Many states have declared so-called tort reforms to limiting medical malpractice awards unconstitutional, finding that such reforms have no demonstrable effect on health care costs.[3] A recent report by the Center for Justice and Democracy found that in the face of an economic downturn, skyrocketing medical costs, and increased premiums of nearly 60 percent, the health insurance industry has enjoyed ever-increasing profits over the last four years and the average salary of its executives have increased annually by $3 million.[4] In *Debunking Medical Malpractice Myths: Unraveling the False Premises Behind "Tort Reform,"* the director for the Center for Justice and Democracy, Geoff Boehm, attempts to demystify the complex and often false issues surrounding medical malpractice and tort reform in the United States. Moreover, Boehm claims that nearly 200,000 avoidable deaths in hospitals attest to the crisis in accountability in medical professions.

HEALTH CARE AND PERSONS OF COLOR

In *Racial Profiling in Health Care: An Institutional Analysis of Medical Treatment Disparities*, René Bowser claims that the U.S. medical establishment engages in racial profiling, causing countless unnecessary losses of lives, particularly among black Americans. One analysis on the issue suggests that more than 886,000 deaths could be prevented if African Americans received the same care as whites.[5] Recently published studies on Medicare patients reveal that significant racial gaps in access to adequate health care in the United States persists, with black persons receiving far fewer operations, tests, medications, and other treatments than whites. As a result, blacks are more likely to suffer the burdens of illness and death. According to one researcher, "these persistent disparities are saying that systematically, based on an individual's skin color, Americans are still treated very differently by our health care system."[6] One of the most striking health disparities in the United States is the infant mortality rate (the number of infant deaths per a thousand live births). The infant mortality rate is an important measure of the state of health of a people because it is directly related to poverty; that is, people living in poverty have high infant mortality rates primarily because poor persons have less access to adequate prenatal and postnatal health care to ensure infant survivability. Persons living in poverty commonly suffer health-related problems unduly when compared to more affluent persons. Government reports on health in the United States reveal that the black infant mortality rate is more than *twice* that of whites, the infant mortality rate for Latinos and Asian Americans falls below that of whites, and the infant mortality rate for American Indians is somewhat higher than that of whites.[7] Black men and women also have lower life expectancies than white men and women. The difference in life expectancy between white men and black men in the United States is 6.3 years with white men having a life expectancy of 75.1 years and black men a life expectancy of 68.8 years. The life expectancy of white women is 80.3 years, and the life expectancy of black women is 75.6 years.[8] The life expectancy of American Indians is further below that of black Americans.[9] Contracting diabetes for American Indians is *three to five times higher* than the rest of the American population, and it is twice as high for Latinos than in the major population. But Latinos account for 20 percent of new tuberculosis cases, and Vietnamese women suffer cervical cancer at nearly *five times* the rate for white women.

WOMEN'S HEALTH ISSUES

Women's health issues in the United States suffer serious neglect. In *Medical Gender Bias and Managed Care*, Vicki Lawrence MacDougall explains that medical gender bias permeates every aspect of the practice of medicine, including medical education, research, diagnosis and treatment decisions, and the administration and effectiveness of pharmaceuticals. Gender bias is particularly pervasive in the treatment of AIDS; heart, lung, and kidney disease; and mental health. Important too are the controversies that continue to plague the health and medicine community surrounding the toxicity of silicone breast implants, the high rate at which physicians perform hysterectomies on women, and the exceptionally high frequency with which physicians perform cesarean sections during childbirth. These controversies seriously affect American women's trust in the federal government and the health care industry to ensure safe medicines and medical procedures. In 1992, for example, the FDA announced a prohibition on any further silicone breast implant surgeries. Despite its own scientific research of a cancer risk to patients with silicone implants, the FDA's ban failed to reveal that risk to 2 million women who had the surgical implants beginning in the early 1980s. Even more astounding is that the American Society of Plastic and Reconstructive Surgery, the American College of Radiology, and the American Medical Association adamantly opposed the government's ban on silicone implants. Dow Corning and Bristol-Myers Squibb corporations had *secret* evidence of the carcinogenicity of silicone implants since the early 1960s, yet they still marketed the implants with assurances of safety. It was only after these pharmaceutical companies manufactured the implants and surgeons had put the implants into patients that the industry admitted there was a cancer risk to patients.

Norplant is no longer available to women as a contraception device, yet scholars argue that the Norplant *crisis* continues to be at the forefront of women's health issues because the product still poses significant dangers to women's reproductive health and freedom.[10] Norplant was an effective contraception that consisted of matchstick-size capsules that released progestin inserted into women's upper arms. Soon after the FDA approved Norplant in 1991, however, several state legislatures considered measures coercing mostly low-income women and women of color convicted of child abuse or drug abuse during pregnancy to use Norplant or serve jail time. Other states considered requiring women receiving public assistance to either use Norplant or lose their benefits. Yet no state governments proposed limiting men's eligibility for social welfare programs or lessening their criminal liability by undergoing vasectomies or using birth control.[11] Gendered racism underscored attempts to coerce low-income women to use Norplant, which is why scholars fear that any newly invented contraception will spark similar social engineering reforms directed toward the underprivileged in U.S. society.

Women of color have limited access to the country's health care industry. Many women of color cannot afford health care services, and few have health insurance. Poor women often have no transportation to health care providers, and still others have language difficulties and cultural differences that keep them from seeking health care services. Without health insurance, many women delay seeking medical treatment, thus worsening their conditions. The American College of Physicians-American Society of Internal Medicine contends that physicians often diagnose women without health insurance at later stages for breast cancer and cervical cancer and observe worse problems from cardiovascular disease and other health problems. Poor women without insurance often forgo mammograms, Pap tests, medicines, and surgery, and pregnant women without insurance are less likely to have prenatal care.[12]

Hysterectomies (removal of the uterus or womb) and castration (removal of all sexual and hormone-producing organs) are the second most frequently performed surgery on women in the United States, with more than 600,000 women undergoing the procedure every year—a rate *five times* higher than in Europe. Often the side effects of the surgery leave women with severe anxiety and depression, weight gain, sexual dysfunctions, and irritability.[13] One reason for so many hysterectomies and castrations is that gynecologists, hospitals, and drug companies earn more than $8 billion a year performing these surgical procedures. Some claim that hysterectomies are routinely recommended for women with various gynecological problems because physicians not only gain financially for performing the procedures, but often they believe the uterus serves no purpose for women past childbearing age and rarely seek alternatives to the procedure.[14] Many physicians perform "radical hysterectomies" believing "that women neither need nor want to have sex beyond a certain age." But physicians go to great lengths "to ensure that a man's sexual integrity remains unscathed in prostate surgeries."[15] One estimate finds that 98 percent of women referred to board-certified gynecologists after discovering they needed hysterectomies actually did not need the procedure when reexamined.[16] Physicians perform 74 percent of hysterectomies on women between the ages of 30 and 54, and by age 65 more than 37 percent of all women in the United States have endured a hysterectomy.

EUGENICS (*GOOD BREEDING*) AND MINORITY STATUS

Most Americans associate human subject medical experimentation with the Nazis during World War II when German physicians experimented mostly on concentration camp prisoners. Among other horrifying conduct, the experiments included "deadly studies and tortures such as injecting people with gasoline and live viruses, immersing people in ice water, and forcing people to ingest poisons."[17] The War Crimes Tribunal at Nuremberg prosecuted the physicians and summarily denied defense arguments of *medical justification* to the "systematic torture, mutilation, and killing of prisoners in experiments." Determining the physicians guilty of "crimes against humanity," the tribunal sentenced several of them to extended prison terms and others to death.[18] Unknown to most Americans is that the U.S. government sanctioned atrocities committed against its own citizens by American physicians long before the Nazis' eugenics program. In fact, Hitler's thinking on eugenics was inspired by the human experimentation practices in the United States.[19]

The eugenics movement began early in U.S. history when most antebellum southern states authorized white slaveholders to castrate slaves as punishment for sexual relations with white women.[20] White slavers often punished slave women for not becoming pregnant and regularly raped slave women to make them pregnant.[21] Female slaves suffered cruel medical experimentation by white physicians who practiced new surgical techniques on enslaved black women, usually without anesthesia, before performing the same procedures on white women. One of the more notorious practitioners was James Marion Sims, who purchased slave women to perfect gynecological surgery.[22] Sims was a plantation physician who experimented on female slaves mostly inflicted with vesicovaginal fistulas, a condition arising during childbirth that involves tears from the vagina to the bladder. In 1845 owners of the Westcott plantation summoned Sims because a young slave woman named Anarcha had been in labor for three days without delivering. Given the prolonged delivery, Anarcha sustained several fistulas that Sims attempted to correct surgically without anesthesia even though it had recently become available. Some argue that Sims may not have known that anesthesia was available at the time, but this is doubtful because Sims used anesthesia on white women undergoing the same surgery. Others explain that Sims believed that, unlike white women, African women had a physiological tolerance to pain. Sims operated on Anarcha more than *thirty times* without anesthesia when postoperative infections frustrated the surgeries. Sims successfully repaired the fistulas after using silver sutures that resisted infection. Sims operated on at least ten other slave women over several years perfecting the surgical technique. He performed surgery on another slave woman named Lucy without anesthesia who almost died from postoperative blood poisoning. Other white physicians commonly used dead slaves for autopsies and stole slaves from graves when cadavers were unavailable.[23]

In the early twentieth century, advocates of the eugenics movement supported sterilizing mentally retarded persons, regarding them as "threatening, dangerous, and a source of criminal conduct or immoral behavior."[24] The U.S. Supreme Court defended eugenics when it supported the involuntary sterilization of Carrie Buck in 1927. In *Buck v. Bell*, the Court ruled constitutional a lower court's sterilization order of Carrie Buck, an unmarried eighteen-year-old girl who officials institutionalized after she became pregnant after a rape. In the decision against Buck, the Supreme Court effectively legitimated compulsory sterilization of "mental incompetent" persons. Justice Oliver Wendell Holmes, an ardent advocate of eugenics, in writing for the Court's majority in *Buck* said that "it is better for all the world, if instead of waiting to execute degenerate offspring for crime, or to let them starve for their imbecility, society can prevent those who are manifestly unfit from continuing their kind."[25] Justice Holmes claimed that since Carrie's mother, Carrie, and Carrie's infant daughter were mentally retarded that "[t]hree generations of imbeciles are enough." Not until 1942, in *Skinner v. Oklahoma ex rel. Williamson*, did the U.S. Supreme Court recognize a person's fundamental right to procreate when it rejected Oklahoma's Habitual Criminal Sterilization Act forcing a habitual criminal to undergo a vasectomy. Still, in *Eugenics and Compulsory Sterilization Laws*, Michael G. Silver explains that even though many states have repealed sterilization laws and many courts have criticized *Buck*, the U.S. Supreme Court has yet to overrule *Buck,* and the lower courts continue to find the involuntary sterilization constitutional.

The Tuskegee Syphilis Study epitomizes the powerlessness of marginalized groups to medical experimentation in the United States. In an experiment lasting from 1932 to 1972 in Macon County, Alabama, physicians with the U.S. Public Health Services deceived six hundred indigent and illiterate black men, mostly poor sharecroppers, into believing that they were receiving adequate and proper medical attention for congenital syphilis.[26] Although the medical establishment understood the complications of congenital syphilis in white people, physicians believed that blacks responded differently to the disease. Thus two major reasons explain why the study was conducted in Macon County. First, there was an above-average percentage of blacks in Macon County infected with congenital syphilis, and second, white physicians found southern blacks easily influenced given their dire impoverishment and ignorance. Public health officials recruited the men without informed consent and outright lied to the men about the medical procedures performed on them.[27] Researchers conducting the experiment had intentionally left the disease untreated, despite the availability of penicillin as an effective therapy, so they could observe the natural progression of the disease on blacks. The national press and medical journals published accounts of the experiment resulting in public indignation and appointment of an advisory panel by the Department of Health, Education and Welfare to ensure prohibitions against medical experimentation. In an effort to redress the Tuskegee Syphilis Study, President Bill Clinton issued a formal apology to the surviving participants of the experiment. But despite the righteous rhetoric of political leaders registering their official remorse for human experimentation and forced sterilization of black people in the United States, it is precisely this type of unconscionable medical racism that, according to law professor scholars, explains why black people distrust the medical establishment even today.

Still, at the height of the eugenics movement some thirty state legislatures enacted compulsory sterilization laws resulting in the forced sterilization of some seventy thousand persons ostensibly feebleminded. More than 60 percent of those sterilized in North Carolina were black, virtually all girls and women. To lower black birthrates, many southern states funded birth control clinics in the 1930s. As late as the 1970s, white physicians regularly made their consent to sterilization a condition for the delivering of babies and the performing of abortions for black women. One survey found that white physicians in teaching hospitals forced medical treatment on poor pregnant black women receiving public assistance.[28] In 1974 an Alabama federal district court discovered that federally funded state programs in Alabama had forced the sterilization of 100,000 to 150,000 poor women annually as a condition of maintaining their public assistance. The U.S. government allowed states to use federal funds for this eugenic sterilization of children until 1978. In fact, more than 300 of the 16,000 women and 8,000 men sterilized using federal government funds were under the age of twenty-one.

The U.S. medical establishment continues to put mostly poor people and persons of color at risk of medical experimentation and forced sterilization.[29] One commentator explains,

> In the past, it was illiterate black men in the South, poor Mexican-American women, orphans and the mentally retarded. Today it might be prisoners, children with incurable diseases, central city toddlers, people with certain gene profiles . . . maybe even people on Medicare. What they have in common is vulnerability, and a need for protection from medical research that could intentionally or unintentionally exploit that vulnerability.[30]

Compulsory sterilization laws remain in effect in seven states, including Arkansas, Delaware, Georgia, Idaho, Mississippi, Vermont, and Virginia. In Arkansas, for example, a state statute allows guardians of persons with mental retardation, mental illness, or other mental incapacity to solicit sterilization petitions. Mississippi law allows for involuntary sterilization of those with "hereditary forms of insanity." In California, the eugenics program was purposely "designed to strengthen the Aryan gene pool," and forced sterilization kept many Mexican and Asian immigrant women and other women of color from having families. In 1977 ten Mexican American women sued a Los Angeles County hospital for attempting to obtain their consent in English to sterilization while the women, who did not speak English, were in labor. Virginia performed more than 2,000 sterilizations, and Oregon forcibly sterilized 2,600 people. California eugenically sterilized more than 20,000 people. One survey found that physicians in Maryland screened 13,000 black women for sickle-cell anemia in 1984 without their consent or counseling.[31]

Indigent patients, poor pregnant women, and mentally retarded children were unwilling subjects of radiation experiments conducted under the auspices of the U.S. government over a thirty-year period from the 1940s to 1970s.[32] Some 400,000 children underwent nasal irradiation therapy for problems with hearing loss during this period.[33] Infant children with Down syndrome were among nine thousand human subjects of radiation experiments conducted by the federal government in this period. Using patients from charity hospitals for black adults and children, researchers conducted radiation experiments in which investigators burned poor whites and blacks on the arms to determine whether blacks suffered more intense burns than did whites after the same levels of exposure. Researchers concluded that blacks are more susceptible than are whites to radiation burning in the case of a nuclear event. Researchers also injected 460 blacks and 770 white patients with a radioactive substance (phosphorus 32) to determine its therapeutic effect on burn patients. In both cases, investigators did not have written or informed consent from the patients. Similarly, as many as three thousand American Indian women per year suffered forced sterilization in Bureau of Indian Affairs health clinics throughout the 1970s and 1980s; accounting for the sterilization of more than 42 percent of American Indian women of childbearing age.[34] Researchers have deliberately infected institutionalized mentally disabled children with isolated strains of hepatitis to develop vaccines. The federal government deliberately destroyed a nuclear-powered rocket over Los Angeles in 1965 to monitor the effects of radiation—putting more than 6 million people at risk of contamination without their informed consent. And in the late 1980s, researchers did not notify parents that one of two measles vaccines given to infants in Los Angeles was experimental. The Center for Disease Control and Prevention (CDC) found developing countries had been using the vaccine and there was an increased death rate among female infants given the vaccine. Los Angeles was the first U.S. city where researchers had administered the drug mostly to black and Latino children.[35]

Medical experimentation continues.[36] A 1993 internal report of the U.S. Agency for International Development shows that the one goal of the U.S. population policy in Haiti is to keep the Haitian people from procreating.[37] The policy targets 200,000 people for conception. A "social marketing component" of the policy is to get 6,000 cycles of birth control pills per month and to establish sterilization facilities. The agency also suggests "the elimination of the practice of requiring physician visits"—thereby denying women access to pelvic examinations and Pap smears. One Haitian women's group in Brooklyn has pointed out that the U.S. government is coercing mostly impoverished Haitians with food and money to undergo sterilization. It markets vasectomies as "reversible" and an AIDS prevention device. They offer clothing to Haitian women who agree to use Norplant even though many women using the contraceptive device report related problems of bleeding, headaches, dizziness, nausea, radical weight loss, depression, and fatigue.[38] Interesting, pharmaceutical companies marketed Norplant to white women in the United States only after they had developed the contraceptive device for poor black women in developing societies.[39]

Even with the hundreds of thousands of Americans subjected to the atrocities of medical experimentation, Congress and the federal courts have done precious little to protect innocent victims. Take the case of James B. Stanley, a master sergeant in the U.S. Army stationed at Fort Knox, Kentucky, who had volunteered in February 1958 to participate in a program ostensibly designed to test the effectiveness of protective clothing and equipment as defenses against chemical warfare. During the testing, military researchers secretly administered LSD to Stanley to study the effects of the drug on human subjects. Stanley suffered hallucinations, incoherence and memory loss, and often he would "awake from sleep at night and, without reason, violently beat his wife and children, later being unable to recall the entire incident." The army discharged Stanley in 1969 and his marriage dissolved shortly thereafter because of the personality changes. In December 1975 Stanley received a letter from the army requesting his cooperation in a study of the long-term effects of LSD on "volunteers who participated" in the 1958 tests. This was the first time the government had notified Stanley of the experiment in which researchers had given him LSD during his time in Maryland. Stanley filed suit under the Federal Tort Claims Act, alleging negligence in the administration, supervision, and subsequent monitoring of the drug-testing program. The U.S. Supreme Court heard Stanley's claim in 1987 but dismissed the case, holding that Stanley was a service member at the time of the experiment and thus could not sue the federal government.[40]

Similarly, military authorities forced American soldiers who participated in the 1990 Gulf War in Iraq to take experimental vaccines. Interesting, federal law prohibits American soldiers from refusing to participate in government medical experiments.[41] Prisoners have also been susceptible to medical experimentation. Between 1963 and 1971 researchers injected radioactive thymidine into the testicles of more than a hundred prisoners at the Oregon State Penitentiary to determine the rate of sperm production when exposed to steroidal hormones. During this same period, researchers subjected state prisoners throughout Alabama to flawed blood-plasma trials. Also during this period, researchers at the California Medical Facility paralyzed sixty-four prisoners with a neuromuscular compound (succinylcholine). Authorities permitted researchers to inject against their will several of the prisoners who refused to participate in the experiment. In 1962 a researcher with New York's Sloan-Kettering Institute for Cancer Research injected nearly four hundred inmates at Ohio State Prison—half of whom were black inmates—with live human cancer cells. That same researcher later injected twenty-two unwitting elderly hospital patients with cancer cells at Brooklyn's Jewish Chronic Disease Hospital. Researchers with the National Institutes of Health extracted blood samples from some seven thousand mostly young underprivileged black boys in Baltimore, Maryland, to screen boys for an extra "Y" chromosome that would predispose them to criminality—a still unproven theory.

The boys' parents had no knowledge nor did they consent to the experiment done on their children. Researchers conducted similar experiment on mostly black boys housed in Maryland state institutions for abandoned or delinquent youth.

ENDNOTES

1. Anthony J. Sebok, "Should Doctors Vote Against John Edwards?" *FindLaw's Writ* (July 26, 2004), http://www.writ.news.findlaw.com. See also *Lakey v. Sta-Rite Industries* (Wake Co. Superior Ct., NC, 1996).
2. See, for example, Mike Malin, "Edwards Should Own Up to His Slimy Work," *Kansas City Star*, August 7, 2004, p. A1; Emily Bazelon, "John Edwards: No Reason to Condemn All Class-Action Lawyers," *Miami Herald*, August 4, 2004, p. A1; William Tucker, "John Edwards and the Damsel in Distress," *The Weekly Standard*, July 29, 2004, http://www.weeklystandard.com/Content/Public/Articles/000/000/004/408jcffq.asp; Kate O'Beirne, "Kate's Take: Crossing Over," *The National Review Online* (February 5, 2004), http://www.nationalreview.com/.
3. Center for Justice and Democracy, *Tort Reforms Are Unconstitutional*, http://www.centerjd.org/free/mythbusters-free/MB_Unconstitutional.htm.
4. Center for Justice and Democracy, *2004 Was the Most Profitable Year Ever for the Insurance Industry* (July 8, 2005), http://www.centerjd.org/free/mythbusters-free/MB_InsProfits2004.htm#_edn1.
5. January W. Payne, "Dying for Basic Care," *Washington Post* (December 21, 2004), http://www.washingtonpost.com/wp-dyn/articles/A13690-2004Dec20.html
6. Rob Stein, "Race Gap Persists in Health Care, Three Studies Say," *Washington Post*, August 18, 2005, p. A01.
7. National Center for Health Statistics. *Health, United States, 2004 with Chartbook on Trends in the Health of Americans*. Hyattsville, MD (2004), http://www.cdc.gov/nchs/data/hus/hus04trend.pdf#exe.
8. Ibid.
9. D. Stanley Eitzen and Maxine Baca Zinn, *Social Problems* (Boston: Allyn & Bacon, 2004), p. 504.
10. Rachel Roth, "No New Babies?: Gender Inequality and Reproductive Control in the Criminal Justice and Prison Systems," *American University Journal of Gender, Social Policy and the Law*, 12 (2004): 391–425; Pamela D. Bridgewater, "Reproductive Freedom as Civil Freedom: The Thirteenth Amendment's Role in the Struggle for Reproductive Rights," *The Journal of Gender, Race and Justice*, 3 (2000): 401–425; Stacey L. Arthur, "The Norplant Prescription: Birth Control, Woman Control, or Crime Control?" *University of California, Los Angeles Law Review*, 40 (1992): 1–101.
11. American Civil Liberties Union, Reproductive Rights, *Norplant: A New Contraceptive with the Potential for Abuse* (January 31, 1994), http://www.aclu.org/ReproductiveRights/ReproductiveRights.cfm?ID=9053&c=225
12. U.S. Department of Health and Human Services, Office of Women's Health, *Minority Women's Health*, http://www.4woman.gov/minority/.
13. Elizabeth Payne, "Breaking the Silence: Putting the Brakes on the Epidemic of Unnecessary Hysterectomies," *Ottawa Citizen*, September 18, 2004, p. 12.
14. See also Lucinda M. Finley, "The Hidden Victims of Tort Reform: Women, Children, and the Elderly," *Emory Law Journal*, 53 (2004): 1263–1314.
15. Payne, "Breaking the Silence."
16. Hysterectomy Educational Resources and Services, "Hysterectomy Alternatives and Aftereffect: Facts About Hysterectomies," http://www.hersfoundation.com/facts.html.
17. Missouri Western State University, Committee on the Use of Human Subject in Research. *History of IRBs*, http://www.mwsc.edu/orgs/human_subs/policies/history.php.
18. Ibid. See also Naomi Schaefer, "The Legacy of Nazi Medicine," *The New Atlantic*, 5 (2004): 54–60.
19. Joe R. Feagin, Clairece B. Feagin, and David V. Baker, *Social Problems: A Critical Power-Conflict Perspective*, 6th ed. (Upper Saddle River, NJ: Prentice Hall, 2006), p. 276–277.
20. Kris W. Druhm, "Comment: A Welcome Return to Draconia: California Penal Law 645, The Castration of Sex Offenders and the Constitution," *Albany Law Review*, 61 (1997): 285–343; Barbara L. Bernier, "Class, Race, and Poverty: Medical Technologies and Socio-Political Choices," *Harvard Black Letter Journal*, 11 (1994): 115.
21. David V. Baker, "Systemic White Racism and the Brutalization of Executed Black Women in the United States," in R. Muraskin, ed., *It's a Crime: Women and Criminal Justice* (Upper Saddle River, NJ: Prentice Hall, 2006).

22. Barron H. Lerner, "Scholars Argue over Legacy of Surgeon Who Was Lionized, Then Vilified," *New York Times*, October 28, 2003, p. F7.

23. Dorothy E. Roberts, *Symposium: Representing Race: Unshackling Black Motherhood*, 95 MICH. L. REV. 938 (1997); see also Roberts, *supra* note 111; Randall, *supra* note 144; G. Barker-Benfield, *The Horrors of the Half-Known Life: Male Attitudes Toward Women and Sexuality in Nineteenth-Century America* (New York: Harper & Row, 1976); D. Axelsen, *Women as Victims of Medical Experimentation: J. Marion Sims' on Slave Women, 1845–1850*, 2 SAGE 10 (1985); B. Lerner, "Scholars Argue over Legacy of Surgeon Who Was Lionized, Then Vilified," *New York Times*, October 28, 2003, p. F7.

24. Lyn Entzeroth, "Putting the Mentally Retarded Criminal Defendant to Death: Charting the Development of a National Consensus to Exempt the Mentally Retarded from the Death Penalty," *Alabama Law Review*, 52 (2001): 911–941.

25. *Buck v. Bell*, 274 U.S. 200, 207 (1927). See also Christopher A. Bracey, "Louis Brandeis and the Race Question," *Alabama Law Review*, 52 (2001): 859–910; Mary L. Dudziak, "Oliver Wendell Holmes as a Eugenic Reformer: Rhetoric in the Writing of Constitutional Law," *Iowa Law Review*, 71 (1986): 833–867; Sheldon M. Novick, *Honorable Justice: The Life of Oliver Wendell Holmes* (Boston: Little, Brown, 1989).

26. See James H. Jones, *Bad Blood: The Tuskegee Syphilis Experiment* (New York: Free Press, 1981).

27. Ronald B. Standler, *Nonconsensual Medical Experiments on Human Beings* (1997), http://www.rbs2.com/humres.htm.

28. Nancy Ehrenreich, "The Colonization of the Womb," *Duke Law Journal*, 43 (1993): 492–587; Lisa C. Ikemoto, "Furthering the Inquiry: Race, Class, and Culture in the Forced Medical Treatment of Pregnant Women," *Tennessee Law Review*, 59 (1992): 487–517.

29. For detailed discussions of the history of eugenics in the United States, see Daniel J. Kevles, *In the Name of Eugenics: Genetics and the Uses of Human Heredity* (Cambridge, MA: Harvard University Press, 1995); Philip R. Reilly, *The Surgical Solution: A History of Involuntary Sterilization in the United States* (Baltimore: Johns Hopkins University Press, 1991).

30. Marilynn Marchione, "Medical Research Re-Examined," *Milwaukee Journal Sentinel* (Wisconsin), May 24, 2004, p. G1. Not all persons subjected to medical experimentation are the disenfranchised. Take the case of Harold Blauer, a forty-two-year-old jet-setting tennis professional and patient at Bellevue Hospital, who admitted himself to the New York State Psychiatric Institute for clinical depression in 1952 and unwittingly became a victim of human experimentation. While at the institute, Blauer inadvertently became a subject in a research experiment classified as secret whose primary purpose was to gather data that the Chemical Corps required for its investigation of mescaline derivatives as potential chemical warfare agents. Physicians injected Blauer with three different mescaline derivatives on five separate occasions. Although Blauer consented to the first injection that physicians fraudulently offered to him as a treatment for his depression, he refused the other four injections because he had adverse reactions. Nurses threatened Blauer that he would be returned to Bellevue Hospital unless he cooperated and continued with the injections. The fifth injection was considerably stronger than the previous injection of the mescaline derivatives and resulted in a stiffening of his body, clenched teeth, and frothing at the mouth for two hours. Blauer eventually lapsed into a coma and died. "The death certificate attributed the death to 'coronary arteriosclerosis; sudden death after intravenous injection of a mescaline derivative.'" Blauer's ex-wife Amy Blauer filed suit for medical malpractice against New York State that operated the institute. In response to the lawsuit and meetings between state and federal lawyers, the government confiscated Blauer's medical records, and they were never produced despite a court order for the documents. Although the physicians, New York State Psychiatric Institute, the State of New York, and the U.S. Army Chemical Corps conspired to conceal evidence and submitted false documents, the lawsuit was settled for $18,000. Twenty-three years after Blauer's death, his daughter Elizabeth Barrett reopened the case with new litigation after the army contacted her about finding the case file in a safe. After a series of lawsuits, a court eventually awarded Blauer's daughter $702,044, although the lawyers involved in the case pocked $1.7 million. See Ronald B. Standler, *Nonconsensual Medical Experiments on Human Beings* (1997), http://www.rbs2.com/humres.htm. See also Lauretta K. Murphy, Mary Ellen Schill, Michael J. Stepek, and Stephen J. Winjum, "*Barrett v. United States:* Absolute Immunity Wrongfully Extended to Assistant Attorney General Defending the State in a Civil Action," *Notre Dame Law Review*, 62 (1987): 286–311; Lieutenant Colonel Carl T. Grasso, "The Statute of Limitations as Applied to Medical Malpractice Actions Brought Under the Federal Tort Claims Act," *Military Law Review*, 117 (1987): 1–152; Jonathan D. Moreno, "Regulation of Research on the Decisionally Impaired: History and Gaps in the Current Regulatory System," *Journal of Health Care Law and Policy*, 1 (1998): 1–21. For a discussion of the government's cover-up of the case, see Leonard W. Schroeter, "Human Experimentation, the Hanford Nuclear Site, and Judgment at Nuremberg," *Gonzaga Law Review*, 31 (1995): 147–263. For a series of cases noted by Standler on the Bauer incident, see *Barrett v. State of New York*, 378 N.Y.S.2d 946 (1976); *Barrett v. Hoffman*, 521 F.Supp 307 (S.D.N.Y. 1981), *rev'd* 689 F.2d

324, *cert. denied*, 462 U.S. 1131, *remanded* 622 F.Supp. 574, *aff'd* 798 F.2d 565; *Barrett v. U.S.*, 660 F.Supp. 1291 (S.D.N.Y. 1987) (awarding $702,044 to daughter); *Barrett v. U.S.*, 668 F.Supp. 339 (S.D.N.Y. 1987), *aff'd* 853 F.2d 124, *cert. denied* 488 U.S. 1041; *Barrett v. U.S.*, 1991 WL 60365 (attorneys billed $1.7 million in these cases).

31. Mark R. Farfel and Neil A. Holtzman, "Education, Consent, and Counseling in Sickle Cell Screening Programs: Report of a Survey," *American Journal of Public Health*, 74 (1984): 373.

32. David L. Wheeler, "Making Amends to Radiation Victims," *The Chronicle of Higher Education*, October 13, 1995, p. A10; "Radiation Probe Taps Records Spanning 30 Years," *The Chronicle of Higher Education*, October 13, 1995, p. A5; Linda Feldmann, "Ethicists Look at Radiation Test," *Christian Science Monitor*, December 31, 1993, p. 2.

33. A Study Is Sought on Cancer Risk of Nasal Irradiation," *Los Angeles Times*, August 8, 1994, p. A3.

34. William Bradford, "With a Very Great Blame on Our Hearts": Reparations, Reconciliation, and an American Indian Plea for Peace with Justice," *American Indian Law Review*, 27 (2003): 1–175, p. 25, note 110.

35. Marlene Cimmons, "CDC Says It Erred in Measles Study," *Los Angeles Times*, June 17, 1996, A11.

36. Jason R. Odeshoo, "Truth or Dare?: Terrorism and "Truth Serum" in the Post-9/11 World," *Stanford Law Review*, 57 (2004): 209–255.

37. Laura Briggs, "Discourses of 'Forced Sterilization' in Puerto Rico," *Contemporary Women's Issues*, 10 (1998): 34–37.

38. Alexander Cockburn, "Real U.S. Policy in Third World: Sterilization," *Los Angeles Times*, September 10, 1994, B7.

39. Dorothy E. Roberts, "Unshackling Black Motherhood," *Michigan Law Review*, 95 (1997): 938, 963. See also Dorothy E. Roberts, "The Only Good Poor Woman: Unconstitutional Conditions and Welfare," *Denver University Law Review*, 72 (1995): 931; Madeline Henley, "Comment, The Creation and Perpetuation of the Mother/Body Myth: Judicial and Legislative Enlistment of Norplant," *Buffalo Law Review*, 41 (1993): 703; Betsy Hartmann, *Reproductive Rights and Wrongs: The Global Politics of Population Control* (Boston: South End Press, 1995); Janice G. Raymond, *Women as Wombs: Reproductive Technologies and the Battle over Women's Freedom* (San Francisco: HarperCollins, 1993).

40. *United States v. Stanley*, 483 U.S. 669 (1987).

41. Harriet A. Washington, "Medical Victims," *Plain Dealer* (Cleveland, Ohio), March 19, 1995, p. 1C.

Debunking Medical Malpractice Myths: Unraveling the False Premises Behind "Tort Reform"

Geoff Boehm

Tort reform lobbyists seeking to limit the rights of victims of medical malpractice through caps on damages often string together various concerns about health care in the United States that are unrelated to, or would not be addressed by, the reforms they seek.

Medical malpractice—negligence and recklessness by hospitals and physicians—injures hundreds of thousands of people each year. In 2000, the Institute of Medicine released a lengthy report, *To Err Is Human*, revealing that preventable medical errors result in up to 98,000 deaths in hospitals annually. Unfortunately, lawmakers and others have focused too much on reducing liability for those preventable errors and too little on reducing their occurrence. As a result, a July 2004 study shows that over a decade in which two-thirds of states passed "tort reform" measures that limit or restrict medical malpractice lawsuits, there was no improvement in safety: The number of avoidable deaths in hospitals alone is now approximately 195,000 per year, not including obstetrics patients. Despite these bleak statistics, when organizations like the American Medical Association (AMA) speak about a malpractice "crisis," they are referring not to the people injured or killed by medical errors or the widespread failure to discipline negligent doctors (including repeat offenders), but rather to doctors' increasing malpractice insurance premiums.

THE UNFOUNDED RHETORIC OF TORT REFORM LOBBYISTS

Tort reform lobbyists seeking to limit the rights of victims of medical malpractice through caps on damages often string together various concerns about health care in the United States that are unrelated to, or would not be addressed by, the reforms they seek. In particular, the insurance industry and other tort reform proponents rely on misinformation and largely anecdotal evidence that the civil justice system is "out of control" and needs to be scaled back. However, the facts reveal a different picture.

First, the number of medical malpractice cases being filed per capita has dropped over the last ten years, as have tort filings

---

Source: Geoff Boehm, from "Debunking Medical Malpractice Myths: Unraveling the False Premises Behind 'Tort Reform,'" in *Yale Journal of Health Policy, Law and Ethics.* 5 (2005): 357–369.

generally. Even in the states that the AMA has labeled "crisis states," the number of cases per capita has been dropping. The vast majority of those injured by malpractice never file a claim seeking to hold the wrong-doers accountable. Even though medical mal-practice kills some 195,000 hospital patients every year and injures many more, only about one in eight of those injured files a claim.

Second, while the claim that medical mal-practice cases tend to be "frivolous" is frequently heard, proponents of that claim have failed to support it with strong empirical support. Politicians, insurance industry exec-utives, and medical society lobbyists often support their claim that the system is filled with "frivolous" malpractice lawsuits by cit-ing the statistic that patients only prevail in their medical malpractice lawsuits about twenty-seven percent of the time. Yet, a 2004 report from the Federal Trade Com-mission and the U.S. Department of Justice found that doctors' own lawsuits against employers and hospitals fare even worse: Doctor-plaintiffs win only fourteen percent of those verdicts. The fact is that some types of cases are difficult to win, even when they are legitimate—that they will have low win percentages is not a reflection of frivolity.

Our civil justice system has various checks and balances to discourage frivolous suits and punish those who file them. Not only can sanctions be imposed on the lawyers respon-sible, but the contingency fee arrangement under which plaintiffs' attorneys work—they only get paid and have their expenses reim-bursed if they succeed in the case—also screens out baseless lawsuits. As far back as 1986, James Gattuso, then of the conserva-tive Heritage Foundation, wrote an article for the Wall Street Journal entitled Don't Rush To Condemn Contingency Fees. He argued that the contingency fee system ensures that injured persons who could not otherwise afford legal representation obtain access to the legal system and "helps screen [baseless lawsuits] out of the system." Even insurance executives, when put under oath, have admitted that frivolous suits are not a problem.

It should also be noted that the issue of "frivolous lawsuits" is a red herring when caps are being considered. By limiting award amounts, caps target the most egregious cases of malpractice and the most severely injured patients—the very opposite of the "frivolous" or "junk" lawsuits that advocates for caps por-tray when they are trying to rile up the public or lawmakers to limit victims' rights. Two recent studies have confirmed that caps on damages in medical malpractice cases, such as California's draconian $250,000 cap on non-economic damages, are most devastating to those who suffered the most heinous injuries, those killed by the defendants' acts, and those who suffered the greatest loss to their quality of life.

In addition to mischaracterizing the quan-tity and quality of medical malpractice suits, supporters of tort reform make unsupported assertions about the impact of medical mal-practice litigation on the quality and availabil-ity of health care. Despite the claims of the AMA and state medical societies, the num-ber of medical professionals is growing. Moreover, these organizations repeatedly aver that doctors are leaving the twenty "AMA crisis states," and even the twenty-four "AMA problem states," in droves because of litigation concerns, resulting in a lack of access to care. However, investiga-tions of such claims by the U.S. General Accounting Office, various reporters, and state agencies have shown the claims to be false or widely exaggerated. To the extent there are access problems, many other expla-nations can be established.

For example, it is true that some rural and impoverished urban areas do not have a suffi-cient supply of health care providers. But it is a fiction to tie that lack of access to malprac-tice litigation or jury awards, or to claim that a cap would make a difference. Such areas often have difficulty attracting or retaining other professionals as well. Moreover, this problem has existed for a long time, even before physicians considered malpractice insurance premiums problematic. In fact, the Council on Graduate Medical Education has stated, "The relative shortage of health professionals in rural areas of the United States is one of the few constants in any description of the United States medical care system." Rural health care shortages occur throughout the world, including places where there is nothing like the U.S. civil justice system in place.

THE TRUTH ABOUT CAPS AND OTHER MEDICAL MALPRACTICE "REFORMS"

The increasing cost of health care in the United States and the high costs of medical malpractice insurance are legitimate and pressing concerns. Unfortunately, caps will do little to address these issues.

First and foremost, costs related to litigation are a miniscule portion of health care spending; according to the United States Congressional Budget Office (CBO), these malpractice costs are less than two percent of total spending. CBO has, in fact, noted that "a cap on noneconomic damages and a ban on punitive damages . . . would lower health care costs by only about 0.4 percent to 0.5 percent, and the likely effect on health insurance premiums would be comparably small."

Tort reform advocates often claim that doctors practice "defensive medicine" because of fears of medical malpractice suits and that this practice, in turn, raises the cost of health care. However, in 1994, the congressional Office of Technology Assessment (OTA) found that less than eight percent of all diagnostic procedures result primarily from liability concerns. OTA found that most physicians who "would order aggressive

diagnostic procedures . . . would do so primarily because they believe such procedures are medically indicated, not primarily because of concerns about liability." Thus, the effects of tort reform on defensive medicine "are likely to be small." The CBO has also reported that "some so-called defensive medicine may be motivated less by liability concerns than by the income it generates for physicians or by the positive (albeit small) benefits to patients. . . . CBO believes that savings from reducing defensive medicine would be very small."

The insurance industry, the U.S. Chamber of Commerce, and corporate front groups such as the American Tort Reform Association have spent many tens of millions of dollars in pursuit of immunity or limitations on liability from wrongdoing. Their efforts include promoting insurance companies' legislative agenda to limit liability for doctors, hospitals, HMOs, nursing homes, and drug companies that cause injury. Moreover, federal and state lawmakers, regulators, doctors, and the general public are being told by medical and insurance lobbyists that doctors' insurance rates are rising due to increasing claims by patients, rising jury verdicts, and exploding tort system costs in general, despite clear evidence to the contrary. Just as caps and other tort reforms do not succeed in significantly reducing aggregate health care costs, they also fail to control individual insurance premiums.

Insurers state that to recoup money paid to patients, they must raise insurance rates or, in some cases, pull out of the market altogether. Since insurers say that jury verdicts are the cause of the current "crisis" in affordable malpractice insurance for doctors, they insist that the only way to bring down insurance rates is to limit an injured consumer's ability to sue in court. However, historically, the cause of skyrocketing rates has little to do with the legal system.

Insurance companies make profits primarily from investment income. Insurance companies take in money in the form of premiums paid and then hold it for some length of time until they need to make a payout to, or on behalf of, a policyholder. In the interim, the money being held, known as the "float," is invested and earns money for the insurance company. When the investment market is strong and/or interest rates high, the companies make a good profit by investing the float and may under-price policies in an effort to attract more premium dollars to invest—this scenario is termed a "soft market." But when investment income falls because of a decline in the markets and/or drops in interest rates, insurance companies will raise their rates or cut back coverage. Such a "hard market" occurred in the mid-1970s, more severely in the mid-1980s, and again between 2002 and 2003. Insurance rates for doctors skyrocketed in each of the hard markets.

Thus, while insurers and other tort reform proponents blame malpractice litigation for the hard market premium increases, they are in fact consistently driven by the insurance companies' response to the broader economic cycle. In fact, claims and payouts stayed flat or declined through each of the "crises" or hard markets. With payouts flat, rising premiums have caused property-casualty insurers' profits to skyrocket. From 2002 to 2003, profits rose 997% and they continue to soar—reportedly doubling between the first quarters of 2003 and 2004. Despite these striking statistics, successful lobbying by interest groups in response to increasing insurance rates for doctors has yielded a wave of legislative activity to restrict injured patients' rights to sue for medical malpractice.

Because insurers target the civil justice system, rather than the economic cycle that leads to periodic "crises," "tort reform" remedies—including caps—pushed by insurance companies and their advocates during each hard market failed to bring down rates. When confronted with a report showing that tort reform does not lead to reduced premi-

ums, the American Insurance Association responded, "Insurers never promised that tort reform would achieve specific savings." Over the past year and a half, insurers continued to raise premiums, even in states where tort reforms were enacted, even though claims and payouts dropped and the investment markets began to improve. It appears we are now entering a soft market: Premiums are beginning to drop or increase more slowly in all lines of insurance, including medical malpractice—in states with and without caps or other tort reforms. While the soft market will bring some relief as premiums drop, if there is no significant increase in regulation of the insurance industry, we can expect that the next downturn in the economy and the market will bring back rising premiums and, predictably, renewed efforts to blame injured patients and seek ineffective and harmful tort reforms, as insurers once again raise their rates to make up for investment losses.

So if one puts aside the unfounded rhetoric that claims to connect a need for caps to rising insurance premiums and health care costs, to a supposedly growing number of frivolous lawsuits, and to alleged movement of doctors among the states, what then are the true motivators for tort reform proponents? First, tort reform efforts (including caps), are based on a mistrust of, or discomfort with, the American institution of civil trial by jury. This fundamental right of ordinary citizens and consumers to hold accountable those with power—including corporations, large institutions, professionals, and even government—is a fulcrum of our democracy. In fact, one reason that several state courts have struck down tort reform laws as unconstitutional is the way in which the laws limit the power of juries to decide cases.

Judges, who have more intimate knowledge of the system than anyone, find such mistrust of juries inappropriate. A 2000 survey sent to one thousand trial judges, including every federal trial judge, revealed that:

- Judges have "a high level of day-to-day confidence in [the jury] system."
- "Only 1 percent of the judges who responded gave the jury system low marks."
- "Nine of every 10 trial judges, those who work closest with the nation's jury system, think the system needs only minor tinkering, at best."
- "Overwhelmingly . . . state and federal judges said they have great faith in juries to solve complicated issues."
- "Nine of 10 judges responding said jurors show considerable understanding of legal issues involved in the cases they hear."

Statistics also show that juries are generally conservative and reasonable, and their decisions rarely differ from what a judge would decide.

RECOMMENDATIONS

Our civil justice system exists to provide those who have been wronged a forum to seek truth and compensation, even to the dismay of those who may have acted negligently, recklessly, or worse. Caps not only limit the liability of wrongdoers, take away the fundamental power of juries to decide adequate compensation, and leave the most severely injured victims without sufficient means of redress, but they do not even address the increasing costs of health care or medical malpractice insurance.

An important solution to avoiding future spikes in premiums is stronger regulation of the insurance industry. Unlike caps and other tort reforms, insurance industry regulation would lower premiums charged to doctors, hospitals, and other policyholders, while protecting the rights of patients and consumers. Given the soaring profits of insurance companies, such

regulation is unlikely to put them in financial harm. State insurance regulators should take the following steps, as suggested by Americans for Insurance Reform—a coalition of over one hundred consumer and public interest groups and a project of the Center for Justice & Democracy—in a recent letter sent to all state insurance commissioners:

(1) Undertake a review of rate levels to determine if rates are excessive in any line of insurance; . . . (2) Initiate an investigation into anti-competitive behavior of insurance companies in making statements and other acts to hold off competition; . . . (3) If any insurer files a rate request in excess of current inflation for that line of insurance, a rate hearing should be called; . . . (4) Begin the process of careful analysis as to what led to this most recent cycle, and your department's role in it by allowing rates to fluctuate between excessive (such as now at the end of the hard market) and inadequate (such as right before the turn in the market from soft to hard); . . . (5) Alert your legislature to the end of the hard market and advise them that there is no need to rush into legislative fixes, such as legal limits on victims' rights; . . . (6) Review successes from other states in averting the same sort of price spikes you may have endured over the last two years. Clearly, insurance rate regulation is one thing that has helped tremendously to prevent large rate increases in some states. Nowhere has this been more evident than in California, a state that in 1988 passed the strongest insurance reform law in the country.

No one denies that there is a broad array of very serious health care issues facing the United States right now—patient safety, rising costs, availability and affordability of health insurance, and, in some places, rapidly rising malpractice premiums (although they are easing as we enter a soft market). But even with these problems, caps are not a solution. Lawmakers and regulators should stop the insurance industry from price-gouging their policyholders, even while the industry's profits rocket upwards. Moreover, doctors would better serve themselves and their patients by directing their anger and efforts regarding rising premiums toward the questionable practices of the insurance industry and the subset of doctors who repeatedly commit malpractice without facing adequate discipline. Seeking to take away patients' rights is not the answer.

STUDY QUESTION

Explain why Boehm contends that caps will do little to address increasing health care costs and the high costs of medical malpractice insurance in the United States.

Racial Profiling in Health Care: An Institutional Analysis of Medical Treatment Disparities

René Bowser

This Article shows that race-based health research fuels a collection of dubious background assumptions, creates a negative profile of Black patients, and reinforces taken-for-granted knowledge that leads to inferior medical treatment. This form of racial profiling is unjust, and also causes countless unnecessary deaths in the Black population.

SEEKING TREATMENT WHILE BLACK: EMPIRICAL EVIDENCE OF RACIAL DISCRIMINATION

A growing body of compelling and disturbing evidence points to inferior medical care for similarly situated Black and White patients. Differences in access to quality medical treatment partly explain the existence of higher rates of death from nearly all diseases among Blacks. Much of the evidence is based on "differential treatment" research. To standardize each patient in all aspects, except race, these studies typically employ multivariate analyses to control for confounding variables like insurance status, socio-economic status, education, and medical condition.

Notwithstanding their importance in highlighting racial disparities, most "differential treatment" studies fail to provide any theoretical framework to understand the racial differences. After discussing the methodology and results, the authors typically relegate a discussion of racial bias or alternative explanations to a few paragraphs. Further, they give no indication of whether the findings of racial disparity in a particular study represent an isolated example or are indicative of a systemic pattern. As one commentator notes: "Researchers sometimes do not know, forget or are unimpressed that Dante reserved the seventh level of hell for those who recognize a problem and do not attempt to do anything to solve it."

The growing body of research that documents significant disparities in patterns of medical use makes it an increasingly difficult problem to ignore. For example, a review

Source: René Bowser, from "Racial Profiling in Health Care: An Institutional Analysis of Medical Treatment Disparities," in Michigan Journal of Race and Law, 7 (2001): 79–133.

prepared for the American Medical Association's Board of Trustees that was restricted to the literature on treatment disparities appearing only in the *New England Journal of Medicine* and the *Journal of the American Medical Association* between 1984 and 1994 filled an alarming sixty-six pages.

POVERTY OF EXISTING EXPLANATIONS OF RACIAL DISPARITY

This section analyzes the three most common alternative explanations for racial disparities in treatment—patient preferences, overuse by Whites, and unconscious racism. It concludes that the available evidence in support of these explanations is insufficient to exclude institutional racism and racial profiling as the primary explanations for the observed racial differences. Even so, the issue of racial bias cannot be resolved in the abstract. History, ideology and institutions all matter in this narrative.

Cultural Preferences

Uncomplicated by the mediating roles of income, education, insurance status and the like, some investigators explain the residual disparity in treatment by speculating that Blacks and Whites may differ in their treatment preferences, with White patients "preferring" more services than Blacks. This argument suggests that the decision to undergo a high technological procedure is influenced by the patient's "perceived risks and benefits of the procedure and other factors, such as one's trust in medical approaches involving advanced forms of high technology." These factors presumably differ by race.

Not much evidence supports this claim. Most of those who advance the patient preferences theory rely on the frequently cited Coronary Artery Surgery Study for support. That study revealed that of those patients whom physicians recommended for coronary

artery bypass surgery, Whites were 13 percent more likely to receive the surgery. The inference is that Black patients who were recommended for surgery declined the surgery because of their "preferences." The study does not, however, state that Black patients expressly refused the surgery. Obviously, there are a host of reasons that could explain the difference, including insurance status and income, factors for which the study did not adjust.

As part of a study of the four-fold racial difference in the use of carotid endarterectomy, a 1998 study evaluated the explanatory role of racial preferences. Based on a small sample of patients hospitalized for stroke or ischemic attack (44 Blacks and 46 Whites), the researchers found a "highly significant racial difference in patients' attitudes toward receiving carotid endarterectomy, a surgery proven to reduce the chance of experiencing a future stroke." Notably, however, more of the Black patients had already experienced a stroke compared to their White counterparts (75 percent versus 33 percent). With this in mind, the researchers conceded that the findings of different racial preferences could be misleading because the Black patients possibly felt they had less to gain from the procedure than White patients who had not yet experienced a stroke.

In contrast, Harvard researchers reported a racial disparity in access to kidney transplantation and rejected the hypothesis that this disparity was the result of patient preferences. The study revealed that in contrast to the small difference in preferences (76.3 percent of Black women wanted a transplant vs. 79.3 percent of White women, and 80.7 percent of Black men vs. 85.5 percent of White men), Black patients were much less likely than White patients to have been referred to a transplantation center for evaluation (50.4 percent for Black women vs. 70.5 percent for White women, and 53.9 percent for Black men vs. 76.2 percent for White men), or to have been placed on a waiting list.

This Harvard study also found that Blacks patients were less likely to report that their primary nephrologist provided all the medical information they desired. This finding is consistent with other studies that report that the Black-White preference differential is related to patient knowledge about a surgical procedure. For instance, Whittle and his colleagues found that Black-White preference differences for coronary artery bypass surgery disappeared when the procedure was explained to Black patients. Furthermore, the study found that Blacks were substantially more likely to give a favorable response to the use of the procedure when the interviewer was Black.

African Americans do share a common legacy with regard to medicine. It is a cumulative experience of several hundred years of pseudoscientific racism and pervasive discrimination in medicine, unethical and often brutal experimentation, and abuse of Black people by both private institutions and government programs in health. Considerations of this sort suggest that, even assuming that some Black patients prefer not to undergo invasive medical procedures, it is a rational decision influenced by a past and historical memory of abuse and an attitude of distrust. If this is the case, there is a logical fallacy in using patient preferences as a variable in explaining disparate medical treatment. Such patient preferences do not explain racial disparities; rather, they demonstrate the consequences of racism. The refusal to undergo treatment is often associated with the fear of abuse and exploitation, and, on a more intimate level, negative experiences with care providers can diminish preferences for robust treatment. Thus, different patient preferences, if they exist, are often a product of racial disparities in medical treatment. They do not explain them.

Overuse by Whites

The second claim is that racial disparities might reflect overuse of medical services by Whites, while Blacks receive the medically indicated and appropriate amount.

Health care is a scare resource. If some groups are receiving more of the resource than required by their medical condition, less is available for other groups, especially in the current environment of cost containment, capitated budgets, and rationing. Assuming that Whites are overusing medical services, a two-tier system of health care exists, in which those in the lower tier receive fewer services, irrespective of insurance status or condition upon presentation. Such a system perpetuates existing inequalities.

In any event, the history of Blacks and medicine makes clear that Black lives have not been as highly valued as White lives. That legacy is carried forward in the current views of Black patients. About 20 percent of Blacks believe that they have been unfairly treated when seeking care specifically because of their race. Twenty-seven percent of Blacks believe a friend has been unfairly treated. A larger number, 65 percent, are concerned that in the future, they or a family member will be treated unfairly when seeking medical care because of their race. Thus, it is unlikely that Black patients are receiving the appropriate amount of care.

Unconscious Racism

The third claim is that medical treatment disparities are the product of unconscious bias. Many studies that attempt to explain racial bias in medical treatment decisions do so in these terms.

While this analysis is fine and highly congenial to explaining a specific treatment decision by a specific physician, it does not answer a number of questions. First, is the pattern of racial disparities in medical treatment the result of an aggregation of specific, particular moments of unconscious racism over the thousands of treatment decisions that occur every day? Second, is unconscious racism in medicine the product of social indoctrination only, or do the history, practices, and attitudes of medicine in some way contribute to the problem?

Medicine is often portrayed as a mirror of society, reflecting prevailing societal attitudes. As Oliver Wendell Holmes states: "[M]edicine, professedly founded on observation, is as sensitive to outside influence, political, religious, philosophical, imaginative, as is the barometer to the atmospheric density."

If this is the case, individual physicians are logically the responsible parties for their unconscious acts of bias. The solution, then, is some form of cultural or sensitivity training, as is often proposed. This explanation, however, privileges a quick and easy remedy and overlooks larger institutional issues.

This Article suggests that ideas about Black patients are transmitted to physicians by the institution of race-based research. Ignoring the role of medical institutions in originating and recreating taken-for-granted knowledge about Black patients renders invisible the relationship between medicine and politics. Medical institutions operate to fulfill the requirements of society. Historically, they have stood ready to supply the "scientific" justifications necessary for social and political needs.

In the following sections, I present a theory of how race-based research creates, legitimates, and sustains negative profiles of Black patients and reinforces taken-for-granted knowledge. This practice, in turn, leads to inferior medical treatment. First, I begin with a brief discussion of New Institutionalism.

THE VICIOUS CYCLE: RACIALIZED RESEARCH, RACIAL PROFILING AND TREATMENT DISPARITIES

Background patterns and understandings are hard to deinstitutionalize, particularly in organized settings. Moreover, as Haney López has pointed out, "individuals often face incentive structures that make it less costly to abide by norms that they disagree with than to act to change them." Researchers who study Black health poten-

tially face publication bias, loss of prestige, and lack of recognition as real scientists if they fail to abide by the norm of using race as a scientific variable. Physicians face incentives in terms of time and cognitive energy that deter them from viewing Black patients individually, reading the literature critically and interrogating their own racial views and prejudices.

Individuals and communities can, of course, alter institutional racism, but not in any precise, easy or predictable way. Medicine can begin the process by becoming more inclusive. As early as the mid-1850s, Dr. John S. Rock (a Black physician) challenged notions of Black inferiority, and explained that the problem with racist science was not what it looked at, but what it ignored. That is, as long as physicians refused to consider how slavery and poverty caused disease, they would only have biological rationales to explain racial differences in health.

Evidence suggests that many Black physicians recognize the intersection of politics and medicine, and have resisted racial profiling. Nickens suggests that physicians of color are "more culturally sensitive to their populations and organize the delivery system in ways more congruent with the needs of a minority population." Moreover, minority consumers actively seek and choose physicians of their own race and ethnicity. As one Black physician explains: "There's a certain relief in their eyes that you can see. I don't know how to translate how that feels—to see another person of color."

The selection of medical students should reflect the type of physicians society needs in the future. In 1997–98, Blacks comprised 8 percent of first year medical students. Projections show that to reach racial and ethnic parity with a managed care-based requirement of 218 physicians per 100,000 population, the number of Black and Latino residents would have to roughly double; the number of Native American physicians would have to triple.

An intensive effort by the Association of American Medical Colleges helped to produce a 36 percent increase in minority enrollment—to 12 percent—between 1990 and 1995. But then the assault on affirmative action began. First, California voters passed Proposition 209, an initiative flatly barring so-called racial or ethnic preferences (even to pursue the goal of diversity) as a factor in admission to the University of California system. In the Fifth Circuit, the decision in *Hopwood v. Texas* had the same effect for university admissions in Texas, Louisiana and Mississippi. These attacks go much further than the landmark *Bakke* case, brought by an unsuccessful applicant to the University of California, Davis, School of Medicine, which stated that race in certain circumstances could be a factor in admissions decisions.

Particularly disturbing is the fact that two-thirds of minority students attending medical schools are enrolled in public institutions. Yet, nearly all of the decline in minority student enrollment has occurred in public medical schools. Public medical schools in California, Louisiana, Mississippi and Texas have been disproportionately affected by this trend; collectively, medical schools in these states accounted for 44 percent of the decrease in the enrollment of people of color in 1996. If these trends continue, and there are strong reasons to believe that they will, enrollment levels will likely return to the levels of the 1970s or worse.

This Article suggests that physicians and biomedical researchers of color are less likely to be affected by the racialized thinking. Increasing the number of such physicians and researchers is a first, albeit small, step in ending racial profiling.

Because of the complexity of the problem, a single solution is elusive and, therefore, the issue must be attacked from multiple fronts. Education is essential and should emphasize the fallacy of using race as a scientific concept and the inherent dangers in practicing racial profiling. Also, because the disparate treatment of Blacks is a civil rights issue, the potential for relief under the civil rights statutes must be pursued.

CIVIL RIGHTS AND RACIAL PROFILING IN HEALTH CARE

Congress enacted Title VI of the Civil Right Act of 1964 to prohibit the expenditure of federal funds on programs and activities that discriminate on the basis of race, color or national origin. Because federal financial assistance includes Medicare and Medicaid funds, and nearly every hospital and nursing home in the United States receives such funds, Title VI applies to the majority of health care institutions. Further, Title VI defines "program or activity" broadly; if any part of an agency or entity receives federal funding, Title VI generally prohibits discrimination throughout the entire entity or institution.

In 1999, the United States Commission on Civil Rights criticized Title VI enforcement efforts in the area of health care; the Commission's report pointed out that the nondiscrimination provisions have not been fully enforced and implemented by the Office of Civil Rights (OCR), the branch of the Department of Health and Human Services charged with enforcement. According to the report, tangible civil rights violations are selectively enforced. Tangible civil rights violations include easily identifiable harms like maintaining segregated hospital and nursing home wards, requiring only racial minorities to pay a deposit for emergency room care, or refusing to admit a patient whose physician does not have admitting privileges at that hospital.

Considerations of this sort suggest that the more complex and intangible violations created by racial profiling present formidable challenges. The poor enforcement history of Title VI naturally gives rise to pessimism regarding the prospects of attaining racial equality in health through this legislation. The political leadership of President Clinton in passing the Minority Health and Health Disparities Act of 2000, and in endorsing other on-going programs to decrease health disparities, however, potentially signals a willingness to change the status quo. Assuming that the current administration continues the policies of its predecessor in this area, this Article suggests that there exists within Title VI potentially promising and unexplored ways to address discrimination generally, including the intangible qualities of institutional racism.

If we are serious about invigorating Title VI enforcement, the cornerstone is the systematic collection of data from each health care provider that receives federal funds on racial disparities in the use of services and the choices of diagnostic and therapeutic alternatives. Indeed, the Commission on Civil Rights recommends this approach:

OCR and other HHS agencies should use existing research outlining disparities in health status and access to health care and incorporate this information in the development of civil rights policies and civil rights enforcement programs. This would include information on . . . the type of treatment offered based on race, ethnicity, and gender. The addition of these factors to data collection instruments could detect, at an earlier phase, potential discriminatory problems at a facility, and secure compliance to remedy such problems before awarding funds. The conceptual basis for data collection by race and ethnicity is simple and appealing. All that is needed is for health care institutions and providers to compile and report the use of specific medical procedures by race and ethnicity. Existing and proposed health care "report cards" offer an existing system for data collection on access, quality, and outcomes. Most have undergone extensive development and review, and need only to be stratified by race.

Under this proposal, civil rights enforcement efforts could be directed at those institutions or facilities that have statistically significant racial disparities in the use of specific medical procedures or referrals to specialists. Optimally, OCR would withhold federal funds from such providers until the racial disparity is either explained or corrected. This would have the advantage of shifting the burden on health care providers to present evidence showing non-discriminatory reasons for the racial disparities in treatment and referrals to specialists.

Such an approach is not without precedent. It is instructive to look at the banking industry, which has historically treated similarly situated Black and White borrowers differently through an ongoing and pervasive practice of lending discrimination and redlining. Since 1990, The Home Mortgage Disclosure Act (HMDA) has required mortgage lenders to reveal demographic characteristics such as the race, gender and income of all mortgage applicants. In this way, evidence of racial disparity is used in the regulatory review process of bank merger and expansion requests.

Statistics are also increasingly being collected to combat racial profiling in criminal law enforcement. In a 1999 speech to the nation, President Clinton criticized race profiling and called for the collection of data on race-based stops. Legislators have also called for such data. Moreover, a federal appeals court recently held that motorists could potentially use statistics to show the requisite discriminatory effect of state police conduct to support their equal protection claims.

Besides the obvious advantage of identifying racial disparities in medical treatment and withholding government funds, data collection potentially compels institutions to think about race. As Sidney Watson has pointed out, "[i]t is only when providers know that something is 'wrong' that they can be motivated to change the status quo to do what is 'right.'"

An internal dialogue should include these questions: Are Black and White patients offered the same options by physicians? Do assumptions about survival affect physicians' recommendations for certain procedures? Do physicians use judgment heuristics and racial profiling because of time pressure? Are physicians' treatment decisions influenced by racialized research that portrays Blacks as different, less likely to respond well to certain treatments, and less likely to adhere to costly treatment regimes?

Such data collection will also improve overall health care quality. Health care quality requires that resources are allocated according to medical need, risk, and benefit, not by alternative standards. Quality improvement experts have emphasized the importance of redesigning systems of care instead of simply identifying individual physicians who provide inadequate care. One way to do this is to implement information systems that provide medical groups and other facilities with timely feedback about treatment decisions, referral rates, and patient satisfaction according to race and ethnic background. Thus, a dialogue on addressing racial disparities and racial bias must be recognized as a serious quality issue.

Another advantage of a facility-level enforcement program is that it obviates the need for an individual plaintiff to identify the wrongdoer or the type of care that should have been provided. Prior to April 2001, there existed an issue as to whether Title VI entailed a private right of action. In *Alexander v. Sandoval*, however, the U.S. Supreme Court held that it did not create a private right of action concerning policies with disparate impact, absent a showing of discriminatory intent. Because of physician discretion, however, an individual claim of disparate medical treatment would have been difficult to prove even if a private right of action had been found. As Bloche explains, clinical variation presents an almost insurmountable obstacle in medical malpractice: "[l]ower intensity care provided to a minority patient can . . . typically be defended as consistent with one or another widely accepted standard of care."

Further, publicly available, institution-specific racial information can conceivably provide an incentive for providers to voluntarily reduce racial and ethnic disparities in care, based on their own economic self-interest. This approach assumes that purchasers of health care will take the existence of racial disparities into account in choosing health care providers. From a policy perspective, employers have been the major forces for change in the health care marketplace. In particular, major corporations, as well as business and health coalitions, are increasingly banding together and using their market power to demand accountability and promote quality as well as cost. From a legal perspective, states have assisted by passing legislation that either permits or encourages the voluntary creation of alliances among purchasers of health care. Thus, major purchasers of health care conceivably have the bargaining power to require a reduction in racial disparities. Whether they have the desire to do so, however, is a much more complicated issue.

In making this case for collecting race-based treatment data, difficult operational issues need to be addressed. For instance, how do we classify races? The Office of Management and Budget provides a uniform classification scheme for data collected by all federal agencies, and those categories are also used by most state agencies, hospital discharge records, and medical record keeping systems. One could argue that these classifications lump heterogeneous groups into one category and, furthermore, present the same problem as using race as a variable in racialized research, namely, they serve to validate socially constructed racial meanings and reinforce White race consciousness and privilege. On this account, then, are there any justifications for perpetuating the use of flawed racial categories?

One might draw a distinction between using the concept of race for research and for civil rights monitoring purposes. Race has served biomedicine badly. Medical research needs to rethink the concept of race as a variable; it might be disaggregated or eliminated altogether in order to account fully for intragroup differences in health outcomes, and to prevent science from ignore the truth that race has no scientific meaning. Some have called for broader measures such as ethnicity.

For purposes of civil rights monitoring, however, the study of racism would be impaired if we abandoned racial categories. Despite the imprecision of our definitions, measurable and substantial disparities exist among groups we label as races. Furthermore, advocates for social equality have long used race-specific statistics in calling for reform. In fact, abandoning racial categories for civil rights purposes would be welcomed by those who are disinclined to address the problems these statistics bring to light. Neoconservatives object to most race-based initiatives, including collecting racial/ethnic data in the United States.

An important legal issue that must be addressed is whether existing civil rights laws prohibit health care providers from collecting racial data. The Office of Minority Health has studied the issue and has concluded that no provision in either the Federal Civil Rights Act of 1964 or promulgated regulations prohibits health insurers or health plans from collecting racial data. Moreover, by law, The Department of Health and Human Services has the authority to obtain racial data from "from any entity that receives funding from DHHS to determine compliance with Title VI law or promulgated regulations on a case-by-case basis." Three states, however, prohibit the collection of such data. The Office of Minority Health is now reviewing these laws and may eventually ask state legislatures to consider revisions that would allow racial and ethnic data collection.

Even if plans are legally mandated to release treatment data by race, additional regulations will be required to provide assurances of confidentiality. For instance, health plans regard referrals to a specialist, one of the most significant indicators of racial bias, as proprietary and a closely guarded competitive secret.

Of course, it would be naive to suggest that HHS can enforce this proposal alone. The history of hospital integration after the passage of Title VI and the enactment of Medicare legislation demonstrates the importance of local organizations. As Smith has pointed out, "a network of local civil rights organizations and health services workers, intimately familiar with the operations of local hospitals, did the 'real work.'" A critical challenge for local and national civil rights organizations, then, is to place the elimination of racial disparities in medical treatment at the top of their agendas and to demand accountability. Indeed, eliminating racial profiling in health care through Title VI enforcement must be pursued with the same vigor that has been directed towards eliminating barriers to other basic civil rights.

CONCLUSION

This Article suggests that medicine is not immune from the injustice of racial profiling. The lives of patients of color are devalued by race-based expectations that arise from the findings and conclusions of flawed racialized research. To the extent that medical judgment is informed by racial categorizations, it is bound to yield racially disparate results.

Three conclusions result from this study. First, medicine needs to rethink research. The publication of the first draft of the human genome project should force an end to research that is arbitrarily based on race. Second, medicine needs to rethink treatment. Education is essential and should emphasize both the fallacy of using race as a scientific concept and the inherent dangers in practicing race-based medicine. Third, society needs to rethink discrimination. By requiring providers who receive federal funds to report data on medical treatment by race and ethnicity, we can identify the extent of the problem, rectify treatment disparities, and, more fundamentally, begin a much-needed dialogue about the meaning of race in medicine.

STUDY QUESTION

What evidence does Bowser put forth to support the conclusion of inferior medical care for similarly situated black and white patients?

READING 7.3

Medical Gender Bias and Managed Care

Vicki Lawrence MacDougall

While there is no empirical data that currently supports the proposition that managed care hurts women more than men, the main goal of this article is to raise the haunting question whether managed care has the built-in propensity to perpetuate—if not sanction and encourage—medical gender bias to the detriment of the health of women enrolled in managed care plans.

MEDICAL GENDER BIAS

The Women's Health Movement began over thirty years ago. The reader might immediately question why it was necessary to have a women's health movement; after all, there is no corresponding men's health movement. The answer lies in history. The historical treatment of women by the medical profession is frightening by today's standards and it reflected the general social, political, and religious attitudes toward women at that time. The historical taint, including the general social attitudes toward women, and scientific ignorance perpetuated the gender discrepancies that still persist in the modern practice of medicine. It was not until the later part of the twentieth century that the medical profession began to recognize gender bias from within its own profession. Recognition of a problem is the first step toward modifications of behavior and paving the way toward a solution. The women's health movement created public awareness and spurred the medical profession toward this introspection.

GENDER DISCREPANCIES IN TREATMENT

Clearly, exclusionary research practices impact the treatment of women by the medical profession. For example, women are prescribed more drugs than men despite the lack of participation by women in research populations. Not surprisingly, women suffer more adverse drug consequences than men. Low fat diets have been encouraged for both men and women. Yet, low fat diets that help men fight

Source: Vicki Lawrence MacDougall, "Medical Gender Bias and Managed Care," Oklahoma City University Law Review, 27 (2002): 781–910.

high cholesterol and heart disease might not be necessary for women. Further, there is some indication that low fat diets may actually hinder a woman's natural ability to fight heart disease. In the context of medical treatment, what is good for the gander might not be good for the goose.

Another example can be seen in the treatment of women suffering from AIDS. Originally, it was believed that only homosexual men contracted the deadly virus. Women were, somewhat understandably, ignored in the early research of the disease. However, researchers continued to ignore women even after women became the largest growing class of patients with AIDS. The progression of the disease in women differs from that of men and women tend to die sooner after the diagnosis of being HIV positive. Yet it was not until 1993 that the most common symptoms in women, cervical cancer, pelvic inflammatory disease, and vaginal yeast infections, were acknowledged by the Center for Disease Control. As a result, women were excluded from participation in many of the experimental treatments and many women were undiagnosed for longer periods of time causing inappropriate treatments of their conditions. Research on women with HIV has been glaringly deficient. Practitioners have not had the advantage of solid research which probably has negatively impacted thousands of female AIDS victims.

Similarly, women were excluded from early research on the effectiveness of autologous bone marrow transplants (ABMT) in conjunction with high-dose chemotherapy (HDC) to fight cancer. As a result, insurance companies denied coverage of ABMT with HDC as a treatment for metastatic breast cancer because its use on women was classified as experimental due to the fact that the original research populations were all male. Currently, women with metastatic breast cancer who are covered by some health insurance providers are forced to fight in court with mixed success for HDC accompanied

by ABMT. Although there appears to be judicial sympathy for the plight of women denied coverage for HDC along with ABMT, courts do not always order health insurance companies to cover the treatment, which means the woman must pay for the treatment out of her own pocket or forgo HDC and ABMT.

However, treatment disparities cannot be blamed entirely on the research industry. Preconceived notions about women by members of the medical profession negatively impact medical treatment. Women are perceived as being more complaining. Women do visit the doctor more than men. Women also might be more descriptive in their symptoms. Further, new research indicates that women might have a lower tolerance for pain than men. For whatever reason, women's symptoms are not taken as seriously by physicians as men's. Doctors are also more likely to assume that a woman's condition is "all in her head." If a man and a woman present to a doctor with the same symptoms, a physician is more likely to search for a physical explanation for the man and is more likely to consider the disorder as psychogenic for the woman and prescribe a psychoactive drug. The origins of attributing physical conditions to psychosomatic illnesses in women can be traced to medical school as well as the personal assumptions by individual doctors based on subjective stereotyping. Empirical studies on the communication gap between physicians and patients show that the communication gap is at its worse when the conversation is between a male doctor and a female patient.

Startling discrepancies in treatment exist for lung, heart, and kidney disease. Part of the disparity is attributed to societal feelings about lung and heart disease. Historically, lung and heart disease was associated with men, not women. At one time, few women smoked and lung cancer became associated with men. As a result, women are not as likely to be properly screened for lung cancer as their male counterparts; men are more than twice as likely to have diagnostic tests ordered as compared with women.

Similarly, heart disease became associated with men. Women were not perceived as potential victims of heart failure because of the prophylactic effects of estrogen. Although estrogen probably does provide temporary protection from heart disease for women, heart disease is, in fact, the leading cause death for women; women just tend to die ten years later of heart disease than men.

As such, there are disturbing differences between the medical care provided to men as compared with women suffering from cardiovascular disease. Women are more likely to be misdiagnosed when suffering from heart disease, women receive fewer invasive procedures (men are twice as likely to undergo a cardiac procedure), with poorer outcomes when invasive procedures are performed, and women are more likely to die sooner after they have a heart attack. Studies suggest that men are 6.5 to 10 times more likely to be referred for cardiac catheterization after an abnormal stress test than women.

The symptoms of angina for a woman may be different than a man which could lead to improper or delayed diagnosis. But research studies show that "women were more than twice as likely to have their symptoms attributed to somatic, psychiatric, or other noncardiac causes as men." Moreover, the lower use of invasive procedures for women, and treatment only through medications, cannot be explained by the medical conditions of women versus those of men. In other words, a man with the same condition would be treated more aggressively by the medical profession. Evidence suggests that there might even be disparities when medications are prescribed to treat cardiovascular disease. Women are less likely to receive thrombolytic therapy, intravenous drugs that dissolve blood clots. "Physicians prescribed nitrates (vasodilators which increase oxygen supply to the heart muscle) and anticoagulation (blood-thinning) therapy more often to men and prescribed diuretics (water pills) more often to women."

Further, the prognosis for women is not as good as for men when an invasive procedure is performed. Originally, equipment was designed for men and was not as well suited for the narrower coronary arteries of women which led to poorer outcomes. The higher death rate can also be attributed to the delay in treatment and the fact that women are usually older than men when they develop heart disease. Again, however, men are more likely to receive coronary angiography, angioplasty, and bypass surgery than women when presenting the same symptoms.

Similarly, a woman suffering from end-stage renal disease has a one-third to one-half chance to receive a kidney transplant compared with a man with the same medical history. The American Medical Association (AMA) cannot explain this phenomena based on any rational medical criteria. The Report of the Council on Ethical and Judicial Affairs of the AMA made the following observation:

> Societal value judgments placed on gender or gender roles may also put women at a disadvantage in the context of receiving certain major diagnostic and therapeutic interventions, such as kidney transplantation and cardiac catheterization. A general perception that men's social role obligations or of their contributions to society are greater than women's may fuel these disparities. For instance, altering one's work schedule to accommodate health concerns may be viewed as more difficult for men than for women. Overall, men's financial contribution to the family may be considered more critical than women's. A kidney transplant is much less cumbersome than dialysis. Coronary bypass surgery, for which catheterization is a prerequisite, is a more efficient and immediate solution to the problem of coronary artery disease than continuous antianginal drug therapy. However, judgments based on evaluations of social worth or preconceptions about the probable roles of men and women are clearly inexcusable in the context of medical decision-making.

Conversely, the medical profession has been criticized for too quickly resorting to surgical solutions for women, particularly in the area of reproductive health.

The mental health field has also been attacked for treatment discrepancies based on gender. Some of the DSM-IV guidelines are attacked as containing sex biases, which could result in a normal woman in our culture easily being misdiagnosed as having various personality disorders. The DSM-IV definition of premenstrual dysphoric disorder (PMDD), commonly known as PMS, is perhaps the most disturbing. The mere inclusion of PMS indicates that a normal biological function for a woman might still be perceived as a disorder. For many in the field of women's health, the PMDD guideline has become a symbolic regression to the historical attitude that a woman's reproductive function was a disease. In response, the mental health field claims that it is a proper criteria and is only used in extreme cases. The danger of abuse of the criteria is just now surfacing with the development of prescription drugs for premenstrual dysphoric disorder.

Concern regarding overuse of prescription drugs by the mental health field, particularly anti-depressants, is well justified. Historically, women and mental illness were perceived as intertwined. During the twentieth century, psychiatrists used surgery as a method to treat mental illness in women. Women were much more likely to have electric shock treatments and lobotomies at the hands of the mental health field. It is certainly not surprising that some accuse the mental health field of much the same behavior through the use of psychotropic drugs instead of surgery.

Women are two to four times more likely to be diagnosed with depression than men and women are prescribed 70 percent of all tranquilizers and anti-depressants. Yet research populations were all male in the development of most of the anti-depressants in use today. There is more and more evidence that some anti-depressants might not be appropriate for women. Further, normal hormonal fluctuations during the menstrual cycle cause a woman to be overdosed at certain times during the month and under medicated at others. The extensive use of anti-depressants has also been challenged because men are less likely to be prescribed anti-depressants when presenting with the same symptoms as a woman. Treatment disparities are likely to continue in the mental health field until medical research provides gender-specific drugs in this area of medicine. Some critics of this field of practice will not likely be pacified until the DSM-IV guidelines are reevaluated to remove the perceived taint of gender bias.

Gender bias has influenced medical practice. Research deficiencies are clearly reflected in the day-to-day practice of medicine. Furthermore, some areas of practice are more tainted than others, such as the treatment of AIDS, heart, lung, and kidney disease, and the mental health field. However, positive steps have been taken by the medical profession as well as the research industry. These steps should indicate a brighter future for the elimination of inappropriate treatment disparities based on gender.

MANAGED CARE'S IMPACT ON WOMEN

Women are the largest group of consumers of health care in America. "Women outnumber men. Women outlive men. Women use more health services than men—they visit doctors more often, undergo more complex procedures, have more laboratory tests, take more medications, and spend more time in hospitals." Any drastic change in the delivery of health care systems will, from a demographic standpoint alone, impact women more than men. Accordingly, any reduction in the quantity or quality of care received as a result of managed care plans will, by definition, impact women's health more than men's health.

Demographics

Many complex factors intertwine to explain why women consume disproportionately more health care services. The mere fact that women utilize medical services during the reproductive process is not a significant factor in the equation. Women consume more medical resources in part due to the "feminization of poverty." The term feminization of poverty refers to the fact that two-thirds of the poor in this country are women. This phenomena was partially caused by the increases in households headed by single women, which are disproportionately poorer than families with both parents. The feminization of poverty has also resulted in the "pauperization of children" who live in female-headed households with single mothers who lack the earning power to support themselves and their children above the poverty line. The "pauperization" extends to older women as well because women live longer than men. "At both ends of life's spectrum, women are reduced to poverty through living costs that escalate in the absence or loss of male support. Regardless of whether their income is supplemented by transfer payments (government benefits (or child support)), the poverty persists."

The feminization of poverty increases health care costs because health problems are caused by "workplace dangers, inadequate sanitation and housing, joblessness, environmental pollution, excessive stress, malnutrition, or violence." Furthermore, "(p)eople with low incomes have more illnesses and die in greater numbers and earlier than people with more income and education." However, poverty is only a partial answer to the question why women consume more health care resources than men.

Women outlive men by approximately seven years, but women also have greater morbidity than men, i.e., more generalized poor health.

Although women are more frequently ill, they suffer from problems that are serious but not life threatening; these conditions lead to symptoms, disability, and medical care, but not death. Men are sick less often, but their illnesses and injuries are more severe; men have higher rates of chronic diseases that are the leading causes of death.

In other words, women live longer sicker lives; men live shorter healthier lives. Furthermore, some diseases, such as Alzheimer's, are more likely to affect women because they live to an older age. As Medicare and Medicaid systems embrace capitated-managed care systems, women will be more affected than men because women are more likely to be beneficiaries under both systems from a purely demographic standpoint.

The Potential HMO Fix for the "Feminization of Poverty"

The government provided incentives for the growth of HMOs to provide health care coverage to larger segments of the population for less money. If more people became insured versus uninsured, health care would improve for society as a whole particularly for the largest class of impoverished and underinsured people, women. Providing coverage to more people which would allow in turn more access to a broader range of health care services, particularly preventative medicine and prenatal care, would benefit women collectively even if individual treatment was not the ultimate medical science would allow.

Originally, managed care was perceived as a partial solution to the "feminization of poverty." In addition to the provision of comprehensive and coordinated care and focusing on prevention and health promotion, premiums and out-of-pocket expenses are usually lower for coverage through an HMO compared with a fee-for-service plan. Furthermore, Medicaid and Medicare beneficiaries under fee-for-service plans often confronted nonfinancial barriers to care, including "inadequate payment levels result-ing in low physician participation, a scarcity of physicians in the impoverished communi-ties where many Medicaid beneficiaries reside, and heavy reliance of fragmented care in hospitals that are often overcrowded and understaffed." Many hoped that Medicare and Medicaid HMOs would curb the rising costs of these programs while mitigating the nonfinancial barriers to access to health care. "Though women consumers have had mixed experiences with nonprofit HMOs, research has shown health outcomes to be quite good. The financial incentives to physician-managers to skimp on care have mostly been balanced by nonprofit HMOs' commitment to reduc-ing costs by keeping people healthy."

However, nonprofit HMOs are no longer the norm and for-profit HMOs have rapidly besieged the market. For-profit HMOs, with their cost-containment mechanisms and per-formance-based incentives, have the arguable propensity to "offer lower quality and fewer services to make larger profits." If the fear that cost-saving techniques will result in denial of or inadequate coverage for important services including specialized care, mental health ser-vices, and long-term care for those suffering from disabling or chronic illness is true, then women as a class will suffer from the for-profit structure of HMOs more than men. "Not surprisingly, critics have dubbed these new for-profit managed care systems 'man-gled care.' Another name could be 'manage-ment care' for a system that provides top management and the doctor-managers of health care corporations with optimum care and compensation, largely at the expense of women."

However, managed care might still have the propensity to help women as a general class. "Managed care has the potential to offer women what they have long desired: comprehensive, coordinated care and an emphasis on preventive services. Studies, for instance, show that women who are HMO members are more likely than women with traditional insurance to receive pap smears and mammograms." However, these are statutorily mandated in some jurisdictions. Managed care is also beginning to routinely screen women for Chlamydia infection. In the one-year period between 1999 and 2000, 72,500 more women than in the previous year were screened for Chlamydia, which if left untreated can cause pelvic inflammatory disease (PID), infertility, ectopic pregnancy, and HIV infection. The same one-year period saw a one-percent increase in breast-cancer screening, saving 130 lives, and an 8 percent increase in pap smears, saving 610 lives. Moreover, many of the larger man-aged care corporations are promoting invest-ments they are making in women's health.

Kaiser Permanente in northern California has a program to identify women at high risk for breast cancer and has contributed to stud-ies on the relationship between hormone replacement therapy and breast cancer. Two of its centers are participating in the Women's Health Initiative, the $625 million study of postmenopausal women's health. U.S. Healthcare is taking part in studies of bone marrow transplants for advanced breast cancer. A handful of plans, including Group Health Cooperative of Puget Sound and Harvard Pilgrim Health Care, are teaching their doctors how to screen women for domestic violence. And Oxford Health Plan is covering a wide range of alternative therapies, an area of special interest to women, and intends to introduce a women's health pro-gram (in 1997).

The Provision of Health Care Services to Women Enrollees

The public promotion of women's health might not be for purely altruistic reasons; MCOs and HMOs are for-profit organiza-tions who realize women are their largest customers. Despite efforts to purvey to women, women in managed care plans still report lower satisfaction with the care provided than women enrolled in other types of plans.

Assuming managed care might have the propensity to further the health needs of women generally (including better preventative services for breast and cervical cancer), fulfillment of the needs of the broader societal interest in women does not necessarily equate to the provision of better care to the majority of individual women within the plan in the treatment or diagnosis of conditions or disease. The managed care system inherited the gender bias that was prevalent within the medical profession and treatment and diagnostic decisions will likely reflect the same biases that were present under the fee-for-service system once prevention fails and a woman-enrollee becomes ill. Any ingrained gender bias would likely become more accentuated because managed care uses cost-containment incentives and physician risk-sharing to curtail specialized services, diagnostic tests, and hospital admissions.

As previously established, gender bias is reflected in the provision of diagnostic tests in the screening for lung and heart disease and in the use of kidney transplantation and invasive procedures to treat cardiovascular disease. Much of this information was compiled while the fee-for-service system predominated. Under a fee-for-service system, physicians make money by ordering diagnostic tests and invasive procedures. The gender bias was sufficiently ingrained to overcome any personal interest in compensation. The AMA opined that the gender disparity in treatment of lung, heart, and kidney disease could not be explained by differences in the clinical presentation of women versus men patients and was most likely explained by subconscious inappropriate gender stereotyping. Under a managed care system with cost-containment incentives and physician risk-sharing, physicians make more money the less doctors order diagnostic tests and costly procedures. Inappropriate subconscious

gender stereotyping would likely be more pronounced when combined with institutional pressures to save money and a subconscious or conscious desire to earn more money by the physician. In other words, women are the likely class of patients that physicians under managed care would be likely to not refer for specialized care, diagnostic, or invasive procedures because women are already not referred for this type of care as a result of the preexisting gender bias prevalent in this area. In fact, one study "found that primary care physicians referred women to specialists less often overall than they did men."

Diagnostic decisions based on physician-patient communication is very likely to be problematic to women-enrollees of HMOs. Women in managed care are more likely than women in fee-for-service systems to assert that their doctor does not spend sufficient time with them.

Quota systems requiring physicians to see a minimum number of patients per day are another aspect of managed care that will affect women's health. Given that forty-one percent of women report changing their physicians because of dissatisfaction about not being heard or taken seriously, volume-based measures of doctors' performance are likely to compromise women's experiences even further.

Physicians are less likely to take a woman's physical complaints as serious as a man's even without consideration of "volume-based measures" of doctors' performance. Studies have shown that men are more stoic in their communicative style; women are more descriptive. Studies also show that physicians are much more likely to take complaints more seriously if they are delivered in a stoic, non-emotional manner. Presentation of symptoms of disease in a stoic fashion is much more compatible with a system where time is limited with patients as in many managed care systems. Seventy-five percent of physicians in managed care feel pressure to see more patients per day (24 percent believed the pressure comprises patient care) and 53.8 percent believe that time spent per patient was either marginal or severely limited.

In a time-restrictive system, physicians are likely to perpetuate the bias that a woman's illness is "all in her head." If a man and a woman present to a doctor with the same physical symptoms, the physician is much more likely to prescribe a psychoactive drug to the woman, assuming her complaint is psychogenic, but will perform diagnostic tests on the man in quest of a physical explanation. Women with symptoms of heart disease are more than "twice as likely to have their symptoms attributed to somatic, psychiatric, or other non-cardiac causes as men." Thus, physicians within managed care systems that are designed with cost-savings disincentives toward specialized care and diagnostic services coupled with a time crunch caused by patient quotas would appear much more likely to misdiagnose women patients due to their non-stoic communicative styles and the preexisting ill-founded bias that women suffer from more psychosomatic illnesses.

The Primary Care Physician and Access to Specialized Treatment

Arguably, the predominate features of most HMOs, the cost-containment and physician-performance incentives of capitation, prospective utilization review, and physician risk-sharing, have the built-in potential to impact women more than men because the goals of all are furthered by gender bias. Further, managed care is designed to limit patient choice and women's health needs might not be furthered by requiring treatment by primary care providers within managed care.

Recent studies suggest that enrollees of managed care are more satisfied with out-of-pocket costs, preventive treatments, and the range of services provided than members of fee-for-service plans. Generally, however, managed care's patients are less satisfied with their choice of doctors, ease of changing physicians, and access to specialized care than fee-for-service patients. Managed care enrollees are six times more likely to be dissatisfied with choice of doctors and the ability to change physicians, and four out of ten women in fair or poor health "were not satisfied with the availability of advice by phone, an area that is particularly important for people in poor health." Further, studies have also established a causal link between poorer health outcomes and enrollment by the chronically ill poor and elderly in managed care plans compared with those in fee-for-service systems.

Many plans allow women to designate obstetrician/gynecologist (OB/GYNs) as their family care provider. However, many times this accommodation was a direct result of state statutes that dictated that women could choose an OB/GYN as their primary care provider. "(M)ost patients of obstetrician/gynecologists see no other practitioner for primary care," yet OB/GYNs are not trained in a quarter of the skills necessary to deliver primary care. Family practitioners have, in fact, the greatest training in delivering the broad range of services required for a "gatekeeper" compared with the training of other specialists, including internists. The training for family practice covers comprehensive care, but its curriculum is based on the male-only model.

Currently, no primary care specialty trains physicians to deliver high-quality comprehensive care to women based on research and clinical training with women. A 1992 survey showed that only twenty-five percent of medical schools offered training in women's health beyond obstetrics/gynecology, and what was offered was elective, rather than mandatory. Consequently, most of the primary care physicians women will visit under managed care plans will have had little or no training in women's health.

Evidence exists that currently primary care providers are neither sufficiently trained in women's health needs nor trained to overcome established practices where gender bias is reflected. "One study found that primary care physicians judged sixty-five percent of women's symptoms, versus fifty-one percent of men's, to be influenced by emotional factors. Perhaps, not surprisingly, women's complaints were more than twice as likely as men's to be identified as psychosomatic."

The Institute of Medicine issued a report in 1996 that concluded that family practitioners and internists did not have some of the skills necessary to perform the myriad of duties they are expected to perform in managed care. The *New England Journal of Medicine* reported that one in four primary care physicians believed that the scope of services they were expected to provide was inappropriate and another study revealed that over one-third felt uncomfortable with some of the procedures they performed in managed care. "Internal medicine residents, for instance, lacked experience in such areas as gynecology and preventive medicine, the supposed bedrock of managed care." A study conducted at Cook County Hospital in Chicago found that 40 percent of internal medicine and family practice residents would not think about providing information regarding family planning or German measles immunizations to a healthy woman. Furthermore, "(g)eneralists were also remiss in counseling women about sexually transmitted diseases, safer sex, and preconception care."

Primary care physicians are also insufficiently trained to render obstetrical/gynecological care. "(S)tudies clearly document that non-gynecologist physicians do an inadequate job of providing pap smears and pelvic and breast exams." Women are allowed to see their OB/GYNs without a referral in about three-quarters of the plans; however, women still need a referral in about half of these plans unless the appointment is for the one "well-woman" check-up allowed per year. Access to OB/GYNs without referrals, even as limited as it is, has been incorporated into plans as a direct response to statutory mandates throughout the country in many instances. "Women whose plans do not designate obstetrician/gynecologists as primary care providers, will need referrals for basic reproductive services. When systems discourage referral, however, doctors designated as primary care providers may take on functions for which they are inadequately trained." Or, a woman with a gynecological or obstetrical problem must first see the primary care provider for a referral and then make another appointment with the OB/GYN, causing delay that in some instances can cause serious harm.

"(P)rimary care is more than just the absence of specialization. It is a specific set of skills that requires appropriate education and training." However, 56.8 percent of primary care physicians responding to one survey reported that participation in managed care did not encourage them to acquire new skills or keep old skills sharp. Further, 67.4 percent did not believe that managed care had increased their interest in keeping up with new developments in their field.

Furthermore, it is feared that HMOs are susceptible to "organizational pathologies" inherent in large organizations that can "impede change, become unresponsive, and limit the appropriate use of discretion by professionals," thereby diminishing personal responsibility and accountability. Again, the structure of the HMO does not appear to be conducive to self-monitoring of proficiency. HMOs do participate in clinical research; however, the research tends to concentrate on effectiveness studies to improve the delivery of health care, not research designed to acquire new medical technologies for providing care. Research is typically designed for short-term benefits for "potential application in that particular MCO and its business objectives." Thus, the research focuses on renovation, not innovation.

Obviously, new discoveries are constantly being made in medicine. In the area of women's health, science is just beginning to appreciate the depth of the gender gap. Research results from including women in research populations with gender analysis of data is likely to increase given the NIH's guidelines and FDA's expectation that women should participate in research studies. The inherent nature of managed care with its tendency to pressure physicians to treat more patients daily would seem to be the antithesis of an environment to remain abreast of current developments.

One danger to women's health is the primary care physicians remaining ignorant of new discoveries particularly in the administering of prescription drugs. It would appear from a layperson's standpoint that primary care physicians have an incredible task as they perform the duties of a full-service physician and must remember from the "all-male model" of medical training the appropriate treatment and medication for the myriad of diseases and conditions they confront on a day-to-day basis. Now, science is injecting the two-model approach with discoveries of differences in the way men and women respond to medications and treatments. Women have more adverse side effects from prescription drugs. Men and women react to some prescription drugs very differently, such as antidepressants and medications for seizures, asthma, allergies, high blood pressure, pain, and heart failure. Furthermore, low fat diets may be appropriate for men, but unnecessary for women. Treatment of cholesterol levels might differ drastically depending on whether the patient is male or female. Further, some studies suggest that moderate consumption of alcohol might help prevent men from having a heart attack, but moderate consumption by women might increase the risk of breast cancer. One has to wonder whether primary care physicians within the managed care system can adapt to the two-model approach to medicine if managed care does not encourage them to keep abreast of new discoveries in their field or acquire new skills as the survey of primary care physicians suggest.

Mental Health Concerns

Overall, women use more mental health services than men. Family practitioners do receive some training in behavioral medicine, which includes problems such as substance abuse, depression, incest, violence, and eating disorders. Once again, however, the training is based on the male model, not a female one. Physicians will likely misdiagnose and mistreat secondary physical illness resulting from violence and sexism if they are untrained in the female model of behavior medicine. In most HMOs, women, in order to receive care from a mental health specialist, must first see the primary care physician in his or her role as gatekeeper who must refer patients, typically following established institutional protocols, for all specialized care, including psychiatric care. But, family care providers are expected to treat rather than refer patients with many psychiatric disorders. However, the primary care physician has insufficient formal training in psychiatry and treatment by the family practitioner could easily result in misdiagnosis or undertreatment. Seventy-three percent of all prescriptions for psychotropic medications are written for women; however, that figures jumps to "an incredible ninety percent when the prescribing physician is not a psychiatrist." Generalists prescribe over seventy percent of anti-depressants.

(S)tudies suggest that they're more likely than psychiatrists to prescribe these drugs at suboptimal doses. They're also more likely than mental health specialists to rely on medication alone—and the wrong medication in many cases . . . . As a result, women with depression who are denied therapy and pushed to use inappropriate drugs won't get the relief they need.

There is also substantial evidence that HMOs have a significant negative impact on the quality of mental health care services received by enrollees. For example, seriously ill patients with depression and schizophrenics treated within an HMO have an additional functional limitation than those treated within a fee-for-service plan. This means that the patient within the HMO might not be able to work around the house or keep a job whereas their fee-for-service counterpart would be able to do so. Furthermore, utilization management has greatly reduced the length of in-patient hospital stays and the number of outpatient treatment sessions. Many plans only cover twenty sessions of outpatient therapy per year, and some will attempt to limit the numbers of sessions even further despite the explicit coverage provision. "(A)lthough men and women have the same rates of psychiatric disorders in any given year, women seek assistance from the health care system more frequently than men and are therefore more affected by policies limiting such care." Further, some mental health concerns predominately effect women.

Many plans, for example, limit coverage to "acute" conditions that are "amenable to short-term resolution." Accordingly, the plans might exclude treatment for bulimia or anorexia, a condition that primarily affects women, because it requires long-term treatment, for example more than twenty sessions, and thus patients with these conditions are not eligible for the benefits under the plan. Further, women are much more likely to be victims of abuse than men. Yet, "victims of rape, incest, or physical abuse require considerably more than a few sessions in order to recover, particularly if they endured prolonged, repeated, or childhood abuse."

It has been suggested that limiting reimbursement to only a small number of sessions per year "makes no sense clinically." One proposed solution combines restricting cost by limiting in-patient care to those patients who are truly a danger to themselves or others while at the same time expanding outpatient plan coverage to a minimum of fifty sessions per year. Further, patients would be required to perform two hours of self-help work per one hour of outpatient treatment to supplement and foster any therapy provided. Appropriate self-help work might include reading appropriate material, participation in self-help groups, viewing educational videotapes, or completing interactive learning computer programs or workbooks. "The challenge of meeting women's mental health needs within a budget can be solved by a combination of focusing managed care interventions more appropriately, using new treatments methods, and enacting legislation" to mandate a clinically appropriate standard of fifty hours of outpatient treatment that would be required of all health care plans.

Surgery and Hospitalization

Managed care companies frequently assert that they are protecting women by limiting access to the surgical procedures that were performed unnecessarily in the past under pay-for-service plans, for example, hysterectomies, and cesarean sections.

What these companies don't say is that while unnecessary or unproven surgeries are being reduced, so are necessary ones. Some managed care companies, for instance, define reconstructive surgery after mastectomy as cosmetic rather than medically necessary and refuse to cover it. Or they pay for the first part of the procedure—the operation to recreate the breast mound—but not subsequent procedures, such as the nipple reconstruction or surgery to adjust the opposite breast so it matches the new one. Even more galling, the same managed care companies that deny breast reconstruction sometimes cover penile implant surgery.

Managed care has been relentless in the reduction of the number of in-patient hospital days. There has been a reduction in in-patient days of forty percent per thousand patients. Notable examples are the famous "drive-by deliveries," outpatient mastectomies, and discharging women after gynecological procedures with catheters in place. However, performance of less-renowned surgical procedures on an outpatient basis or reduction of the recuperative time spent within the hospital will also have a disproportionate impact on women inasmuch as surgery is performed on women 50 percent more often than on men.

The trend toward outpatient care, lowering hospital admissions, combined with the reduction of the amount of in-patient days caused a financial crunch in many hospitals. Many hospitals responded by reductions in staff which resulted in registered nurses no longer delivering care, but instead supervising less-trained personnel. Nurses fear the reduction of staff and delivery of care by personnel other than nurses impacts the quality of care delivered within hospitals. One survey reported that 57 percent of registered nurses believed that the quality of nursing care did not meet professional standards.

One hidden cost of shortening the length of time spent in hospitals is the cost to family members who become surrogate nurses when patients are discharged. Most people who provide surrogate nursing will be women.

Interestingly, however, studies advocating early discharge fail to consider the impact—financial or otherwise—on family caregivers. When studies suggest that reducing length of stay saves money, costs incurred by family caregivers are almost never factored into cost-benefit analyses. These costs are very real and include time taken off work, job losses related to family caregiving burdens, emotional stress, and physical illnesses that may result from shouldering this burden.

Managed care's quest to reduce cost through limiting length of hospital stays and increasing outpatient treatment has directly impacted more women than men because

women are the largest consumers of health and surgical care. Furthermore, women are just as importantly impacted indirectly by virtue of the fact they are forced to assume surrogate-nursing duties as the usual caregivers when patients are discharged earlier than in the past.

Impact on Sub-Populations

There is no definitive study that shows a reduction in the overall quality or effectiveness of medical care in managed care systems. Yet "evidence suggests that managed care may adversely affect the health of some vulnerable subpopulations" based on socioeconomic, racial, and ethnic disparities. Moreover, institutional quality control has inadequately invested in efforts to collect data, monitor, and address disparities in the health care of subpopulations.

The progression of disease can differ drastically between different subpopulations. For example, Caucasian women have the greatest incidence of breast cancer, but African-American women have higher mortality rates. Native Hawaiian women have an unusually high death rate, while American Indian women in New Mexico have the lowest rate of incidence of breast cancer and the lowest death rate. Asian-American women have a higher incident rate of invasive cervical cancer than Caucasian women, with Vietnamese women having a five times higher rate of incidence than in Caucasian women. African-American women are the most at risk for death from heart disease (there are 147 deaths per 100,000 compared to 88 for Caucasian women). Asian-American/Pacific Islander women age sixty-five or older have the highest suicide rate of all women. African-American women have the highest rate of obesity, while Alaska Native women have the highest smoking rate. Seventy-seven percent of all women with AIDS are African-American or Hispanic, with AIDS being the second leading cause of death of twenty-five to forty-four year-old African-American women.

These disparities could indicate difference in rates of early detection of disease, treatment protocols, cultural, or lifestyle factors. In addition, there could exist an undiscovered physiological explanation for some of these disparities, that science has yet to discover. The exclusion of women from research studies created a large void of information regarding women's health, but it also created a similar void for racial/ethnic and socioeconomic subpopulations. Both the NIH and FDA have addressed racial/ethnic analysis of data as well as gender analysis. Research clearly reveals a racial/ethnic/socioeconomic disparity in the treatment and progression of some diseases and that some subpopulations require tailored support plans to allow effective treatment of their diseases. Compared to more affluent women, lower-income women have a "higher incidence of chronic conditions such as arthritis, hypertension, diabetes, or limitations in activities" and are more "likely to report anxiety or depression, suicidal thoughts, and dissatisfaction with their lives or have low self-esteem," compounding their health problems. As a result, access to specialized care is more important to lower-income women as a class because they usually have more chronic health needs.

Yet, studies of managed care systems establish that lower-income women have low levels of satisfaction with their plans in key areas. One-third of low-income women and women in fair to poor health rated their access to specialty care as fair to poor, an area that particularly affects these subpopulations because their need might be greater overall for specialized care due to their chronic health needs. "Women with incomes below $25,000 were more likely to be dissatisfied with the clinic hours, waiting time to get a routine appointment, availability of emergency care, waiting time to get care in an emergency, and access to specialty care."

Low-income women, despite generally poorer health status and lower access rates than higher-income women, were "more susceptible to access constraints," meaning that lower-income women might have more difficulty maneuvering utilization controls within managed care systems or those constraints create an undue burden to access for lower-income women. Further, studies have shown differences in the quality of care of subpopulations within the managed care system; for example, poorer health outcomes for the elderly and the chronically ill poor have been linked to enrollment in managed care plans as compared with more traditional health care plans. If managed care has the propensity to perpetuate gender bias and if the cost-containment efforts and performance incentives impact the health of women enrollees more than men, the negative impact of managed care might be magnified toward vulnerable subpopulations, as recent studies suggest, resulting in a decrease in the quality of services rendered with corresponding negative health outcomes.

CONCLUSION

The genesis of medical gender bias can be traced to scientific ignorance and the patriarchal structure of our society. The male-centeredness of our society caused physicians, during the primal period of the development of medicine as a science, to perceive women as inherently pathological with all illness springing from her reproductive organs. The early practitioners also created the perception that normal biological functions of women were diseases causing illness and mental instability. As science and society matured, twentieth-century doctors abandoned the concept that the uterus, as the root of all disease, was the controlling organ in a woman's anatomy. Instead, "modern medicine" gave us the male model of treatment with the assumption that men and women were biologically the same, with the exception of reproductive organs, and the progression of disease, responses to pharmaceuticals, and diagnostic and treatment decisions would be the same for both men and women. The health needs of women were studied and approached as if women were small men with breasts, uteruses, and vaginas.

Research until the last decade of the twentieth century was conducted on all-male research populations due to protectionism of women and their unborn children, to enable more readily validated research by having research populations as homogeneous as possible, and as a result of the fear of liability if an unborn child was unwittingly injured as a result of the mother's participation in a research study. Research results derived from all-male research participants were simply extrapolated and applied to the remainder of the population under the assumption that women would respond to disease and treatment the same as men. The women's health movement brought awareness of medical gender bias to the forefront which caused the medical and scientific communities to acknowledge its presence and the resulting negative impact upon women's health.

Science is now awakening to the disparity in differences of the health needs of men and women as more and more evidence of the gender gap is revealed. However, medicine is only as good as the science on which it is based. Prior to 1993, federal regulatory policy excluded fertile people from participation in research studies to protect women and their potential fetuses from research and protect the research industry from liability to women and their children. Although NIH guidelines in 1986 encouraged researchers to include woman participants, the guideline was rarely implemented nor enforced. The NIH's Revitalization Act of 1993 requires the inclusion of sufficient women to assure valid gender analysis of data in most clinical trials unless the inclusion is inappropriate from the

standpoint of the health of the participant, the nature of the research, or there is a clear and compelling rationale for the exclusion. Thus, research studies funded by the NIH can still exclude pregnant women or pregnable women if the research poses an "unacceptable risk for women of childbearing potential." The FDA removed the federal impediment to the inclusion of women in clinical trials in 1993; however, FDA guidelines still require that female participants are not pregnant and will avoid pregnancy during the trial.

Both the NIH and FDA policies are positive moves for women's health. However, both can easily be criticized as not going far enough to provide sufficient meaningful data of gender differences. The FDA policy expects that women be included in clinical trials with proper gender analysis of data but does not mandate inclusion. The FDA should mandate the inclusion of women in clinical trials. Arguably, pharmaceutical companies face more liability for excluding women from research and subsequently injecting a product without sufficient testing on women into the stream of commerce than for inclusion of women in research studies. Further, firmly established principles of self-autonomy support the principle that a woman, even if she is biologically capable of becoming pregnant, has the right to decide for herself whether to participate in a research study with acceptance of any accompanying unknown or unknowable risk of harm to her future reproductive capabilities or her future progeny, as men currently have the right to accept.

Participation by pregnant women in research trials is more controversial. However, courts would probably decide that a pregnant woman has the right to consent to experimental treatment if the treatment has therapeutic value to herself or her fetus, even if the treatment is accompanied by a potential risk of harm. The right of self-autonomy supports the right for the pregnant woman to weigh the therapeutic value of any treatment against the potential harm to her fetus and decide whether the treatment is in the best interest of herself and the future of her family. Accordingly, pregnant women should not be excluded from research trials assuming the research has therapeutic value, to herself or to her fetus. Some non-therapeutic research poses no danger to a pregnant woman or to her fetus. Exclusion of pregnant women from participation in any non-therapeutic research is simply overbroad and the NIH and FDA guidelines should not exclude pregnant women from non-therapeutic research if the risk of in-vivo injuries is minimal.

Inclusion of women in research is essential to the provision of improved medical care for women. Granted, the thought of women of childbearing potential, especially pregnant women, participating in clinical research is a frightening prospect to many in our society. More frightening, however, is the continued practice of women consuming prescription drugs when neither the medical profession nor the pharmaceutical industry knows the true impact on women due to clinical testing on only male participants.

Research deficiencies regarding women's health clearly impacts the treatment provided by physicians. However, the research industry cannot be blamed entirely for the treatment disparities. Preconceived biases possessed by some members of the medical community also perpetuate gender bias. Women are perceived differently from men by physicians. Women's complaints are not taken as seriously and physicians are more likely to consider a woman's physical symptoms as having a psychogenic origin than a man presenting the same physical symptoms. Women are more likely to be prescribed a psychoactive drug than a man with the same symptoms. In some areas of practice, doctors are much more likely to misdiagnose women and are much less likely to order diagnostic tests or invasive procedures for a woman as compared with a man. There is no medical explanation for the treatment differences. The AMA has recognized

the presence of gender bias within the medical profession and encouraged doctors to examine their own attitudes to assure that biases did not impact treatment and that gender was not used as an inappropriate criteria for clinical decision-making.

Managed care entered the forefront of the health care arena at approximately the same time as significant inroads were being made in the area of women's health. Managed care utilizes capitated payments, prospective utilization review, physician risk-sharing, and primary care providers to screen referrals for diagnostic tests, hospitalization, and specialized care. Performance-based incentives and cost-containment mechanisms are designed to reduce the rising cost of medical care. However, there is growing consumer concern regarding the quality of care rendered and the impact of managed care on women's health.

Women are the largest consumers of health care in this country and any impact that managed care has on quality will impact women more than men from a demographic standpoint. Originally, managed care was perceived as a partial solution to the "feminization of poverty" because managed care had the potential to provide health-care coverage to broader segments of the population for less money and offered ostensibly better preventative and prenatal care. Today there is some evidence that managed care is having a negative impact on women enrollees, especially socioeconomic or ethnic subpopulations, despite the lack of empirical support that managed care has eroded the overall quality of care. The legislative response to the quality of care rendered by MCOs and HMOs indirectly acknowledges that quality issues dealing with managed care are more likely to impact women. Evidencing the presence of gender bias within managed care systems is the fact that legislation was perceived as necessary to allow a sufficient hospital stay for childbirth, assure pap smears and mammograms would be provided, allow sufficient recuperative time following a mastectomy, and assure that the resulting reconstructive surgery would be provided.

Subconscious gender stereotyping, already proven to influence diagnostic decisions and referrals for diagnostic tests and invasive procedures, are likely to become more pronounced in managed care given the institutional pressures created by physician risk-sharing, cost-containment measures, and prospective utilization review to save money. Quota systems designed to force physicians to treat more patients per day might impact women more than men because of differences in communicative styles. Indeed, recent studies of women enrollees of managed care show that women are not as satisfied with their choice of physicians or access to specialized care as fee-for-service patients.

The primary care physician acts as a gatekeeper to the managed care system. Specialized care, hospitalization, and diagnostic testing must first be approved by the primary care physician. Yet, very few primary care physicians have training in women's health other than a basic course in obstetrics and gynecology. Studies suggest that primary care providers are not sufficiently trained in the myriad of duties they are expected to perform and might not be sufficiently schooled in women's health to overcome the built-in gender biases of attributing a woman's physical symptoms as psychosomatic and not treating women the same as men in referring women for diagnostic tests and invasive procedures to treat certain conditions. Concern is also raised that the primary care physician will not be able to readily adapt as the research industry provides new information of gender differences in response to disease and treatment in a system that has been criticized by physicians as not fostering physicians to keep abreast of new developments.

One reform of the managed care system to assure women's health is not sacrificed by the performance-based incentives and cost-containment mechanisms is to require primary care physicians to receive formal educational training in women's health. Primary care providers should include all physicians who provide primary health care services to women enrolled in managed care plans, including internists and OB-GYNs. Managed care could require that primary care physicians complete a medical school course in women's health as a condition of the provider contract. Primary care providers already within the system could be required to participate in continuing medical education courses regarding women's health. Managed care setting the requirement would have the added byproduct of forcing the addition of women's health courses in all medical schools and the creation of a more extensive market in continuing medical education courses.

Primary care physicians are not sufficiently trained in mental illness, yet many times they treat patients suffering from mental illness typically with a heavier reliance on the use of antidepressants, often prescribing lower doses than needed. Further, primary care providers may act as a gatekeeper to mental health services within the system. Women are the largest consumers of mental health services and any restriction to mental health services impacts women as a class more than men. Coverage of outpatient sessions is restricted to only a limited number of sessions by the terms of some plans or by de facto prospective utilization review in other plans. Expanding outpatient sessions to fifty outpatient sessions per year is clinically sound and would allow more effective treatment of the serious conditions that need more prolonged therapy. Expansion of mental health outpatient coverage would benefit women because women are more likely to suffer from conditions necessitating prolonged outpatient treatment.

The eradication of gender bias within the medical community will take years. The litigation system will not be a very likely method to indirectly attack the problem of gender bias, particularly given the presence of ERISA, although certainly the legal system might provide compensation for women who were treated by physicians who failed to use the standard of care other doctors would have used under the same circumstances. If litigation is probably not an effective way to attack the problem, the only other avenues would appear to be consumerism and legislation.

Women need to become more aggressive in demanding medical research, medical treatment, and health plans consider women's health a top priority. Expanding research and the inclusion of more women in clinical trials is critical to the development of a mode of practice that is clinically sound for women and to bypass the traditional all-male model to the practice of medicine. Further, women need to be more vocal in their demands of managed care. Most cost-containment measures revolve around the primary care provider. The starting point to avoid the preservation of the status quo with its inherent gender bias is enlightening primary care physicians in women's health. Consumerism is one avenue of change. Managed care might respond to consumer pressure from women because women are the largest consumers of health care and managed care has been solicitous to women in the past. If managed care fails to respond and if "customers become sufficiently discontented, they will eventually call on legislatures to act on their behalf."

STUDY QUESTION

Does MacDougall adequately support her contention that there is a propensity in managed care to perpetuate medical gender bias to the detriment of the health of women enrolled in managed care plans? Explain.

Eugenics and Compulsory Sterilization Laws: Providing Redress for the Victims of a Shameful Era in United States History

Michael G. Silver

This note . . . discusses the historical background of the American eugenics movement, the rationale behind the Buck decision, and its implications vis-à-vis state sterilization statutes; . . . the paradox that has gripped this area of law since the 1940s; . . . why those whom the states sterilized under eugenics-based laws suffered constitutional violations; outlines the victims' efforts at obtaining judicial and legislative redress; . . . [and] argues that Congress and the states should act legislatively to recognize and compensate the victims because of the legal system's inability to address their grievances.

THE EUGENICS MOVEMENT AND *BUCK V. BELL*

The eugenics movement arose in the early twentieth century as a result of a primitive understanding of genetics and its relation to the nation's social policies. The movement's proponents soon persuaded legislatures in approximately thirty states to enact compulsory sterilization laws. The Supreme Court, confronted with a constitutional challenge to Virginia's law in 1927, upheld the statute and thus gave legal sanction to the sterilization of tens of thousands of American citizens.

The Rise of the Eugenics Movement

Proponents of eugenics argued that forced sterilization of the "undesirable" and "feeble-minded" could cure America's social ills.

Scientifically, the movement grew out of Gregor Mendel's findings about the heritability of physical traits. Francis Galton, a European geneticist, defined eugenics as "the study of the agencies under social control that may improve or impair the racial qualities of future generations either physically or mentally." Building upon Galton and Mendel's work, eugenicists studied the inheritance of social behaviors, intelligence, and personality and "carried out elaborate research programs to determine the type of inheritance these traits exhibited."

Eugenics proponents "develop[ed] a taxonomy of human traits," categorizing some people as "normal" and "healthy" and others as "abnormal" and "unhealthy." Harry Laughlin, a leading American eugenicist, defined "socially inadequate" people to include the "feebleminded," the "inebriated

Source: Michael G. Silver, "Eugenics and Compulsory Sterilization Laws: Providing Redress for the Victims of a Shameful Era in United States History," George Washington Law Review, 72 (2004): 862–891.

or the drug addicted," the blind, deaf, or deformed, the "dependents" (i.e., orphans), and the homeless. The "accepted view" was that these groups "were reproducing more quickly than normal people, thus posing a significant threat to society." There also was a racial and ethnic component to the "science" of the eugenics movement.

Eugenics gained popularity largely as a reaction to social and economic currents of the time period, which included rapid industrialization, labor strife, urbanization, and vices associated with urban population growth (such as alcoholism and prostitution). Progressives, along with notable intellectuals, businessmen, and politicians, embraced eugenics policies as tools of social reform. Eugenics "fit perfectly with Progressive ideology" because eugenicists "were scientifically trained experts who sought to apply rational principles to solving the problems of anti-social and problematic behavior by seeking out the cause, in this case poor heredity."

As a result of widespread intellectual acceptance of eugenics thought, proponents of social policy reform influenced state legislatures to pass sterilization laws "directed at the mentally retarded, mentally ill, epileptic, and criminal populations." Indiana passed the first such law in 1907. By 1925, twenty-three states had followed suit.

Buck v. Bell

In the Supreme Court's first attempt at judging the legality of the state sterilization laws, the Court upheld a Virginia statute in *Buck v. Bell*. A Virginia appellate court had affirmed a county court decision to order the sterilization of Carrie Buck an eighteen-year-old female institutionalized at the Virginia State Colony for Epileptics and Feeble Minded. Buck challenged the Virginia statute on substantive due process and equal protection grounds under the Fourteenth Amendment.

An eight-justice majority upheld Virginia's law. Writing for the Court, Justice Holmes

opined that "[i]t is better for all the world, if instead of waiting to execute degenerate offspring for crime, or to let them starve for their imbecility, society can prevent those who are manifestly unfit from continuing their kind." Justice Holmes analogized the "sacrific[e]" of the "feebleminded" in undergoing sterilization to that of "the public welfare . . . call[ing] upon the best citizens for their lives." As he succinctly and chillingly remarked, "[t]hree generations of imbeciles are enough." By upholding the statute on eugenics grounds, the Court "articulat[ed] the accepted liberal view."

Justice Holmes also utilized a public health rationale in ratifying the Virginia law. He relied on a 1905 Supreme Court case that upheld a Massachusetts law providing for compulsory smallpox vaccinations. As he explained, "[t]he principle that sustains compulsory vaccination is broad enough to cover cutting the Fallopian tubes."

Finally, Justice Holmes emphasized that the Virginia authorities had followed proper procedures. As he asserted:

> [S]o far as procedure is concerned the rights of the patient are most carefully considered, and as every step in this case was taken in scrupulous compliance with the statute and after months of observation, there is no doubt that in that respect the plaintiff in error has had due process of law.

Buck was a "radical departure from existing Supreme Court medical jurisprudence." The case "was the first and only instance in which the Court allowed a physician, acting as the agent of state government, to perform an operation . . . neither desired nor needed by the 'patient.'"

Buck erased any doubts about the constitutionality of eugenics-based sterilization laws. In the ensuing ten years after the decision, twenty states passed such laws, many closely patterned after Virginia's statute. Nationally, from 1929 through 1941, more than 2,000 eugenics sterilizations were performed each year. By 1963, various states had sterilized over 60,000 persons pursuant to these laws.

The sterilization programs often targeted individuals as young as ten years old. According to David Smith, a coauthor of a book about Carrie Buck, the eugenicists sought out people whom they considered "poor white trash" or individuals who merely "came to the attention of someone, a judge or social worker or someone who would diagnose them as being misfits." At the time, such authority figures could designate anyone as "'feebleminded'—a catchall term for real and imagined disabilities." Often, these authorities never actually tested the victims for mental disability. Beyond the psychological trauma, sometimes the operations had devastating physical consequences. In North Carolina, for example, recently unearthed records of the state's Eugenics Board reveal that several patients died from the surgery.

The "benevolent" intentions of the Social Progressives who championed eugenics resulted in legislation in over thirty states. Tens of thousands of sterilizations ensued, usually involving the poorest and least protected members of society. The Supreme Court, through Buck, validated such practices and contributed to the movement's peak in the 1930s. During and immediately after World War II, however, courts, science, and public opinion began to frown upon eugenics.

THE PARADOX OF POST-*BUCK* POLICY AND JURISPRUDENCE

Fifteen years after Buck, the Supreme Court struck down an Oklahoma sterilization statute pertaining to habitual criminals in *Skinner v. Oklahoma ex rel. Williamson*. After the tragic excesses of the Nazi sterilization regime were exposed, state courts and legal commentators started to question the viability of *Buck*. States soon began repealing their eugenics- based sterilization statutes.

Yet, sterilizations continued in many states until the 1970s. Rather than overrule *Buck*, the Supreme Court cited it as an example of the limits to the constitutional right to privacy. State courts that adjudicated constitutional challenges to sterilization laws struggled to reconcile their distaste for eugenics with the Supreme Court's silence on the issue after *Skinner*. The courts often struck the statutes down on procedural grounds but invariably ignored the broader constitutional questions. In this area, perhaps, jurisprudence evolved more slowly than policy and scientific developments.

Skinner v. Oklahoma ex rel. Williamson

In 1942, the Supreme Court, in *Skinner v. Oklahoma ex rel. Williamson*, struck down on equal protection grounds an Oklahoma statute providing for involuntary sterilization of "habitual criminals." Upon first glance, Skinner appeared to repudiate Buck, as the Court described the far-reaching and intrusive nature of compulsory sterilization. Justice Douglas opined that "[t]his case touches a sensitive and important area of human rights. Oklahoma deprives certain individuals of a right . . . basic to the perpetuation of a race—the right to have offspring." Acknowledging the dangers of negative eugenics, Douglas noted:

> The power to sterilize, if exercised, may have subtle, far-reaching and devastating effects. In evil or reckless hands it can cause races or types which are inimical to the dominant group to wither and disappear. There is no redemption for the individual whom the law touches. Any experiment which the State conducts is to his irreparable injury. He is forever deprived of a basic liberty.

Thus, for the "first time the Supreme Court described reproductive prerogatives as 'fundamental rights.'"

Despite its lofty rhetoric, the Court did not overrule Buck. On the contrary, both the majority and two concurrences distinguished Buck from Skinner. In their views, sterilization laws pertaining to the "feebleminded" did not contain the same constitutional infirmities. Writing for the Court, Justice Douglas made a very subtle distinction:

In *Buck v. Bell*, the Virginia statute was upheld though it applied only to feebleminded persons in institutions of the State. But it was pointed out that "so far as the operations enable those who otherwise must be kept confined to be returned to the world, and thus open the asylum to others, the equality aimed at will be more nearly reached." Here there is no such saving feature. Embezzlers are forever free. Those who steal or take in other ways are not.

Although Douglas did not explicitly rely on eugenics grounds for distinguishing the two cases, the Justice's personal notes indicated such a cognizance.

Chief Justice Stone, in his concurrence, argued that the Court should have struck down the statute on due process grounds. Unlike the majority, he explicitly distinguished *Skinner* from *Buck* on eugenics grounds:

Science has found and the law has recognized that there are certain types of mental deficiency associated with delinquency that are inheritable. But the State does not contend—nor can there be any pretense—that either common knowledge or experience, or scientific investigation, has given assurance that the criminal tendencies of any class of habitual offenders are universally or even generally inheritable.

Justice Stone thus believed that science supported the Court's decision in *Buck*, but not Skinner.

Justice Jackson viewed *Buck* similarly. He explained that the Oklahoma statute presented "constitutional questions of gravity," noting that there are "limits to the extent to which a legislatively represented majority may conduct biological experiments at the expense of the dignity and personality and natural powers of a minority—even those

who have been guilty of what the majority defines as crimes." But, referring to Buck, he added:

This Court has sustained such an experiment with respect to an imbecile, a person with definite and observable characteristics, where the condition had persisted through three generations and afforded grounds for the belief that it was transmissible and would continue to manifest itself in generations to come.

Justice Jackson thus endorsed the eugenic scheme outlined in *Buck* as being scientifically legitimate. Moreover, by relying on the "fact" that the "condition had persisted through three generations," he sanctioned Justice Holmes's erroneous findings regarding Carrie Buck and her family. His concurrence again demonstrated the Court's reluctance to apply its important and prophetic views on "fundamental rights" to a group it considered unworthy of them.

Eugenics Movement Exposed, But Sterilizations Continue

In the years following *Skinner*, the eugenics movement declined because of a confluence of factors. After World War II, the American public became aware of the extensive Nazi sterilization program. Around the same time, the scientific community began to debunk the theories behind eugenics. By the 1960s and 1970s, most states that had experimented with eugenics had repealed their sterilization laws. Nonetheless, coercive sterilizations continued on a large scale in several states as late as the mid-1960s. And in a handful of states, involuntary sterilization laws remain on the books.

The downfall of the Third Reich and subsequent Nuremberg Trials brought to light the Nazis' extensive use of eugenics policies. Eugenics "was central to the entire Nazi enterprise, joined with romantic nativist and racist myths of the purebred Nordic." In 1951, the Central Association of Sterilized People in West Germany estimated that the Nazi programs had sterilized 3.5 million persons.

The American eugenics movement directly influenced Nazi sterilization policies. Both the State of Virginia and the Nazis based their sterilization laws on the Model Eugenical Sterilization Law proposed by Harry Laughlin, a well-known eugenicist. Laughlin's newsletter, Eugenic News, praised the Nazi law: "One may condemn the Nazi policy generally, but specifically it remained for Germany in 1933 to lead the great nations of the world in the recognition of the biological foundations for national character." In Nazi propaganda, "the United States became the main point of reference, by reason of its specific combination of ethnic and eugenic racism . . . [and] the extent to which information on American eugenics was available in Germany." At the Nuremberg Trials after World War II, the accused Nazi doctors cited Buck as legal precedent for the Nazis' race purity programs.

In addition to its identification with Nazi Germany, other forces served to discredit the eugenics movement. In the late 1930s and 1940s, geneticists "firmly rejected the eugenics thesis that feeblemindedness was a Mendelian disorder." In 1936, the American Neurological Association Committee for the Investigation of Eugenical Sterilization issued a statement opposing eugenic sterilization, as did an American Medical Association committee a year later. In 1940, a leading British scientist wrote an influential book which asserted that "the idea that social inefficiency can be prevented on the basis of genetical theory is essentially invalid." It became clear that the focus that eugenics places on determinism (i.e., that the presence of the gene guaranteed the expression of the trait) was its fatal flaw.

As a result, during the 1950s and 1960s, the pace of state-sponsored sterilizations slowed significantly. Many states repealed their eugenics-based statutes. A significant development occurred in 1978, when the U.S. Department of Health, Education, and Welfare issued final rules prohibiting the use of federal funds to sterilize persons under twenty-one, mentally incompetent persons of any age, and institutionalized persons of any age. In 1979, California and the District of Columbia banned the sterilization of any person under the government's care.

Many of the sterilization statutes, nonetheless, persisted. The "decline that began with the onset of World War II was a gradual one that lasted two decades and was by no means uniform." During the mid-1960s, "long after most sterilization programs were thought to have ended, a few states were still sterilizing several hundred retarded persons each year." By 1968, for example, twenty-seven states retained eugenic sterilization laws in some form. From 1970 to 1974, twenty-three sterilizations were performed in state institutions in North Carolina, usually at the request of a relative who was worried that an inmate would become impregnated involuntarily.

As of 2004, seven states still have laws on the books that provide for involuntary sterilization: Arkansas, Delaware, Georgia, Idaho, Mississippi, Vermont, and Virginia. Arkansas's statute permits guardians of certain mental "incompetents" to file sterilization petitions encompassing (rather broadly) those "incapable of caring for [themselves] by reason of mental retardation, mental illness, imbecility, idiocy, or other mental incapacity." Mississippi's law, originally enacted in 1948, allows for involuntary sterilization of those with "hereditary forms of insanity." Some of these remaining statutes have been amended and now require procedural due process protections for those individuals whom the states decide to sterilize.

Compulsory Sterilization Statutes Violated the Fundamental Substantive Due Process Rights of over 60,000 Americans

Although the Supreme Court has not ruled on sterilization laws since Skinner and has not afforded stricter constitutional scrutiny to laws affecting the mentally retarded, the Court did establish a constitutional right to privacy that bestowed a liberty interest which state involuntary sterilization policies violate. Consequently, the victims of eugenics-based compulsory sterilization laws suffered constitutional violations.

The Supreme Court: Development of the Right to Privacy

The Supreme Court's "development of the doctrine of reproductive privacy in the 1960s and 1970s [affects] the constitutional analysis of sterilization laws." These decisions brought about new solicitude for individual liberties as they pertained to procreation and family. Consequently, this area of Supreme Court jurisprudence supports the notion that the states violated the "fundamental" rights of those whom they sterilized under eugenics-based laws.

In *Griswold v. Connecticut*, the Court held that a Connecticut statute prohibiting the use of contraceptives violated the privacy rights of married couples. The case established that matters of family and reproductive autonomy ordinarily trigger special constitutional consideration. In *Eisenstadt v. Baird*, the Court held that this privacy right applied to individuals as well. Justice Brennan wrote that the right to privacy encompassed the "free[dom] from unwarranted governmental intrusion into matters so fundamentally affecting a person as the decision whether to bear or beget a child."

Roe v. Wade completed the right to privacy continuum. Justice Blackmun found the right to terminate a pregnancy implicated a "fundamental right" grounded in "the Fourteenth Amendment's concept of personal liberty and restrictions upon state action." Regulations on such rights are justified "only by a 'compelling state interest,' and [such] legislative enactments must be narrowly drawn" to accommodate the state interest.

In 1992, the Court revisited *Roe* in *Planned Parenthood of Southeastern Pennsylvania v.* *Casey*. *Casey* reaffirmed *Roe's* central holding that the Fourteenth Amendment protects a woman's right to have an abortion. As Justices O'Connor, Souter, and Kennedy explained:

> It is settled now, as it was when the Court heard arguments in Roe v. Wade, that the Constitution places limits on a State's right to interfere with a person's most basic decisions about family and parenthood, as well as bodily integrity. . . . Our law affords constitutional protection to personal decisions relating to marriage, procreation, contraception, family relationships, child rearing, and education.

In doing so, the Court rejected as too rigid Justice Blackmun's trimester formula, however, and replaced the strict scrutiny regime with a more rigorous "undue burden" standard.

Significantly, *Casey* reaffirmed the underpinnings of the right to privacy cases and, unlike *Roe*, did not cite *Buck* as a limitation on the individual's substantive due process rights. Indeed, the Court subtly criticized *Buck* by noting approvingly that *Roe* prevented states from engaging in eugenics-based population control.

Most recently, the Court struck down Texas's sodomy law as a violation of the substantive Due Process Clause of the Fourteenth Amendment. In holding that homosexual adults had the right to engage in private, intimate sexual acts in the confines of their homes, the Court relied on the *Griswold-Roe-Casey* line of cases. Justice Kennedy presciently stated that "times can blind us to certain truths and later generations can see that laws once thought necessary and proper in fact serve only to oppress. As the Constitution endures, persons in every generation can invoke its principles in their own search for greater freedom." As in *Casey*, the Court did not cite *Buck* as a limitation on the right to privacy.

The right to privacy cases showed the paramount importance of protecting collective and individual choices associated with reproduction. Sterilization, by definition, robs the individual of the right to "bear and beget a child," thus implicating that person's "fundamental" rights. The Court has viewed the Fourteenth Amendment liberty component as an evolving right, one able to protect those who suffered at the hands of pernicious laws—such as compulsory sterilization statutes—mistakenly thought to be "necessary and proper" at the time of enactment.

EFFECT OF ESTABLISHING A CONSTITUTIONAL VIOLATION

The determination that involuntary sterilization laws implicated fundamental rights does not, by itself, establish a constitutional violation. Such a determination merely triggers the Supreme Court's two-part "strict scrutiny" test. A state may justify regulations on such "fundamental" rights only by proffering a "compelling state interest." The government also must narrowly tailor the law to accommodate the state interest. Whether the law is "narrowly tailored" depends on whether the state ignored less-restrictive alternatives in effectuating the statutory goals.

State governments have offered various "compelling state interests" in defending the involuntary sterilization of mentally retarded individuals. According to the Minnesota Court of Appeals:

> Several compelling interests have been advanced to justify this type of court-ordered sterilization: the perceived harm caused to society by the presumed inability of a retarded person to serve as a parent [and] the burden on families . . . willing to care for their retarded children at home but are unable to care for grandchildren that may result without reproductive control . . . .[Also,] popular birth control methods . . . can have troublesome side effects.

The "compelling" interests proffered thus ranged from social utilitarian (e.g., "perceived harm caused to society") to practical considerations (e.g., "[t]he State has a compelling interest in ensuring that those in its care do not use birth control methods that are injurious to their health").

Under a strict scrutiny analysis, two arguments could refute a state's contention that sterilization serves a compelling government interest. First, a challenger to the statute could argue that the state-asserted interests are merely pretexts for administrative convenience or cost effectiveness. As the court noted in *In re Hillstrom*, the fundamental right involved "must be safeguarded to assure that sterilization is not a subterfuge for convenience and relief from the responsibility of supervision." Second, even if the state can establish that involuntary sterilization is necessary to promote a compelling state interest, such state actions may fail because they are not narrowly tailored (i.e., they ignore less restrictive alternatives). In the case of a mentally retarded female, for example, the plaintiff or her proxy could show that alternative methods of birth control or greater supervision could prevent pregnancy without resort to sterilization.

Planned Parenthood of Southeastern Pennsylvania v. Casey clarified the level of scrutiny afforded to state regulations on reproductive privacy, substituting the "undue burden" standard for that of strict scrutiny. Generally, this standard allows more regulation to survive constitutional scrutiny. As the Court explained:

> A finding of an undue burden is a shorthand for the conclusion that a state regulation has the purpose or effect of placing a substantial obstacle in the path of a woman seeking an abortion of a nonviable fetus. A statute with this purpose is invalid because the means chosen by the State to further the interest in potential life must be calculated to inform the woman's free choice, not hinder it.

Compulsory sterilization laws likely would not pass constitutional muster under this standard. Sterilization surely places an "undue burden" on one's right to procreate, as the procedure almost always is irrevocable. The Court did recognize that a state, for policy reasons, could enact "persuasive measures" that favor one reproductive decision over another. Forcible surgical invasions of the body by the state, however, are not "persuasive" in the same manner as a waiting period or dissemination of materials promoting nonabortive options.

Plaintiffs who challenge involuntary sterilizations as violations of their substantive due process rights conceivably could win under either the undue burden standard of *Casey* or the less taxing strict scrutiny test. Their constitutional claims are strong. Unfortunately, procedural obstacles and practical considerations continue to stand in the way of such plaintiffs even getting into court.

The Victims: Current-Day Struggles for Recognition and Redress

The Supreme Court's reproductive privacy cases, combined with state court jurisprudence in the area of sterilizations, support the notion that eugenic sterilization laws violated the fundamental rights of the 60,000 victims of compulsory sterilizations in the United States. Unfortunately, those who desire redress for these constitutional violations face obstacles in the legal arena. The governors and legislatures in several states recently apologized for and began to investigate their states' programs, but practical concerns continue to make it difficult to identify the victims and provide them meaningful relief.

State Recognition and Apologies

Although the legal system has not yet recognized the rights of the sterilization victims, policymakers have begun to acknowledge their suffering. During the past year, governors in five states (Virginia, North Carolina,

Oregon, South Carolina, and California) formally apologized to the victims of their states' compulsory sterilization programs.

Virginia Governor Mark Warner offered the Commonwealth's "sincere apology for Virginia's participation in eugenics," noting that, "the eugenics movement was a shameful effort in which state government never should have been involved." The Governor's statement was read at a Charlottesville event honoring the memory of Carrie Buck.

In December 2002, North Carolina authorities apologized for the state's sterilization program after the Winston-Salem Journal ran an extensive weeklong series of articles about the state's experience with eugenics. North Carolina's program claimed over 7,600 victims between 1929 and 1974; by the late 1960s, more than sixty percent of those sterilized were black, and ninety-nine percent were female. After the apology, the state's governor appointed a Eugenics Study Committee to investigate the state's eugenic sterilization program. The Governor plans to implement measures proposed by the committee, such as forming a nonprofit group to locate those whom the state sterilized; utilizing volunteers to assist the victims in navigating through medical records so as to verify their claims; providing health care benefits to the victims through Medicaid or the state health plan; building a memorial; and implementing information about eugenics in the state university's history curriculum.

In Oregon, Governor John Kitzhaber expressed his regrets regarding a state eugenics law that stood from 1917 to 1983 and allowed more than 2,500 people to be sterilized without their consent. Kitzhaber told a group of the victims: "Our hearts are heavy for the pain you endured. The time has come to apologize for misdeeds that resulted from widespread misconceptions, ignorance and bigotry."

In March 2003, California Governor Gray Davis formally apologized to the more than 19,000 victims of the state's sterilization program, the largest of its kind in the nation. Davis said:

> To the victims and their families of this past injustice, the people of California are deeply sorry for the suffering you endured over the years. Our hearts are heavy for the pain caused by eugenics. It was a sad and regrettable chapter in the state's history . . . [—]one that must never be repeated again.

Some criticized the California apology as tepid, noting that unlike North Carolina or Virginia, Davis neither invited survivors or disability groups to the announcement nor ordered a committee to probe details of California's eugenics program.

Reparations and the Repeal of Sterilization Laws

The legal obstacles described above have made it difficult for the victims to obtain relief in the court system. One idea that circumvents such obstacles is reparations. As a sixty-one-year-old man sterilized under Oregon's law and present at Governor Kitzhaber's apology said, the Governor's statement did not "erase what happened"; therefore, he and other sterilized Oregonians should be compensated. He claimed he had difficulty finding an attorney willing to sue the state, and the Governor's spokesperson confirmed that no such lawsuits have been filed in Oregon.

North Carolina has taken the clear lead on reparations. On April 17, 2003, Governor Mike Easley signed legislation repealing the state's sterilization law. State Representative Larry Womble also proposed a bill that would set up a legislative research commission to investigate the feasibility of reparations and counseling programs for the victims.

Daunting challenges remain, even for North Carolina. The state's health and human services secretary commented that it would be a "herculean task" to track down victims

and their families, as state officials could not access more than 150,000 pages of information because of patient confidentiality rules. As for reparations, even supportive politicians acknowledged that budgetary limitations could stymie such proposals.

California legislators will face similar hurdles in any attempt to follow North Carolina's lead. At the time of the Governor's announcement, a spokeswoman for the state's health and human services agency had not yet verified the year when California had discontinued its compulsory sterilization program. Moreover, both the agency and a spokesperson for the Governor said patient confidentiality rules shielded records from review, making it difficult to ascertain details about the program and to locate survivors.

Significant legal and practical considerations continue to make it difficult for individuals sterilized against their will to be identified and compensated for the constitutional wrongs they suffered. Statutes of limitations and lack of standing prevent legal redress. And the states that have begun to acknowledge the wrongs of their experience with eugenics have encountered practical difficulties identifying and reaching the victims. Because of these concerns, the victims who desire acknowledgment or some modicum of compensation cannot rely upon the states or the legal system alone.

Congress Should Apologize for the National Scope of the Eugenics Movement, and the States, Acting Pursuant to Congressional Incentives, Should Identify and Compensate the Victims

Congress should pass a resolution officially apologizing to those whom the states sterilized under eugenics-based laws. Thus far, five states have apologized to victims of their respective programs via legislative resolution or gubernatorial pronouncement. At a minimum, the other twenty-five or so states that had (or still have) such laws on the books should do the same. A resolution from Congress would acknowledge the national scope of this problem. Moreover, such a statement would atone for the fact that the federal government, speaking through the Supreme Court in Buck, facilitated the enactment of the state laws.

Congress should enact legislation that provides financial incentives for states to identify and compensate victims of their former sterilization programs. This is a carrot-type approach, aimed at inducing states to take the steps to fully account for their experiments with eugenics. Under this scheme, the victims would receive tangible compensation for the constitutional violations of their rights rather than the symbolic justice of a resolution or gubernatorial apology. The reparations themselves would serve as a substitute (albeit a modest one) for the legal damages the victims of constitutional violations ordinarily are entitled to.

To address the practical concerns of such a scheme, as Paul Lombardo has suggested, Congress first should stipulate that any state reparations programs be targeted narrowly and exclusively at victims who are alive, rather than their relatives or the relatives of victims who have since died. Second, Congress should provide incentives for states to better identify and reach the victims themselves. For instance, Congress could provide seed money to hire additional archivists to search through medical records repositories and to computerize databases of sterilization victims.

Such a proposal raises constitutional questions, as Congress may not possess the power to effectuate such a law. It is unclear whether Congress could act pursuant to the Commerce Clause, as the Rehnquist Court has significantly scaled back the scope of the clause in recent decisions. The use of Congress's spending power may give more latitude in this area.

Lastly, irrespective of Congressional enticement, the states should investigate their programs, listen to the victims' stories, work with universities that sponsored eugenics research, explore reparations schemes, and, if necessary, repeal sterilization statutes remaining on the books. North Carolina is a model in this regard. The states should also make a narrow exception to their patient confidentiality rules in order to streamline the process of opening up the archives and identifying the victims.

Admittedly, no changes in law or policy can mitigate the loss the sterilization victims suffered in terms of experiencing the joys of childrearing. Nor could they erase the stigma associated with the state unfairly or inaccurately labeling the victims as "feebleminded."

Nonetheless, such actions would serve three vital purposes. A Congressional apology would acknowledge the national scope of the eugenics movement and the hand the Supreme Court played in validating the various state laws. State repeal of sterilization statutes would forever remove from the record the influence of eugenicists such as Harry Laughlin, who lobbied vociferously for the passage of such laws. And good faith efforts at identifying the victims and setting aside modest funds for reparations would show concern for their dignity and provide a modest substitute for the legal damages they otherwise would have been entitled to under constitutional law.

CONCLUSION

In the name of progressive social policy and "science," the application of sterilization laws in more than thirty states denied over 60,000 Americans the "fundamental" right to procreate. The Supreme Court, as the federal government's proxy, validated these laws in *Buck*. State and lower federal courts subsequently criticized the decision, and many (but not all) state legislatures repealed such sterilization laws. The Court's unwillingness to overrule *Buck*, however, forced the other courts to avoid the substantive constitutional issues raised by the plaintiffs in their challenges to the various laws.

Today, our understanding of genetics, constitutional principles, and dignitary concerns compel us to recognize the fallacies of the eugenics theory and condemn the sterilization policies that resulted from it. Yet, procedural obstacles have prevented, and will continue to constrict, the legal system from creating avenues of redress for the victims. The survivors of these programs are caught between a legal rock and a hard place.

Fortunately, Congress and state policymakers are in a position to act. These legislative actors should heed the precedent set recently by North Carolina and by Congress in a somewhat similar context. In 1988, the United States formally apologized to the Japanese-Americans placed in internment camps during World War II and established a $1.25 billion trust fund to make reparations to the survivors and their beneficiaries. There, the government denied fundamental rights to American citizens, and the Supreme Court upheld the practice against constitutional attack. Likewise, the over 60,000 American citizens sterilized as part of a social engineering experiment suffered grave constitutional wrongs, and they deserve recognition and redress as well.

STUDY QUESTION

Describe the three approaches identified by Silver that would provide tangible and symbolic relief to the aggrieved parties in eugenics cases.

CHAPTER 8

Inequality in Communities of Color

INTRODUCTION

The readings selected for this chapter reveal the extent to which structural inequality permeates communities of color in the United States. Unfortunately, communities of color disproportionately suffer from societal problems. As law professor and social critic Derrick Bell explains, racism is inevitable in American society—where majority rule can effectively maintain control of an ideological framework that defines minorities as expendable.[1] In communities of color, white racist society protects majority group interests by compromising minority interests in their own communities. In this chapter, we focus on some of the more important concerns in which the white majority continues to compromise minority communities: the depiction of minorities in media programming; white Americans' continued victimization of persons of color; the structural perversions of homelessness; the state of civil rights in the United States; and a growing judicial vindication of past injustices by white supremacists.

THE MEDIA AND RACIST IDEOLOGY

The racist ideology entrenched in media broadcasting is a powerful source of social inequality in U.S. society. Popular television programs usually consign persons of color to stereotypical roles that reinforce the notion of minority persons as unintelligent, shiftless, criminal, and culturally inferior. Film and television producers portray communities of color as impoverished, dilapidated, and crime ridden. Since its inception in the 1930s, television and films have portrayed persons of color as threatening to the white middle class. Today, although some television shows and films appear to have broken some of the more commonly held stereotypes, television broadcasting and films have yet to address the issues of institutional racism and poverty.[2] Racist stereotypes in the media include the pernicious portrayal of Arab, Muslim, South Asian, and Middle Eastern persons as radical fundamentalists and outright terrorists. Media broadcasting glorifies Euro-American culture by disenfranchising minority persons. For example, even though Latinos are the most rapidly growing population in the United States, the portrayal of Latinos in television broadcasting has regressed significantly since the early 1950s. A report by the National Council of La Raza found that the number of Latinos in television programming dropped from 3 percent in the 1950s to 1 percent in the 1990s. The percentage of black television characters increased from 3 percent to 17 percent over the same period as that measured for Latinos. Whites are 75 percent of all television characters.[3]

White stereotypes of black men as hypersexual and dangerous have resurfaced. The events surrounding the death of Nicole Brown Simpson and the subsequent murder trial of O. J. Simpson, the Clarence Thomas confirmation hearings and debate over sexual harassment, accusations against Michael Jackson over child sexual abuse, Mike Tyson's subsequent rape conviction, and the sexual assault allegation by a white woman against Kobe Bryant illustrate a political climate in U.S. society that continues to vilify black males. *Time* magazine darkened O. J. Simpson's police photograph and made it look far more sinister for its cover after his arrest in the killings of Nicole Brown Simpson and Ronald Goldman. One commentator points out that these cases provide opportunities for the media to utilize racist stereotypes to violate, degrade, and debase black men.[4]

The media also portrays its racial bias against black men often far more deceitfully. For example, a deep-rooted stereotype in U.S. society that often goes unchallenged by the media is that "[i]f you have to make something sound bad, blame it on a black person, because white people will believe it."[5] The black community condemned the media for *uncritically* reporting Susan Smith and her nationally televised pleas for the safe return of her two young sons in South Carolina, whom she claimed a black man had kidnapped at gunpoint in a carjacking. The national news media televised a composite drawing of the suspect. Yet nine days after an extensive federal and state manhunt for the black kidnapper, Smith confessed to murdering her sons.[6] The case of Charles Stuart in Massachusetts stands out as another example of white vilification of black men in U.S. society. There, Charles Stuart, a white man, accused a black man of killing his pregnant wife and two sons. Police reacted to Stuart's claim by raiding nearby housing projects, questioning black men, and eventually making an arrest. Stuart later committed suicide after his brother informed police that Stuart was the actual killer. Racial hoaxes in the context of the *criminal black man* are frequent. One scholar identified 67 racial hoaxes over a ten-year period in which 47 cases involved white fabrications of black crimes, and 7 cases involved black crime fabrications by police or court officers.[7] To law professor N. Jeremi Duru, the image of the "bestial black man" has grave consequences for the black community. In his piece on *The Central Park Five, the Scottsboro Boys, and the Myth of the Bestial Black Man*, Professor Duru traces the historical development of the mythic bestial black man and examines the judicial system's support for the myth within the context wrongful convictions of innocent black men in the Scottsboro and Central Park cases. Unfortunately, the myth continues—and the myth will persist until the American people recognize and confront its vicious cruelty and arrant ugliness.

HATE CRIMES

Hate crime is not new to U.S. society; racial, ethnic, and religious violence has a long history in America. The genocidal policies of the federal government since the earliest periods of American colonial history brought about the wholesale slaughter of some 15 million American Indians.[8] White lynch mobs killed thousands of blacks during Reconstruction, Jim Crow, and the early civil rights period. Lynch mobs preyed on Jewish and Chinese merchants, Mormon missionaries and Catholic priests, Italian sugarcane workers and Latino cowhands.[9] White terrorist mobs lynched nearly six hundred Mexicans mostly in California and Texas from 1848 to 1928.[10] Racial violence remains a pervasive artifact of U.S. society today, more so than what most people realize.[11] The most recently publicized incidences of bias-motivated violence are the 1998 gruesome murders of James Byrd Jr. and Matthew Wayne Shepard. Three white men named Lawrence Russell Brewer, Shawn Allen Berry, and John William King picked up James Byrd Jr., a black man, who was hitchhiking down a country road in Jasper, Texas, after attending his niece's bridal shower. The three white men took Byrd to an isolated area, beat him, chained him by the neck to the back of a pickup truck, and then dragged him two miles down a winding country road—tearing off his head, part of his neck, and his right arm. Sheriff's deputies found Byrd's wallet, keys, and dentures scattered along the road and his torso a mile from the rest of his body. The ordeal so badly disfigured and dismembered Byrd's body that authorities could only identify him by fingerprints. Officials later linked Byrd's murderers to white supremacist groups in eastern Texas. In 1998 Russell Henderson and Aaron McKinney robbed, brutally pistol-whipped, tied to a fence post, and left Matthew Wayne Shepard, a gay University of Wyoming student, to die. Besides the killings of Byrd and Shepard, 105 other bias-motivated murders and non-negligent manslaughters have occurred in the United States since 1995.[12]

In 1990 Congress enacted the Hate Crime Statistics Act (HCSA) requiring the Justice Department to collect and publish data on crimes based on race, religion, sexual orientation, or ethnicity from law enforcement agencies across the country. Congress expanded the HCSA in 1994 to include crimes based on disability in the Violent Crime Control and Law Enforcement Act. Bias-motivated crimes include offenses committed against individuals, institutions, and businesses. The Church Arson Prevention Act of 1996, for example, makes it a crime to damage, destroy, or deface a church because of its religious character. One commentator defines hate crimes as involving "a heightened sense of tension and fear about demographic changes in the region, the recession, population growth and a declining level of civility and concern for others in our society."[13] The Uniform Crime Reports on bias-motivated (hate) crimes known to police show that in 2003 some 7,489 hate crime incidents in 2003 involved 8,715 separate offenses, 6,934 known offenders, and the victimization of 9,100 persons because of their race, ethnicity, religion, sexual orientation, or disability.[14] The Southern Poverty Law Center's Intelligence Project counted 762 active hate groups in the United States in 2004, with the majority of these hate groups located in South Carolina, Georgia, Florida, Texas, and California.[15] Also, since the September 11, 2001, terrorist attacks, hate violence against Arab Americans, Muslims, Sikhs, and Middle Eastern persons have more than doubled. Hate violence against Anti-Other Ethnicity or National Origin categories that include Arab Americans has increased by nearly 425 percent.[16] A recent study by the Council on American-Islamic Relations reveals that the rise of anti-Muslim hate crimes is attributed to rising Islamophobic rhetoric in U.S. society—especially the anti-Muslim rhetoric of political, religious, and media figures. Most recently, this emotionally charged rhetoric barred singer Cat Stevens and Islamic scholar Tariq Ramadan from entering the United States.[17]

Our understanding of the pervasiveness of bias-motivated crimes is purely conjectural because official criminal justice data on hate crimes are incomplete and inaccurate. For example, official statistics on bias-motivated violence do not include figures on hate literature and rallies, graffiti in public places, name-calling, and epithets not associated with assaults and other threats. Moreover, compliance with the HCSA is voluntary; as a result, many law enforcement agencies fail to report any information on hate crimes. National hate crime statistics for 2003 reveal, for instance, that only 71 percent of the more than 17,000 law enforcement agencies in the United States provided data on hate crimes to the Uniform Crime Reporting Program. What is more, the U.S. Commission of Civil Rights points out that President George W. Bush's backpedaling on civil rights includes his failure to support legislation protecting women, gay men and lesbians, or persons with disabilities from hate crime. Accordingly, "*race-neutral, gender-neutral*, or otherwise *unspecific terms* that the President uses dilute the symbolic significance of bias-motivate crimes against traditionally victimized groups."[18]

Whites are the most frequent perpetrators of race violence in the United States. Whites are 42 percent of all suspected offenders of hate crimes. In contrast, blacks are 12 percent, American Indians are 0.5 percent, and Asian Americans are 0.7 percent of bias-motivated offenders. The remaining percentages of suspected hate-crime offenders include multiracial groups and those of unknown race. Hate-crime data reveal that whites are *three times* as likely to victimize blacks, nearly *four times* as likely to victimize American Indians, and nearly *ten times* as likely to victimize Asian Americans as are persons in these groups to perpetrate crimes against whites. In her essay written especially for this volume, criminologist Barbara Perry contends in *Normative Violence: Everyday Racism in the Lives of American Indians* that the most striking theme emerging in her study of white ethnoviolence toward American Indians living near or in reservations is its *normativity*.

HOMELESSNESS

The homeless are perceived in the public's mind as lazy, dirty, drug addicts, alcoholics, and mentally ill; in short, they are regarded as societal dropouts and as public nuisances who violate public space by sleeping in alleyways and doorways. But this depiction of the homeless belies the societal realities of homelessness. Most studies on homelessness reveal that the problem is not simply an artifact of individual disabilities and pathologies but results from a complex set of structural problems in U.S.

society. Homelessness results from growing shortages of affordable rental housing, increasing poverty rates, unemployment, declines in public assistance programs, lack of affordable health care, increases in the prevalence of single-parent families, the lack of support services for mentally ill persons, substance abusers, and prison releases.[19] The Urban Institute has found that about 3.5 million people, of whom 1.3 million are children, are likely to experience homelessness in a given year.[20] Most homeless persons are single and young, but increasing numbers of the homeless are women, children, and the elderly.[21] Many of the homeless are not limited to living in large metropolitan areas; rural communities are experiencing homelessness as well. Families of color are 62 percent of homeless—38 percent are white, 43 percent are black, 15 percent are Hispanic, 3 percent are American Indian, and 1 percent are of other races.[22]

About half of the homeless population are families comprising single mothers with two to three children with incomes well below the poverty level. Homeless families need help finding jobs and affordable housing. Social services to homeless persons are largely clothing, transportation assistance, and help in getting public benefits. Only about a fifth of homeless families actually receive help finding housing. And in many cases, social service agencies require families to undergo a transitional period before housing placement. This is particularly a problem for families fleeing domestic violence or where the head of the household is undergoing residential treatment for drug or alcohol abuse.[23] Studies show that homeless single mothers generally loathe homeless shelters in which to live with their dependent children because shelter rules exacerbate parental authority. Many homeless mothers spend much of their time trying to find permanent housing and rely on social networks to help themselves and their children.[24]

A 2004 survey shows that demands for emergency shelter and food in the United States have increased significantly over the past years.[25] The survey reveals that in some of the largest cities nationwide, requests for emergency food aid increased by 13 percent and demands for emergency shelter rose by 6 percent. Of the adult population requesting food assistance over the last year, 34 percent were employed. Families with children are 40 percent of the total homeless population in the United States, and they comprise 56 percent of all recipients of food assistance. Still, about 20 percent of all requests for food assistance go unmet because of state and federal cutbacks in social welfare programs directed toward the poor. The unmet food need of homeless families is far worse in some American cities. Social services in New Orleans and Los Angeles reject some 66 percent of food requests. In Boston, the rejection rate for food requests exceeds 50 percent. About 23 percent of all emergency shelter needs across the country go unmet. Yet officials expect demands for shelter and emergency food to increase dramatically over the next several years. One commentator suggests that "what emerges from the survey is a devastating portrait of the human cost of American society's unprecedented level of social inequality."[26]

Indigent and low-income people frequently use public housing programs to obtain adequate and affordable housing. Yet Human Rights Watch recently found that public housing authorities commonly deny homeless persons public housing because of "one-strike" policies that automatically prevent poor people access to public housing that have felony convictions. Housing authorities established these rigorous policies for public safety concerns, but in many cases, the policies exclude persons for minor offenses that have no impact on public safety; "unfortunately, the criteria for exclusion are needlessly overbroad and can exclude certain offenders for life—regardless of evidence of their rehabilitation." Although there is no nationwide data on the number of people excluded because of past criminal offenses from public housing, Human Rights Watch estimates that hundreds of thousands of poor people are likely ineligible for public housing given the 650,000 people that leave prison each year and the 3.5 million persons convicted of felonies within the past five years.[27]

With increasing frequency, many of the country's homeless are experiencing hate crimes and violent acts involving extreme brutality. The National Coalition for the Homeless reports that since 1999 perpetrators have committed 281 hate crimes and violent acts against people experiencing homelessness, murdered 131 homeless persons, and committed another 150 nonlethal attacks against homeless people. Sadly, the ages of the victims range from as young as four months to the elderly. Most victims are male, but many are women. In one instance, for example, three men beat a forty-one-year-old homeless Minneapolis woman with baseball bats, and in another instance, four teens (while laughing) attacked seven homeless people with a 50,000-volt stun gun shocking their victims' genitals, kicking them, and urinating on them. Still, federal and state laws do not recognize crimes against the homeless as hate crimes.[28]

Unquestionably, hate crimes and violent acts against the homeless relate to a growing trend of community intolerance toward homeless persons generally. One measure of the mounting social bigotry against homelessness in the United States is the widespread *criminalization of homelessness* through "selective enforcement of existing laws, arbitrary police practices, and discriminatory public regulations."[29] Criminalizing the activities of people experiencing homelessness often results in civil rights violations involving unlawful detainments, arrests, and physical violence by police. For decades, the Los Angeles Sheriff's Department has "dumped" homeless and mentally ill persons from surrounding cities to Los Angeles's downtown skid row district.[30] In many cases, the criminalization of homelessness stems from redevelopment schemes of community business elites and city governments attempting to transform public space.[31] Yet these communities fail to provide sufficient housing and social services needs for homeless persons. A recent national survey found that more than two thirds of the 147 communities surveyed across the country had passed city ordinances prohibiting homelessness. San Francisco, California, for example, is one of the "meanest cities" in one of the "meanest states" for homeless people to live. In a single year (2000–2001), San Francisco officials issued more than 27,000 citations to homeless people for sleeping or camping in the park, trespassing, or disobeying park signs, and spent nearly $31 million incarcerating the homeless.[32] Maya Nordberg explains in *Jails Not Homes: Quality of Life on the Streets of San Francisco* that the process of criminalizing homeless people effectively moves them from the streets through the jails and back to the streets. To correct this revolving-door approach to homelessness, Nordberg suggests that San Francisco divest its homeless outreach programs from law enforcement and the court to permanent housing and expanding social services.[33]

Is Civil Rights Law Dead?

President George W. Bush promised the American people in his inaugural address in January 2001 to protect civil rights by reforming education, immigration and election policies, and promoting unity and opportunity. The U.S. Commission on Civil Rights has recently concluded, however, that the Bush administration has failed in civil rights reform.[34] In its September 2004 report, the commission held that on the issues of voting rights, equal educational opportunity, affirmative action, fair housing, environmental justice, racial profiling, hate crimes, immigration, women's rights, and gay rights, the Bush administration has unsuccessfully met federal efforts to eradicate entrenched discrimination in America, to expand and protect rights for disadvantaged groups, and to promote access to federal programs and services for traditionally underserved populations. Accordingly, the Bush administration has done precious little to improve equal opportunity, the administration has appointed cabinet members who openly oppose civil rights protections, and the administration has not funded civil rights programs required to further social, political, and economic equity.

Regarding the Bush administration's aversion to eradicating entrenched discrimination in the United States, the Civil Rights Commission details persistent segregation and legal discrimination that continue to impede equal opportunity in education, employment, housing, public accommodations, and people's voting ability. The commission contends that the administration's policies in these areas have departed from well-established civil rights protections. For example, many eligible Americans remain disenfranchised from their fundamental right to vote because the administration has not moved to ensure congressional appropriation of the funds required to implement the Help America Vote Act (HAVA) of 2002. As a result of the administration's inaction in election reform under the act, state and local voting precincts were unable to correct for many of the same problems that hampered the 2000 presidential election and further disenfranchised eligible black voters in the 2004 presidential election.

The Bush administration has touted the No Child Left Behind program as a major educational reform designed to hold state and local educational systems responsible for the academic progress of children. The Civil Rights Commission points out, however, that the program is so flawed that it will actually inhibit equal educational opportunity and fail to close the educational achievement gap between advantaged white children and disadvantaged children of color. According to the commission's report, students with limited English proficiency, students from low-income families, and students with disabilities more often attend schools that do not have adequate resources to provide them with the tools required for academic achievement. Thus government regulators are more likely to define these students as low performers and impose sanctions on school districts affecting future funding under the program.

The commission contends that the administration has demonstrated poor leadership in affirmative action. The administration has challenged affirmative action programs for disadvantaged businesses and education by promoting "race-neutral alternatives" that the commission claims are ineffective in maintaining diversity. Although the Bush administration denies entrenched discrimination in awarding federal contracts, non-minority-owned businesses receive fifty times as many construction loan dollars as black-owned businesses, and women-owned businesses receive only 48 cents for every dollar of work that comparable male-owned businesses receive from contracts with the federal government. Without affirmative action in the awarding of federal contracts, the commission believes that the disparity in minority-owned business participation in winning federal contracts will significantly increase. When the U.S. Supreme Court revisited affirmative action in higher education in 2003, the Bush administration challenged contentions that "affirmative action remains a valuable tool to providing equal opportunity" for disadvantaged persons of color who otherwise are unlikely to attend and graduate from college.

Inadequate housing opportunities plague many poor families and families of color in the United States. Instead of alleviating the strain on inadequate housing opportunities for disadvantaged groups living in distressed communities, the commission argues that the federal government has instituted housing polices that have diverted billions of dollars from programs to help low-income and disabled persons pay for housing with rent vouchers. Instead, President Bush has favored *home purchasing programs* that are hampered by insufficient funding and fail to relieve the unrelenting affordable housing crisis.

The Bush administration has failed to eliminate discriminatory environmental pollution policies that unduly affect poor neighborhoods and communities of color. Environmental pollution polices overburden minority and low-income communities with exposure to life-threatening hazardous conditions from industrial sites. Industries have located incinerators, oil refineries, power plants, landfills, and diesel bus stations largely in minority and low-income communities. Yet the Bush administration refuses to acknowledge environmental injustice. As a result, the administration has not implemented environmental justice safeguards under its proposed Clear Skies Act that repeals many established pollution control measures. It is significant that President Bush signed legislation designed to revitalize abandoned and contaminated industrial sites for commercial and residential use, but "white communities experience faster cleanup, better results, and harsher assessment against those failing to clean them up as expected, despite that many abandoned industrial sites exist in minority and low-income communities."

The administration made assurances to the American people that it would end racial profiling in law enforcement. Yet the administration has implemented regulations that have furthered racial profiling. Responding to the terrorist attacks of September 11, 2001, law enforcement nationwide have increasingly targeted South Asians, Arab Americans, Muslims, and other persons of Middle Eastern descent, resulting in involuntary detentions, forced registration, and extensive monitoring of these persons. The administration has also failed to support legislation strengthening hate-crime protection in the face of increasing violence directed against Middle Eastern and Arab persons since September 11. Immigration policies and practices put into effect by the administration have circumvented legitimate claims and maltreatment of Haitian asylum seekers and Arab and Muslim immigrants. The Department of Justice has detained more than eleven hundred Middle Eastern and South Asian men without revealing who it had detained, the reasons for detention, where detainees were held, or even contacting family members of the detainees. Many of these detainees continue to complain of prison guard mistreatment. Officials have interviewed some five thousand people of Middle Eastern and South Asian ancestry about their religious practices, attitudes toward the federal government, and immigration status. To the Civil Rights Commission, "changes to the nation's policies under the Bush administration have left immigrants unprotected and unfairly treated."

Regarding disadvantaged groups, President Bush has inadequately funded the housing needs of American Indians, and his administration's inability to fund American Indian education and health needs adequately promises to maintain their substandard living conditions. The federal government has underfunded tribal colleges and universities, terminated funding for educational programs directly benefiting American Indians, and failed to provide the funding required to meet the goals of the No Child Left Behind program in Indian country. President Bush also terminated tribal law enforcement and court programs.

Women's rights have also faltered under the Bush administration. Government officials have withdrawn guidelines on sexual harassment in schools, ended distribution of information on women's workplace rights, and abolished the Equal Pay Initiative. Regarding the rights of gay and lesbians, the administration has called for a constitutional amendment banning same-sex marriages, removed Web site documents pertaining to sexual orientation discrimination in the federal government, and opposed the Employment Non-Discrimination Act and Hate Crimes Prevention Act that included protection for gay and lesbians. Although the administration has touted faith-based and community initiatives as a means of curbing discrimination against religious organizations and allowed religious groups to receive federal funds, the Civil Rights Commission is concerned that the initiatives allow for employment discrimination against persons based on religion.

In *The Struggle for Civil Rights: The Need for, and Impediments to, Political Coalitions Among and Within Minority Groups*, Kevin R. Johnson, a professor of law and Chicano studies at the University of California at Davis, explains that the relevant question concerning civil rights is not whether civil rights law is dead but "whether the political struggle for civil rights in the United States is alive and well." Conceding that these are indeed difficult times for the civil rights struggle in the United States, Johnson believes that to keep civil rights alive we must build coalitions of color that challenge racial hierarchy and white dominion in American society. Yet a daunting challenge to the civil rights struggle is the racism within communities of color directed at other communities of color. He writes, "Unfortunately, racism among minority communities is a social problem that thwarts collective action. Rather than condemn yet ignore it, those committed to social justice must acknowledge the problem and struggle with its solution."

SUMMARY

This chapter addresses some of the more substantive issues confronting communities of color in the United States today: namely, the perpetuation and consequences of negative media images of persons of color; white hate violence waged against persons of color; the criminalization of homelessness; the failure of the U.S. government to eradicate the segregation and legal discrimination as impediments to equal educational, employment, housing, public accommodations, and voting opportunities; and the collective action to compel state and federal justice systems to vindicate decades-old racial murders of activists by white supremacists. By no means is this an exhaustive list of the institutional inequities facing communities of color. For example, many people would agree that environmental pollution is one of America's most critical national dilemmas. Toxic chemicals, air and water pollution, and waste and disposal continue to threaten not only the environment but the lives of people as well. Yet environmental pollution does not threaten all people equally; it has a disproportionate effect on the nation's poor, persons of lower socioeconomic status, and persons and communities of color. White society in the United States maintains political, economic, and cultural dominion over communities of color community through various institutional devices. The readings adopted for this chapter illustrate how white society maintains its dominance over communities of color.

ENDNOTES

1. Derrick Bell, "Racism Will Always Be with Us," *New Perspectives Quarterly*, 8(3) (1991): 44–48.
2. Robert Staples and Terry Jones, "Culture, Ideology and Black Television Images," in Adalberto Aguirre Jr. and David V. Baker, eds., *Sources: Notable Selections in Race and Ethnicity* (Guilford, CT: Dushkin Publishing Groups), pp. 313–324.
3. National Council of La Raza, *Out of the Picture: Hispanics in the Media* (August 1994), http://www.nclr.org/content/publications/detail/1404.
4. Jack Lule, "The Rape of Mike Tyson: Race, the Press, and Symbolic Types," *Critical Studies in Mass Communication*, 12 (1995): 176–195.
5. LaMont Jones, "Media's Portrayal of Minorities Called Biased," *Pittsburgh Post-Gazette*, October 1, 1995, p. A19.
6. Katheryn K. Russell, *The Color of Crime: Racial Hoaxes, White Fear, Black Protectionism, Police Harassment, and Other Macroaggressions* (New York: New York University Press, 1998).
7. Ibid. See also Katheryn K. Russell, "The Racial Hoax as Crime: The Law as Affirmation," *Indiana Law Journal*, 71 (1996): 593–621; Gregg Barak, Jeanne M. Flavin, and Paul S. Leighton, *Class, Race, Gender, and Crime: Social Realities of Justice in America* (Los Angeles: Roxbury, 2001), p. 209.
8. David D. Stannard, *American Holocaust: The Conquest of the New World* (New York: Oxford University Press, 1992).
9. W. Fitzhugh Brundage, *Lynching in the New South: Georgia and Virginia*, 1880–1930 (Urbana: University of Illinois Press, 1993), p. 91; William D. Carrigan, "The Lynchings of Persons of Mexican Origins or Descent in the United States, 1848 to 1928," *Journal of Social History*, 37(2) (2003): 411–440.
10. William D. Carrigan, *The Making of a Lynching Culture: Violence and Vigilantism in Central Texas, 1836–1916* (Urbana: University of Illinois Press, 2004); see also Carrigan, "The Lynching of Persons of Mexican Origin."
11. Leadership Conference on Civil Rights Education Fund, *Cause for Concern: Hate Crime in America* (August 2004), http://www.civilrights.org/publications/reports/cause_for_concern_2004/index.html.
12. Federal Bureau of Investigation, Uniform Crime Reports, *Hate Crime Statistics*, //www.fbi.gov/ucr/ucr.htm.
13. Combating Hate," *Los Angeles Times*, May 17, 1994, p. A9.
14. U.S. Department of Justice, *Sourcebook of Criminal Justice Statistics Online*, http://www.albany.edu/sourcebook/pdf/t3114.pdf.
15. Southern Poverty Law Center, Intelligence Report, *Active U.S. Hate Groups in 2004*, http://www.splcenter.org/intel/map/hate.jsp.
16. U.S. Commission on Civil Rights, Office of Civil Rights Evaluation, Redefining Rights in America: *The Civil Rights Record of the George W. Bush Administration, 2001–2004*, Draft Report for Commissioners' Review (September 2004), p. 91, http://www.usccr.gov/pubs/bush/bush04.pdf.
17. Muslims Cite a Rise in Hate Crimes," *Los Angeles Times*, May 12, 2005, p. A16.
18. U.S. Commission on Civil Rights, Office of Civil Rights Evaluation, *Redefining Rights in America: The Civil Rights Record of the George W. Bush Administration, 2001–2004*, Draft Report for Commissioners' Review (September 2004), p. 95, http://www.usccr.gov/pubs/bush/bush04.pdf.
19. National Coalition for the Homeless, *Why Are People Homeless?* (September 2002), http://www.nationalhomeless.org/causes.html.
20. The Urban Institute, *A New Look at Homelessness in America* (February 1, 2000), http://www.urban.org/url.cfm?ID=900302. See also National Coalition for the Homeless, *How Many People Experience Homelessness?* (September 2002), http://www.nationalhomeless.org/numbers.html.
21. The United States Conference of Mayors, *Hunger and Homelessness Survey: A Status Report on Hunger and Homelessness in America's Cities* (December 2003), http://www.usmayors.org/uscm/hungersurvey/2003/onlinereport/HungerAndHomelessnessReport2003.pdf.
22. National Alliance to End *Homelessness, Homelessness: Programs and the People They Serve* (December 1999), http://www.endhomelessness.org/back/hudreport.htm.
23. National Alliance to End Homelessness, *A Snapshot of Homelessness*, http://www.endhomelessness.org/pub/tenyear/demograp.htm.

24. Shirley P. Thrasher and Carol T. Mowbray, "A Strengths Perspective: An Ethnographic Study of Homeless Women with Children," *Health and Social Work*, 20 (1995): 93–110.

25. The United States Conference of Mayors, *Hunger, Homelessness Survey: A Status Report on Hunger and Homelessness in American Cities*, December 2004, http://www.usmayors.org/uscm/hungersurvey/ 2004/onlinereport/HungerAndHomelessnessReport2004.pdf.

26. Rick Kelly, *Hungry and Homeless Ranks Swell in U.S. Cities*, World Socialist Web Site (December 17, 2004), http://www.wsws.org/articles/2004/dec2004/hung-d17_prn.shtml.

27. Human Rights Watch, *No Second Chance: People with Criminal Records Denied Access to Public Housing* (November 2004), http://hrw.org/reports/2004/usa1104/usa1104.pdf.

28. National Coalition for the Homeless, *Hate, Violence, and Death on Main Street USA: A Report on Hate Crimes and Violence Against People Experiencing Homelessness 2003* (June 2004), http://www .nationalhomeless.org/hatecrimes/fullreport.pdf.

29. National Coalition for the Homeless, *Illegal to Be Homeless: The Criminalization of Homelessness in the United States* (August 2003), p. 5, http://www.nationalhomeless.org/civilrights/crim2003/report .pdf; see also Judith Lynn Failer, "Homelessness in the Criminal Law," in William C. Heffernan and John Kleinig, eds., *From Social Justice to Criminal Justice: Poverty and the Administration of Criminal Law* (New York: Harvard University Press, 2000), pp. 248–263.

30. Cara Mia DiMassa and Richard Winton, "Dumping of Homeless Suspected Downtown," *Los Angeles Times*, September 23, 2005, pp. A1, A28.

31. Adalberto Aguirre Jr. and Jonathan Brooks, "City Redevelopment Policies and the Criminalization of Homelessness: A Narrative Case Study," *Research in Urban Sociology*, 6 (2001): 75.

32. National Coalition for the Homeless, *Illegal to Be Homeless: The Criminalization of Homelessness in the United States* (August 2003), http://www.nationalhomeless.org/civilrights/crim2003/report.pdf.

33. Maya Nordberg, "Jail Not Homes: Quality of Life on the Streets of San Francisco," *Hastings College of Law*, 13 (2002): 261–305.

34. U.S. Commission on Civil Rights, Office of Civil Rights Evaluation, *Redefining Rights in America: The Civil Rights Record of the George W. Bush Administration*, 2001–2004, Draft Report of the Commissioners' Review (September 2004), http://www.usccr.gov/pubs/bush/bush04.pdf.

The Central Park Five, the Scottsboro Boys, and the Myth of the Bestial Black Man

N. Jeremi Duru

This article seeks to explain the judicial travesty in the Central Park case by contextualizing it in view of the myth of the Bestial Black Man: a myth, deeply imbedded in American culture, that black men are animalistic, sexually unrestrained, inherently criminal, and ultimately bent on rape.

On August 23, 2002, a convicted rapist and murderer named Matias Reyes signed a sworn statement confessing to a rape with which he had not previously been connected. After crossing paths in a New York correctional facility with Kharey Wise, who was serving time for the rape Reyes committed, and who was having difficulty coping with incarceration, Reyes began to feel guilty about Wise's imprisonment. Having decided to "do one thing right in [his] life," Reyes approached prison officials and admitted to committing the rape attributed to Wise. He stated that on April 19, 1989, he raped a woman jogging in Central Park.

On that day, a stock broker named Trisha Meili embarked on her standard after-work jog. She ran from her Manhattan apartment into Central Park and onto the Reservoir Path, a popular Central Park jogging route. When she reached the northern reaches of the park, she was attacked, raped, severely beaten, and left to die alone in the dark. Passers-by discovered her body three and a half hours later, and she was rushed to the hospital. Miraculously, although her body temperature dropped to eighty-four degrees and she lost 75 percent of her blood, she survived. That same evening, thirty or more young black and Latino teenagers were in the park, and some were involved in assaults on various park-goers. Several of these teenagers were quickly rounded up and interrogated in connection with the rape. Among those interrogated were fourteen-year-old Kevin Richardson, fourteen-year-old Raymond Santana, fifteen-year-old Yusef Salaam, fifteen-year-old Antron McCray, and sixteen-year-old Kharey Wise. After interrogations which lasted as long as twenty-eight hours, each of the youngsters confessed to involvement in attacking and raping Meili. None confessed to actually raping her, but each said he had held or hit her, and each blamed the actual rape on one or more of the others. Although each of the defendants later maintained his innocence, insisting that the confessions were coerced, all five were convicted and sentenced to prison terms of between five and fifteen years. The incident lives as one of the most

Source: N. Jeremi Duru, "The Central Park Five, The Scottsboro Boys, and the Myth of the Bestial Black Man," Cardozo Law Review, 25 (2004): 1315–1365.

racially divisive in recent American history, and until January 2001, the case was considered closed.

Reyes' confession, however, changed that. After Reyes confessed, authorities ordered DNA tests which revealed that semen and pubic hair found at the crime scene—unattributable to any of the five convicted of the rape—was Reyes.' Manhattan District Attorney Robert Morgenthau immediately launched an investigation, scrutinizing both Reyes' confession and the 15,000 pages of testimony and evidence presented during the Central Park rape trial. Morgenthau found that Reyes' confession accurately described the crime scene and the jogger's injuries, while the youths' confessions were inconsistent with each other and with the physical evidence. Further, Morgenthau found that Reyes had confessed with precision to several other rapes for which he was never charged. On December 5, 2002, upon concluding his investigation, Morgenthau filed with the court a fifty-eight-page recommendation that the convictions of the Central Park Five be vacated. Just two weeks later, on December 19, 2002, New York State Supreme Court Justice Charles Tejada followed the recommendation and vacated the convictions. Justice Tejada's order was issued too late to save the Central Park Five from their punishments, coming four months after Wise, the last of the Central Park Five serving his rape sentence, was released from prison.

Despite the revelations suggesting the youths' innocence, some detectives, police officials, and members of the press remain convinced of the youths' involvement in the attack. Few seriously argue that Reyes was not involved, as the evidence of his involvement is overwhelming. Still, some officials insist that the youths participated, citing as support their confessions to other attacks in the park that night, as if such involvement would necessarily implicate them in the attack on the jogger. Some insist that the youths attacked the jogger, but at a different time of the evening than

did Reyes. Others suggest that the youths participated in the rape along with Reyes.

These arguments suffer under scrutiny, as the vacation of the convictions implies inaccuracy in the youths' confessions to the rape, and thus suggests the need to re-examine their confessions to other assaults in Central Park that night. Even assuming, arguendo, that all of the youths were involved in other assaults that night, their involvement in those assaults certainly does not translate into involvement in attacking Meili. Indeed, available evidence strongly indicates the youths' non-involvement in Meili's attack:

- The youths' involvement is largely premised on the argument that Reyes alone could not have inflicted the "head-to-toe" damage Meili suffered. The theory relies on the youths having been primarily responsible for the beating that drained the majority of Meili's blood from her body, yet none of her blood was found on any of the youths, their clothes, or their shoes.

- The only item of physical evidence connecting the youths to the crime at the time of trial were strands of hair found on Richardson and believed to have come from Meili. DNA analysis conducted in the aftermath of Reyes' confession reveals that the hair does not match Meili's.

- Unlike Reyes, who was able to identify the location of the crime scene with precision thirteen years later, the youths, when confessing a day after the rape, claimed that the attack took place blocks from where it actually occurred.

- The youths' descriptions of the crime were wildly inconsistent, differing with respect to every significant facet of the crime.

- The path created when Meili was dragged into the woods was between sixteen and eighteen inches wide, a path "more consistent with a single attacker dragging an inert form than with a group," according to Nancy Ryan, Morgenthau's Chief of Trials.

• Despite the leniency parole boards afford inmates who are contrite, none of the four youths whose prison records can be accessed has admitted to the rape since the original confessions, costing each opportunities for early release.

The substantial evidence indicating the Central Park defendants' non-involvement, Reyes' confession, and Judge Tejada's decision to overturn the convictions force society to query how a case some considered "rock-solid" could have resulted in the wrongful conviction and imprisonment of five teenagers. Journalists and commentators largely agree that the case was poorly handled. One newspaper enumerated the respects in which authorities erred in pursuing the prosecution: "Botched record-keeping. Mishandled evidence. Incomplete legwork by detectives. Faulty conclusions by zealous prosecutors. This is the legacy of the Central Park jogger case." The Central Park case is certainly characterized by all of these things, but they do not tell the whole story. Exploration of American history, the place of black men in that history, and a similar case with a tragically similar outcome half a century earlier, reveal that the Central Park case was squarely about race and injustice. The true legacy of the Central Park case is the illumination of the festering existence of racial hatred and virulent stereotyping traceable to the days of chattel slavery. Indeed, the Central Park rape case has exposed the extent to which American society is only narrowly removed from its most shameful days.

This article seeks to explain the judicial travesty in the Central Park case by contextualizing it in view of the myth of the Bestial Black Man: a myth, deeply imbedded in American culture, that black men are animalistic, sexually unrestrained, inherently criminal, and ultimately bent on rape. An examination of the myth's foundations, its historical impact on the dispensation of extra-legal and legal punishment against black men, its stubborn perseverance in modern America, and the public discourse surrounding the apprehension of the Central Park Five indicate that the myth impacted the Central Park convictions.

Part I of this article explores the creation of the mythic Bestial Black Man. Part II traces the growth of the myth in Reconstruction and post-Reconstruction America and explores the extra-legal means employed to attack the black men perceived as personifying the myth. Part III examines the legal system's complicity in supporting and promoting the myth of the Bestial Black Man. Part IV explores the 1931 Scottsboro cases, in which nine young black men in rural Alabama were wrongly convicted of rape, and the way in which the mythic Bestial Black Man impacted the cases. Part V examines the legal revolution that occurred in the wake of the Scottsboro trials and in the following decades, as well as the persistence of the mythic Bestial Black Man in spite of the reforms spurred by that revolution. Part VI analyzes the Central Park case in view of the myth of the Bestial Black Man as expressed in America's history generally and in the Scottsboro cases in particular. This part further explores the extent to which the myth potentially impacted the Central Park convictions, despite a trial free of openly race-based prejudice. Part VII examines the consequences of allowing the Bestial Black Man myth to impact rape convictions. Finally, the piece concludes that society's examination and confrontation of the myth of the Bestial Black Man, rather than a regime of legal reforms, provides the best hope of eradicating the influence of the myth on the criminal justice system.

THE BESTIAL BLACK MAN ON TRIAL

As mobs executed lynchings throughout America, a modest movement against lynching gained steam. In the 1920s and 1930s, anti-lynching legislation was proposed in Congress.

The legislation was hotly debated, but ultimately did not pass. Still, the specter of federal intervention, together with increased popular opposition to lynching, served to modestly chill the lynching epidemic, meaning that more blacks accused of rape were able to reach the courtroom. A black rape suspect fortunate enough to survive until his day in court, however, did not often fair much better than one attacked and killed by mobs. Such a defendant was usually subjected to what law professor Randall Kennedy terms a "legal lynching." A legal lynching, as Kennedy defines it, is: "an execution sanctioned by the forms of judicial process absent the substance of judicial fairness." Legal lynchings occur when the threat of extra-legal lynching at the hands of violent mobs is so great that the legal system takes the place of the mob in an attempt to cloak the punishment with legitimacy. Kennedy offers as an example the rural Mississippi rape trial of three black men—Issac Howard, Ernest McGhee, and Johnnie Jones:

> The courthouse where the trial took place was surrounded by barbed wire, machine guns, and more than three hundred National Guards equipped with gas masks and fixed bayonets. At one point during the trial of all three men, a mob of several thousand whites attempted to overcome the court's defenses. Against the backdrop of this intimidation, the jury deliberated only six minutes before returning the foreordained guilty verdict.

As soon as the guilty verdict was handed down, the presiding judge sentenced the defendants to death by hanging. In a move that revealed the transparency of the legal proceeding, the judge then ordered whites in the courtroom to calm mob members and explain that the men would be hanged. He reasoned that any extra-legal lynchings would serve as support for the anti-lynching legislation on Capitol Hill, which could lead to its passage and the consequent destruction of "'one of the South's cherished possessions—the supremacy of the white race.'" In courtrooms such as this one, "legal lynching" replaced extra-legal lynching as the primary weapon aimed at the mythical Bestial Black Man.

Even when not surrounded and threatened by murderous mobs, American courts have supported and promoted the concept that black men are prone to raping white women and, in doing so, have strengthened the myth of the Bestial Black Man. Courts have done so by the very rules employed in resolving criminal matters. A line of Alabama cases is particularly instructive. In 1908, the Alabama Supreme Court heard *Pumphrey v. State*, an appeal from a conviction of "assault with intent to ravish." The defendant was black and the alleged victim was white. The appellate court focused on the factors the jury could legitimately consider in inferring intent. Ultimately, the court affirmed the conviction, and in doing so, announced a rule that would endure in Alabama law for decades. The Court found that "'social customs founded on race differences,' and the fact that [the alleged victim] was a white person and the defendant a negro" were properly considered in determining the defendant's intent regarding rape. Alabama courts applied the Pumphrey rule for decades, paving the way for Alabama jury members to import racial stereotypes and myths, such as the myth of the Bestial Black Man, into their calculus regarding intention to rape. Indeed, in commenting on the rule's application in the 1953 case of *McQuirter v. State*, Jennifer Wriggins writes, the customs founded on racial differences "which the jury was to consider included the assumption that Black men always and only want to rape white women . . . " Although Alabama courts have not applied the rule since McQuirter, it remains a valid part of Alabama common law. Notably, Alabama courts are not anomalous in the application of the rule the Alabama Supreme Court announced in Pumphrey. Indeed, the Pumphrey Court borrowed the rule directly from Georgia law.

In the absence of doctrine such as the Pumphrey rule serving to usher the myth of the Bestial Black Man into the courtroom, the myth has often crept into courts via lawyers' remarks based on, and promoting, the stereotype that black men are destined to rape. To illustrate this phenomenon, the late jurist and scholar Leon Higginbotham presents two cases in which courtroom comments clearly relying on stereotypes of the Bestial Black Man, and clearly aimed at frightening court members, went unchallenged by trial courts.

In *Garner v. State*, a Mississippi court tried a black man for raping a white woman. In closing, the prosecutor made the following statement: "Ah! It is nothing now days [sic] and not uncommon to pick up a paper and see where some brute has committed this crime. . . . You see it South, North, and East, where a brute of his race has committed this fiendish crime." The defendant's attorney objected to the statement. Despite the obvious prejudicial nature of the statement and the appeal to fears of the mythic Bestial Black Man, the trial court overruled the objection. The defendant was later convicted of rape.

In neighboring Arkansas some years later, a state court tried a black man for raping a black woman in the case of *Kindle v. State*. In his summation, the prosecutor, at one point, seemed unconcerned with the victim's plight, instead implying that if not convicted, the defendant could go on to rape a white woman. In stating to the jury, "Gentlemen, you don't know that [the defendant] will rape the same color the next time," the prosecutor essentially asked the jury to convict the defendant, not for the rape of a black woman—the rape for which he stood trial—but to prevent the potential future rape of a white woman. Aside from relegating the black woman's rape to little more than a warning sign that the defendant might later commit an "important" rape, the comment presented jury members with the specter of the Bestial Black Man and implied that he might one day

come for them and theirs. The defendant was convicted and the appellate court affirmed.

America's preoccupation with, and detestation of, the mythic Bestial Black Man has been as present in sentencing as it has been in conviction. The grossly disproportionate number of black men executed for rape highlights the extent to which the judicial system has considered a black man's rape of a white women singularly appalling. Since 1930, 455 men have been sentenced to death and executed for rape. Four hundred and five of these men have been black. The race of the victim is not irrelevant. In the years between 1930 and 1967, the state executed 36 percent of black men convicted of raping white women, while executing a mere two percent of rape convicts when any other racial combination of convicted rapist and victim existed. Notably, no rapist of any race has ever been sentenced to death for raping a black woman, sending an unmistakable signal that rapes of white women have historically been deemed more tragic in America than rapes of black women. In the midst of this climate of extra-legal lynchings and legal lynchings, of legal doctrines presuming the bestiality of black males and courts willing to accept racially prejudicial and inflammatory perspectives, nine black teenagers who would come to be known collectively as the Scottsboro Boys went on trial for their lives.

LEGAL REFORMS AND THE PERSISTENCE OF THE MYTHIC BESTIAL BLACK MAN

In the years following the Scottsboro tragedy, America experienced a movement theretofore unprecedented in the nation's history. Justice-minded people of all races challenged a presumption central to early American history—that people of African descent are inferior to people of European descent and are therefore entitled to fewer of America's coveted rights. The challenges were manifest in various forms. Some marched peacefully in protest of America's relegation of blacks to second-class citizenship. Others engaged in civil disobedience, sitting at lunch counters from which they were prohibited because of race and riding in portions of buses reserved for whites. Still others asserted their equality more forcefully, insisting on the observance of their human rights and defending themselves against attacks on those rights. The nation bled. And, eventually, the law shifted.

In 1954, the Supreme Court reexamined its segregationist "separate but equal" rule, established nearly sixty years prior. In *Brown v. Board of Education*, the Supreme Court established that "separate educational facilities are inherently unequal," striking a fierce blow to institutionalized legal segregation upon which the entire Jim Crow system was based. In the years that followed, legal reforms directed at curing the nation's racial ills were plentiful. The Civil Rights Act of 1964, the Voting Rights Act of 1965, and the Fair Housing Act of 1968 all contributed to the tide of legal change meant to secure for black Americans true equality of citizenship. Then, in 1977, the Supreme Court found executions for rape unconstitutional, eliminating America's most racially disproportionate use of the death penalty, and ensuring that no other group of wrongly convicted young men would ever face state-sanctioned death for rape as the Scottsboro Boys did.

All of these reforms have provided meaningful progress toward racial equality in America. Their impact must not be understated. Still, these and other reforms are powerless to eradicate the deeply seeded presumptions about race upon which America was based from its inception. As such, their impact must also not be overstated. There is no question that despite progressive legislation and jurisprudence and the evolving perspectives of Americans, presumptions based on race endure and people continue to act on those presumptions. To believe otherwise would be naïve. In his groundbreaking article exploring subtle racism, law professor Charles

Lawrence explains that racism is deeply imbedded in our history and culture. As he notes, "Americans share a common historical and cultural heritage in which racism has played and still plays a dominant role. Because of this shared experience, we also inevitably share many ideas, attitudes, and beliefs that attach significance to an individual's race and induce negative feelings and opinions about non-whites."

Under a regime of laws designed to promote racial equality and discourage racial discrimination, however, racist presumptions and ideas are less likely to be expressed overtly. The absence or relative infrequency of overt racial discrimination and prejudice does not translate into the absence of racial discrimination and prejudice. As law professor Angela J. Davis explains, "when state actors openly expressed their racist views, it was easy to identify and label the invidious nature of their actions. But today, with some notable exceptions, most racist behavior is not openly expressed." Further, deeply seeded prejudice often resides in the subconscious, meaning that even the person affected by it may be oblivious to its impact. So, as Lawrence explains, "[i]n a society that no longer condones overt racist attitudes and behavior, many of these attitudes will be repressed and prevented from reaching awareness in an undisguised form." Consequently, "well-intentioned people who would be appalled by the notion that they would be seen as behaving in a racist or discriminatory manner," may unconsciously engage in racism. The consequence is a strain of racism no less virulent than overt racism, but certainly less visible.

In an America where racism is more often subtle than overt, and even when subtle, is often unconsciously expressed, the myth of the Bestial Black Man does not live in the forefront of American life as it once did. No reputable journalist in today's America would endorse lynching 1,000 black men a day to prevent rapes from occurring. Indeed, few Americans would openly endorse the lynchings of blacks for any reason. And it is difficult to imagine any person in today's America calmly admitting to participation in a lynching and then describing the victim being forced to eat his genitals. Although racially offensive movies occasionally spring forth from Hollywood, no Hollywood studio would produce a film such as *Birth of a Nation,* in which the heroic Ku Klux Klan seeks to save a damsel in distress from an animalistic black man. If such a film were produced, no President of our country would publicly endorse it. No judge would get away with sentencing three black men to death moments before asserting in open court that white supremacy is one of the South's most cherished possessions. And if the Alabama Supreme Court had occasion to revisit the Pumphrey rule it established in 1908, it would most certainly find that "social customs, founded on race differences, and the fact that [the alleged] victim was a white person and the defendant a negro," are not properly considered by a jury in determining intent to rape.

Like race-based presumptions generally, the myth of the Bestial Black Man is currently expressed more subtly than it had been through the first half of the twentieth century, and likely with little conscious connection to the origin and historical perpetuation of the myth. Its existence, however, is undeniable. Just as was the case in the early days of slavery, conceptions of black men as animalistic, inherently criminal, and intensely sexual abound.

THE MODERN MYTHIC BESTIAL BLACK MAN

The conception of blacks as uncivilized animals perseveres. And just as it did during times when explicit racism was more acceptable, these images have infiltrated the courts. Indeed, lawyers' in-court use of animal imagery to describe black men in the post-civil rights movement era has not been uncommon.

Lawyers have referred to black male defendants as "laughing hyenas out to kill someone," "vultures," "tigers," "mad dogs," and "animals in the jungle."

No recent case is more famous in this regard than the trial of officers accused of using excessive force against Los Angeles motorist Rodney King. The case was replete with animal imagery and the suggestion that the brutalized King was sub-human. Most famously, King was described as emitting "a bear-like yell" and "groan[ing] like a wounded animal," as he was beaten. Defense lawyers relied on references to King's sub-human strength and the images of animalism to suggest that the brutality the officers heaped on King was necessary to control him. Although packaged more artfully than similar descriptions of black men in this nation's history, this description of King, as animalistically immune to traditional forms of restraint, was nothing more than "the old story of blacks as beasts and animals."

The myth of inherent black criminality has remained just as stubbornly entrenched in American consciousness. As law professor Katheryn Russell explains in The Color of Crime, her groundbreaking book exploring the intersection of race and crime, "the picture that comes to mind when most of us think about crime is the picture of a young Black man." Indeed, as recently as the 1970s, under the guise of testing for anemia, the United States government tested the blood of thousands of black youths for indications of innate violent criminality. The perception is widespread and often subconscious. For instance, studies reveal that ambiguous behavior, when committed by a black person, is perceived as more threatening than similar behavior committed by a white person. The results from one University of California, Davis study are particularly telling. In that study, students were asked to observe arguments between two people in which one eventually pushed the other. Different students were assigned to observe different mock altercations in which the people portraying the arguers were of different races. Where the person who did the pushing was black and the recipient was white, 75 percent of observers considered the push to be "violent" behavior rather than an episode of "playing around." In sharp contrast, when the pusher was white and the recipient was black, 17 percent of observers perceived the push as "violent."

Cynthia Kwei Young Lee, in her incisive discussion of perceived black criminality, illustrated the real-world application of the California, Davis study by examining a 1995 fatal altercation in San Francisco between a black college student and a white construction worker. In that case, Patrick Hourican, the white man, damaged the car of Louis Waldron, the black man, as he bicycled past. Waldron chased Hourican down and asked that Hourican compensate him. Hourican punched Waldron and left again. Waldron again gave chase and when he reached Hourican again demanded compensation. Hourican then allegedly directed a racial epithet toward Waldron. Waldron responded with a punch. Hourican fell, hit his head, and died. Waldron, who had never previously been arrested for, or charged with, any crime, was arrested and charged with first degree murder. Outraged, his attorney asserted that if Waldron were white, he would not have been charged with anything, much less with first degree murder, in connection with the incident. Recent San Francisco history supported the attorney's assertion. Two months earlier, in a bar fight in the same jurisdiction, one white man delivered a single punch against another. The latter fell and died. The former was charged with no crime.

The extent of perceived inherent criminality among blacks is further reflected by the ease with which the public accepts unfounded criminal allegations leveled at blacks and the intensity of the consequent reaction. After Charles Stuart called the Boston police in October of 1989 exclaiming that a black man

shot and killed his pregnant wife, the city flew into a rage. Authorities swooped into black neighborhoods and black men were accosted and strip-searched in the streets. The terror abated several days later when authorities arrested a black man named William Bennett. Bennett, of course, had nothing to do with the crime. It later surfaced that an adulterous Stuart had previously plotted to kill his wife and on this occasion shot her in hopes of receiving life insurance benefits.

Stuart is not alone in blaming a black man for his gruesome crime in hopes of escaping suspicion. In 1992, Jesse Anderson, a white man, claimed two black men ambushed him and his wife as they left a Milwaukee area restaurant, and that they stabbed and killed his wife. In actuality, Anderson killed his wife and was later arrested and convicted for it. In 1994, Susan Smith, a white South Carolinian woman, frantically alerted police that a black man had carjacked her and kidnapped her two young sons. In the days following the report she pled on television for her children to be strong. The case produced national and international concern. A week and a half later, she confessed that she had strapped her children into the car herself and pushed it into a lake so that they would die. In 1996, a white Marylander named Robert Harris claimed to police that a black man attacked him and his fiancée, shooting his fiancée to death. Some days later Harris confessed to hiring a hit man to kill his fiancée so that he could recover life insurance benefits.

Whether they did so consciously or subconsciously, each of these individuals relied on the prevalence of the perception of the inherently criminal black man. As Lee explains, the assailants chose to blame black men because they "knew that others would be most likely to believe their false claims if they attributed their crimes to Black men."

Some suggest that the fear of black violence and the perception of black criminality is justified in light of studies, such as the Sentencing Project's 1995 report, indicating that blacks are over-represented in the criminal justice system. While over-representation does exist, the same report revealed that "the majority of arrestees for violent offenses are white." Indeed, as of the issuance of the Sentencing Project's report, black violent crime arrestees represented less than one percent of all blacks and less than two percent of all black males. Although these numbers belie the myth that blacks are inherently criminal, the myth persists.

The perception of black men as intensely sexual persists as well. In her 1994 book on modern white perceptions of blacks, Rose Finkenstaedt explores the continued existence of the image of the black man as "an inexhaustible sex-machine with oversized genitals and a vast store of experience." This conception continues to support presumptions of black men as prone to engage in unacceptable sexual behavior. Considered in concert with the perception that blacks are inherently criminal, the stereotype of the super-sexed black man leads to the continued belief that black men tend to be sexually predatory. Certainly, this belief is expressed more subtly than it was during the days of forced segregation and frequent lynchings. As a result, although fears of black male sexuality remain with us, they "have gone underground." Consequently, black men charged with rape continue to face an uphill battle in asserting innocence. Indeed, despite decades of legal reforms there continues to be a public willingness "to believe accusations [of sexually deviant behavior] against black men because of racist beliefs about their uncontrollable and 'animalistic' sexuality."

It is clear, then, that the three salient characteristics of the mythic Bestial Black Man—animalism, inherent criminality, and unrestrained sexuality—survive in modern American life. As Jennifer Wriggins observes, "[t]he patterns that began in slavery and continued long afterwards have left a powerful legacy that manifests itself today in several ways." The perseverance of the mythic Bestial Black Man is certainly one such manifestation.

CONSEQUENCES OF WRONGFUL CONVICTION

The consequences of reliance on the myth of the Bestial Black Man and consequent rush to judgment are dire. Historically, for many black men, the consequence has been execution, perhaps the most unforgiving of all consequences. For others, such as the Scottsboro Boys, the primary consequences have been prolonged loss of liberty and slandered reputations. The consequences of wrongful convictions, however, run deeper still, both for the wrongfully convicted and for others. While all of the consequences of a wrongful conviction may be too extensive to enumerate, or too subtle to perceive, some consequences are frightfully evident. In addition to the consequences suffered by the wrongly convicted, consequences exist for the victim of the crime, and for potential future victims of the true assailant. Consequences of each sort flowed following the wrongful convictions in the Central Park case.

The Wrongly Convicted

On top of being incorrectly labeled a rapist and unjustly jailed, the wrongly convicted must adjust to the shame heaped upon one accused and convicted of a ghastly crime as well as the helplessness associated with a futile quest to assert innocence. In addition, the wrongly convicted are sent to fend for themselves in often inhumane penal institutions. America's prisons are plagued with violence and operate under an unforgiving regime of strong dominating weak. Dominance is often asserted through male-on-male rape, a dehumanizing and horrific experience for the victim. Sexual assault convicts are often the most assiduously pursued victims of prison rape, making wrongly convicted rapists particularly vulnerable. Aside from the physical and emotional pain of prison rape, the act carries with it a possible death sentence by way of HIV infection. American prisons have an HIV infection rate six times the rate outside prison walls, making contraction through prison rape a significant possibility. When released, the wrongly convicted are certainly damaged. Whether they dominated or were dominated in prison, released prisoners almost universally find reintroduction into society daunting. With America's shift away from the rehabilitative model of incarceration, a convict is unlikely to acquire skills that would aid him in becoming a contributing member of society when released. Rather, the convict often returns to society deeply scarred as a consequence of the incarceration. If the prisoner dominated in prison, it is hard for him to temper the aggression that was central to his survival while incarcerated. If the prisoner was dominated, it is possible that his spirit will never revive, leaving him a shell of the person who entered prison. In the alternative, he may seek to dominate people on the outside in an attempt to regain the self-esteem he felt he lost while incarcerated.

Although none of the Central Park Five have spoken publicly about their experiences in prison, the young men certainly suffered many consequences of wrongful conviction. All of them have struggled under the stigma of being rapists and have had difficulty gaining employment once released. After being released, one of the youths, Raymond Santana, resorted to selling drugs and was returned to jail. Even before trial, Wise was assaulted in prison and according to Reyes he did not fare much better as his sentence dragged on. Indeed, as noted above, Reyes' confession was sparked in part by Wise's plight. Wise's mother lamented that when Wise was finally released in August 2002, he was emotionally damaged. Indeed, according to her, as of December of that year, he had not smiled since his release. With few employment options available to Wise, Wise's mother made a public plea, asking that anybody in need of a person to mop floors consider hiring her son.

McCray, Salaam, and Richardson have emerged with less noticeable scars and have been able to partially reconstruct their lives. McCray is a married father of three, has a steady job in a factory, and hopes to attend college. Salaam, also a father, is pursuing his bachelor's degree in computer science. Richardson, too, is pursuing a bachelor's degree, his in social services, while working as a night-watchman.

Although some of the Central Park defendants have patched their lives together following their wrongful convictions and incarcerations, all were most certainly damaged by the experiences, perhaps irreversibly so. The cost to society of this damage remains untold.

The Crime Victim

The rush to judgment almost certainly damages the rape victim as well. Rape is a devastating experience for the victim, with long-term, and often permanent physical and psychological effects. To the extent that a rape victim is able to gain any closure upon conviction of those charged with her rape, that closure may be shattered if it is discovered that the real rapist is someone other than the person or people convicted.

Miraculously, Trisha Meili was able to recover from the horrible attack and live her life. She is now married and working at a nonprofit organization in Connecticut. Although she cannot remember the attack and she continues to suffer its physical effects, such as poor balance and eyesight and ineffective olfactory senses, she has triumphed over her horrid experience and believes that having experienced what she did, she "can recover from anything." As she writes in her 2003 book recounting her recovery, "the attack, meant to take my life, gave me a deeper life, one richer and more meaningful than it might have been." She has even been able to overcome any resentment she may have once felt toward the youths convicted of her rape. However, having reached the stage at which she was able to write a book about her experience and was preparing to reveal her identity, she was forced to contend with the reality of Reyes' confession and with the consequent reintroduction of her story to the national and international media. This proved devastating for Meili. Upon learning that Reyes confessed to the rape and that the Central Park Five had their convictions vacated, Meili was anguished: "I was living the horror as I had not lived it before, since I had been beaten into a coma the first time around." She was "too stunned to respond" when she initially learned of Reyes' confession and then grew haunted by it. She explains, "Reyes became real to me in a way that the five had not. I didn't want to see him in the papers or hear him talk on television. . . ." Reyes' confession caused Meili trauma, reopening what Meili believed was a closed chapter. This trauma is a direct consequence of the wrongful convictions.

Potential Future Victims

Finally, by convicting innocents and closing a case, the judicial system leaves society to fend for itself against the real rapist. Realizing that others have been apprehended for his crime, and that authorities are not searching for him, the real rapist is free to unleash further terror on unsuspecting people. Because the alleged victims in the Scottsboro case were not actually victims and there was no rape, society in that instance was spared this consequence. Tragically, in the case of the Central Park rape, society was not. According to authorities, after the Central Park Five were arrested, Reyes continued to commit serious, violent crimes in New York City. In the days between Meili's attack and Reyes' eventual arrest several months later, Reyes inflicted at least five rapes, beatings, and robberies on unsuspecting New Yorkers. Among these was the rape of a pregnant woman in the presence of her children. Had officials stemmed the rush to judgment and investigated the possibility that someone other than the five teenagers upon whom they were focusing committed the

Central Park rape, some or all of these victims may have been spared their attacks.

CONCLUSION

History has taught us that the myth of the Bestial Black Man is not easily cordoned or defeated. Imbedded in American culture during slavery, the myth of the Bestial Black Man triumphed even as chattel slavery died. America's fear of, and desire to destroy, the mythic Bestial Black Man has endured as well, causing black men throughout this country, particularly those accused of raping white women, untold trouble and torture. In post-slavery America, the attack on the mythic Bestial Black Man came largely at the hands of lynch mob members. Black men accused of rape who managed to get to the courthouse frequently fell victim to "legal" lynchings in which proponents of extra-legal lynching explicitly or implicitly encouraged courts to convict the defendants and sentence them to death. In the absence of mobs, courts have employed presumptions suggesting the guilt of blacks accused of raping white woman and have stood silent as prosecutors have imported the myth of the Bestial Black Man into the courtroom. Although the reforms spurred by the Scottsboro case together with general reforms granting blacks the right to equality in various realms of life have certainly served to decrease the prevalence of the myth, it endures. Whether conscious or subconscious, the myth perseveres, gaining exposure, predictably, when black males face rape charges, as they did in the Central Park rape case.

Faced with the myth of the Bestial Black Man and its impact on the criminal justice system, talented lawyers and legal scholars may propose reforms designed to block the myth's access to the judicial mechanism. Indeed, to battle wrongful convictions influenced by race, one might recommend various reforms, such as mandating the videotaping of police interrogations, mandating that juries contain some persons of the defendant's race, or holding prosecutors civilly or criminally liable for blatant prosecutorial racism. While these and other similar reforms may serve to reduce the myth's impact on dispensation of justice, legal reforms alone are not the answer. Indeed, to focus on legal reforms alone as the solution is to ignore the genesis of the problem. The myth of the Bestial Black Man was born of misguided perception, unfounded fear, and a philosophy of superiority among the races; it was not born of law. And it persists despite the evaporation of the legal framework that once supported it. Law was not the myth's Alpha and will not be its Omega.

The substantial reforms following the Scottsboro tragedy did not protect the Central Park Five, so there is little reason to believe reforms instituted in the wake of the Central Park tragedy would necessarily protect the next group of black men falsely accused of rape.

Only when members of American society broadly confront the existence of the mythic Bestial Black Man will the myth begin to crumble. Until then, the myth will continue to persevere and by doing so will continue to discover entries into the criminal justice system.

STUDY QUESTION

Discuss N. Jeremi Duru's examination of the modern myth of the bestial black man.

Normative Violence: Everyday Racism in the Lives of American Indians

Barbara Perry

What I offer here are some preliminary data and observations about the dynamics of hate crime against Native Americans in three distinct regions: the Four Corners area, the upper Midwest, and the northern plains.

Over the past four years, I have spent many hours, many days in fact, listening to stories that had previously gone untold. I have provided an outlet for voices long silenced by inhibitions ranging from fear of violence, to forms of personal denial, to perceptions of official apathy. I am speaking here of stories of racist victimization experienced by Native Americans. In the first project of its kind, I have travelled to American Indian reservations and contingent border towns to gain some insight into the experiences of the Native American people living there. While my focus was on hate crime victimization, I was also very much interested in how that aspect of oppression was embedded in other corresponding forms of discrimination.

My observations across venues as diverse as Northern Wisconsin and Northern Arizona have revealed some remarkably consistent patterns of experiences and perceptions. However, to date, the most striking theme that is emerging is the apparent normativity of racial violence and harassment. Consequently, in this paper, my intent is to highlight the multiple and complex ways in which this perception has presented itself. I begin with a brief overview of the scholarly context of my work, followed by an explicit consideration of this theme of normativity. By way of conclusion, I consider the impacts—as identified by my participants—of these everyday forms of violence.

THE FORGOTTEN VICTIMS OF ETHNOVIOLENCE

Scholarly attention has historically been devoted to the historical and contemporary victimization of American Indians as nations. Equally important is the corresponding victimization of American Indians as individual members of those many nations. A review of the literature on Native Americans and criminal justice, and even a similar review of the narrower literature on ethnoviolence reveals virtually no consideration of Native Americans as victims of racially motivated violence. Bachman's examination of violence on Native American reservations is silent on the question of inter-group violence. Nielsen and

Source: Barbara Perry, "Normative Violence: Everyday Racism in the Lives of American Indians," An original essay written for this volume.

Silverman's anthology on Native Americans, crime and justice likewise makes no mention of Native Americans as victims of racially motivated crime. Barker's journalistic account of the murders of Native Americans in Farmington, New Mexico, touches on the issue of hate crime, but provides no concrete data or analysis. It is this void that this paper begins to address. What I offer here are some preliminary data and observations about the dynamics of hate crime against Native Americans in three distinct regions: the Four Corners area, the upper Midwest, and the northern plains.

I situate this exploratory study within the broader and well-developed literature on the historical and contemporary oppression of Native Americans. I see ethnoviolence nested within a matrix of social processes that have long produced and reproduced the subordinate status of Native Americans in the United States. The collective victimization that American Indians have so long experienced are by now well documented. However, what remains unexplored is whether their oppression is also manifest in individual experiences of ethnoviolence or hate crime.

That is not to say that the collective and individualized mechanisms of oppression are unrelated. On the contrary, ethnoviolence is at once part of and symptomatic of larger patterns of intergroup conflict, and especially of subordination. Ethnoviolence is, in fact, a social practice embedded in the context of the "birdcage" of oppression which systematically restricts the capacities and autonomy of its victims. Young operationalizes oppression in a way that provides a very useful framework for contextualizing ethnoviolence, and especially that perpetrated against Native Americans. She articulates five inter-related "faces of oppression" by which we might characterize the experiences of minority groups: exploitation (e.g., employment segregation); marginalization (e.g., impoverishment); powerlessness (e.g., underrepresentation in political office); cultural imperialism (e.g., demeaning stereo-

types); and violence (e.g., hate crime). The first three of these mechanisms reflect the structural and institutional relationships which restrict opportunities for minority groups to express their capacities and to participate in the social world around them. It is the processes and imagery associated with cultural imperialism which supports these practices ideologically. Together, structural exclusions and cultural imaging leave minority members vulnerable to systemic violence, and especially ethnoviolence.

Ethnoviolence, then, is much more than the act of mean-spirited bigots. It is embedded in the structural and cultural context within which groups interact. It does not occur in a social or cultural vacuum, nor is it over when the perpetrator moves on. Hate crimes must be conceived of as socially situated, dynamic processes, involving context and actors, structure and agency. Specifically, ethnoviolence refers to acts of violence and intimidation, usually directed toward already stigmatized and marginalized groups. As such, it is a mechanism of power, intended to reaffirm the precarious hierarchies that characterize a given social order. It simultaneously recreates the dominance of the perpetrator's group, and the subordination of the victim's group. Ethnoviolence is a mechanism to intimidate a group of people who "hold in common a single difference from the defined norm—religion, race, gender, sexual identity."

The disempowerment of Native Americans, together with their construction as the deviant Other provides the context for anti-Indian *violence*. The former makes them vulnerable targets, the latter makes them "legitimate" targets. As noted previously, the collective victimization of American Indians is well documented. Stannard's work is an encyclopedic survey of the atrocities perpetrated against the indigenous peoples of the America's. Similarly, the extensive works of Churchill frequently return to the theme of Native American genocide. In addition, the many accounts of state persecution of AIM members (e.g., Leonard

Peltier, Russell Means) attest to the use of state power to suppress Native dissidents and activists. What these accounts fail to address, however, are the "mundane" everyday experiences of "random, unprovoked attacks on their person or property, which have no motive but to damage, humiliate or destroy the person."

THE PROJECT

The primary aim of this ongoing study is to conduct the first large scale empirical exploration of hate crime against American Indians. To date, I have conducted three legs of the research: a 1999 pilot study undertaken in the Four Corners region (funded by the Office of Intramural Grants at NAU); a campus hate crime survey of Native American students at NAU; and a 2002/2003 protocol study in the upper Midwest, and the northern plains region (funded by USDA).

During visits to American Indian reservations and nearby border towns, we conducted a series of semi-structured interviews canvassing Native American experiences of ethnoviolence.

There is widespread consensus among scholars who work with Native American communities that face-to-face interviews must be the primary means of soliciting insights from Indigenous Peoples. For the most part, these communities are grounded in an oral tradition. Interviews, therefore, allow information to be gathered in a narrative, story-telling mode that is familiar to participants. Moreover, the utility of surveys is limited, first by the suspicion with which many Native American participants regard the written word. As Marianne Nielsen has expressed it, written surveys "are far too reminiscent of broken treaties." On the basis of her extensive research among Indigenous Peoples in Canada, the United States, New Zealand and Australia, Nielsen concludes that,

> Many Indigenous cultures emphasize oral tradition, and have little regard for written

documents. This can manifest itself in a number of ways. The author has been told by older people, for example, that it is disrespectful to take notes during an interview. It may also mean that people will simply refuse to fill out the questionnaire, thereby biasing the non-response rate by excluding people with more traditional values. Because of its highly structured nature, a survey design may also lose the nuances of the data, or miss getting an answer, altogether.

Practically, the use of surveys is also restricted by the fact that many Native Americans on reservations—particularly elders—have little to no proficiency in reading or writing English. The interview process, then, ensured the most extensively nuanced responses possible. And, in all likelihood, such an approach maximized participants' willingness to share their stories.

It is also important to note that, in each region, I hired an American Indian Research Assistant, who assisted in the development and conduct of a culturally sensitive interview. In addition, they helped to ensure that the key concepts could be translated into the Native languages. The presence of Native American Research Assistants, typically from the areas in question, undoubtedly helped to bridge the cultural distance between the Native American participants and the non-Native researcher. In addition to the on-site interviews, I also conducted a survey of Native American students at NAU, which tapped their experiences of racial violence and discrimination on campus.

By its very nature, ethnoviolence is a controversial subject of inquiry. It forces consideration of individual trauma and suffering (physical and psychic), intergroup tensions and conflicts, and chinks in the armor of democracy and egalitarianism. This research faced additional barriers because of the nature of the population involved. Colleagues warned me that I would have great difficulty in gaining access to the Native American community; and that Native American people would be unwilling, even afraid to talk openly about their experiences and perceptions of racial discrimination and violence. Fortunately, we found the opposite to be true. In all but one of the sites that I have visited, participants were genuinely eager to share their experiences of racial violence and discrimination. In one town, those approached consistently refused to participate. Typically, they would decline saying that it would be a waste of time. There appeared to be a widespread sense that whatever was said would have little impact on the lives of individuals or their communities. More typical, however, were those who gladly shared their perceptions and experiences. At one location, we literally had people lined up out the door of the office we were using to conduct interviews. Especially rewarding were those interviews in which participants expressed gratitude for our efforts to uncover what seemed to them to be the invisible and hidden practices of violence. These expressed the following sentiment:

> I'm glad you're here. I think this is really important work that no one has wanted to do before. Your questions are welcome here; the answers, I hope the answers will help us here and other Indian tribes too.

The interviews addressed the dynamics of violent and nonviolent victimization. Thus, they reflected the following concepts: hate crime (e.g., verbal insults, harassment, physical violence, dynamics, location); oppression/discrimination (e.g., chronic unemployment); reporting of ethnoviolence; and recommendations for responding to hate crime. Moreover, I was especially interested in the extent to which violence is perceived to be motivated by recent or current activism on the part of local Native American communities. Additionally, a great deal of time in these interviews was devoted to the question of policies and practices that might enhance relationships between communities, and thus drive down the incidence of hate crime.

The interviews were conducted in seven states: Arizona, New Mexico, Utah, Colorado, Minnesota, Wisconsin, and Montana. Respondents were drawn from seven American Indian tribes: Apache, Navajo, Hopi, Ojibwe, Crow, Blackfeet, and Northern Cheyenne, representing over a dozen reservations. To date, I have interviewed or surveyed approximately 220 Native Americans.

Given the wide dispersal—geographically and demographically—of what might be called "Indian Country," conducting all of the interviews in the homes of subjects was not a viable option. The travel costs and time required were prohibitive. In addition, there exists no accurate census of Native Americans that could have been consulted to create a random sample. Consequently, I employed a combination of convenience and snowball sampling. My Research Assistants and I spent anywhere from one to two weeks in or near the Native American communities in question, where we solicited volunteers in a number of public locales, ranging from Indian Centers, to government offices, to public libraries. Others were arranged or suggested by participants and other contacts in the field. Many of these interviews were, in fact, conducted in the homes of participants. For the most part, then, subjects were in a relatively familiar and unthreatening setting.

NORMATIVE VIOLENCE

In my journeys, I have uncovered dramatic instances of all the components of oppression noted earlier. All are apparent from the visible socio-economics of the communities I visited, from archival materials, from newspaper and television news stories, and from the stories of the people who live there. For example, myriad forms of employment discrimination are evident (e.g., exploitation of Native American craftspeople), as are practices that constitute cultural imperialism (e.g., Indian logos, racial slurs, the absence of American

Indians in school curricula). However, I was especially struck by the empirical validity of the conceptual observation that Native Americans live with the "daily knowledge . . . that they are *liable* to violation, solely on account of their group identity." In other words, the American Indians who spoke with me reported a lifetime's worth of microaggressions, "a term used to describe racial assaults, subtle, stunning, often automatic and non-verbal exchanges which are 'put-downs' of Blacks by Whites," and one might say, of Native Americans.

What I am referring to here are the everyday acts of omission and commission that remind minority group members of their "place." These often include discriminatory acts by criminal justice representatives—racial profiling, or disparate sentencing, for example. But they also include the daily onslaught of thoughtless acts by lay people—surveillance of Native American shoppers by store employees, crossing the street when approaching a young Native American male, or the use of insulting labels and language. Bell hooks attests to the violent potential inherent in the game of racial accountability. She observes that the daily violence experienced by so many black people

> . . . is necessary for the maintenance of racial difference. Indeed, if black people have not learned our place as second-class citizens through educational institutions, we learn it by the daily assaults perpetuated by white offenders on our bodies and beings that we feel but rarely publicly protest or name . . . Most black folks believe that if they do not conform to white dominated standards of acceptable behavior they will not survive.

As many Native American or black or Asian or Latino people know, the white gaze is upon them, judging them against their own whiteness, but also against those imposed standards to which hooks refers. Racial violence, then, is but one mechanism along the continuum of microaggressions that underlie the

contemporary racial hierarchy that seeks to maintain the relative disempowerment of Native Americans and other racial minorities.

Across state and tribal lines, it is distressingly clear that racial violence and harassment are normative parts of the everyday lived experience of Native Americans. Of the more than 200 Native Americans that were interviewed, the majority had either themselves been victims, or knew of someone close to them who had been victims, of some form of hate crime—ranging from verbal harassment to pushing and shoving to brutal assaults with knives and lighter fluid. By far the most common incidents were various types of name-calling and verbal harassment on the street and in commercial establishments. Nonetheless, there were also a small number of physical and property offenses. Among the most vicious attacks were two cases in which perpetrators bit their victims. In one of these cases, a small piece of the victim's ear was bitten off; in the other, the tip of the victim's tongue was lost. Some participants further reported that they had been victimized by police officers, which might help to explain why so few victims in general reported their experiences.

One category of offences that I had not anticipated had to do with property crimes in the ranching communities of Montana. Several participants mentioned the common acts of vandalism and sabotage that occurred when white ranchers lost their lease on Native owned land. Some of these leases had been operative for fifty years or more. When the current Native owners refused to renew the lease—often so they could ranch the land themselves, or offer the lease to other Native American ranchers—the white ranchers became incensed. Apparently, it was not uncommon for them to retaliate by damaging the new lessee's farm equipment, or even to set the fields alight.

While the property crimes noted above seemed to be restricted to Montana, other forms of violence appeared to be more universal. Virtually without exception, high schools were described as very unwelcoming places for Native American youth:

Over the last few years the confederate flag and the white t-shirts have come on a lot. Just the other night Friday night, our homecoming game, someone who plays on the football team, I was coming down to watch, it and a young man in a truck—I didn't recognize the truck—drives by me with two big huge confederate flags blowing off the back of his truck. They have hung them from the fence during football game, leave them up there until some staff member goes over and gets ready to tear them down then they come in.

Is the racially, you were talking about the racist hate mail, the racial hate mail . . .

Yeah . . .

Can you elaborate a little more?

It seems to have been generated from the high school which again the high school is a mixture of Native Americans and non-Native Americans. Certainly it's in a facility off reservation and one of them was this individual who had signed on for a . . . I don't know if it was a chat room or where—out looking for other people to meet and had given information that, you know, clearly said that he hated Native Americans and "what do you do on your spare time off? Bash them every chance I get." Supposedly it is a group of white t-shirt boys, these guys are known for just wearing white t-shirts even in just winter time. To display their racial superiority in their eyes and certainly their group.

Nor are adults strangers to violence and harassment:

Is there much violence today, still that you notice that goes on in the communities and either way it doesn't just have to be like white on Indian violence, violence in general?

Hum, I suppose yes. I know that there's . . . actually my son and some of his friends went to a bar in, might have been a bar I'm not sure, in Minocqua and they got into a fight with some white guys because they're, they said because they were Indian and those guys started in on them. Could be, you know probably, yeah it still happens.

Actually come to think about it I was on a pool league with my sister and brother-in-law and in this one bar in Woodruff because that is

where pool leagues are in bars right? So we were in after everyone was done and we stayed to play a couple games before I went home and this one couple came in there and I had given my sister a dollar and we all pitched in a dollar to play the jukebox. This guy comes in and he is sitting on this long table right by the jukebox and he is just saying shit to her. Then he goes up to the bar "she won't give me my dime back, I put in a dime and she is playing all my music." Pulled out a dime in my pocket "Here is a dime. God! Take it." So he took the dollar went and settled and just was on her saying stuff to her you know. Finally I went over and said to him "you got your dollar back; can't you leave her alone?" "What the fuck did you say to me bitch?" and he threw an ashtray at me, and I was so stunned I was like "Oh my God!" My sister told him "What did you do to my sister, what did you do?" I was standing there just watching. I was just . . . couldn't believe it and then he comes up and punched me in the side of the head and I said "Well what the fuck did you do that for?" and, Christ he was pulling my hair and this must be. . . I'm 5'6" and he's probably 6' 2" and probably 350 pounds and I couldn't believe it. I was like "Man!" So the cops were called and they interviewed them and they said no they don't want to press charges—of course, because it was their fault! Gees, so yeah it's because we were Indian and they weren't.

Nothing in recent years compares to the harassment and violence that occurred at the Wisconsin boat landings in the closing years of the 20th century. Participants shared some remarkable tales of their experiences at the time:

I was out by the boat landing one night where there was over a thousand people chanting racial things; it got so they wouldn't allow our boats to come off the lake, so we had to take our trucks around, and boat trailers, to another landing. And I said, well, I'll take one, and another guy too. We did our ceremonies and everything before we left, and we did our water ceremonies when we were there. The stories that came out of that, especially the ones . . . how people would prepare themselves to be there at night. There was spear guns, there was pipe bombs, there was airguns, there was slingshots. One day we were setting the nets and they were throwing rocks and they were shooting, shooting wrist rockets, sling-shots with ball bearings. One hit Sarah in her side, and knocked her to the bottom of the boat. I got hit too.

I've actually had rocks thrown at me, I've been spit at, I've been sworn at. I've been called filthy names. On all 12 nights of spearing I was at the landings in some capacity or another. I have heard men teaching their teenage sons to "look at the timber niggers, they're fat and ugly and lazy." Prejudice is actually being taught.

My husband's had rocks thrown in his face, and I've had rocks thrown at me. Unfortunately, one of the big rocks hit our motorman in the back, almost crippled him that one night. His wife wouldn't let him go out again.

We had people chase us, we had people fol-low us. We had threats, we had people pushing. When we would stand at the landings they would come up behind us and they would push the backs of our knees, and they would throw lit cigarettes at us. They would spit on us, throw rocks. Death threats. My son—nuts were loos-ened on his tires on his van. He was coming home and he thought he had a flat tire, because his car started wobbling. So he stopped and all the lug nuts were loose. A lot of them too were slashed at the landings.

What landing was that I lost my hearing? They were all bad. We went out, me and my husband, we walked out towards the lake. We were all clustered at this boat landing and we thought, let's see if there's a better area by the lake where we can congregate. So there was all protestors through here, but we walked through, and we went down to the water, said some prayers by the water, and when we were coming back they parted and he (my husband) was walking ahead of me they parted. He did-n't know but when he went past they closed up and they blocked me off. So I was standing down here, and this lady starts yelling "You wanna buy a button?" She had these STA but-tons "Stop Treaty Abuse." "You wanna buy a button? They're only a dollar." And this guy says, "Oh, the only thing she has a dollar for is a beer at a bar." And they started circling around me screaming, they were all screaming. They had me, and they were blowing whistles in my ear, so all the rest of th night . . . I didn't want to put my hands on my ears 'cause I didn't want them to know that they were doing anything to affect me, so I just stood there. And all that night my ear was, like, totally numb, it was really numb. And then the next day my ear

starting aching, and aching really bad so I went to the doctor, and it wouldn't go away. They sent me down to the clinic over here, to the ear doctor there. And they tested and I had lost hearing; I had lost a lot of hearing in this ear from those whistles, 'cause they would stand right behind you and lean and blow.

While the tension around spear fishing has subsided, the violence and harassment have not disappeared. Rather, it continues and, to those with whom I spoke, the violence seems unremarkable. Often, when asked if they per-ceived racial violence to be a problem in their communities, participants would respond with an almost dismissive, "Oh yeah. Of course." One participant responded to the question, saying "Yeah, racial attacks are common in Indian Country, and of course Indian people have become calloused over the years, and when it happens, they don't think anything of it. It's just the way life is here." That violence per-meates the lives of Native Americans is also evident in the fact that most complained of multiple victimizations over the course of their lives. Rarely did they describe violent victimiza-tion as "one off" affairs that touched them once and never again. There was always the sense, the fear, the expectation, that in the presence of non-Native Americans, they were vulnerable to harassment and attack: "It's always there. I don't want to say it's a norm, but we get so used to it, we never know what's coming next, or where it's coming from. That's what it's like to be an Indian around here."

Ironically, so common is the violence and harassment perceived to be that many claim to have ceased to pay attention:

We get so used to it—some of us, most of us, just ignore it, let it wash away.

I get used to it, so I ignore it. It happens so often that if you pay attention, it gets overwhelming.

You don't really notice it, it's so common. It's like an itch that's always there. After a while, it's just another irritation.

Ya 'hafta' ignore it, or it makes you so angry. People stare at me, follow me, call be things every day when I'm off the reservation. I can't respond to every time.

Perhaps one of the most telling statements in this context comes from a Lame Deer resident who observed that he is

> . . . so used to it, when it's absent you don't know how to act. You are so used to the harassment and name calling being around, you don't notice it until it is gone.

He described for me his experiences in towns and cities away from the reservation, away from the state, where his reception was much warmer than in nearby border towns. He explained how he didn't feel the same animosity; how he was able to relax without fear of harassment. It was in those situations, he claimed, that he realized how bad things were on the reservation and local communities.

I found this story to be especially revealing. It highlighted for me how incessant and oppressive the reservation and border climate must be for so many Native Americans. So, too, does the following observation by a Wisconsin participant:

> That racism is commonplace in the lives of the Native communities. It is almost like the sky. It is always there, right above everything that goes on, influencing your mood and your day, bearing down on you and inescapable.

The experiences of this community are not unlike the women in Dekeseredy et al.'s study of women in a Canadian public housing development. Many of them also reported their perceptions of "routine oppression" whereby they lived in constant fear of harassment or worse. While seemingly minor, the very pervasiveness of those petty actions— name calling, being followed, etc.—itself represents a violent form of oppression. Moreover, it is not readily apparent which of these acts might be the prelude to a more serious assault or beating.

Another telling indicator of the constancy of racial violence and harassment was the sense of immutability expressed by so many members of the Native American community. There is a distressing fatalism in the general acceptance of the permanence of racism. That is, participants expressed their belief that racism and its attendant forms of violence and harassment were so deeply embedded in their relationships with non-Natives that it would never cease to exist for them. Its presence had become as commonplace and "natural" as the earth; racism was seen as an unchanging an unchangeable daily reality, regardless of what efforts might go into altering relationships:

> We talk about it, and we talk to people like you, and nothing ever changes. It won't change; it will just always be the same.
>
> Racism is not going away in my generation and not in my grandchildren's generation. It's part of our history, and I think it will always be a part of our future, too.
>
> Q. What do you think can be done to reduce the problems in your community, to make Native Americans safer?
>
> A. It doesn't matter; we've tried this and that—cultural events, education, other get-togethers. And nothing changes. I'm still afraid sometimes, to go some places. I still get harassed, and watched, and called names. It's never gonna be any different. That's just what being an Indian is like for us.
>
> It's bred in their genes. We were just born and they hate us. So you don't have to do anything to them really. There is nothing that I have to do to anyone, they are still gonna hate me, and they are still gonna hate Indians. You know, that's the way it is.

Such resignation to the durability of racism and harassment is especially disturbing to the extent that it signifies the "taken-for-grantedness" of everyday violence. It has come to be expected—and accepted—as an intrinsic part of life for many Native Americans, as resistant to change as the flow of a river. As Feagin has described the African American experience, being Indian in U.S.

society "means always having to be prepared for anti-[Indian] actions by whites—in most places, at most times of the day, week, month, or year."

In short, racial violence and the potential for racial violence are normative in Native American communities and reservation border towns. It has become an institutionalized mechanism for establishing boundaries, both social and physical. Violence is one means by which to remind Native Americans where they do and don't belong. Moreover, it is clear that there are social or political contexts in which Native American fears are most likely to be realized—in particular, times when those carefully crafted socio-political boundaries are challenged. As stated by one participant, "You don't wanna stand up, like I always do, or you get trouble." In other words, efforts toward empowerment are commonly met with equally steadfast reactionary mobilizations. In particular, rights claims have triggered hostile and frequently violent reprisals from what might loosely be called an anti-Indian movement.

While few tribes have been spared anti-Indian backlash, the effects have perhaps been felt most keenly by those occupying lands in the Pacific Northwest, the Northern Plains, the Upper Midwest and the Great Lakes regions. Ostensibly premised on the notion of "equal rights for all," opponents have denied the legitimacy of Native American rights claims. Moreover, they have engaged in quite tangible violations of Native American *human* rights, through ongoing harassment and violence against the tribal government and individual American Indians. The spearfishing conflicts of the upper Midwest provide evidence of this. Many of the participants I interviewed there had been involved in these conflicts. I noted earlier some of the experiences of these activists. Many had been shot at, spit at, bounced around in the wake of speed boats, and had been the recipients of death threats. Unfortunately, the posture of entitlement taken by Native American activists are often seen as an affront to white dominance, in that the activists are perceived to be violating the anticipated rules of behavior. Instead of accepting their subordination, they resist it. In such a context, incidents of racial violence often escalate in retaliation. To paraphrase, from the perspective of those sympathetic to the anti-Indian movement, the only good Indian is a quiet Indian. Should Native Americans step outside the permissible boundaries that define "a good Indian," they become vulnerable to retaliatory violence. Seen in this light, hate crime can be seen as a reactionary tool, a resource for the reassertion of whiteness over color.

Even in the most extreme cases, violence against Native Americans remains unmarked and unremarkable. In part, this is itself a hallmark of the normativity of violence: it is so constant, so deeply embedded in American Indian lives that it hardly warrants reporting. More significant, however, is the fact that victims see little use in registering complaints with an unsympathetic white justice system, or even with tribal law enforcement authorities. In other words, some participants pointed to an enabling climate in which racial violence is allowed to flourish. This view was expressed by a participant who observed that "There's a lot of incidents that never get reported—who ya' gonna file a complaint with: The County? The State? The Feds? Nobody trusts them, they're a big part of the problem."

In the upper Midwest, this has been evident in the role of politicians and law enforcement in their reaction to the spearfishing conflicts:

> My husband was arrested along with another man for holding up the Plains Indian flag at a boat landing. Well, we forgot to tell you the whole point of that story, which is: the protestors had ordered the police to arrest them! And as it turned out, they had them in a back of a squad car, and there was frantic radio communication back and forth to try to find something to charge them with! They ended up successfully suing the county and various law enforcement entities. AND a friend and treaty rights

supporter was also arrested at a joint PARR/ STA rally at Torpy Park in Minocqua for holding up a sign reading People Already Racist (and) Radical (PARR) and we were ALL there and the PARR speakers actually ORDERED the law enforcement to arrest her even though all she was doing was silently standing there holding up a sign! And the police, at PARR's direction, did arrest her! We passed the hat and got money to bail her out. The main points are that in those times the police were actually being manipulated by the anti-Indian groups! And very openly, as the man who called for her arrest did so by microphone from a stage.

However, Native Americans also perceive problems with law enforcement beyond the boat landings. There is a widespread perception that law enforcement will not by sympathetic to Native American complaints:

Q: Is there some reluctance to report victimization?
A: I think so, because, the perception based on experience this time, is that—first of all, you're going into a system that you have no control over—and they have their ways. You file a complaint—it doesn't necessarily or usually get acted upon, a lot of times they aren't. It is pretty rare that there was any satisfaction with the way things were handled. However, on the flip side, were you to do something— you better believe you know where you're going! They'll be right there on your tail. It's just a matter of how much you're gonna pay or how long you're gonna have to sit it out. I think that's still true.
A classic colonial relationship. The latter group determines all the rules and all the means and the former must struggle to fit in. This is seen in the fact that there is a lot of racism and discriminatory treatment in the law and law enforcement. The cops discriminate a lot as do judges in sentencing. They both view Native individuals as examples of their culture and society.

In light of such perceptions, it should come as no surprise that American Indian victims fail to report victimization to police. As the visible and uniformed face of the "dominant society," law enforcement agents—even American Indian officers—bear the brunt of this suspicion. Native Americans are not likely to freely initiate contact with officers who represent a state or a culture that has so often betrayed them. Moreover, this lack of trust is not misplaced. One participant highlighted the frustration that inhibits reporting victimization to police:

When Indian people become a victim, they don't know where to go or who to see to remedy the situation. So at that point, Native people become angry and frustrated, and that particular situation does not get resolved, and the Native people say, "Oh, what the heck!" When Native people do get an opportunity to file a complaint, it's always a negative reply. Native people don't trust the White system, because it's always in their favor, so they figure it's a losing battle right from the start.

At one extreme is the "petit apartheid" of which Georges-Abeyie writes: the minor, ongoing, daily forms of harassment to which minorities—including Native Americans—are subject, the stop and search, the racial profiling, the racial epithets, the surveillance and suspicion, all of which are facts of life for many Native Americans. At the other extreme is the exercise of violence:

There's a lot of violence, but police don't do anything. It's worse than that, because the cops are really bad. They beat Indians real bad sometimes, and follow them, thinking they're always up to no good, or in gangs. They'll go out of their way to pick up Indians if they see a tribal plate.

On a related note, participants also observed how being "Indian" seemed to absolve police from the responsibility of responding to victimization:

We had two deaths, unfounded deaths here in the community. Two girls have been killed. I called the tribal chairman and I asked what was going on with that. I said the white girl, which a lot of white girls are beaten and killed by men, and they continued a upspeeded investigation to find out who did it. That hasn't happened with the Indians. We still have two unsolved murders. The murderers are walking around on our reservation, it that's what it is.

We started going down to the boat landing, we got about half way down there. It was a really long, dark road, a couple miles. And then there were some people coming behind us. They were saying things, like "let's get 'em" and "we can get 'em now; it's really dark." And they were threatening us. So we turned around and went back in the dark, and we got to the car and he (my husband) wasn't with us. So I go to the cop "My husband is halfway down there and there's a group of guys that was threatening us. Can you help me?" He asked what's your husband's name, and I told him, and he says "what's he wearing?" then he says wait a minute. So then he says, go tell this officer that. So he goes, what's your husband's name, what's he wearing. And I go, "Will you please help me? They could be hurting him." And he goes, "maybe this guy could help you. You know the landings closing, we're going to close it because of the violence down there. We're gonna be clearing out the landing. People are going to be coming out." I said, "Do you know my husband could be dead. He could be lying there dead in the woods and you guys aren't helping me." He goes, "Go talk to this guy" and he takes me to the third cop, who's, like, "what's your husband's name, what's he wearing?" The cops were playing with us. I was frantic and they wouldn't help, they wouldn't help us!

See, they never really did anything when my nephew got killed, and all the other stuff like when the white people got killed. They didn't go to any great lengths to find who did it, or anything. Now, this white couple gets killed and they wanna do something; now they say there's a violence problem around here. What they mean is, now the white folks are in danger, we got a problem.

Ironically, the comments of white police officers that were also interviewed lends credibility to the observations of tribal members. One officer stated quite frankly that,

Much of the distrust between communities is the fault of the Native people, who think everyone is racist and is discriminating. The Tribe brings stereotypes upon themselves, and use stereotypes. They use the notion of the "White Man" as a political ploy to get tribal votes.

Another officer was a little more subtle, though no less racist in his comments. In spite of the extent of violence and harassment revealed in the interviews, this officer claimed that violence was not widespread, and that

Most people feel safe and this is for the people here that are the tribal members here on the reservation and from what I see over the years. I've lived here and worked here or lived or outside the reservation, worked inside the reservation. The majority of people just want to get along. Go about their business, live their lives, don't want any problems and they won't do anything of a prejudiced nature of, that wouldn't be considered a hate crime because they wouldn't want to get involved in something like that. They're overall just good law-abiding citizens, there are just a few bad apples that love to instigate a little problem and looking for a scapegoat in life and it is always easy to blame one race no matter which race it is. Blaming another for some type of problem.

In light of such willful blindness, it is no wonder that tribal members have little faith in local law enforcement.

THE CUMULATIVE EFFECTS OF NORMATIVE VIOLENCE

Not surprisingly, the cumulative effect of anti-Indian activity takes its toll. Those I have interviewed describe an array of individual and collective reactions, many of which were indicative of the aggregate impact of normative, systemic victimization. One participant stated the impact very simply: "A lot of it is petty stuff. But it's the petty stuff that gets to you after a while, because it's all the time." This corresponds to Feagin's (2001: 196) observation that

For any given individual, repeated encounters with white animosity and mistreatment accumulate across many institutional arenas and over long periods of time. The steady acid rain of racist encounters with whites can significantly affect not only one's psychological and physical health, but also one's general outlook and perspective.

Among my Native American participants, there were many whose stories supported Feagin's contention, especially with respect to "outlook and perspective." Indeed, there was a generalized sense of feeling weighed down, oppressed by the ongoing threat of harassment and other racist actions:

> You just get tired. You don't want to have to face it anymore. After a while, you hate to go into town, 'cause ya'know as soon as you cross that line, somebody's gonna do something—yell at ya,'curse ya,' maybe chase you back across the river. Sometimes it's just too much.
>
> You get so used to it, you have to try to ignore it. It's when I'm paying attention or letting it get to me that I get overwhelmed.
>
> It wears us down, ya' know? We don't have to do anything. We're just there and someone calls us a "lazy Indian," or an "Indian whore," and maybe they throw stuff, or, one time someone spit on me—I didn't do anything! It's that stuff everyday or every week that gets to me. I just don't wanna' have to face any white people.
>
> I think we must be crazy, or stupid, or something! Folks just keep knockin' us down—with words or with, I don't know, bats and fists—and we keep getting back up. Some say that's brave, I say it's nuts. How many times can you fall down before you don't wanna' get hit again?

The perception of recurrent threats and harassment leaves its victims feeling disempowered. It is, as many expressed it, "overwhelming," or "tiring", or "wearing." Even those who try to ignore or deny their daily realities feel embattled by that effort. For some, the constancy of the fear is almost paralytic. At the very least, it limits their desire to interact with white people. For others, it limits their movements and their perceived options, resulting in withdrawal. It creates "more borders," said one participant, in that people become fearful of moving out of the relative safety of the reservation. They "stay here for all their lives, because they're afraid

to go "out there" because of what's going on, for all of these reasons." Very similar sentiments were expressed by others:

> That's why people don't leave, why they don't go into the towns to look for a job. They're afraid to go there, so they stay inside. They know—from their experience, or their family's, or their friends—what can happen. There's too much risk out there.
>
> People don't like to go over to Cut Bank, because they don't get treated right, in the stores, in the restaurants, on the streets. While you're there, ask people what they think about Browning—they'll tell you how we can't be trusted, we'll steal in the store, we're drunk. And they say all that makes insulting us, or even shoving us out of the store okay . . . And then, on top of it, we'll get harassed by police. As soon as we leave the rez, they're waiting for us. So why would we want to go there?

For too many American Indians, the perception, if not the reality of "what's out there" has its intended effect of keeping people in their place. It reinforces the boundaries—social and geographical—across which Native Americans are not meant to cross. It contributes to ongoing withdrawal and isolation; in short, it furthers historical patterns of segregation Through violence, the threat of violence, or even through the malevolent gaze, Native Americans are daily reminded that there are places in which they are not welcome:

> This is an incredibly racist area, in spite of or because of the high number of Native Americans, the number and size of reservations in the area. I am a little different because I have money and status in the town, and people still follow me around; I still don't feel welcome, as if this is my home and my land. There is always an arm's length relationship between Indians and whites, between tribal communities and the city of Bemidji. People here don't see tribal members as citizens or members of the same community.
>
> There were places you just didn't want to go. Like Mercer and all—that's where the head of the Ku Klux Klan lives. That's only 14 miles from here. There's just places you don't wanna

go, you don't feel safe. Really you don't fell safe when you go off the rez.

It's (racism) a part of our everyday experience, memory. My mom's 73; when she went to school and lived here, it was kinda like our communities were separate. And I'm 49 and back here and it's still separate, but far from equal.

There is just places where you get in you know you are not supposed to be in there. I guess there is, there's a kind of sense, places—for Indians and non-Indians in the communities around here—there is an idea that Indians have a certain place; that there is a certain way that they are supposed to behave when they are on the communities. And like in the South compared to this area is the deep North you know. The whole sense of maintaining one's place and one's position in society is the kind of feeling that Indian people get around here.

Another damaging cumulative effect of the daily threat of harassment is the cultivation of anti-white sentiment, and ultimately, anti-white violence. Several participants spoke of the way that their harassment exacerbates anger toward and distrust of whites.

I just get so mad sometimes. Why do they have to do that? Why do they follow me and call me names? Or try to scare me? It makes it so I don't want to have nothin' to do with them. Why would I? They hate me so I kinda feel the same way.

'Cause it's everyday, you don't forget. It was worst during the spearing, but it keeps going, people still say things, and sometimes throw things at us. And I can't forgive or forget—maybe I'm just the wrong kind of person, that I can't forgive. I know it's sad, but now I feel prejudiced.

For some, the anger spills into action. Some reported hearing of, witnessing, or engaging in retaliatory violence against whites. Again, it was the daily barrage of insults, slights, harassment, and surveillance that engendered bitterness that some were unable to contain: "For many of the Native people, we hit a boiling point of pent up frustrations and anger at the racism and ignorance and the fact that we feel powerless to

fight and we explode." One educator described her perception of retaliatory violence in the schools:

It goes both ways. The Indian kids come here, maybe from the reservation schools, or at least from the reservation. And they're already angry when they get here, so it doesn't take much for them to react when someone calls them "Chief," or tells them to go back to the reservation, or bumps into them—intentionally or not—in the hall. These kids live with it everyday, and at some point, some of them turn around and give some back.

A mother tells the story of how her daughter "gave some back:"

My kids are going through the same thing, just like I did . . . My daughter got in a fight last week, and she ended up leaving because that's what the guy said, kept saying, "ya' Indian, ya' fuckin' Indian," "You girls are nothin' but Indian whores," "You need to go back to your reservation where you belong," "I wish you were all dead." She just went off. She ended up fighting with him, and then I had to go to the school and she ended up being suspended. I had to take her out of that school because this is happening all the time.

Another participant related his own biography:

I grew up on the reservation, and as a kid, and now it was always the same. I didn't trust white people, because I felt like they were always hassling me and my friends and family—everybody. Or they were ignoring us. Either way we were treated racist. Sometimes I ignore it, but sometimes I fight back. I call names, I've even hit people who crossed the line, especially when they hollered at my wife or something. I'm not proud of it, but dammit, I do have to get even sometimes.

And yet another speaks to the cyclical nature of anti-Indian/anti-white violence, and what he sees as likely consequences:

Out there, it's hatred against Native Americans. The Cheyenne, we're prejudiced against whites because of distrust, not hatred . . . And when we act against the constant slurs, we sometimes react with violence, and then we go to jail. That doesn't happen to the whites.

The last observation is especially enlightening. The speaker attests to the reality—and basis—of anti-white retaliatory violence. But he also alludes to one unfortunate consequence of such retaliation—it inadvertently reinforces white perceptions of Native American criminality. Rather than treat such violence as part of a provocative cycle, white culture and often the white criminal justice system reacts in a way that must further embitter Native Americans. And so the cycle of distrust begins anew.

Not surprisingly, many of the reactions to the normative violence described by participants are negative. That is, they are characterized by withdrawal, anger, or even retaliation. However, there are those who react in a constructive manner. Some use harassing moments as opportunities to educate. One student in a campus hate crime survey tells this tale:

> The first incident was in a class with a professor who did not know I was Native American and made some condescending remarks about Native Americans. I immediately raised my hand and told him that I had a 4.0 GPA, was in the Honors program, never drank, smoked, or had sex and I did not appreciate his stereotype. That was the only comment he ever made.

Other examples of people standing up to and correcting bigotry were plentiful. A particularly memorable one occurred on a bus trip:

> This lady was sitting in back of the bus driver, and I was sitting in the other front seat. And they started to talk about things, and the subject of spearing came up, and about all those fish that are thrown in the dump and why do they take them. And he was kinda half agreeing with her. After they got through talking, I said, "Can I interject something here?" And I told them, "I don't know if people realize it or not,

but those aren't fish that are thrown in the dump. It's the hide and the skeleton of the fish. The meat is taken out of it." "Oh" he says, and she didn't say nothin.' She got off in Minocqua! It's all these misconceptions, and lies—they're just ignorant.

Most remarkable, perhaps, is the strength and resilience of Native Americans in the face of the everyday violence described here. In fact, they currently enjoy a resurgence of numbers and of nationalist identity. As Frideres puts it, "with the emergence of Native identity, the sense of alienation experienced by many Natives has been dispelled by a new sense of significance and purpose." The activism which has been at the root of so much violence, and the backlash associated with it, has engendered a renewed pride in American Indian identity, and with it, a recognition of the need to pursue that which is theirs by right. In short, it has mobilized Native Americans around their cultural identity and political sovereignty.

> One thing that this whole treaty battle brought about was a resurgence of traditions and people's appreciation for a traditional way of life. That's why we moved back here. My husband's from Milwaukee and we were living down there, renting a house and we had been down there for 21 years, and all of a sudden because of this we just gave notice and we packed a U-Haul truck and we moved up here, and we didn't have any place to live when we got here. Because we thought we were spiritually called to come home. And so the first night we stayed at a motel an the next day they found us this house. . . . And that's what happened to a lot of people. It brought us back spiritually and physically. It made people stronger in their heritage.
>   A lot of people—this has been my experience anyway—even among Indian people there were people saying "Don't!" Because when you're told you're bad for doing something, and told a thousand times, sometimes you start to believe is. And there were others that weren't quite sure, but became supportive. People who don't go to meetings were coming to meetings. People who went about their lives—they wanted, they really needed to learn—what are

these treaties about, how did they occur, you know. And they developed the sense that it was a birthright for future generations. That was exciting. That was a very positive outcome of the conflict, that will have contributions for years to come.

It is these sorts of reactions to the normativity of violence that will ultimately present the greatest defense. To use the moment of victimization to confront and challenge oppression speaks volumes. In particular, it says to the perpetrator that Native Americans refuse to "stay in their place," but will instead fight for a reconstructed definition of what that place is. Moreover, such resistance also sends a powerful message of strength and solidarity to American Indian communities as well.

CONCLUDING THOUGHTS

The Rodney King beating. The dragging death of James Byrd. The sodomization of Abner Louima. The shooting death of Balbir Singh Sodhi. These dramatic acts of racial violence make the headlines. What remains unpublicized are the unremarkable acts of racial violence that occur everyday. We hear or see little of the pervasive racism and violence that characterizes the daily lives of those who live with the constant knowledge that they might—at any moment—because become a victim of racial violence or harassment. The stories I have told here begin to illustrate the normativity of violence as experienced by Native Americans living in or near American Indian reservations in the United States.

What I have attempted to offer here is space to listen to the lived experiences of, perceptions of, and reactions to everyday harassment. This is very much in contrast to the "usual strategy that authors adopt in books about racism (which) is to silence the voices of the victims, neglect their feeling, ignore their conclusions." These are precisely the patterns that I have sought to counter. Instead, I share here narratives offered by those who know best—those American Indians whose days are shaped by racism and violence.

STUDY QUESTION

How does Barbara Perry define the concept of "normative violence"?

Jails Not Homes: Quality of Life on the Streets of San Francisco

Maya Nordberg

[T]his note discusses quality-of-life violations, tracing the history and means of implementation, specifically with reference to homeless individuals; [it] details San Francisco's recent, current and proposed application of quality-of-life citations and prosecutions; [and it] outlines non-punitive, community-based alternatives to quality-of-life enforcement policies.

For more than a decade, urban centers in the United States have engaged in a social experiment to clean up city streets, sweeping away the visibly homeless and acts associated with poverty and disorder, such as loitering, sleeping in public, sitting on sidewalks, and camping in parks. As an extension of "community-oriented" policing, cities have focused on the importance of "order-maintenance." Cities prohibit and prosecute relatively minor acts of disorder, perceived as diminishing a community's quality-of-life, in an effort to prevent more serious crime and overall neighborhood decay. Residual effects of minor crime or infractions, such as broken windows and other minor evidence of community inattention, are perceived as "indications of disorder," and if left un-remedied, "demonstrat[e] a loss of public order and control in the neighborhood and thus breed more serious criminal activity."

Vagrancy Laws

For hundreds of years, vagrancy statutes criminally penalized individuals for visible indigence, the appearance of poverty, or failing to demonstrate a "visible means of support." Various laws and court decisions cast vagrants and migratory poor as threats to safety, public health and economic stability. The Articles of Confederation guaranteed "the privileges and immunities of free citizens in the several states" for all "free inhabitants," but deliberately excluded paupers and vagabonds from that grant of liberty and protection. In 1837, the Supreme Court opined: "We think it as competent and as necessary for a state to provide precautionary measures against the moral pestilence of paupers, vagabonds, and possibly convicts; as it is to guard against the physical pestilence. . . ." Merely because of their economic status,

Source: Maya Nordberg, "Jails Not Homes: Quality of Life on the Streets of San Francisco, Hastings College of the Law, 13 (2002): 261–305.

those without means could be legally excluded, castigated and imprisoned. In contrast to most criminal statutes, vagrancy laws punished the poor for their impoverished or transient status rather than any specific acts.

Communities implemented vagrancy laws as a means of controlling undesirables, prohibiting the status of those perceived as potentially causing future crime. In 1812, Congress amended Washington, D.C.'s city charter to include a provision requiring that those perceived as likely to become paupers and those lacking permanent housing pay a monetary deposit "for their good behaviour" meant to "indemnify the city for their support." Those "vagrants, idle or disorderly persons" unable to pay the security deposit were confined and required to perform forced labor for up to a year. Vagrancy laws were legislatively enacted "quasi slavery. In 1865, for example, Alabama broadened its vagrancy statute to include 'any runaway, stubborn servant or child' and 'a laborer or servant who loiters away his time, or refuses to comply with any contract for a term of service without just cause.'" Vagrancy laws criminalized perceived poverty, effectively controlling and incarcerating poor people based on their employment or housing status.

Beginning in 1972, with *Papachristou v. City of Jacksonville*, the Supreme Court held that vagrancy and loitering laws were unconstitutionally vague, violating the Due Process Clause of the Fourteenth Amendment. Writing for a unanimous court, Justice Douglas concluded:

> The implicit presumption in these generalized vagrancy standards—that crime is being nipped in the bud—is too extravagant to deserve extended treatment. Of course, vagrancy statutes are useful to the police. Of course, they are nets making easy the roundup of so-called undesirables. But the rule of law implies equality and justice in its application. Vagrancy laws . . . teach that the scales of justice are so tipped that even-handed administration of the law is not possible. The rule of law, evenly applied to minorities as well as majorities, to the poor as

well as the rich, is the great mucilage that holds society together.

The Court held that the vagrancy ordinance at issue in *Papachristou* was unconstitutionally vague in failing to provide adequate notice of prohibited behavior and "encourag[ing] arbitrary and erratic arrests and convictions." Among other prohibited acts, the Court concluded that begging, living off the wages of others, nightwalking, wandering "around from place to place without any lawful purpose or object," and habitual loafing were "normally innocent" activities, "historically part of the amenities of life as we have known them." The presumption that these acts suggested "future criminality" did not support banning all indicia of "vagabondage." Due process prohibited the *Papachristou* vagrancy law that equated poverty, immorality and criminality because the ordinance failed to provide notice and lead to unfettered police discretion.

In the 1980s, the emergence of the "broken windows" theory of community policing, which linked minor disorder to larger crime and urban decay, breathed new life into vagrancy laws. The concept of quality-of-life crimes developed out of "broken windows," building a foundation on the centuries-old legal tradition of criminalizing acts associated with poverty and homelessness.

Generally, quality-of-life ordinances avoided sweeping prohibitions of the status of homelessness. In the 1962 decision of *Robinson v. California*, the Supreme Court held that criminalizing an involuntary status violates the Eighth Amendment, imposing a cruel and unusual punishment. The Court qualified Robinson in 1967 with *Powell v. Texas*, holding that communities may prohibit acts associated with status instead of the status itself, such as proscribing drug use rather than drug addiction. Recent quality-of-life ordinances have passed Constitutional muster, with specifically tailored legislation that prohibits acts and avoids both Papachristou vagueness challenges and Robinson status challenges.

Prevailing Trend: Distinguishing the Status of Homelessness from the Act of Being Homeless

While perhaps counter-intuitive, many courts have distinguished a person's homeless status from the acts committed because a person is homeless. In drafting specifically tailored legislation, communities are constitutionally permitted to prohibit individual acts, even if those acts are intrinsically linked to status.

In one example, Santa Ana, California, in 1988, formed a "vagrancy task force" to implement a quality-of-life enforcement campaign targeted at the community's homeless population. As described by the California Court of Appeals, this amounted to a "harassment sweep." Santa Ana intended to clarify "a policy that the vagrants are no longer welcome," with a stated "objective [of] cleaning up its neighborhoods and forcing out the vagrant population." The city commenced sweeps, where homeless people were "handcuffed, transported to an athletic field for booking, chained to benches, marked with numbers, and held for as long as six hours before being released at another location, some for crimes such as dropping a match, a leaf, or a piece of paper or jaywalking." After Santa Ana stipulated to refrain from similar sweeps, the city enacted an anti-camping ordinance, assessed by the California Court of Appeals as a continuation of "the city's war on its own weakest citizens."

In *Tobe v. City of Santa Ana*, the California Court of Appeals issued the homeless petitioners a writ of mandate, forcing the city to halt its anti-vagrancy campaign. The court found for the petitioners on the basis that "[a] minority may not be entirely suppressed in the name of otherwise laudable public purposes." The court held that the city's campaign violated the right to travel. Further, the court applied the jurisprudence of "status" crimes and the Eight Amendment's proscription of Cruel and Unusual Punishment, declaring that "homelessness, like illness and addiction, is a status not subject to the reach of the criminal

law; and that is true even if it involves conduct of an involuntary or necessary nature, e.g., sleeping." The court briefly considered the city's attempt to characterize petitioners as "voluntarily homeless," and dismissed this as "a somewhat frivolous lawyer's gambit we thought Anatole France had long since put to rest anyway: 'The majestic egalitarianism of the law forbids rich and poor alike to sleep under bridges, to beg in the streets, or to steal bread.'" The court concluded by quoting United States Supreme Court Justice William O. Douglas: "'How can we hold our heads high and still confuse with crime the need for welfare or the need for work?'"

The California Supreme Court reversed the appellate court's decision in *Tobe*. The court held that the anti-vagrancy campaign and the challenged anti-camping ordinance were facially valid. "Unlike the dissent, [the majority] cannot conclude that the city intends to enforce the ordinance against persons who have no alternative to 'camping' or placing 'camp paraphernalia' on public property." The court found Santa Ana's policies reasonable regulations of public spaces, holding that "a city not only has the power to keep its streets and other public property open and available for the purpose to which they are dedicated, it has a duty to do so." The court stressed that the ordinance was neutral on its face, and due to procedural defects, did not rule on the ordinance as applied. The dissent criticized this decision as ignoring the purpose and effect of the ordinance, which effectively exiled indigent homeless people to locations beyond the city limits. Ultimately, Santa Ana, like cities elsewhere, gained judicial approval of the validity of juxtaposing public order with the fundamental human necessity of shelter.

Anomaly: Quality-of-Life Ordinance Invalidated as an Unconstitutional Prohibition of Status

Not all courts have viewed quality-of-life ordinances as specifically tailored, constitutionally permissible prohibitions of acts. In one example, Miami, Florida enforced a quality-of-life ordinance that failed constitutional analysis on multiple grounds. Miami began homeless sweeps as a response to perceived negative effects on business, tourism and the downtown area. Miami police officers "arrest[ed] thousands of homeless individuals from 1987 to 1990 for misdemeanors such as obstructing the sidewalk, loitering, and being in the park after hours." Confiscation and destruction of property often accompanied the arrests. In some instances, police officers and other city officials removed belongings with "front-end loaders and dump trucks." On two occasions, "officers awakened and handcuffed [homeless] class members, dumped their personal possessions—including personal identification, medicine, clothing and a Bible—into a pile, and set the pile ablaze."

The district court held that Miami's program of arrests and property destruction punished the plaintiffs for their homeless status, and thus violated the Eighth Amendment's proscription of Cruel and Unusual Punishment. Further, the program violated the Due Process Clause of the Fourteenth Amendment, the right to travel, and the Fourth Amendment right to be free from unreasonable searches and seizures. The court discussed the involuntary nature of homelessness and focused on the 700 shelter beds available to meet the needs of a population estimated at 6000. In conclusion, the court held "that plaintiffs have established that the City has a [constitutionally impermissible] policy and practice of arresting homeless individuals for the purpose of driving them from public areas."

"Doing Something" About Homelessness

Quality-of-life prosecutions continue the trend documented in *Pottinger* and *Tobe*: cities arrest, cite, move and harass homeless people, often destroying their property, as a short-term fix to the problem of merchant and resident demands that city officials "do

something'" about public poverty. In 1999, George Kelling, co-author of the Broken Windows theory, echoed the sentiments: "I don't advocate a high number of arrests. I do advocate doing something about the behavior." "Doing something" is the call to action triggering homeless sweeps and other "misguided" political gestures that clean away "the visible symptoms of homelessness but not its underlying causes."

Policies of the late 1980s candidly explained quality-of-life enforcement as a means to rid certain neighborhoods of homeless people and to assert that "homeless people are unwelcome" in city limits. In 1997, New York Mayor Rudolph Giuliani demonstrated the continued political currency of this cleansing sentiment, explaining to reporters that "it would be a 'good thing' if poor people left the city . . . 'That's not an unspoken part of our strategy. That is our strategy.' " Cities no longer appear to officially describe quality-of-life programs in express terms of homeless removal or targeted arrest campaigns, abandoning the publicized attempts to require housing as a pre-requisite to remaining in any given community. But officials continue to explore methods of "doing something." These articulated goals demonstrate that while ordinances may purport neutrality, the legislation and requisite enforcement are designed to remove visible poverty, not abate the underlying causes of homeless within communities.

Crime Reduction

Quality-of-life enforcement programs have failed to deliver anticipated results. Crime rates declined in cities with quality-of-life programs, but not more so than in those cities without quality-of-life programs. The decline is consistent with dropping national rates and likely caused by a number of factors. The spokesman for California Attorney General Bill Lockyer assessed recent reductions in crime rates, noting: "Anyone who tells you that they know why crime rates go up and down is lying." One scholar agreed, stating: "We don't know to what extent it's police activity, to what extent it's the booming economy . . . to what extent it's the act of God." New research undermines even the basic assumptions of quality-of-life enforcement efforts, analyzing "whether the main premise—disorder increases fear, crime, and deterioration—is correct after all . . . [T]he premise of these methods has been exaggerated, they have been overused, and they have overshadowed other problem-solving and community-oriented strategies." The link between anti-disorder campaigns and the reduction in serious crime appears tenuous.

Realities of Implementation

Cycles of Incarceration

Quality-of-life citations perpetuate cycles of incarceration. A 1996 study conducted in Austin, Texas, suggested that "a revolving prison door is a better metaphor for Kelling's theory than a broken window." The study detailed the 5612 arrests for quality-of-life violations in Austin made during a four-month period. "A third of the arrests . . . were of repeat offenders, of whom two-thirds were homeless.'Clearly, those who have no permanent residence and those suffering from addiction are particularly prone to commit these types of crimes, and circulate in and out of the municipal justice system.' " A 1999 national study of clients of homeless assistance programs revealed that while eighteen percent of the homeless clients spent time in a state or federal prison, almost half, forty-nine percent, spent five or more days in a city or county jail in their lifetime. The study suggests that the high rate of jail time might be attributable to incarceration for performing life-sustaining acts in public.

The cycle of incarceration begins when law enforcement officials "catch" homeless people in the act of living without housing. Discretion and local ordinances determine the extent of

police intervention and the debt the individuals must repay for their wrong-doing. An example of extreme quality-of-life enforcement tactics occurred in New York City as a part of Mayor Giuliani's zero-tolerance anti-crime policies. Quality-of-life offenders were "arrested, handcuffed, booked, transported, strip-searched, jailed, and given a criminal record for a minor misdemeanor offense." More common are techniques in other communities, which include issuing citations for violations of minor infractions with court summonses requiring offenders to appear at a later court date. If the individual misses that court date, the court issues a warrant for that person's arrest. If police officers later question the individual about a minor infraction, such as suspected littering or loitering, the officers will conduct a routine records check. After discovering the outstanding warrant, the officers will either take the person to jail or explain the potential for arrest, instructing the individual to "move on." The officers' request that the detainee leave the area or cease specific activities may not have originally been enforceable, but now the person must comply or go to jail for the past offense. A minor municipal citation, initially punishable by fine or through community service, transforms into a permanent arrest record and probable jail term.

Enhanced Surveillance

In both encounters discussed above, the initial violation and the later suspected violation provide police officers with opportunities for "enhanced surveillance" of the offender. Quality-of-life violations, from obstructing the sidewalk to panhandling, establish particularized and reasonable suspicion, justifying brief investigatory detentions and subsequent protective pat-down searches. The Fourth Amendment prohibits detentions, searches and seizures based only on officers' hunches. Available circumstances coupled with officers' inferences must amount to "some objective manifestation that the person stopped is, or is about to be, engaged in criminal activity." Detention and search of homeless people just because of status would be constitutionally impermissible; the status is non-criminal. But the constitutional assessment changes if the individual engages in status-related criminal activities, such as sleeping in a park or blocking the doorway of a closed business in the middle of the night. Such status-derivative acts open the door to array of police interventions.

Minor infractions convert otherwise illegal, unconstitutional violations of a person's right to privacy, into permissible police investigations. Quality-of-life encourages police to seek out and detain individuals based on appearance, perceived economic status, or ability to blend into an otherwise homogenous neighborhood. "These mechanisms have little to do with fixing broken windows and much more to do with arresting window breakers—or persons who look like they might break windows, or who are strangers, or outsiders, or disorderly." Visible poverty and lack of housing amount to the requisite manifestation of criminal activity, justifying increased police inquiry, citation and potential incarceration.

Discriminatory Enforcement

Kelling and Coles, in *Fixing Broken Windows*, acknowledged that, "while it does not have to, order-maintenance policing can enforce a tyranny of the majority, a repression of minority or marginal elements within the community." Discretion in enforcing quality-of-life codes determines patterns of both police presence and disregard in particular communities. "A community policing model tends to empower those who want more policing at the expense of those who want more control of the police." White, middle class constituencies more often capitalize on the benefits and opportunities of community-oriented policing programs. "Meanwhile, those who are most disproportionately the

objects of police enforcement of quality of life laws are young black men."

How do we define minor disorder? Clearly, we are not talking about arresting those who pay their house keeper in cash to knowingly benefit from IRS underreporting, or who pay their nannies under the table. The quality-of-life initiative focuses instead on the type of minor offenses—loitering, fare-beating, and panhandling—that affect the poorer members of society, which, tragically, include a disproportionate number of minorities. Who gets to define disorder? By handing over the informal power to define deviance to police officers and some community members, we may be enabling the repression of political, cultural, or sexual outsiders in a way that is antithetical to our conceptions of democratic theory or constitutional principles.

As applied, the policing of minor neighborhood disorder concentrates police surveillance and action on marginalized "others." One author suggests "[n]on-enforcement of low-level criminal laws, though it encourages a certain disrespect for the law, is less troubling than discriminatory enforcement." Groups of "others" experience disparate treatment inconsistent with ideals of equal protection and the notion that laws should apply equally regardless of race, gender, sexual orientation, or otherwise minoritized status. Enforcing otherwise neutral ordinances primarily against those perceived as sources of deviance and disorder creates de facto vagrancy codes, where social and economic status determine the degree of policing, punishment and constitutional protections.

SAN FRANCISCO'S QUALITY-OF-LIFE ENFORCEMENT

Candidate positions on homelessness make or break elections in San Francisco. Issues of homelessness occupy mainstream policy discussions in San Francisco without interference from "compassion fatigue" or "disorder fatigue." In 1999, San Francisco spent $57 million of locally generated funds on homeless services, more so than any other city in the United States. In 2001, that number increased to over $82 million. But arrests of homeless people for sleeping, loitering and other quality-of-life offenses continue to increase.

The San Francisco Tradition

Jordan's Matrix

In 1991, city voters elected former police officer Frank Jordan as Mayor, based in part on a platform dedicated to addressing "aggressive panhandling" and "cleaning up" homeless encampments. Jordan's administration adopted the nationally endorsed criminalization efforts, using local sales as public and legal justification for Matrix, a policy of "homeless sweeps" and orchestrated arrests. Matrix directed police officers to vigorously enforce specific quality-of-life ordinances and issue citations to homeless people for publicly "performing life-sustaining acts," such as sleeping in doorways or parks, or urinating in public. Citations required the payment of a seventy-six dollar fine within three weeks as punishment for violating the local ordinance. Most citations did not result in immediate arrest, though failure to pay multiple citations could result in arrest. Underlying this program was the goal of deterring behaviors that "make San Francisco a less desirable place in which to live, work or visit."

In the legal battle that ensued, the federal district court found that the Matrix arrests did not punish homeless individuals for their status but rather for acts derivative of their homeless status, and thus did not violate the Eight Amendment's prohibition against cruel and unusual punishment. The court doubted whether homelessness even constituted a status under Eighth Amendment jurisprudence. Further, the court held that the Matrix arrests did not violate the Equal Protection Clause, impermissibly burden the

homeless plaintiffs' due process rights, nor interfere with their right to travel.

Brown's Sweeping Efforts

In 1995, a five-way mayoral debate focused on criticisms of Jordan's Matrix program, the quality-of-life plan intended to right the wrongs of homeless-oriented disorder. The San Francisco Chronicle, the city's highest circulating daily newspaper, endorsed Jordan expressly on the basis of Matrix. With a vow to end Matrix, Willie L. Brown, Jr. won the San Francisco mayoral election, defeating incumbent Frank Jordan. During the campaign, Brown described Matrix as "persons in uniforms operating as if they are occupational officers in a conquered land."

In February 1996, Brown publicly requested that the Police Chief suspend Matrix and its targeted quality-of-life ordinance enforcement. A week later, the Police Chief issued a bulletin affirming the rights of homeless people, and on April 15, 1996, the Police Chief issued a memorandum announcing the official end of Matrix-related law enforcement efforts. The next day a San Francisco Municipal Court judge dismissed all Matrix citations and recalled all Matrix-related warrants. While Matrix officially ended with the beginning of Brown's first administration, the Mayor's subsequent "acts and words have created uncertainty as to whether the change is nominal or substantive."

Mayor Brown replaced the orchestrated sweeps of Matrix with an unpublicized policy of aggressive enforcement of quality-of-life ordinances and prosecution of individual homeless people caught violating those ordinances. The San Francisco Police Department's quality-of-life enforcement officially devolved into general "law enforcement," or specific responses to complaints as they arise. Though Mayor Brown publicly declared a departure from Jordan's highly publicized and controversial Matrix program, officers continue to "disperse" loiterers from public spaces and cite people for sleeping in parks. As applied, Brown's policies may differ from Jordan's more in rhetoric than substance. "He might have dropped Matrix in name, but that is still what is happening."

Mayor Brown did not tout an organized criminalization campaign in the media, and yet quality-of-life citations have doubled since the initiation of Matrix. Over 11,000 citations in 1994 (during Matrix) increased to over 16,000 in 1996, and escalated to over 23,000 in 1999. Officers gave these tickets to homeless people for sleeping, camping, urinating, trespassing, and drinking alcohol in public.

This increased citation rate may be attributable in part to economic factors. The improved economy of the late 1990s prompted downtown revitalization projects and business improvement plans, and introduced upscale housing, consumers, and money into run-down inner-city neighborhoods. With the influx of wealth, San Francisco enforced quality-of-life violations in an effort to increase perceptions of safety and cleanliness. The increased wealth of many city residents encouraged a bottom-line emphasis on "order," leading to the dispersal and "clean-up" of homeless people. The union of "tough love" and "law and order" rationalizes the use of police officers and citations to force homeless people off the streets, sometimes "banishing" them from the city. Paul Boden, board member of the National Coalition for the Homeless and executive director of the San Francisco Coalition on Homelessness, explained: "There is an attitude that with unemployment at record lows, with the stock market at record highs, if you're poor, it's your own damn fault." Additionally San Francisco is home to one of the toughest housing markets in the nation, with a vacancy rate of less than one percent. Economics have changed the character of homelessness in San Francisco and fueled the soaring quality-of-life citation rate.

The increasing citation rate may also be partially due to police officers' perceptions about the efficacy of the citation process.

With the vigorous enforcement of quality-of-life offenses beginning in January of 2000, the San Francisco City Attorney's Office demonstrated a commitment to following through with these citations. In cities across the country, "police officers, knowing now that there is a system to deal with these offenses, are issuing more charges." Further, quality-of-life citations allow officers to conduct broad investigations with "enhanced surveillance." Citations and the accompanying searches, seizures and warrant checks of minor offenders lead to increased harassment and institutionalization for life-sustaining acts which are legal when performed by housed people.

Prosecutors in Traffic Court

From January 2000 to June 2001, Mayor Brown gained the cooperation of city agencies in issuing an ultimatum to homeless offenders of quality-of-life ordinances: pay fines or accept deals from prosecutors. As an alternative to fines, homeless people who violated quality-of-life ordinances could opt to perform community service or add their names to the city's extensive wait lists for housing and social services.

In January 2000, Mayor Brown and City Attorney Louise Renne responded to merchant and resident complaints about loitering, drinking in public, and public urination by assigning two attorneys to represent the city in prosecutions of these quality-of-life violations in traffic court. The Mayor's budget provided this prosecution program with $250,000, but did not allocate additional funds to the agencies responsible for delivering the housing, shelter, mental health, and substance abuse services to the homeless population. District Attorney Terrence Hallinan deputized the two Deputy City Attorneys to represent the city in this "law enforcement" or "criminal prosecution" capacity. Initially, at least, Hallinan would not take city funds for this "nuisance" prosecution program. "I did not feel it was appropriate for my office. The City Attorney volunteered to undertake this responsibility and I agreed to swear in their deputies as long as I retained oversight." The attorneys worked through the City Attorney's office, with permission to prosecute conferred by the District Attorney's Office.

The deputy City Attorneys in traffic court ensured that homeless people accused of committing quality-of-life infractions would no longer be "let off without penalty." The stated purpose of this quality-of-life initiative was to connect homeless people with social services. Renne explained: "Everyone talks about decriminalizing homelessness. That's what we've done. . . . This is a completely civil program. People go through it and get services." The deputy City Attorneys approached alleged quality-of-life offenders before the traffic court Commissioner called their cases. The deputy City Attorneys were authorized to make deals and prosecute these infractions. In lieu of fines, offenders were offered the option of performing community service or enrolling in social service programs, depending on the infraction. These services were intended to act as "rehabilitation program[s] for offenders . . . to address the underlying causes of the violation[s]."

If the alleged offender accepted the deal, the city waived the monetary fine pending the individual's completion of a service program managed by the Pre-Trial Diversion Program, a private, non-profit organization that finds community service and social service placements for defendants. The City Attorney's Office publicized the following as among available services: volunteer work, temporary shelter, "English as a Second Language" courses, computer classes, alcohol counseling, substance abuse treatment, and mental health services.

The prosecution program embraced coercion as a means to influence the decisions of homeless people. If the accused refused the proffered deal, the deputy City Attorney prosecuted the infraction. Appearing in front

of the traffic court Commissioner, the attorney would present the city's case, "call" the officer who made the initial report, and question the officer and alleged offender. The Commissioner asked the accused individuals for their plea and explanation.

Though non-compliance or failure to appear at court dates, compulsory community service, or social service appointments lead to an arrest warrant and potential incarceration, Mayor Brown and other local policy makers envisioned the program as a constructive approach to homelessness. "'We think it's an opportunity for the city to make sure that additional people get connected with social services,' said Marc Slavin, spokesman for the city attorney's office. 'We're not taking a punitive approach.'"

The San Francisco Bay Guardian described one case from February 2000, early in the city's prosecution efforts, apparently when neither prosecuting attorney made an appearance:

Robert Stenet, who is homeless, was given a $68 ticket for sleeping in Golden Gate Park. There was no deputy city attorney prosecuting at his Feb. 3 hearing. Stenet was more punctual than the judge, appearing at 10:30 on the dot, ruddy from exposure.

When Judge Pauline Sloan asked him how he pled, he said, "No contest with an explanation, your honor."

"OK, so you plead not guilty, right?" she replied, reaching for her "dismissed" stamp.

Stenet kept talking. It was pouring rain, he explained, and he was trying to find a dry spot. "I wasn't even really sleeping," he told the judge. "I just had my eyes closed."

Sloan dismissed his case immediately, but he apologized anyway. "I'm sorry," he said. "I won't make that mistake again, your honor."

After leaving the courtroom he told the Bay Guardian, "I was going to tell her: I was trying to get into a shelter, but I couldn't. It's been raining."

Initially, many of the citations were poorly documented by the reporting officers and were later dismissed by the deputy City Attorneys, who worked to get better police reports. The traffic court Commissioners continued to dismiss some citations either because the city failed to substantiate the violation, or the Deputy City Attorneys made deals with many quality-of-life offenders. Many more citations proceeded to arrest warrants when individuals failed to appear for their court appointments.

In June of 2000, District Attorney Terrance Hallinan informed the San Francisco Board of Supervisors and City Attorney Louise Renne that as of August 1, 2000, he would withdraw permission for the Deputy City Attorneys to continue with these prosecutions. "I think it's appropriate that my office do it. . . . We're the prosecutors and we can do it at half the price." The Board of Supervisors allocated over $151,000 to the District Attorney's Office to continue the quality-of-life initiative with one lawyer and one paralegal for the 2000–2001 fiscal year. Beginning in August 2000, the District Attorney's office assumed complete control of the program, prosecuting homeless people for quality-of-life citations in traffic court. The District Attorney's office did not position attorneys in traffic court to punish non-homeless offenders of these or other minor local ordinances.

The "Success" of Citation and Prosecution Process

The process of deal-making or subsequent prosecutions in traffic court raised fundamental questions of fairness. The City Attorney's Office established this deal-or-prosecution program to specifically target homeless individuals for quality-of-life citations. The attorneys made their offers outside of courtrooms and outside the presence of the traffic court Commissioners. The prosecuting attorneys suggested deals one-on-one to the accused with no advocates present, creating an environment of limited alternatives. One person, alleged to have

violated a quality-of-life ordinance, described the deal-making process as coercive: "This guy here tried to intimidate me. . . . I think it's an intimidation tactic. A lot of people are ignorant of the law."

In California, persons charged with infractions are not subject to imprisonment and are statutorily precluded from the right to counsel and the right to jury trial; infractions result in fines or community service in lieu of fines. Some individuals, ticketed with quality-of-life citations, were arrested and incarcerated at the San Francisco County Jail over night because of warrants arising from these citations. These individuals were generally released on the next court date with "credit for time served." This incarceration credit cancelled out the individual's debt for committing an infraction that could not lead to time in jail. Even though an individual cannot be jailed for minor ordinance violations such as sleeping in a park, the reality remains that the individual faces potential incarceration with repeat offenses and the issuance of warrants. If the individual accused of a quality-of-life violation refused to take the deal, then the attorney prosecuted the case. The combined effect of education, experience and authority presented by the prosecutor, police officer and judge created an environment of intimidation.

Jail Time

Even if homeless people appeared at scheduled court dates, the possibility of losing remained. Oftentimes, these individuals were technically guilty of acts they perform publicly because of inadequate alternatives. Individuals agreeing to complete diversionary community service continued to risk an arrest warrant for failure to complete any step in the process, from initial court appointment to final discharge from the program. Many times, homeless people missed the original court date and arrest warrants issued. Faced with the ordeal of defending themselves in court for an act they in fact committed, many people resigned themselves to an arrest warrant and an eventual night in jail.

Wasted Resources

Quality-of-life enforcement, including arrests, court appearances, and sanctions, results in unintended consequences. Oftentimes, homeless individuals are forced to leave belongings unattended: separated from their possessions, records and medications. Facing a court date or arrest on a warrant leads to missed housing, job, and medical appointments, and loss of public benefits or any semblance of a safety net.

Many police officers balk at citing or arresting homeless people for acts associated with living in public. The trivial "transgressions" of quality-of-life violations are viewed as distracting time and effort away from their "proper duties." Police and correctional officers often do not have the training or resources to provide referrals or supervision to individuals who may need specialized services for mental illness or substance abuse. Contemporary society demands that officers expand their professional repertoire beyond mere enforcement of laws, increasing their responsiveness to crime prevention and community life. Conflict arises because police officers often do not want to and are not adequately trained or prepared to perform "social work," while concurrently, "the police and jails appear to be among the most frequent providers of services to the population [of homeless people]." Police departments, jails and courts are not prepared to deal with the specialized and intensive needs of homeless people, "which raises critical questions related to the costs and benefits of such a diversion—questions that must be resolved not only in economic but also in humanitarian terms." We are asking too much of our police officers, prosecutors and court system. Since January 2000, San Francisco has spent over

$400,000 prosecuting quality-of-life citations. These prosecutions "take up an inordinate amount of court time since they get re-docketed numerous times due to the failure of homeless people to appear or because the person does not have the funds to pay the fine."

Estimated costs of enforcing quality-of-life codes vary, but uniformly exceed the estimated costs for housing. "In 1993, the average cost of detaining one person for one day in jail in the U.S. was over $40, excluding the police resources utilized in the arrest process." But that figure did not incorporate court and prosecutorial expenses. In 1995, prosecuting a typical quality-of-life violation in New York, from initial detention to final court appearance and compliance with the court-ordered remedy, was estimated to "cost[] upwards of $2000." A realistic local cost approximation may be reflected in the numbers cited by then-San Francisco Supervisor, Angela Alioto, in a Resolution proposed in 1993 and adopted in 1995: "Urging the mayor to redirect police activities from the enforcement of quality of life infractions in light of the United States Justice Department's declaration that such acts violate the Eighth Amendment of the U.S. Constitution because they constitute cruel and unusual punishment." The resolution denounced the Matrix program, estimating that average quality-of-life arrests cost between $226 and $584 each. By comparison, "the cost of providing transitional housing, which includes not only housing and food but also transportation and counseling services was approximately $30.90 per person per day." Whether $40 a day, $226 for an arrest, or $2000 for the whole process, quality-of-life enforcement costs more than providing comprehensive services to homeless persons.

Legal advocacy organizations sometimes represent homeless individuals at quality-of-life infraction hearings in traffic court. That representation counters the resources, legitimacy, and education of the prosecutors and

Commissioners. Attorneys may make traffic court appearances on behalf of their homeless clients, ensuring that the quality-of-life citations do not become warrants. However, these pro bono attorneys cannot accept settlement proposals of community or social service assignments from prosecutors "without the participation of the accused." Because of this constraint, some indigent offenders are sentenced to pay fines that they have no means of paying. These unpaid fines lead to arrest warrants. But many homeless people cited for quality-of-life violations candidly admit, that without advocacy, they would not make the initial court appearance and the citation would have lead to an arrest warrant anyway.

Current Policies and Proposals

Prosecutors Out of Traffic Court: Old Procedures, New Violations

In July 2001, the District Attorney officially ended the publicized quality-of-life prosecution program. Since that time, homeless people penalized for living in public face no formalized prosecution, confronting only the usual citation experience: paying fines or challenging tickets, a process that involves making court appearances, disputing the testimony of police officers, and asking for mercy before court commissioners. Another development includes the expansion of prosecutorial efforts. Instead of confronting prosecutors in traffic court, homeless people are now often charged with homelessness-related misdemeanors in Superior Court.

Community Courts

San Francisco District Attorney Terrance Hallinan proposed prosecuting quality-of-life violations via the District Attorney's Community Court Initiative. Community courts are a national phenomenon based on the model of New York City's Midtown Community Court which opened in 1993. The New York court attempted to promote "broken windows theory, community empowerment, and problem solving . . . combin[ing] punishment with help . . . to address[ ] social problems."

Community courts began in San Francisco as a means to empower community members in devising local solutions, providing restitution to the community and victims. "The purpose of San Francisco Community Court is to discourage quality of life violations within the city by sanctioning the offenders with financial and/or community service." Loitering, littering, open alcohol container violations, "and other miscellaneous quality of life crimes" may be heard before these courts. Offenders may opt for this Alternative Dispute Resolution program as an informal alternative to Traffic Court. Neighborhood residents and merchants form judicial panels to hear cases, deliberate, and decide sentences. Penalties include community service, anger management classes, drug and alcohol counseling, restitution and mediation. Currently, few if any, homeless people charged with quality-of-life violations choose to appear before these courts. But there have been suggestions that the District Attorney may divert some, or all, quality-of-life cases from Traffic Court to community courts.

Assessment: Enforcers of Quality-of-Life

A limited definition of community undermines this proposed policy of diverting homeless quality-of-life offenders to community courts. These courts both forestall long-term solutions to homelessness, and further criminalize homeless individuals by tying services to punishment.

When San Francisco reacted to community concerns about restitution and control over sentencing, the city included only residents and merchants in its definition of "community." Homeless people, though they may have significant, long-term ties to the area and concerns about sentencing, are not included in this concept of "community." Community courts perpetuate the division between the community, i.e. those with a residence or property, and the sources of community disorder, i.e. those without residences or property. Homeless people are not included in community courts except as offenders, and their interests in safety, restitution, and alternatives to criminal punishment remain officially unrecognized.

Unlike New York, San Francisco's Community Court Initiative did not expand access or funding to local social services. In New York, service providers are physically located within the Midtown Community Court complex, facilitating referrals for education, job training, drug and alcohol treatment, mediation, health care, counseling and community service. In San Francisco, Pre-Trial Diversion makes referrals to local service providers. But as discussed above, the waiting lists for housing, mental health and substance abuse treatment are prohibitive barriers that the services of the Pre-Trial Diversion do not overcome.

When implemented to penalize homeless people for living in public, San Francisco community courts represent a variation on the theme of criminalizing homelessness. These quasi-judicial community panels are not designed to view homeless people as neighbors and penalties will likely reflect this residency bias. Homeless people are not entitled to any representation in Community Court, facing a panel of neighborhood resources and legitimacy but receiving no advocacy. Without additional funding for social services, the referrals of Pre-Trial Diversion are moot. Homeless quality-of-life offenders leave Community Court with no more access to housing or treatment than they entered with, and they continue loitering and drinking alcohol in public, because they have nowhere else to go. Community courts divert funds into a system of punishment that could otherwise be implemented for the services the community

courts intend to provide. Finally, community courts reinforce the idea that police officers, citations, and court systems are appropriate responses to homelessness. Solutions to homelessness require complex community remedies that are not patrolled and enforced by the police or court systems.

Quality-of-Life: Obscuring Real Solutions

Quality-of-life enforcement presents the debate about social services for homeless people in terms of false alternatives. The prohibition of acts intertwined with homelessness, "significantly lowers any standards of acceptable survival conditions, converting the debated living options into jail versus the streets, instead of the streets versus a shelter, or a shelter versus housing." Either society issues and prosecutes citations, with court-enforced services, or we "do nothing," leaving homeless people with no services and our streets in disarray.

Advocacy for the rights of homeless people becomes "reactive" to these false alternatives. Energy is wasted preventing a cycle of incarceration for basic acts of living. Daily, resources are spent challenging incarceration, begging for a return to "benign neglect." Success in these attempts only translates to "negative rights," where homeless people are not punished for poverty, residency status and illness. Attorneys are forced to quibble with the officers' reporting on citations, rather than address their clients' underlying needs and the reasons prompting recidivism.

Real solutions, based on economic justice, call for a very different kind of advocacy. . . . [A]dvocates should be arguing for "rights to a job [,] . . . the economic means to survive . . . and decent affordable housing" rather than "the right to sleep in the park and to beg in the subway . . . and for the placement in neighborhoods of mass shelters that no one (including homeless people) reasonably wants to live in or near." The economic and social costs of arrest, prosecution, and court-enforced service planning are high. Ultimately, this short-term reactive advocacy obscures and effaces long-term solutions to homelessness.

CONCLUSION

Contrasting the order and safety of public spaces with the rights and needs of homeless people who live in those same spaces presents a false dichotomy. Safe and clean public spaces are vital for the entire community, including people with permanent housing and those without. Policy makers need not prioritize the interests of tourism and other commercial enterprises over the rights and needs of homeless people. Maintaining public spaces is a universally popular and laudable goal that does not necessitate criminalizing individuals for homelessness.

The police department and the court system should not be the primary providers of social services to homeless people. Delivering specifically tailored, high quality services to homeless people is a vital component of any solution-oriented approach to homelessness. But the costs are high and the outcome poor when society demands that the police and courts solve the problems of homelessness through assessment, referral or delivery of social services. We are asking too much of our officers and attempting to turn our courts into social service agencies.

Real solutions demand comprehensive, community-based efforts to increase the availability of safe, affordable housing, jobs, and substance abuse, mental health and other social services. San Francisco's investment in policing and prosecuting acts associated with homelessness is irrational and wasteful. The cycle of jail time, from initial police contact through warrants and probable incarceration, does not change a homeless person's permanent housing status. After receiving citations, appearing for or missing court appearances, completing community service or complying with waitlists, homeless offenders of quality-of-life ordinances, are still homeless. In theory, the city mandated criminalization as a prerequisite to otherwise unavailable housing and community services. In practice, housing and services remained unavailable and homeless people received citations in succession without meaningful community intervention or alternatives. Rather than spending limited resources on permanent housing or expanding social services, San Francisco's process of criminalization moves homeless people from the streets through the jails and back to the streets without long-term improvement. To provide effective solutions to homelessness, San Francisco must begin by divesting its homeless outreach programs from the police department and the courts.

STUDY QUESTION

Why does Maya Nordberg argue that delivering comprehensive services to homeless people is more effective and cheaper than resorting to police and courts?

The Struggle for Civil Rights: The Need for, and Impediments to, Political Coalitions Among and Within Minority Groups

Kevin R. Johnson

[C]oalitions are necessary to fully understand and attack racial hierarchy and white supremacy in the United States.

The ominous title of this conference—"Is Civil Rights Law Dead?"—is in no small part a sign of the times. The last few years have seen dire setbacks in civil rights law, including but not limited to attacks on affirmative action, passage of restrictionist immigration legislation and welfare reform, imposition of limits on civil rights litigation, and the creation of legal roadblocks to remedy the influence of race on the criminal justice system. Since September 2001, the "war on terror" also has had significant negative civil rights impacts.

The security measures taken by the federal government in response to September 11, although primarily targeting Arabs and Muslims, will likely have civil rights impacts on many minority communities for years to come. One of the most visible products of September 11, the USA PATRIOT Act, which, among other things, expanded the power of government to conduct electronic and other surveillance, clearly will have long term civil rights impacts on citizens as well as noncitizens. It is difficult to divine what impacts the new

Department of Homeland Security will have on civil rights in the United States, although immigration matters within the new department might well be handled with a security tilt.

In my mind, the relevant question, however, is not whether civil rights law is dead, but instead whether the political struggle for civil rights in the United States is alive and well. Like the national economy, law has a cyclical quality to it, depending on, among many other things, the political composition of the Supreme Court. Political struggle for social justice is particularly necessary when the courts turn a deaf ear to civil rights grievances. Ultimately, the struggle for hearts and minds will determine the fate of civil rights in the United States.

For that reason, my focus on the movement for civil rights, rather than civil rights law, is intentional. It is important, especially for lawyers and law professors immersed in the letter of the law, to recall that civil rights law cannot be relied on exclusively—or even primarily—in the struggle to ensure respect

---

Source: Kevin R. Johnson, "The Struggle for Civil Rights: The Need For, And Impediments To, Political Coalitions Among and Within Minority Groups," Louisiana Law Review, 63 (2003): 759–783.

for the rights of all Americans. As the civil rights movement of the 1960s taught, political, as well as legal means, are necessary to move us toward a more racially just nation. As no less an icon than *Brown v. Board of Education*, which outlawed *de jure* segregation but left intractable *de facto* segregation in its wake, exemplifies, law and litigation alone are unlikely to bring about the desired social change. Indeed, as critical theorists have observed, resort to law may in certain circumstances reinforce racial hierarchy. Only sustained political struggle will allow for lasting change of the racial status quo.

Even with civil rights litigation gains in the 1960s and beyond, the status of minorities in the United States has not changed as dramatically as one might expect or hope. Segregation remains at high levels in neighborhoods and schools across the nation, with "hyper-segregation" the norm for African American and Latina/o students. Employment discrimination and wage disparities between minority groups and whites remain an enduring social problem that legal rules and regulations have not fully remedied. Employment discrimination has evolved with the racial demographics of workers in the global economy.

As to the question whether the political struggle for civil rights in the United States is "dead," I offer an emphatic "no." Consider events just within a few months of this March 2003 symposium. Civil rights advocates and others participated in a growing anti-war movement as the United States engaged in war to topple the Iraqi government. Nascent political coalitions among Asian American, Latina/o, and other groups protested the treatment of Arab and Muslim noncitizens subject to special registration requirements imposed by the federal government as part of the "war on terror." The filibuster of the judicial nomination of Miguel Estrada, a Latino nominee prominent in conservative circles but who refused to fully share his legal views with the U.S. Senate, prevented his confirmation. Political pressure forced Trent Lott,

who waxed fondly before television cameras about how the nation would have avoided its racial "problems" if it had only elected as President a candidate running on a segregationist third party ticket, to relinquish his leadership role in the U.S. Senate. Last but not least, a wide array of advocacy groups in early 2003 filed amicus curiae briefs supporting affirmative action in the University of Michigan cases and rallied on the steps of the Supreme Court during oral argument in the cases to show support for affirmative action. In sum, many signs point to the vitality of the political struggle for civil rights.

Given that the courts in these times are not likely allies in the quest for racial justice, reinvigorated forms of political action should be investigated. Professor Adrien Katherine Wing's paper "Civil Rights in the Post 9–11 World: Critical Race Praxis, Coalition Building, and the War on Terrorism" moves us forward in thinking about the struggle for civil rights in this most challenging era. Known for her influential Critical Race Theory and Critical Race Feminist scholarship, Professor Wing brings much to analyzing the U.S. government's responses to the tragedy of September 11 and the political opportunities created as a result.

Although the political struggle for civil rights in my view is far from dead, I very much agree with Professor Wing about the need for "a thorough reconceptualization [of civil rights] in the 21st century." Changes over recent decades require precisely such a reconceptualization and complete redefinition of the goals of the struggle for civil rights, as well as the desired means to achieve them. The growth of the Latina/o population across the country, including the Midwest and South, has shifted the balance of civil rights concerns, adding to longstanding ones. Asian migration, which has increased significantly since 1965, has similarly affected the civil rights agenda. Changing racial demographics have expanded the scope of civil rights to include matters not necessarily thought of as traditional civil rights issues, such as immigration, language regulation, and even access to driver's licenses.

In addition, old issues have been recognized as having "civil rights" implications because of their impacts on minority communities. For example, the field of environmental justice, which grew from environmental law, is of relatively recent origin as activists and academics have come to appreciate the impacts of environmental hazards on communities of color. Immigration law and its enforcement has increasingly been viewed as implicating civil rights concerns. Similarly, voting rights scholarship has focused on race and its impacts on electoral politics, with even the racially disparate impacts of campaign finance reform recognized to a certain extent as a civil rights issue.

As this brief review suggests, "civil rights" are not static and fixed but dynamic and ever-changing. In this vein, the aggressive efforts of the federal government in the "war on terror" have created an entire new set of civil rights challenges, with the Arab and Muslim communities being most directly and immediately affected. However, immigrants and citizens from a variety of backgrounds also have suffered—and will continue to suffer for the indefinite future—from the various security measures taken in the name of national security.

In analyzing the political struggle for civil rights in the United States, Professor Wing builds on two fundamental tenets of Critical Race Theory: (1) race is a social construction, a product of our collective minds rather than a biological truth; and (2) tying critical theory to practice, which often is referred to in Critical Race Theory parlance as "critical race praxis." Both Critical Race Theory teachings shed much light on the civil rights controversies of the times in which we live, thus demonstrating Critical Race Theory's theoretical and practical utility.

As has occurred in different forms with other minority groups, society has racialized and demonized Arabs and Muslims as, among other things, religious fanatics bent on terrorism. This racialization, evident in a diverse array of sources ranging from popular culture to special legal rules and regulations, including "secret evidence" hearings in which the government denied Arab and Muslim noncitizens the evidence allegedly justifying their deportation, existed long before September 11. The events of that day, however, strongly reinforced the negative stereotypes already in place and facilitated the nation's aggressive actions toward Arabs and Muslims.

In hopes of tying theory to practice, Professor Wing advocates political coalitions among racialized communities to combat old and new forms of discrimination and civil rights deprivations. Such coalitions, she contends, are necessary to the political struggle for civil rights in the post-September 11 era. This essay focuses on this aspect of Professor Wing's article and analyzes the efficacy of multiracial coalitions in the political struggle for civil rights.

Part I of this essay argues that, despite the growing minority population in the United States, coalitions between communities of color will be necessary to displace white domination of the electoral process in this country. Part II addresses two formidable barriers to coalitions of color, both racism within minority communities toward other minority communities and intra-minority group tensions. These issues, often avoided because of their sensitivity, must be addressed if the hopes of creating multiracial coalitions are to be fully realized.

THE NEED FOR POLITICAL COALITIONS BETWEEN RACIAL MINORITIES

In recent works, prominent commentators, such as Lani Guinier, Gerald Torres, Robert Williams, and Eric Yamamoto, have expressed optimism about the potential for multiracial coalitions. Coalition is a fundamental tenet of the growing body of critical Latina/o theory scholarship. This is a politically pragmatic approach based on the old maxim that "there is power in numbers." Others, including Richard Delgado and Haunani-Kay Trask, are more pessimistic. Fears of coalitions run the gamut from diluting a group's particular message and goals to co-optation, with the bottom line being that the costs of collective action outweigh any benefits.

In my estimation, coalitions are necessary to fully understand and attack racial hierarchy and white supremacy in the United States. Racism against minority groups is related in direct and indirect ways. Indeed, the relationships of many different sorts of subordinations give rise to the potential for coalition. Coalitions between diverse communities, however, require much care and attention. As Angela Harris has emphasized, "solidarity is the product of struggle, not wishful thinking; and struggle means not only political struggle, but moral and ethical struggle as well."

The popular press has paid much attention to the future population projections showing that minorities will comprise a majority of the nation's population later this century. Even with the changing demographics, political coalitions between minority groups will remain important. Alliances between and among minority groups are essential, even in parts of the United States where minorities comprise a high proportion of the population. For example, although the demographics of California, perhaps the most diverse state with one of the highest concentrations of minorities in the country, are rapidly changing, that does not necessarily translate into changing electoral outcomes.

Voter eligibility and low turnout remain significant issues for African Americans, Latina/os, and Asian Americans. Voter turnout traditionally has been lower among minority communities than white communities. Intimidation and discouragement of minorities from voting at times continue to occur.

Importantly, a significant number of Latina/os and Asian Americans in California and other states are immigrants who, as noncitizens, are not eligible to vote. Some academics have embraced extension of the franchise to lawful immigrants. That, however, has not been seriously advocated in the political arena for decades. The result is that part of the greater community—a significant part in many locales—is denied the right to vote.

The disenfranchisement of convicted felons also has significant impacts on Latina/o and African American voter eligibility because of the disparate impact of the criminal justice system on those communities. Through felony disenfranchisement, the operation of the criminal justice system effectively diminishes the electoral power of African Americans and Latina/os. Consequently, race-based law enforcement, which has been the subject of sustained attack in recent years, is a voting rights as well as a criminal justice issue.

Victor Valle and Rodolfo Torres discuss the formidable impediments to the exercise of political power by Latina/os in Los Angeles, which they dub the "Latino Metropolis," despite their growing numbers. Latina/os failed to elect a progressive Latino for mayor in 2002 and not until the 1990s was a Latina/o elected to the powerful Los Angeles County Board of Supervisors. Los Angeles did not have a Latina/o mayor the entire twentieth century and elected a Latina to the Los Angeles County Board of Supervisors only after successful voting rights litigation in 1990.

A recent study demonstrates the need for coalition between minorities in racially-diverse California: By 2040, whites are projected to be little more than one-third of the adult population of California. However, if the citizenship and [voter] turnout rates of Asians and Latinos remain at their 2000 levels, whites will still make up a majority (53 percent) of the voting population.

Thus, in light of the limits on minority electoral power even with increasing numbers, coalitions among minority communities will be essential if the hope of destabilizing white privilege is to be realized.

The need for coalitions among minorities should not be surprising. In nations around the world, coalition governments, often, but not always, composed of different racial and ethnic groups, are a necessary fact of political life; governments and heads of state fall when coalitions crumble. This dynamic in certain respects may represent the future of the United States. With the end of Anglo numerical superiority will come the need for coalitions for progress and social justice. In fact, coalitions in all likelihood will be necessary to govern at all.

Ultimately, the demographic changes offer both opportunity and danger, for progress and retrenchment, for equality and oppression. Nothing is predetermined.

IMPEDIMENTS TO COALITION EFFORTS

Two issues may affect the ability of coalition formation among racial minority groups. First, a reconceptualization of an inclusive notion of "civil rights" is necessary. Times and racial demographics have changed. The conception of civil rights must as well.

Second, racism between and within minority communities must be addressed. Although far easier to sweep under the rug than to attempt to constructively address, racial divides must be bridged or any lasting efforts at political alliances are doomed.

The Need for the Reconceptualization of "Civil Rights" for the Twenty-First Century

Serious impediments stand in the way of multiracial coalitions. Importantly, as the nation has become increasingly multiracial over time, civil rights have become more complicated. Perhaps most important, the notion of "civil rights" as an issue pertaining to the treatment of African Americans by whites has changed as the presence of Asian Americans, Latina/os, Native Americans, and other minority groups in the United States has become increasingly evident and acknowledged.

Successful multiracial coalitions have worked in the past. For example, Asian Americans and Latina/os worked together to devise a redistricting scheme in Monterey Park, a Los Angeles suburb. Affirmative action has been an issue in which multiracial coalitions have been effective.

Civil rights issues are changing with the times, a period of high immigration and globalization of the world economy. Coalitions will need to be built around new as well as old civil rights issues.

To this end, abandonment of the traditional view that civil rights are exclusively Black/white issues mediating relations between African Americans and whites will be essential. Along these lines, different minority groups must not see civil rights as a zero-sum game. If viewed in that way, tensions will almost inevitably flare and coalitions likely will crumble. Rather, racial justice for all groups should be viewed as the common goal. Justice is not a scarce resource, but the minimum degree of respect that all communities deserve.

Beyond Black and White

One important barrier to inter-group cooperation has been the traditional understanding of civil rights matters as almost exclusively Black and white in nature and scope. It is true that, as Professor Wing mentions, a case can be made for "black exceptionalism," with the brutal legacy of slavery, lynchings, and Jim Crow, all central to the shaping of the African American community as we know it today. But even assuming that claim to be true, other minority groups have suffered serious civil rights deprivations and continue to suffer them.

The struggle of African Americans for civil rights is the one most familiar to many

Americans. The 1950s and 1960s have forever imprinted on the national psyche the courage and persistence of the efforts to desegregate the Jim Crow South, as well as the violent resistance to those efforts. Such struggles, however, were not the only ones. Chicana/os, Asian Americans, and Native Americans have engaged in their own civil rights struggles for many years.

Most knowledgeable observers today appreciate that the struggle for civil rights is considerably more complicated than Black/white. Burgeoning bodies of scholarship analyzing Latina/o, Asian American, and Native American civil rights issues have grown substantially over the last few decades.

Along with African Americans, Asian Americans, Latina/os, Native Americans, and other groups press for recognition and redress of civil rights grievances. Some of the pressing civil rights issues of these communities differ in important respects from those central to African Americans. Latina/o civil rights issues include such matters as immigration and language policy and rules. Asian Americans share some similar issues. A growing multiracial community also has appeared on the national scene, with the complexities of the mixed race population brought into the public consciousness by the racial classification controversy surrounding Census 2000. The question then becomes how to approach the complexities of the emerging civil rights concerns so that practical action can be taken.

At a minimum, dialogue and discussion will be required in any effort to hash out common ground on the modern conception of civil rights. Immigration has been a dividing line between minority groups at various times in U.S. history, with poor African American, and often white, workers pitted against immigrant labor. Difficult issues of race and class plague the debate. Despite its difficulty, the answer is not to avoid addressing these issues, as has often been the case, but to attempt to discuss them and determine whether common ground can be identified.

As Professor Wing alludes to in her contribution to this symposium, the measures taken in the "war on terror" allow a ready opportunity for political coalitions among different racial minority groups pursuing a civil rights agenda. The focus on the war has been on Arab and Muslim noncitizens, who as presumed terrorists have been subject to surveillance, interviewed and interrogated, detained, required to submit to "special" registration, and have been the focal point of no less than a nationwide dragnet based on racial, national origin, and religious profiles. In the long run, however, the harms caused by the measures enforced in the war on terror will not be limited to Arabs and Muslims. Immigration reform measures will affect communities with large immigrant populations, such as Asian and Latina/o communities. The law has tightened generally on immigrants, not simply "terrorists"; many Mexican immigrants already have suffered and more will in the future, which is precisely what occurred as a result of the 1996 immigration reforms enacted by Congress in the name of fighting terrorism. Moreover, citizens of certain national origin ancestries are likely to be affected as well.

Racial profiling, which appeared to be on its deathbed at the turn of the century, made a comeback as part of the "war on terror" and will likely influence law enforcement measures affecting African Americans, Latina/os, and Asian Americans, as well as Arabs and Muslims for years to come. These interrelated civil rights injuries create opportunities for coalition if the different groups fully appreciate the convergence of interests. Unfortunately, the interrelationships may not always appear to be self-evident. African Americans, Asian Americans, and Latina/os at first glance may consider it irrelevant that "those" Arabs and Muslims are being profiled, detained, interrogated, and worse. However, the logic of the security measures, based on statistical probabilities that have been used by defenders of racial profiling in criminal and immigration law enforcement, likely will affect all minority groups. Similar reasoning may be used to justify race-based traffic stops and immigration stops.

Given common ground among civil rights issues, possible coalitions exist on a variety of matters. Racial minorities share common cause, for example, in seeking to eliminate racial discrimination in the workplace, public education, and the criminal justice system, and in the pursuit of economic justice. To build coalitions, however, we must recognize that African American, Asian American, and Latina/o communities have interests that at times may diverge. Differences must be discussed candidly and honestly to discern whether coalitions are possible. The need will be to focus on the building of coalitions on specific issues.

CIVIL RIGHTS IS NOT A ZERO-SUM GAME

Related to the Black/white binary view of civil rights is the view that "civil rights" is a zero-sum game, with one minority group losing when another gains. When viewed in that way, tensions will inevitably result between minority groups pursuing the "scarce resource" of civil rights. In recent years, for example, African Americans at times have felt threatened by Latina/o and Asian American electoral gains. In the long run, infighting among, and fragmenting of, minority communities could result in racial minorities failing to satisfy the potential for positive civil rights reform.

In zero-sum games, groups fear conflict and betrayal; in that mindset, cooperation, by definition a prerequisite for successful coalitions, is unlikely. Unfortunately, that is how some minorities have viewed civil rights. Not surprisingly, conflict has resulted. Consequently, the struggle for civil rights must work to both expand the conception of civil rights to comport with modern realities facing minority communities and view the struggle for civil rights not as a zero-sum game, but an instance in which the civil rights of all groups can be recognized and protected.

This will not be an easy task. Many, perhaps most, of us are conditioned to view the world as one of scarce resources and inherent limits. Such constraints unquestionably exist in certain circumstances. However, we have not—nor should we—view "equality" and "racial justice" as limited resources. No one views First Amendment rights of free expression and religious freedom in that way, for example. Racial equality is no different. Rights of membership in society for all groups should not be viewed as a scarce resource to be allocated among groups.

Conflict Among Minorities

Coalition opportunities exist between various minority groups on certain issues. However, such possibilities need sustained commitment to cooperation rather than competition. Coalitions are fragile and require care and attention. In addition, we must begin to address a fundamental division—racial discrimination—between minority groups.

Racism within minority communities is a rarely-discussed barrier to multiracial coalitions. Anti-African American sentiment exists in the Latina/o community, just as it exists among certain segments of the Asian American community. Unfortunately, integration and assimilation of certain immigrants groups into U.S. society with whites has at times meant adoption of racist attitudes toward African Americans. At the same time, some African Americans have embraced xenophobic views toward Latina/os and Asians. Although such racism is decried, its roots and impacts have gone largely ignored. Racism within communities of color causes tension that hinders political cooperation, generates suspicion, and flares up in times of social turmoil. Those communities must squarely address such racism or take the risk that it will undermine the struggle for civil rights.

Consider an example. Los Angeles has been said to be the place for development of the progressive politics of the future, in part because the 2001 mayoral election saw a runoff between a white liberal and progressive Latino. However, the mayoral race also revealed simmering tensions between African Americans and Latina/os. Campaign advertisements of the white candidate supported heavily by African Americans played on racially-charged themes directed at the Latina/o candidate, with bad blood remaining after the election.

Moreover, conflict within communities of color also exists. Latina/os, African Americans, and Asian Americans are in actuality a diverse community of communities. This is often ignored by whites who essentialize minority groups as well as by minority groups hoping to provide a united front in hopes of maximizing their political power. Efforts to ignore these tensions, however, may well worsen them, with an eruption of discontent almost inevitable.

Conflict Between Groups

There has been much publicized interethnic conflict between minority groups, as well as with the Anglo population. In the wake of the Rodney King violence of May 1992, African American and Korean American conflict grabbed the nation's attention. This is true even though many of the people involved in the violence were Latina/o. Thus, the violence in south central Los Angeles in May 1992 was a complex, multiracial outburst of discontent.

Conflict between minority groups has been sensationalized and arguably has been over-emphasized. In major civil rights litigation, for example, minority activist organizations historically have cooperated. Future cooperation will require work on some major issues, such as discrimination, immigration, employment, criminal justice, and voting rights. Conflict exists, however, even if it simmers just below the surface.

To increase coalition and cooperation, minority groups will need to address racism within their communities toward other minority communities in order to form long-lasting bonds and alliances. To this point, little has been done in this regard, although few deny that racism within minority communities exists to some degree.

Given this and other divides, the future of multiracial coalitions is far from certain. Reminiscent of the Republican Party's current efforts to court Latina/o voters, whites can be expected to attempt to forge political alliances with minority groups. At times, blacks and whites have joined forces to support restrictionist immigration measures that have damaged Latina/os and Asian Americans. Occasionally, Latina/os and Asian Americans have identified as "white" and sought to gain the benefits of white privilege.

In light of history and physical difference, coalitions with whites appear more likely for Latina/os than for Asian Americans and African Americans. However, Latina/os have historically been discriminated against in U.S. social life and, consequently, segments of the community have a well-developed racial consciousness. Richard Delgado has suggested that minority groups should bargain with each other rather than try to cut the best deal with whites.

Latina/os could serve as a bridge to other groups and assist in the building of multiracial coalitions. That may or may not come to be. Whatever the impetus, work among minority groups will be necessary to bring about change.

Conflict Within Groups

In addition to tensions between communities, intraethnic conflict within minority communities is an issue. Although often viewed by whites as monolithic, Asian Americans and Latina/os are extremely heterogeneous populations. National origin, class, and other differences may divide Latina/os and Asian

Americans. Similarly, class and other cleavages may divide the African American community; the burgeoning Black middle class may not share the class-based concerns of poor and working class African Americans. Consequently, efforts must be made to build coalitions within as well as among minority communities.

Intragroup conflict to a certain extent already has emerged in the political process. In 1992, two prominent African American politicians (Yvonne Braithwaite Burke and Diane Watson) fought a no-holds-barred campaign to become the first African American on the Los Angeles County Board of Supervisors. One reason for the ferocity of the campaign was that "Watson [saw] herself as a genuine part of the South L.A. community [long a center of the African American community in greater Los Angeles] and Burke as a carpet-bagger." In 2002, a Latino Los Angeles city council candidate accused opponent Antonio Villaraigosa, a progressive Latino politician who had failed in a run for mayor, of being a "pocho," a derogatory term for a person of Mexican ancestry deemed to be too assimilated or too "white." Along these lines, the Asian American community is so heterogeneous that building lasting pan-Asian political coalitions has proven difficult.

Intra-group conflict can be seen with respect to high profile federal judicial nominations, such as conservative African American Clarence Thomas's appointment to the Supreme Court and the nomination of Honduran-born Miguel Estrada to a coveted court of appeals position. Both were opposed by some portions of their communities, which generated considerable national controversy.

Intra-Latina/o tensions erupted in *Cano v. Davis*, in which the Mexican American Legal Defense and Education Fund accused the California Legislature, with a record number of Latina/os, of diluting Latina/o voting power in violation of the Voting Rights Act in the state's congressional redistricting scheme.

This visible conflict within the Mexican American community, which is generally more cohesive than the greater Latina/o community, suggests the possible splintering of Latina/os along political, national origin, and other lines. In the long term, for example, one could envision a voting rights claim by Central Americans, who comprise a significant percentage of the Latina/o population in Los Angeles County, contending that they are being locked out of the electoral process by politicians of Mexican ancestry, who comprise the vast majority of Latina/os in state and local elected offices in California. Similar occurrences might happen among different Latina/o national origin groups in New York and Florida, which have diverse Latina/o populations like California's.

To this point, intra-community fissures within the Asian American, African American, and Latina/o communities have generally gone ignored. The fault lines are evident among Latina/os who differ socioeconomically and politically along national origin lines. Asian Americans also are far from a monolithic community with national origin, political, and class differences. This is true even though Latina/os and Asian Americans often face discrimination as "foreigners."

In sum, intra-group cooperation cannot be assumed in the multiracial politics of tomorrow. Rather, coalition within, as well as between, minority communities must be built carefully and with sensitivity. This will become an increasingly important issue in the years to come, as immigration continues to diversify the U.S. population and internal divides continue to emerge within, as well as between, minority groups.

CONCLUSION

These are difficult times in the struggle for civil rights in the United States. New challenges face minority communities across the nation. Ultimately, political struggle, as well as resort to law and the courts, will be necessary.

As has been well-documented, civil rights law has not been particularly helpful to racial minorities in recent years. Consequently, the time is right to re-examine the strategies for political struggle given the demographic and other changes occurring in the United States. It is unclear, however, whether the predicates exist for the multiracial coalitions necessary for successful political action between communities of color.

To build coalitions, concerted efforts are necessary to reconceptualize civil rights for the twenty-first century in a multi-racially diverse America. The antiquated two dimensional view of civil rights must give way to a multidimensional view that comports with the modern demographics of the nation. Importantly, social justice cannot be viewed as a zero-sum game in which one minority group loses when another gains. Such an approach likely will result in tensions, barriers to coalitions, and frustration of efforts to bring about social change.

Moreover, and perhaps most importantly, we must begin to address racism within minority communities directed at other communities of color if we hope to build coalitions among those communities. Unfortunately, racism among minority communities is a social problem that thwarts collective action. Rather than condemn yet ignore it, those committed to social justice must acknowledge the problem and struggle with its solution. In the long run, this likely will prove to be a formidable challenge to the struggle for civil rights.

STUDY QUESTION

What is Kevin Johnson's answer to the question of whether the political struggle for civil rights in the United States is "dead," and how does he answer that question.

Index